Gabriele Cornelli (Ed.)
Plato's Styles and Characters

Beiträge zur Altertumskunde

―

Herausgegeben von Michael Erler, Dorothee Gall,
Ludwig Koenen und Clemens Zintzen

Band 341

Plato's Styles and Characters

Between Literature and Philosophy

Edited by
Gabriele Cornelli

DE GRUYTER

The publication of this book has been supported by the International Plato Society, the Archai UNESCO Chair / Universidade de Brasília and the CAPES/ Coordenação de aperfeiçoamento de pessoal de nível superior/ Ministry of Education/Brazil.

ISBN 978-3-11-057817-1
e-ISBN (PDF) 978-3-11-044560-2
e-ISBN (EPUB) 978-3-11-043654-9
ISSN 1616-0452

Library of Congress Cataloging-in-Publication Data
A CIP catalog record for this book has been applied for at the Library of Congress.

Bibliographic information published by the Deutsche Nationalbibliothek
The Deutsche Nationalbibliothek lists this publication in the Deutsche Nationalbibliografie; detailed bibliographic data are available on the Internet at http://dnb.dnb.de.

© 2016 Walter de Gruyter GmbH, Berlin/Boston
This volume is text- and page-identical with the hardback published in 2016.
Printing and binding: Hubert & Co. GmbH & Co. KG, Göttingen

♾ Printed on acid-free paper
Printed in Germany

www.degruyter.com

To Samuel Scolnicov† (1941–2014)

Table of Contents

Introduction —— 1

Plato's Literary Style

Samuel Scolnicov
Beyond Language and Literature —— 5

Raúl Gutiérrez
The Three Waves of Dialectic in the *Republic* —— 15

Mary Louise Gill
Plato's Unfinished Trilogy: *Timaeus–Critias–Hermocrates* —— 33

María Angélica Fierro
The Myth of the Winged Chariot in the *Phaedrus:* A Vehicle for Philosophical Thinking —— 47

Lucas Soares
Perspectivism, Proleptic Writing and Generic *agón*: Three Readings of the *Symposium* —— 63

Graciela E. Marcos de Pinotti
Plato's Argumentative Strategies in *Theaetetus* and *Sophist* —— 77

José Trindade Santos
"Reading Plato's Sophist" —— 89

Other Genres and Traditions

Michael Erler
Detailed Completeness and Pleasure of the Narrative. Some Remarks on the Narrative Tradition and Plato —— 103

Dino De Sanctis
The meeting scenes in the *incipit* of Plato's dialogue —— 119

Gilmário Guerreiro da Costa
The Philosophical Writing and the Drama of Knowledge in Plato —— 137

Marcus Mota
Comic Dramaturgy in Plato: Observations from the Ion —— 157

Mario Regali
***Amicus Homerus:* Allusive Art in Plato's *Incipit* to Book X of the *Republic* (595a – c)** —— 173

Fernando Muniz
Performance and Elenchos in Plato's Ion —— 187

Mauro Tulli
Plato and the Catalogue Form in *Ion* —— 203

Fernando Santoro
Orphic Aristophanes at Plato's Symposium —— 211

Álvaro Vallejo Campos
Socrates as a physician of the soul —— 227

Silvio Marino
The Style of Medical Writing in the Speech of Eryximachus: Imitation and Contamination —— 241

Esteban Bieda
Gorgias, the eighth orator. Gorgianic echoes in Agathon's Speech in the Symposium —— 253

Beatriz Bossi
Plato's Phaedrus: A Play Inside the Play —— 263

Plato's Characters

Gabriele Cornelli
He longs for him, he hates him and he wants him for himself: The Alcibiades Case between Socrates and Plato —— 281

Debra Nails
Five Platonic Characters —— 297

Francisco Bravo
Who Is Plato's Callicles and What Does He Teach? —— 317

Michele Corradi
Doing business with Protagoras (*Prot.* 313e): Plato and the Construction of a Character —— 335

Marcelo D. Boeri
Theaetetus and Protarchus: two philosophical characters or what a philosophical soul should do —— 357

Christian Keime
The Role of Diotima in the *Symposium:* The Dialogue and Its Double —— 379

Contributors —— 401

Citations Index —— 407

Author Index —— 411

Subject Index —— 419

Introduction

The significance of Plato's literary style to the content of his ideas is perhaps one of the central problems in the study of Plato and Ancient Philosophy as a whole. As Samuel Scolnicov pointed out in this collection, many other philosophers have employed literary techniques to express their ideas, just as many literary authors have exemplified philosophical ideas in their narratives, but for no other philosopher does the mode of expression play such a vital role in their thought as it does for Plato. And yet, even after two thousand years, there is still no consensus about the reason why Plato expresses his ideas in this distinctive style. Selected from the first Latin American Area meeting of the International Plato Society (www.platosociety.org) in Brazil (20 – 24th August, 2012), the following collection of essays presents some of the most recent scholarship from around the world on the wide range of issues related to Plato's dialogue form. The meeting was organized by Archai Unesco Chair on The Plural Origins of Western Thought of the University of Brasilia (www.archai.unb.br) and the Platonists Brazilian Society (www.platao.org), with a generous support of the International Plato Society, University of Brasilia and the Coordination for the Improvement of Higher Education Personnel (CAPES) of the Brazilian Ministry of Higher Education.

Scholars in Platonic studies gathered together at this conference and explored new paths of research in the field, despite the divergence of opinion among the participants, at the end. There is a lot to be learnt from a closer examination of Plato's literary art of writing philosophy in its cultural and historical context. Understanding how Plato turned the various styles and devices of his predecessors into elements of his own writing is a key step in assessing the real singularity of his writing and the conception of philosophy it conveys. Plato's use of characters is one of the exciting fields of research now on the table. As central feature of Plato's way of writing philosophy, it that needs to be understood in its singularity in comparison to others genres of writing also using characters before him – poetry, history, etc.

The contributions can be divided into three categories. The first addresses general questions concerning Plato's literary style. The second concerns the relation of his style to other genres and traditions in Ancient Greece. And the third examines Plato's characters and his purpose in using them.

Samuel Scolnicov, Raúl Gutiérrez, and Mary Louise Gill address the general question of the dialogue form for Plato's thought. María Angélica Fierro and Lucas Soares explain Plato's use of specific literary devices, such as myth, allegory, perspective, and prolepsis. And Graciela E. Marcos de Pinotti and José Trindade Santos reflect upon Plato's use of language in the development of his arguments.

Michael Erler and Dino De Sanctis provide comparisons of the dialogues with other narrative styles of the time. Gilmário Guerreiro da Costa, Marcus Mota, Fernando Muniz, Mario Regali, Mauro Tulli, and Fernando Santoro address the relation of Plato's thought and writing to Ancient Greek poetry. Álvaro Vallejo Campos and Silvio Marino explore the use of medical terminology and ideas in the dialogues. Esteban Bieda and Beatriz Bossi discuss Plato's complex relation towards the use of rhetoric in philosophic teaching.

Gabriele Cornelli, Debra Nails, Francisco Bravo, and Michele Corradi address the question of the relation between Plato's characters and the historical individuals they represent, while Marcelo D. Boeri and Christian Keime examine the purpose of the characters in the dialogues.

Through these essays readers will have an understanding of the complexity of issues surrounding Plato's combination of literature and philosophy. They will also be able to access the most recent developments on these topics from various approaches – from the 'analytic' to the 'continental', from the established traditions in Europe and North America to the emerging Platonic scholarship in South America.

I would like to express my deepest gratitude to the Archai team for help me to organize the venue in such an effective way, and especially to Nicholas Riegel, who worked very hard on the revision of the papers here published.

A last remark is very much needed. Samuel Scolnicov, one of the authors of this book, died in August 13, 2014, while this book was being prepared. Samuel was born on March 11, 1941 in Brazil and immigrated to Israel in 1958. His outstanding scholarly productivity is very well known: he wrote not only in English, but also in his native Portuguese and in Hebrew. He was between the small group of international Plato scholars who founded the International Plato Society in 1989, and served as its President from 1998–2001. Samuel truly embodied the ideals of the IPS, moving easily among numerous languages and cultures, and among the diversity of approaches to Platonic studies. Dedicating this book to him seemed the most natural thing to do. *Saudades*, Samuel.

Gabriele Cornelli
President of the International Plato Society

Plato's Literary Style

Samuel Scolnicov
Beyond Language and Literature

Literary forms have often been used to develop philosophical positions. In fact, as far as we know, written prose was first developed for history and philosophy by Herodotus and Anaximander and a few others. Aphorisms were used by Heraclitus and Nietzsche, essays by Montaigne, monologues by Augustine and Descartes, and hierarchically numbered propositions by Wittgenstein. These were, each at its time, a novel form of philosophical discourse, intrinsically connected with the philosophical positions presented.

Time and again, dialogue has been used in philosophical writing as a literary façade. Cicero did it, and so did later, among many others, Galileo and Berkeley.[1] But their dialogues are little more than confrontations of ideas thinly veiled behind names of speakers that are mere personifications of philosophical positions. Salviati is mostly a spokesman for Galileo himself and Simplicio is, as expected, an aristotelian. Berkeley's Hylas is the materialist, as his name implies, and Philonous is 'the lover of mind', to wit: Berkeley himself. Their philosophical positions could be and were developed also apart from the literary form in which they were presented in these dialogues.

A platonic dialogue, by contrast, is real drama, with developed characters, personality clashes, in most cases with an elaborate setting, even ostensibly precise dramatic date.[2] What happens in it is not just a conflict of ideas, but a full confrontation of individuals,[3] with all their complexities, intellectual as well as emotional and moral. Drama can carry ideas, and often does. This was done by Ibsen and Bernard Shaw, as had been done much before by Aristophanes and many others to this day. But these are dramas in which ideas are *exemplified*; particular cases are explored in the interest of general ideas. But Plato's dialogues are not dramas *engagés* just as they are not plain philosophical treatises. Although his dialogues deal with ideas *directly*, these are explored not 'objectively', but from the points of view of the characters involved in the conversation at each of its stages.

There were antecedents to Plato's dialogues, by now well known. There was, after the death of Socrates, a spate of *logoi sokratikoi*;[4] Plato was apparently not

---
1 Galileo 1632; Berkeley 1713.
2 But Plato's chronology is notoriously inconsistent. See below, p. 7.
3 With few exceptions, such as the boy in Meno, the Eleatic Stranger of the *Sophist* or the Athenian of the *Laws*.
4 See Giannantoni 1983.

the first to write such *logoi*. But this is immaterial to our present interest. Whatever his historical position in this respect, he certainly brought the genre to its perfection – with an important difference to boot, which will occupy us as we go along. The other *logoi sokratikoi* exhibited Socrates' *modus philosophandi* and, at most, conveyed a moral message detachable from the dialogical form, or were of merely protreptic intent. As a matter of fact, if anything can be said about the historical Socrates, his intent seems indeed to have been mostly protreptic.

However, for our purposes, we are interested not in the historical Socrates, whoever he may have been, but in the Socrates of Plato's dialogues. Yet, Socrates in the *Republic* says things that in the *Apology* he would not say, or flatly contradicts them: immortality of the soul (whatever that means), ideas, etc. This is not a chronological distinction, not the venerable one corresponding to the 'early' and 'later' dialogues, respectively. It is rather the distinction between the aporetic Socrates, such as that in *Laches* or *Euthyphro*, and the 'positive' Socrates, such as the one in *Phaedo* or the *Republic*. Socrates of Plato's dialogues is a complex figure. Elsewhere, I have called these two strains of Socrates of the dialogues 'Plato's Socrates' and 'the platonic Socrates': the agnostic, aporetic, and the pythagorizing, mythologizing, metaphysical Socrates. In the same dialogue both may be there at different times. *Euthydemus, Phaedrus*, even *Phaedo* and the *Republic* have both. Traits of the first appear also in 'later' dialogues, such as *Theaetetus*, and of the second also in 'early' dialogues, as *Protagoras*. Here, I am interested mainly in the platonic Socrates, although I shall be referring occasionally to Plato's Socrates. The difference should be clear from the context. Neither of these is necessarily Plato's mouthpiece. Socrates often says different things in different dialogues and even sometimes, if we take his words at face value, contradicts himself from one dialogue to another and even in the same dialogue.

One might say that, as in good drama, Plato is behind *all* of his characters and, what amounts to the same, in none of them. Or perhaps he is in his characters not only as their creator but also as voicing through them views that he himself held or, at least, considered. Shakespeare did not put part of himself into Iago, but Callicles may have a good claim to a part of Plato, or so the argument goes.

A playwright does not commit himself to consistency over different pieces. It does happen sometimes, particularly when the author has a social or political agenda, but this is certainly not the rule. The same has been sometimes said of Plato: each of his dialogue is to be read on its own, without taking over ideas from one to another. But Plato himself quotes from one dialogue in another, even if sometimes he does it not quite accurately or straightforwardly misleading.

Plato's dialogue form is not just a beautiful outer shell but part and parcel of the philosophical matter. As it has often been remarked but seldom paid attention to sufficiently, Plato's philosophy is dialogical. In most cases, this has been taken to mean that Plato uses dialogue as a pedagogical or philosophical method, the results of the enquiry being either merely protreptic or else independent of the didactical process. Romantics favoured the search itself over its possible results, while others, more dogmatically or analytically oriented, strove to surface from the dialogues with explicit 'doctrines'.[5] To my mind, both these readings of the dialogues fall short of giving a satisfactory explanation of the full significance of this peculiarly platonic literary and philosophical form.

Plato's dialogues do not seem, at first look, to be all merely protreptic and exploratory, at least not such dialogues as the *Symposium* and the *Republic* – and even these were not always above suspicion; even the 'later' dialogues have sometimes been said to be merely tentative. Perhaps, then, there are, nevertheless, philosophical doctrines in Plato? Of course, in *Phaedo, Symposium, Republic* and other dialogues, there are the ideas, the immortality of the soul (whatever that means), the distinction between *doxa* and *episteme*. Are not these firm doctrines to be learned from those dialogues? *But*, of these supposed doctrines, the first two are presented as provisional hypotheses,[6] and the third seems to be gratuitously assumed and it is by no means evident; Protagoras, for once, negated it squarely. *Parmenides* and *Euthydemus*, to mention only two dialogues, put these doctrines in serious doubt. And do, *e.g.*, the *Sophist* and the *Laws* go back on them? The chronology of *Timaeus* was hotly disputed because it explicitly held them.[7]

If we cannot make much headway with the content of the dialogues, let us try another approach: let us investigate their *form*. On the literary level, Plato's dialogues may be classified as either diegetic, *i.e.* narrated, or mimetic, *i.e.* directly presented. Some, like *Theaetetus* or *Parmenides*, are mixed and some are in the form of a narration framing a direct dialogue. In the *Republic*, Plato prefers narration to *mimesis*.[8] Narration interposes the narrator between the content narrated and his audience, thus allowing the author to distance himself from the *prima facie* veracity of the content.

---

5 *E.g.*, Crombie 1962. For a variety of approaches, see now Press 1993.
6 See *Phaedo* 107b.
7 Cf. Owen 1953 and Cherniss 1957.
8 *Republic* iii 394d ff.

In both cases, Plato's dialogues are *incomplete*. Aporetic dialogues are such by their own nature. But, narrated or not, his dialogues contain purposeful inconsistencies in chronology or other disturbing details precisely in order to warn us against taking at face value all that is said. And one should never forget that the narrator is himself a *dramatis persona*. As such, he has his own interests and point of view and his report is never to be taken without more ado as narrating things as they presumably were.

But, one may say, when Socrates is the narrator, he is surely to be trusted. – Or is he? Take the case of *Euthydemus*. Twice in the course of the dialogue, Socrates is on the verge of admitting that his story is not well told. At the third time, Crito himself challenges Socrates' narrative to the point that Clinias – Socrates' young respondent, credited by him of quite unlikely answers – immediately drops out of the dialogue altogether.[9]

Euthydemus teaches us something important about Socrates' method. While the two sophists, Euthydemus and Dionysodorus, put their questions from their own point of view, without any preparation of their interlocutor,[10] Socrates argues dialectically. In this dialogue as in all the other dialogues, he starts always from the point where his interlocutor stands and aims at disproving him and sometimes, if possible, at leading him gradually to change his views. In so arguing, Socrates is necessarily being ironical. He takes on positions that are not his, but his method brings him to develop them only for the sake of the argument. One should, thus, be very careful when ascribing to Socrates views that he presents during the conversation.

In *Meno* 80, Plato introduces his hypothetical method, to be fully explained in Phaedo 100–101.[11] This method, inspired by the geometrical method of analysis, starts from an accepted conclusion and looks for the minor premise that will support it. For Plato, philosophy is not primarily a deductive science. Against the rules of good logical reasoning, accepted at least since Parmenides, the conclusion is taken to be stronger than its premises. The hypothetical method goes 'the wrong way':[12] it goes from the conclusion to the premise, which is now the *desideratum*.

The source of that premise is irrelevant. It could be a few lines from a poem, an accepted scientific theory, a myth (invented *ad hoc* or pre-existing), a purported dream. If that premise is not consistent with other opinions accepted by the interlocutor, either it or the opinions that conflict with it are to be discarded as

---

9 *Euthydemus* 293b-end.
10 *Euthydemus* 274d-e.
11 Cf. Scolnicov 1975.
12 Cf. Cornford 1932.

false;[13] if no such contradiction is found, that premise is considered provisionally true until proved otherwise and is now itself in need of support 'in the same way'.[14]

One consequence of the hypothetical method is directly relevant to our present concerns: it can be successfully applied only in dialogues in which the interlocutor shares with Socrates the primary intuition expressed by the desired conclusion. Meno, as a matter of fact, is not convinced that learning is reminiscing and asks to hear from Socrates what he has to say on the matter, rather than find the truth for himself; the dialogue with him fails. Simmias and Cebes are well predisposed towards *philosophia* and the dialogue can proceed to a positive outcome, even if provisional and in need of further support.[15]

Plato's fundamental intuition is the primacy of ethics, *i.e.* of *philosophia* as he understood it, continuing Socrates' rejection of the unexamined life. All his effort is directed at supplying *philosophia* its foundation. Even in *Parmenides*, the question of *philosophia* is there in a crucial passage.[16]

This means that the platonic Socrates is preaching to the converted or to youngsters as yet unformed and uncrystallized. With others he is a dismal educational failure. But this is a necessary consequence of Plato's method of hypothesis. If the method takes its start from accepted conclusions, going 'upwards' from them to their premises, it is inevitable that for those who do not share, not even for the sake of argument, those conclusions, the hypothetical movement has no starting point.

On the other hand, socratic-platonic dialectic is essentially ironic, especially in the elenctic dialogues. The dialectical procedure starts from where the interlocutor stands. Socrates accepts the interlocutor's view *pro tempore* and only *argumenti gratia*. Otherwise, dialectic cannot proceed. But, then, this means that Socrates' initial positions cannot ever be trusted as his own.

How much of Plato's irony is Socrates'? Again, I try strenuously not to say anything about the 'historical' Socrates. By 'Socrates' I mean Socrates of Plato's dialogues. Yet, if Socrates (even the 'historical' one, for once) asked questions and refused to answer – this is all the irony we need for a start. Xenophon's Socrates gives good advice and is very useful to have around. That Plato is ironical

---

13 *Phaedo* 92c, 100a, 101d.
14 *Phaedo* 101d.
15 Cf. *Phaedo* 107a.
16 *Parmenides* 135c5.

goes without saying. Is Socrates' irony all of it Plato's? Not impossible, but I personally find it hard to believe.[17]

Yet, socratic irony never discloses what Socrates means. It only makes exceedingly clear what he *does not* mean. In this, it is not like ordinary irony, or antiphrasis, which says the opposite of what is meant.[18] Nor is it like romantic irony, or Vlastos's complex irony, which leaves us undecided between 'yes' and 'no'.[19] It is *open irony*, in which the opposite pole is never given.[20]

Socratic irony *cannot* tell us, not even indirectly, Socrates' meaning. Socratic irony involves a different understanding of the very words used. Using other words would be of no avail. Language is essentially ambiguous, as *Euthydemus* and *Cratylus* teach us. Time and again, Socrates' argumentation brings us back to what seems to be the accepted virtues.[21] The words are the same, but, for Socrates, they bear a different meaning, for which there are no other words than the ones he and everybody else use.

Here an important distinction is in order: the distinction between *utterance* and *proposition*. An utterance is a unit of speech, long or short, the actual token of words emitted by the speaker at a given moment, essentially dependent on him as the speaker. A proposition is the content expressed in the utterance, independent of him who produced it or of the language in which it was produced. (For our purposes, the modern distinction between sentence and proposition is irrelevant.) The dialogue format presents us with purported utterances, not with propositions. All that is said is dependent of he who says it and in which context and is inextricable from the sayer and from its context.

In *Euthydemus*, Plato makes a firm stand on the view that words have no meaning in themselves. He is careful not to say that such is the meaning of this word; instead he says that people *use* this word to convey such a meaning. Words are *tools*[22] used by the speaker to convey what he wants. Any word can bear any meaning. I may, of course, use 'dog' to mean cat, if I disregard the risk of being misunderstood. The meaning of the words is not in themselves but in the soul of the speaker (and of the hearer).[23]

---

17 Holger Thesleff, in private correspondence, pushed me towards taking a stand on this question.
18 Quintilianus 9.2.44.
19 Vlastos 1991.
20 On Socrates' open irony, see Scolnicov 2004.
21 Cf. Desjardins 1988.
22 *Cratylus* 388c ff.
23 *Euthydemus* 295b5, e8.

Thus, dialogue is absolutely necessary. Without it, we can never know whether our words were properly understood.[24] And, *a fortiori*, the written word is little less than useless – again, if the reader is not among the converted. But, if he is not, how can he ever be won over? First, by trying to disabuse him of the meaning he attaches to his words; then, by guiding him, very slowly, to grasp the meaning Socrates attaches to *his* words, with no guarantee of success. After much time spent together, a spark leaps from soul to soul, if it ever does, and kindles a fire that will now nourish itself.[25]

This is not a matter of unwritten doctrines[26] that could be put in words and one must be careful not to disclose them to the uninitiated. The philosophical core of Plato's thought cannot be put in words, since words can never be trusted. This is true not only of the written word. What cannot be written cannot be said either. Words, written or spoken, can teach us only what we already know, or little else.[27] A spark leaps, not through words.

One could say, then, as it has been said more than once, that all of Plato's dialogues are merely protreptic. Indeed, it is not the death of Socrates one should mourn, but the death of the *logos*, if it comes to pass. This is Socrates' last will and testament, in the all-important central excursus of *Phaedo*: 'Keep the *logos* alive!'[28] But there are in the dialogues no 'gaps' to be filled in oral discussion. This is not to say that no discussion or clarification followed their first 'publication', whatever that was.[29] His dialogues were not, most of them, written to be read by all. But, in them, Plato said exactly what he wanted to say. The written (or spoken) platonic dialogue goes as far as Plato believed language can go. But the rest is not silence. The rest is a *Gestalt* switch. True, an inner circle of initiated would be more likely to undergo that switch than the ordinary man-in-the-street. And even that is doubtful, as the end of *Euthydemus* shows. But if they could understand him, this was not because they had more information, rather because they shared, at least partially, Socrates'/Plato's view on *nous* and *philosophia*.

This *logos* to be continued, in Plato's interpretation, is not an open discussion. It has a very definite direction. To keep the *logos* alive is to 'save' it, to give it its metaphysical foundation, so that it can withstand the attacks of Demo-

---

24 *Euthydemus* 295c.
25 *Seventh Letter* 341c.
26 As held, in modern times, among others by Krämer 1959 and Szlezák 1993.
27 Hoffmann 1947.
28 *Phaedo* 89b. The place of the passage in the almost exact middle of the dialogue is a prime example of 'pedimental structure', as it called by Thesleff 1966, in Thesleff 2009, 28 and *passim*.
29 Thesleff 2000, 241–550.

critus' mechanicalism and Protagoras' relativistic ethics. If a real distinction between *doxa* and *episteme* cannot be supported, Protagoras won the day. Plato (as well as his own Socrates of the 'early' dialogues) had a positive view about the normativity of reason, but, due to the constraints of language, he could not have possibly put it in words other than those in common use, with a different meaning, understandable only to those who shared his views. No convincing the unconvinced. No esotericism either. Just a profound mistrust of language.

The fulcrum of Plato's thought is beyond language. Its meaning cannot convincingly be put in words. Nor can it be proved, for a proof would have to be based on some more primitive assumption, which would, again, be open to the same difficulty. That archimedean point has to be *directly* intuited. But it is not a matter of mysticism or extra-sensory perception. There is nothing mysterious about it. The *arkhe anupothetos*, or the idea of the Good, or the Beautiful of the *Symposium* are not irrational; on the contrary, they are emphatically brought up as the pinnacle of rationality. But the object of that primary intuition is not, as it has sometimes been assumed, the unhypothetical beginning. If it were, philosophy would be a deductive affair, as it was for Parmenides, with all its ensuing *aporiai*. That *arkhe* comes, paradoxically, at the *end* of the dialectical process and once achieved, all hypothetical steps leading to it are confirmed – but not until then. Until the principle is achieved – if it ever is – all these steps only have the epistemic status of opinions (*doxai*).

Therefore, if the distinction between *doxa* and *episteme* is to be kept, the idea of the Good, even if it is the result of an hypothetical procedure, cannot be a mere idea in the kantian sense. It cannot be only a postulate of reason, or else we are thrown back onto a transcendental[30] variation of Protagoras' *homomensura*, only this time not relative to the individual man but to a transcendental subject, as Kant has it – a price Plato could not be prepared to pay.

That mainspring of Plato's philosophy cannot be dependent on language nor can it be an intuited but unsupported premise of a series of deductions. The starting point of the philosophical enterprise, faithful to Plato's hypothetical method, must be an intuition of the *conclusion*, not of the first principle. It must be *outside* the dialogues, since dialogues are inevitably tied up with language and can go no further than the utterances pronounced by the participants in a particular occasion. That starting point, which demands the conviction of the participants in the philosophical enterprise, cannot be summarized in a proposition, discursively stated. That necessary basic conviction is elicited by an *event* outside the dialogues.

---

30 In a kantian sense, as distinct from transcendent.

The formative event in Plato's thought is Socrates' death. Those present at Socrates' death understood what he meant by saying that 'the unexamined life is not worth living for man'. Socrates made these words meaningful on his own person. For those who were not there, Plato (like other Socratic authors) tried to convey the significance of the moment and the emotion attached to it, as best he could, in the last scene of *Phaedo*.

All of Plato's dialogues go back to that event. Socrates is present in all of them, if not personally, at least by implication. Socrates' death shows us what meaning *he* gave to his words, as Plato saw it. A life in which reason is the servant of the passions or of mere empirical utility is not worth for man to live it. Not the death of Socrates should be mourned, but the death of the *logos*, if he dies and we cannot save it.

The unexamined life is not worth living for man. Was this just Socrates' private opinion? Those present *felt* its truth. But that opinion needs a metaphysical basis that can vouch for it, that can support it and turn it into real *episteme*. Plato's metaphysics from *Phaedo* onwards is the salvation of the *logos*; it is Socrates put on what was, for Plato, a secure basis.

For Socrates, as Plato understood him and portrayed him, reason was *normative*, in and of itself. The rational examination of one's life needs no justification. Reason is its own justification, and a human life without reason as the supreme criterion of goodness is not worth living. Not for Plato; not the Socrates of *Phaedo* or the *Symposium*. But that is already matter for another paper.

Works Cited

Allen, R E (ed.) 1965, *Studies in Plato's Metaphysics*, Routledege & Kegan Paul, London.
Berkeley, George 1713, *Three Dialogues between Hylas and Philonous*.
Cherniss, H F 1957, 'The relation of the Timaeus to Plato's later dialogues', in Allen 1965.
Cornford, F M 1932, 'Mathematics and dialectic in the Republic vi-vii', in 1965.
Crombie, Ian M 1962, *An Examination of Plato's Doctrines*, Routledge & K. Paul, London.
Desjardins, Rosemarie 1988, 'Why dialogues?', in Griswold Jr. 1988, 110–15.
Galileo Galilei 1632, *Dialogo dei due massimi sistemi del mondo*.
Giannantoni, Gabriele 1983, *Socraticorum reliquiae*, Bibliopolis, Roma.
Griswold Jr., C.L. (ed.) 1988, Platonic writings / Platonic readings Routledge, London.
Hoffmann, Ernst 1947, 'Die literarische Voraussetzungen des Platonsverständnisses', Zeitschrift für philosophische Forschung 2, 465–480
Krämer, Martin 1959, Arete bei Plato und Aristoteles, Heidelberg.
Owen, G E L 1953, 'The place of the Timaeus in Plato's dialogues', in Allen 1965.
Press, Gerald A 1993, *Plato's dialogues: New studies and interpretations*, Rowman & Littlefield, Lanham, Md.
Quintilianus, Marcus Fabius, *Institutio oratoria*.

Scolnicov, Samuel 1975, 'Hypothetical method and rationality in Plato', *Kant-Studien* 66, 157–162.
Scolnicov, Samuel 2004, 'Plato's ethics of irony', in Maurizio Migliori (ed.), *Plato ethicus* Academia Verlag, St. Augustin, 289–300.
Szlezák, Thomas A 1993, *Platon lesen*, frommann-holzboog, Stuttgart.
Thesleff, Holger 2000, 'Plato and his public' (2000), *Studies in the styles of Plato*, 241–250.
Thesleff, Holger 2009, *Platonic patterns: A collection of studies*, Parmenides Publishing, Zurich.
Thesleff, Holger 1966, *Studies in the styles of Plato* (1966), now reprinted in Thesleff 2009, 28 and passim.
Vlastos, Gregory 1991, 'Socratic irony', in *Socrates: Ironist and moral philosopher*, Cambridge University Press Cambridge, 21–44.

Raúl Gutiérrez[1]
The Three Waves of Dialectic in the *Republic*

The alleged lack of unity of the *Republic* has become increasingly questioned. There are several strategies to show that this unity exists. One of the most common ones is to recognize in *Republic* I the anticipation of positions that will not be developed thoroughly until further on.[2] Thus H.-J. Krämer (1959, p. 53 ff.) has recognized in Socrates' three final arguments in *Republic* I – the arguments about *pleonexia* (348b8–350c11); about cooperation (350c12–352d2); and about the relationship between natural or artificial beings, their *arete* and function (352d2–354a7) – an anticipation of the fundamental ontological positions developed in the following books. However, if we change perspective, one might claim that those arguments are nothing more than a draft and, thus, an image of different aspects of the notion of justice.[3] Accordingly, the correspondence between natural or artificial beings, their *arete* and their function, can be understood as an image of the correspondence between a *physis* and an *ergon*,[4] since this correspondence is, in turn, explicitly qualified by Socrates not only as an *eidōlon* of psychic justice (443c4–5), but also as an *archē* and a *typos* of his project of forming citizens for the just city (443c1), which, as such, leaves its stamp on the soul of the receiver, that is, on the soul of someone

---

[1] I would like to thank Alexandra Alván for translating this paper and Peter Simpson for carefully reading the translation. My aim here is to explain in more detail what I presented in Gutiérrez, R. (2009). So I set to one side questions about the *koinōnia* of Ideas and the *Parmenides*. I had already in the cited paper considered the three waves as hypotheses, each of which relied on a superior hypothesis that explained it. Here I further develop the analysis of the third wave following closely Benson's (2008) analysis of the third wave. I was not aware of Benson's paper when I wrote my earlier paper.
[2] Cf. Kahn, C. (1993); Wilson, J.R.S. (1995). Wilson presents Thrasymachus as an illustration of the *thymoeides*. The starting point for his argument is *R.* 411e1, where, as at 439b4, he is said to be ὥσπερ θηρίον, referring, according to Wilson, to the *thymoeides* (59). In the first passage, however, the soul's trichotomy has not yet been fully developed (the *epithymētikon* is not mentioned), and it is not until the 439b4 passage that this characterization is referred to the *epithymētikon*, the determinant one. The reference to Thrasymachus' "leonine" aspect and to his search of εὐδοκιμεῖν and φιλονικεῖν (338a6–7), which are without doubt present in Thrasymachus, favours Wilson's interpretation, but it seems to me that both his calculating and spirited parts appear in him as subordinated to his desiring part.
[3] Cf. Gutiérrez, R (2013, 2015).
[4] Cf. *inter alia* 370a; c3–5; 374a5–6.

who embarks on the process of formation presented in the allegory of the cave. Finally, the definition of justice as 'doing one's own thing' –τὸ τὰ αὑτοῦ πράττειν– implies that it is understood as an image of the intelligible order, a *kata logon* order, that is, an order in accordance with reason and, thus, in accordance with the foundation which is the Idea of Good. The order, therefore, is one in which none of its members, Ideas, either do injustice to each other or suffer it at the hands of each other (οὔτ' ἀδικοῦντα οὔτ' ἀδικούμενα ὑπ'ἀλλήλων) (500c2–5), which means that they are just and, consequently, that each one minds his own business –occupies his place– according to the correspondence between *physis* and *ergon*.[5] This multiple articulation of the discourse on justice responds to the Platonic conception of the "art of conversion" (τέχνη τῆς περιαγωγῆς), an art whose aim is to educate individuals "most easily and efficiently" (ῥᾷστά τε καὶ ἀνυσιμώτατα, 518d). For if one wants justice to dwell in all the members of a community (433d ff.), one must articulate it in a language that is comprehensible to its different interlocutors and, for this reason, one must even turn to the use of images that aid in the comprehension of it.[6] Hence, after considering this ascending development in the Republic in the first section of this paper, I will try to show that the image of the three waves (τρικυμία), introduced in Republic V and concluded in Republic VI, constitute an image of dialectic and an example of it put into practice.

I

After examining the conventional conceptions of justice, and after offering as an alternative the image of his own conception of justice in the final section of *Republic* I, Plato makes Glaucon and Adeimantus ask about the nature of justice and injustice, as well as about the power (δύναμις) that they have by themselves due to their presence in the soul (358b4–6; 366d7-e9). The investigation focuses,

---

5 That psychic justice is an image of intelligible justice is justified by the exhortation to the philosopher to imitate and make himself like (μιμεῖσθαί τε καὶ μάλιστα ἀφομοιοῦσθαι) the intelligible order, so that he becomes "ordered and divine" and is in a condition to put "what he sees there into the dispositions of men, both in private and in public" and thus to act as a *demiurge* of virtue (500c5-d8).

6 Not only is the third argument above mentioned (the one concerning the correspondence between natural and artificial beings and their *arete* and function) explained this way, but so also is the comparison in general of justice with *technē* in Republic I, cf. R. 335c5–334b6; 335b2-d13; 340d1–342e11; 345c7–347a6; 349d13–350c11. A justification for this interpretation of *Republic* is offered by Phaedr. 277b-c.

then, on psychic justice. However, since they have not been persuaded by Socrates' arguments, Glaucon and Adeimantus decide to take on the role of devil's advocates and defend Thrasymachus' position. They ask Socrates, who has dedicated his whole life to examining justice, to undertake the defence of justice (367d8-e1). Socrates proposes then, in accordance with the mentioned art of conversion, the analogy between *polis* and *psychē* (368c7–369a3). For, according to him, someone who cannot see sharply enough (368c8) so as to examine justice in the soul directly ought to study it there where it can more easily be learnt (ῥᾷων καταμαθεῖν, 368e8; cf. 435d8), namely in something bigger (368e7), in the polis. So the investigation of political justice is introduced with the aim of studying psychic justice, since, as more precisely stated later, the former is conceived as an image (εἴδωλον) of the latter (443c4–5). Such a procedure –resorting to an image to study its original– is characteristic of *dianoia* (cf. 510b; 511a), but one should not leave out of sight the fact that right up to *Republic* IV, 434d-e the investigation focuses on the genesis of the polis. Only after that is the proposal pursued of translating to the individual what has been made evident in the polis.[7] However, although it is easier to investigate in bigger letters a thing that is seen further away and in smaller letters, the place where these bigger letters are found (as is signalled by Socrates with a clear reference to the inside of the cave and so to the sensible region) seems "hard going and steeped in shadows" (δύσβατος καὶ ἐπίσκιος), "dark and hard to search out" (σκοτεινὸς καὶ δυσδιερεύνητος, 432c7–8).[8] Nevertheless, Socrates adds, it is manifest that justice is present somehow (πῃ, 432c1) and that now, after the foundation of the city in *Republic* II, they have found the "track" (ἴχνος, 432d3) of justice, namely the correspondence between *physis* and *ergon* (433a4–9). Moreoover, when in *Republic* IV 434d we are invited to transfer to the individual what has been established about the polis, we are also warned that they (that is, the original and the image) must be "rubbed" against each other, in order to see if there is a correspondence (ὁμολογία, 434d4; e3–4) between them. Although resort to an image to study the original is characteristic of *dianoia* (510b; 510d), yet it brings with it a limitation to the investigation, the lack of accuracy (435d1). A "longer and further road" (μακροτέρα καὶ πλείων ὁδός) is required, a road which, in regard to the study of soul, will not be followed here (435d). The reason is that the criterion according to which one could establish firmly the similitude between just city and just man is the Idea of justice itself (κατ'αὐτὸ τὸ τῆς δικαιοσύνης εἶδος, 435b1–2),

---

[7] Cf. *R.* 434d3: ἐὰν μὲν ἡμῖν καὶ εἰς ἕνα ἕκαστον τῶν ἀνθρώπων ἰὸν τὸ εἶδος τοῦτο ὁμολογῆται καὶ ἐκεῖ δικαιοσύνη εἶναι, συγχωρησόμεθα ἤδη. 434e3: ὃ οὖν ἡμῖν ἐφάνη, ἐπαναφέρωμεν εἰς τὸν ἕνα, κἂν μὲν ὁμολογῆται, καλῶς ἕξει.

[8] I have followed Bloom's translation (1991²), but often with some changes.

which, at least up to this point, has not yet been fully considered.[9] Instead, reference is made to what has been obtained through the analysis of the structure of the polis and its virtues, and therefore Socrates and his interlocutors are only going to investigate if the soul has "these three [same] forms in it [as the polis] or not" (435b-c; e). Nonetheless, we find here a change in perspective, or the properly dianoetic turn, for the investigation about the structure of the soul itself has recourse to a hypothesis according to which "it is clear that the same thing won't be willing at the same time to do or suffer opposites with regard to the same and in relation to the same thing".[10] Thus, instead of proceeding dialectically, Socrates relies on this principle as a hypothesis, a principle which, after the manner of mathematicians, he takes as an assumption and as an assumption that will allow him to establish if in each and every case we act as a result of one species or if, since there are three species, sometimes we act as a result of one of them, and sometimes as a result of another (436a8-b3). And if the trichotomy can be deduced from that hypothesis assumed as a principle, then it will be possible to analyse in the individual the same virtues as in the city (435c). Now if, using the method so far, Socrates refers to analogy, his investigation must be insufficient to reach the desired accuracy, since this investigation of the original will continue to be conditioned by the image. An adequate dialectical analysis is required, which, as we have already pointed out, is not given here.[11] But the resort to a hypothesis, which is assumed as a principle and criterion for the division of the soul, suggests that, from this point on, the method being applied is that described in the segment of the line that corresponds to *dianoia*. This method allows for the establishing and separating of the soul's species in such a way that the analysis of the virtues can then be undertaken.

Now, the coincidence of this method with the hypothetico-deductive method is manifest in the very terms used. In both cases they start (1) with a hypothesis

---

9 Just like the proposal of the analogy between *polis* and *psychē* in *Republic* IV, the resort to the Idea of justice at this point of the argument shows, it seems to me, that Socrates, the guide in the dialogue, is always one step ahead of his interlocutors. In *Republic* IV the analogy is proposed, which is a procedure characteristic of *dianoia*, but the investigation focuses first on the polis; likewise our passage here refers to the Idea of justice and to dialectic, but now the procedure is immediately dianoetic.

10 R. 436b8–9: Δῆλον ὅτι ταὐτὸν τἀναντία ποιεῖν ἢ πάσχειν κατὰ ταὐτόν γε καὶ πρὸς ταὐτὸν οὐκ ἐθελήσει ἅμα. Cf. 436e8–437a2.

11 We must bear in mind that, in the *Republic*, Socrates expressly restricts his consideration of the soul to the way in which "we now see it" (ὥσπερ νῦν ἡμεῖς θεώμωθα), "in the present" (ἐν τῷ παρόντι), "maimed by community with body and other evils", but not "as it is in truth" (οἷον δ'ἐστὶν τῇ ἀληθείᾳ) "when it has become pure" (οἷον ἐστιν καθαρὸν γιγνόμενον), 611b10-c7. Cf. Szlezák, T.A. (1976).

(ὑποθέμενοι, 437a6; cf. 510c3, 6; ἐξ ὑποθέσεων) – mathematical beings and the principle of non-contradiction or opposites – and proceed to their respective conclusions, that is, about the topic of their investigation – the properties of mathematical beings and the division of the soul. And they both assume (2) their hypotheses as manifest (δῆλον, 436b8; φανερῶν, 510d1). In the simile of the line the practitioners of the method are said to act as though they knew these hypotheses and had no need to give any account of them to themselves or to others (510c6–7). To use the language of *Republic* IV, they do not feel compelled to go through all the objections or to spend a long time making sure they're not true (437a4–6), nor are they scared or persuaded by the objections (436e8–9). Furthermore, these two methods both seek (3) the agreement of thought with itself (ὁμολγήσαντες, 437a6; ὁμολογουμένως, 510d2), that is, consistency between the hypotheses and the consequences, such that "if it should ever appear otherwise" we shall have to admit that "all our conclusions based on it [the hypothesis] will be undone" (437a7–9, Bloom). Finally, (4) just as in the case of *dianoia*'s resort to images (510b; d), we should not forget that the analysis of the division of the soul is still conditioned by the analogy and, hence, by the reference to political justice as an image of justice in the soul. Now, at the very beginning of the examination of the soul's structure, it was said that one ought to rub the soul and the polis against each other to see if, in regard to justice, there was a correspondence (ὁμολογία, 434d4; e3–4) between them. Something else is also added that somehow makes point (3) clearer, that is, that if there is correspondence between justice in the polis and justice in the soul, the argument would be consistent, but if something else shows up in the individual, then justice in the polis will have to be examined again (434e4–5). Anyway, there's an important change of perspective here. The resort to political justice in order to study psychic justice has a pedagogical purpose, to make the study of the latter "easier" (434d9; 368e8). However, although the image is considered in *Republic* IV, the examination of the soul's structure itself takes as starting point a principle that is formulated for the first time within and by the reflection of the soul on itself, namely the principle of contradiction (or, according to some, of opposites), whose clarity and evidence (436b8) is, without doubt, greater than that of political justice studied so far. Certainly, the analysis of the soul's structure and of justice as based on this principle is intended to provide greater clarity than the analysis based on the analogy between polis and soul, but it does not allow one to achieve the accuracy that is apparently only possible through dialectic. In this sense, in contrast to the dark and shadowy place where political justice is examined, a place is said to have been reached by the end of the investigation of psychic justice where we can attain a most clear vision (σαφέστατα, 445b6); we have ascended (ἀναβεβήκαμεν) to a height of *logos* from which, as from a lookout, we can observe that there is only "one form for excellence and an unlimited number for vice, but some four among them are also worth mentioning" (445c).[12] That clarity, however, does not amount to as much as one could supposedly attain with dialectic.

II

Republic IV concludes with Socrates' explicit recognition of the ascent that has been made by thought up to that point. And at the beginning of *Republic* V Socrates intends to continue the dialogue with a presentation of the deficient forms of government and souls, but he is detained by Polemarchus and Adeimantus, who think he has "faultily" (φαύλως, 449c4) examined one entire aspect of the issue, and they want him to do it "sufficiently" (ἱκανῶς, 449e7). The issue in question is the community of women and children among the guardians of the polis (449d4). And the reason for the faultiness is a lack of foundation: λόγου δεῖται (449c7–8). If one limits the sense of *logos* here to a simple explanation of the community in question one is failing to consider (1) that Socrates declares that he had already foreseen the first time he brought this issue up that it would unleash a "swarm of arguments" (ἑσμὸν λόγων, 450b1), by which image he undoubtedly means to refer to dialectic;[13] (2) that the required explanation must be *sufficient* and that, thus, it takes us to a series of arguments that must be developed "in due measure"(μετρίων, 450b5). And Glaucon adds: "For intelligent men, Socrates, the proper measure of listening to such arguments is a whole life."[14] This means that those who have understood what is at stake, and how fundamental and decisive the dialectic exercise is, will not doubt to dedicate their entire lives to it.[15] The term μετρίων is, thus, understood in a strong sense, and ultimately leads us back to the absolute measure, to the corresponding Ideas in each case and, in general, to the Idea of Good.[16] This is,

---

12 R. 445c5–6: ἓν μὲν εἶναι εἶδος τῆς ἀρετῆς, ἄπειρα δὲ τῆς κακίας, τέτταρα δ'ἐν αὐτοῖς ἄττα ὧν καὶ ἄξιον ἐπιμνησθῆναι.
13 Cf. Halliwell, S. (1998, p.135, note *ad loc.*)
14 Cf. 450b6–7: Μέτρον τοιούτων λόγων ἀκούειν ὅλος ὁ βίος νοῦν ἔχουσιν.
15 See the corresponding note by Leroux, G. (2000, pp. 619–620, n. 5). Cf. *R.* 498d, where Socrates even claims the possibility of continuing with the philosophical dialogue after death. See also *Gorg.* 511c-513a; *Theaet.* 173c and *Pol.* 283c.
16 Cf. 504c1–3: "My friend, a measure in such things, which in any way falls short of that which *is*, is no measure at all (μετρίως). For nothing incomplete is the measure of anything." ('Ἀλλ', ὦ φίλε, μέτρον τῶν τοιούτων ἀπολεῖπον καὶ ὁτιοῦν τοῦ ὄντος οὐ πάνυ μετρίως γίγνεται· ἀτελὲς

therefore, the required foundation. Finally, one should also consider (3) that the reference to the foundation keeps perfect symmetry with the return to the examination of the deficient forms of government and souls in *Republic* VIII. For Socrates points out there that they will try to proceed as adequate judges (ἱκανοὶ κριταί, 545c5) so that observation and judgement can take place in accordance with the foundation (κατὰ λόγον, 545c6–7) laid down in the central books.[17]

Now, as we know from the simile of the line, dialectic also starts from hypotheses that, as in the case of dianoetic procedure, serve to explain the issues proposed. In this sense, dialectic proposes a hypothesis and examines if it has as a consequence the answer to the formulated question. But, unlike *dianoia*, it does not consider hypotheses as principles, but as actual hypotheses that, as such, require in turn an explanation and foundation (511b4–5). That is why dialectic considers hypotheses as steppingstones or springboards (οἷον ἐπιβάσεις τε καὶ ὁρμάς) that lead to the unhypothetical and first principle of the whole and to contact with it (511b6–7). This ascending road is followed by a descending one that, again in contrast to *dianoia*, does not resort to sensible images, but only to Ideas (511b7-c1; cf. 476a; 596a). The image of steppingstones and springboards toward the principle is understood in *Republic* 533c7-d1 in terms of an *anairesis* of hypotheses, that is, in terms of an overcoming of their merely hypothetical character by means of successive superior hypotheses that allow one to reach solid ground in the ultimate principle, that is, actual presence in the principle. In *Republic* 534b8-c3 it is added, furthermore, that the dialectician ought to be able (1) to offer a definition of the being (λόγος τῆς οὐσίας) of everything, even of the Idea of Good, distinguishing it from everything else (ἀπὸ τῶν ἄλλων πάντων ἀφελών); (2) to soar above all the objections (διὰ πάντων ἐλέγχων), as in a battle; and (3) trying to refute them (ἐλέγχειν) not according to *doxa*, but according to essence (κατ' οὐσίαν), and to run along all these roads with invincible argument. Worth noting is that, in this manner, the *elenchus* becomes an integral part of the dialectical method and constitutes, as we shall see, a way of confirming the respective hypothesis. Finally, in 537c7 the dialectician is described as one who is able to reunite multiplicity in and through unity (συνοπτικός),[18] and in 454a5–7 there is reference to the complementary procedure of

---

γὰρ οὐδὲν οὐδένος μέτρον)". The last sentence refers to the "longer way" just mentioned (504b2) as much a to its goal, the Idea of the Good.

17 Cf. Gutiérrez, R. (2003).
18 See the implicit reference to συναγωγή in 507b2–7 and to the σύνοψις of mathematics in 537c2–3.

division (κατ'εἴδη διαιρούμενοι).¹⁹ In this sense, the distinction and the *koinōnia* between the unity of each Idea and its multiple appearances, be these intelligible or visible (475e9–476a7),²⁰ can be understood as the ontological condition for the possibility of these procedures. Anyway, we must not forget that Socrates expressly points out that he will not reveal all that he understands as dialectic (532d8-e1); instead he will only submit himself to an image (εἰκόνα, 533a3) of dialectic.²¹ And such an image of dialectic is what, according to our proposal, is precisely put into practice in *Republic* V–VI.

III

As we know, *Republic* V is structured according to the image of a sequence of three waves (τρικυμία, 472a4), each one bigger and more difficult to overcome than the previous one,²² so much so that even the help of a dolphin, or of any other extraordinary form of rescue, is required to get one through them (453d9–11). It seems to me that the *trikymia* is part of a wide variety of *images* of dialectic.²³ So, the first wave examines the community (κοινωνία) of functions between men and women, the second examines the community (κοινωνία) of women and children, and the third examines the feasibility of the just city. What is examined is whether these things are possible or not (450c-d; 452e5; 456c4; 457d9; 471c6–7). We are facing, then, a sequence of issues to be examined. And the first one is: "whether female human nature can share in common with the nature of the male class in all functions or in none at all, or in some things yes and in others no, particularly with respect to war" (453a1–4). The hypothesis that serves as a starting point for the examination of this issue is the agreement established in *Republic* II-IV regarding the correspondence between one *physis* and one *ergon*: "you yourselves agreed that each one must mind his own business according to nature".²⁴ Further, the hypothesis is the notion

---

19 Against this see Halliwell, S. (1998, p.148): "It is hard to deny a connection altogether (...). Yet the *Rep.* itself contains no statement of the collection-and-division method (...); so it is implausible that P. already has a fully developed concept of the method." How can we know such a thing? The expression κατ'εἴδη διαιρούμενοι is expressly referred to the Ideas by Penner, T. (2006, pp. 243–244); Szlezák, T.A. (2004, p. 37). Cf. Gutiérrez, R. (2009).
20 For a justification of the discourse on sensible and intelligible appearances see: Ferrari, F. (2000). Cf. Gutiérrez, R. (2009).
21 See Szlezák, T.A. (2004, pp. 24–35).
22 Cf. 457b7; c4–5; 472a3–4; 473c6–7.
23 Cf. Halliwell, S. (1998, p.135, note to 450b1).
24 Cf. 453b4–5: ὡμολογεῖτε δεῖν κατὰ φύσιν ἕκαστον ἕνα ἓν τὸ αὑτοῦ πράττειν.

of justice itself (453d–e), which is at this point without doubt the most solid or unyielding.²⁵ However, an attempt is made to refute the hypothesis, based on a certain way of understanding the terms of the hypothesis: "Can it be that a woman doesn't differ in her nature very much from a man?" (453b2–3). If women do differ – as is initially admitted –, they couldn't undertake the same functions, which means that he who holds this hypothesis is mistaken and contradicts himself in thinking that the community of functions of men and women follows from the aforementioned hypothesis (453b10c1). It is precisely then by introducing the maritime images of dialectic, that we are invited to start swimming, be it amid the biggest sea or in a little swimming pool (453d5–7)²⁶. Consequently it is not accidental that this is followed by a *diairesis* between the arts of disputation and of dialectic, the first of which proceeds on the basis of merely nominal distinctions (κατὰ τὸ ὄνομα, 454a7), while the second on the basis of eidetic distinctions (κατ' εἴδη διαιρούμενοι, 454a6).²⁷ It is necessary, then, to determine in what sense we speak of identity and difference of natures when we speak of the correspondence between *physis* and *ergon*, whether we are speaking in absolute or relative terms (οὐ πάντως, 454c7–8). Evidently the word *physis*, when said in relative terms, is only being used, specifically with regard to occupations (τὸ πρὸς αὐτὰ τεῖνον τὰ ἐπιτηδεύματα, 454d1), to mean "natural aptitude" to carry out a function in a better and easier way than others (370a-c). On the other hand, if we were to understand the identity and difference of natures in absolute terms, the bold and the hairy would have opposing natures and could not share the same occupations, which is absurd (454c); but keeping the relative sense in mind, a man and a woman endowed with the ability for medicine would share the same nature or "natural aptitude", and not so a physician and a carpenter (454c–d). Neither does the biological difference between men and women spoil the consistency between the hypothesis and the community of functions (454d–e). There will only be a difference regarding the strength and weakness of men and women, though not in the aspects that concern the exercise of their different occupations, that is, the skill to learn, good memory and the bodily conditions that are adequate for the development of thought

---

25 Cf. *Phaid.* 100a3–7: καὶ ὑποθέμενος ἑκάστοτε λόγον ὃν ἂν κρίνω ἐρρωμενέστατον εἶναι, ἃ μὲν ἄν μοι δοκῇ τούτῳ συμφωνεῖν τίθεμι ὡς ἀληθῆ ὄντα [...], ἃ δ' ἂν μή, ὡς οὐκ ἀληθῆ. It seems that this is the method applied in what follows, cf. Benson, H.H. (2008). However, the difficulties that the comparison of this stage of the method with that described in 101d3–5 generate, mainly due to the meaning of συμφωνεῖν, are well known; on this matter see: Gentzler, J. (1991, p. 267); Kahn, C. (1996, p. 316); Kanayama, Y. (2000, pp. 62–66).
26 Cf. *Phdr.* 264a5; *Prm.* 137a5–6.
27 Cf. *Phaedr.* 265d ff. See *supra* p. 7 and note 18.

(455b4-c2). Furthermore, Socrates suggests that the male sex excels the female sex in every sense, but by introducing the comparison he is showing that "there is no practice of a city's governors which belongs to woman because she's woman, or to man because he's man; but the natures are scattered alike among both animals; and woman participates according to nature in all practices, and man in all, but in all of them woman is weaker than man" (455d6-e2). In this way, with a clear reference to the Platonic conceptions of justice and injustice, it is precisely stated that while the proposed legislation is *kata physin*, the current institutions are constituted *para physin* (456c; cf. 444d–e). Consequently, by being in accordance with nature, the community of functions is also possible (457c1–2). Now, those who are best by nature, be they male or female, will be educated in the same way with the purpose that they achieve the greatest excellence, which is, in turn, what's best for the polis (456e). In conclusion, as Socrates states, "the argument is in agreement with itself in that it says what is both possible and beneficial" (πῃ τὸν λόγον αὐτὸν αὑτῷ ὁμολογεῖσθαι ὡς δυνατά τε καὶ ὠφέλιμα λέγει, 457c1–2), that is, that the community of functions follows directly and immediately –without resorting to sensible experience– from the hypothesis of the correspondence between nature and function. Or put in terms of the description of the dialectician (534c1–3), Socrates refutes the attempt of refutation of the hypothesis by basing himself not on *doxa*, on which the refutation attempt is most definitely based, but on *ousia*.

Now, this community of functions of women and men requires the community of women and children, for it is from this "lineage of guardians" (466c–d) that those who share the same nature ought to be chosen, and so they will be able to share their functions. The first community, then, demands selective marriages and the abolishment of the traditional family. So, after explaining how that community can be implemented, the second wave examines whether the community of women and children follows (ἑπομένη, 461d7) from the hypothesis presupposed by the proposed constitution.[28] And the hypothesis –the ἀρχὴ τῆς ὁμολογίας, 462a2– is that the greater good for the polis is "what binds it together and makes it one" and the greatest evil, what "splits it and makes it many instead of one" (462a9–b3). It is this hypothesis that the legislator must bear in mind as he establishes his laws and he must examine whether the political or-

---

[28] The previous section, 458c-461e, is limited to the examination of the organizational aspect, that is, "how the rulers will arrange these things when they come into being" (458b4), while the 462a-466d section examines its possibility. Halliwell already notices that the latter "will be eventually construed as concerned with the ultimate conditions (the *sine qua non*: philosopher rulers [that is, the third wave, R.G.]) needed to put such a scheme into practice", Halliwell, S. (1998, p. 157, commentary to 458b3–5).

ganization proposed harmonizes with the tracks of good or evil (462a2–7). Once again, as with the first wave, the hypothesis agrees with the already mentioned Platonic conception of justice. For, conceived as *idiopragia*, it establishes a harmonic order, a perfect unity out of what is multiple (παντάπασιν ἕνα γενόμενον ἐκ πολλῶν, 443e1), both in the political and psychic communities. This is the reason why it is said that the best governed polis is that which resembles most a man whose community of body and soul form a unique order governed by a unique guiding principle, in such a way that the whole of it feels and suffers simultaneously even if only one part is afflicted (462c-d). Hence, what binds the city together is the community of pleasure and pain, and what splits it apart is their particularization (462b). And that is only possible in a city where people say "my own" and "not my own" in the same way and with respect to the same thing (462b-c).

Once this similarity between a just city and a just man is established, the next step is to examine whether the consequences that follow from the hypothesis –τὰ τοῦ λόγου ὁμολογήματα– match Kallipolis to a greater degree than other cities (462e). The same community of women and children also follows from the hypothesis for this reason, that while in other cities rulers consider their colleagues as relatives or strangers, in Kallipolis guardians see them as brothers or sisters, fathers or mothers, sons or daughters, descendants or ancestors (463b10-c7).[29] And in accordance with this, the corresponding praxis will be prescribed (463c-d). Thus in Kallipolis, more than in any other city, citizens will agree in saying whether they are doing well or not and will unanimously say: "my own affairs are doing well or badly" (463e3–5). The aforementioned community of pleasures and pains will follow from this way of thinking and speaking. Certainly, the immediate cause (αἰτία) of this community is the community of women and children, which, in turn, depends on the hypothesis that unity is the greatest good for the polis (464b1–7). The consequences then are the abolishment of property (464b8–c4), unity of opinion, and the orientation of all towards one same goal (464d3–5); as well as the disappearance of the different forms of conflict (464d7–465b4) and, consequently, the instauration of complete peace (465b5–10). The happiness of the guardians is, ultimately, the result of this, "a life more blessed than that most blessed one the Olympic victors live" (465d). This way Socrates is able to respond to the only objection that comes up in this wave, that is, that "being able to have it all", the guardians of Kallipolis

---

[29] These changes at the lexicological level also include the disappearance of certain denominations, e.g. δεσπότας and δουλός, etc., which evidently reflect a transformation in power balance, cf. 463a-b.

"have nothing"; for, in this way, they will be happier than the rest of the citizens, since they will be provided with "everything necessary to life –both they themselves and their children as well", they will receive honours from the State and a worthy burial (465e–466b). Finally, legislation about war, the education of children (466d6–469b4) and the fostering of the PanHellenic ideal (469b5–c3) are also established. In general, the laws deduced from the hypothesis reach such a level of concreteness that one might be able to forget Socrates' insistence on the fact that the paradigm of the good State he has proposed is only a model drawn in arguments or speech (τῷ λόγῳ, 473a5–b1), something that we should not forget, since the entire legislation of Kallipolis should, according to the method, be derived from the hypothesis.[30]

However, having already pointed out in the second wave that the just city is similar to the just man, Socrates recognizes now that the latter is nothing else than the closest possible approximation to what justice is and that the just man participates in it to a greater degree than the rest (472b7–c3),[31] for, in the end, it is justice itself alone that constitutes the true paradigm (472c3–4).[32] The second wave has definitely picked up the argument from *Republic* II–IV regarding the similarity between the just polis and the just man, but only now, in the transition from the second to the third wave, the difference between the Ideas and the instances that participate in them is established, configuring in this way the normative and paradigmatic role of the Ideas.[33] So, the result of the investigation of *Republic* II-IV, the definition of psychic justice, conditioned initially by the reference to political justice as its image, is recognized as a hypothesis in the first and second waves, and, from now on, it will be referred to the original, the Idea of justice, which, as we will see as the third wave unfolds, returns us to a third form of community (κοινωνία), the community of the intelligible order as the authentic paradigm of justice. This way, which was announced, though not developed, in *Republic* IV 435b, namely the need to rely on the Idea of justice as a criterion to decide about the similarity between city and soul, starts to reveal itself as an argument.

The third wave examines what the previous wave had assumed and what is expressly recognized as the *sine qua non* of all goods, including the community of functions of men and women, and the community of women and children

---

30 Cf. 472d9–473b2.
31 Cf. 472b7-c3, especially c1–3: ἢ ἀγαπήσομεν ἐὰν ὅτι ἐγγύτατα αὐτῆς ᾖ καὶ πλεῖστα τῶν ἄλλων ἐκείνης μετέχῃ; Οὕτως, ἔφη· ἀγαπήσομεν.
32 Cf. *R.* 472c4–5: Παραδείγματος ἄρα ἕνεκα ... ἐζητοῦμεν αὐτό τε δικαιοσύνης οἷον ἐστι.
33 Cf. Vegetti, M. (2000, p. 85, n. 105).

among the guardians[34]: "I see that, if it should come into being [such a political regime], everything would be good for the city (...), they would be best at fighting their enemies too because they would least desert one another, these men who recognize each others as brothers, fathers and sons", obviously due to the community of women and children; and in virtue of the community of functions of men and women, "if the females join in the campaign (...), they would be unbeatable. And I see" –Socrates adds– "all the good things that they would have at home and are left out in your account. Take it that I agree that there would be all these things and countless others if this regime should come into being..." (471c8–e2). The third wave is then the greatest and most difficult, being, in a certain way, the superior hypothesis (472a). Socrates had already recognized this by the beginning of the second wave, since he compared himself to people of idle spirit, who consider what they want as something already real, and please themselves by reviewing what they will do once their wish is granted; in this same sense, he postpones the examination of the feasibility of the just polis, assuming it as possible, and commits himself to the examination of 1) how rulers would organize it once it came to be, and 2) how, already having come to be, the community of women and children is the most agreeable for the city and for the guardians (458a–b). Actually, there is a greater display of dialectic procedure in the third wave. For this wave is not only limited, like the previous ones, to identifying a hypothesis –in this case, whether philosophy and political power coincide (473c11; d1–2; d2–3)– from which it is possible to deduce what was proposed in the first place –whether Kallipolis is possible–,[35] but it also proposes a superior hypothesis within the wave, a hypothesis that ought to serve as an explanation for the initial hypothesis. The new hypothesis refers to the nature of philosophy (472a–480a), for "if we should come to an adequate agreement about that, we'll also agree that the same men [philosophers] possess both [sets of qualities]" (ἐὰν ἐκείνην ἱκανῶς ὁμολογήσωμεν, ὁμολογήσειν καὶ ὅτι οἷοί τε ταῦτα ἔχειν οἱ αὐτοί) necessary and sufficient to rule and "that there should be no other leaders of cities than these" (485a4–8; cf. 474b3–c7). Agreeing sufficiently on these matters means that the hypothesis of the coincidence between philosophy and political power follows directly from the hypothesis

---

[34] Cf. 458a-b.

[35] There is evidently here a reciprocal conditionality, for if philosophy and political power coincide, then Kallipolis would be possible, but, in turn, that coincidence would only be possible if Kallipolis were possible. However, as Benson observes, Socrates focuses his attention on the coincidence of philosophy and political power, cf. Benson, H.H. (2008, pp. 95 and 110 n. 34).

about the nature of philosophy and, consequently, that Kallipolis would be possible.[36]

Now, in the third wave, the issue of the feasibility of the proposed political regime is examined assuming as hypothesis the coincidence of philosophy and political power. This is the necessary and sufficient condition for the possibility of a just polis.[37] Its foundation requires considering the nature of philosophy. However, we will not examine here the thoroughly discussed final section of *Republic* V,[38] instead, we will only refer to the summary presented at the beginning of *Republic* VI. Socrates says there that philosophers can attain the knowledge of what behaves always in the same way and according to itself, that is, of the Ideas; of the *philodoxoi*, on the other hand, he says that they only have opinions and "wander among what is many and varies in all ways". This distinction leads to the question about which of them should govern (484b3–6). It's plain that if the aim is for them "to give laws about what is fine, just and good, if any need to be given, and as guardians to preserve those that are already established" (484d1–3), philosophical knowledge turns out to be necessary for just political power, and, consequently, philosophers will be called upon to govern. From the start, philosophers surpass the *philodoxoi* on the main issue, knowledge, but they ought not to "lack experience or fall short of the others in any other part of virtue" (484d5–7). Knowledge and virtue are then the necessary and sufficient conditions for authentic political power. But the question then is whether knowledge is sufficient for virtue (485a1–2). And that is precisely what is examined in the following section (485a10–487a8). Thus, just as he whose desires are weakened for everything else is dragged by desires towards only one thing,

---

[36] It seems to me that Benson, H.H. (2008) has convincingly shown that the 471c-502c section constitutes a clear illustration of the dialectic method in the same sense in which we have been reading the first two waves, though it is more amply developed in the third. So, Benson distinguishes two phases in the dialectic process, 1) the identification of the hypothesis (471c-473e) and 2) the confirmation of the hypothesis; this second phase has, in turn, two moments, 2.1) the argument that accounts for the hypothesis through a superior hypothesis (473e-487a) and 2.2) the argument that confirms the hypothesis in confrontation with its *alleged* or apparent consequences. From now on we shall be following Benson closely.

[37] Socrates refers to the sufficient condition when he says he could show that Kallipolis is possible by changing only one thing that would change everything (473c2–4), and to the necessary condition when he says that "unless the philosophers rule (...) there is no rest from ills for the cities, nor I think for human kind, nor will the regime we have now described in speech ever come forth from nature" (473c11-e2). Cf. Benson, H.H. (2008, p. 95).

[38] There's ample bibliography on this topic. I have expressed my former view in Gutiérrez, R. (2009). The dissertation of Hartenburg, G.J. (2011) has allowed me to correct my view in a fundamental way, mostly on the idea of "soothe and gently persuading" the lover of sights and "disguising from him that he is not healthy" (476e1–2).

(485d6–7), so in the case of the philosopher as lover of truth, if he loves her entirely (πάσης, 485b5; d3) and truly (τῷ ὄντι, 485d3), his desires will be oriented exclusively towards "learning and all that's like it", that is, towards "the pleasure of the soul itself with respect to itself" (485d10–11). Evidently, from such a conception of philosophy, moderation and not the love of money follows naturally (485d6–e6). Magnificence, instead of pettiness, follows from the philosopher's permanent aspiration for the whole and for the integrity of the divine and human (486a1–7); courage, from his contemplation of all time and all being, for he will not fear death (486a8–b5); and from all of that, justice and tameness (486b6–13), facility for learning (486c1–6), memory (486c7–d3) and, finally, measure and grace (486d4–12). These virtues are present as natural dispositions in the future philosopher, and once perfected by education and age, they will be indispensable to the exercise of political power (486e1–487a8).

Having so deduced the possibility of the coincidence of knowledge and virtue, of philosophy and political power, from the hypothesis concerning the nature of philosophy, the attempt to confirm the hypothesis by refuting possible objections follows in the 487a–502c section. So, Adeimantus, admitting that he cannot oppose the argument (λόγῳ, 487c5) itself, denies the conclusion to be true in deed (ἔργῳ, 487c6), considering the current situation of cities.[39] As with the previous waves, one might say that, in this section, the dialectician Socrates faces, as in a battle, the attempts at refutation directed against him. The dialectician must be able to refute possible objections, though not based on appearances, but on essence: διὰ πάντων ἐλέγχων διεξιὼν μὴ κατὰ δόξαν ἀλλὰ κατ'οὐσίαν προθυμούμενος ἐλέγχειν (534c1–2). The *elenchos* constitutes a moment in the confirmation of the hypothesis. This way, according to Adeimantus and following the opinions of ordinary people, those who dedicate themselves to philosophy past their youth usually turn out to be a) quite queer, not to say completely vicious; or b) at best, useless to the polis (487c–d). Socrates does not deny that those are the facts in current cities, which, according to him, are unjust,[40] but he responds with the image of the ship to show that it is not due to philosophy that current philosophers are useless, but it is due to the blindness of the *demos* and due to demagogues, "who claim to practice such things", but spread the opinion that most philosophers are "vicious and the most decent useless"; this, and not philosophy, would be, according to Socrates, the cause (αἰτία) of the uselessness of these philosophers (487d–489d). Next he explains why

---

[39] In 472e6–473b3 Glaucon accepts Socrates request not to force him to show in deed what he has described in his argument.
[40] Cf. 487d10, 489b3, d5, 495c8. Cf. Benson, H.H. (2008), p. 111 n. 42.

most philosophers are vicious and why philosophy is not the cause (αἰτία) of it (489d10–12). According to him, it is rather due to the fact that, despite possessing a philosophical nature with the innate mentioned dispositions, they are corrupted by traditional education (492a5–493a5), Sophists (493a5–495b7) or relatives, friends or other flatterers (494a11–495a3). This is the cause (αἰτία) of the deterioration of philosophical natures and, thus, of the way in which they practice philosophy (495a4–7). From men with such natural gifts then come both the worst evils as well as the best goods, depending on the education received (495b). This being so, if natures apt for philosophy do not concern themselves with it, men who lack the necessary natural aptitudes take their place, allowing for the reproach that of "those who have intercourse with her, some are worthless and the many worthy of bad things" (495c4–6), for, instead of approaching what really is and joining it, begetting intelligence and truth, and attaining knowledge, nutrition and true life (490b), they only beget sophisms that lack nobility and true intelligence (496a). Very few, then, will those be who can dedicate themselves to philosophy with dignity, and they will doubtless be unnoticed (496a11–e2). Finally, with the purpose of carrying his demonstration to the end (τέλος ἡ ἀπόδειξις, 497e1), and in spite of the existing conditions in current political regimes, Socrates examines the way in which the city ought to deal with philosophy in order not to succumb, which way is, from a start, qualified as opposite to the current one (497d8–9; e6–7).

It's interesting that in the final section of the third wave Socrates picks up from where he left them some of the themes of the first wave, underlining in this way the continuity of the *trikymia*; for he seems to refer once again to the distinction, examined in the first wave, between the art of disputation and dialectic, as well as to lifetime dedication to the quest for the foundation. Thus, by contrasting the way in which philosophy is "currently" (νῦν) practised and the way in which it ought to be practised in Kallipolis, he points out that while adolescents abandon the hardest part of philosophy, dialectic (τὸ περὶ τοὺς λόγους, 498a3), when they have barely come close to it, in Kallipolis the opposite should take place; for even though they must be given an education and a philosophy adequate to childhood as children and adolescents in order to intensify philosophical exercises as they reach maturity, it will not be until bodily force yields and they are excluded from political and military duties that they will be "let loose to graze and do nothing else" but philosophy (498b–c). Expression is even given to the hope of carrying out this commitment after death, a period of time that is "no time at all if you compare it to the whole" (498d). Most people, however, are not persuaded by what has been said so far, neither "have they given an adequate hearing to fair and free speeches of the sort that strain with every nerve in quest of the truth" –a reference to dialectic– and abandon themselves "to the subtleties and contentious quibbles that strain toward nothing but opinion and contention" (499a4–8) –a reference to eristic. Ordinary people, then, must be shown that the philosopher, instead of participating in these disputes, directs his thought to "things that are set in a regular arrangement (τεταγμένα) and are always in the same condition (κατὰ ταὐτὰ ἀεὶ ἔχοντα), things that neither do injustice to one another nor suffer it at one another's hands (οὔτ' ἀδικοῦντα οὔτ' ἀδικούμενα ὑπ'ἀλλήλων), but remain all in order according to reason (κατὰ λόγον)" (500c).⁴¹ In this way, by picking up on the final section of *Republic* V about the nature of philosophy, Socrates now confirms that he was referring then to a third type of *koinōnia*, not only that between Ideas, bodies and actions, but to a more fundamental one, the *koinōnia* of Ideas amongst themselves (476a6–7), a community that, unlike the political and psychic ones, constitutes an intrinsically just order. This order is just since each one of its elements fulfils its function in accordance with its own nature. And it fulfils it *kata logon*, that is, not only in accordance with thought, but also, and precisely because of it, in accordance with the foundation, that is, with the Good. That is the foundation that was said to be lacking (λόγου δεῖται, 449c7–8) at the beginning of *Republic* V and that will be made explicit, though only through an image, in the development of Kallipolis' educational project in books VI and VII. In any case, it is this order governed by the Idea of Good that is the one that the philosopher ought to imitate and make himself like in the measure that it is possible for man to do so.⁴² This is, then, the condition for the possibility of the coincidence of philosophy and political power, for, only in this way, if necessity arises, will he act as a demiurge of moderation, justice and every civic virtue, both in the private and public realms (500d4–8). Only in this way will the coincidence of philosophy and political power make sense. Finally, he recognizes that the proposed legislation "is best, granted it's possible" and that, although "it is hard for it to come to be, [it is] not, however, impossible" (502c5–7; 499c2–5; d4–6). Thus, the three waves, not only the third, reach their *telos* (502c9). And although the reference to the foundation is clear, and thus also to the Idea of the Good, a *logos tēs ousias* is not offered, only an image of it. As Socrates says then, quite a bit is being left out on this occasion (509c7–10).⁴³

---

41 It is remarkable that Benson, H.H. (2008) does not mention this passage, nor the *homoiōsis theōi*, which are *conditiones sine qua non* to explain the coincidence between knowledge and virtue, and, consequently, the feasibility of Kallipolis.
42 Cf. 500c5–7: ταῦτα μιμεῖσθαί τε καὶ ὅτι μάλιστα ἀφομοιοῦσθαι. ἢ οἴει τινὰ μηχανὴν εἶναι, ὅτῳ τις ὁμιλεῖ ἀγάμενος, μὴ μιμεῖσθαι ἐκεῖνο; Ἀδύνατον, ἔφη.
43 Cf. Szlezák, T.A. (1985, pp. 271–326); Szlezák, T.A. (2004, pp. 1–43).

Works Cited

Adam, J. 1963[2], *The Republic of Plato. Edited with Critical Notes, Commentary and Appendices by J.A.. With an Introduction by D.A. Rees*, 2 vol., Cambridge University Press, Cambridge.

Benson, H.H. 2008, "Knowledge, Virtue and Method in *Republic* 471c-502c", *Philosophical Inquiry* XXX, 3–4, pp. 87–114.

Bloom, A. 1991[2], *The Republic of Plato. Translated with Notes and Interpretive Essay by A.B.*, Basic Books, New York.

Ferrari, F. 2000, "Teoria delle idee e ontologia", in: M. Vegetti (ed.), *Platone. La Repubblica*, Vol. IV. Libro V, Bibliopolis, Neaple, pp. 365–391.

Gentzler, J. 1991, "'Συμφωνεῖν' in Plato's *Phaedo*", *Phronesis* 36, pp. 265–276.

Gutiérrez, R. 2003, "'The Logic of Decadence': On the Deficients Forms of Government in Plato's *Republic*", *The New Yearbook for Phenomenlogy and Phenomenological Philosophy* III, 85–102 (Spanish original in: *Estudios de Filosofía* 2002, 26, pp. 43–61.

Gutiérrez, R. 2009, "Dialéctica, Koinonía y Unidad. República V y las hipótesis I y II del *Parménides*", in: M. Perine (org.) *Estudos Platônicos. Sobre o ser e aparecer, o belo e o bem*, E. Loyola: Sao Paulo pp. 113–135.

Gutiérrez, R. (2013), "Disputas sobre las sombras de la *eikasía* y las estatuas de la *pístis*" , in: Gutiérrez, R. (ed.), Μαθήματα. *Ecos de Filosofía Antigua*, Fondo Editorial Pontificia Universidad Católica del Perú: Lima, 231-251; also in: Radice, R. & Tiengo, G. (eds.) 2015, *Seconda Navigazione. A cura di R.R. & G.T.*, Vita e Pensiero: Milano, 293-310.

Halliwell, S. 1993, 1998, *Plato: Republic 5, with an introduction, translation and commentary by S.H.*, Aris & Phillips: Warminster. Reprinted with corrections.

Hartenburg, G.J. 2011, *"A Somewhat Lengthy and Difficult Argument". The Metaphysics and Epistemology of Plato's* Republic *476e-480a"*. Doctoral Dissertation, University of California-Irvine, ProQuest: Ann Arbor.

Kahn, C. 1993, "Proleptic Composition in the *Republic*, or Why Book I was never a separate dialogue", *Classical Quarterly*, New Series, Vol. 43, Nr. 1, pp. 131–142.

Kahn, C. 1996, *Plato and the Socratic Dialogue*, Cambridge University Press: Cambridge.

Kanayama, Y. 2000, "The Methodology of the Second Voyage and the Proof of the Soul's Indestructibility in Plato's *Phaedo*", *Oxford Studies in Ancient Philosophy*, pp. 41–100.

Krämer, H.-J. 1959, *Arete bei Platon und Aristoteles. Zum Wesen und zur Geschichte der platonischen Ontologie*, Carl Winter: Heidelberg.

Leroux, G. 2000, *Platon, République. Traduction et présentation par G.L.*, Flammarion: Paris.

Penner, T. 2006, "The Forms in the *Republic*", in: G. Santas (Ed.) *The Blackwell Guide to Plato's Republic*, Blackwell: Malden/Oxford/Victoria, pp. 234–262.

Szlezák, T.A. 1976, "Unsterblichkeit und Trichotomie der Seele im zehnten Buch der Politeia", *Phronesis* 21, pp. 31–58.

Szlezák, T.A. 1985, *Platon und die Schriftlichkeit der Philosophie*, W. De Gruyter: Berlin/New York.

Szlezák, T.A. 2004, *Das Bild des Dialektikers in Platons späten Dialogen*, W. de Gruyter: Berlin/New York.

Vegetti, M. 2000, *Platone. La Repubblica. Traduzione e commento a cura di M.V.* Vol. IV, Libro V, Bibliopolis: Neaple.

Wilson, J.R.S. 1995, "Thrasymachus and the Thumos: A Further Case of Prolepsis in *Republic* I", *Classical Quarterly*, New Series, Vol. 45, pp. 58–67.

Mary Louise Gill
Plato's Unfinished Trilogy:
Timaeus–Critias–Hermocrates

Plato announced two trilogies he did not finish, the *Sophist–Statesman* culminating in the missing *Philosopher*, and the *Timaeus–Critias* culminating in the missing *Hermocrates*. I examined the first series in a recent book,[1] and my work on that series encouraged me to ask about the other great unfinished trilogy, whose second member *Critias* breaks off in mid-sentence. We can be fairly sure that the missing dialogues were not written and lost, because ancient lists of Plato's works survive, and all works listed (including spuria) have come down to us. The *Philosopher* and *Hermocrates* receive no mention.[2] Did Plato simply lose interest and turn to other projects or die before he could finish? Some scholars have urged that Plato terminated the *Critias* in mid-sentence because he could better demonstrate the origins and functioning of a well-ordered state in the manner articulated in the *Laws*.[3]

I believe that Plato had special reasons for promising the *Philosopher* and *Hermocrates* and leaving them unwritten. In my recent book I argue that he advertised the *Philosopher* but did not write it to stimulate his audience to construct the portrait it would have contained.[4] He did not leave his audience to their own devices but established a trajectory in the existing dialogues indicating how to

---

[1] M. L. Gill (2012).
[2] Diogenes Laertius (early third century C.E.) in his *Lives of Eminent Philosophers* 3.56–62 (= Hicks 1925) discusses several ancient editions of Plato, including the important one of Thrasyllus (early first century C.E.) arranging Plato's works in tetralogies (see Tarrant 1993), and that of the earlier grammarian Aristophanes of Byzantium (librarian in Alexandria in the early second century B.C.E), who organized some of Plato's dialogues in trilogies. We have all the works Diogenes lists in the editions of Aristophanes and Thrasyllus, plus several works they rejected as spurious.
[3] Cornford (1937, pp. 6–8), C. Gill (1977, pp. 301–302), Nesselrath (2006), Sattler (2007).
[4] M. L. Gill (2012, 'Introduction', pp. 1–17). Many scholars have addressed the question about the *Philosopher*—e.g., Campbell (1867, 'Introduction to the *Statesman*', pp. lvi-lix.), Cornford (1935, pp. 168–169), Skemp (1952, pp. 20–22), Friedländer (1969, vol. 1, pp. 152–153; vol. 3, pp. 281 and 525 n. 5), Klein (1977, pp. 4–5), Guthrie (1978, vol. 5, pp.123–124), Dorter (1994, pp. 235–237), M. Frede (1996, pp. 146, 149–151), Notomi (1999, pp. 23–25, 238–240, 287–288, 296–301), and Miller (2004, p. 10). Wyller (1972) argues that the *Parmenides* is the *Philosopher*, a view criticized by Panagiotou (1973), and Davidson (1993, p. 193) suggests that the *Philebus* took the place of the *Philosopher*. For discussion of efforts to identify the *Philosopher* with various existing dialogues, see Taylor (1926, p. 375 n. 1) and Wyller (1972).

continue the series. Not only that: he gives the audience the means to dig out the main pieces of the project and to combine them into a portrait of the philosopher. I will contend that the *Timaeus–Critias* establishes its own trajectory and similarly indicates how to complete the series, though I believe that the two series serve entirely distinct purposes.

Let me begin with the series I have worked on before, because some features of that group extend to the other series, and differences between the two series are instructive. The *Sophist* and *Statesman* present themselves as members of a larger group starting with the *Theaetetus*, Plato's investigation of knowledge, defined (I argue) as expertise, a cognitive capacity exercised in acts of knowing. Knowledge so defined then serves as the wide kind divided dichotomously in the search for the special expertise of the sophist and statesman.[5] Expertise would also serve as the wide kind to be divided in the search for the special expertise of the philosopher. Both the *Sophist* and *Statesman* link themselves dramatically to the *Theaetetus* by presenting that conversation as having occurred the previous day (*Sph.* 216a1–2, *Stm.* 258a3–4), and the *Theaetetus* links itself to them with Socrates' farewell invitation to meet again in the same place tomorrow (*Tht.* 210d4). The three dialogues feature the same dramatic characters—Socrates, Theodorus, Theaetetus, and Socrates the Younger. An unnamed visitor from Elea accompanies Theodorus on the second day, replacing Socrates as the main speaker in the *Sophist* and *Statesman*, and he undertakes to define the sophist, the statesman, and the philosopher (*Sph.* 216d3–217b4; *Stm.* 257a1–c5, 258b1–c2). The series belongs to a yet larger group. Cross-references in both the *Theaetetus* (*Tht.* 183e5–184a2) and *Sophist* (*Sph.* 217c3–7) to Socrates' long-ago meeting with Parmenides portrayed in the *Parmenides* alert the audience to the relevance of that discussion for the present one, though the *Parmenides* stands outside the series. Thus three dialogues—*Theaetetus*, *Sophist*, and *Statesman*—group themselves into a series, herald the *Philosopher* as a fourth member, and assert their reliance on the *Parmenides*.

The second part of the *Parmenides* presents a philosophical exercise, introduced as the first step in a larger philosophical program. Having performed an exercise about oneness in the second part of the *Parmenides*, Parmenides advises the student to repeat it taking other topics as his subject-matter: likeness, unlikeness, change, rest, being, not-being, and similar entities (*Prm.* 136b1–c5). I argue in my book that the dialogues leading up to the anticipated but missing *Philosopher*, though they reach some substantive conclusions, are themselves

---

5 Starting with the wide kind, each division yields two kinds, one of which is further divided with the aim of locating the target expertise at the tip of one branch of the divided tree.

philosophical exercises of various sorts designed to train students in dialectic, the philosopher's method; and that a second version of the *Parmenides* exercise, closely patterned on it, spans parts of the *Theaetetus* and *Sophist* and brings the philosopher into view. That is the exercise about *being*, the subject-matter studied by Plato's philosopher. Plato hides the pieces of the puzzle and its solution in plain sight, forcing his students (and us modern readers) to dig them out and reconstruct the project. In finding the philosopher through the exercise, the student becomes a philosopher by mastering his methods, and thus the target of the exercise is internally related to its pedagogical purpose. Plato withheld the *Philosopher* because he would have spoiled the exercise had he written it for us.

Like the *Sophist* and *Statesman*, the *Timaeus* and *Critias* repeatedly herald a third dialogue, the missing *Hermocrates*, and like the other series, they link themselves to a previous dialogue, the *Republic*, Socrates' account of the ideal political state. Socrates claims that yesterday he presented a static picture and today wants to see the city in motion, engaged in some great contest that will reflect the character of the citizens and the training they received (*Ti.* 19b3–c8). Speaking directly to Critias and Hermocrates (*Ti.* 19c8–9), he says that he himself is unable to sing adequate praise of the city and its citizens in action, and that the poets and sophists have also proved unsuccessful. He therefore assigns the topic to those assembled, persons with the right character and training (*Ti.* 20a1–b1). Critias claims that ancient Athens exemplifies the ideal city in motion, and to prove his point he tells the story of Atlantis, an island kingdom, whose imperial ambitions were blocked by the glorious deeds of Athens 9000 years ago. After Critias finishes his tale about Atlantis and ancient Athens, he lays out the plan for today's feast (*Ti.* 27a2–b6). First, Timaeus will use his expertise in astronomy and cosmology to describe the origin of the world and conclude with the emergence of human beings. Then having learned from Timaeus about the origin of humans and from Socrates how some of those people became distinguished, Critias will spell out the details of the Atlantis story and show in detail that the citizens of Socrates' ideal city were in fact the citizens of ancient Athens, saviors of the whole world from the unjust greed of Atlantis. No mention of Hermocrates here (*Ti.* 27b), but when Socrates first described each man's credentials to give him a feast in exchange for his, he praised Hermocrates as well-qualified to deal with these matters, saying that his fitness became evident the day before when Hermocrates asked Socrates to discuss matters of government. According to Socrates, no one is better equipped to give the follow-up speech—no one but Hermocrates could present our city pursuing a war in a manner appropriate to her (*Ti.* 20b1–7). Thus we expect the *Hermocrates* to continue a discussion started by Critias about Athens and her conduct in times of war.

The *Critias* reminds us that Hermocrates will speak third (*Critias* 107d8–108c7). Critias asks for and is granted indulgence, claiming that in describing the actions of humans he faces harsher judgment than Timaeus, because people know more about humans than they do about the gods and cosmology, and therefore will notice mistakes. Socrates in granting the indulgence says that he will extend this favor also to Hermocrates, who will doubtless make the same entreaty. Hermocrates agrees and accepts the indulgence in advance. These advertisements increase our expectation that the *Hermocrates* will follow the *Critias* and somehow elaborate Critias' discussion of human action.

The *Timaeus* and *Critias* are puzzling in several respects, and an adequate interpretation of the truncated series should address the puzzles. First, the *Timaeus* begins very oddly with Socrates saying: 'One, two, three—but where, my dear Timaeus, is the fourth of yesterday's guests, today's hosts?' to which Timaeus responds, 'He has come down with some illness, Socrates, for he would not willingly have missed this meeting' (*Ti.* 17a1–5). Apparently the missing fourth person would have had something to add to today's feast in exchange for that of Socrates the previous day. Who is the missing fourth person, and what might he have contributed to the discussion?

A second puzzle: Socrates summarizes yesterday's conversation (*Ti.* 17c1–19a9), clearly recalling some main points in the *Republic*, and yet—unlike the *Philosopher* series tying itself to the *Theaetetus*—the cast of characters, with the exception of Socrates himself, is totally different: Timaeus, Critias, and Hermocrates replace Glaucon and Adeimantus, Socrates' interlocutors in *Republic* II–X. Plato relaxes the connection with the *Republic* even further by staging that conversation on a day celebrating the goddess Bendis in the Piraeus, whereas today's conversation celebrates Athena, the patron goddess of Athens (*Ti.* 21a1–3), festivals scholars separate by two months.[6] Increasing the distance between the *Timaeus* and *Republic*, Socrates summarizes yesterday's discussion but omits numerous important topics. While focusing on the best sort of political organization (*politeia*) and the sort of men composing it (17c1–3), he mentions the principle of specialization from *Republic* II (each person performs one task for which he is properly suited), the physical and cultural education of the citizens, training of women comparable to the training of men, no private property but attention to virtue, and much detail based on Spartan practices from *Republic* V: the status of woman, marriages by lot, and the procreation of children. At the end of his summary Socrates asks Timaeus if he left anything out, and Timaeus replies 'Not a thing—those were the exactly the things said, Socrates'

---

6 Nails (2002, p. 326).

(*Ti.* 19b1–2). This reply provokes the reader to ask: What about the many topics in the *Republic* arguably vital to its main project, such as justice, its principal focus? What about the separation of the guardians from the rest of the warrior class?[7] What about the tri-partite soul in Book IV? the higher studies of the philosopher-rulers in Books V–VII? the treatment of degenerate constitutions in Books VIII–IX? and so on?[8] The *Timaeus–Critias–Hermocrates* series evidently has a more tenuous link to the *Republic* than the *Sophist–Statesman–Philosopher* to the *Theaetetus*. Why invoke the *Republic* and focus almost exclusively on political arrangements inspired by Sparta?

Third, some controversy surrounds Plato's choice of dramatic characters in the *Timaeus–Critias* and consequently scholars disagree about the dramatic date and aim of the series. Socrates describes Timaeus, Critias, and Hermocrates as well-equipped by nature and training to take part in both philosophy and politics at once (*Ti.* 19e2–8). We know of Timaeus exclusively from the *Timaeus–Critias*, described by Socrates as a renowned political leader of well-governed Italian Locri and master of the whole field of philosophy. The Neoplatonist philosopher Iamblichus, perhaps relying on the *Timaeus*, lists him twice in his catalogue of Pythagoreans.[9]

The identity of Critias is contested. Many scholars identify him as the Critias in the *Protagoras*, who advises against taking sides in a dispute between Socrates and Protagoras and exhorts them to continue the discussion (*Prt.* 316a5, 336d6–e4). He is also a main speaker in the *Charmides*. A frequent companion of Socrates, Critias wrote political essays and admired all things Spartan, a stance that recommends him to put the static Spartan-inspired picture Socrates summarizes at the start of the *Timaeus* into motion in the account of ancient Athens in the Atlantis tale and *Critias*.[10] Critias also wrote poetry and drama, but he was mainly remembered in the fourth century as leader of the Thirty Tyrants, a brutal Spartan-backed oligarchy that governed Athens for nine months in 404 B.C.E. after Athens' defeat in the Peloponnesian War. A kinsman of Plato born around 460, Critias was killed in 403 during the restoration of democracy.

---

[7] According to the summary in the *Timaeus*, the guardians should be gentle with their own subjects and harsh with enemies, and they should be both spirited and philosophical (*Ti.* 18a). These characteristics recall *Rep.* II, 375a–376c, and describe the guardians before the full guardians have been separated out. Not until the end of *Rep.* III (414b) are the full guardians distinguished from the warrior class, after which members of the warrior class are called auxiliaries.
[8] Cf. Clay (1997, pp. 50–51).
[9] *Lives of the Pythagoreans* 267 (catalogue quoted by Diels & Kranz 1951–1952, vol. 1, pp. 146–148, as 58 A). See also Nails (2002, p. 293).
[10] Cf. C. Gill (1977, pp. 294–295) and Tuozzo (2011, esp. pp. 59–66).

Contrary to this scholarly trend, Debra Nails and others have argued that Critias in the *Timaeus* is Critias III, the grandfather of Critias the tyrant (= Critias IV), born around 520 and died around 429. (See Stemma Plato.)[11] Critias in the *Timaeus* says he got the Atlantis story from his grandfather Critias (if we are talking about Critias III, this would be Critias II who lived from ca. 600 until 510). That Critias got it from his father Dropides (= Dropides II, archon ca. 593/2), who got the story from Solon, whose source was Egyptian priests with records to prove the truth of the tale. In telling the Atlantis story, Critias refers to Dropides as his great grandfather (*Ti.* 20e1–3). This identification recommends Critias III, the grandfather of Socrates' contemporary. If instead the dramatic character is Critias the tyrant, he must telescope two generations of his ancestors when he speaks of Dropides, since Dropides was his *great-great-great*-grandfather.[12]

Scholars generally agree about Hermocrates, identified by Proclus in his commentary on the *Timaeus* (on *Ti.* 20a7–b1) as the famous Syracusan general during the last third of the fifth century (born ca. 455 and died 408/7).[13] Thucydides in his *History of the Peloponnesian War*, Book VI.7, describes him as a brave and intelligent man and puts into his mouth a speech (IV.58–64), delivered to an assembly of Sicilian states in 424 B.C.E., advising them to make peace with one another and to prepare for Athenian aggression.[14] In Book VI Thucydides describes the role of Hermocrates in defeating the Athenians in their misguided Sicilian Expedition, an effort to dominate the island of Sicily in 415–413 B.C.E. while in the midst of the Peloponnesian War with Sparta at home.[15] The identity of Hermocrates seems to me crucial in determining the content of the missing dialogue. Hermocrates will have much to say about Athenian conduct during the conflict in which he took part.[16]

Debra Nails lists the *Timaeus–Critias*, along with the *Republic*, as dialogues with problematic dramatic dates.[17] To fit the chronology including an aged Critias III, she suggests that the *Timaeus* took place around 429 B.C.E., at the start of the Peloponnesian War, when Critias III would have been about 90 years old. The old man displays a remarkable memory, recalling in the *Critias* precise details about Atlantis—the building projects, exact dimensions of bridges and canals, and so on—all of which he learned at age 10 from his grandfather, himself

---

11 Nails (2002, p. 244).
12 Cf. Nails (2002, pp. 106–11).
13 Proclus (= Diehl [1903] 1965, pp. 17, 16–20).
14 Thucydides (= Jones & Powel 1942).
15 Cf. Thucydides II.65 (= Jones & Powell 1942), C. Gill (1977, p. 298).
16 Cf. Clay (1997, pp. 53–54).
17 Nails (2002, pp. 324–327).

Plato's Unfinished Trilogy: *Timaeus–Critias–Hermocrates* — 39

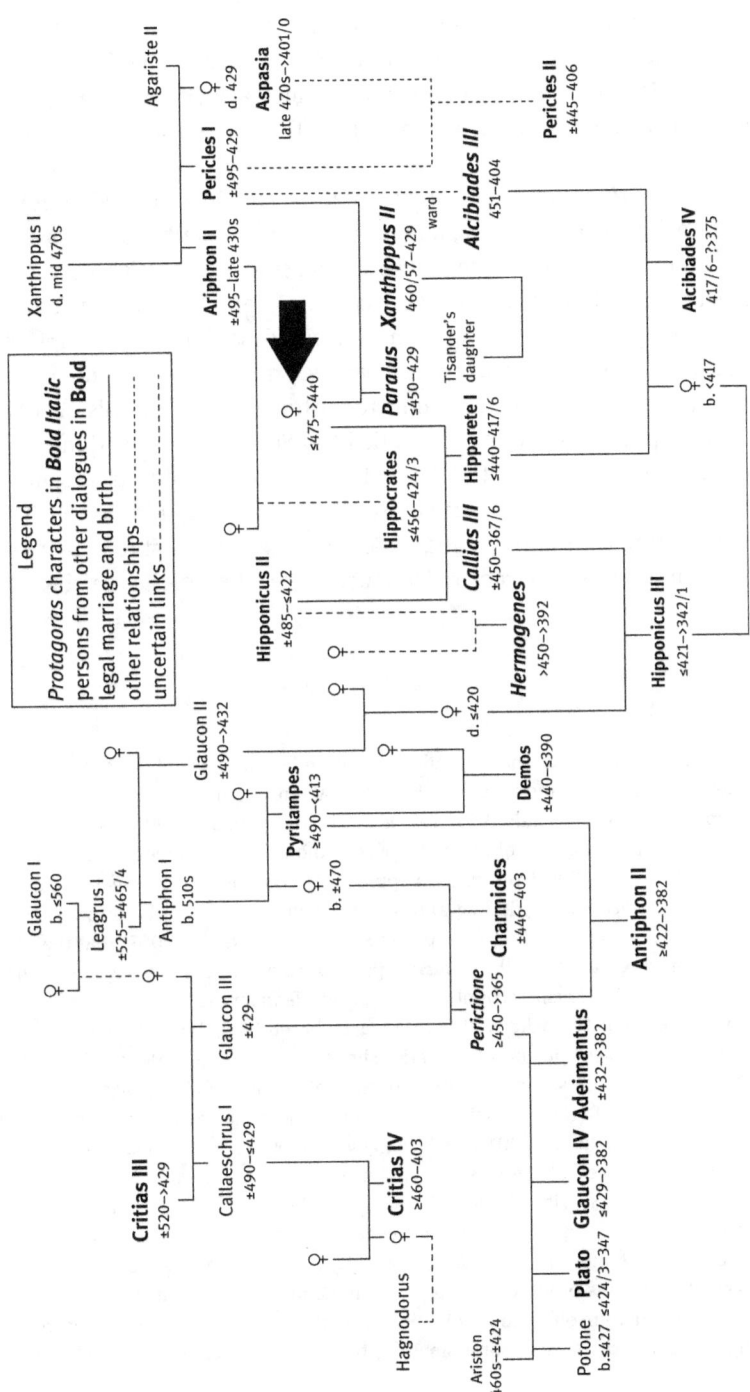

Fig. 1: Plato, Protagoras, abridged stemmata

close to 90 at the time (*Ti.* 21a8–b1). A dramatic date for the *Timaeus–Critias* in 429, in time to include an aged Critias III, poses an obstacle for my interpretation, since that date is too early to accommodate the message of the larger series, including the *Hermocrates*, as I understand it. I set this issue aside for the moment.

The *Timaeus* and *Critias* establish a temporal trajectory, from the indefinitely distant past before the creation of time, a precosmic chaos described by Timaeus in the middle of the *Timaeus*, when he makes a fresh start at 47e3. Earlier in the narrative the Demiurge establishes time (*Ti.* 37c6–38c3), and then time marches forward toward the present, beginning with Timaeus describing the origins of the cosmos down to the emergence of human beings. Critias in the next dialogue starts to flesh out the Atlantis story and aims to portray the noble deeds of Athens 9000 years ago, putting in motion the static ideal Socrates presented the day before.[18] Continuing that temporal trajectory, Hermocrates should discuss Athens of the more recent past, and given who he is, one expects him to tell the tale of Athens repeating the hubris of Atlantis in her greedy attempt to annex Sicily in 415–413, an attempt blocked by Syracuse under the able leadership of Hermocrates himself.[19]

---

18 C. Gill (1977, pp. 294–295) argues that the Atlantis story relies on elements of the Persian Wars, especially at the time of Marathon (490 B.C.E.), when Athens repulsed a much larger Persian army: see Herodotus VII.139 (= Hude 1993). Yet, as C. Gill also points out, Athens in the Atlantis story is unlike Athens at the time of the battle of Marathon, and much more 'a picture of Sparta lodged in an Attic locale'. It is, he thinks, an appropriate vision for the pro-Spartan Athenian, Critias, to give. For objections to finding allusions to Marathon in the Atlantis story, see Broadie (2012, pp. 131–132 and n. 32). I agree with Broadie (cf. Vidal-Naquet 2007) that the Atlantis story (and its truncated version in the *Critias*) is pseudo-history, but in my view the pseudo-history is a set-up for an historical account in the missing *Hermocrates*.

19 See Hermocrates' speech at Thucydides VI.76 (= Jones & Powell 1942). Wilamowitz-Moellendorff (1959, p. 466), briefly presents a view of the series similar to mine. Cf. Cornford (1935, p. 2), C. Gill (1977, p. 298), Johansen (2004, pp. 11, 184), and especially Clay (1997). I disagree with C. Gill's suggestion that the unwritten sequel might have depicted a Spartanized Athens defeating an Athenian Atlantis (cf. Vidal-Naquet 2007, p. 27): in my view it would have reenacted the historical account Thucydides gives of Syracuse defeating an Athenian Atlantis. Sattler (2007) states that Nesselrath (2006, p. 53) rightly rejects Wilomowitz' view, because the Egyptian priest tells Solon in the *Timaeus* that most of its inhabitants were killed in a natural catastrophe before they had a chance to degenerate. But on Wilamowitz' side, the Egyptian priest carefully tells Solon that the race of Athenians of 9000 years ago was not entirely wiped out. He says: 'This is the race from whom you yourself, your whole city, all that you and your countrymen here today, are sprung, thanks to the survival of a small portion of their stock' (23b–c, trans. Zeyl 2000).

Timaeus takes up some of the topics overlooked in Socrates' summary of the *Republic*, for instance, the tri-partite soul and the bodily locations of its three parts. Other missing topics should guide our reading of the trilogy, and especially the degeneration of persons and states in *Republic* VIII and IX. The *Republic* describes how, after many generations, the ideal city could degenerate through timocracy and oligarchy to democracy and final tyranny. Degeneration is a recurrent theme in the *Timaeus–Critias*: the *Timaeus* ends with an account of the degeneration of unjust and cowardly men first into women and then over generations into various sorts of animals (*Ti.* 90e1–92c3), and the *Critias* describes the effects of erosion on the land around Athens over long periods (*Critias* 110d5–d8).

The *Critias* describes great Atlantis, a city that preserved her self-control for generations and recognized that honoring wealth would diminish one's virtue (*Critias* 120d6–121a6). But then in the final paragraph of the dialogue, before it abruptly ends, Critias tells us that the people of Atlantis over-reached, and as the divine element in them became faint and their human character gained control, they could no longer bear their good fortune and became bloated with unjust greed (*pleonexias adikou*) and power (*dunameos*) (*Critias* 121a7–b7). For this excess Zeus will exact punishment: He convenes an assembly of gods to declare that punishment (*Critias* 121b7–c5). The sentence breaks off before Zeus speaks, but we know from the story of Atlantis in the *Timaeus* the form this punishment will take: virtuous Athens will block her aggression (*Ti.* 24d6–25c6), and then the island of Atlantis will sink below the sea and disappear, leaving behind a layer of mud near the surface obstructing navigation (*Ti.* 25c6–d6). The flood will also destroy Athens, though a few stout souls living in the mountains will survive and regenerate the city (*Ti.* 22c1–23d1). As I read the series, the *Hermocrates* would have revealed that in the 9000 years since Athens' greatness, she has declined into the new Atlantis, the aggressor seeking to dominate the world.

Plato presents pieces of the final dialogue, as well as the continuation of the *Critias*, at the start of the series.[20] The Atlantis story in the *Timaeus* has already outlined the major contours of the trilogy, and in its talk of recurrent fire and flood has emphasized the theme of recurrence: For the content of the missing *Hermocrates*, simply read 'Athens' for 'Atlantis' and 'Syracuse' for 'Athens'. Plato evokes recent history without explicitly telling it, and that should suffice,

---

20 Clay (1997, p. 52) points out that Plato has prepared us for something missing and elliptical from the start by the absence of the fourth guest from the day before (17a), and by Solon's failure to complete his *Atlantis* (21c–d). In Clay's view—and I agree—Plato intended the *Timaeus–Critias–Hermocrates* to stop in mid-sentence: the series is finished but intentionally incomplete.

especially since his fourth-century audience can read a full account of the disastrous Sicilian Expedition in Thucydides' *History* Book VI. The series *Timaeus–Critias–Hermocrates* would have contained a powerful political message about the corruption of Athens, a message Plato left to his audience to reconstruct. Cities once great eventually become greedy, fall away from justice, and decline finally into tyranny. Such degeneration need not happen, of course, but to avoid it people should cultivate and maintain their rational powers through studying the orderly cyclical motions of the heavenly bodies discussed in the *Timaeus*.[21]

How can my reconstruction be right, calling as it does for the *Timaeus* series to take place in the late 400s after the invasion of Sicily and before the death of Hermocrates in 408/7? Some scholars argue that authors of Plato's time remembered Solon as having lived several generations later than he actually did, thus allowing Critias the tyrant to be the main speaker.[22] I believe that Plato exploited that misconception and intended his audience to identify Critias as the notorious contemporary of Socrates. But Debra Nails has convinced me in her detailed work on Plato's family tree that Plato probably knew his family history well enough to recognize that too large a gap separated Critias the tyrant from Solon for historical accuracy.[23] Indeed, having Critias speak so explicitly of Dropides as his great grandfather seems designed to rule out the infamous Critias as a speaker in the series.

Yet what perfect camouflage to obscure Plato's political message should any authority ask! By including the detail about Dropides, Plato forces his critics to interpret the *Timaeus* trilogy as taking place much earlier, before Plato was born, and with a pleasing message about Athens, still great at that time. But the trilogy sends the opposite message to Plato's intended audience. Socrates' contemporary Critias is the right person to recount the deeds of glorious Athens of the distant past but with a disturbing undertone. Evidently Socrates and Plato both respected his character and politics until his greed and power corrupted him (*Ep.* VII, 324b8–325c5).[24] By selecting Critias, Plato reinforces his theme of degeneration.

---

[21] On education in the *Timaeus* that could avert such degeneration, see *Ti.* 88b5–90d7, and Sattler (forthcoming). The higher education of philosopher-kings in the *Republic* also bears on this question. See Burnyeat (2000).
[22] For a full discussion, see Nesserath (2006, pp. 43–50).
[23] See Nails (2002, pp. 106–107 and 244: Stemma Plato, reproduced above, p. 39).
[24] Tuozzo (2011, esp. pp. 52–85), discussing the *Charmides*, a dialogue featuring Critias, argues that Plato's attitude toward Critias is more nuanced than that of many ancient authors who sided with the restored democracy (such as Xenophon). For instance, Plato may have approved of the

I end with the question about the missing fourth person, whose absence Socrates notes in his opening statement in the *Timaeus*. The fourth person is ill, says Timaeus; otherwise he would not willingly have missed the meeting. Consistent with my reading of the series and its temporal trajectory, the fourth person should be someone competent to judge the political situation of the present day. How much further has Athens fallen since the invasion of Sicily? Think of Critias and his bloody junta in 404–403 and the unjust trial and death of Socrates himself in 399 carried out by the restored democracy. The missing fourth person needs to have outlived the speakers in the *Timaeus–Critias* to tell of Athens' further corruption involving them. If I am right about the content of the *Hermocrates* and the theme of recurrence, that fourth speaker could also have told the tale of Syracuse after its own shining moment stopping Athenian aggression. In Plato's lifetime that great city degenerated into tyranny under the rule of Dionysius II, events detailed in the *Seventh Letter*, written either by Plato or by someone intimately acquainted with Plato's hopes and disappointment in Sicily when he tried and failed to transform Dionysius II into a philosopher-king. Like Atlantis and Athens, Syracuse too awaits the punishment of Zeus.

Plato need not spell out the particular differences between Atlantis, Athens, and Syracuse, glorious cities in their prime and their eventual corruption.[25] Plato can again rely on his fourth century audience to have read Thucydides' *History*. In stating his methods and aims, Thucydides admits that details of his account may be inexact, because he often had to rely on conflicting second-hand reports. The specific details do not matter; he wishes to convey a universal message: given human nature, the events he describes will occur again (*History of the Peloponnesian War* I.22). I suggest that the missing fourth person is Plato himself, who witnessed the continued decline of Athens and knows first-hand the degeneration of Syracuse.[26]

---

project of the oligarchy while disapproving their methods. Tuozzo argues that Critias was a conservative, deeply attached to aristocratic ideals, and an admirer of all things Spartan.

25 Cf. Johansen (2004, p. 11), who thinks that Hermocrates is present in the *Timaeus–Critias* to remind us of the '*general* phenomenon of unjust aggression against justified self-defence'.

26 I am by no means the first person to suggest Plato as the missing fourth person: Proclus (= Diehl [1903] 1965, pp. 20, 9–21) attributes the view to Dercyllides and dismisses it; Taylor (1928, p. 25) says the view has sometimes been revived in modern times but finds the idea so ridiculous that he does not cite the relevant sources, saying only that the idea is based on nothing more than Plato's absence from the death-scene in the *Phaedo* because of ill-health. Cf. Archer-Hind (1888, p. 55), who also cites no sources. Cornford (1935, pp. 3–4) thinks there is no ground for any conjecture as to the identity of the fourth person, and that the most sensible remark is that of Atticus, preserved by Proclus (= Diehl [1903] 1965, pp. 20, 21–27), that the fourth person would have been another visitor from Italy or Sicily, since Socrates asks for news of him—that is, he asks why the fourth person is absent today.

He gives us a nice clue: on one other occasion Plato missed an important date—Socrates' final day depicted in the *Phaedo*—and for the same reason: he was ill (*Phd.* 59b10).

Works Cited

Archer-Hind, R. D. 1888, *The Timaeus of Plato*, with Introduction and Notes, MacMillan, London. Reprinted by Arno Press, 1973.
Broadie, S. 2012, *Nature and Divinity in Plato's Timaeus*, Cambridge University Press, Cambridge.
Burnet, J. 1900–1907, Platonis Opera, 5 vols., Clarendon Press, Oxford.
Burnyeat, M. F. 2000, 'Why Mathematics is Good for the Soul', in T. Smiley (ed.), *Mathematics and Necessity*, The British Academy, London, pp. 1–81.
Campbell, L. 1867, *The Sophistes and Politicus of Plato*, a Revised Text and English Notes, Clarendon Press, Oxford.
Clay, D. 1997, 'The Plan of Plato's *Critias*', in T. Calvo & L. Brisson (eds.), *Interpreting the Timaeus–Critias*, Academia, Sankt Augustin, pp. 49–54.
Cornford, F. M. 1935, *Plato's Theory of Knowledge:* the *Theaetetus* and the *Sophist* of Plato translated with running commentary, Routledge & Kegan Paul, London.
Davidson, D. 1993, 'Plato's Philosopher', in T. H. Irwin & M. C. Nussbaum (eds.), *Virtue, Love & Form* [Essays in Memory of Gregory Vlastos], Academic Printing & Publishing, Edmonton, pp. 179–194.
Diehl, E. [1903] 1965, *Procli Diadochi: in Platonis Timaeus Commentaria*, Hakkert, Amsterdam.
Diels, H. & Kranz, W. 1951–1952, *Die Fragmente der Vorsokratiker*, 3 vols., 6th edn., Weidmann, Berlin. (Original work by Diels published 1903.)
Dorter, K. 1994, *Form and Good in Plato's Eleatic Dialogues: The Parmenides, Theaetetus, Sophist, and Statesman*, University of California Press, Berkeley.
Duke, E. A. et al. 1995, *Platonis Opera*, vol. 1, Clarendon Press, Oxford.
Frede, M. 1996, 'The Literary Form of the *Sophist*', in C. Gill & M. M. McCabe (eds.), *Form and Argument in Late Plato*, Clarendon Press, Oxford, pp. 135–151.
Friedländer, P. 1969, *Plato*, 3 vols., Princeton University Press, Princeton.
Gill, C. 1977, 'The Genre of the Atlantis Story', *Classical Philology*, vol. 72, no. 4, pp. 287–304.
Gill, M. L. 2012, *Philosophos: Plato's Missing Dialogue*, Oxford University Press, Oxford.
Guthrie, W. K. C. 1978, *A History of Greek Philosophy* (6 vols.), vol. 5: *The Later Plato and the Academy*, Cambridge University Press, Cambridge.
Hicks, R. D. 1925, *Diogenes Laertius: Lives of Eminent Philosophers*, 2 vols., Loeb Classical Library, Harvard University Press, Cambridge.
Hude, K. 1993, *Herodotus Historiae*, 2 vols., 3rd revised edn., Clarendon Press, Oxford.
Johansen, T. K. 2004, *Plato's Natural Philosophy: A Study of the Timaeus–Critias*, Cambridge University Press, Cambridge.
Jones, H. S. & Powell, J. E. 1942, Thucydides, Historiae, 2 vols., Clarendon Press, Oxford.

Klein, J. 1977, *Plato's Trilogy: Theaetetus, the Sophist, and the Statesman*, University of Chicago Press, Chicago.
Miller, M. 2004, *The Philosopher in Plato's Statesman*, repr. with suppl. material, Parmenides Publishing, Las Vegas. (Originally published 1980.)
Nails, D. 2002, *The People of Plato: A Prosopography of Plato and other Socratics*, Hackett, Indianapolis.
Nesselrath, H.-G. 2006, *Platon: Kritias, Platon Werke* VIII, 4, translation and commentary, Vandenhoeck & Ruprecht, Göttingen.
Notomi, N. 1999, *The Unity of Plato's 'Sophist': Between the Sophist and the Philosopher*, Cambridge University Press, Cambridge.
Panagiotou, S. 1973, 'The *Parmenides* is the *Philosopher*: A Reply', *Classica et Mediaevalia* 30: 187–210.
Sattler, B. 2007, review of Nesselrath, *Platon: Kritias*, *Bryn Mawr Classical Review*, 2007.01.43.
Sattler, B. forthcoming, 'Planetary Motions—a Guide through Human History? Plato's Astronomy and Philosophy of History in the *Timaeus*'.
Skemp, J. B. 1952, *Plato: The Statesman*, Routledge & Kegan Paul, London.
Tarrant, H. 1993, *Thrasyllan Platonism*, Cornell University Press, Ithaca.
Taylor, A. E. 1926, *Plato: The Man and his Work.* Methuen, London.
Taylor, A. E. 1928, *A Commentary of Plato's Timaeus*, Clarendon Press, Oxford.
Tuozzo, T. 2011, *Plato's Charmides: Positive Elenchus in a "Socratic" Dialogue*, Cambridge University Press, New York.
Vidal-Naquet, P. 2007, *The Atlantis Story: A Short History of Plato's Myth*, trans. by J. Lloyd, University of Exeter Press, Exeter. (Originally published in French, Belles Lettres, Paris, 2005.)
Wilamowitz-Moellendorff, U. von 1959, *Platon: sein Leben und seine Werke*, Weidemann, Berlin.
Wyller, E. A. 1972, 'The *Parmenides* is the *Philosopher*', *Classica et Mediaevalia*, vol. 29, pp. 27–39.
Zeyl, D. 2000, *Plato: Timaeus*, Hackett, Indianapolis.

María Angélica Fierro
The Myth of the Winged Chariot in the *Phaedrus:* A Vehicle for Philosophical Thinking

> One should achieve one of these things: learn the truth about these things or find it for oneself, or, if that is impossible, adopt the best and most irrefutable of men's theories, and, borne upon this, sail through the dangers of life as upon a raft (*schedía*), unless someone should make the journey safer and less risky upon a firmer vessel (*óchēma*) of some divine doctrine.
>
> Phd. 85d (Grube's translation)

Plato's abundant use of myth and his general reflections on poetry suggest that, though to be condemned when uncritically used,[1] story-telling is valued and well-considered if it is put at the service of philosophical teaching. In general terms it can be said that in Plato's philosophy the myth either suggests through images something not susceptible at present to a complete conceptual explanation or expresses what is not in itself expressible by means of a philosophical argument on its own,[2] as is the case with the eschatological myths of the *Phaedo*, *Gorgias* and *Republic* 10 and the creational myth of the *Timaeus*.[3] Here I will examine the different functions that the myth of the winged chariot simultaneously

---

[1] In *Republic* II myths are condemned when they misrepresent the real nature of the gods. Superficial rationalistic interpretations of myths are also rejected for example at *Phdr.* 229c ff. through Socrates' critical reflections on sophistic exegesis of the story of Boreas and Orithuia. As he says at *Phdr.* 275b-c, in the end what really matters in relation to any story is whether the tale expresses something true or not. On this point see also Halliwell (1993, p. 27, n. 32) and Szlezák (1993, pp. 96–97).

[2] Thus *mýthos* represents what *lógos* fails to explain. Halliwell (1993, p.17) follows this kind of interpretation regarding the final myth of *Republic*. Vasallo 2011 offers a detailed examination of the structure of the palinode. Werner 2012: chap. 3 gives an analogous approach of the palinode to what I develop in the last two sections. In his excellent work Vallejo Campos 1995 prefers to focus on other myths.

[3] In consequence a *mýthos* as a whole can potentially be rendered as *lógos*. See esp. *Gorg.* 523a. However, because of its power of communicating the truth in an intuitive form, *mýthos* preserves its own characteristics and advantages over *lógos* (see Szlezák 1993, p. 98). Some scholars have even suggested that through myths, such as the one of *Republic* 10, Plato means to present alternative/opposite views to the ones developed through the philosophical arguments so that the reader has to arrive at his own conclusion regarding these debatable matters (see McCabe 1992).

fulfills in the *Phaedrus*. I will show that this winged chariot has the purpose of being an efficient "vehicle" of philosophical thinking.⁴

In Socrates's second speech itself there are some clues about the grounds for the development of the myth of the winged chariot. First of all, before the mythical account of what the soul's *idéa* and *páthī* are, it is stated that this explanation will be human and shorter, instead of divine and longer, as well as rendered through a comparison of what the soul is like:

> [Regarding the soul] to say what kind of thing it is would require a long exposition, and one calling for utterly superhuman powers; to say what resembles requires a shorter one, and one within human capacities (*anthrōpínes kaì eláttonos*). Phdr. 246a

Afterwards, there is a more specific warning that here the god is depicted as a living organism with soul and body due to the limitations of human understanding on this topic and its incapacity for formulating a rational argument about it:

> ...immortal it is not, on the basis of any argument which has been reasoned through (*ex henòs lógou lelogisménou*), but because we have not seen or adequately conceived of a god we imagine a kind of immortal living creature which has both a soul and a body, combined for all time. But let this, and our account of it, be as is pleasing to the god. Phdr. 246c⁵

Finally, at the end of Socrates's discourse he states that his poetic fashion of speaking about *érōs* was designed to suit Phaedrus's frame of mind.

> This, dear god of love, is offered and paid to you as the finest and best palinode of which I am capable, especially given that it was forced to use somewhat poetical language because of Phaedrus (*toîs onómasin īnagkasménī poiītikoîs tisin dià Faîdron*). Phdr. 257a

If we take into account these three indications, independently of the particular contexts in which they are pronounced, the following reasons for Plato's use of this myth as a resort in the *Phaedrus* can be devised:
1) An account of what something is *like*, instead of what something *really is*, allows making a shorter presentation of contents which would require a longer development.
2) It also allows the expression in human terms about something which it is not possible to speak in divine terms, that is to say, through a clear grasp of the subject and on basis of an argument or *lógos*.

---

4 Translations from *Phaedrus* are taken from Rowe 1988; text (with references) from Burnet 1900–1907.
5 On this point see also *Ti.* 28c, 29cd, 30d.

The Myth of the Winged Chariot in the Phaedrus — 49

3) In addition, it stimulates a sympathetic attitude for its contents in people who are more inclined to poetic ways of expression than to a purely dialectical argument.

Corresponding with these hints, which are given in the text itself, I intend to show here that the myth of the winged chariot simultaneously meets more specifically the following purposes:

a) Along the lines of 1) above, it brings together different views on the human condition which are to be found in other Platonic dialogues: the *Symposium*'s theory of *érōs*; the *Republic*'s tripartite model of the soul; the *Phaedo*'s *psychī–sōma* dualistic conception. In this sense it summarizes something which would require a longer dissertation.

b) Along the lines of 2) above, it describes not only our present, incarnated existence but lets us speculate about a possible existence without a mortal body and envisage it as part of a continuous process of life and death pertaining to the whole universe within the perspective of eternity. Thus it gives an account about something which human reason is not able to fully understand.

c) Along the lines of 3) above, it provides an attractive account of these topics, as well as of other issues, which makes it understandable by an interlocutor who has a Phaedrus-like psychological type.

In addition to this, I mean to give evidence that this myth not only fulfills these three functions but also articulates these different issues appropriately. At first sight it seems that the myth tackles quite dissimilar topics: the three anthropological conceptions mentioned above at a); the *Meno*'s and *Phaedo*'s theory of *anámnēsis*; the *Stateman*'s dialectical method of division and collection; surreptitious hints to the *Timaeus*' cosmological theory; an account of the Ideas analogous to the description of them in the middle dialogues; a detailed phenomenology of the state of being in love. Besides, the mythical account is inserted in the wider context of Socrates's palinode to Eros, which is loosely organized according to a classification of the forms of *manía* and also includes a dialectical "proof" of the immortality of the self-moving soul (*Phdr.* 245b–246a). Such a jumble of issues would contradict the ideal of producing discourses with their sections assembled in a way similar to the parts of a living organism (*Phdr.* 264c). Thus, the myth would deserve the same reproach for lack of structure and disproportion as could be adjudicated to the dialogue as a whole.[6] I intend to

---

[6] The dialogue has two parts with quite different topics and styles (a first part which consists of

show that, at least regarding the topics concerning to a) –c) mentioned above, the literary strategy of the myth of the winged chariot actually allows the integration of different elements in an organized whole. In this way it works as an efficient *óchēma* for the understanding of philosophical matters.

Articulation of three anthropological models through the mythical account

In Socrates' second speech, right after the division of *manía* into four classes and the demonstration of the immortal nature of the self-moving soul, the human, shorter account (*anthrōpínes kaì eláttonos*) of the "form"—*idea*—of the soul and what it is like—*hoîon ésti*—is rendered through the simile—*hōî éoiken*—of the winged chariot which is described in the following terms:

> Let it then resemble the combined power (*dýnamis*) of a winged team of horses and their charioteer. Now in the case of gods, horses and charioteers are all both good and of good stock; whereas in the case of the rest there is a mixture. In the first place our driver has charge of a pair; secondly one of them he finds noble and good, and of similar stock, while the other is of opposite stock, and opposite in its nature; so that the driving in our case is necessarily difficult and troublesome. *Phdr.* 246a–b

In this section I aim to show that this image does not juxtapose[7] but concisely articulates three conceptions of the human condition which are developed at length in dialogues focused on other topics and placed in other dramatic contexts.

Firstly, as usually pointed out, the symbolism of the two horses and the charioteer can be easily traced back to the tripartite theory of the soul designed in *Republic* 4 and particularly taken up again in Books 8 and 9. The black horse would represent the appetitive part of the soul or the *epithymītikón*, which thoughtlessly goes for its objects, independently of their goodness or badness, and diverts reason from its aiming at truth and the real good (see R. 4.439b, d and 4.442a). The white horse would symbolize the spirited part or the *thymoeidés*, from which aggressiveness emerges and which loves victory and hon-

---

three speeches on Eros and a second part which develops a dialectical discussion on rhetoric and the art of producing discourses) and extension (the first part is quite longer and, besides, Socrates's speech much longer than any other part). For this reason it can be described as a sort of bicephalus monster whose heads have quite different sizes (see Rowe 1986, p. 106).
7 For this view, see Ostenfeld 1982, pp. 228–234.

our (see *R.* 4.439e, 2.375a–b, 9.581b). Finally, the charioteer would personify reason or the *logistikón* which, as lover of learning and wisdom (see *Rep.* 582d, 581b), ideally should lead the entire soul towards what really is.

Secondly, in the same passage mentioned above, another element is included: the "wings" of the soul which represent the rising *dýnamis* of Eros.

> The natural property (*dýnamis*) of a wing is to carry what is heavy upwards, lifting it aloft to the region where the race of the gods resides. *Phdr.* 246d

Both horses possess wings, in a Pegasus-like way, whose *dýnamis* -the power of desire- pulls the soul, under the guidance of the charioteer, towards the plain of the truth where beauty shines out.[8] The picture of Eros uplifting the soul towards beauty itself clearly evokes the conception of *érōs* in the *Symposium* which drives the soul through the different steps of the *scala amoris* (210a–212a).

Thirdly, the human soul whose wings are not strong enough to take it in the journey with the gods towards the eidetic realm must adopt an incarnated existence in a mortal *sōma*:

> (...) but before it was possible to see beauty blazing out, when with a happy company they saw a blessed sight before them –ourselves following with Zeus, others with different gods– and were initiated into what it is right to call most blessed of mysteries, which we celebrated, whole in ourselves, and untouched by the evils which awaited us in a later time, with our gaze turned in our final initiation towards whole, simple, unchanging and blissful revelations, in a pure light, pure ourselves and not entombed in this thing which we now carry around with us called body, imprisoned like oysters (*asīmantoi toútou ho nŷn dī sōma periférontes onomázomen, ostréou trópon dedesmeuménoi*). *Phdr.* 250b–c

Thus, the soul, which is imprisoned in a mortal body as in a tomb, loses its purity and splendor and forgets about the divine things, that is to say, about its travel together with the divine caravan towards the Ideas. This depiction immediately brings to mind the couple *psychī–sōma* which is the characteristic description of the human condition in the *Phaedo*.[9]

I intend to show here that the myth of the winged chariot does not just jumble these three anthropological conceptions but rather provides a dynamic artic-

---

8 However, Plato may also have in mind a winged charioteer as some representations of the time suggest This is the case of the theme "Eos on a chariot" who is "shown both with and without wings" and "sometimes the horses have wings" (see Matheson 1995, p. 209, actually Plato is probably conceiving the whole soul as capable of acquiring wings, that is to say as by Eros cf. *Phdr.* 251d.
9 In the *Phaedo* the body is characterized as an "obstacle" (*empódion*) to noetic activity (*Phd.* 65a, 66b-d) and as a "prison" (*eirgmós*) (*Phd.* 82e). See also *Cra.* 400c and *Grg.* 493a.

ulation of them. Firstly, it should be noted that *érōs* in the *Phaedrus* is able to adopt in the case of human beings two opposite directions. On one hand, *érōs* can be "upwards" and elevate the soul towards the eternal reality – the Ideas. On the other hand, there is a "downwards" *érōs*, not explicitly mentioned in the palonide, which is the soul's desire for what is mortal and corruptible. The wings of the soul which raise the chariot symbolize Eros the god, that is to say, *érōs* in its most perfect expression. This kind of *érōs* participates in the divine (*Phdr.* 246d) and nourishes with the truth (*Phdr.* 248b–c), that is to say, with the contact with the eidetic realm (*Phdr.* 247d). Notwithstanding, many souls do not achieve the "beatific visions", have their wings trampled, lame and ruined (*Phdr.* 248b) or even lose them so that they fall down on earth and takes hold of a mortal *sōma* (*Phdr.* 248c). Thus, in the case of non-divine souls, their upwards *érōs* which aims at the truth is resisted and even cancelled by a downwards *érōs* which aims towards mortal and bodily objects of desire. These two possible directions of *érōs* are clearly mentioned at *Phdr.* 246b–c:

> Now when it is perfectly winged, it travels above the earth and governs the whole cosmos; but the one that has lost its wings is swept along until it lays hold something solid, where it settles down, taking on an earthly body, which seems to move itself because of the power of the soul...

In the *Symposium* Socrates-Diotima's speech also depicts *érōs* as able to flow into different directions. Here *érōs* is a *daímōn-metaxý*, that is to say, an "intermediary" between the mortal realm and immortal realm (see Fierro 2007). Its utmost expression is being a *philósophos*, especially in the description of the ascent towards beauty itself in the Higher Mysteries (*Smp.* 210a–212a). However, *érōs* usually runs into other directions and, thus, originates other forms of existence, insofar as some people love (*erân*) wisdom but others love business, physical training or honours (*Smp.* 205a–206a). In other words, although everybody shares *érōs*' lacking-resourceful condition and is a lover of the good, some are able to procreate *katà to sōma*, others procreate *katà tīn psychīn* and only a few climb the *scala amoris* towards beauty itself and procreate true virtue. In addition to this, some conclusions on the different, even opposite, directions of *érōs* can also be inferred from some details of the dramatic context. Insofar as the fictional date of the *Symposium*'s opening narration should be placed around 403 BC, this means that Alcibiades had already met his tragic end. On the other hand, at Agathon's party, whose fictional date should be placed around 416 BC, Alcibidades makes clear his refusal to be driven by Socrates towards a philosophical way of life and his preference for the flatteries from the many (*Smp.* 216a-b). He constitutes, then, an example of how *érōs* can steer the existence of a person not only in a different track from philosophy but even into an opposite and destructive route (see Fierro 2010).

Secondly, the image of the winged chariot, which is led by the charioteer towards the eidetic realm, pulled into that direction by the white horse but unbalanced by the black horse stands for how opposite forces of desire create an intrinsic lack of equilibrium within non-divine souls. This picture displays, indeed, how the direction and strength of the drive which comes from each of the two horses and represent different kinds of desires or parts of the soul help to fortify or weaken the two fundamental directions of *érōs* mentioned above. It shows, then, how the *Symposium*'s theory of *érōs* and the *Republic*'s tripartite theory of the soul can be articulated (see Fierro 2008; Sassi 2007). Let us examine this point with more detail.

According to the hydraulic image of the soul at R. 485d-e there are two different streams of desire within the soul which clearly correspond to two of its parts: on one hand, the stream which flows towards wisdom and can be identified with reason or the *logistikón*; on the other hand, the stream which runs towards the bodily pleasures and can be identified with the appetites or the *epithymītikón*. Similarly, in the *Phaedrus* the black horse works as a force of opposite direction to the track into which the charioteer wishes to pull the soul. The only difference is that while in the *Republic* the *epithymītikón* refers to all kinds of appetites, in the *Phaedrus* the black horse mainly represents the sexual appetite which drives the soul in opposite direction to reason's guidelines. As it follows from *Phdr.* 253e–254b, the black horse is deaf (*kophós*, *Phdr.* 253e) and unbridled (*hýbreōs kaì alazoneías hetaîros*, *Phdr.* 253e), that is to say, as the appetitive part in the *Republic*, it is irrational or *alogistón*, insofar as it pounces on the beautiful beloved in a beastlike way and is unable to reflect on what is good or bad to do and to impose to itself appropriate limits. The black's horse yearning for bodily pleasures makes it "heavy" and "robust" (*polýs*, *Phdr.* 253e) and, thus, counteracts reason's effort to lead the soul upwards, that is to say, towards the truth. Only if the black horse were educated within appropriate limits, its negative influence within the soul could be reduced.[10] The charioteer, in the fashion of the *logistikón* in the *Republic*, represents that aspect of the soul able to establish what is best to do, in this case not to assault the beloved and look for mere sexual satisfaction, and, if possible, to evaluate the right action on the grounds of full knowledge of the real good (*Phdr.* 254b–c). Through this knowledge the mind strengthens itself and achieves

---

[10] See *Phdr.* 254e y 247b. Cf. *R.* 3.403e and ff.; 8.559a and ff.

its maximum expression as *noûs* (*Phdr.* 247c–d).[11] In other words, both the winged *érōs* and the charioteer – reason – grow stronger by means of the same kind of nourishment, that is to say, the spectacle of truth:

> The cause of their great eagerness to see the plain of truth where it lies is that the pasturage which is fitting for the best part of the soul comes from the meadow there, and that the nature of the wing which lifts up the soul is nourished by this. *Phdr.* 248b–c

Thus, it is clear that in both the *Phaedrus* and the *Republic* there are references to two opposite "streams of desire" within us: the motivations of the appetitive part of the soul and reason's desire for wisdom and the real good.

In addition to this, the third part of the soul – the spirited part – is symbolized by the white horse whose own desire – the love for honour (*Phdr.* 253d) –, as in the *Republic*, also plays its part in the interaction with the streams of desire within the soul. The white horse represents, similarly to the black horse, an irrational – beast-like – psychological force which is unable to orient itself towards the real good, that is to say, the Ideas, but needs reason's help for this. However, unlike the case of the black horse, its nature is essentially good and of good elements and docile to the charioteer's directions (*Phdr.* 246b). Thus, although, as we learn from *Republic*, the spirited part can be corrupted and finally dragged into the stream of the appetites (see, for example, *Rep.* 590b), its ideal condition is, as it is depicted in the *Phaedrus*, to work as an auxiliary of the charioteer and provide its strength for the achievement of reason's goals (cf. *Rep.* 441a). Then, the white horse is described in the *Phaedrus* as a "lover of honour" but "with moderation and shame" (*metà sōphrosýnes te kaì aidoûs*) and also as a "lover of true renown" or "true opinion" (*Phdr.* 253d), insofar as, as in the *Republic*, if appropriately trained, it should fight for the right convictions which reason holds (cf. *Rep.* 442b).

Thirdly, the *Phaedrus*'s description of the human condition through the image of the winged chariot allows the inclusion of the *Phaedo*'s characteristic pair *psychī-sōma* (see Fierro 2014). As seen above at *Phdr.* 246 b, the force from the black horse, which opposes reason's love for the truth, arises within the soul due a yearning for a mortal *sōma* through which its earthly desires could be fulfilled (Broadie 2001: 297). This attraction for what is mortal and perishable is the original cause of the different types of incarnated existence which results from a combination of the choice of each soul and the fate allocated to each of them (*Phdr.* 248e, 249b). Thus, as in the *Phaedo*, in our present existence soul and body are "intermingled" and due to their mutual association the soul

---

[11] As said at *Phdr.* 247d only the *noûs* can contemplate the Ideas.

reveals not only its essential desire for the intelligible reality but also other desires and emotions related to its somatic condition (*Phd.* 66b–e). Similarly, at *Phdr.* 250b–c it is stated that, even if in primeval times our souls lack a mortal embodiment, were pure and had full knowledge of the Ideas, now and here they are buried in the sepulcher of their mortal *sōmata*. On the other hand, in the *Phaedrus*, as in the *Republic*, the soul's somatic desires are distributed between the two irrational parts, although there is a special emphasis on the disruptive effect of the black horse's sexual craving for the beautiful beloved. The task of philosophy is here described, in similar terms to the *Phaedo* and the *Symposium*, as a "purification" and "initiation" in the mysteries which takes place when *érōs* moves from the beautiful body of the beloved towards beauty itself. In other words, falling in love triggers the *anámnīsis* and helps us recall not only the Idea of beauty but also the rest of the Ideas (*Phdr.* 250c–d). If possible, this process should take place not only in the lover but also in the beloved, whose love for truth would be awakened through the right kind of loving relationship. In both cases *érōs* heads for wisdom only if, as the *Republic* states, the three parts of the soul or sources of motivation are appropriately arranged. It is even speculated that, if a soul is able to lead a philosophical kind of life, that is to say, to purify itself from the bodily and refrain its appetitive part, have the spirited part as an ally and develop its love for the truth, it may escape forever, or at least for ten thousand years, from reincarnation (*Phdr.* 249a). Nevertheless, apparently, this does not mean that the soul will abandon a somatic condition but rather acquire a new kind of *sōma* which, being a "vehicle" or *óchīma*, allows the soul an unobstructed performance of intelligent, orderly actions (*Phdr.* 247a) and so constitutes an immortal living organism similar to the gods.

The mythical account of our human condition: our present existence and the existence *ante nativitatem* and *post mortem* in a cosmic context

As seen above, three different anthropological conceptions are brought together through the image of the winged chariot. In addition, this mythical discourse offers an explanation of our present existence which is part of a more general speculation of the avatars of an *ante nativitatem* and *post mortem* existence within the framework of the whole universe.

Firstly, let us examine the *ante nativitatem* condition and the first forms of embodiment of non-divine souls. At the start of the cosmic cycle of ten thousand years the human souls lack a mortal *sōma* and travel in their chariots together with the gods (*Phdr.* 248e). Right at the beginning of the first one thousand years all non-divine human souls are carried away through the heavens by the revolution and try to follow the divine souls to the place outside the heavens.[12] According to how successful they are in seeing the "plain of truth", the non-divine souls can be classified into three groups (*Phdr.* 248c–e, 249b):

Type 1: Those souls which poke out their heads into the *hypeouránios tópos* and uneasily (*mógis*)[13] catch sight of true reality.
Type 2: Those souls which also poke out their heads but are able to see only a fraction of true reality due to the pulls of their black horses.
Type 3: Those souls which try to ascend but fight between each other, cannot see anything at all and nourish exclusively from *dóxa*, insofar as they become wingless and lame.

The fact that all types of non-divine souls yearn for the sight of the eidetic realm evokes the Socratic-Platonic assertion of the universal desire for the good. However, it is not altogether clear what concrete reference corresponds to each type of non-divine souls. If we take into account the clues in the text, the following hermeneutic options seem to be open to us:

–**Type 1** are second-rate divinities (*daímones*) and/or human souls which do not reincarnate insofar as they have become divine in the previous cosmic cycle of ten thousand years. However, insofar as their desire for the mortal realm is not fully annihilated, they might reincarnate in subsequent cosmic cycles (*Phdr.* 248c).
–**Type 2**, which catch sight only of sections of the prairie of truth, should be either exclusively the human souls which reincarnate in the best ways of life (a philosopher, devotee of beauty or good lover) or all human souls whose rank of reincarnation depends on how much each of them sees of true reality.[14]
–According to how **Type 2** is taken, **Type 3** are either the human souls which adopt lives lower in rank to the philosopher or the souls of animals.

---

12 On the hermeneutic problems regarding the first fall of the souls see McGibbon 1968.
13 On *mógis* in Plato see Steinhal 1993.
14 The main hermeneutic problem is how to combine the assertion that the souls whose first reincarnation is in human forms of existence are those who do not see the Ideas (*Phdr.* 248c) and the assertion that the possibility of embodiment in a human kind of existence requires some previous acquaintance with the Ideas (*Phdr.* 249b). I interpret that *Phdr.* 248c implies that all the souls who adopt any human form of existence or at least those who lead a philosophical life do not have full knowledge of the eidetic realm but have seen only a fraction of it.

For all non-divine souls their chance of taking a peek at the place outside the heavens, the scope of their vision and the regularity of their access to truth depend on how much strength the wings of their *erōs* have gathered, that is to say, as stated above, what kind of interaction they have achieved between their different streams of desire. Thus, to a certain extent, every non-divine soul is responsible for its first embodiment, insofar as the acquisition of this condition is linked to its effort and ability to ascend towards the truth (see also R. 10.617e). In fact, the text underlines that in their subsequent periods of embodiment and disembodiment the non-divine souls which have experienced a human life have a choice in their next forms of existence. On one hand, if someone chooses three times the life of a philosopher, devotee of beauty or good lover, after three cycles of one thousand years, he can abandon his mortal embodiment and join the heavenly procession (*Phdr.* 249a). On the other hand, according to their choices, the rest of these non-divine souls go to the heavens or places under the earth in their disembodiment periods and, afterwards, adopt different kinds of embodied existences.

The myth also offers a significant parallelism between the *ante nativitatem* and *post mortem* condition for human souls and our present life which is explained, in fact, as a consequence of our previous forms of existences (*Phdr.* 250d–252a). Here and now our soul faces the same inner fight between its streams of desire, insofar as the black horse (the appetitive part) also drags the soul in opposite direction to the charioteer (reason)'s commands and the pulls of the white horse (the spirited part) (*Phdr.* 253e–254a). Here and now the wings of desire can grow in our soul and lift us towards beauty itself, if *erōs* does not get stuck in a mere sexual craving for the beautiful beloved (*Phdr.* 250d–252b). In the same way, here and now, even those who lead a philosophical kind of life "partially" and "harshly" (*mógis*) recall beauty itself and, more generally, the eidetic realm (249e, 250b). Similarly, the soul has a choice to develop a virtuous kind of life (*Phdr.* 248e) here and now, not only in previous and subsequent embodiments.

As to how each human soul tries to emulate a god, a parallelism can also be traced between our embodied existence and our disembodied existence (*Phdr.* 247b, 248a–b, 250b–c). In both cases the god clearly represents a psychophysical paradigm which each human soul tries to follow, as far as possible. The divine souls are always constituted of good "horses" or irrational aspects which are amenable to follow the charioteer (reason)'s directions. Insofar as all the streams of desire flow in them in the same direction, their wings of *erōs* are always strong enough to uplift them easily towards "the prairie of truth". Thus, the god has a unified soul without conflicts as well as a body which is a perfect vehicle of its intelligent performance, while human souls can only attempt to achieve a similar condition to different degrees of success. The role of the gods as a paradigm for human beings explains why they are described in anthropomorphic terms and, in fact, identified with the gods of the Olympic pantheon,[15] although the divine is ultimately conceived in different terms from the traditional religion.[16] In addition to this, not only here and now but also after death, the *homoíōsis theoî*[17] expresses itself in different forms, insofar as, according to his/her erotic-psychological idiosyncrasy, each person, being a lover or a beloved, imitates and follows a different god (*Phdr.* 252c–253b), that is to say, each human being replicates the gods under different patterns.

Being an archetype of the best kind of life to which a human being can strive is not the only role of the gods. Although their description cannot be directly related to any astronomical or astrological explanation of the time,[18] many features suggest that the gods in the *Phaedrus* refer to the heavenly bodies. Firstly, they seem to be in charge of the orderly movements of the universe, insofar as they are portrayed as "travelling above the earth" and "administering the entire world" (*Phdr.* 246bc). In addition, Zeus, who is "the great leader in heaven" who "goes first, ordering all things and caring for all of them, and is followed by an army of gods and daemons" (*Phdr.* 246e–247a), seems to represent something like either the soul of World in Plato's *Timaeus* or the movement of the outer circle of the fixed stars.[19] Moreover, their *diéxodoi*[20] within the heavens, and the circularity of these movements,[21] suggest the orbital courses of the heavenly bodies. As to Hestia, who does not move with the rest of the gods but stays at home, evokes the belief that the Earth has a fixed position in relation to the circling

---

15 Such as Zeus, Hestia, Ares, Hera and Apollo (*Phdr.* 246e – 247a, 252c, 253b).

16 In spite of his criticisms of many anthropological features of the Homeric gods, in the *Phaedrus* Plato retains the traditional view that the divine condition constitutes a projection of the human aspirations to rise above our mortal restrictions. However, at the same time, in agreement with Plato's censure of traditional religion, their anthropomorphic characteristics are ultimately removed and the gods are identified with the heavenly bodies, as we can see in the *Timaeus*. For further development on this point see Fierro 2013 and Brisson 2003.

17 See Annas 1998, pp. 52–71 and Sedley 1999.

18 See Hackforth 1952, pp. 71–4 and Poratti 2010, pp. 357–64.

19 See Robin 1954 on *Phdr.* 247a; also Ostenfeld 1982, p. 234. By contrast, for Eggers Lan 1992, Zeus is just a moral paradigm and does not stand for the World-soul. See also Griswold 1996, pp. 84, and 259 nn. 13 and 15.

20 *Phdr.* 247a4: *diéxodoi* often refers to the paths of the heavenly bodies. See Rowe 1988 ad loc. and Hackforth 1952, p. 73 n. 3. At the same time this also alludes in mythical terms to the 'excursion' of the gods (see LSJ s.v. *diéxodos* III.2.)

21 According to *Phdr.* 247c, 'the revolution carries them round' (*periágei hē periforá*). See also *Phdr.* 247d, where it is also said that 'the revolution brings them back again to the same place in circles'.

starry heaven.[22] Finally, the regular access of the gods to the place "outside the heavens" (*Phdr.* 247b–c) can be understood as an anthropomorphic representation of the full eidetic knowledge that the gods possess in a unmediated way according to which each of them "performs his own task' (*Phdr.* 247a) – that is, executes orderly astronomical movements. Thus, the mythical account also allows an explanation of the human existence within a cosmological background which is represented by the movements of the traditional gods. The dialectical argument at *Phdr.* 245a–e explains why every soul, being a self-mover, is immortal (*Phdr.* 245b–246a). If this constant and eternal movement of the soul could be identified with the erotic strength which propels every living creature in the universe, the human souls, who are responsible in any kind of existence for the growth or decay of their wings of desire, would actively take part in the development of the universe for the whole eternity. Those who are able to follow the astral gods join efforts with them in the nourishment of the uplifting *érōs*. On the contrary, those who nourish the *érōs* of opposite direction contribute to stop a positive cosmic expansion. Thus, every person must consider himself/herself as a direct contributor to or detractor of the increase of the desire for truth and the real good at all levels.

The mythical account as the appropriate speech for a Phaedrus-like soul

According to the second part of the *Phaedrus* true rhetoric is not only an expertise in the usual rhetorical devices which should be based on dialectical knowledge but also a *psychagōgía*. This last requirement implies that a good speech must be suitable for the kind of soul to which it is addressed.

Regarding Phaedrus his psychological profile is clearly traced in the introduction and consistently kept along the dialogue. He is a fan of the trendy intellectuals of the time, in this particular case, the famous *logográphos* Lysias (see, for example, *Phdr.* 272a). His main interest lies on displaying their productions in order to appear before his peers as a well informed man about the last novelties of the moment.[23] It is clearly stated that the poetic richness and multicoloured forms of expression in Socrates's second speech, particularly in the mythical section, are wittingly designed to impress Phaedrus (*Phdr.* 257b). And, in fact, there

---

22 See Hackforth 1952, p. 73.
23 For an excellent account of this point see Ferrari 1990, ch.1.

are clear signs that Socrates succeeds in his attempt to do so, as read at 257c as Phaedrus asserts:

> For some time I have been amazed at how much finer you managed to make your speech than the one before; so that I'm afraid Lysias will appear wretched to me in comparison, if he really does consent to put up another in competition with it.

However, it must be noted that, as shown above, the speech is also an appropriate vehicle to encapsulate some key notions about human nature and the universe whose knowledge is indispensable for someone who wishes to undertake the commitment of becoming a good orator and dialectician and, more importantly, to acquire real knowledge about herself/himself (see Grinswold 1986). A real understanding of these notions in the myth certainly requires a hermeneutic effort which Phaedrus, for example, may not be able or willing to do. Nevertheless, this written mythical account might luckily find appropriate readers who could grasp its meaning and even revive it through the most authentic form of dialectics, that is, a living discussion.[24]

Conclusion

Here I have shown that the myth of the winged chariot is not a heterogeneous mixture of diverse concepts but cleverly designed to offer an overall picture of how different philosophical notions are connected. The description of the chariot which is led by the charioteer and dragged by a pair of winged horses of opposite nature allows us to understand how three anthropological descriptions are linked together. The narration of the fabulous voyage of the chariots towards the top of the heavens and back to earth also offers an understanding of the human condition not only about our current situation but also in a hypothetical *ante nativitatem* and *post mortem* existence as well as in the context of the eternal becoming of the universe. The mythical account also works as a good summary on these matters and others[25] which are mentioned but not developed in the reflections about rhetoric, dialectics and the value of written speeches in the second part of the dialogue. Finally, non-philosophers like Phaedrus can

---

[24] On how in the *Phaedrus* dialectics should ultimately be understood as a "living discussion" see Rowe 1986 and McKenzie 1982.
[25] Some of the other topics which the myth addresses are mentioned here in the introductory section above. Unfortunately it is no possible to develop here how they could also be understood in connection with the rest of the issues of the mythical account.

easily be captivated by its poetic charm. Thus, it can be said that the myth constitutes a powerful example of how the combination of knowledge and literary skills in the use of words are able to propel human souls towards the search for truth.

Works Cited

Annas, J. 1999, *Platonic Ethics: Old and New*, Cornell University Press, Ithaca.
Brisson, L. 2003, 'Le corps des dieux', in J. Laurent (ed.) *Les dieux de Platon*, Caen Cedex, Normandie, pp. 1–23.
Burnet, I. 1905–1907, *Platonis Opera*, 5 vols., Oxford University Press, Oxford.
Broadie, S. 2001, "Soul and body in Plato and Descartes", *Proceedings of the Aristotelian Society* no. 101, pp. 295–308.
Cooper, J.M. (ed.) 1997, *Plato. Complete Works*, Hackett, Indianapolis-Cambridge.
Cornford, F.M. 1937, *Plato's Cosmology*, with transl. and comm., Kegan Paul, London.
De Vries, G. J. 1969, *A Commentary on the Phaedrus of Plato*, Hakkert, Amsterdam.
Eggers Lan, C.E. 1992, "Zeus e anima del mondo nel *Fedro*", in L. Rossetti (ed.), *Understanding the Phaedrus*. Sank Agustin, pp. 40–46.
Ferrari, G. 1990, *Listening to the Cicadas*, Cambridge University Press, Cambridge.
Fierro, M.A. 2007, "El concepto filosófico de *metaxý* en el *Banquete* de Platón" en J. Martínez Contreras (ed.), *El saber filosófico*, México, Siglo XXI, pp. 249–254.
Fierro, M.A. 2008, "La teoría platónica del *éros* en la *República*", *Diánoia*, vol. LIII, no. 60, pp. 21–52.
Fierro, M.A. 2010, "La concepción del *éros* universal en *Fedro*", en J. Labastida & V. Aréchiga (eds.), *Identidad y diferencia*, tomo 2: *El pasado y el presente*; Sección: *Antigüedad y Medioevo*, Siglo XXI, México, pp. 11–25.
Fierro, M. A. 2013, "Two conceptions of the body in Plato's Phaedrus", G. Boys-Stones, C. Gill & D. El.Murr (eds.), *The Platonic Art of Philosophy*, Cambridge University Press, Cambridge: 27–50.
Fierro, M.A. 2014, " Alma encarnada – cuerpo amante en el *Fedón* de Platón", Benítez Grobet, Laura & Velázquez Zaragoza, Alejandra (eds.), *Platonismo y neoplatonismo en la modernidad filosófica*, Universidad Autónoma de México & Ediciones Torres Asociados, México DF: 25–58.
Griswold, Ch. L. (1986), *Self-Knowledge in Plato's Phaedrus*, Pensylvannia State University, New Haven-London.
Hackforth, R. 1952, *Plato's Phaedrus*, transl. with introd. And comm., Cambridge University Press, Cambridge.
Halliwell, S. (1993). *Plato: Republic 10*, transl. and comm., Aris & Phillips Ltd., Warminster.
Heath, M. 1987, "The Unity of Plato's *Phaedrus*", *Oxford Studies in Ancient Philosophy*, pp. 150–173.
McCabe, M.M. 1992, "Myth, allegory and argument in Plato", *Apeiron* 25, pp. 47–67.
McGibbon D. 1968, 'The Fall of the Soul in Plato's *Phaedrus*', *Classical Quaterly*, vol. 14, no.1, pp. 56–63.

McKenzie, M.M. 1982, "Paradox in Plato's *Phaedrus*", *Proceedings of the Cambridge Philological Society*, 28, pp. 64–76.

Ostenfeld, E. N. 1982, *Forms, Matter and Mind. Three Strands in Plato's Metaphysics*, Martinus Nijhoff, The Hague-Boston-London.

Ostenfeld, E.N. 1987, *Ancient Greek Philosophy and the Body-Mind Debate*. Aarhus University, Dinamarca.

Poratti, A. 2010, Fedro. *Platón*, Akal, Madrid.

Robin, L. 1954, *Platon. Ouvres Complètes. Tome IV. 3e Partie*. Phèdre, Greek text and annotated transl., Les Belles Lettres, Paris.

Rowe, C.J. 1986, "The Argument and Structure of Plato's *Phaedrus*", *Proceedings of the Cambridge Philological Society* 32, pp. 106–25..

Rowe, C.J. 1986, *Plato. Phaedrus*, trad. con introd. y com., Aris & Phillips Ltd., Warminster.

Sedley, D. 1999, "The ideal of godlikeness", in G. Fine (ed.), *Plato 2. Ethics, Politics, Religion and the Soul*, Oxford, pp. 309–328.

Steinthal, H. 1993, "*Mógis* und *exaíphnes:* Platon über die Grenzen des Erkennens", in *Festschrift für W. Heilman zum 65. Geburstag*, pp. 99–105.

Szlezák, Th. A. 1976, "Unsterblichkeit und Trichotomie der Seele in zehnten Buch der *Politeia*", *Phronesis* 21, pp. 31–58.

Sassi, M.M. 2007, "Eros come energia psichica", M. Migliori, L. Napolitano Valditari & A. Fermani (eds.), *Interiorità e anima: la psyché in Platone*, Vita e pensiero, Macerata, pp. 275-95.

Vallejo Campos, A. 1993, *Mito y persuasión en Platón*, Suplementos. Er, Revista de Filosofía, Sevilla.

Vasallo, C. 2011, "La palinodia tra retorica e metafora. Alcuni problemi di struttura in Phdr. 244a3-257b6", G. Casertano (ed.), *Il "Fedro" di Platone: struttura e problematiche*, Loffredo Editori, Casoria, pp. 327-352.

Werner, D. 2012, *Myth and Philosophy in Plato's Phaedrus*, Cambridge University of Press, Cambridge.

Lucas Soares
Perspectivism, Proleptic Writing and Generic *agón:* Three Readings of the *Symposium*

Traditional readings of the *Symposium*[1] generally reduce Platonic erotics to the Socrates-Diotima discourse, relegating the five prior discourses and the last by Alcibiades to a secondary philosophical role. The devaluation of these discourses runs parallel to the canonization of the Socrates-Diotima discourse as a privileged place through which Plato supposedly reveals his only and true thought as to the nature of love. This primacy given to the Socratic eulogy tends to be supported by the key distinction that Socrates establishes as a criterion, in standing as a guarantor of the truth in relation to the erotic issue before pronouncing his discourse.

With this traditional reading of the dialogue in mind, in the present work I am interested in proposing a reading of the *Symposium* based on three mutually-correlative philosophical-literary currents. As regards the first current, and against the backdrop of dramatic-philosophical polyphony that characterizes the dialogue, I start from the assumption that the erotic issue, as Plato presents it in the *Symposium*, cannot be grasped unidirectionally, but through seven theoretical perspectives in harmony. The second current is concerned with analyzing the extent to which Plato puts into practice in the *Symposium*, as in no other dialogue, a kind of proleptic writing, in the sense that each eulogy contains fragmentary foretastes of topics that, through a subtle play of rectification and complementation, will be taken up again in later discourses. This proleptic writing is related to the perspectivist reading, as each discursive position is constituted from its dialogical-philosophical counterpoint with the remaining theoretical perspectives. As for the third current, I am interested in taking the agonal char-

---

[1] To quote some representative names of what we call "traditional reading", see Bury (1932, pp. lii-liii), Brochard (1940, pp. 49–59), who reads the five first speeches as parodies of living authors; Rosen (1968, p. xxxvi), Cornford (1974, pp. 139–146), Grube (1983, pp. 154–167), Guthrie (1990, pp. 371–380), White (1989, pp. 149–157), Osborne (1994, p. 101), Kahn (1996, pp. 267–281), and Reale (2004, p. 34). For the problem of the meaning of the first speeches, cf. especially Corrigan-Glazov-Corrigan (2004, pp. 46–50). It is however also worth nothing that in recent decades works have appeared such as those of Nussbaum (1995, pp. 252–268), Brisson (1998, pp. 51–54) and Reeve (2006, p. 124–146), who underlined the philosophical relevance of Alcibiades' discourse within the body of the dialogue, without subordinating it –as is usually done- to the Socrates-Diotima discourse.

acter typical of the Greek mentality in this period, approaching dialogue in the light of an *agón* between discursive genres, an aspect related to this play of counterpoints that the discourses establish between them.

I. Perspectivist reading

The primacy that is traditionally given to the Socratic eulogy is based, as mentioned above, on the key distinction that Socrates himself makes a criterion, in standing as a guarantor of the truth in relation to the erotic issue before pronouncing his discourse (*Smp.* 198d7–199a3, 199b2–5). For this image of Socrates as a mouthpiece for truth, it is interesting to recall a passage from the *Gorgias* in which, on seeing the difficulties that the character of Polus has in refuting Socrates' position, Socrates states: "Not merely so, Polus, but impossible; for the truth is never refuted (*tò gàr alethès oudépote elénchetai*, *Grg.* 473b10–11)". In establishing himself, then, in the Symposium as a mouthpiece not of *one* but of *the* truth about love ("Not at all, my dear Agathon. It is rather that you are unable to contradict the truth, since it is not at all hard to contradict Socrates ", *Smp.* 201c8–9), all that is said about *Éros* in the first five discourses Socrates places on the side of the pure *dóxa* or appearance of truth, so that in his eulogy it would be necessary to situate –if we follow the traditional interpretation– the theoretical core of the dialogue. One of the problems with this reading is that it ultimately devalues prior discourses in terms of simple rhetoric exercises, stylistically attractive but of little philosophical substance,[2] ignoring that a large part of the Socratic conceptual platform is forged through the appropriation and reformulation of some of the topics put forward in these discourses. To quote a couple of examples: from the discourse of Eryximachus and Aristophanes, Socrates takes up the conciliatory role of *Éros*; from that of Agathon he takes its methodological precept as to how a eulogy should be done, etc. As in all dialogue, there are points about which the interlocutors agree and others about which they do not. But what is important, in philosophical terms, is that precisely in the context of this agreement and confrontation of positions the complex physiognomy of the erotic phenomenon is gradually revealed in the *Symposium*, taken each time from a different perspective or point of view.

With this traditional reading of the dialogue in mind, the question that arises is whether the first five discourses and the last (and unexpected) one by Alci-

---

[2] Bury (1932, pp. xxv-xxvii, xxxvi), to quote just one example, subscribes to this position in regards to the discourses of Phaedrus, Pausanias and Agathon.

biades do not also partly contribute, in their way, to the configuration of the Platonic theory of love. Starting from the dramatic-philosophical polyphony that forms the backbone of the dialogue, and borrowing a term from the Nietzschean philosophical lexicon,[3] I am interested in proposing here, in contrast to the traditional interpretation, a reading of the *Symposium* in perspectivist terms. This stems from the assumption that the erotic issue cannot be grasped unidirectionally (as if the truth about *Éros* could only be approached from the perspective of the Socrates-Diotima discourse, or as if this could *exceed*, in Hegelian terms of annulment and preservation, the other discourses), but through seven theoretical perspectives in harmony. The *Symposium* would thus imply a perspectivist way of accessing the nature of love; a way in which all discourses are –to use Kierkegaard's words (2000, p. 108)– "like a sliding telescope, the one presentation ingeniously merges into the other". Under this proposed reading approach, each of the seven theoretical perspectives contains a partial grain of truth about the erotic phenomenon. As if Plato, faced with the question of how love is understood by the intellectual elite of his era embodied in the orators of the symposium, said to us: if there is a truth about love, this can only be revealed through the combination of perspectives put forward. This is not to minimize the claim for truth (tied specifically to interaction between *éros* and philosophy as supported by the theory of the Ideas) implied in the discourse of Socrates-Diotima, but rather to approach and measure the partial grains of truth which the other discourses reach (underestimated generally in traditional readings of the dialogue), which, through a subtle play of rectification and complementation orchestrated by Plato, contribute to enlightening areas of meaning of the erotic experience that the Socratic discourse does not allow us to grasp. If, as Nietzsche states (1983, p. 120), Plato lifted Socrates out of the street "to exhibit him in all his own disguises and multiplicities", in the *Symposium* that is masked behind seven discursive perspectives to offer a typology or thought in spiral form (hence the choice of indirect style) about love.

Let us bear in mind that Plato could –following the discursive register cultivated by some sophists– have written a treatise on love, approaching its nature from a single perspective. But it is clear that he preferred to dialogue with all the avatars that a conversation among a group of people entails (abrupt interruptions, changes in order, oversights, ironic comments, silences, humorous passages, hiccoughs, sneezes, etc.) where each orator makes his small contribution to the reflection on love. Each discourse thinks and translates the erotic phenom-

---

[3] For the notion of 'perspectivism' in the Nietzschean corpus, cf. especially Nietzsche (1992, p. 87; 1990, pp. 245–246).

enon in its own way and according to the discursive genre (rhetoric, medical, poetic, philosophical, etc.) on which each is based, while demonstrating the impossibility of reducing it to an unambiguous concept. In other words, each orator says in his own way not the truth (as Socrates states: "Regard this speech, then, Phaedrus, if you want to, as spoken in eulogy of *Éros*", *Smp.* 199b2–4) but a foreshortening of truth about love. As Barthes notes in this regard (1982, p. 225): "What the guests try to produce are not proved remarks, accounts of experiences, but a doctrine: *Éros* is for each of them a system". Plato presents to us a framework of theoretical perspectives through which he comes to tell us that regarding the nature of love there is no explanation that can be sustained precisely: hence perhaps the subsequent conceptual reformulation of his erotics in the *Phaedrus*, where *Éros* ceases to be a *daímon* in order to regain his status as a god: "What Plato shows us," Lacan states (2003, p. 54) "in a fashion that will never be unveiled, which will never be revealed, is that the contour that this difficulty outlines is something which indicates to us the point at which there is the fundamental topology which prevents there being said about love something which hangs together." The diversity and complexity of the erotic phenomenon thus exceed in the *Symposium* any conceptual attempt to establish its ultimate sense –as noted in traditional readings–within the narrow limits that *one* discourse implies. Apollodorus' tale implies not just spoiled pieces of ribbon, but also different musical versions of the same theme.

The perspectivist approach of the erotic issue is then, diametrically opposed to the readings that go out of their way to find in Plato a systematic will. That which could be a defect turns out to represent one of the central virtues of the dialogue. Because the *Symposium* is a perfect work in that it refuses to reduce the nature of love to a closed conceptual whole, in that rather than seeking to close, it seeks to put forward the perspectives of a given problem:

> If –as Heidegger argues (2000, pp. 181–182)– we scrutinize the traditional configuration of Plato's philosophy as a whole we notice that it consists of particular conversations and areas of discussion. Nowhere do we find a "system" in the sense of a unified structure planned and executed with equal compartments for all essential questions and issues. Various questions are posed from various points of approach and on various levels, developed and answered to varying extents.[4]

---

[4] See, along the same lines, Dover (1978, p. 160, n. 9): "It was not Plato's practice to reconcile what he said in one work with what he had said previously in another work, hence it is often difficult to decide if he has changed his mind or if he is expressing different aspects of the same problem".

The very choice of the dialogue format expresses the way that Plato finds to communicate the impossibility –inherent to the philosophical job in hand– of saying something (whether it be about love, the soul, poetry, etc.) that can be sustained definitely. The discourses can be read in this sense as *interventions* on love, which in not being able to give an unambiguous meaning, ultimately take on the obdurate multiplicity that characterizes the human erotic experience. Starting from this first current we can see the complex erotic scheme of the dialogue in the light of an incessant play of seven discursive perspectives correcting and complementing each other. As in no other work, in the *Symposium* Plato refines the point of view technique, no longer placed –as in most of the dialogues– in two archetypal characters (Socrates and those interlocutors on hand) but fragmented among seven figures (not counting the two narrators, Apollodorus-Aristodemus). The *Symposium* thus involves a choral structure of diverse tonalities that, only through their counterpoint, produce the sought after philosophical effect.

II. Proleptic writing and dialogic-philosophical counterpoints

In the *Symposium* Plato puts into practice like in no other dialogue a kind of proleptic writing (*prólepsis:* in advance, foreshadowing), in the sense that each eulogy contains fragmentary advances of topics that, through a subtle play of rectification and complementation, will be taken up again in posterior discourses. This proleptic writing is connected to perspectivist writing, as each discursive position is made up from its counterpoint with the other theoretical perspectives. Let us see some examples of this discursive counterpoint, through which Plato develops wisdom about love in the *Symposium*. In his eulogy, Pausanias rectifies the indivisible concept of Phaedrus' *Éros* in favour of a dual concept (the older and motherless *Éros* of Uranus, and the younger, more common Pandemus) but follows the young orator in the estimation of the *Éros* of older origin (Uranus), which contrasts at that time with the position taken by Agathon, who conceives of *Éros* as the youngest and most delicate of the gods, in order to distance him from the area of Necessity (*Anánke*), violence and discord in which the Hesiodic genealogy drawn up by Phaedrus had placed him. Although Eryximachus picks up the dual concept of the *Éros* opened by Pausanian, he does so within a nominal resignification (an "ordered" *Éros* that instils harmony and health, in contrast to an "excessive" type that engenders discord and disease) and a solid expansion of its area of influence (limited in the case of Pausanias to the plane of human souls) and to a micro and macro cosmic level, at the core of which *Éros* operates over all things human and divine through a harmonizing role (*Smp.* 187b4–6). With the dual concept of the god displaced to the plane of ancient human nature, the cosmic power of Eryximachus' *Éros* is recovered from another perspective in the discourse of Aristophanes and in that of Socrates-Diotima. In the former, this recovery is carried out not only from the doctor or curer-restorer role that Aristophanes' *Éros* takes on, but also in the context of the cosmic explanation (the sun as the father of the male gender, the land that of the female, and the moon of the androgyne) of the descendents of the three sexual genders that characterise our primitive spherical being. In the discourse of Socrates-Diotima, this recovery can be seen in the intermediary (*metaxý*) and cohesive role of the *Éros-daímon*, whose power allows it to establish community (*homilía*) and contact (*diálektos*) between gods and men (*Smp.* 202e3–203a4).

The strategy of mythical justification of *paiderastía* ("attraction to boys") from the Uranus *Éros* (motherless), as read in Pausanias' discourse, foreshadows somehow Aristophanes' strategy in relation to the sexual tendencies (heterosexual, homosexual and lesbian) of his spheres, once divided by the divinity. The restrictive perspective that the Aristophanic discourse establishes around the possibility of restitution of our old original half ("the fortune that falls to few in our day", *Smp.* 193b5–6) reappears, from another conceptual perspective, in Socrates' discourse in the light of the restricted character that Diotima assigns to the understanding of the final revelation (Idea of beauty) at the end of her erotic initiation: "I doubt if you would approach the rites and revelations to which these, for the properly instructed, are merely the avenue" (*Smp.* 210a1–2). The trilogy of debauchery, disease and pain that Aristophanes works from, as a consequence of the original iniquity of primitive human nature, can be understood as a response to the trilogy of harmony, health and love as communicated in Eryximachus' discourse. And, in turn, we can think of an erotics of the mutilated body in Aristophanes' discourse, because in Eryximachus' discourse it was possible to introduce previously the perspective of a double erotics of the body, whose devaluation in Pausanias' discourse became patent through the association between Aphrodite Pandemos and carnal love.

The methodological precept that Agathon sets out at the start of his discourse foreshadows the enunciation that will follow that of Socrates-Diotima, as well as the relationship that this establishes between his *Éros* and the cardinal virtues (justice, bravery, moderation and wisdom) ultimately is reconfigured in Alcibiades' discourse around the figure of Socrates as the cause of such virtues in men. In the Socratic refutation of Agathon's discourse, Plato not only foreshadows in terms of structure and form the relational character (*Éros* is desire for something), lacking character (*Éros* is desire for that which is lacking) and intermediary character (*Éros* is neither beautiful nor ugly, nor good nor bad) which the conceptual pair of *Éros-daímon* will have in the Socrates-Diotima discourse, but also this refutation constitutes a foreshadowing of that which Diotima will do to Socrates, who until the encounter with the priestess thought –like Agathon and the other orators– that *Éros* was a great god and that, therefore, had to be put in the place of the loved (*Smp*. 201e2–7).[5]

In light of these examples, which we mention here to illustrate the proleptic writing that Plato applies in the *Symposium*, I believe it is easier to see in what sense the perspective taken by Socrates does not imply, at the time of its appearance, a new concept in radical terms, given that his discourse is unthinkable when separated from the play of counterpoints that is taken on with the remaining interventions, which are important within the conceptual architecture of the dialogue in revealing partial aspects of the erotics issue. To put it in the terms with which Kant (1984, p. 16) referred to Hume's legacy: "If we begin from a well-grounded though undeveloped thought that another bequeaths us, then we can well hope, by continued reflection, to take it further than could the sagacious man whom one has to thank for the first spark of this light". This play of rectification and complementation, of continuity and antagonism among the seven discourses is overshadowed in what we call the traditional reading of the *Symposium*, as the latter approaches the work from the narrow antinomy of *dóxa* (five first discourses) – *alétheia* (discourse of Socrates-Diotima). In keeping with the dialogical character that his philosophy takes on, Plato would be saying, through the choral or polyphonic structure that informs the *Symposium*, that the truth about a given matter (such as, in this case, that of *éros*) is constructed –and is only possible– through a dialogical-philosophical counterpoint.

III. An agón of discursive genres

The *Symposium* begins with a joke (*paízon*, *Smp*. 172a1–5)[6] and concludes with an apologia of the true artist as artist of tragedy and comedy. This fact, which

---

[5] An exhaustive analysis of the Socratic refutation of Agathon's discourse can be read in Payne (1999, pp. 235–253).
[6] One of the most interesting analyses of the joke that begins the dialogue can be read in Stokes (1993, p. 128). The *Cratylus* also starts with a joke: one character (Cratylus) says to another (Hermogenes) that his name is not his name. Leading from the etymology of his name ("of the stock –*genos*– of Hermes", interpreter of divine will, god of commerce and theft), Cratylus maintains that Hermogenes has an incorrect name as this does not reflect his reality characterized by the

tends to be overlooked, is not a minor matter within the conceptual architecture of the work. From beginning to end in the *Symposium* Plato makes all the most renowned discursive genres (rhetoric, scientific, comic, tragic and philosophical) of his era interact around a reflection on love. But to better understand this one must bear in mind the agonistic mentality running through democratic Athens, the intellectual capital of Greece since the mid 5th century BC, the most prestigious city in wisdom and power, according to Plato's testimony, and the city with the greatest freedom of speech (*Ap.* 29d7–8, *Grg.* 461e1–3). Deleuze and Guattari (1993, p. 10) cast light on this relationship between the agonistic mentality and the Athenian democratic *polis* as a community of both free men and rivals (citizens):

> It is in this first aspect that philosophy seems to be something Greek and coincides with the contribution of cities: the formation of societies of friends or equals but also the promotion of relationships of rivalry between and within them, the contest between claimants in every sphere, in love, the games, tribunals, the judiciaries, politics, and even in thought, which finds its condition not only in the friend but in the claimant and the rival (the dialectic Plato defined as *amphisbetesis*. It is the rivalry of free men, a generalised athleticism: the *agón*.

Along similar interpretative lines, Cassin (1994, p. 12) stresses that the Greek *agón* ultimately refers to the meetings and tournaments that took place for the purpose of a 'game', a 'combat', a 'trial' or a 'theatrical performance'; these constitute the four possible types of antagonism among competitors, wrestlers, plaintiffs and actors. With regards to the erotic *agón*, there is nothing more eloquent than the words of Pausanias on the forms that pederastic love takes in Athens:

> Now our law has a sure and excellent test for the trial of these persons, showing which are to be favoured and which to be shunned. In the one case, accordingly, it encourages pursuit, but flight in the other, applying ordeals and tests (*agonothetôn*) in each case, whereby we are able to rank the lover and the beloved on this side or on that (*Smp.* 183e6–184a4).

Basing his argument on a key passage from the start of the dialogue, in which Agathon says to Socrates "A little later on you and I shall go to law (*diadikasómetha*) on this matter of our wisdom, and Dionysus shall be our judge" (*Smp.* 175e7–9), Hadot (2008, p. 87) interprets that the *Symposium* as a whole could have been titled *The Judgement of Dionysius*, thus underlining the agonal character of the work in relation to the *sophia*. Such is, in short, the situation

---

lack of resources and skill with words, hence in his case the name is not seen to fit the reality, which is the subject of the dialogue (*Cra.* 383a4–384c6).

that is the setting for Plato's *Symposium*, and that, it might be said, reflects the agonal character of the Greek mentality itself in the era: as a result of the victory of the poet Agathon in a tragic contest, we witness the celebration of an *agón* among seven theoretical perspectives of love, the revealing of which implies in turn, in the last section of the dialogue, an erotic *agón* between Socrates, Alcibiades and Agathon.[7]

If we then approach the *Symposium* from the mentality of the *agón* or, rather, as a combat of arguments (*agón lógon*) or "symposium of discourses" (*tôn lógon hestíasis*, *Ti.* 27b7–8)[8] around the problem of love, we should not be surprised by the proposal to read the dialogue in the light of an *agón* among discursive genres, or in other words, as a regulated exchange of discourses (*lógoi*) around a subject (*éros*) which implies, like all agonal space, hints of tension and anger among the interlocutors. This accounts for passages such as the following, in which, after Aristophanes' discourse and with the expectancy generated among the diners over his imminent discourse on *Éros*, Socrates says to the doctor Eryximachus:

> Eryximachus, made a fine hit (*egónisai*): but if you could be where I am now—or rather, I should say, where I shall be when Agathon has spoken—you would be fitly and sorely afraid, and would be as hard put to it as I am (*Smp.* 194a1–4).

Those "prose plays" (*Po.* 1447b10–15), to put it in Aristotelian terms, that are the Platonic dialogues, only put those characters on the stage whose main mission is to *personify* different discursive points of view. Or, to put it another way, they are at the service of a *lógos* that represents them and they submit to the play of dialogue exchange. A dialogue between *lógoi* rather than between characters, to the extent that Plato sometimes goes to the extreme of personifying a reasoning or argument (*lógos*).[9] The very choice of the dialogue form aims, as Nussbaum claims (1995, pp. 36, 133), to show us a confrontation of positions, the different aspects of a given problem, and to highlight the loss that any "solution" can entail:

---

[7] For the subject of the competition of the discursive genres and the role of philosophy in relation to them, see Mársico, among others (2002, pp. lxxvi-lxxxi).

[8] Cf. also *Lg.* I 640b7–8, where symposia are defined as "meetings of friends who share in peace a good disposition towards friends". Unlike Plato, in his *Symposium* Xenophon does not let the flautist, dancer and zither player go, but they accompany the diners throughout the evening. See in this regard *Prt.* 347c3-e1, where Plato draws a counter position between the symposia of upper-class, educated men and those of ordinary men.

[9] See, among other examples, *Phd.* 87a7–9, 89b9-c4, *Rep.* 457c1–2, 461e7–8, 503a7-b1, and *Sph.* 238b4–5.

> Plato uses the dialogue to motivate a view, to make us feel the force of a problem and to explain the practical roots and implications of a solution. The plan is to show us diverse responses to a problem, allowing them to be 'examined' as the dialogue progresses. If this is done properly, by the end we will clearly see both the nature of the problem and what options are within our reach.

Ultimately, what is left standing at the end of the *Symposium* are seven theoretical perspectives through which Plato seeks to show the complex nature of the erotic problem. As if in writing the dialogue he told us that to speak of love it is not enough to be a philosopher, but also a rhetorician, a physician, a poet (tragic and comic), a politician.

Although the "Socratic dialogues"[10] as a literary genre are not a creation of Plato's, it is Plato who unlike other disciples of Socrates raises the dialogue format –as can be seen in the *Symposium*– to an exceptional artistic level, converting this mixture of literary form and philosophical content into the instrument *par excellence* of philosophy. The Platonic dialogue thus becomes a framework of literary procedures and argumentative strategies that, as Nietzsche discerned in the 19th century, leads to the prototype of a new form of polyphonic art;[11] an amalgam that condenses within it registers belonging to different discursive genres of the period (poetry, scientific and historic treatises in prose, rhetoric, philosophy, etc.):

> If –Nietzsche claims (1973, pp. 120–121)– tragedy had absorbed all preceding artistic genres, the same can be said, in an eccentric sense, of the Platonic dialogue, which was created by mixing all available styles and forms together so that it hovers somewhere midway between narrative, lyric and drama, between prose and poetry, thus breaking the strict older law about the unity of linguistic form. The Platonic dialogue was the boat on which the older forms of poetry, together with all her children, sought refuge after their shipwreck. Plato really did bequeath the model of a new art-form to all prosperity, the model of the *novel*.

This Nietzschean interpretation turned out to be the precursor of contemporary reading of the Platonic dialogical genre as "intertextuality", "polyphony" or "conversation" among traditional discourse genres, subscribed to by interpreters

---

10 Cf. with Aristotle, *Po.* 1447b11.

11 For aspects relating to the issue of structure and function in Platonic discourse, the unity between literary form and philosophical content, the use of argumentative and literary techniques, and the various hermeneutic problems that the dialogue form entails, cf., among other works, Vicaire (1960, pp. 77–149, 158–192), Santa Cruz (1996, pp. 11–24), and Cossutta & Narcy (2001).

such as Gadamer (1977, pp. 636–637), Nussbaum (1995, pp. 179–181, 183), and Nightingale (1995, pp. 1–12), among others.

But the Platonic dialogue not only implies a complex and polyphonic dramatic structure, but also a break with traditional genre distinctions. Different "voices" operating in Plato's dialogues can be explained by the "conversation" that Plato maintains with traditional discourse genres.[12] Within his intellectual project, this polyphonic form of philosophy, as well as incorporating said genres into his dialogues, allows Plato to redefine philosophical work as a specialized, discursive and social practice, opposed to the traditional (pre-Platonic) concept of philosophy as "intellectual formation" in the broad sense. Although he defines the philosophical register as opposed to that of traditional discourse genres, through the dialogue format Plato manages to appropriate and intertwine procedures connected to those same genres he criticises. Hence, even when the dialogic form is sought to stand as an alternative to the discursive genres with which he enters into a critical discussion (as can be read in *Lg.* VII 817a-e, in the mouth of the character of the Athenian), he still incurs a positive debt with them.

In this perspective, if Plato contradicts himself it is because –to paraphrase Walt Whitman– his dialogues contain a multitude of voices. Precisely because understanding of the polyphonic dimension of the dialogue and of the Platonic concept of philosophy condition each other, the reflection on love which can be taken from the *Symposium* cannot be taken from the different discursive registers that dealt with this topic, hence Plato configures his erotics by dialoguing between genres. In other words, Plato is fully conscious that to approach the nature of love it is essential that there be an interaction between the different intellectual representations reflected in the most renowned discursive genres of his day. Rather than revealing the truth about love through *one* discourse in particular, this dialogue concentrates on a perspectivist approach of the erotic experience, whose truth can be deduced from the dialogic-philosophical *agón* between such genres. The *Symposium* is, in this respect, the best and the clearest example of Plato's philosophical-literary versatility,[13] and one of the dialogues that best illustrates the mix of genres that characterises his work.

---

[12] For the definition of "discursive genre" as a "way of thinking", "system of the imagination" or "grammar of things" capable of constructing a coherent model of the world, see especially Nightingale (1995, p. 3).

[13] Cf. in this regard Rosen (1968, p. xxxvi). On the polyphonic structure of the Platonic dialogue, see also Migliori (2005, pp. 11–46).

Works Cited

Barthes, R 1982, *Fragmentos de un discurso amoroso*, Siglo XXI, México.
Brisson, L 1998, Platon, *Le Banquet*, GF – Flammarion, Paris.
Brochard, V 1940, 'Sobre el *Banquete* de Platón', in *Estudios sobre Sócrates y Platón*, Losada, Buenos Aires, pp. 42–81.
Burnet, J 1900–1907, *Platonis Opera*, Oxford Classical Texts, Oxford, 5 vols.
Bury, RG 1932, *The Symposium of Plato*, W. Heffer and Sons, Cambridge.
Cassin, B 1994, *Nuestros griegos y sus modernos. Estrategias contemporáneas de apropiación de la antigüedad*, Manantial, Buenos Aires.
Cornford, FM 1974, 'La doctrina de *éros* en el *Banquete* de Platón', in *La filosofía no escrita*, Ariel, Barcelona, pp. 127–146.
Corrigan, K & Glazov-Corrigan, E 2004, *Plato's Dialectic at Play: Argument, Structure, and Myth in the Symposium*, The Pennsylvania State University Press, Pennsylvania.
Cossutta, F & Narcy, M 2001, *La forme dialogue chez Platon. Évolution et réceptions*, Jérôme Millon, Grenoble.
Deleuze, G & Guattari, F 1993, *¿Qué es la filosofía?*, Anagrama, Barcelona.
Dover, KJ 1978, *Greek Homosexuality*, Duckworth, London.
Dover, KJ 1980, Plato, *Symposium*, Cambridge University Press, Cambridge.
Gadamer, HG 1977, *Verdad y método* I, Sígueme, Salamanca.
Grube, G 1983, *El pensamiento de Platón*, Gredos, Madrid.
Guthrie, WKC 1990, *Historia de la filosofía griega*, Gredos, Madrid, vol. IV.
Hadot, P 2008, *Elogio de Sócrates*, Paidós, Barcelona.
Heidegger, M 2000 [1961], *Nietzsche*, Destino, Barcelona, vol. I.
Juliá, V 2004, Platón, *Banquete*, Losada, Buenos Aires.
Kahn, CH 1996, 'The object of love', in *Plato and the Socratic Dialogue. The Philosophical Use of a Literary Form*, Cambridge University Press, Cambridge, pp. 258–281.
Kant, I 1984 [1783], *Prolegómenos a toda metafísica futura que pueda presentarse como ciencia*, Charcas, Buenos Aires.
Kierkegaard, S 2000 [1841], *Sobre el concepto de ironía, en constante referencia a Sócrates*, in *Escritos*, Trotta, Madrid, vol. I.
Lacan, J 2003, *El seminario de Jacques Lacan. Libro 8: la transferencia*, Paidós, Buenos Aires.
Liddell, HG, Scott, R & Jones, HS 1968, *A Greek-English Lexicon*, Clarendon Press, Oxford.
Mársico, CT 2002, 'Estudio preliminar al *Banquete*', in Platón, *Banquete*, Altamira, Buenos Aires, pp. lxxvi–lxxxi.
Martínez Hernández, M 1986, Platón, *Banquete*, in Platón, *Diálogos*, Gredos, Madrid, vol. III.
Migliori, M 2005, 'La struttura polifonica del Fedro', in *Quaderni Bombesi*, Rivista Semestrale di Filosofia e di Scienze Umane della scuola di Alta Formazione Filosofica "B. Spaventa", Bomba, I, pp. 11–46.
Nietzsche, F 1973 [1872], *El nacimiento de la tragedia*, Alianza, Madrid.
Nietzsche, F 1983 [1885], *Más allá del bien y del mal*, Alianza, Madrid.
Nietzsche, F 1992 [1884–1888], *Fragmentos póstumos*, Norma, Colombia.
Nietzsche, F 1990 [1887], *La ciencia jovial*, Monte Ávila, Caracas.
Nightingale, AW 1995, *Genres in Dialogue. Plato and the Construct of Philosophy*, Cambridge University Press, Cambridge.

Nussbaum, MC 1995, *La fragilidad del bien. Fortuna y ética en la tragedia y la filosofía griega*, Visor, Madrid.
Osborne, C 1994, *Eros Unveiled. Plato and the God of Love*, Clarendon Press, Oxford.
Payne, A 1999, 'The Refutation of Agathon: *Symposium* 199c-201c', *Ancient Philosophy*, vol. 19, no. 2, pp. 235–253.
Radice, R 2003, *Lexicon: Plato*, Electronic edition, Biblia, Milano.
Reale, G 2004, *Eros, demonio mediador*, Herder, Barcelona.
Reeve, CDC 2006, 'A Study in Violets: Alcibiades in the *Symposium*', in JH Lesher, D Nails & FCC Sheffield (eds), *Plato's Symposium: Issues in Interpretation and Reception*, Center for Hellenic Studies, Washington, DC, pp. 124–146.
Rosen, S 1968, *Plato's Symposium*, Yale University Press, New Haven.
Rowe, CH 1998, Plato, *Symposium*, Aris & Phillips Ltd, Warminster.
Santa Cruz, MI 1996, 'Formas discursivas en la obra escrita de Platón', in J. Aguirre Sala (ed), *Las formas discursivas en la obra de Platón*, Universidad Iberoamericana, México, pp. 11–24.
Stokes, MC 1993, 'Symposium 172a-c: a Platonic phallacy?', *Liverpool Classical Monthly* vol. 18, no. 8, p. 128.
Vicaire, P 1960, *Platon: Critique littéraire*, Klincksieck, Paris.
White, FC 1989, 'Love and Beauty in Plato's *Symposium*', *Journal of Hellenic Studies*, vol. 109, pp. 149–157.

Graciela E. Marcos de Pinotti
Plato's Argumentative Strategies in *Theaetetus* and *Sophist*

In *Theaetetus* and *Sophist*, Plato accomplishes a construction operation of his adversaries which leads him to associate doctrines regularly attributed to Heracliteans or Eleatic thinkers with different sophistical positions. However, his primary purpose is not to refute historical positions, but to assert fundamental theses and principles of his own philosophy. So I am not interested here in evaluating the legitimacy of such associations, or "dialectical combinations", as Cornford (1935, p. 36) calls them. I will focus instead on the peculiar kind of argument he employs for the refutation of both kinds of opponents. This is a sort of peculiar argumentation, as I will try to show, which does not appeal to the existence of the Forms but to the conditions of the possibility of language.

In *Theaetetus*, Plato associates Protagoras' doctrine with the Heraclitean thesis. His main arguments against these positions assume there is a meaningful use of language and certain conditions which make it possible. Plato's opponent uses language, but he does not accept some of the conditions his practice entails. He tacitly admits that there is meaningful language as long as he is ready to communicate his position, but the content he disseminates is incompatible with that admission. Heracliteans, for example, claim that everything is in flux and that nothing stays. But since total instability would make the language practice impossible, their thesis, which is refuted as soon as it is made known, appears intrinsically incoherent. Protagoras –I mean the Protagoras Plato transmits– also contradicts himself: his thesis that the truth is relative to each one becomes false as soon as it is asserted. A similar strategy is adopted in *Sophist*, where it is Parmenides' figure that gains relevance. The sophistic denial of falsehood is related there to the Parmenidean denial of speaking or thinking of that which is not. Plato means Parmenides contradicts himself when declaring that non-being is unthinkable and not to be spoken of or uttered in the discourse, and the Monist does so as well when he uses the name to claim that 'one alone is'. Those who deny the possibility of any kind of blending or combination also contradict themselves, as the mere assertion of their thesis forces them to combine names in the discourse. In all these cases, there would be a contradiction between what is said and what for Plato is implied in saying it. His arguments would therefore respond to a similar strategy intended to bring to light some necessary premises without which, what we say, or what we want to be capable of saying, could not be said.[1]

In this paper I attempt to show that resorting to the *factum* of language rather than to the assumptions of the Forms is not a flaw in these arguments. On the contrary, this assures them a greater scope than the one of those arguments which Socrates proposes to his followers in *Phaedo* or *Republic*. The arguments I have chosen to analyse try to persuade every speaker (*a fortiori* the philosopher) who is ready to accept certain premises that Plato deemed necessary for our language practice.

1. The Factum of Language in *Theaetetus*. Refutation of Heracliteanism and Self-Refutation of Protagoras

1.1. The Heraclitean thesis is introduced in *Tht*. 152c as Protagoras' secret doctrine, implied in his theory of man as the measure of all things. Such a thesis claims that "nothing is one thing just by itself, and that you can't correctly speak of anything either as some thing or as qualified in some way" (*Tht*. 152d2–4). As a result of movement, change, and mixture with one another, "all the things which we say are –which is not the right way to speak of them– are coming to be" (*Tht*. 152d7–8). The attribution of being to things conceals their flowing nature and it provides them with some firmness and determination which they do not have. Hence the need to reform our language, which, in a world which is subject to changes in all respects as the Heracliteans describe it, would become useless. If their thesis is true,

> We should exclude 'be' from everywhere (...) nor ought we to admit 'something', 'someone's', 'my', 'this', 'that', or any other word that brings things to a standstill. We ought, rather, to use expressions that conform to the nature of things, and speak of them as coming to be, undergoing production, ceasing to be, and altering; because if anyone brings things to a standstill by what he says, he'll be easy to refute in doing that (*Tht*. 157b3–c2).[2]

---

[1] The Platonic strategy is in a way similar to the one used by Aristotle in his defense of the Non-contradiction principle in *Met*. IV, often characterised as trascendental. On the nature and scope of trascendental arguments see Cabrera (2007).
[2] Pl., *Theaetetus:* translated by McDowell (1973).

The Heracliteans, convinced that everything is unstable, suggest reforming language, producing one which is foreign to any kind of permanency. If everything comes down to movement, possessive and demonstrative words would be avoided, since, as they denote stability, they turn out to be inappropriate to refer to something which is subject to constant change and which does not preserve its identity throughout time.[3] Instead, we are forced to resort exclusively to verbs which express such processes. Otherwise, we would be refuted: facts would deny what is said.

However, later on, the idea of radically reforming language is abandoned and the thesis of universal flux, according to which *everything* is changing in *all* respects, is refuted. It is now understood that such a position, far from offering support to the definition of knowledge as a sensation, or to the Protagorean *dictum* of man as the measure of all things, leads to the fact that "every answer, whatever it's about, is equally correct" (*Tht.* 183a5–6). Concerning the new language, in keeping with the universal flux, which it seemed necessary to produce in accordance with the Heraclitean doctrine, it is now uncertain whether there is one which is indefinite enough to fit in that position. Some kind of permanency is the *sine qua non* of the meaningfulness of language, so that if the assertion "nothing is, everything is changing" makes sense, it is false, since some sort of stability is possible.[4] The *factum* of language shows that the extreme Heracliteans cause the collapse of what they presuppose when asserting their thesis whose truth would prevent saying something meaningful.[5] This is among those positions which condemn their followers to silence, or, if they decide to

---

[3] For Sedley (2003, p. 8), "such modes of discourse are intended as fully in the spirit of Heraclitus himself, and arguably, far from being and abandonment of truth, as representing the one way in which language *can* capture the truth about the world". According to Boeri (2006, p. 107, n. 97 *ad loc.* 157b-c), if the Heracliteans are right, "no queda claro cómo se podría comunicar a los demás la teoría del cambio perpetuo. Platón vuelve sobre este problema (en 183a-b) y, como se verá, el punto constituye un detalle decisivo para hacer posible la reducción al absurdo de la doctrina heraclítea".

[4] See *Tht.* 181b-183c. The problem is to determine whether Plato's argument entails that there is certain stability in the physical world, or that there must be something stable somewhere and this something stable is the Forms. In my view, Plato never accepted the extreme Heraclitean doctrine claiming that all sensibles are in constant flux. His argument against this doctrine of total instability in *Tht.* requires stability in sensibles.

[5] Sedley (2003, pp. 8–9) argues that radical flux does not lead to the collapse of language, but of dialectic. If "every answer, whatever it's about, is equally correct" (*Tht.* 183a4–6), there can be no dialectic, and, more specifically, no definitions, so Theaetetus' definition of knowledge really does undermine itself.

express it, they are condemned to self-refutation: its mere stating makes the speaker contradict himself.

At this point, we wonder whether the assumption of the existence of the Forms is necessary to give sense to this argument, or whether we have to do our best to understand it without resorting to the hypothesis of the Forms. Actually, the reading of *Theaetetus* as a whole confronts us with this dilemma. In the case of, at least, the argument against the extreme Heraclitean doctrine, it results from it that (i) nothing can have any description applied to it (182d4), (ii) all answers are equally right (183a5) and (iii) all existing language is useless except perhaps the phase "not so" (183b4). These consequences are introduced by Plato as obviously unacceptable[6] and sufficient for anyone, *not only the supporters of the Forms* to reject the thesis in question. Therefore, reading the argument without resorting to the existence of those realities assures it, as far as I can see, a greater scope than in the other case.

1.2. An argumentative strategy resorting again to language and to what is involved in it is used by Plato in order to accuse Protagoras of refuting himself. I refer to the argument known as *peritropḗ*[7] or self-refutation (*Tht.* 171a6–d8). The passage describes a hypothetical dialogue between Abdera's Sophist and a majority opposing his doctrine, for whom the opinions are not always true – as would follow from the man-measure *dictum* – but could be true or false instead. Protagoras, by agreeing that everyone judges something which is, somehow admits that their opponents' belief is true. But as soon as he does so, he has to concede that his own belief is false. While his opponents do not admit being wrong, Protagoras, "according to what he has written", has to concede that they are right.

Regardless of whether this criticism is valid or not, which has been greatly discussed by *Theaetetus'* scholars, I am interested in focusing on the contrast between the theses supported by the Platonic Protagoras and what he is *forced* to concede to his opponents in virtue of his own admissions. Examples of the former are that man is the measure of all things, "that no one is better at discriminating someone else's experience than he is", that every opinion is true or "that everyone has in his judgments the things which are" (171a9). Examples of the latter are "that their opinion is true –that is, the opinion of those who believe that what he thinks is false", or "that his own opinion is false" (171b1–2). In the first

---

[6] According to Robinson (1950, p. 9), "we are tacitly given to understand that these consequences are obviously false and therefore the view which entails them must be false too".
[7] From Sextus Empiricus (*P.* 2, 128a1): turning an opponent's arguments against himself (LSJ).

case, we have Protagoras' general statements in which the notion of truth is involved. They are introduced here by *homologeîn*, which implies peace and agreement, leaving aside any kind of constraint or violence.[8] Instead, in the second case, Plato uses *synchoreîn*, a verb which has a strong nuance of involuntariness, of reluctant acceptance.[9] In *Tht.* 171a8, b1, b12 and c1, it expresses the concessions Protagoras unwillingly makes to his opponents. The difference is analogous to the one between what has been agreed or explicitly acknowledged and what is implied in it. Since we are not always willing to accept what follows from our assertions, these uses of *homologeîn* and *synchoreîn* would allow making a distinction between giving our immediate consent to something and accepting it unnaturally, forced to acknowledge what follows from our assumptions.[10]

By referring to Protagoras' work, Plato wants to suggest that he, simply by trusting his truth to writing and making his doctrine known, considers it true not only for himself, otherwise, he would not have made it public. When subjecting his truth to the opinion of the rest of men, the Sophist ends up setting up the other's point of view, off which denial the thesis of man as the measure of all things feeds, at least under Plato's individualistic reading. The conclusion is that Protagoras' doctrine is disputed "by everyone, beginning with Protagoras himself" (*Tht.* 171b10–11), so his truth "isn't true for anyone: not for anyone else, and not for Protagoras himself" (*Tht.* 171c5–7).

The conflict that Plato intends to highlight is between Protagoras and his *own*, not others', admissions, rather than the conflict that confronts him with the opinion of the majority. His doctrine carries the germ of its own ruin. Whether Protagoras admits it or not, when the aim for the truth which encourages his formulation is disputed, the doctrine proclaiming the impossibility of such judgment refutes itself.[11] The moral of the Platonic argument, interpreted as such, is

---

8 It means *agree with, say the same things as* (LSJ). See *Tht.* 171a9: *homologôn tà ónta doxázein hápantas*; 171b2: *homologeî alethê eînai*; 171b7: *homologeî kaì taúten alethê tèn dóxan*.
9 See Thucydides, *I*, 140, cited in LSJ.
10 See Marcos de Pinotti (2006, pp. 214–218), where I argue that in *Tht.* 171a-c *synchoreîn* does not exactly mean admitting what the other has said, but what follows from one's own admissions. The difference is crucial: one refers to the other's right to mistrust my assertions, whereas in the other, the conflict is posed to oneself. The uses of *synchoreîn* in *Tht.* 166b2 and 169d6 are particularly clear in this sense. Out of the multiple uses recorded by LSJ, where *synchoreîn* refers to the moment in which a weakened army has to give up territory, see p.e. *Phd.* 94b, 100a (*accede, assent to, acquiesce in*); *Rep.* 383a, c, 489d, 543b, *Euthphr.* 13a, c (*concede or grant in argument*); *Cra.* 435b (*agreement, consent*) and *Phdr.* 234e (*one must concede*).
11 See Narcy (1994, p. 340, n. 231 *ad loc. Tht.* 171a): "En face d'un Protagoras isolè par son propre principe, ceux qui ont l'opinion contraire sont nécessairement plusieurs. Voilà donc

that there are no speakers who do not challenge Protagoras' doctrine. Whoever wants to express how things are just for him has nothing better to do than to remain silent. It is not by chance that the fertile land to refute Protagoras, as well as the Heracliteans, is that of *lógos* as the oral expression of what is thought. This reappears in *Sophist*, to which I will refer below, where the resorting to language becomes even more relevant.

2. The Factum of Language in *Sophist*. On How to Refute Those Who Deny Something "Absolutely"

This dialogue, devoted to the problem about falsehood, in which Plato discusses several positions of Eleatic roots, offers more examples of the refutation strategy that we have found in *Theaetetus*. At least three times Plato faces his opponents, taking advantage of inconsistencies between what they say and the speech itself, trying "to show that what is proposed and how it is proposed are inconsistent and incompatible" (Wilmet 1990, p. 97).[12] But the peculiarity of the arguments of *Sophist* is that they are addressed against explicitly denying positions, which try to deny something (not-being, or multiplicity, or combination) *absolutely*. However, Plato perceives that no absolute denial can thrive in the field of language. The following arguments are addressed against positions which Plato considers untenable because the truth of what they deny is a *sine qua non* of the meaningfulness of that denial.

2.1. The first example belongs to the discussion about what is not anything at all, a non-existent which has no entity, not even the necessary one to be able to think or say that it is *not*. The expressions with which we try to refer to it do not succeed in saying it, and, thus, do not manage to reach the status of names. In turn, nothing which is can be ascribed to that which has no sort of being. The number, as a unity or as plurality, is among the things which are, therefore, it cannot be added to what has no being at all. The problem is that

---

una opinion qui n'est pas celle de celui-là *seul* à qui apparît, et qui suffit, par son existence même, à invalider le principe énoncé par Protagoras".

12 Such a method, Wilmet adds, "is already implicit in the early, 'definition' dialogues, where Socrates forces someone to say what he thinks, i.e., forces him to *speak*, and tries to derive from that sole speech either inconsistencies or conclusions that the speaker is *not* ready to endorse. It becomes all the more explicit in later dialogues, especially *Theaetetus* and *Sophist* (...)".

just by saying 'things that are not', or 'that which is not', we are illegitimately adding the number –either plurality or the unity respectively– to what has no being at all, and consequently no determination at all.¹³ No expression we might coin could escape this fate. Language is condemned to think, express, pronounce and say what is. It forbids any kind of reference to what is not anything at all. The conclusion is that which is not at all not only "is unthinkable, not to be spoken of or uttered or expressed" (*Sph.* 238c10–11),¹⁴ but cannot even be spoken of as unthinkable or being incapable of being spoken of or uttered or expressed. When trying to do so, we contradict ourselves. In order to speak correctly about the non being (*perì autoû*, 239b10), we should neither ascribe unity nor plurality to it, but without doing so, it is not possible to make a statement about something. The conditions a statement about what is not anything at all should meet are incompatible with those which any statement as such has to meet. The attempt to express something about what has no being at all is futile. To what extent then did Parmenides not contradict himself when denying the possibility of thinking of or speaking of that which just simply is not? The subtle Platonic argument, though in the beginning it seems to confirm the Eleatic prohibition,¹⁵ implies that Parmenides could not even formulate his own *dictum*. When saying that the non-existent cannot be thought of, expressed, etc., he contradicted himself (Malcolm 1967, p. 136).

2.2. In the same direction goes the Monism refutation in *Sph.* 244b ss. In the first part of the argument Plato resorts to the *factum* of language again. The Monists say there is nothing else except one. However, the mere proposition 'one alone is' cannot be uttered without admitting the existence of two names. Plato alleges that this would imply that the only thing existing is complex, it consists of that 'one' thing and its existence, i.e., it is not really one. We should notice that names are not understood here as mere conventions, in which case, the Monist would not be prevented from accepting them. Parmenides, as we

---

13 On the impossibility of thinking of or speaking of something "apart from number" see *Sph.* 238b6–8. In *Tht.* 185c4-d1, unity and numbers in general (as well as being, not being, likeness and unlikeness, sameness and difference, and so on) are included among the common terms (*koiná*) that apply to everything.
14 Pl., *Sophist*: translated by Cornford (1935).
15 For Cornford (1935, p. 208), in *Sph.* 237b-239c "Plato is not criticising, but confirming" Parmenides' doctrine about not-being (p. 203). The conclusion that the very words 'the non-existent' (absolute nonentity) cannot be uttered at all without self-contradiction "is not urged against Parmenides, and could not be urged without descending to captiousness. In all this section on 'the totally non-existent' Plato is rather confirming Parmenides and accepting his warning".

know, admitted their existence and that mortals used them in order to express something that was nothing else than an opinion. But names are viewed here as an expression of what things really are. That there exist two names, as Crombie (1963, p. 393) explains, must mean something like "that there exist *grounds* necessitating the use of two non-synonymous words", or "that the one substance contains two aspects". Furthermore, the Monists cannot even admit the existence of a name. If the name is the same as the thing, it will not be able to name it, and if it is different from it, it will be in fact affirming the existence of *two* things. Consequently, the Monists are limited to silence or to a mere verbalism (Guariglia 1970, p. 75). As soon as they try to communicate their thesis, they deny there is only one thing. Once more the Platonic argument shows that a philosopher's thesis can be intrinsically incoherent. Plato focuses on the inconsistency between the content of what is said and the speech itself, between the thesis that is communicated and the language that expresses it. Such a thesis falls apart and, somehow, the effort made to refute it becomes unnecessary. This is clearly emphasized in the next passage of the *Sophist* that I have selected.

2.3. *Sph.* 252c6–9 occurs in a context where Plato discusses several alternatives with regard to the possibility and the extent of combination. The first one is that "nothing has any capacity for combination with anything else for any purpose" (*Sph.* 251e9). Against this view Plato argues that if no combination was possible, then (i) there would be nothing, as nothing would participate in Being, and (ii) those who said that e.g. 'Motion is' would be saying nothing (*légoien àn oudén*, *Sph.* 252b5).[16] The truth of the separatist thesis would then carry out the ruin of philosophy, depriving of sense everything that was said by the ancient philosophers reflecting upon Being. In fact, in *Sph.* 259d9–e2, "the attempt to separate everything from every other thing" will be described as non philosophical (*aphilosóphou*). Even more, the greatest absurdity involved in the separatist thesis affects those who try to defend it. In fact, (iii) those who say that no combination is possible, according to Plato, refute themselves in propounding their thesis, because

> in referring to anything they cannot help using the words 'being' and 'apart' and 'from the others', and 'by itself' and any number more. They cannot refrain from these expressions or from connecting them in their statements, and so need not wait for others to refute them;

---

[16] Taken literally this means that those who say that Motion is would not make a statement. But 'say nothing' can also be understood to mean 'say what is false'. Heinaman (1983, p. 177) poses the question of what the combination or communion, i.e. the communion of Forms, explains. It is unclear whether it accounts for the meaningfulness or the truth of statements.

the foe is in their own household, as the saying goes, and, like that queer fellow Eurycles, they carry about with them wherever they go a voice in their own bellies to contradict them (*Sph.* 252c6–9).

The difficulty evokes the aporia to which the attempt to deny what is not anything at all led us. Just as we could not say it was unthinkable or unsayable because when doing so we were contradicting ourselves, those who do not admit any kind of combination cannot express this without refuting themselves, either. They say that there is no blending, that nothing combines with anything. But if it actually were so, Plato argues, that nothing combines with anything could not even be uttered. The sole propounding of this thesis demands the combination of terms in statements (*synáptein en toîs lógois*, *Sph.* 252c5), showing that some kind of combination is possible.

Once more, the position with which Plato is confronted is condemned to irreparable falseness and his supporters, to silence. The separatist denial of all blending –as well as the Parmenidean denial of not being, the Monist denial of multiplicity, and, in general, any position that tries to deny *something absolutely*– appear as untenable. Whoever supports such a position is forced to remain quiet or, if he decides to speak, to contradict himself, because of implicitly accepting that the thing which, he says, is not anything at all, in a sense *is*. Plato can see that no absolute denial can thrive in the field of language, in which it becomes inconsistent since everything about which we can utter words, even if we did so to deny it, somehow is (*pós eînai*). It is possible to deny that something is so that this denial makes sense and, even more, so that it is true. But we need to lessen the strength of 'no' and admit that when saying that something is *not*, we, in fact, say so because it is not obvious that it is not. We do not refer to what is not in *any* sense or in *any* way whatsoever, absolutely and undeniably, in which case denying it would be unnecessary, but to something about which there is no lack of reasons in favour of it being, even if we say it is not.

Prm. 160b5–163b6, within the framework of the discussion of the hypothesis "if unity is not", is especially clear in this sense. There Plato argues that unity, if it is not, "must have a share of being in a way" (161e).[17] Since we claim to speak truly, i.e., to say things which are, "it seems that unity is, if it is not" (162a); "unity, since it is not, must share in being in order not to be" (162b). We must provide it with some kind of being and also with the difference with respect to the other things. Otherwise, saying "unity is not" would not differ from saying something completely opposite, 'not unity is not', or that any other thing is not

---

[17] Pl., *Parmenides:* translated by Allen (1983).

("largeness is not", "smallness is not") (*Parm.* 160b6–c5). So, although we add not being to the unity –or rather, just because we add not being *to the unity*, expressing that the unity, not any other thing, is not– we are inevitably determining it. When calling it "unity" we silently and implicitly acknowledge that it differs from the other things and that these, in turn, differ from it. When ascribing the difference to it, we ascribe the necessary reality to deny it and not any other thing. In contrast with the unity that (we say) is not of *Prm.* 160b5 ss. and in general, in contrast with all that of which we can think or say it is, so that what is thought or what is said makes sense, the absolute not being giving birth to the aporia of *Sph.* 237b7–239c3, as well as the multiplicity which the Monist denies, or the combination that the separatists claim impossible, cannot be denied consistently. The way in which our language is structured prevents that.

In this sense, as we can see, even if the examples of *Theaetetus* and *Sophist* examined here respond to quite a similar refutation strategy, focused on the contradiction between what the opponent says and what is implied in the speech itself, there are differences between them. The peculiarity of the arguments in *Sophist* is that they aim at positions which are explicit and absolute negations, while, in the arguments offered in *Theaetetus*, the denial is just implicit.[18] Yet the target of Plato's criticism is the same. In all the cases, he tries to show that the use of language commits us to admitting that all that about which we speak, even if we do so in order to deny it, is in a sense, and it has certain determinations without which it could not become an object of discourse. We are also committed to admitting that not everything that we say is similarly true. Plato believes that no speaker can avoid these commitments that language imposes on him. Consequently, as soon as he asserts a thesis whose content is incompatible with any of the premises without which nothing could be said, he gets caught in a contradiction.

To conclude, I would like to emphasize once more that the resource to the conditions of possibility of language rather than to the thesis of the existence of the Forms is not a defect of the argumentative strategy displayed in the passages of *Theaetetus* and *Sophist* analyzed here. On the contrary, such resource gives rise to a special type of argument that tries to persuade every language user and not only those who defend the Forms. Despite this, Plato's reader will inevitably find veiled references to these realities in almost all of them.

---

18 When affirming that everything is in flux, the Heraclitean thesis denies any form of permanency, while Protagoras' thesis about every opinion being true denies falseness.

Works Cited

Allen, R E, 1983, *Plato's Parmenides. Translation and Analysis*, Oxford, Basil Blackwell.
Boeri, M, 2006, Platón, *Teeteto. Introducción, traducción y notas*, Buenos Aires, Losada.
Cabrera, I, 2007, 'Argumentos trascendentales o cómo no perderse en un laberinto de modalidades', in I. Cabrera, I. (comp.), *Argumentos trascendentales*, México, UNAM, pp. 7–29.
Cornford, F M, 1935, *Plato's Theory of Knowledge. The* Theaetetus *and the* Sophist, Londres, Humanities Press.
Crombie, I, 1963, *An Examination of Plato's Docrines*, vol. II, London, Routledge & Kegan Paul.
Guariglia, O, 1970, 'Platón, *Sofista* 244b–245e. La refutación de la tesis eleática', *Diálogos* vol. 7, nº 19, pp. 73–82.
Heinaman, R, 1983, 'Communion of Forms', *Proceedings of the Aristotelian Society*, vol. 82, pp. 175–190.
Liddell, H. G. and Scott, R. Revised and augmented throughout by Jones, H. S. (LSJ), 1996, *A Greek-English Lexicon.With a revised supplement*, Oxford, Clarendon.
McDowell, J, 1973, Plato, *Theaetetus. Translated with Notes*. Oxford, Clarendon Press.
Malcolm, J, 1967, 'Plato's Analysis of *to on* and *to me on* in the *Sophist, Phronesis*, 12, pp. 130-146.
Marcos de Pinotti, G E, 2006, 'En defensa de Platón. Notas al argumento de auto-refutación de Protágoras (*Teet.* 171a–c)', in M. C. Di Gregori & M. A. Di Berardino (comps), *Conocimiento, realidad y relativismo*, México, UNAM, pp. 209–227.
Narcy, M, 1994, Platon, *Théétète*. Trad., introduction et notes, Paris, G-F Flammarion.
Robinson, R, 1950, 'Forms and Error in Plato's *Theaetetus*', *The Philosophical Review* vol.49, nº 1, pp. 3–30.
Sedley, D, 2003, 'The Collapse of Language? *Theaetetus* 179c-183c', *Plato* 3 (on line), pp. 1–11. *The Internet Journal of the International Plato Society*. URL: http://gramata.univ-paris1.fr/Plato/spip.php?article38
Wilmet, R, 1990, 'Platonic Forms and the Possibility of Language', *Revue de Philosophie Ancienne* vol. 8, nº 1, pp. 97–118.

José Trindade Santos
"Reading Plato's Sophist"

I

Plato's *Sophist* explores a cluster of philosophical interconnected problems, namely those of truth/falsity and being/not-being. Highlighting some key passages in Plato's dialogues in which these problems are approached I come to the *Sophist* where they are brought together and solved.

1. The elenctic dialogues

In the elenctic dialogues Socrates uses the *elenchos* to test the consistency of any given answer to the "What is X" question he presents his interlocutor with. This strategy relies on the strong presupposition that infallible *epistêmê* is granted to anyone who successfully manages to survive the test of stating what anything is with a *logos*[1].

Contrary to some well-established positions on the subject,[2] I think this methodological procedure dispenses with a proper theory of truth. Such a conception of dialectics should be understood in an agonistic context, in which, through question and answer, any candidate comes to be or not to be recognized as a *sophos*[3].

2. The dialogues on the Theory of Forms

Quite differently, when the method of question and answer is used in a cooperative search for *epistêmê* the focus no longer lies on the *logoi* offered by the participants in the ongoing search, but on the object of the enquiry.

---

1 *Epistêmê* should be understood as the cognitive state in which one "in the strict sense knows" something (Aristotle *DA* B5,417a28–30); or knows "in itself that which is cognizable and true" (Plato *VII Letter* 342b1). This perspective dispenses with the alternative between "objective and subjective knowledge" (Chr. Gill 1996, 284–286), for while our "knowledge" can only be understood as a dual process, *epistêmê* is a cognitive state of the soul.
2 G. Vlastos 1994.
3 As Ch. Gill (1996, 290) suggests "Socrates" reacts to an incompatibility in his opponents' positions by refuting them.

The *Phaedo* (72e–76e; 100a–103c) and the *Republic* (VII 523a–525) take pains to explain how, guided by the hypothesis of Forms and in association with *anamnêsis*, *epistêmê* may be attained. Two different epistemic objects and not one, according to the cognitive competences involved (*R.* V 477c–d), should be considered. One, grasped by intelligence, is the Form or Forms relative to the particular topic (*hekaston: Phd.* 101c) of the quest; the other is whatever perceptible objects relate to it, configured through the cooperation of sense-perception, *anamnêsis* and thought expressed by the complex of *doxa* (*Phd.* 100e–103a).

But the *state* of *epistêmê* can never be attained through any kind of dialectical *process* despite the nature and number of cognitive competences used to achieve it. The *Seventh Letter* (344b) tries to overcome this gap promising a "sudden burst of the light of intelligence" produced by "rubbing together names, definitions, visions and sense-perceptions". The *Timaeus* (37a–c) explains how the circles of the Same and the Other cooperate to generate true beliefs and knowledge. But the aporetic ending of the *Theaetetus* makes it clear that, with or without the assistance of *logos*, true belief and *epistêmê* shall always be incommensurable.

3. The Theaetetus

At 188a–c in quick succession Socrates shows that if one can only know or not know there is no way for any known thing to be not known (*eidenai*) and vice-versa. Other approaches, as from being or not being, perceiving or not perceiving, lead to the same result (188c–189b).

This conclusion is subsequently confirmed from the varying perspectives of *allodoxia*, the block of wax and the aviary (189b–200c), and reaffirmed in the last section of the dialogue, which shows that the gap between *doxa* and *epistêmê* cannot be bridged by *logos* (206d–210d). Though this aporetic conclusion may be interpreted in a number of ways[4] I suggest Plato advances it as a *reductio* of *epistêmê*.

---

4 There is the possibility of interpreting the aporetic conclusion as a consequence of the non admission of Forms by the argument (Mi Kyoung-Lee 2008, 414).

4. The Sophist I

Such *reductio* explains why the search for *epistêmê* is abandoned in the *Sophist* and replaced by a quest beginning (236e) and ending (259b) with being, not-being and being and not-being[5]. The Guest (EG) affects being puzzled by the fact that each Greek cosmologist has used several names and expressions to refer to one single entity: "being" ("the all": 244b; "the one": 244b–c; "the whole": 244d), thus attaching different descriptions to it (243b–c). He then asks what could these people have meant[6] when they used the term 'being' (243b, 244a–b).

4.1 The Sophist II

And yet, up to this point the reader is being told quite a different story, for most of the dialogue has been focused on the protean figure of the sophist. How is it possible that a man who, to his pupils, appears to be wise in all things ends not being wise at all (233c, 234e–235a)? How can he:

> truly possess the knowledge of all the things about which he seems to be able to argue[7] (235a)?

The answer to this questions lies in the scandalous dialectical device through which he manages to turn every argument topsy-turvy. By using Parmenides' prohibition against saying that "things that are not are" (B7.1), the sophist manages to avoid falsity and contradiction with the allegation that:

> [what is not] is inconceivable, inexpressible, unspeakable and irrational (238c, 241a).

Plato denounces this dialectical strategy in two other dialogues – the *Euthydemus* (283e–284c, 285d–286b) and the *Cratylus* (429d–430a) – without attempting to refute it. Apparently in the *Sophist* he sets his mind on disarming it once and for all, and with good reasons. For the sophist's resistance to contradiction made

---

[5] Plato approaches the study of reality through the criticism of the relevant Greek doctrines on the nature of being (242c-249d), from which he elicits his own position on the topic (247d-e; 249c-d).
[6] In order to express this new approach Plato resorts to an unusual succession of verbs in a relatively short passage (243c-244b): *legô, dêloumai, phthengomai, tithêmi, kaleô, sêmainô*.
[7] H. N. Fowler's translation of the dialogue, published in the Loeb series (translations of other dialogues are mine).

him the next best candidate to the status of wise man, explaining the success he enjoys not only with his disciples, but also among occasional listeners at his public exhibitions (*Euthd.* 276b–c, 303b; *Sph.* 232d, 240a–b).

Nevertheless, a straight refutation of the argument on which the sophist's dialectical strategy stands is not easily worked out. For, as long as truth and falsity are equated with being and not-being, respectively (237b sqq.), the very possibility of falsity demands that *in a way* not-being must be and being not be (241d). This requires a clarification of what being and not-being are and how they relate to each other.

Being envelops all kinds: namely Motion and Rest, all of them related through the Same and the Other. As none of these is the others, if Being is what everyone of them is, Not-Being is what all and each one of them are not. Consequently, Not-Being is the contraposition (*antikeimenon antithesis*) of Being to any of its parts[8] (258b).

This result comes as a consequence of the reformulation of the meaning of the negative from contrary to different (257b–259b), paving the way to a novel approach to the interconnected problems of *logos* and truth/falsity[9].

4.2 The Sophist III

Though it comes about as a kind of epilogue to the search, in fact it is through its association with the preceding subsection on being and not-being that the strategy of the sophist is put to an end. We find it in Euthydemus' version of Parmenides B7.1, in Plato's *Euthydemus*:

> "nobody ever says *the* things that are not" (*ta ge mê onta legein*: 284c3–4), for he would be making something".

By all means this is an extraordinary claim! If any *logos* must be of what is, then it can only be read as its name[10]. Therefore no *logos* can say what is not, for, by

---

8 The same applying to any kind in contraposition to its difference (257e).
9 In Parmenides B2, the negative separates the two opposite ways "for thinking" (B2.2). The opposition is composed by their qualification as the "authentic" and the "unknowable anonymous path" ("of research": B8.15–18; vide B2.2, B6.3, B7.2). Being only two (B2.2), the denial of one immediately leads to its opposite (B2.3b; B2.5b).
10 If whatever is said about something is true, just because it was said, *logos* cannot state anything about it, but only refer to it in the way a name does (this interpretation explains Cratylus' denial of false names: *Cra.* 429b; on the other hand, if "what is" is the only true name, "everything is in the same way to everybody at the same time and always" – *Cra.* 386d – definitely abolishing the pos-

saying it, it would *make* what is out of what is not (*Euthd.* 284c3–5). The sophism commences by advancing an ontological claim – saying gives being to a thing (283e9–10) –, then gives it a logical twist: saying "one thing" that is is telling the truth (284a7).

Such a devious argument justifies the pains the EG takes to establish *logos* as "an interweaving" (*symplokê*: *Sph.* 259e, 262c) of name and verb (262d). Only after "an action or inaction, being or not-being" are attributed to anyone or anything (262c) comes the key assertion according to which *logos* does not merely name, but, through the interweaving of name and verb, manages to "conclude something" ("accomplish": *perainei ti:* 262d). As only in *logos* there is "assertion and negation" (263a–e), only *logos* may be true or false. Therefore, the association of being with truth and not-being with falsity is dismissed.

4.3 The Sophist IV

There remains yet one tenet in the core of the *Sophist:* being and the way *einai* is used in the subsection devoted to the Five Greatest Kinds (250a–259b). Even before, from the moment the argument tackles with the nature of images (236e–237a; 240a–b), the reader notices something running amiss in the way the verb 'be' should be understood. For example, in order to describe the nature of images different types of propositions are required: any image is ("exists), though (it is) not truly, as it is not the very thing it is the image of (240b2–13).

In order to interpret these sentences the reader must understand them in three different ways: stating existence ("the image exists"), truth ("it is not truly") and identity ("it is not the thing..."). Later the EG legitimates predication when "things that are or are not" are stated *of* and *about* some named entity (263a).

As in each one of these sentences whatever is said states "something that is" about "what is", the entity 'being' (i.e., "being", "any being" or "what is") is the ultimate reference of all discourse[11]. Therefore, if the name 'being' (244a–d) has one definite meaning each one of the four types of sentences listed above must be distinguished and separated from the others.

---

sibility of contradiction). Plato reacts to this quibble. Either name is, and it is other than the thing (named), or it is not (being the same as the thing), and it is either the name of nothing or the name of a name (*Sph.* 244d; notice the EG's criticism of the *opsimatheis:* 251b-c).

11 See P. Curd's thesis of "predicational monism" in Parmenides and Plato: "each thing that is can only be one thing; it can hold only one predicate, and must hold it in a particularly strong way" (1991, 242–243; related to Plato: 257, 263–264).

In order to "disambiguate" them Plato presents the reader with standard cases in which they can easily be distinguished (as in the examples above). However, in order to be able to perform this task the EG is forced to develop a long argument.

Its first steps are noticed in the abandonment of the strict dualism supported by the "friends of Forms" (248a–b, 252a), entailing the communion of Movement and Rest in Being (248e–249d). Subsequently the opposition of one to many is resolved through the intermingling of Forms (252b), supported by the interrelation of the Five Greatest Kinds (252d ff.).

It is a moot point whether Plato is successful in fully distinguishing these types of the sentences in which *einai* is used. He commences by establishing 'participation' as the communion of different kinds (250b). This done, sentences expressing identity are explained through the participation of their elements in the Same (254d); existential sentences as participation in Being[12] (256a1). Predicative ones express participation or communion between any two or more different kinds in one another (252b, 253a–b). Finally the veridical reading of the verb is separated from *ousia* as truth and falsity are explained as "qualities of *logos*" (263b, d, 264a–b).

II Reading the *Sophist*

1. Form and content

I aimed at showing how Plato's *Sophist* may be approached from the joint perspectives of form and content. Embracing Plato's conception of "an open ended search" I proposed a no less open ended interpretation of the dialogue.

As inter-textual connections are not explicitly allowed by Plato such proposal implies a number of unwarranted, hardly consensual assumptions. And yet, they are necessary to catch a glimpse of the underlying program of the dialogue, if we suppose Plato is trying to establish the basic concepts on which philosophical research depends.

The dialogue form captures this program through the interchange of the participants. Three levels may be distinguished. While at the "authorial level" Plato hides behind the Eleatic Guest's questions and answers, at the "reception level",

---

[12] Following J. Acrkill's proposal (1957, 251–259; 1965, 207–218), despite the criticism his interpretation has received (G. Owen 1999, 440, n. 46, 446; L. Brown 1999, 455, 470–472; 2008, 440–441).

Theaetetus' responses act as guidelines to the points the reader should accept in order to understand what is going on in the investigation. Finally at the "fictional level" a number of "characters" are used to introduce conceptions required to unfold the argument.

This particular strategy is manifest in the mention of fictional characters whenever the course of the investigation is altered. Three key passages are paradigmatic of this practice. Integrating the sophistic readings of B7.1 the "assault on Parmenides" (241d) is used as a bridge allowing the transit from the problem of how falsity stands to truth (237d–241b) to the quest on the nature of being and not-being (242c–246a). The argument against the "friends of the Forms" rejects the strict dualism of the Middle Dialogues (248d–249d) allowing the EG to introduce Motion and Rest in "being and the all" (249d). The criticism of the "late-learners" (251b–c) allows the move to the problem of predication, required to prompt the solution advanced through the commingling of genera (253b–c).

In this perspective the *Sophist* is read as synthesis, from the points of view of philosophical content as well as style. Plato uses the methodology applied in the elenctic dialogues in a different approach. Instead of testing Theaetetus' "knowledge" he uses it to create a dialectical context suited to the sharing of opinions. The understanding connecting both searchers acts as the model the reader is referred to in order to follow the unfolding of the argument, both representing the inner dialogue of soul with itself (*Theat.* 189e-190a; *Sph.* 263e–264a).

2. The "program" of the dialogue

In the introduction to the central section of the dialogue (232b–236c; 236c–259b) the EG confesses his bewilderment at the success enjoyed by the sophist. He then proceeds to justify it with the effect caused by the sophist's strategy of refutation. This he shows is prompted by the combination of Parmenides' argument with the double equation of being/not being with truth/falsity (238d, 240c).

If 'the veridical is' should be understood as "whatever is really" and the "altogether not veridical" as its contrary (240b), then 'falsehood' is "what is not" (240d–e). Such conclusion manages to capture in contradiction anyone who admits that there is such a thing as "false opinion". For, he who sustains that "some opinions are false" either says "what is not", states that what was said "is not" or both (236e–237a, 240e; vide *Euthd.* 283e–286e; *Cra.* 429d: *Teaet.* 167a–d, 170d), thereby violating Parmenides' prohibition (B7.1: *Soph.* 237a).

The analysis of the core of this dilemma reveals that the knot of the problem lies in the collapse of two distinct levels of falsehood: one of the thing said, the other of the statement asserting it. The way out of it is found only when the argument establishes that, as "qualities" of discourse (263b–d), "truth/falsity" are no longer applicable to things. In fact from "things that are" truth or falsity may follow. Of "things that are not", when 'not' means the opposite, nothing can be said (258e).

Perhaps surprisingly this interdiction confirms the previous sophistic allegation that in this sense "what is not" is "unspeakable" (etc.: *vide* 239a, 241a). But with his move the EG managed to undo the double equation (of being with truth and not-being with falsehood) on which the sophist's dialectical acumen stands (236c–237a).

However, such conclusion cannot be reached until the meaning of the negative is reformulated, indicating that 'not' signifies "something different from the words it is prefixed to" (257b-c). This thesis generalizes the preceding one, that Not-Being:

> ... is not the opposite of Being, but only something different (257b).

And yet, to get to this conclusion the EG previously had to reject two other theses. One is the "late learners'" denial of the predicative strength of statements, by which one may "call many names to a single thing" (251b). The other thesis is Plato's own. According to the *Republic* V 479 (*vide Phaed.* 78d) there is no generation in being, for "it is always unchanged and the same" (*Soph.* 248a). However, should this thesis be accepted, it would follow as a consequence that this cosmos consists of two incommunicable worlds (*Parm.* 133a–135a).

3. The structure of the dialogue[13]

The argument above should set philosophy on the right track and put the sophist in his place. But it is not enough if both objectives are to be attained. It will therefore be necessary to ground the exposition and resolution of the problems of Being/Not-Being and truth/falsity on the structure on which philosophical research depends.

This work is done in the core of the central section of the *Sophist* (236c–264b). In it Plato follows his ultimate proposal of exposing his conception of di-

---

13 I use 'structure' to point to the unity of the different parts in the central section of the dialogue (237–264). I give 'program' a broader meaning relating the *Sophist* to those dialogues in which Parmenides' arguments are prominent. These fall in two headings: the sophists ("the school of Protagoras"), in the *Euthydemus*, the *Cratylus*, and the *Theaetetus*; and Plato himself, in the *Phaedo*, the *Republic* and the *Parmenides*.

alectics (253d–e) embracing Being (254d–257b) and Not-Being (256d–258e) as parallel (250e) conceptions until the relation uniting them finally comes forth (259a–b). This is Plato's answer to the question he addressed to the doctrines the EG takes as representative of Greek philosophical tradition. What were these men thinking whenever they used the notion of 'being' to refer to the cosmos (242c–243b)? Whatever is implied in any statement which asserts that something "is" (243d–e; vide 243d–244b)?

The greatest innovation contained in this conception of dialectics consists in the previous separation and subsequent combination of the ontological and epistemological perspectives on reality[14]. While the three first Greatest Kinds – Being, Movement and Rest – refer to what exists, the Same and the Other provide the dialectician with the ability to relate them using different kinds of statements: existential, identitative and predicative ones (this last one exploring the participation of Forms in one another: 255a–b, 256a).

Plato's theory of Being shows how this kind includes all the others granting them 'existence' (Being is everything that is, seen in itself). In his conception of Not-Being he starts by making manifest the function played by the Other as 'difference' (Not-Being is Being seen from the perspective of any other kind: 255d, 256d–e). He then proceeds to condense in the idea of 'contraposition' (257d–258c) the role played by Not-Being in the generation of ontological hierarchies. In these each grade is what it is, in contraposition to all the others it is not, but in relation to which it is and is said by discourse (258d–259b).

4. Conclusion

Does this reading of the *Sophist* show how form and content relate in the composition of the dialogue? To me such a well-knit structure suggests that Plato departed from a previously sketched out plan, he then proceeded to turn into a dialogue. For structure is the key to understanding the *Sophist*. It allows the reader to grasp its program and understand where it is heading.

Opposed to a structural composition, the transcription of an oral conversation writes itself. Take for instance the elenctic dialogues: the *Lysis* or the *Charmides*. They may be seen as the record of actual debates. There seems not to be a particular reason for any option in the exchange between Socrates and Critias on

---

[14] In the *Phaedo* or the *Republic* Epistemology and Ontology are tied together, for each one of the two cognitive competences "is related to" its own content – "being" or "opinion" – and "effects" its product: "knowledge" or "belief" (*R.* V 477d ff.).

the nature of *sôphrosynê*; nor for the short conversation with Lysis precisely in the place we read it. As no definite answer is found, these dialogues might linger on forever.

The problem with structure is that any views on it hardly are consensual. For any approach to structure depends on intertextual connections relying on presuppositions that divide the interpreters. This might, however, be what was in Plato's mind when he chose to write dialogues.

It is difficult to imagine the program of the *Sophist* in the form of a conference but the *Timaeus* shows this is not impossible. The philosopher Plato might go on hidden from his audience. But would the readers miss any relevant hint? I think they would. With Theaetetus gone, the constant counterpoint of his presence, the assurance, hesitation or evasiveness in his answers would be lost. The point of his presence is the actual learning, for the *Meno* has made it clear that something is taught only when someone is there to understand it ("learning" and "knowing": *manthanein*).

Works Cited

Ackrill, J. (1957/1965), "Plato and the Copula: *Sophist* 251–259", 1957 (rep. in *Studies in Plato's Metaphysics*, R. E. Allen (ed.), 1965, 207–218).

Aristotle. *On the Soul, Parva naturalia, On Breath,* Translation by W. S. Hett. Harvard, Cambridge. 1975.

Brown, L. (2012), "Negation and not-being: Dark Matter in the *Sophist*", *Presocratics and Plato: A Festschrift in honour of Charles Kahn*, R. Patterson, V. Karasmanis, A. Hermann (eds.), Parmenides Publishing, Las Vegas 2012, 233–254.

Brown, L. (2008), "The *Sophist* on Statements, Predication and Falsehood", *The Oxford Handbook of Plato*, G. Fine (ed.), Oxford, 437–462.

Brown, L. (1999), "Being in the *Sophist*: A Syntactical Enquiry", *Plato I*, Gail Fine (ed.), Oxford, 455–478.

Curd, P. (1991), "Parmenidean Monism", *Phronesis* XXXVI/3, 241–264.

Denyer, N. C. (1991), *Language, Thought and Falsehood in Ancient Greek Philosophy*, London 1991.

Gill, C. (1996), "Afterword: Dialectic and the Dialogue Form in Late Plato", *Form and Argument in Late Plato*, Chr. Gill, M. M. McCabe (eds.), Oxford Clarendon P., Oxford, 283–311.

Kahn, C. (1973), *The Verb 'Be' and its synonyms, The Verb 'Be' in Ancient Greek, Philosophical and grammatical studies* edited by W. M. Verhaar, Dordrecht/Boston 1973.

Kahn, C. (2003), "Introduction", "The Greek Verb 'Be'…", 2003^2.

Kyoung-Lee, M. (2008), "The *Theaetetus*", *The Oxford Handbook of Plato*, G. Fine (ed.), Oxford, 412–436.

Owen, G. (1970/1999), "Plato on not-being" *Plato I*, G. Vlastos (ed.), Garden City 1970, 223–265 (repr. in *Plato I*, Gail Fine (ed.), Oxford, 1999, 416–454).

Plato. Translated by W. R. M. Lamb, H. N. Fowler, P. Shorey, R. G. Bury. Harvard, Cambridge. 1914–1935.
Vlastos, G. (1994), *Socratic Studies,* M. Burnyeat (ed.), Cambridge U. P., Cambridge.

Other Genres and Traditions

Michael Erler
Detailed Completeness and Pleasure of the Narrative. Some Remarks on the Narrative Tradition and Plato[1]

Introduction

In the 'Preface' of his novel *Der Zauberberg* Thomas Mann claims that pleasure results from the completeness of a narrative.[2] In doing so he reacts to a differentiation between history and philosophy, which is propagated by Schopenhauer.[3] But he also follows a tradition which goes back to antiquity, that is to Homer[4], and also to the Platonic dialogues, as I shall argue. In the following I shall dwell on Plato as narrator.[5] Plato, of course, never narrates a dialogue in his own person. Even in his dialogues with a framing narrative he always ascribes the role of primary narrator either to Socrates or to someone else.[6] On the other hand it is characteristic of the Platonic *Sokratikoi logoi* – some even call this characteristic an invention by Plato[7] – that Plato shows strong concern with character types, as well as with historical and detailed historical settings of the conversations he describes. Already in antiquity Plato was admired for his ability to describe situations in a realistic manner, conveying to the reader the feeling of being in a theatre.[8] Often Plato reminds the reader of the sources of the stories and describes the character of narrators in detail.[9] By doing so, he emphasizes the truth of the setting in a way that reminds one of the strategies employed by historians to prove the authenticity of a real conversation – recall

---

[1] A slightly modified version of this contribution in German will appear in S. Föllinger, Müller (Hgg.), "Der Dialog in der Antike. Formen und Funktionen einer literarischen Gattung zwischen Philosophie, Wissensvermittlung und dramatischer Inszenierung" 2013, 349–364.
[2] Th. Mann, Gesammelte Werke in dreizehn Bänden, Frankfurt a.M. 1974, III, 10; see Reents 1998, p. 66.
[3] See Reents 1998, p. 66.
[4] See Kannicht 1988, p. 10–15.
[5] Halperin 1992, p. 94; Morgan 2004; Hunter 2006; Halliwell 2009.
[6] See Erler 2007, p. 73 sqq.:
[7] Cf. Clay 2000, p. 10; Blondell 2002, p. 31sqq.; Rossetti & Stavru 2010, p. 11 sqq.
[8] About the mimetic character of Plato's dialogues cf. Halliwell 1997, pp. 313–332; Halliwell 2002, p. 37–71; Büttner 2000. Plato's critique of poetry and his own dialogues as poetry are discussed in Erler 2013.
[9] See Blondell 2002, p. 31 sqq.

the prooemia of the *Symposium*, the *Parmenides* or the beginning of the *Timaeus*.[10] Plato plays the game so well that his dialogues sometimes were read as historical documents.[11] Plato the narrator, it seems, aims at completeness of his narrative in order to entertain the reader. One wonders how this fits into what Plato, the philosopher, has to say about his search for a unity which lies behind the plurality of the phenomena and overcomes the plurality of the sensible world. One could try to explain it as a strategy. The 'historical' setting and personae of the dialogue function as a sort of evidence and as support for what is being argued for.[12] I wish to focus on Plato's way to narrate his stories in the dialogues, because the rhetoric of completeness Plato illustrates and practices, very much resembles what we find as early as in Homer.[13] For like Homer the narrator Plato presents us with the figure of the narrator in dialogues, which combine dramatic and narrative elements[14], which offers the same kind of rhetoric of completeness and which in addition to that reflects on what they think that the audience might expect of their narration. These reflections point to the poetical discussions of Plato's times and can be understood – or so I shall argue – as kind of poetical self-commentaries and as a hermeneutical device.

To prove my case I mainly shall refer to two dialogues, the *Phaedo* and the *Symposium*. I shall suggest reading some passages in the light of the narrative tradition before Plato and in view of what Plato has to say in the *Republic* on poetry. I shall argue that Plato's comments on his dialogues not only transform traditional concepts as they often do[15] and that he takes position in a poetical debate about what a narration should be like, but also that he offers hermeneutical clues for a better understanding of some peculiarities of his own dialogues.

---

10 For the prooemium see Muthmann 1961. See also (for the *Timaeus*) Erler 1997.
11 For anecdotes concerning dialogues like the *Gorgias* or the *Phaidon* see Athen. 11, 505d-506a = Anecd. 37 Riginos; vgl. Diog. Laert. 3, 35 = anecd. 17 Riginos; cf. Erler 2009a, pp. 61–64.
12 See Erler 2009b.
13 Cf. *Od.* 3, 267 sq.; 4, 17 sq.; 8, 73–82.
14 For Platonic analysis of different kinds of narratives cf. Pl. *R.* 392d-394c and Erler 2007, pp. 71–75. Whether Plato's categories can be applied to his own dialogues (so for instance de Jong 1987, pp. 2–5) his been doubted by Halliwell 2009, p. 19 sqq.
15 For the tradition of narrative in antiquity see de Jong 1987; de Jong, Nünlist & Bowie 2004; Schwinge 1991, pp. 482–512; Radke 2007; Köhnken 2006.

Examples from Plato's dialogues

Let us turn to the *Phaedo* first. In the introductory conversation[16] of the *Phaedo*, Echecrates asks *Phaedo* to tell him about what happened in Socrates' last hours. For, as he says, he had not heard anything about Socrates' death, whereas Phaedo – as it turns out – was present at this moment. Since Echecrates wishes to hear what happened, he asks Phaedo to report what Socrates said and how he died. In fact, nobody had been present of those able to recount clearly what Echecrates wishes to be told. So he asks Phaedo to describe the whole situation in detail, the discussions that took place during Socrates's last hours in prison and everything he and his friends did say and do.[17] Phaedo, of course, is well prepared to tell the story, because – as he explains – to think of Socrates for him is most pleasurable:

> I will try to give you an account of what happened. There is nothing I like better than thinking about Socrates, whether I am talking about him myself or listening to someone else (*Phd.* 58d; transl. Bluck).

This little conversation at the beginning of the dialogue is remarkable for two reasons. First, when Echecrates insists that Phaedo should tell both "what was said" and "what was done" during Socrates' last day[18], Plato closely links the dramatic and the pragmatic aspects of the dialogue – Socrates' pursuit of truth by arguments and his behaviour – and engages the reader in the search for truth by considering what has been said and what has been done. Second, it becomes clear also that a factual report is expected which is based on accuracy and is elaborated. At the same time these qualities are the reason why the report will be enjoyed by the narrator– Phaedo – and the recipient of the story – Echecrates.

Let us turn now to a second example of a narrator in a Platonic dialogue. At the beginning of the Symposium we observe quite the same situation. The opening part is composed in dramatic manner.[19] Apollodoros offers a report about the banquet in honor of Agathos and his victory. Apollodoros thinks he is well prepared for this narration. For only recently – he says – he told an acquaintance – Glaukon – this very story as well. Now this Glaukon had heard the very story from somebody else. But he was in doubt whether the report was accurate at

---

16 See Erler 1992 and Erler 1994.
17 Cf. *Phd.* 57a-59c. Translation: Bluck 1955.
18 Cf. *Phd.* 58c.
19 Cf. Phaed. 58c and Gallop 2001, p. 281.

all, because the chronology of the meeting which was told did not seem to be correct to him. Yet Apollodoros claims that he had taken care to know exactly what Socrates said or did on that occasion. By doing so, Apollodoros signals – as did Echecrates in the *Phaedo* – that he is also very much interested in the historical aspect of the report, for instance when he assures his audience that he had checked what was said turning to Socrates several times and asking him for confirmation. This proves how much he was concerned to check the sources of what he was told.[20] It seems that Plato creates here what could be called a 'Beglaubigungsapparat'[21], that is, a feature which will later become typical in the tradition of ancient novel and in historiography.[22] Apollodoros' narrative is not just about *logoi* concerning philosophy, but pretends to be called *historia*.

So again we observe that accuracy and detailed completeness of the story is what narrators in Plato are longing for and what is expected of them by their audiences. This is an expectation which Plato himself obviously tries to meet when he gives his dialogues the flavor of historical testimonies by telling stories about Socratic conversations in great detail and in historical settings.

Another example can be found in other dialogues as well. Very interesting in this respect is the *Theaetetus*.[23] Here again a narrator – Eucleides – is well prepared to report a conversation which Socrates once had with Theaetetus. This narrator was not present in person at the discussion. He therefore tries to get information from others, takes notes, asks Socrates for confirmation and additional information, and notes down the whole discussion completely and accurately as a dialogue in writing. Again it becomes clear that the report of Eucleides is intended to be plausible, complete, detailed and authentic. More than that: It is expected, that exactly these qualities, this 'rhetoric of completeness', is what the audience expects and what it takes pleasure in, just like Apollodoros who says in the *Symposium* that when he talks about philosophy or listens to others he thinks that he enjoys it very much.[24]

Let us keep in mind then: The narrators in Plato – as far as we have seen – all aim at detailed completeness, authenticity and plausibility in their narrations, and by doing this, they obviously think, that stories told that way are regarded to be beneficial and enjoyable by the audience.

---

20 Cf. Halperin 1992; Erler 2011.
21 Cf. *Smp.* 172b-e; 173b.
22 Cf. Erler 2007, p. 192 sq. See Pl. *Prm.* 126a sqq. or *Ti.* 25d sqq.
23 Hunter 2006.
24 Cf. *Tht.* 143b sqq.; Erler 2007, p. 79; cf. Halliwell 2009, p. 16 sqq.; Tulli 2011.

Tradition

The expectation of Apollodoros that the report about what happened at the symposium will be pleasurable and useful, and the expectations of other narrators and audiences in the dialogues, indeed are interesting.[25] For they remind one of the discussions held in Hellenistic times about the *utile* and *dulce* as effects of poetry and narrations. This discussion culminates in what Horace has to say in the *ars poetica* about poets that wish to benefit or to please, or to speak what is enjoyable and helpful.[26] Some authors like Eratosthenes[27] indeed argued, that poets aim at *psychagogia* and do not wish to teach their readers; others like Aristotle argued, that didactic poems lecture and just because of that are not to be regarded as poems. According to Horace, Homer's poems offer both pleasure and instruction. At least this is what Horace himself experienced – or so he claimed – when reading Homer at Praeneste.[28] I would like to argue, that these alternatives of experiences and expectations – foul or fair, beneficial or edifying or both – point to a tradition which forms the background for what Apollorodoros or Echecrates have to say about what they expect from a narrative in Plato's dialogues. Let us remind us for a moment of what we can learn about the relationship, or rather about the *palintonos harmonia*, of the concepts of the beneficial or enchantment – of *prodesse* or *delectare* – concerning poetry or the narrative from Homer onwards.[29]

Now, while reading Homeric epic we indeed get interesting information about what the audience expected from a singer and what he was prepared to offer.[30] Most of the evidence comes from the *Odyssey*. Here Odysseus for instance makes compliments to the divine singer Demodokos. His song causes delight (*terpein*) because he produces a kind of song about the *klea andrôn* as if he was present at the events he is talking about, or as if he had heard about them from others. Demodokos obviously produces a kind of song which was liked by his audience, because the Phaeacians were delighted by his verses as was Odysseus in his praise of Demodokos in the *Odyssey*.[31] And later on Odysseus asks the singer to tell the story of the building of the wooden horse, and

---

25 cf. *Smp.* 173c.
26 Cf. Hor. *ars* 333f.: *aut prodesse volunt aut delectare poetae/ aut simul et iucunda et idonea dicere vitae* cf. Brink 1971, p. 352sqq.; Cf. Hunter 2006, p.301
27 Cf. Eratosthenes bei Str. 1, 1, 15.
28 Cf Hor. *epist.* 1, 2, 3f.
29 cf. Kannicht 1988, p. 13ff.
30 Cf. *Od.* 1, 337 sqq..; cf. Kraus 1955.
31 Cf. *Od.* 8, 487–98.

again he asks for a very detailed story (*katà moîran kataléxēs*) and was moved to tears.³²

It becomes clear that 'To tell a story aright' as Odysseus sees it, obviously means not lo leave out any detail, and to seek completeness and authenticity thanks to the inspiration of an authentic eyewitness. This suggests that a story like the one sung by Demodokos could be regarded as a kind of history, for it follows rules, to which later historians would stick. In fact, this is exactly what Alkinoos asks him to do, i.e. to report accurately or undistorted. And later Alkinoos confirms, that Odysseus offers a story which is reliable, detailed and in order. Indeed Odysseus does aim at authenticity when he tells his story, for instance when he makes use of what could be called a "Beglaubigungsapparat" – very much like the one we find in Plato's dialogues. A good example of this kind of proof of authenticity can be found in the *Odyssey*, when Odysseus narrates how the cattle of Helios were slaughtered on the island of Helios by Odysseus' comrades, how Lampetie rushed to Zeus to reveal to him what happened, how Zeus got angry and convoked the assembly of the gods and promised that all ships would be destroyed.³³ Now it is interesting that Odysseus, the narrator, thinks it necessary to explain, where he got this story from. And quite understandably so, because the story he told happened in heaven, where no mortal was allowed in. He therefore was no eyewitness of what happened there. Yet Odysseus is able to confirm that his story is true because he was told it by someone who got it from an immortal eyewitness.³⁴ Again we realize that Odysseus, the narrator in the epic, strives for completeness and authenticity – as does Homer, the author – and that by doing so he obviously meets the expectations of their audiences. Odysseus practices what indeed has been called a ‚rhetoric of completeness', a kind of narration which also was used by a singer like Demodokos and – we may say – was also practiced by the author of the *Odyssey* – and *Ilias* – himself when he performed his epic.³⁵ Obviously this rhetoric of completeness was regarded to create *terpsis* in the audience, because this kind of narration was instructive and entertaining at the same time. The more comprehensively and exactly a story was told, the greater was the *terpsis* attained by the singer.³⁶

---

32 Cf. Alkinoos in *Od.* 11, 363 sqq.
33 Cf. *Od.* 12, 260–402 , esp. 390; cf. *Il.* 2, 484–87.
34 Cf. *Od.* 12, 389 sq.
35 Cf. *Od.* 10, 14–16. See also A. R. 1, 20–22, and Hunter 2005, pp. 156–162; Fantuzzi & Hunter 2002, pp. 311–12.
36 Cf. Maehler 1963, pp. 15, 27–31, 34; cf. Latacz 1966, pp. 208–214.

This is confirmed by the famous song of the sirens in the *Odyssee*. Odysseus was advised to protect himself against the demonic enchantment of the song of the sirens. Now, the sirens indeed claim that whoever passes past them would be entertained and well instructed.[37] For the sirens know everything – for instance about Troy and everthing that Argives and Trojans endured in Troy.[38] Here we have the poetic concept of the Homeric singer: knowledge and pleasure as specific effects of narration – the more exactly the song is narrated, the more it will be enjoyable. R. Kannicht drew attention to the fact that here we can observe a kind of an "immanent narrative theory"[39], and in my opinion he argues convincingly that in Homeric epic – and beyond – pleasure and knowledge are closely connected with each other, and the effect of a narrative. A story which is narrated completely and thoroughly is regarded to be entertaining, because it makes the audience richer in knowledge. Now, all this already points to what we have observed in the Platonic dialogues. I claim that this forms the horizon of expectations of audiences also in the dialogues –and one may wonder whether this is true also as far as Plato's dialogues as narrations are concerned. Before turning back to Plato I think it is worth reminding us for a moment of what happened to the concept of rhetorical completeness after Homer.

Hesiod still seems to share the concept of a combination of enchantment and knowledge as effect of narrative and poetry. In his *Works and Days*, however, it becomes clear that he was convinced that only the person will go home more enchanted, who participates in the useful knowledge about the world he had to offer. It also becomes evident that in Hesiod the aspect of usefulness becomes more and more important, and that there was a gap between the two aspects. After Hesiod there is a dispute 'knowledge *versus* pleasure'. In that debate the category of literature's usefulness became the more prominent one.

In fact, usefulness seems to be the essential determination of literature, i.e. the criterion of poetry, in Solon as well as in Xenophanes. For Xenophanes poetry's uselessness is proven by the fact that the poet lies about the gods.[40] Solon[41] expects that poems should have a social effect – for instance, to tell the audience what really matters. Protagonists of utility were poets like Tyrtaios, and later some Sophists – and finally Aristophanes, who in the Frogs of 405 BC

---

37 Cf. Kannicht 1988, 14.
38 Cf. *Od.* 12, 189–91.
39 Cf. Kannicht, 1988, 14.
40 Cf. Primavesi 2009, p. 113 sq.
41 Cf. Solon *frg.* 1 Diehl=13 West; cf. Kannicht 1988, pp. 17–19.

presents us with the figure of an Aeschylus, who wishes the poet to teach his audience the right behaviour – a position which obviously Aristophanes shared.[42]

The contrary position, that is, that poetry should just be edifying, also was propagated – most of all by Gorgias, whose epistemological nihilism only allows for a paraphrase of the *phainomena* which in his view cannot be more than an enchanting description.[43] The arousal of emotions is therefore the only effect literature will and should have, as he tries to show in his Helena. Interpretation of poetry can therefore be pleasurable, but cannot teach anything.

Narrative Tradition and Plato's dialogues

It seems to me that this very development and the growing emphasis on the aspect of entertainment is of importance for what Plato has to say about the effects of poetry in his dialogues in general.[44] For it prompts Plato to be dismissive of the traditional poetry in the *Republic* and to regard traditional poetry like the one of Homer as useless and dangerous just because it stirs up emotions in the irrational part of the human soul. Furthermore, it causes pleasure and pain and hinders the rule of reason in the soul of the recipient. But it should not be overlooked, that Socrates also has to say something about the conditions which would or could allow for the acceptance of poetry even in Kallipolis. Socrates seems to accept poetry if there would be advocates who are no poets but lovers of poetry to plead poetry's cause and would be able to show that literature or poetry is delightful and beneficial.[45] But – as we see – this only is possible under the condition that poetry proves to be pleasant and beneficial for the government and the life of man. So let us keep in mind: For Socrates the combination of pleasure and usefulness is the *conditio sine qua non* which makes poetry acceptable, i.e. Plato wishes to rejoin again the two elements, the *delectare* and the *prodesse* – which were combined in Homer, but got separated afterwards. We also saw that in Plato's and Socrates' times the aspect of pleasure was prominent amongst Sophists, whereas the aspect of utility was propagated for instance by Aristophanes.

Seen before this background some features of narrative in the dialogues gain profile: Echecrates asks for a story about Socrates, because he finds this kind of story pleasant, and that Apollodoros hopes for entertainment and benefit from

---

[42] Cf. Ar. *Ra.* 686 sq.; *Ach.* 658; Schwinge 1997.
[43] Vgl. Gorgias *Helena* DK 82 B 11; cf. Kannicht 1988, pp. 21–24.
[44] Vgl. Pl. *R.* 598d7 sqq.; 606e sqq.; 607d; 599c sqq.
[45] Vgl. *R.* 607d.

narrations about philosophical conversation. Both expect stories which are detailed and thorough. For the reader often is reminded of the sources of the discussion and that the narrator has been doing research in order to fill in gaps if some information seems to be missing. As in Homer we are confronted with a 'rhetoric of completeness' that Plato describes, and which causes pleasure in the audience.

So let us pause for a moment and resume: In narrative situations within some of his dialogues, Plato obviously illustrates a way of storytelling which seems to be traditional in that it combines the aspects of completeness, of benefit and pleasure. When for instance Apollodoros expects benefit and pleasure from a narration[46] he seems to share the position of Socrates in the *Republic* whose close friend he obviously is. So one wonders whether Apollodoros and Echecrates represent a position, which Socrates would subscribe to and Plato follows himself in his detailed dialogue-stories.

Plato's understanding of utility

Though this might seem plausible at first sight, doubts remain. One wonders whether Plato's Socrates really has in mind the 'completeness' of a story and a sort of 'historical record' each time he postulates that a narration should be beneficial and entertaining. It is telling that Apollodoros[47], although he is a close friend of Socrates and prefers philosophical conversations of rich people, does not make any difference between Socratic discussions and philosophical conversations in general. In addition to this, it is not clear to me whether Socrates would share his view on what makes a story beneficial and useful. One wonders whether Plato's Socrates really expects a detailed and complete account and 'historical record' also when he postulates that a narration should be beneficial and entertaining. Now, it is true, a detailed account of what happened in the sense of historical completeness is what Apollodoros is hoping for and what he appears to enjoy most, very much as Echecrates does in the *Phaedo*. This fits well with what we have learned about the narrative in Homer.

In fact Plato, the author, seems to join this tradition by presenting in his dialogues personal which offer stories which strive for detailed completeness, but

---

[46] Cf. *Smp.* 173c.
[47] The figure of Apollodoros is well discussed by Schirren 1999; for Apollodoros and Socrates cf. Erler 2009c.

also by composing his dialogues as historical narratives and by making use of a rhetoric of completeness.

What, then, about Plato the philosopher? There are doubts if Plato the philosopher shares the view that this way of story-telling is beneficial in a philosophical understanding. For in the dialogues it becomes also evident that even a very detailed account of what happened and was said, cannot guarantee a kind of philosophical insight which alone Plato would regard as beneficial.[48]

Plato makes this clear in the *Symposium*. In this dialogue Alcibiades believes he would know who Socrates really is just because he is familiar with every detail of his appearance and behaviour. But it turns out, that Alcibiades does not know anything about who Socrates really is.[49] This is confirmed at the beginning of the *Politikos*. Here it is shown that detailed description of man's behaviour or appearance provides knowledge which is beneficial. According to Plato, knowledge which really is useful and enjoyable can be only gained by reaching out for the noetic area and by a method which Plato calls dialectic.[50] Now, it is interesting that Plato in his dialogues illustrates what kind of story could provide an effect which he would regard as beneficial even from a philosophical point of view. In the dialogue named after him, Phaedo not only reports a Socratic conversation and explains that he enjoyed remembering this conversation very much. He also describes and analyses the very special effect that the conversation with Socrates had on him – an effect that could be called beneficial. Phaedo tells us that to his surprise he felt no pity appropriate to the death of a good friend, but a strange mingling of pain and pleasure. Phaedo indicates that this was not only the case for himself, but also for his friends:

> Well, when I arrived I had an extraordinary sensation. I did not feel *pity*, as might have been expected of one who was present at the death of a friend. The man seemed to me to be wonderfully gifted, Echecrates, in temperament no less than in speech; he died so fearlessly and nobly. It struck me that even on the point of his departure for the other world Providence was guiding him, and that even when he reached it, if anyone there has ever enjoyed blessings, then he would. Consequently, I had none of the sensations of pity that you might expect a man to have on so sad an occasion. Nor again did I derive pleasure from the fact that we were engaged in our usual philosophical discussions – for that was the nature of the conversation. It was simply a rather strange feeling, an unusual mixture of pleasure and pain combined, which came over me when I reflected that in a very short while he was

---

[48] Cf. Pl. *R.* 379b11; 608e4; *Ap.* 24e10; *Euthphr.* 13b-c; *Prt.* 333d sqq.; *Euthd.* 280b-c; *Grg.* 499d; *Men.* 87e sqq., 96e.
[49] cf. Pl. *Smp.* 213b sqq. and see Erler 2010, pp. 49–54.
[50] cf. *Phd.* 69d Cf. Kullmann 1974, p. 132 sqq.

going to die. All of us who were present were affected in much the same way, sometimes laughing, at times crying (transl. Bluck).⁵¹

Now, what Phaedo says about his emotions is striking indeed. For this disappearing of emotion and the controlled mingling of pain and pleasure, exactly corresponds to the reaction Socrates predicted when analyzing what true philosophical virtue is. It seems that true virtue causes a kind of *katharsis* of pleasure and pain. "Perhaps really, in actual fact, temperance and justice and courage are a sort of consummated purification of all such sensations, and wisdom itself is a sort of purificatory rite".⁵²

Indeed, in the *Phaedo*, Socrates behaves according to the philosophical understanding of virtues like bravery or prudence.⁵³ He is presented as an almost flawless figure without any affection, someone who even sends away his family in order not to be affected by their emotions. He behaves not like a common man, but more like a hero – but not like a tragic hero who is affected by great emotions.⁵⁴ His heroism rather is anti-heroic – it seems – in that he behaves in every aspect in a self-controlled, rational manner, without misapprehension and with total control of affections like pleasure or pain. Socrates is well aware that the Athenian people would interpret the circumstances of his death in a different way if he were to behave with the conviction of a tragic man – as he says. Socrates himself therefore reminds us of this contrast in that he distances himself from a tragic view of the world⁵⁵ and thereby signals that Plato wishes us to have this contrast in mind. But there is more to it. For we now can observe that the flawless figure of Socrates has an impact on his friends, and especially on Phaedo, which confirms the impact that according to Socrates' argument in the *Phaedo* true virtue has on other people. Phaedo claims that the reason for this was the way Socrates behaved when reacting to Phaedo's observations.

His analysis is of interest also if one wishes to understand better what Plato's Socrates means when he speaks of the benefit of listening to philosophical conversation. He obviously means by benefit of a narration about Socrates that Socratic virtues can unfold their cathartic effect and dry up or mitigate emotions. We should understand that there is pleasure and benefit to be gained by listening to the report of a Socratic conversation because such a report has a kind of thera-

---

51 *Phd.* 58e–59a.
52 *Phd.* 69b-c (transl. Bluck).
53 Cf. Halliwell 2002, p. 106 sqq.
54 Cf. *Phd.* 59a; Erler 2011.
55 Cf. *Phd.* 115a.

peutic effect on the recipient. As we can see in this concept, pleasure and benefit are united again.

Of course, poets before Plato like Hesiod or Pindar[56] were well aware that *logoi* can mitigate pain or pleasure, i.e. might have a therapeutic effect on the audiences. Plato obviously follows this traditional view, but he transforms the tradition he decides to join in; for he seems to be convinced, that real benefit cannot be gained by detailed completeness of the story but by the virtues represented by Socrates. In this – new and Platonic – sense a story about what Socrates did or said provides the audience with pleasure and real – i. e philosophical – benefit.

Conclusion

In his dialogue Plato the author illustrates different ways of communications and communicators, and among them narratives and narrators. He also describes different attitudes of the story-teller to his tale and different attitudes with which the audience receives the tale. It turns out that the story teller strives for detailed completeness to create pleasure and benefit in the audience. It might be attractive to ask whether this poetical statement of a person in his dialogues also might be understood as a hermeneutical device for a better understanding of Plato's dialogues as narratives themselves. Indeed there are – or so I think – good arguments for this. For we have other examples for this kind of hermeneutical devices in Plato's dialogues like the beginning of the *Theaetetus* I was referring to at the beginning of this paper. Here[57] Plato not only illustrates how a detailed and complete story about Socrates is composed. He also describes how this narrative is turned into a dramatic dialogue. For Eucleides decides to transform the dihegematic report into a dramatic dialogue because this form is much more entertaining – as it is argued. Now, it is remarkable that all later dialogues following the *Theaetetus* are in dramatic form. The beginning of the *Theaetetus* looks like an explanation the author is giving us for this fact. In this paper I wanted to suggest that the illustration of narrators and narratives as well as the expectations of the audience can be interpreted as Plato's reflections about narrations, narrated dialogues, and the effects these are supposed to have on the audience. It seems that Plato signals that he wishes to take a stand in the ongoing poetical discussion about what a good story is for – it

---

56 Cf. Hes. *Th.* 98 ff.; Pi. *N.* 8, 49 sqq.; Dalfen 1974, pp. 32; 262 sqq.
57 Cf. *Tht.* 142c–143a.

should provide pleasure and benefit. Plato the philosopher, it seems, kind of distances himself from this tradition of historical completeness as being useful, in that he replaces the traditional concept of usefulness by his philosophical one. The famous passage in the *Phaedo*, where Plato informs us that he was not present at the prison at that day[58], might be taken as a confirmation of this position. This position foreshadows the Hellenistic concern with the *utile* and the *dulce* in literature. I suggest that there are more passages like the ones we were dealing with in Plato's work, which can be regarded as poetical advices which Plato himself applied, all of which form part of what I would like to call the implicit poetics of Plato's dialogues, and which once again prove that Plato was a *poeta doctus* avant la lettre.[59]

Works Cited

Blondell, R 2002, The play of character in Plato's dialogues, Cambridge University Press, Cambridge.
Bluck, RS 1955: Plato's *Phaedo:* a translation of Plato's Phaedo with introduction, notes and appendices, Routledge, London.
Brink, CO 1971, Horace on poetry: The Ars Poetica, Cambridge University Press, Cambridge.
Büttner, St 2000, Die Literaturtheorie bei Platon und ihre anthropologische Begründung, Francke Verlag, Tübingen.
Clay, D 2000, Platonic Questions, Pennsylvania State Univ. Press, University Park.
Dalfen, J 1974, Polis und Poiesis, Fink, München.
Erler, M 1992, 'Anagnorisis in Tragödie und Philosophie: Eine Anmerkung zu Platons Dialog "Politikos"', *Würzburger Jahrbücher für die Altertumswissenschaft*, no. 18, pp. 147–170.
Erler, M 1994, 'Episode und Exkurs in Drama und Dialog: Anmerkung zu einer poetologischen Diskussion bei Platon und Aristoteles', in A Bierl, P von Moellendorff (eds), Orchestra. Festschrift für H. Flashar, Teubner, Stuttgart/Leipzig, pp. 318–330
Erler, M 1997, 'Ideal und Wirklichkeit: Die Rahmengespräche des Timaios und Kritias und Aristoteles Poetik', in Th Calvo & L Brisson (eds), Interpreting the Timaeus-Critias: Proceedings of the IV. Symposium Platonicum, Academia Verlag, Sankt Augustin, pp. 83–88.
Erler, M 2003, 'To Hear the Right Thing and to Miss the Point: Plato's Implicite Poetics', in A Michelini (ed), Plato as Author: The Rhetoric of Philosophy. Acts of the Sample Symposium of the Cincinnati Classics Department 1999, Brill, Leiden/Boston/Köln, pp. 153–173.
Erler, M 2007, 'Platon', in H Flashar (ed), Grundriss der Geschichte der Philosophie. Begründet von Friedrich Ueberweg. Völlig neu bearbeitete Ausgabe. Die Philosophie der Antike, 2/2, Schwabe Verlag, Basel.

---

58 Cf. *Phd.* 59b.
59 Cf. Erler 2003.

Erler, M 2009a, 'Kontexte der Philosophie Platons', in Ch Horn, J Müller & J. Söder (eds), Platon-Handbuch, Metzler, Stuttgart, pp. 61–99.

Erler, M 2009b, '"The fox knoweth many things, the hedgehog one great thing": the relation of philosophical concepts and historical contexts in Plato's Dialogues', *Hermathena*, no. 187, pp. 5–26.

Erler, M 2009c, "Denn mit Menschen sprechen wir und nicht mit Göttern": Platonische und epikureische epimeleia tês psychês, in D Frede & B Reis (eds), Body and Soul in Ancient Philosophy, de Gruyter, Berlin/New York, pp. 163–178.

Erler, M 2010, 'Charis und Charisma: Zwei Bilder vom Weisen und ihre Diskussion in Platons Dialogen', in D Koch, I Männlein-Robert & N Weidtmann (eds), Platon und das Göttliche, Attempto, Tübingen, pp. 42–61.

Erler, M 2011, 'Die Rahmenhandlung des Dialoges (57a-61b, 88c-89a, 102a, 115a-118a)', in J Müller (ed), Platon: *Phaidon*, Akademie-Verlag, Berlin, pp. 19–32.

Erler, M 2013, 'Plasma und Historie: Platon über die Poetizität seiner Dialoge', in M Erler, J.E Heßler (eds), Argument und literarische Form , Berlin/New York 2013, pp. 59–85. (in print).

Fantuzzi, M & Hunter, R 2002, Muse e modelli, Editori Laterza, Rome/Bari.

Gallop, D 2001, 'Emotions in the Phaedo', in: A Havlicek & F Karfík (eds), Plato's *Phaedo*, Oikumene, Prague, pp. 275–286.

Halliwell, St 1997, 'The *Republic's* two critiques of poetry (Book II 376c-398b, Book X 595a-608b)', in O Höffe (ed), Platon, Politeia, Akademie-Verlag, Berlin 1997, pp. 313–332.

Halliwell, St 2002, The Aesthetics of Mimesis. Ancient Texts and Modern Problems, Princeton University Press, Princeton (New J.).

Halliwell, St 2009, 'The theory and practice of narrative in Plato', in A Rengakos, J Grethlein (eds), Narratology and Interpretation: The content of the narrative form in ancient texts, de Gruyter, Berlin/New York, pp. 15–41.

Halperin, DM 1992, 'Plato and the erotics of narrativity', in JC Klagge & ND Smith (eds), Methods of interpreting Plato and his dialogues, Clarendon Press, Oxford, pp. 93–130 (now in ND Smith (ed), Plato: Critical assessments, Routledge, London/New York 1998, vol. 3, pp. 241–272.

Hunter, R 2005, 'Generic consciousness in the orphic Argonautica?', in M Paschalis (ed), Roman and Greek imperial Epic, Rethymnon Classical studies 2, Crete University Press, pp. 149–168.

Hunter, R 2006, 'Plato's *Symposium* and the traditions of ancient fiction', in JH Lesher, D Nails, FCC Sheffield (eds), Plato's Symposium: Issues in Interpretation and Reception, Harvard University Press, Cambridge (Mass.)/London, pp. 295–312.

de Jong, IJF 1987, Narrators and Focalizers: the presentation of the story in the Iliad, Grüner, Amsterdam.

de Jong, IJF, Nünlist, R & Bowie, A 2004 (eds): Narrators, Narratees, and Narratives in Ancient Greek Literature: Studies in Ancient Greek Narratives 1, Brill, Leiden/Boston.

Kannicht, R 1988, The Ancient Quarrel between Philosophy and poetry, University of Canterbury, Christ Church.

Köhnken, A 2006, Darstellungsziele und Erzählstrategien in antiken Texten, de Gruyter, Berlin/New York.

Kraus, W 1955, 'Die Auffassung des Dichterberufs im frühen Griechentum', *Wiener Studien*, no. 68, pp. 65–87.
Kullmann, W 1974, Wissenschaft und Methode, de Gruyter, Berlin.
Latacz, J 1966, Zum Wortfeld "Freude" in der Sprache Homers, Winter, Heidelberg.
Maehler, H 1963, Die Auffassung des Dichterberufes im frühen Griechentum bis zur Zeit Pindars, Vandenhoeck & Ruprecht, Göttingen.
Morgan, KA 2004, 'Plato', in IJF De Jong, R Nünlist, A Bowie (eds), Narrators, Narratees, and Narratives in Ancient Greek Literature: Studies in Ancient Greek Narrative, vol. 1, Brill, Leiden, pp. 357–374.
Muthmann, F 1961, Untersuchungen zur 'Einkleidung' einiger platonischer Dialoge, Diss. Bonn.
Primavesi, O 2009, 'Zum Problem der epischen Fiktion in der vorplatonischen Poetik', in U Peters & R Warning (eds), Fiktion und Fiktionalität in den Literaturen des Mittelalters, Wilhelm Fink, München, pp. 105–120.
Radke, G 2007, 'Die poetische Souveränität des homerischen Erzählers', *Rheinisches Museum*, no. 150, pp. 8–66
Reents, E 1998, Zu Thomas Manns Schopenhauer-Rezeption, Königshausen und Neumann, Würzburg.
Riginos, AS 1976, Platonica: The anecdotes concerning the life and writings of Plato, Brill, Leiden.
Rossetti, L & Stavru, A 2010, Introduction, in L Rossetti, A Stavru (eds), Socratica 2008: Studies in Ancient Socratic Literature, Levante editori, Bari.
Schirren, Th 1999, 'Apollodoros manikos: Ein textkritisches Problem in Platons Symposion 173d8 und dessen Konsequenzen', *Göttinger Forum für Altertumswissenschaft*, no. 2, pp. 217–236.
Schwinge, E-R 1991, 'Homerische Epen und Erzählforschung', in J Latacz (ed), Zweihundert Jahre Homerforschung, Teubner, Stuttgart, pp. 482–512.
Schwinge, E-R 1997, Griechische Tragödie und zeitgenössische Rezeption: Aristophanes und Gorgias. Zur Frage einer angemessenen Tragödiendeutung, Joachim Jungius-Gesellschaft der Wissenschaften, Hamburg.
Tulli, M 2011, 'Il proemio del Teeteto e la poetica del dialogo', in M Tulli (ed), L'Autore pensoso, Fabrizio Serra editore, Pisa/Roma, pp. 121–133.

Dino De Sanctis
The meeting scenes in the *incipit* of Plato's dialogue

In a dense succession of allusions and explicit reminiscences, motifs deriving from the *epos*, lyrics, paeans and theatre are woven together in the dialogue[1]. Plato draws on these motifs in order to create a new lite prary genre, capable of reproducing the ever-open συνουσία between master and pupil[2]. In this complex process critics nowadays perceive a testimony marked by maturity and awareness, along the lines of *Kreuzung der Gattungen*, as Michael Erler highlighted in outlining the image of Plato as *poeta doctus* with whom subsequent Hellenistic poetry would come into close and fertile contact[3]. Therefore it is possible to say that Plato continuously dialogues with the system of literary genres and significantly anticipates its developments in Hellenistic period. It is no wonder then that the meeting scenes between Socrates and his interlocutors assume a particular importance in this process, from which emerge useful premises for understanding the meaning of the dialogue itself[4]. As well as creating an expertly conceived horizon of expectation for the addressee, in these scenes Plato mostly evokes the meeting place, a recognizable place in Athens, as well as the time of the meeting, often 'today', 'νῦν, or 'yesterday', χθές[5]. The opening of the *Republic* fits very well into this perspective, as a sort of paradigm. In any case, in the complex genesis of the dialogue, the *Republic* imposes itself as a synthesis carrying particular weight in the λόγος Σωκρατικός, as a type of highpoint, according to Charles H. Kahn· on the dialectical and pedagogical level in Plato's literary experience[6]. It follows that this *incipit* becomes an important point of reference for the proemial technique that Plato has inherited from tradition[7].

---

1 On the so called *Gattungsmischung* in the Plato' s dialogue, see Nightingale (1995).
2 The dialogue is the crucial form able to pick up the legacy of past literary tradition in a new perspective: see Andrieu (1954, 304–308).
3 For a specific discussion, see Erler (2007, pp. 80–82) and Murray (1996, pp. 12–14).
4 See Burnyeat (1997) on the value and significance of the *incipit* in Plato' s dialogues as anticipation of general themes.
5 In this regard, I make reference to the systematic study by Morgan (2004, pp. 346–368), with a comprehensive overview of time in the dialogue.
6 Kahn (1996, pp. 292–296).
7 On this technique from Homer to Hesiod, see Thalmann (1984, pp. 33–77).

At the beginning of the dialogue, Socrates, as is known, gives an account of a recent journey in the first person, the well-known descent to Pireaus on the occasion of the festivities for Bendis, a new Thracian goddess to Athens (327a1–b5)[8]:

Κατέβην χθὲς εἰς Πειραιᾶ μετὰ Γλαύκωνος τοῦ Ἀρίστωνος προσευξόμενός τε τῇ θεῷ καὶ ἅμα τὴν ἑορτὴν βουλόμενος θεάσασθαι τίνα τρόπον ποιήσουσιν ἅτε νῦν πρῶτον ἄγοντες. καλὴ μὲν οὖν μοι καὶ ἡ τῶν ἐπιχωρίων πομπὴ ἔδοξεν εἶναι, οὐ μέντοι ἧττον ἐφαίνετο πρέπειν ἣν οἱ Θρᾷκες ἔπεμπον. προσευξάμενοι δὲ καὶ θεωρήσαντες ἀπῇμεν πρὸς τὸ ἄστυ. κατιδὼν οὖν πόρρωθεν ἡμᾶς οἴκαδε ὡρμημένους Πολέμαρχος ὁ Κεφάλου ἐκέλευσε δραμόντα τὸν παῖδα περιμεῖναί ἑ κελεῦσαι. καί μου ὄπισθεν ὁ παῖς λαβόμενος τοῦ ἱματίου, Κελεύει ὑμᾶς, ἔφη, Πολέμαρχος περιμεῖναι.

For a while now critics have identified here an intentional reference to καταβαίνειν, a motif that permeates the archaic *epos* starting with the *Nekyia* in the *Odyssey* and continuing up as far as Parmenides' Περὶ φύσεως, by way of Orphism[9]. In Plato, therefore, this is a refined example of allusive technique, as shown in Giorgio Pasquali's crucial study, a technique indeed that is necessary and precious for every poetic style[10]. In Plato therefore, a deeper poetic strategy may be perceived in every allusion that his work offers. It is no coincidence that Mario Vegetti has dedicated memorable pages to the beginning of the dialogue, highlighting the underlying function they take on within a narrative structure where, little by little, a process of *Kallipolis* takes shape in the guise of δικαιοσύνη, the wished-for model of the perfect society. In this way the opening the *Republic* with Socrates' *Katabasis* anticipates in a polarized manner the principal acquisition of knowledge in the dialogue: an *anabasis* after the descent[11]. Consequently it comes as no surprise that, in a excellent monograph dedicated to the link between Plato and poetry, Mario Regali has returned to the *incipit* of the *Republic*, and he skilfully sets down, in my opinion, the plentiful and functional presence of literary motifs that characterize it in a closely-argued and certainly programmatic link with the *Timaeus*. On the occasion of the meeting between Socrates and the Polemarch and Socrates' subsequent visit to Cephalus' abode, the philosophers' society now experiences the beginning of its consolida-

---

[8] Campese (1998, pp. 105–116), examines closely the cult of Bendis in Athens connected to the Bendideia.
[9] On the motiv of *katabasis* from *epos* to Plato see now Männlein-Robert (2013, pp. 243–244).
[10] Pasquali (1968², pp. 275–282).
[11] In order to have the right *modus vivendi*, i.e. an *anabasis*, it is necessary an ascent to the light, made possible by the knowledge dialectics offer, with the guidance and paideutic support of φιλόσοφος at its center. See Vegetti (1998, pp. 93–104).

tion which, in the fiction of the *Timaeus*, will reach its apex right in the λόγοι held between Hermocrates, Timaeus, Critias and Socrates (17a – 18c)[12].

Taking this as a starting point, which is useful in order to understand the meaning that must be grasped in the *incipit* of the *Republic*, I believe it is fitting to reconsider some of the elements present in the scene. First of all, the time-element in the story: the walk down to the city of Piraeus, narrated by Socrates, is collocated in a precise chronological dimension, almost ostentatiously so. The opening of the dialogue κατέβην χθές dominates, and it is no coincidence that it is clearly in *positio princeps*, as Diskin Clay has clarified[13]. Then the setting: the part of Piraeus where Socrates has decided to go in order to observe the Bendideia is near Athens, but outside the centre of the town. And finally the occasion: the ἑορτή for the goddess, with a procession, the beautiful πομπή that the people of the place have painstakingly prepared. The brief journey, in the company of Glaucon, son of Aristodemus, comes to an end when, on the orders of the Polemarch who from afar has spotted Glaucon and Socrates, a young slave tugs Socrates' cloak and invites him to stop. The path of the φιλόσοφος is therefore blocked, but this obstacle in its turn leads to a decisive result: the young man who clutches Socrates' cloak actually hinders – or at least delays – the return to the city for the φιλόσοφος. In the framework of the *Republic*, it is a moment of intense of realism, by no means isolated in the great panoply of events and situations that confer such a special aura to the dialogue. The reference to this same cloak in the *Protagoras* (335d2–5), for instance, is just as realistic; Aristophanes' hiccups and the sneeze advised as a remedy by Eryximachus, or the cockcrow that inaugurates a new day in the *Symposium* (185d2–3 e 189a), Charmides' headache in *Charmides* (157b–c). And, of course, just as for the cloak, the sneeze and the headache, so too does Socrates' break along the road to Piraeus in the *Republic* end up revealing a more complex motivation. This lengthy break does not represent a useless indulgence, rather does it open up the road to an unexpected opportunity: observing the evening spectacle of an atmospheric procession in honour of Bendis, which is a novelty that cannot be passed up, just waiting to be discovered after dinner and the subsequent discussion in the Polemarch's house[14].

---

12 Regali (2012, pp. 71–78) suggests that in the *incipit* it is evident the complex literary genre of *Timaeus* through a special characterization of his protagonists.
13 In this regard see the detailed exam in Clay (1992).
14 On the link between the candlelit procession for Bendis and that by the Panathenaeas in honor of Athena, see Gastaldi (1998, pp. 117–131).

In the poetic geography of the Piraeus therefore, the Polemarch's house is immediately identifiable as a place of particular substance[15]. Here Socrates finds a community of men ready to start up an intense dialogue with him, beginning with the courteous host, Cephalus, who is seated and has been crowned after a sacrifice. He is keen to tell how old people often get together with him to complain about their lost goods, but not before he clarifies, following the symmetry of the *incipit* of the dialogue, that Socrates does not often come down to the Pireus and visit him in his house, Ὦ Σώκρατες, οὐ δὲ θαμίζεις ἡμῖν καταβαίνων εἰς τὸν Πειραιᾶ (328 c6–7)[16].

The opening of the *Republic* shows how complex the narrative technique is that distinguishes the meeting scenes described by Plato. It is my intention here to highlight the role played by Athens in some of these, as it is a crucial frame for the συνουσία between Socrates and his interlocutors[17]. In the dialogue – but above all in the *incipit* – Athens is in fact seen like an immense theatrical *scenario* in which Socrates is the main focus. In this dialogue Athens opposes the outside world, the world beyond the walls, because it represents the quintessential place wherein Socrates carries out his investigations, his ζητεῖν, and makes them paradigmatic. It is in this sense that the opening of *Crito* is moving, when Crito visits Socrates in prison in Athens (43a–43b). It is very early, dawn is just breaking. The guard has given permission for this meeting because Crito has at this stage become his friend, since he visits Socrates so frequently. So far Crito has admired Socrates, sleeping and alone[18]. It is in this sense that the opening of *Euthyphro* (2a1–2b10) also deserves to be recalled: Euthyphro asks Socrates why he has left the διατριβαί in the Lyceum and has come to the Porch of the King[19].

The judicial problem emerges immediately, which is centred on δίκη and γραφή, what emerges above all is the portrait, ambiguous and sarcastic, of the young and unknown Meletus: there are no facts about this man in Athens, but he came originally from the Pithus deme and his beard is not yet fully grown[20]. Certainly, it is in this sense that the opening of the *Gorgias* should also be considered (47a1.5), then Socrates asks Callicles if he has come late to the feast and politely attributes the blame to Chaeraphon for spending, διατρί-

---

15 As a maritime locality, the Pireus is by no means immune to the risks of brine-filled air and foreign commerce as Plato recalls in the *Laws* (IV 704a-715e): see Schöpsdau (2003, pp. 137–145).
16 For Cephalus' profile in the *Republic*, see in particular Blondell (2002, pp. 165–175).
17 In this regard, see Morgan (2012, pp. 415–437).
18 On this *incipit* see Burnet (1924, pp. 254–255).
19 For the *Euthyphro*' introduction and his legal problems, see Walker (1984, pp. 62–64)
20 See Nails (2002, p. 201).

βειν, too much time in the ἀγορά[21]. These are all examples that point to a special relationship between Socrates and Athens. A bond that can be recognized in the tone of the opening in the *Charmides* (135a1–b4)[22]:

Ἥκομεν τῇ προτεραίᾳ ἑσπέρας ἐκ Ποτειδαίας ἀπὸ τοῦ στρατοπέδου, οἷον δὲ διὰ χρόνου ἀφιγμένος ἀσμένως ᾖα ἐπὶ τὰς συνήθεις διατριβάς. καὶ δὴ καὶ εἰς τὴν Ταυρέου παλαίστραν τὴν καταντικρὺ τοῦ τῆς Βασίλης ἱεροῦ εἰσῆλθον, καὶ αὐτόθι κατέλαβον πάνυ πολλούς, τοὺς μὲν καὶ ἀγνῶτας ἐμοί, τοὺς δὲ πλείστους γνωρίμους. καί με ὡς εἶδον εἰσιόντα ἐξ ἀπροσδοκήτου, εὐθὺς πόρρωθεν ἠσπάζοντο ἄλλος ἄλλοθεν· Χαιρεφῶν δέ, ἅτε καὶ μανικὸς ὤν, ἀναπηδήσας ἐκ μέσων ἔθει πρός με, καί μου λαβόμενος τῆς χειρός, Ὦ Σώκρατες, ἦ δ' ὅς, πῶς ἐσώθης ἐκ τῆς μάχης;

What emerges strongly from the details evoked in this scene is the joy on the part of the person who has been away from his own city and now returns: Socrates. The lively ἥκομεν, *we reached*, introduces a sudden account, almost a fairy tale, set at evening time in the gymnasium of Taureas[23]. The long time spent away from Athens, at war, is concentrated in the διὰ χρόνου. Socrates' happiness, and the happiness his return occasions, derives from the chance to frequent again the places designated for discussions, the συνήθεις διατριβαί[24]. The scene is immediately animated by a merry crowd, ready for dialogue: they experience this great joy in the opening ἀσμένως for Socrates, ἠσπάζοντο for Socrates' friends. Therefore, what unfolds in the opening lines of the *Charmides*, well before the actual encounter, is a scene of return: this return places Socrates, the φιλόσοφος, in a dimension close to that of Odysseus, the ἥρως. For that again, just as Odysseus confronts a νόστος in order to re-appropriate his place in Ithaca, which has been temporarily lost on account of the Trojan War, in the same way Socrates' return is finalized in such a way as to rekindle a wished-for διαλέγεσθαι, which had been interrupted by the War in Potidaea[25]. And the link between the φιλόσοφος and the ἥρως, at the beginning of the dialogue, is even more substantial, if one thinks of Socrates' entrance into the gymnasium (135b–c). Here, everyone wants to quiz him and Socrates immediately satisfies his friends' curiosity about the war with his answers, until they tire of this

---

[21] For the proverbial opening of *Gorgias*, see Sansone (2009, pp. 631–633).
[22] See now Tuozzo (2011, pp. 101–110).
[23] The *Charmides*' opening recalls the motive of gymnasium as crucial in *Lisis*. In this regard, see Penner, Rowe (2005, pp. 231–236).
[24] In *Charmides* the διαλέγεσθαι with Socrates is the new kind of poetry. See Tulli (2000, pp. 259–264).
[25] On *Charmides* as a return-dialogue and for the problems linked to its fictive chronology, see Lampert (2010, pp. 145–15).

topic. This scene definitely seems to have been modelled on the account that Odysseus gives the Phaeacians at Scheria, when Alcinous, on discovering the identity of the castaway that has arrived at his table, puts a series of questions to Odysseus, to which he will answer with the μεγάλη διήγησις of the *Apologoi* (*Od.* IX – XIII), a long narration structured, in fact, around the dialectic device of question-answer[26].

Therefore, it is now easy to understand why for Socrates, whatever is far from the city becomes useless, inconvenient, often lacking in anything attractive, indeed caught up in διατριβή, and silent compared to the great and beneficial διαλέγεσθαι. In any case, as he reveals before the judges in the *Apologia*, like a second Heracles[27], in order to discover and locate somebody who is truly wise, Socrates has to wander from place to place in his city, cope with weariness, here understandably called πόνοι, after having ascertained the oracle's answer (22a – b)[28]. Far from the streets of Athens, Socrates instead is bewildered. At the beginning of the *Phaedrus*, near Ilissus, the countryside opens out before the eyes of Socrates and Phaedrus, but in the *Phaedrus* the countryside does not figure as an attractive place. Little by little, in the fresh country greenness of the grass and the sun- and cicada-filled trees, the flames of a dangerous ambiguity are ready to crackle, if there is no-one present that knows how to converse properly. This perspective already emerges at the beginning of the meeting proper between Socrates and Phaedrus with which the dialogue opens (227a1 – b1)[29]:

{ΣΩ.} Ὦ φίλε Φαῖδρε, ποῖ δὴ καὶ πόθεν; {ΦΑΙ.} Παρὰ Λυσίου, ὦ Σώκρατες, τοῦ Κεφάλου, πορεύομαι δὲ πρὸς περίπατον ἔξω τείχους· συχνὸν γὰρ ἐκεῖ διέτριψα χρόνον καθήμενος ἐξ ἑωθινοῦ. τῷ δὲ σῷ καὶ ἐμῷ ἑταίρῳ πειθόμενος Ἀκουμενῷ κατὰ τὰς ὁδοὺς ποιοῦμαι τοὺς περιπάτους· φησὶ γὰρ ἀκοπωτέρους εἶναι τῶν ἐν τοῖς δρόμοις.

After the greeting, Ὦ φίλε Φαῖδρε, a question gets the discussion under way, ποῖ δὴ καὶ πόθεν. Socrates shows that he is interested in knowing where his friend has arrived from. The answer coincides with the focus being placed on Athens: Phaedrus has come from Lysias' house, who is staying with the orator, Epicrates, in a house that used to belong to Maricus, near the temple to Olympic Zeus

---

26 On central dialectic device in *epos* and in particular after the *Apologoi*, see Sammons (2010, pp. 51 – 56).
27 Clay (2000, pp. 51 – 59) analyzes Socrates as epic hero.
28 On Chaerephon's question to Pythian Oracles in *Apology*, see de Strycher, Slings (1994, pp. 74 – 82).
29 Rowe (1986, p. 135) supposes that "this long introductory section sets the tone of the whole dialogue".

(227b4–5). Phaedrus then adds that he is taking a walk outside the walls because walking along these streets is less tiring than walking under the city's porch, as recommended by Acumenos. Immediately, in the *incipit* of the dialogue, Plato shows his interest in the urban geography of Athens with a deliberateness and realism that recall the comedy by Aristophanes, where certain glimpses of the city emerge with great clarity. In this regard, think of Strepsiade's house in *The Clouds* (32–33) or that of Agathon in the *Thesmoforiazusae*, which stands out from the front door, Ὁρᾷς τὸ θύριον τοῦτο; / Νὴ τὸν Ἡρακλέα οἶμαί γε (25–26)[30]; think too of the empty Pnyx from whence in the countryside a disconcerted Dicaeopolis arrives early in the morning in the *Acharnians*, ὡς νῦν, ὁπότ' οὔσης κυρίας ἐκκλησίας / ἑωθινῆς ἔρημος ἡ πνὺξ αὐτηί (19–20)[31].

But this is not all. The opposition that Phaedrus recalls, between walks within the city, περίπατοι ἐν τοῖς δρόμοις, and the roads outside, περίπατοι ἔξω τείχους, has an obvious function: that of clarifying the pertinent places appropriate for Socrates, and those that are more appropriate for Phaedrus, who wishes for peace and quiet and a silent read. The τόπος now reveals an ἦθος, but for it to be clear, it is necessary, as in the *Republic*, for Socrates to take some time out in a different dimension to Athens. In the *Phaedrus*, therefore, the περίπατοι ἔξω τείχους become the setting for a walk between Socrates and Phaedrus. Socrates in fact deviates from his preference at his friend's suggestion and, with a σχολή in his possession, decides to accompany Phaedrus on his relaxing stroll outside the walls in order to listen to a speech by Lysias on love[32]. In this way they leave Athens behind them and the countryside enters the scene. At first sight this countryside is luxuriant, sunny and bewitching. Bit by bit, however, with regard to such lush countryside, Socrates, citizen *par excellence*, betrays decided embarrassment. Despite the spectacle being so charming, for Socrates the scenery around Ilissus provokes his irony, because it is a place where man's presence fades, and along with it, therefore, any kind of research into understanding him. Socrates is desirous of learning, he is a φιλομαθής: while the countryside and the trees are not capable of teaching, διδάσκειν, Socrates reminds us that teaching can only come from men who live in the city, οἱ δ' ἐν τῷ ἄστει ἄνθρωποι (230d3–5)[33].

It is no wonder then that Phaedrus, as soon as Socrates decides to stop under a plane tree, idyllic *locus amoenus*, perceives in his interlocutor a man who is ἀτοπώτατος, once he finds himself outside Athens (230c6–d2)[34]:

---

[30] The image of θύριον the often used in comedy: in this regard see Austin, Olson (2004, p. 60).
[31] Olson (2002, p. 72).
[32] The σχολή is crucial also for the cicadas' myth in *Phaedrus*: see Ferrari (1987, pp. 14–15).
[33] In this regard, see Heitsch (1993, pp. 71–76).
[34] On Socrates' ἀτοπία, see Hadot (1987, pp. 77–116).

{ΦΑΙ.} Σὺ δέ γε, ὦ θαυμάσιε, ἀτοπώτατός τις φαίνῃ. ἀτεχνῶς γάρ, ὃ λέγεις, ξεναγουμένῳ τινὶ καὶ οὐκ ἐπιχωρίῳ ἔοικας· οὕτως ἐκ τοῦ ἄστεος οὔτ' εἰς τὴν ὑπερορίαν ἀποδημεῖς, οὔτ' ἔξω τείχους ἔμοιγε δοκεῖς τὸ παράπαν ἐξιέναι.

Once he leaves Athens' walls, Socrates increases his ἀτοπία, he seems to lose his elected place, his τόπος, together with all the characteristics that connote him in the city, until he resembles a foreigner being guided by others. Socrates is not a ἐπιχώριος in the countryside, because he never carries out the ἀποδημεῖν of his city[35].

The initial question that opens the dialogue arouses interest in the meeting scene between Phaedrus and Socrates: ποῖ δὴ καὶ πόθεν. It arouses interest, in fact, because what is recognizable here, in any case, and as we shall see immediately, is a precise metrical sequence: a spondee followed by a dactyl. A musical and calculated echo from a world that feels itself close to poetry. This question turns up again at the beginning of the *Lysis*, when Socrates meets a groups of youths led by Hippothales, Ctesippus and Hieronymus (203a1–b1)[36]:

ἐπορευόμην μὲν ἐξ Ἀκαδημείας εὐθὺ Λυκείου τὴν ἔξω τείχους ὑπ' αὐτὸ τὸ τεῖχος· ἐπειδὴ δ' ἐγενόμην κατὰ τὴν πυλίδα ᾗ ἡ Πάνοπος κρήνη, ἐνταῦθα συνέτυχον Ἱπποθάλει τε τῷ Ἱερωνύμου καὶ Κτησίππῳ τῷ Παιανιεῖ καὶ ἄλλοις μετὰ τούτων νεανίσκοις ἀθρόοις συνεστῶσι. καί με προσιόντα ὁ Ἱπποθάλης ἰδών, Ὦ Σώκρατες, ἔφη, ποῖ δὴ πορεύῃ καὶ πόθεν;

Socrates is returning from the Academy to the Lyceum on the road that runs along the outside walls of the city: he has just arrived at the small door where Panopea's well is situated. Here Hippothales exclaims, "ποῖ δὴ πορεύῃ καὶ πόθεν;" "O Socrates, where are you going and whence do you come?" In this case, indeed, with the verb πορεύῃ, Hippothales' question takes on the rhythm of an iambic trimeter[37]: Both in the *Phaedrus* and in the *Lysis*, the question ποῖ δὴ (πορεύῃ) καὶ πόθεν therefore evokes a continuous πλάνη, carried out by Socrates and his interlocutors in a city, Athens, that was in continuous motion. For ποῖ δὴ (πορεύῃ) καὶ πόθεν, in any case, it is not difficult on a literary level to identify a clear model that may be traced back to Homer, a model that underlines the meeting between a character and a foreigner[38]. Think, for example, of the welcome given by Telemachus to Mentor, in whose likeness Athena arrives on Ithaca, τίς πόθεν εἰς ἀνδρῶν; πόθι τοι πόλις ἠδὲ τοκῆες; (*Od.* I 170), – interestingly, Alcinous asks Odysseus the same question when he is shipwrecked on Scheria (*Od.*

---

35 Tulli (1990, pp. 97–105) highlights the irony in the description of *locus amoenus* in *Phaidrus*.
36 See Martinelli Tempesta (2004, pp. 229–232).
37 See Capra (2003, pp. 190–191).
38 On the identification of the guest see de Jong (2001, pp. 25–26).

VII 238) –[39]; consider the words that Circes says in front of Odysseus and his companions, who have reached her magical and mysterious abode, ὦ ξεῖνοι, τίνες ἐστέ; πόθεν πλεῖθ' ὑγρὰ κέλευθα; (*Od.* IX 252). The paradigm does not come across as odd in the *Odyssey*, where the motif of the journey amounts to what is practically a constant and pervasive presence. It must certainly be said that its recurrence in comedy and tragedy was to be frequent. The following represent some of the many examples: in *The Birds* (407–408), Euelpides reassures Pisthetaerus, who fears he is going to die during the tricky task he is about to undertake. At this point the coryphaeus approaches Hoopoe and asks for some information about the couple, τίνες ποθ' οἵδε καὶ πόθεν. Hoopoe's answer is eloquent, ξένω σοφῆς ἀφ' Ἑλλάδος[40]. Apart from Aristophanes, there is above all Euripides. *Electra* offers a significant instance (779–785):

ἰδὼν δ' αὐτεῖ· Χαίρετ' , ὦ ξένοι· τίνες
πόθεν πορεύεσθ' ἔστε τ' ἐκ ποίας χθονός;
ὁ δ' εἶπ' Ὀρέστης· Θεσσαλοί· πρὸς δ' Ἀλφεὸν
θύσοντες ἐρχόμεσθ' Ὀλυμπίωι Διί.
κλύων δὲ ταῦτ' Αἴγισθος ἐννέπει τάδε·
νῦν μὲν παρ' ἡμῖν χρὴ συνεστίους ὁμοῦ
θοίνης γενέσθαι·

At the beginning of the third episode, after Orestes and Pylades have killed Aegisthus, a messenger tells Electra of the death of her violent stepfather, usurper of Agamemnon's kingdom. The messenger formulates his tale in a mimetic manner, reproducing the banter between Aegisthus and Orestes. After seeing the foreigners approaching the garden where he has been trimming a myrtle branch for himself, Aegisthus greets the men that are approaching him with χαίρετε, and asks them who they are, where they are headed, and from what country they hail, τίνες / πόθεν πορεύεσθ' ἔστε τ' ἐκ ποίας χθονός. After Orestes' deceitful answer that he is a Thessalian that has come to offer sacrifice to Olympian Zeus, Aegisthus invites the small army to meet up in his house for a banquet.

This type of meeting, which Plato dramatizes between Socrates and his interlocutor in the *Phaedrus* and the *Lysis*, seems to take on the features of a typical dialogical situation, at this base of which it is right to perceive a consistently poetic input. In any case, the same question that we observed in the ποῖ δὴ (πορεύῃ) καὶ πόθεν, even if in part varied, opens the *Protagoras*, when Socrates'

---

39 For this question, similar in *Odyssey* XIX (104–105), see Garvie (1994, p. 212).
40 Various corrections for an acceptable metrical scheme have been made for this section: see Dunbar (1995, pp. 291–294).

friend, to whom the story about the meeting with the Sophist will be told, believes that Socrates is returning from a hunt with Alcibiades, πόθεν, ὦ Σώκρατες, φαίνῃ; (309a1). But it also opens the *Menexenus*, {ΣΩ.} ἐξ ἀγορᾶς ἢ πόθεν Μενέξενος; (234a1), in order to underline the sudden appearance of Menexenus returning from Buleuterius. Here too in these dialogues, in preparation for the subsequent theme that will unfold, the *incipit* focuses on the space of the scene as if on the stage of some immense urban theatre[41].

A testimony in this sense also reaches us from the opening of *Ion*, which has at its centre the meeting between Socrates and a rhapsode[42]. After a special greeting, τὸν Ἴωνα χαίρειν, the repartee comes fast and furious (530a1–b3)[43]:

{ΣΩ.} Τὸν Ἴωνα χαίρειν. πόθεν τὰ νῦν ἡμῖν ἐπιδεδήμηκας; ἢ οἴκοθεν ἐξ Ἐφέσου; {ΙΩΝ.} Οὐδαμῶς, ὦ Σώκρατες, ἀλλ' ἐξ Ἐπιδαύρου ἐκ τῶν Ἀσκληπιείων. {ΣΩ.} Μῶν καὶ ῥαψῳδῶν ἀγῶνα τιθέασιν τῷ θεῷ οἱ Ἐπιδαύριοι; {ΙΩΝ.} Πάνυ γε, καὶ τῆς ἄλλης γε μουσικῆς. {ΣΩ.} Τί οὖν; ἠγωνίζου τι ἡμῖν; καὶ πῶς τι ἠγωνίσω; {ΙΩΝ.} Τὰ πρῶτα τῶν ἄθλων ἠνεγκάμεθα, ὦ Σώκρατες. {ΣΩ.} Εὖ λέγεις· ἄγε δὴ ὅπως καὶ τὰ Παναθήναια νικήσομεν. {ΙΩΝ.} Ἀλλ' ἔσται ταῦτα, ἐὰν θεὸς ἐθέλῃ.

This *incipit* is redolent of a real stichomythia. Three questions mark the pace of the dialogue: Socrates asks where Ion has come from, if the inhabitants of Epidaurus have set up a race for Asclepius, and whether Ion has won this race. Socrates' questions alternate with the rhapsode's answers, until Socrates hopes for future victories at the Panathenaea games and Ion accepts this good wish, placing himself in the hands of the god, ἐὰν θεὸς ἐθέλῃ[44]. In *Ion* too, the opening with the question, πόθεν τὰ νῦν ἡμῖν ἐπιδεδήμηκας, tends to highlight space and time. In this dialogue, however, we are not dealing – as in *Lysis* and *Charmides* – with a specific place in Athens[45]. The impression is that Socrates meets Ion, who has just arrived, on the city streets and that Ion brings with him a geographical element, which is simultaneously both *recherché* and idiosyncratic. Ion comes from Ionia, which is geographically far from Athens and his name car-

---

41 Tsitsiridis (1998, pp. 129–130).
42 Flashar (1958, pp. 17–21) identifies here the particular elements of a *typische Dialogsituation*. In general for the problems in this dialogue important observations in Verdenius (1943, pp. 233–262) and Liebert (2010, pp. 1779–218).
43 On the greeting in *Ion*, see Rijksbaron (2007, pp. 121–125). See also in general on the dialogue's *incipit* Battegazzore (1969, pp. 5–13).
44 Centrone, Petrucci (2012, pp. 314–315).
45 In the *Protagoras* (309d3), in order to indicate the arrival of the Sophist, who has been in the city for three days, Plato uses the verb ἐπιδημέω with which *Ion* opens. See Denyer (2008, pp. 65–67).

ries an echo of this. Furthermore, Ion boasts of an important statute. Indeed, Socrates greets his interlocutor in an formal tone, τὸν Ἴωνα χαίρειν: this tone is justified when in the presence of someone of very elevated rank. But this is not all: Socrates underlines his interlocutor's foreign identity. He immediately asks if the rhapsode has come from Ephesus, his native city. Ion's answer is decidedly, if not deliberately, negative, as the use of the adverb οὐδαμῶς highlights, a resolute adverb, which almost seems to prove the rhapsode's scorn when faced with the idea that a man as important and busy as Ion could have enough free time to spend in his homeland. Ion is always travelling around, from contest to contest, as the initial repartee in the dialogue leads us to believe[46].

This behaviour on the part of Ion emerges again when he is asked another question: when Socrates asks Ion if he is an expert only on Homer, or also on Hesiod and Archilocus, νῦν δέ μοι τοσόνδε ἀπόκριναι· πότερον περὶ Ὁμήρου μόνον δεινὸς εἶ ἢ καὶ περὶ Ἡσιόδου καὶ Ἀρχιλόχου; (531a1–2), the rhapsode's scorn flares up again, as may be seen in the locution "absolutely not", given that Ion's δεινότης is exclusively focused on Homer, οὐδαμῶς, ἀλλὰ περὶ Ὁμήρου μόνον· ἱκανὸν γάρ μοι δοκεῖ εἶναι (531a3)[47].

From the very opening of *Ion* Plato shows a substantial difference between Socrates and the rhapsode in regard to the problem of their πλάνη, despite the fact that both of them are completely caught up in a life of wandering. While Socrates' πλάνη, it could be said, has developed for Athens, Ion is taken up with a journey that makes no allowance for rests, from Ephesus to Greece, from Epidaurus to Athens and then, as may be easily imagined, from Athens to other cities. During his city journey, Socrates' quest runs along the lines of ζητεῖν. Ion's journeying however is different in nature: Ion does not move towards knowledge, rather does he take for granted that he knows. Indeed, on his busy journey from Ionia to Greece, Ion shows that he possesses a traditional store of poetry and knowledge, obsessively static and circumscribed only to Homer in a limiting and infantile manner. In light of this, the etymological game that Plato, I believe, advances at the end of the dialogue on the rhapsode's name is very significant[48]:

{ΣΩ.} Τί δή ποτ' οὖν πρὸς τῶν θεῶν, ὦ Ἴων, ἀμφότερα ἄριστος ὢν τῶν Ἑλλήνων, καὶ στρατηγὸς καὶ ῥαψῳδός, ῥαψῳδεῖς μὲν περιιὼν τοῖς Ἕλλησι, στρατηγεῖς δ' οὔ;

---

46 Kahn (1996, pp. 110–113) analyzes the argumentation until the beginning of *Ion* as clear evidence of socratic *elenchus*.
47 On nexus "Homer, Hesiod and other poets" in Plato's dialogues, see Arrighetti (1987, pp. 13–15).
48 Regali (2012, pp. 258–275), analyzes etymological games in Plato's dialogues.

Socrates is about to unmask Ion's useless knowledge: the knowledge that the rhapsode has gained from Homer ought to make him among the best strategists in Greece, just as he is effectively one of the best rhapsodes. In actual fact, Ἴων – despite being the best in both fields, ἀμφότερα ἄριστος ὤν – continues to travel among the Greeks only as a rhapsode, ῥαψῳδεῖς μὲν περιιών[49]. In this game that is cultivated and shows great awareness, Ἴων – ὤν – περιιών, all the weakness inherent in Ion's τέχνη emerges. It is no coincidence that the περιιέναι is fitting for Socrates too, after all; but this wandering is conjugated by φιλόσοφος in a different manner and with different ends compared to the rhapsode. This perspective is evident for instance in the *Apology* (23a–b), when Socrates says that he goes around Athens, his one and only pole of interest, in order to evaluate among its citizens and foreigners who the wisest man is, in this way bringing enmity, calumny and rancour down on his head, ταῦτ' οὖν ἐγὼ μὲν ἔτι καὶ νῦν περιιὼν ζητῶ καὶ ἐρευνῶ κατὰ τὸν θεὸν καὶ τῶν ἀστῶν καὶ ξένων ἄν τινα οἴωμαι σοφὸν εἶναι (23b4–6).[50]

The epichoric character of Socrates' περιιέναι is reinforced in the *incipit* of *Ion* by his profound ignorance with regard to anything happening outside Athens, which is very evident at the beginning of the dialogue: in any case, Socrates knows nothing of what has happened in nearby Epidaurus and has to listen to Ion in order to get more precise information. But even when he gets the news about Epidaurus, Socrates is still focused on his own city: it is no coincidence that he hopes Ion's victory will come to pass during the Panathenae games, to the advantage of his fellow citizens and Athens, ἄγε δὴ ὅπως καὶ τὰ Παναθήναια νικήσομεν (530b1)[51]. Actually, if one looks closely, Socrates underlines this advantage emphatically by associating himself, by means of νικήσομεν, with the victory he wishes for the rhapsode, as if he too must be the creator of this victory, if not the only protagonist; this points to the dialectic victory that in a short time Socrates will gain over Ion. Despite the absence of a specific place in Athens, the urban horizon is also outlined icastically in *Ion*, reaching its apex in the ἡμῖν, the *we*, which refers to the city as a whole. In this sense, it is useful to remember the beginning of the *Hippias Major* (281a1–b1)[52]:

{ΣΩ.} Ἱππίας ὁ καλός τε καὶ σοφός· ὡς διὰ χρόνου ἡμῖν κατῆρας εἰς τὰς Ἀθήνας. {ΙΠ.} Οὐ γὰρ σχολή, ὦ Σώκρατες. ἡ γὰρ Ἦλις ὅταν τι δέηται διαπράξασθαι πρός τινα τῶν πόλεων, ἀεὶ ἐπὶ

---

[49] This game has also been well grasped by Padilla (1992, pp. 124–125), testifying to a more static Socrates and an Ion who is in continuous movement.
[50] Heitsch (2002, pp. 91–92).
[51] Capuccino (2005, pp. 109–115).
[52] On the general Hippias' character, see Blondell (2002, pp. 137–154).

πρῶτον ἐμὲ ἔρχεται τῶν πολιτῶν αἱρουμένη πρεσβευτήν, ἡγουμένη δικαστὴν καὶ ἄγγελον ἱκανώτατον εἶναι τῶν λόγων οἳ ἂν παρὰ τῶν πόλεων ἑκάστων λέγωνται

Like Ion, Hippias, Socrates' new and special interlocutor, is encountered suddenly on the city streets. Significantly, Socrates cries: Ἱππίας ὁ καλός τε καὶ σοφός, and immediately remembers that after a long absence the Sophist has finally returned to Athens for us, ὡς διὰ χρόνου ἡμῖν κατῆρας εἰς τὰς Ἀθήνας. Indeed, as Hippias confirms in a tone that is almost smug and yet resigned, Elis, his homeland, has constant need of his services and when it has to interact with the other cities, it always calls on the Sophist before any other citizen, since Hippias is the most suitable judge and messenger that Elis has[53]. Both Ion and Hippias appear in the *incipit* of the dialogue as strangers who have come to Athens, men engaged in important business, business that leaves them with little time, and who are ready to give crucial help to whatever communities they arrive in[54]. This help will, however, reveal itself to be useless in relation to the higher and more demanding work that Socrates is trying to carry out. In this way the rhapsode and the Sophist are united by a desire to know many beautiful things, πολλὰ καὶ καλά, but also by the fact that they have no actual personal experience of them[55].

Before bringing this brief and partial analysis to a conclusion, I would like to briefly touch on Greek poetry, insofar as it is the second part of the literary diptych, together with the *epos*, tragedy and comedy, with which, as I have recalled, Plato was in close contact. In the meeting scenes in the dialogue, the mimetic component is highlighted by a greeting, an urban space, and realistic gestures of intimate and ordinary familiarity. Intentional signals of a nuance-filled world, which Plato offers the reader by means of the delineation of his Socrates. A similar problem mediated by literary fiction and a learned blend of elements also emerges from the idyll of Theocritus, whose links to the *epos*, comedy and dialogue certainly represent an acquisition for critics of no little significance. Here, between the urban and pastoral settings, Theocritus often falls back on the mimetic component in order to create, with the highest possible quantity of literary elements, a lasting impression of spontaneity. One thinks of the pre-dialogic frame for the meeting between Lycidas and Simichidas in the bucolic

---

[53] On the characterization of Hippias in this dialogue, see Woodruff (1982, pp. 123–132).
[54] Note also the similarity between Ion and Hippias on the level of looks: both are lovers, so to say, of luxury and make-up (535d1–3 e 289e6). On irony toward Hippias as sophist without σοφία at the dialogue's beginning, see Centrone, Petrucci (2012, p. 43).
[55] On nexus πολλὰ καὶ καλά see Corradi (2012, pp. 164–165).

poem known as *The Harvest Feast* (VII 7–26)[56]; or of the *Syracusan Women* (XV 1–10) with the question by Gorgo, who wants to know if Praxinoa is at home, as well as the opening of the dialogue with its wealth of barbed repartee between the two women[57]; or, above all of the meeting between Aeschines and Thyonicus (XIV 1–7)[58]:

{ΑΙΣΧΙΝΑΣ} Χαίρειν πολλὰ τὸν ἄνδρα Θυώνιχον.{ΘΥΩΝΙΧΟΣ} ἄλλα τοιαῦτα
Αἰσχίνᾳ. ὡς χρόνιος. {ΑΙ.} χρόνιος. {ΘΥ.} τί δέ τοι τὸ μέλημα;
{ΑΙ.} πράσσομες οὐχ ὡς λῷστα, Θυώνιχε. {ΘΥ.}ταῦτ' ἄρα λεπτός,
χὠ μύσταξ πολὺς οὗτος,ἀυσταλέοι δὲ κίκιννοι.
τοιοῦτος πρώαν τις ἀφίκετο Πυθαγορικτάς,
ὠχρὸς κἀνυπόδητος· Ἀθαναῖος δ' ἔφατ' ἦμεν.

The dialogue opens with a greeting with a formal tone: the χαίρειν πολλά now recalls the χαίρειν in *Ion* that introduces a meeting between two young friends that haven't seen each other for a long time, as the adjective χρόνιος indicates, and it closely resembles the διὰ χρόνου present both in the *incipit* of the *Hippias Major* and in the *incipit* of the *Charmides*[59]. It is immediately obvious how thin and unkempt Thyonicus is, on account of the suffering the narrator protagonist has undergone: it is the theme of the idyll, which realistically tackles the problem of youthful love and its consequences. It is certainly not possible to state that Theocritus has Plato's dialogue in mind as a model for this scene, or only Plato's dialogue: comedy from Aristophanes to Menandros also plays a crucial role in the composition and poetics of the idylls, as well as Sophron's mime, which was appreciated by Plato himself[60]. What is certain however is that on account of the *Gattungsmischung* that unfolds in the dialogue and to which I alluded at the beginning of this article, it is not unlikely to think that Plato, by creating in the dialogue a literary space of compelling and modern originality, gave a remarkable stimulus to the consolidation of a mimetic genre, such as Theocritus' idyll is, which is sensitive to the need to unite form and content in an elegant and cultivated blend[61].

I would like to conclude with a well-known judgement from the Peripatetic School. In the *Academicorum Index* Philodemus, in his biographical reconstruc-

---

[56] On fictional world of Theocritus, see Payne (2007, pp. 49–91).
[57] Klooster (2011, pp. 108–110) analyzes the spatial references in this Idyll.
[58] Principal debt of Idyll XIV is to comedy: realism is a good proof of *mimesis*. In this regard, see Hunter (1996, pp. 110–123).
[59] Gow (1965, pp. 247–248).
[60] For a discussion on this relationship, see Hordern (2004, pp. 26–29).
[61] Giuliano (2005, pp. 21–135).

tion of the Academy, cites an *excerptum* by Dicaearchus (*PHerc*. 1021, col. I Dorandi). According to Dicaearchus, Plato, by means of the εὐρυθμία that infuses the dialogue with grace, was capable of bringing the φιλοσοφία to an apex of perfection, even to its dissolution. So these words, as suggestive as they are partially elusive, may be reconsidered. Indeed they can, because the καταλύειν, the dissolution to which Dicaearchus alludes, coincides perhaps with the beginning of a new poetic style – or renewed, a poetic style to which Plato as a conscious innovator, offered opportunities for development that were decisive, crucial and ineluctable[62].

Works Cited

Andrieu, J 1954, *Le dialogue antique. Structure et présentation*, Les Belles Lettres, Paris.
Arrighetti, G 1987, *Poeti, eruditi e biografi. Momenti della riflessione dei Greci sulla letteratura*, Giardini, Pisa.
Austin C, Olson S D 2004, *Aristophanes. Thesmophoriazusae*, Oxford Clarendon Press, Oxford.
Battegazzore, A M 1969, *Platone. Ione*, Paravia, Torino.
Blondell, R 2002, *The Play of Character in Plato's Dialogues*, CUP, Cambridge 2002.
Burnet, J 1924, *Plato's Euthyphro, Apology of Socrates and Crito*, Oxford Clarendon Press, Oxford.
Burnyeat, M F 1997, 'First Words', *Proceedings of the Cambridge Philological Society* 43, pp. 1–19.
Campese, S. 1998, 'Bendidie e Panatenee', in M Vegetti (ed), *Platone – Repubblica*, Volume I, Bibliopolis, Napoli, pp. 105–116.
Capra, A 2003, 'Poeti, eristi e innamorati: il *Liside* nel suo contesto', in S Martinelli Tempesta & F Trabattoni (eds), *Platone. Liside Volume 2*, LED, Milano, pp. 173–231.
Capuccino, C 2005, *Filosofi e rapsodi. Testo, traduzione e commento dello Ione platonico*, CLUEB, Bologna.
Centrone, B, Petrucci, F 2012, *Platone. Ippia maggione, Ippia minore, Ione, Menesseno*, Einaudi, Torino.
Clay, D 1992, 'Plato's First Words', *Yale Classical Studies* 29, pp. 113–129.
Clay, D 2000, *Platonic Questions. Dialogues with the Silent Philosopher*, The Pennsylvania State University Press, University Park.
Corradi, M 2012, *Protagora tra filologia e filosofia. Le testimonianze di Aristotele*, Serra, Pisa-Roma.
de Jong, I J F 2001, *A Narratological Commentary on the Odyssey*, CUP, New York.
de Strycher E, Slings S R 1994, *Plato's Apology of Socrates. A Literary and Philosophical Study with a Running Commentary*, Brill, Leiden-New York.
Denyer, N 2008, *Protagoras. Plato*, CUP, Cambridge.

---

[62] Gaiser (1988, pp. 326–328).

Dunbar, N 1995, *Aristophanes. Birds*, Oxford Clarendon Press, Oxford.
Erler, M 2007, *Platon, Grurdriss der Geschichte der Philosophie, Die Philosophie der Antike*, Schwabe, Basel.
Murray, P 1996, *Platon on the Poetry: Ion, Republic 376e-389b, Republic 595–608b*, CUP, Cambridge.
Nails, D 2002, *The People of Plato. A Prosopography of Plato and Other Socratics*, Hackett Publishing Company, Indianapolis-Cambridge.
Ferrari, G R F 1987, *Listening to the Cicadas. A Study of Plato's Phaedrus*, CUP, Cambridge.
Flashar, H 1958, *Der Dialog Ion als Zeugnis platonischer Philosophie*, Akademie Verlag, Berlin.
Gaiser, K 1988, *Philodems Academica*, Friedrich Frommann Verlag, Stuttgart.
Garvie, A F 1994, *Odyssey. Books VI-VIII*, CUP, Cambridge.
Gastaldi, S 1998, 'Bendidie e Panatenee', in M Vegetti (ed), *Platone – Repubblica, Volume I*, Bibliopolis, Napoli 1998, pp. 117–131.
Giuliano, F M 2005, *Platone e la poesia. Teoria della composizione e prassi della ricezione*, Academia Verlag, Sankt Augustin.
Gow, A S F 1965, *Theocritus, edited with a Translation and Commentary*, I-II, CUP, Cambridge.
Hadot, P 1987, *Exercices spirituels et philosophie antique*, Albin Michel, Paris.
Halliwell, S 2002, *The Aesthetics of Mimesis. Ancient Texts and Modern Problems*, Princeton University Press, Princeton.
Heitsch, E 1993, *Platon Phaidros. Übersetzung und Kommentar*, Vandenhoeck & Ruprecht, Göttingen.
Heitsch, E 2002, *Platon Apologie des Sokrates. Übersetzung und Kommentar*, Vandenhoeck & Ruprecht, Göttingen.
Hordern, J H 2004, *Sophron's Mimes. Text, Translation and Commentary*, Oxford Clarendon Press, Oxford–New York.
Hunter, R 1996, *Theocritus and the Archeology of Greek Poetry*, CUP, Cambridge.
Kahn, C 1996, *Plato and the Socratic Dialogue. The Philosophical Use of a Literary Form*, CUP, Cambridge
Klooster, J 2011, *Poetry as Window and Mirror: Positioning the Poet in Hellenistic Poetry*, Brill, Leiden-Boston.
Lampert, L 2010, *How Philosophy Became Socratic. A Study of Plato's Protagoras, Charmides and Republic*, University of Chicago Press, Chicago-London.
Liebert, R S 2010, 'Fact and Fiction in Plato's Ion', *American Journal of Philology* 131, pp. 179–218.
Männlein-Robert, I 2013 'Katabasis und Höhle. Philosophische Entwürfe der (Unter-)Welt in Platons Politeia', in N Notomi & L Brisson (eds), *Dialogues on Plato's Politeia (Republic). Selected papers from the IX Symposium Platonicum*, Academia Verlag, Sank Augustin, pp. 243–244.
Martinelli Tempesta, S 2003, *Liside. Platone, edizione critica e commento filologico*, Volume 1, in S Martinelli Tempesta & F Trabattoni (eds), *Liside. Platone*, LED, Milano.
Morgan, K A 2004, 'Plato', in I J F de Jong, R Nünlist, A Bowie (eds), *Narrators, Narratees and Narratives in Ancient Greek Literature*, Brill, Leiden-Boston, pp. 357–376.
Morgan, K A 2012, 'Plato', in I J F de Jong (ed), *Space in Ancient Greek Literature*, Brill, Leiden, pp. 415–437.

Nightingale, A W 1995, *Genres in Dialogue. Plato and the Construct of Philosophy*, CUP, Cambridge.
Olson, S D 2002, *Aristophanes. Acharnians*, Oxford Clarendon Press, Oxford.
Padilla, M 1992, 'Rhapsodic Plato? Ion' s Re-presentation', *Lexis* 9–10, pp. 121–145.
Pasquali, G 1968², 'Arte allusiva', *L' Italia che scrive* 25, 1942, pp. 185–187, now in *Pagine stravaganti di un filologo, II, Stravaganze quarte e supreme*, Le lettere, Firenze, pp. 275–282.
Payne, M 2007, *Theocritus and the Invention of Fiction*, CUP, Cambridge.
Penner T, Rowe C J 2005, *Plato' s Lysis*, CUP, Cambridge
Regali, M 2012, 'Hesiod in the Timaeus: the Demiurge addresses the Gods', in G R Boys-Stones & J H Haubold (eds), *Plato and Hesiod*, Oxford University Press, Oxford, pp. 259–275.
Regali, M 2012, *Il poeta e il demiurgo: teoria e prassi della produzione letteraria nel Timeo e nel Crizia di Platone*, Academia Verlag, Sankt Augustin.
Rijksbaron, A 2007, *Plato. Ion. Or: On the Iliad*, Brill, Leiden-Boston.
Rowe, C J 1986, *Plato. Phaedrus*, Aris & Phillis, Warminster.
Sammons, B 2010, *The Art and the Rhetoric of the Homeric Catalogue*, Oxford University Press, Oxford.
Sansone, D 2009, 'Once again the Opening of Plato's *Gorgias*', *Classical Quarterly* N S 59, pp. 631–633.
Schöpsdau, K 2003, *Platons Nomoi, Buch IV-VII, Übersetzung und Kommentar*, Vandenhoeck & Ruprecht, Göttingen.
Thalmann, W G 1984, *Conventions of Form and Thought in Early Greek Epic Poetry*, John Hopkins University Press, Baltimore-London.
Tsitsiridis, S 1998, *Platons Menexenos. Einleitung, Text und Kommentar*, Teubner, Stuttgart.
Tulli, M 1990, 'Età di Crono e ricerca sulla natura nel *Politico* di Platone', *Studi Classici e Orientali* 60, pp. 97–115
Tulli, M 2000, 'Carmide fra poesia e ricerca', in T M Robinson & L Brisson (eds), *Plato. Euthydemus, Lysis, Charmides. Proceedings of the V Symposium Platonicum. Selected Papiers*, Academia Verlag, Sankt Augustin, pp. 259–264.
Tuozzo, T M 2011, *Plato's Charmides. Positive Elenchus in a "Socratic" Dialogue*, CUP, Cambridge.
Vegetti, M 1998, 'Κατάβασις', in M Vegetti (ed), *Platone – Repubblica*, Volume I, Bibliopolis, Napoli 1998, pp. 93–104.
Verdenius, W J 1943, 'L'Ion de Platon', *Mnemosyne* III S 11, pp. 233–262.
Walker, I 1984, *Plato' s Euthyphro*, Scholars Press, Chico.
Woodruff, P 1982, *Plato. Hippias Major*, Blackwell, Oxford.

Gilmário Guerreiro da Costa
The Philosophical Writing and the Drama of Knowledge in Plato

To Ligia

1.

By virtue of a remarkable irony, attempts to defend Plato against accusations of dogmatism often assert the ambiguous and rich nature of his writing. This issue is precisely the rejected trait in *Phaedrus* (275a) which is now endowed with greater strength and persuasion. In other words, the philosopher meets his other, the artist. To a great extent, this phenomenon is due to the fact that in Plato's dialogue we read the great drama of knowledge and research, a great achievement of the Greek culture. The present essay tries to discuss some explanatory and comprehensive possibilities of this phenomenon in the platonic text. We will focus on three elements closely related to each other: the singularity of his writing, its artistic feature, and the critical and ambiguous gesture with which he establishes his thematic and formal relation with the tragedy.

The writing of the dialogues moves a textual scene in which it deploys, with a peculiar feature, the most different problems of the philosophy. Such a procedure displays the disquieting nature of the thinking in its search of the truth. Regardless of the higher or lower success in this pursuit, the thinking ended indelibly marked. The marks left are the result of a deep pedagogical zeal, under the effigy of the great master, Socrates, as well as of devices built with rare art in the weaving of the dialogues.

The writing reunites in this challenge with its other – the reader, whose behaviour is ambiguous, in a mixture of interpretation and interpellation. He reads the text, but also participates in the textual play, reacting to it and giving a meaning for it. It is in the movement manner and temporality of the writing that it calls for the approach to the eternity of Ideas. The paradox may be apparent – which does not fade the dramatic frame of this project.

2.

Platonic reflection either by its textual configuration, or by the themes which it faces, proves to be especially useful in order to encourage a dialogue between philosophy and literature. To express it in a hermeneutic way, the writer Plato often rearranges the data of this "approximation in the distance", putting in the proscenium certain questions that will be obsessively incorporated all over the history of philosophy.

In the interplay between literature and philosophy one must insure oneself against some methodological pitfalls, especially the presumption of extracting from the literary work some general philosophical truths, as if the literary text would be nothing more than a simple illustration of those ideas. In a rare gesture of lucidity and humbleness, Benedito Nunes admitted that he incurred in similar misconception when he wrote his first book about Clarice Lispector:

> Assim, nesse primeiro estudo, intitulado *O mundo de Clarice Lispector*, apresentei a ficção da romancista de *A paixão segundo G.H.* como uma ilustração do pensamento sartriano. Eis o parco rendimento – ou rendimento nulo? – da Crítica desenvolvida como paráfrase filosófica. (Nunes, 1993, p. 197–8)[1]

Among the more specific literary features which the author states he had forgotten, we can highlight the character's building, the peculiarities of the language, and the relations between history and discourse. By serving up the example of Walter Benjamin, Nunes says that the only way of bringing justice to the demands of truth regarding the relationship between literature and philosophy would be to provide the necessary attention to the truth of the work *as fiction*, as literature.

According to Professor Nunes, the required dialogue between philosophy and literature would make hermeneutics a proper methodological exercise capable of overcoming misunderstanding and arbitrariness. In this context, he strongly questions the legitimacy of an exhaustive scientific analysis of the literary work (Nunes, 1993, p. 198). We will stress a bit later how much the statement of inexhaustibility of the literary texts reaches the Platonic writing as well. It is the requirement to do justice to the Greek philosopher: to protect him from accusations of dogmatism. Such a proposal addresses the guidelines of the proper Platonic text – the dialogue as a mobile effigy of persistence in the pursuit of philosophical truth in its dramatic, uncertain hue.

In a paper full of suggestions and investigative paths, Jeanne Marie Gagnebin focuses on the analysis and interpretation of what she calls "the literary

---

[1] "Thereby, in this first study, entitled *The world of Clarice Lispector*, I introduced the novelist's fiction of *The passion according to G. H.* as an illustration of the Sartrean thought. Here is the meager income – or thought an null income? – of the critic developed as a philosophical paraphrase."

forms of philosophy" (2006). This frame, according to her, has the advantage of resisting a plan which is merely normative: "Tal recorte tem a vantagem de não colocar de antemão uma questão normativa sobre as diferenças, os direitos, os domínios respectivos dos discursos literários e filosóficos" (Gagnebin, 2006, p. 201)[2]. She deems it necessary, as a preparatory test, that one revisit the problem of the interplay between form and content. There is in this item a remarkable Benjaminian substratum: "não só quais "conteúdos filosóficos" estão presentes ali, mas como são transformados em "conteúdos literários"." (Gagnebin, 2006, p. 201)[3]. Often the distinctions between form and content show ineffectiveness and insufficient procedures to take either philosophy or literature into consideration.

The characterization of the craft of the writer and the philosopher disseminates lots of clichés, such as the assertion of laying with the philosopher the responsibility for thinking, and with the writers, for written expression. With regard to philosophy these stereotypes express suspicion with rhetoric. The text in a broad sense is used only as a tool: "Até no próprio meio filosófico, por exemplo, na academia, reina certa desconfiança em relação aos aspectos formais mais apurados de uma palestra oral ou de um texto escrito de filosofia." (Gagnebin, 2006, p. 202)[4].

Nonetheless, a closer examination of this issue reveals the inadequacy of the dichotomous statement that emerges from these commonplaces. According to Gagnebin, in an insightful affirmation, thought is not elaborated without language, "sem o tatear na temporalidade das palavras" (Gagnebin, 2006, p. 202)[5]. Language is poured into metaphors and rhetoric, and philosophical writing makes use of this heterogeneous matter, consciously or not. It follows the emphasis on the interplay among form, exhibition, and knowledge linked to these considerations. They intertwine internally so that the shape resists being merely an adornment.

The study of the form-dialogue in Plato, in this context, is emblematic. It would explain the apparent inconsistencies and deadlocks of the Platonic philosophy. The complex movement of life unveils itself in the dialogues. Doing

---

[2] "Such frame has the advantage of not putting in advance normative questions about differences, rights, the respective domains of the literary and philosophical discourses."
[3] "not just which "philosophical contents" are there, but as well in which way they are turned "literary contents"."
[4] "Even in the very philosophical middle, the academy, prevails suspicion of a more accurate presentation of an oral or a written text of philosophy."
[5] It translates as follows: "without groping in the temporality of words."

an amazing mimesis they extract in their form a moving picture of the human existence reality, of knowledge, or rather, the drama in the pursuit of knowledge:

> Se levarmos a sério a forma *diálogo*, isto é, a renovação constante do contexto e dos interlocutores, o movimento de idas e vindas, de avanços e regressos, as resistências, o cansaço, os saltos, as aporias, os momentos de elevação, os de desânimo etc., então percebermos que aquilo que Platão nos transmite não é nenhum sistema apodítico, nenhuma verdade proposicional, mas, antes de mais nada, uma *experiência:* a do movimento incessante do pensar, através da linguagem racional (*logos*) e para além dela – "para além do conceito através do conceito", dirá também Adorno (Gagnebin, 2006, p. 204).[6]

The mimesis, supposedly expelled during the representation of the content of life, meddles in the webs of the very formal constitution of the dialogues. This is also an experience of thinking, wherein not only Socrates' interlocutor, but also the readers are invited to attend.

3.

In a model essay written about Goethe's Elective Affinities, Walter Benjamin puts forward a dual contribution that interests us. The first binds to the status of the interplay between form and content. Seeming to fail due to an excessive dichotomy, he replaces the terms at issue by the concepts of truth content (*Wahrheitsgehalt*) and material content (*Sachgehalt*). His interest lies in underlining the immiscibility of these elements in the work of art. He draws up a sort of law of literary writing: "plus la teneur de vérité d'une oeuvre est significative, plus son lien au contenu concret est discret et intime" (Benjamin, 2000, p. 274–5). This is the affirmation of the truth of the work as fiction. In an apparent paradoxical gesture, it is by pretending in its configuration that the artistic weaving allows us to discern the intimate reading of reality, of what goes beyond it. On the other hand, such a text confines and grants the gift of its idiosyncratic intelligibility, intrinsically poetic.

The second Benjaminian contribution binds to what he calls *expressionless*. He delineates the problem this way: "C'est lui qui brise en toute belle apparence

---

[6] "If we take seriously the dialogue-form, i.e., the constant renewal of the context and of the interlocutors, the movement of comings and goings, advances and returns, resistances, fatigue, the jumps, the deadlocks, the movements of elevation, of dismay etc., then we realize that what Plato conveys is by no means an apodictic system, no propositional truth, but an *experience:* of the ceaseless movement of thought through rational language (logos) and beyond it – beyond concept through concept, as Adorno would say."

ce qui survit en elle comme héritage du chaos : la fausse totalité, celle qui s'égare – la totalité absolue. N'achève l'oeuvre que ce qui la brise, pour faire d'elle una oeuvre morcelée, un fragment du vrai monde, le débris d'un symbole." (Benjamin, 2000, p. 363) The dialectical finesse crafts this passage. The work results from the chaos that it tries to exorcise in organizing itself as a cosmos. In doing so, it sought to erase the traces of the process, pretending settle any debt that hinted. However, language keeps with itself the memory of this proud deletion of the origin. That is what Benjamin calls *expressionless*. The legitimate offer of the totality is served by the very impossibility of the work. It ends to direct it to the fragments which border the chaos, and thus donate the portion of truth that is due to this entire process. It uncovers a kind of a revelation of the tragic debt of the writing. This is especially true in the Platonic dialogues. It seems to us legitimate to approach this sort of analysis with some considerations on the figure of the instant, *exaiphnes* (156 d–e), as it lies in a passage of the *Parmenides*, by Plato. It comes out during the course of a debate about the relationship between motion and rest:

> For there is no change from rest while resting, nor from motion while moving; but the instant, this strange nature, is something inserted between motion and rest, and it is in no time at all; but into it and from it what is moved changes to being at rest, and what is at rest to being moved. (Plato, 1997, 156d–e)

The instant is characterized as something of a "strange nature" (*physis atopos*), without a place (*a-topos*). Such a peculiarity enables it to function as an intermediary (*metaxy*) between motion and rest. Although the term does not have a conceptual formulation, it suggests an appreciation for the temporality. It gives some clues to transcend critically the deadlocks to which the dialogue had led. Its role in this sense is especially important to ensure a bond between *one* and *many*.

Fernando Rey Puente (2010) claims that the figure of time in Plato would lead to resistance either to Neoplatonic interpretations, or to Nietzschean ones. In the same order they both use such categories of transcendence and eternity in the analysis of the theory of ideas. The observation made by the author becomes more vigorous when he analyses the function played by this temporal figure, the instant, in the broader context of the Platonic philosophy. In referring to the passage of the allegory of the cave, when the prisoner is suddenly (*exaiphnes*) freed from his bonds, Puente states: "Esse "salto epistemológico" é como que o resultado produzido subitamente depois de longa e paciente frequentação e exercitação." (Puente, 2010, p. 53)[7]. In the specific case of the *Parmenides,* the instant is precisely the figure which shows suspicion with regard to a supposed intransigent dualism in the thought of the Greek philosopher: "Platão parece estar, na verdade, muito mais interessado nos *metaxý* do que em uma transcendência radical[8]." (Puente, 2010, p. 57). The instant thus gives rise to a double *productive interruption:* in the context of knowledge, when the subject is allowed to reach a more advanced level of the understanding of the world; and of the ontological bond between the multiplicity of forms and phenomena.

Monique Dixsaut claims the focus of this passage is the quest to explain the change: "*Si donc changer, on ne peut le faire sans changer, quand change-t-on?*" (Dixsaut, 2003, p. 140). In this sense, it would not connect eternity and time, as held in the Neoplatonic interpretation of the *Parmenides*. This remark seems to be correct. And yet, the instant (*exaiphnes*) appears to work as a figure of this relationship. It approaches the eternity on this point: they both suspend time. Nonetheless, they differ in that the eternal returns to itself, in the unity of its recollection, of all things extraneous to becoming, while the instant only prepares a new round of confrontation of the coming-to-be in the multiplicity and immerses in the vicissitudes of time. From the safe return (paradoxically temporary) to the eternal, to the subjection to the will of the tragic game in the world.[9]

In any case, the fundamental a-topic character of the instant should be stressed: it is not in time precisely because it means the interruption of time, allowing for change and becoming: "*Le changemente est cet événement pur qui interrompt le cours et la succession du temps qui s'avance*" (Dixsaut, 2003, p. 140). It could be asked if the very texture of the Platonic dialogue, on the threshold of silence that often surrounds it, could not bear exactly this kind of interruption. Would some of the allure of the Platonic writing not lie in this – not only in the temporality of enrollment in the debates, but also in the silence of its recurrent interruption in the unusual way in which he ends (often *an ending without end*) his works?

---

[7] "This "epistemological leap" comes as a sudden result after long and patient attendance and exercises."

[8] "Plato seems to be actually much more interested in the *metaxý* than in a radical transcendence"

[9] Such are recurring figures in the modern lyric poetry. Take, for example, these verses of Salvattore Quasimodo: "*Ognuno sta solo sul cuor della terra / trafitto da un raggio di sole: / ed è súbito sera*" (QUASIMODO, 1999, p. 18–9). Here it is delineated a kind of interruption which suggests tragic contours, due to a state of things disinterested in human, extraneous to the intelligent sensitivity (*logopoetic*) of poetry and philosophy.

4.

A study of textuality in the Platonic dialogues may benefit from some aspects of the hermeneutical research of Paul Ricoeur. In his essay "The hermeneutical function of distanciation", he aims at articulating two elements frequently regarded as irreconcilable: to respect the living and multiple core of existence, but, at the same time, to avoid the loss of meaning by dispersing and becoming. It thus implies to resist a kind of abstraction that provides us with a cognisable structure of reality, but void of strength, and an innocent immersion of becoming, which, if on the one hand it offers considerable vitality, notwithstanding it imposes considerable obstacles to the intelligibility of these phenomena.

Consistent with this project, the philosopher presents his thesis: he aims at overcoming the traditional opposition between explanation (*explication*) and understanding (*compréhension*). Such a gap between the two procedures stems from the struggle of hermeneutics, especially with Wilhelm Dilthey, to protect human phenomena from the causal uniformity peculiar to the researches in natural science in his time. Through a way of investigation different from this type of scientific procedure, which is based on logical and causal explanation, understanding, as defended by Dilthey, would be more consistent with the specificity of the human sciences. In these sciences, rather than separation, we find the empathy of the subject in front of an other that, far from being objectifiable, also emerges as a subject to whom we interpret, and from whom we are interpreted and questioned as well.

Although representing an important step in safeguarding the peculiarity of human study, such distinction would lead to deadlocks and excesses. In the case of Hans-Georg Gadamer, the tension between the two methodological operations leads to antinomy. The title of his masterpiece, *Truth and method*, according to Ricoeur, should be changed to *Truth or method*.

However, does this separation correspond effectively to the destination of hermeneutics and of the human sciences? Ricoeur denies it firmly. The several extracts analyzed by him highlight various plans of distanciation which could not be attributed to the explanatory conduct of the natural sciences. In some way, men experience in their own spirits' operations the distanciation. Now it is not something imposed from outside through an abstraction resulting from methodology. Precisely because it emerges from the game of empathy and distanciation, the link between understanding and explanation reveals itself not only possible, but necessary as well (Ricoeur, 1982).

It will be with the notion of text that the philosopher introduces some paths to overcome the aforementioned antinomy. The text is "the paradigm of distanciation in communication", it is "communication in and through distance" (Ricoeur, 1982, p. 131). The next step will then explain the criteria of textuality from which he serves in order to present his study: "the realization of language as *discourse*"; "the realization of discourse as *structured work*"; "the relation of *speaking to writing* in discourse and in the works of discourse"; "the work of discourse as the *projection of a world*"; "discourse and the work of discourse as the *mediation of self-understanding*" (Ricoeur, 1982, p. 132). These last three elements concern us most directly here.

The written text is not confined to the intentions of its author. It reaches autonomy, giving to *Verfremdung* a positive accent which it did not manifest in Gadamer's hermeneutics. Furthermore, the work transcends its psychosocial context, opening up to multiple readings. Its movement goes from a decontextualization to a recontextualization effect by the act of reading. The distantiation thus reveals as constitutive of the work, it is both what must be overcome, and what limits the interpretation as well. In a remark which should not be indifferent to Plato's readers, the French philosopher maintains that from these mechanisms come the changes in *the functioning of reference*: "The passage from speaking to writing affects discourse in several other ways. In particular, the functioning of reference is profoundly altered when it is no longer possible to identify the thing spoken about as part of the common situation of the interlocutors." (Ricoeur, 1982, p. 140). More specifically, literature leads the question of reference to another level – destruction of the world to achieve it in its innermost essence. Its critical potentiality lies in this – it opens fissures through which one can still think. In this aesthetic space is evidenced not only a epistemological, but also an ethical and political demand:

> The role of most our literature is, it seems, to destroy the world. That is true of fictional literature – folktales, myths, novels, plays – but also of all literature which could be called poetic, where language seems to glorify itself at the expense of the referential function of ordinary discourse. (Ricoeur, 1982, p. 141)

This investigation indicates important and active tasks for the reader. Self-understanding in front of the work becomes not a rational act of imposition, but of exposure. In an enlightening paradox, we can only find ourselves as readers, if we lose ourselves: "As reader, I find myself only by losing myself. Reading introduces me into the imaginative variations of the *ego*. The metamorphosis of the world in play is also the playful metamorphosis of the *ego*." (Ricoeur, 1982, p. 144). It reveals the insufficient character of appropriation as obliteration of distance: in the world of the work we distance ourselves from ourselves.

The study of Platonic argumentation, as carried out by Franco Trabattoni, seems to strengthen such an investigative thread. There would be in the Greek philosopher a precocious hermeneutic consciousness, especially the bottomlessness of language: "Nisso, manifesta-se, de fato, uma característica estrutural e não eliminável do pensamento e da linguagem, ou seja, sua infinita declinabilidade, sua substancial falta de fundo." (Trabattoni, 2010a, p. 17)[10] This movement would have been silenced by Aristotle, being responsible for concealing a fecund way of research about the dialogues, as the author argues in a provocative moment (2010a). In this endless stream of possibilities in language, the Platonic dialogues weave strategically the circular and endless motion of thinking. It stands out a picture of a philosopher against dogmatism, turning unjustified one after another criticism brought against him by sections of the so-called postmodern thought. It is a bold thesis, one cannot deny it.

From this reasoning follows the necessary care with the Platonic writing, stressing its hermeneutical substrates, weaved in a precarious way, as it is common to the very act of writing. Rhetoric, far from being the opposite of logos, may be the medium in which the drama of knowledge spreads. The dialogues would be a way of representing the non-exhaustiveness of the world in which man lives, what the author calls "vicariousness". This is precisely, according to him, the meaning of the theory of ideas. The Platonic reminiscence configures the assertion of the endless wandering of thought:

> Essa situação é expressa por Platão por meio da metáfora (mesmo que, talvez, não se trate só de uma metáfora) da doutrina da reminiscência, segundo a qual conhecer é recordar: um recordar que, evidentemente, se desenvolve por rastros, lampejos e resíduos, logo não pode mais reunir o estado de exaustividade a que uma definição gostaria de aspirar. (Trabattoni, 2010a, p. 14–5)[11].

Within this stream of questions and inquiries, philosophy outlines its most fertile ways of improvement and progress. Nonetheless, one does not do justice to Plato if, when resisting the accusations of dogmatism, we turn his thought into a pure skeptical play or into relativist complacency. For this is exactly what the dialogues do not do. Aware of these risks, Trabattoni claims to be peculiar to Platonism the commitment to the interplay between unity and multiplicity: "a unidade

---

10 "It manifests itself, in fact, a structural and non eliminable feature of thought and language, i.e., its endless deviation, its substantial bottomless."
11 "This situation is expressed by Plato through the metaphor (though perhaps this is not just a metaphor) of doctrine of reminiscence, according to which knowledge is remembering: a remembering that of course develops through traces, glimpses, wastes, therefore it can no longer gather the state of completeness to which a definition would aspire."

do múltiplo" (2010a, p. 22).[12] The Socratic question, in this sense, does not intend to reach the absolute truth, but rather to stage the universal: "põe em evidência o terreno do universal em que move o logos" (2010a, p. 23).[13] The deconstrutive maelstrom in its obsession with difference would be intelligible only if articulated to Platonism, this alleged *other* against which it launched so many criticisms. Nevertheless, the defense of such articulation between unity and multiplicity does not mean that its possession is something peaceful, easy. Otherwise, it becomes evident exactly the precariousness of the search.

The Platonic argumentation, its textual craft, resists at one stroke dogmatism and skepticism[14]. These are the essential conditions for building a dialogue, or at least the expectation of its possibility. The élan of this *approach in the distance*, made possible (or at least desired) through dialogue, relies on expectation of a genuine encounter, under the sign, although still imprecise, of the truth. If someone has the truth, suspends time, and dictates the way to follow; but if this approach is impossible, conversation becomes a vain game. Such are the demands of dialogue, in particular, and of philosophy, in general. It is ascribe to Plato the boldest convergence between the two instances.

5.

Showing that when preparing a hypothesis, rigor can pay tribute to the beauty, Jeanne Marie Gagnebin argues that, as Homer in the exercise of offering eternal glory to his heroes, Plato also would weave similar frames in his dialogues: a monument to the glory of Socrates. It is a reminiscence that is stated in the precariousness of the poetic word:

---

12 "the unity of multiple".
13 "It points out the universal's ground in which logos moves".
14 In an important research on the subject of politics in the Platonic philosophy, Mario Vegetti emphasized an element of interest to this discussion: the defence of the polysemy of the Platonic text: "Esforços hermenêuticos orientados podem, diria, devem ser levados a cabo, porque um excesso de tolerância acarreta um pressuposto de irrelevância teórica da interpretação, mas é igualmente verdade que estes esforços devem, por outro lado, aceitar uma margem irredutível de polissemia do seu objeto: o pensar filosófico de Platão – pela mesma forma textual em que é representado – não pode ser reduzido a um sistema unívoco de significados." (VEGETTI, 2010, p. 272-3) ["Oriented hermeneutical efforts oriented can, I would say, should be carried out, because an excess of tolerance implies a presumption of theoretical irrelevance of interpretation, however it is equally true that these efforts must, on the other hand, accept an irreducible margin of polysemy of its object: Plato's philosophical thinking – due to the textual form in which it is represented – cannot be reduced to a system of univocal meanings."]

o impulso para filosofia em Platão – em particular para *escrever* diálogos filosóficos, apesar de suas numerosas críticas à escrita –, provém não só de uma "busca da verdade", meio abstrata, mas também da necessidade, ligada a essa busca, de defender a memória, a honra, a glória, o *kléos* do herói/mestre morto, Sócrates. (Gagnebin, 2006b, p. 196)[15]

This hypothesis aims at strengthening itself through analysis of some dialogues, especially the *Apology*. When Socrates reflects on his choice of a life dedicated to the truth, even under the most different risks, he is inserted in the affirmative framework of his peculiar heroism: "Nesse contexto, podemos também dizer que Platão assume, em relação ao mestre morto, a mesma função que cabia ao poeta em relação aos heróis mortos: lembrar suas façanhas e suas palavras para que a posteridade não se esqueça dos seus nomes e de sua glória." (Gagnebin, 2006b, p. 196)[16] Such a project will require the Greek philosopher to care for the texture of the dialogues, which is characterized by the effort to provide that "exemplary image" of Socrates. Fiction in this sense would not be the reverse of truth, but its pursuit by other means: "Todos os estudiosos de Platão que analisam, por exemplo, as encenações iniciais dos diálogos, sabem dessas construções complexas (para não dizer... sofisticadas!)." (Gagnebin, 2006b, p. 198)[17]

It is necessary to understand, in this scenario, the reasons for the author's absence as subject of the utterance of the dialogues. According to Gagnebin, this is justified by the pursuit of guaranteeing objectivity (Gagnebin, 2006b, p. 198–9). The answer is, in general, correct. However, it is insufficient. Moreover, it seems to us that Plato absents himself so that the drama (the scene) may emerge, thereby ensuring strength to the scene's exhibition – of which also result the writing's precariousness and temporality.

But is he absent at all? Is this his intent? He operates the drama chosen by him. Fiction strengthens truth. At the same time, through the combination of stability and precariousness of the writing, he stages the living and risky character of this search. The heroic act celebrated in the Homeric poems has its perfect counterpart in the dialogue's weaving, taking Socrates' life as its object. Still concerning the "exemplary death" of Socrates, as it was built in the dialogues, some

---

15 "The drive to philosophy in Plato – in particular to write philosophical dialogues, despite his numerous criticisms of writing – stems not only from a "search for truth", kind of abstract, but also from the necessity, connected to that search, to defend the memory, the honour, the glory, the *kléos* of the dead hero/master, Socrates".
16 "In this context we can also say that Plato assumes, regarding the dead master, the same function that was incumbent on the poets to do with regard to dead heroes: remembering their exploits and words so that the posterity does not forget their names and their glory".
17 "Every Plato' scholar who examines, for instance, the dialogues' initial staging, know these complex constructs (not to say... sophisticated!)".

additional considerations. It seems that the assembly of *Apology*, *Crito* and *Phaedo* provide evidence of a bold Platonic procedure of writing: he works on metaphors of death, and death as a metaphor, a gesture constitutive of human culture, to which Plato's writing gave an unforgettable shape.

6.

Aristide Valentin is a character of detective stories created by G. K. Chesterton. In a melancholic moment, when he compares his work with that of criminals, he remarks to himself: "*The criminal is the creative artist; the detective only the critic*" (Chesterton, p. 15) The critic and the reader in search of traces and clues left by the text – the criminal as an image of transgression, and the detective as an hermeneutist of transgression, and at the same time who restores the order, which is expressed in the temporality of reading. To let us utilize the beautiful title of a Martha Nussbaum's book, it is a kind of "fragility of reading".

Hans Robert Jauss wrote in 1977 a text in a similar direction on the aesthetic pleasure, entitled "The aesthetic pleasure and basic experiences of poiesis, aesthesis and catharsis" (Jauss, 2011). Initially, he does a retrospection of the main theorists who addressed the issue. He makes them dialogue with each other and then presents his own perspective, a part on which we will focus on here.

Human action in aesthetic activity moves under three functions: *poiesis*, *aesthesis*, and *katharsis*. The first binds to "obra que nós mesmos realizamos" (Jauss, 2011, p. 100)[18] In turn, the *aisthesis* configures the pleasant reception, the renewed and intensified vision. Regarding the *catharsis*, it refers to the liberating transformation of the everyday automatism:

> Designa-se por *katharsis*, unindo-se a determinação de Górgias com a de Aristóteles, aquele prazer dos afetos provocados pelo discurso ou pela poesia, capaz de conduzir o ouvinte e o espectador tanto à transformação de suas convicções quanto à liberação de sua psique." (Jauss, 2011, p. 101)[19]

These three functions find themselves in a dynamic exchange, overlapping and connecting to each other. The author gives us good example, which also points to intertextual elements, by stressing the moment when the *aisthesis* would turn

---

[18] "the work that we ourselves performed"
[19] "By joining the determination of Gorgias with Aristotle, catharsis is designated as that pleasure of affections caused by speech or poetry, capable of conducing both the listener and the spectator either to transform their believes or to release their psyche".

into *poiesis*, as the reader, realizing the presumed incompleteness of the *asthetic object*, may "sair de sua atitude contemplativa e converter-se em co-criador da obra, à medida que conclui a concretização de sua forma e de seu significado." (Jauss, 2011, p. 103)[20] The text concludes with a luminous quotation by Goethe:

> Há três classes de leitores: o primeiro, o que goza sem julgamento, o terceiro, o que julga sem gozar, o intermédio, que julga gozando e goza julgando, é o que propriamente recria a obra de arte. (Jauss, 2011, p. 103)[21]

The act of reading thus reveals remarkable complexity. Far from being a mere texts' decoding, it assumes the risks of creative participation in the aesthetic process. And it is in the experience of aesthetic pleasure that the dichotomy of enjoyment and judgment has more consistent opportunities to be overcome. Reading loses innocence, but it now claims the right to create. It is not satisfied with being the inferior double of the texts' world, rather it intends to question them and recreate them under the sign of the highest demands of their time.

And the requirements made by the Platonic writing are high. Its dramatic character, akin to theatre, demands of readers an active procedure, similar, as Nussbaum points out, to the spectator's movements in the tragedy: "Like the spectator of a tragedy, the dialogue reader is asked by the interaction to work through everything actively and to see where he really stands, who is really praiseworthy and why." (Nussbaum, 2001, p. 126–7) The *dialogue-form*, as the author explains, encourages critical judgment. It represents not only the interlocutors' scene, but also the virtual scene of the readers' intervention. As we see it, the silence of reading is similar to "a silent inner conversation of the soul with itself" (Plato, 1921, 263e).

According to Nussbaum, however, comparison to tragedy should not overlook the many differences between the two genres, especially by their effect, since the Platonic writing moves to respond the intellect's appeal. Even myths bind to a philosophical account, leading to a progressive abstraction: "He is using it not to entertain in its own right, but to show forth general philosophical truths for which he has already argued" (Nussbaum, 2001, p. 131). But some considerations about the place of imagination in these myths seem to lack in this study, particularly in its metaphorical content. Ricoeur thus conceives the act

---

[20] "get out of his contemplative attitude and become a co-creator, as he completes the achievement of its form and its meaning".
[21] "There are three classes of readers: the first, who enjoys without judgment; the third, who judges without enjoying; and the second, who judges enjoying and enjoys judging, is that which exactly recreates the work of art".

of imagining: "Imagining is to be absent in entire things" (Ricoeur, 1992, p. 155). The French philosopher's approach is phenomenological. His impulse, nevertheless, matches the aspirations of the Platonic philosophy, the writing of it, in its materiality, leads to the purification of dealing with everyday objects so as to achieve them, paradoxically, in its absence, in the deepest level of understanding. Imagining and thinking imply each other, and shines through the seductive scene of the Platonic language.

In this context, some passages of the *Symposium* can be enlightening. The dialogue opens with the representation of the reminiscence plan which unfolds throughout the book. In these multiple narratives, one inside the other, such as the satyrs' statues mentioned by Socrates, we find a fictionist's art. Aristodemus had told the story he had witnessed to Apollodorus, and from this to his listeners in the dialogue: "Si donc il me faut, à vous aussi, faire ce récit, allons-y" (Platon, 2011a, 173c), not only to the partner, but also to the readers. In the traces of reminiscence, the strength and fragility of the Platonic knowledge's drama is insinuated. Apollodorus, in the very beginning, confesses: "Il faut dire qu'Aristodème n'avait pas un souvenir exact de ce que chacun avait dit, et moi non plus je me souviens pas de tout de qu'il a raconté" (Platon, 2011a, 177e). It is worth mentioning, in this way, the memory's productive character – and of the reading. In a passage filled with irony, Guimarães Rosa wrote: "The book may be worthy due the things that could not be in there" (Rosa, 1994, p. 526). In the interstices of the *Symposium*, on the level of remembrance, a bet of seduction lies: that the readers may accept the invitation to enjoyment and thinking. To judge by the Rosa's note, the value of this work relies on similar intervention.

We referred above to figures of Plato's interruption. The comic upheavals in *Symposium* are quite suggestive in this regard. Primarily, Socrates' delay, immersed in his thoughts (174d–175c). A little further on, before Aristophanes could deliver his speech, he had begun to hiccup (185d–e). Both scenes make someone crack a smile, albeit a discreet one, akin to the enjoyment of the spirit's identity with itself, even from the contradictions of an event. Gesture opposed to reverence, thus preparatory to philosophy. There are also two other interruptions, at Alcibiades' arrival (212c–d), and the entry of the revelers (223b). These events break certain expectations of order, thereby the text moving theatrically. Here a closed argument is not enough – it is also necessary to please, to arouse pleasure.

The construction of the sophist's image in the *Sophist* is similar to such a gesture, moved by great art of drafting and mordacity, through definitions with which dialectics pays tribute to irony and humour. Let us take some examples. At first, the sophist is presented with a hunter's properties, distinguished by his prey, namely, young rich: "But the other turns towards the land and to rivers of a different kind – rivers of wealth and youth, bounteous meadows, as it were – and he intends to coerce the creatures in them" (Plato, 1921, 222a). The second characterization binds to the merchant's art: the sophist imports knowledge (*mathematopolike*) and virtue (224c). He does not deal with knowledge, but with its appearance, because he is only interested in profit and ostentation: "Then it is a sort of knowledge based upon mere opinion that the sophist has been shown to possess about things, not true knowledge" (Plato, 1921, 233c), points out the Stranger in dialogue with Theaetetus. The sophist thus offers *doxa*, not *episteme*.

Another piece in this representation, recurrent in the Platonic work, and articulated here in double voice, combines sophistic procedures and imitation. His words, filled with deception, simulate a reality which effectively constitutes only a distorted doubling (234d). If someone advocated the dualism, that would be, in practice, the sophist, not Plato. It is the sophist who produces through simulacra (*phantasma*) the world's deceitful double. For this reason, "he must be classed as juggler and imitator" (Plato, 1921, 235a).

Notwithstanding, one might as well submit the Platonic questioning the similar suspicion that the sophist image's construction is made by means of an art equally mimetic. By refuting the legitimacy of the philosophical and pedagogical work of these men due to the fact that it is established through imitation, Plato does it with resources which turn out to be mimetic as well. One might object that this exercise does not produce simulacra, but the actual image of these thinkers. If so, there would be a legitimate mimetic art – that emerges not exactly from the content of the debates, but from the very form of dialogue. Yet the tension (dramatic?) seems to establish.

7.

There are not many philosophers, like Plato, who give such great importance to the effect of an artistic work on the public. Highlighting the risks to which we are exposed in the proximity to art, he takes very seriously the expressive strength of poetry, especially the tragic one. It is a remarkable and ambiguity care that seeks to warn us about the dangers of something, but in the end awakes interest precisely for this kind of experience. Furthermore, it allows us to glimpse fissures in the anthropological project based on the control of the so called soul's upper part – *upper* not rarely subjected to the inferior part's vagaries.

Something similar is noted in this passage of the *Cratylus,* which surprises us in admitting the irresistible force of desire: "Socrate – Je vais te dire mon impression. Dis-moi, quel est le lien le plus fort qui oblige un être vivant à demerer quelque part: est-ce la contrainte ou le désir? *Hermogène* – C'est de beaucoup le désir." (Platon, 2011b, 403c). This concern is recurrent in several passages of the *Republic*, especially in Books III and X. In the former there is a warning against fables since some of them might undermine courage – and the virtues' development in general: "Then it seems we must exercise supervision also, in the matter of such tales as these, over those who undertake to supply them and request them not to dispraise in this indiscriminating fashion the life in Hades but rather praise it, since what they now tell us is neither true or edifying to men who are destined to be warriors" (Plato, 1937a, 386b–c). Furthermore, the Greek philosopher has a suspicion regarding the enchantment's effect of the poetic language: "the more poetic they are [some passages from Homer] the less are they suited to the ears of boys and men who are destined to be free" (Plato, 1937a, 387b). Lamentations over the dead should be avoided as they may bring out excessive fear of death.

It is recurrent in the text the intent to investigate the means to strengthen temperance (*sophrosyne*) and self-control, often neglected, according to Plato, by the Homeric poems. However, these criticisms are often accompanied by hesitations regarding the excellence of the Greek poet: "But, for Homer's sake (...) I hesitate" (Plato, 1937a, 391a). He dedicates to a critical revision of the concept of god and hero consistent with his metaphysical and pedagogical presuppositions, especially regarding their attributes: "For we proved, I take it, that for evil to arise from gods is an impossibility" (Plato, 1937a, 391e).

It is important maintain caution in respect to violent laughter, motivated by ethical considerations: "they must not be prone to laughter. For ordinarily when one abandons himself to violent laughter his condition provokes a violent reaction" (Plato, 1937a, 388e). The difficulty of this section can be measured if we compare it with the use of irony and humour in several passages of the Platonic work. Take, for instance, the moment in the *Sophist* when Socrates handles the delimitation of the sophist's work (Plato, 1921, 222a–231e). The scene is quite well constructed, and unfolds, by ridicule and laughter, the sophist's halting step. This does not come to be a contradiction, but reveals the care of the philosopher in the treatment of some topics, respecting its complexity. In any case, the asymmetry between the philosophical content plan, and the artistic-formal production of the dialogues is suggestive enough to raise doubts and suspicion about this question.

Then we come to the study of imitation (*mimesis*), whereby is made an initial distinction between literary genres. The peculiarity of epic, tragedy, and comedy is investigated. The first interplays narrative and dramatic forms, the other two only a dramatic form, which is, according to Plato, the imitative weaving *par excellence* (Plato, 1937a, 395a). Imitation, in contrast to narrative, is defined as someone pretending to be someone else: "But when he [the poet] delivers a speech as if he were someone else, shall we not say that he then assimilates thereby his own diction as far as possible to that of the person whom he announces as about to speak?" (Plato, 1937a, 393c). In Book III, it is accepted the narrative poetry. This approach changes in Book X, on the occasion of the famous invective against poets. It now deals with the foundation of the ideal city and the status of poetry in relation to politics and education. In inquiring critically this object, not only an alleged animosity emerges. It raises also the suspicion that the philosopher, through his painstaking work, ends by granting to poetry precisely its importance. It is refused in this way the mimetic poetry: "In refusing to admit at all so much of it as is imitative; for that it is certainly not to be received is, I think, still more plainly apparent now that we have distinguished the several parts of the soul" (Plato, 1937b, 595a).

The first criticism is addressed to the fact that the mimetic works divert us from the knowledge of truth: "that kind of art seems to be a corruption of the mind of all listeners who do not possess as an antidote an knowledge of its real nature" (Plato, 1937b, 595b). Furthermore, it deviates us three degrees from truth. The poets imitate craftsmen who, in turn, imitate the natural craftsman, God. It is, therefore, an imitation of appearance, not reality, as the example of the three beds shows. In this context, Plato presents the hypothesis that tragedy would owe a lot to Homer. It is an insightful hypothesis that could come only from one who knew the tragedy intimately. That it is articulated by its outspoken critic is a remarkable piece of irony: "tragedy and its leader Homer" (Plato, 1937b, 598d). A little further, he sees Homer as "the most poetic of poets and the first of tragedians" (Plato, 1937b, 607a). Not only in this passage, but throughout Book X the Greek philosopher, in the ruthless evaluation of poetry in general, and tragedy in particular, shows such a great knowledge of the intricacies of this art that he often risks convincing us precisely of the opposite of what he intends, i.e., of the immeasurable importance of poetry, and the inexhaustibility of its signs.

Also problematic is the fact that the poets do not know what excellence (*arete*) is: "Shall we, then, lay it down that all the poetic tribe, beginning with Homer, are imitators of images of excellence and of the other things that they 'create', and do not hold on truth?" (Plato, 1937b, 600e). Not knowing what it is, they are not able to act in accordance with its demands; even when sometimes they seem to do it, this action reveals to be not consistent whatsoever.

Often, the more Plato denies poetry, the closer he is to its essence, and to the affirmation of its relevance. It is what is observed when he associates it with a game, and claims that it leads to the rapture, to go astray: "the imitator knows nothing worth mentioning of the things he imitates, but that imitation is a form of play, not to be taken seriously" (Plato, 1937b, 602b). An observation which does not lack sharpness. Nevertheless, it is not enough to establish reasons for the abandonment of this activity. Rather, poetry moves in its game on a route similar to that of philosophy: it resists to utilitarian demands, relying solely on its free faculty of expression. Contrary to what he had intended, the Greek philosopher opened a rich route of research whose tailpiece is a consistent defense of artistic creativity in the most different kinds of authors, among which we may mention Johann Huizinga and Hans-Georg Gadamer. Art is a game. Would not be philosophy a game as well?

The critique of the rapture sent by poetry belongs to a section devoted to the praise of calm, for its accordance to law and identity: "the intelligent and temperate disposition, always remaining approximately the same" (Plato, 1937b, 604e). It is a beautiful and difficult quality to imitate. The poet's action is quite different. He pretends to suffer what he is not suffering at all: "For the representation imitates a type that is alien to them" (Plato, 1937b, 604e). By resisting to the calm, it produces a radical difference in the subject towards himself. Contradictory feelings divert him from the reason's axis.

This entire critique of the mimetic character of poetry achieves his logical outcome in the poet's expulsion from the Platonic ideal city (Plato, 1937b, 607a). It is now appropriate, given some philosophical precepts, that men deal with issues and tonalities capable of fostering temperance and respecting gods. Now it focus on values that are conducive to the care of the soul's immortality (Plato, 1937b, 608e). In this time and space is introduced the myth of Er. A real nice outcome: following the poet's expulsion, the Greek philosopher weaves with rare gift a prose characterized exactly by form and poetical imagination.

These Platonic hesitations were well examined by a contemporary scholar (Rutherford, 1995). They are of two kinds. 1. The assertions present in the *Republic* are not made without the necessary reconsideration of their consistency. The fear of excessive confidence, the *hybris* regarding knowledge, is accompanied by a temperate meditation, in a combination of Socratic wisdom and diligence. In Book VII, in discussions about the good in itself, we read: "Have a care, however, lest I deceive you unintentionally with a false reckoning of the interest" (Plato, 1937b, 507a). Questions are expressed a little further with regard the image in words offered by Socrates to Glaucon in Book VII (533a). Rutherford notes: "We may suppose that Plato is concerned to preserve, even in the vast exposition of the Republic, the original modesty and admissions of ignorance which were surely typical of Socrates; yet the preoccupation with the limits and imperfections of his methods and words seems to go deeper still." Soon after he concludes: ""It seems that the exposition in the *Republic* is partial and tentative; the gap between what Socrates has achieved and what the poets can do is not so vast as we at first anticipated." (Rutherford, 1995, p. 235). 2. On the other hand, poetry which is not submissive to magic is frequently encountered in philosophy, in which the seduction of literary writing is insinuated through dialogues: "Plato is the greatest critic of Homer and tragedy; but he also learns from them and seeks to rival them. To put it in another way, Plato uses the arts of literature in the service of philosophy" (Rutherford, 1995, p. 237). Despite the questionable character of this instrumental function of literary art, the remark has the merit of pointing margins of hesitation present in the Platonic reasoning. Even the art of dialectics, with its sophisticated rationality, demands the creative action of its actors (Dixsaut, 2003, p. 168).

One can forward a concern about these writing's fluctuations and deviations. The exalted defense of philosophy leaves the impression of an essential gap: a deficit in the symbolic work with the world due to the abandonment of poetry. This is a theme of a huge education concern, whose examination should not be absent in philosophical thinking concerning the essence of an ideal city. An important part of this Platonic reasoning is moved in an intense poetic weaving text, which demonstrates the complexity of this issue, by means of an effort to express the pursuit of knowledge in dramatic configuration.

If these hesitations did not turn Plato into a tragic author, they at least offer nuances to the alleged superiority of the philosophical discourse with respect to tragedy. One cannot assure knowledge without the mishaps that occur in the human ways full of dilemmas and instability. If the failure of the pursuit in search of the Ideal is staged, that would lead to the Ideal's abandonment – it only displays the scar of the search. Like his master, the Plato writer frequently also only knows that he does not know.

Works Cited

Bailly, Anatole. Le grand Bailly – dictionnaire grec-français. Hachette: Paris, 2000.

Benjamin, Walter. "Les affinités electives de Goethe". Trad. Maurice de Gandillac In Oeuvres I. Trad. Maurice de Gandillac, Rainer Rochlitz et Pierre Rusch. Paris: Gallimard, 2000.

Chesterton, G. K. "The blue cross". In Father Brown: selected stories. London: Collector's Library, 2003.

Dixsaut, Monique. Platon: le désir de comprendre. Paris : Librairie Philosophique J. Vrin, 2003.

Gagnebin, Jeanne Marie. "As formas literárias da filosofia". In Lembrar escrever esquecer. São Paulo: Ed. 34, 2006a.

—— "Platão, creio, estava doente". In Lembrar escrever esquecer. São Paulo: Ed. 34, 2006b.

Jauss, Hans Robert. "O prazer estético e as experiências fundamentais da poiesis, aisthesis e katharsis". In LIMA, Luiz Costa. Org. e trad. *A literatura e o leitor: textos de estética da recepção*. 2ª. edição revista e ampliada. Rio de Janeiro: Paz e Terra, 2011.

Nunes, Benedito. No tempo do niilismo. São Paulo: Ática, 1993.

Nussbaum, Martha. The fragility of goodness: luck and ethics in Greek tragedy and philosophy. Revised edition. Cambridge: Cambridge University Press, 2001.

Plato. *Parmenides*. Trad. R. E. Allen. Revised Edition. New Haven: Yale University Press, 1997.

—— *The Republic:* Books I-V. Trad. Paul Shorey. Cambridge: Harvard University Press; London: William Heinemann LTD, 1937a. (Loeb Classical Library)

—— *The Republic:* Books VI-X. Trad. Paul Shorey. Cambridge: Harvard University Press; London: William Heinemann LTD, 1937b. (Loeb Classical Library)

—— *Theatetus, Sophist*. Trad. Harold N. Fowler. London: William Heinemann LTD; Cambridge: Harvard University Press, 1921. (Loeb Classical Library)

Platon. "Banquet". Trad. Luc Brisson. In Oeuvres completes. Org. Luc Brisson. Trad. Luc Brisson et. al. Paris: Flammarion, 2011a.

—— "Cratyle". Trad. Catherine Dalimier. In Oeuvres completes. Org. Luc Brisson. Trad. Luc Brisson et. al. Paris: Flammarion, 2011b.

Puente, Fernando Rey. "O súbito (exaíphnes) em Platão". in Ensaios sobre o tempo na filosofia antiga. São Paulo: Annablume, 2010.

Ricoeur, Paul. "The hermeneutical function of distanciation". In Hermeneutics and the human sciences. Org. e trad. John B. Thompson. Cambridge: Cambridge University Press, 1982.

—— "O processo metafórico como cognição, imaginação e sentimento". In SACKS, Sheldon. Trad. Leila Cristina M. Darin et. al. São Paulo: EDUC/Pontes, 1992.

Rosa, Guimarães. Ficção completa. Rio de Janeiro: Nova Aguilar, 1994. Vol. 2.

Rutherford, R. B. The art of Plato – ten essays in Platonic interpretation. Cambridge, Massachusetts: Harvard University Press, 1995.

Trabattoni, Franco. "A argumentação platônica". ARCHAI: Revista de Estudos sobre as Origens do Pensamento Ocidental. Brasília, n. 4, p. 11–27, jan. 2010a.

—— Platão. Trad. Rineu Quinalia. São Paulo: Annablume, 2010b. (Coleção Archai: as origens do pensamento ocidental, 2)

Vegetti, Mario. Um paradigma no céu: Platão político, de Aristóteles ao século XX. Trad. Maria da Graça Gomes de Pina. São Paulo: Annablume, 2010. (Coleção Archai: as origens do pensamento ocidental, 4)

Marcus Mota
Comic Dramaturgy in Plato: Observations from the Ion

One of the evident but difficult-to-characterize aspects of Platonic writing is its relationship to comic tradition. This relationship is expressed in the use of comic procedures; a Platonic text is organized based on the appropriation and transformation of these procedures. The text alludes to production contexts and practices which, although recorded in writing, become comprehensible, effective, and best understood in performance.

The difficulty in identifying such procedures in Platonic writing lies initially in the interpreter's familiarity with the comic tradition that determines them. Since comedy is materialized in performative, intersubjective situations, such as in contact and face-to-face exchanges, a hermeneutic model that takes into consideration the specificities of its productive context is needed to correlate textuality to performative acts.

Again, this is not about pointing out comic portions or moments of humor in the Platonic text[1]. To understand comedy in action, an important methodological step is to not restrict oneself to the effects, namely, to mere laughter.[2] The breadth of the production process in comedy demands integration strategies, or overtaking of isolated instances. The decentralization regarding laughter allows the perception of complexity in the production of comedy because the acts produced become distinguishable; correlated, diverse acts of composition, performance, and reception spring from them. The focus on the response and the reception in laughter postulates reduction of the breadth of the interpretation to perceive how comedy operates.

In the *Ion*, a type of integral dramaturgy, which is explained in the correlation between composition, performance, and reception, is found not only in the organization of the text but is also discussed in the characters' speeches. Consequently, the dialogue presents an exceptional wealth of data and questions for the understanding of the appropriation and transformation of the comic tradition developed by Plato, as well as for the discussion of this comic tradition. In other words, the *Ion* is a document that witnesses an experiment of expression

---

1 As seen in Jones s/d.
2 Another strategy is to approximate Platonic works from other genres, such as old comedy, but without questioning what genre, as a concept, is understood to be, as in Charalabopoulos 2012, Puchner 2010, and Nightingale 2000.

dealing with comic tradition; for this exact reason, it enters comic tradition as a modality, or a type of comic production. Moreover, the *Ion* belongs to the histories of philosophy and comedy.

Therefore, the philosophical dialogue the *Ion* and even philosophical dialogue in general are better understood as types of writing that use existing performative traditions. The dialogue itself does not exist to record people's verbal exchanges. The dialogue's dialogic quality lies in its interactions with situations mediated other than through words. Since comedy is manifested in its breadth by productive context and by its generalized corporeality, the approximation between comedy and the philosophical dialogic quality enables a better understanding of the ways performative traditions are reprocessed.

Consequently, the comedy of the Platonic dialogue is not a theme itself: as understood in its production context, the comedy substantiates the way the game of the text is perceived within performative traditions. Comedy indicates the materiality of the performance in the text or the performative contextualization of the dialogue. Thus, it is possible not only to discuss comedy but to exploit it.

Ion is organized in the asymmetrical interaction between two personative agents, Ion and Socrates.[3] The minimalism of the dialogue, which is restricted to only two speakers, links the text to the procedures of doubles, or comic pairs, as present in the most diverse performative traditions. Aristophanes, a contemporary of Plato, initiates many of his comedies using dialogues between pairs, showing the formalization and popularity of the procedure.[4]

In the *Ion*, however, the comic pair is not limited to merely a few scenes: the action between Ion and Socrates takes place through continuous dialogue. In this section, the procedure is expanded and redefined within the scope of the dialogue. The act between Ion and Socrates supports the length of the dialogue. The comic pair is simultaneously the only source and the conduit of the scenes.

Because comedy is a procedure with high productivity, the comic pair, at the time it is introduced by the writer, draws together an unfolding set of expectations: the pair simultaneously updates what is expected of a comic pair in general and what it as a specific pair presents in the present moment. Thus, the banter between the comic pair is conducted in tension between completeness and incompleteness, as the role and characterization of each of the two participants depends on the role of the other. In other words, a comic pair only exists in the offering of figures that depend on one another: each one is incomplete if isolated

---

[3] For a discussion of terms, see Mota 2006 and Mota 2008.
[4] As in the beginning of *The Frogs*, *The Wasps*, *The Birds*, *Peace*, and *Thesmophoriazusae*.

and viable only in the presence of its counterpart. The pair plays a game of need and attachment. The oppositions are not abstract and not reduced to a list of ideas: the comic pair uses differences and confrontations to manifest the integration of its component parts.

In the *Ion*, Plato uses the recourse of the comic pair to add other nuances. The common asymmetry between the members of the pair is much more stressed than in other types of characterizations and is simultaneously hidden: the famous performer Ion cannot show his abilities during the time that Socrates dominates the dialogue verbally. However, Socrates is concerned with making Ion show his cognitive deficit instead of his knowledge of his art form. Such asymmetry destabilizes the expectations surrounding the overall type of the comic pair; these expectations, even based on the disparity of the attributes of the characters, manifest a solidarity horizon and an attachment between the participants.

More specifically, according to the data by John Bremer, the following statistics apply to the *Ion*:
1) Number of speeches in the text: 171
2) Number of speeches delivered by Socrates: 86
3) Number of speeches delivered by Ion: 85
4) Number of words in the dialogue: 3,859
5) Number of words spoken by Socrates: 3,155
6) Number of words spoken by Ion: 704
7) Number of syllables in the text: 7,776
8) Number of syllables spoken by Socrates: 6,377
9) Number of syllables spoken by Ion: 1,399

Based on the linguistic materiality of the text, we see, at first, that the balance between the participations seems to be equal. This is convenient for a comic pair, giving them having equal opportunities to introduce themselves and to show their material: Socrates and Ion split almost evenly the total number of speeches in the text.

By forwarding and detailing these numbers, we begin to quantify this participation and to match the traditional performative model of the pairs with its recreation by Plato. In its linguistic materiality, the figure of Socrates in his speeches manifests an arithmetic disproportion: of the total number of words uttered in the dialogue, Socrates is responsible for 82% of them. Thus, Socrates speaks more words and longer sentences, constituting a hegemonic dominance over the text, an orientation center of the dialogue.

These linguistic data point to some conclusions in the way Plato uses the comic-pair characterization archetype. First, to speak more is to occupy more time. Again referencing the data by Bremer, assuming a constant speed in the rhythm of speech, the dialogue of the *Ion* could be performed in 30 minutes, of which Socrates would speak for 24 minutes and 36 seconds and Ion would only speak for 5 minutes and 24 seconds.

Due to the disproportional speaking time assigned to Socrates by Plato, a disproportional focus of interest falls to Socrates. Time and focus are completed in performative events. By manipulating the magnitude of the presence of the interlocutors, the members of the comic pair, Plato offers a risky experiment: he disrupts the solidarity of the pair and the expectation that the performers will have equal opportunities to show their abilities. At the end, the dialogue is organized almost as a monologue, presenting a one-dimensional event.

But who is interested in this Platonic *monodialogue?* Why redefine the organizational and expectational structures of a comic archetype to the point of disfiguring it, putting at risk the possibility of its own existence? What kind of extreme experiment has Plato enacted by creating a pair that is not truly a pair?

To better answer these questions, we must expand our knowledge of the repertoire in comic scenarios linked to the comic pair, knowledge that is fundamental in the production of comedy. In doing so, we follow the implications of dealing with multidimensional events that are not only defined by acts of integration and interaction but also demand such acts from its interpreters.

In reality, the comic pair is not a pair. The complicity of its participants involves another correlated party, namely, the audience. The game between the two halves of the pair alternates with the game played by the audience. The face-to-face interaction takes place between the members of the pair and between the pair and the immediate audience. This interaction is referred to as *triangulation*.[5] The participants that compose the comic pair, as well as those in other genres and comic traditions, do not attempt to hide that they are in front of a group that observes them and participates in the performance. The comic agents perform their routines in the continuity of this *in loco* observational context. Thereby, the actions of the comic agents sometimes manifest possibilities of action and expectations from the audience and other times redirect such expectations.

Triangulation involves an unfolding of the pair, providing a finish, a broad horizon of the comic procedure. Such an unfolding from that audience is corre-

---

[5] This term has been further explained in the reference to the clown game with its audience (see Padilha 2011), although the recourse is present in the formation of several comic forms such as circus and street theater. In some of today's contexts, the term appears in opposition to an acting model that assumes a deliberate lack of immediate contact with the spectator (i.e., the fourth wall), as seen in Sofredini 1980. For an account of contact with the triangulation experience, see Soffredini & Pace 2010.

lated to the unfolding of the broader audience: the reception role involves not only having another audience than merely that of the participants of the comic pair to one another, with both members of the pair reacting to each other's actions. Such a dynamic of reception between agents and audience proclaims acts of interaction and attachment, making performers and the public occupy the same time and space.

To return to the *Ion*, the overly asymmetrical interaction indicates a resurgence of triangulation in the orientation of material for consumption by the public. If the solidarity between Socrates and Ion is disrupted with Socrates appearing as the orientation center in the dialogue, the figure of Socrates poses an overload to the receptive function. He becomes responsible for most of the actions in the dialogues and for the solidarity nexus with the audience. The audience in this dialogue is defined by the game that would attach them to one of the participants in the pair. The exorbitant level of hegemony of Socrates yields a much more favorable reception from the audience of one of the participants in the pair. The excess of the figure of Socrates, shown in his dominance in speeches and in his recurrent action of seeking recourse by degrading Ion, links the reception of this piece to a type of solidarity among the audience with Socrates.

Excesses respond to excesses: the change that Plato brings forth in the archetype of the comic pair results in correlated changes to the piece: if its composition changes, its reception changes. The dialogue of the *Ion* is organized in an exaggerated asymmetry that projects a diminutive space for one figure and an exponentially greater space of importance for the other. Such imbalance produces a reduction of solidarity between Ion and Socrates and, proportionally, reduces the attachment between the audience and the figure of Socrates. Thus, that which Socrates attributes to Ion reinforces and confirms that which the audience agrees is true of Socrates.

The manipulation of the archetype of the comic pair by Plato in the dialogue of the *Ion* ultimately removes the figure of Socrates from that of Ion and reinforces the complicity between Socrates and the audience (in this case, the Platonic circle). In light of this, Ion becomes the target of satire. The degradation of Ion reinforces the attachment and solidarity between Socrates and the audience. As such, it is necessary to dedicate time to dissect the character of Ion, to parse his actions.[6]

---

[6] For a counterpoint, see the discussion in Mota 2011 regarding the Pythagorean community and the formation of its horizon of expectations.

Consequently, the satiric procedure performed here shows dual facets: the degradation of the observational target is linked to its knowledge. Satire ambivalently depends on the game of proximity and on the distance between audience, satirist, and observational target.

Part of the time in which Socrates takes focus in the dialogue is dedicated to showing what he knows of Ion's activities. The Platonic satire, as in the use of pairs, is also diverse because it does not restrict itself to mocking a historic personality or a single individual. What matters to Plato is not the rhapsode Ion, but, based on the activity of Ion, the breadth of the performance in its dimensions of composition, performance, and reception.

This shift deals with the Athenian tradition of satire performed publicly in comedies. In his discussion about the satire of public figures in the years between 432/431 and 405/404 in Athens, Alan Sommerstein concluded that those who were the targets of comic degradation (*komodoumenoi*) presented characteristics that made them known to the public. Due to the activity or functions of the targets, their family prestige, or their instantly obtained prestige, their notoriety reveals itself in an ambivalent manner: these individuals achieve social advancement[7]. However, their trajectories are simultaneously counterbalanced by public appreciation, which is expanded and redefined in the comedic spectacle.

In the case of the *Ion*, no actual public figure is the target of satire, to our knowledge. The character of Ion is an amalgamation of characteristics assigned to his profession. Platonic differences lie in the shift of the publicist aspect of the comedic satire to the specific dimension of the Platonic group. In reception sociology, we see that the shift of the public figure known by his stereotype complements the passage of the comedic audience's heterogeneity to the homogeneity of the Platonic group. The characteristics chosen by Plato in constructing the figure of Ion are not confined to the particular sphere of one individual. For Plato, what matters most is to demonstrate wide negation unrestricted to characterization.

In this sense, the first block of Socrates' speech is understood (503 BCE), which identifies the activity of Ion by merely suggesting the development of his appearance in front of the public: his shape, physical complexion, and facial features. Plato identifies these integrating elements of the rhapsode's activity and stresses them, with the purpose of contrasting them. Stressing elements of characterization shows that Plato is not interested in the particular figure of Ion but in what he does. Consequently, Plato does not degrade the individual but an observational target assigned to him. While amplifying the comic degradation of the individual figure to a dimension simultaneously more open and

---

7 Sommerstein 1996.

easily identifiable (i.e., a stereotype), Plato produces a comedy that he offers to whomever takes part, in opposition between the degraded figure and another archetypal rhapsode.

In this sense, Plato understands well that the type of satire practiced is related to the type of community to whom the satire is directed. Plato appropriates a type of recourse from comic tradition based on the reception of the:community, which configures the selection of the content recorded in the dialogue. Thus, when reading the *Ion*, perceiving how the text records changes in the procedures of comic tradition, we can better understand this tradition and the functioning of the Platonic circle. The record of the parody of Ion results in clarifying the horizon of the reception of the community to which the parody is directed. One of the things Plato did while using the comic elements present in face-to-face interactions was to change his reception horizon from the public space of exchanges to the convivial space among the participants of the pro-Plato group. Thus, the text of the *Ion* is geared towards a homogenous and specific public, in the sense that it is comprised of people who share certain productions and transmission of knowledge practices.

Matters of reception are fundamental for the *Ion*. Initially, we see the comic pair, which manifests well-marked reception roles several times: most often, Ion is the audience in the persuasion spectacle enacted by Socrates.[8] This situation, as built, subverts the expectations marked in the opening of the text, in which the meeting with a famous and skillful rhapsode projects an imminent opportunity for Ion to show his skills publicly. On the contrary, Socrates will refuse to be Ion's audience and will play the role of rhapsode himself. Such disruption of the expectations involving the meeting with Ion imposes the centrality of the figure and attributes of Socrates. From Ion's spectacle, we move to the display of Socrates' abilities. To whom does Socrates present himself? To whom is a detained rhapsode, incapable of performing, considered to be a worthy citizen? Why interrupt the winning career of Ion? Socrates crosses the path of the rhapsode and determines another way of relating to performative events.

Secondly, the issue of reception is explained in the ring theory, or magnetic theory, of the performing arts. According to this theory, a network of links exists between the agents of an interactive creative process, starting with a process-generator moment (i.e., the Muses) until reaching its extreme point of effect in the audience. A graphical, linear image arranged as follows depicts these links:

---

[8] *Ion*, 530d , 536e.

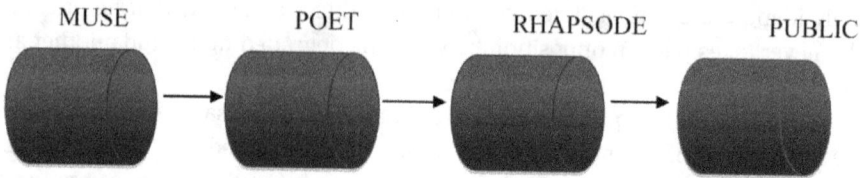

Fig.1: Plato's Magnetic Theory of Art

According to this theory, to draw an analogy with the strength of the magnet, which attracts iron rings and infuses the power of attraction in them, the maintaining and originating cause of a performance does not lie in the face-to-face interaction between the rhapsode and the audience but in the extrapersonal impulses experienced by the participants of the reception and production chains: the muse inspires the poet-author, the interpreter-rhapsode adds no textual content but sheds light on the meanings over the work of the poet-author, and the audience attaches itself to the inspiration of the poet-author by means of the work of the interpreter-rhapsode. Such phenomenology of the composition-reception process of performative events not only deconstructs and describes its functions but also values them. The interpreter-performer-rhapsode interaction is negatively marked, hence the proposition of a hierarchy, of an order of values with cognitive implications.

However, such cause-and-effect structure applied to the production and reception of performative events possesses well-outlined contours. The role of the interpreter, the performer, the person immediately attached to an effective context of exchange, is the lowest link in the chain. If strict linear logic is followed, the last degree of the chain, namely, that of the public, would have the lowest cognitive index, the least value, because it is furthest from the causal source, namely, the Muse.[9] However, Plato manipulates the geometric scheme and situates the rhapsode, the second-to-last position, as the breaking point of the tension of the chain. While imposing logic to the described order, regarding the phenomenology of concrete performative events, Plato demonstrates that the choice of hierarchy is preliminary. Ion and his art are, beforehand, enamored of models contrary to those which Plato and his circle support (i. e., anti-models). The analogy of the iron rings kept together by the strength of the magnet is only effective in the Platonic discourse.

Thus, we see that Plato builds his argument through an analogy that is not verified in its total application. Thereby, the analogy only works if accepted by

---

[9] *Ion* 535 e.

the group that shares the same references and dispositions of the person who proposes it. That is, the effectiveness of the analogy depends on the assumption shared between the figure and his audience; to produce such consensus, a previous agreement is needed. Thus, the degradation of the figure of Ion, his abilities, and the entire set of references related to his activities precede the text of the *Ion*: these features defined the Platonic group.

Hence, if the text of the *Ion* is the record of group assumptions involving Plato, the degradation of the rhapsode explains what is considered negative and positive by this community. If Plato applies an analogy to ratify his previous positions, the practice of the group is conducted in this distinction by assumption. If Plato uses hierarchy to degrade the rhapsode, the interpretative activity of the group uses hierarchical models, with their axiological and cognitive implications.

At present, the crooked logic of this distorted argument is justified due to the group's choice, or the reception horizon of the Platonic circle. For the cohesion of the group, it is necessary to establish distinctions, or markings that identify who does or does not belong. The partial transference of attributes from the magnet to the rhapsode's activity, although at first belittling to the performer, contributes to the process that is basic to Socrates and to Ion, namely, persuasion—the adherence completes something that is greater than common and individual understanding.[10]

The reinforcement of the group that derives from degrading an observational target is a technique used widely in the comic tradition.[11] Such connection uses incongruities that are shared and experimented with by members of the audience. Some of the persuasion or maintenance of the bonds between the participants in the Platonic circle arises from these cognitive games, from the juggling that unites fun, discussion, and criticism of the polis. The strengthening of the group is proportional to the degradation of the observational target, based on the interpretative practices that may appear to be simplifying and partial but which reach their plenitude in this exact confusion, in this coexistence between what I deny and what I perceive as being mine.

Hence, if instead of discussing the coherence of the Platonic argument, we move towards incorporating these cognitive games into the routines and strategies of group cohesion, we can move forward with the data that the *Ion* makes available about the productivity of comedy inside Platonic circles.

---

10 Perks 2012.
11 Bakhtin 1987.

When posing the rhapsode as a weak link inside a reception-production chain of performative events, the Platonic argument puts forth that the performer's (supposed) inferiority constitutes the deficit. If the observational target is thus defined, the identity of the group is posed as well, proportionally to it. In this moment, Ion progresses in another common procedure, namely, disguise, or the game of assuming the traces of the one(s) whom legitimacy I deny.

Such a procedure is fundamental to reemphasize the problem regarding Plato's comedy; the reception horizon of his group is not purely intellectual. Socrates, after degrading Ion, takes the place of the rhapsode. In a dialogue that opens and is extended with the imminent display of the abilities of the itinerant artist, we have an inversion of roles: Socrates, rather than the rhapsode Ion, will present Homer's parts.[12] However, Socrates meets Ion, who is performing in a victorious tour. After complimenting the rhapsode, Socrates starts to restrict Ion's activity to dialectical exercises. After rejecting Ion's performance twice, Socrates requests and allows that the rhapsode present verses of Homer but in a reduced context, illustrative of the dialectic application. Later, Socrates interrupts this reduced performance and starts to present Homer's texts within the justifications of the persuasive activity already initiated.

What we have then is a Socrates-Ion, a juxtaposition between a reduced rhapsodic performance and the exercise of the Socratic dialectic. The effects of such juxtaposition between opposites are interesting: how does one approximate things that are presumptively taken as opposites? This disguise by Socrates explains the asymmetry in the dialogue, as shown by the superior status of Socrates and the degradation of the rhapsode; Socrates can take Ion's turn but not vice-versa. When Ion attempts to assert himself in his answers, which are not acts of ventriloquism despite Socrates' insistence, he ultimately appears ridiculous and incongruent.[13] The resulting argument by Plato is sublimated by adherence to persuasive tactics; however, the positions assigned to the rhapsode in this dialogue are incomprehensible, consenting, or unreasonable. Ion proves himself to be someone who does not adhere to the Socratic methods and who will not integrate into the Platonic community.

Again, Socrates does not change into Ion in this disguise. Acting as a rhapsode, Socrates gives a reduced performance with neither the traces of characterization nor the audience that are normally linked to the rhapsode's activity. However, the interpretation of parts of the Homeric work is linked to the exercise of the Socratic dialectic.

---

12 *Ion* 538b–539e.
13 *Ion* 539e,540d. V. Goldblatt 2006.

The personified parody projects Socrates into acting, to manifest the possibility of Socrates acting like someone he is not. Such a procedure is dangerous: it falls at the border of denying whom he does not want to be and becoming what he denies. In any event, such danger is normalized due to the effects of the simultaneity: abstract logic of thoughts and cohesion of actions do not matter. Socrates' acting is directed to his audience, to strengthen the bonds among the members of the Platonic circle. Socrates-Ion shows the community as residing between performative practices, the dialectic, and the rhapsode, even when the lattermost is the target of parody and degradation in the dialogue.

The performative dimension of the Socratic circle is then manifested in acts of appropriation and transformation of other social performances, of which prestige and hegemony are placed under revision. Even if I become another, I act within the horizon of the expectations of my group; thus, I intend to reassert the assumptions of my community. When I do what others do, I do it better.

The performative dimension of the Platonic dialogue and circle finds a scope for its understanding in the study of comic procedures. If Plato juxtaposes what he refutes with what he asserts, other procedures taken as "creations" of the Socratic method become comprehensible in performative and even in comic-performative traditions. As an example, we have the Socratic interrogation and the organization of the dialogue in discontinued blocks.

The Socratic interrogation is a recurring attempt at recourse in the asymmetrical acting ability between Socrates and the rhapsode. In general, it deals with a series of questions that attempt to test the consistency of the ideas of the interlocutor. However, from the content of the dialogue, we see that its interactivity and formalization draw more attention than its assumed intellectual purpose.

From the beginning, the Socratic interrogation occurs in a context of false dialogue: the questions guide and restrict the activity of the interlocutor. The interlocutor ultimately agrees mechanically with the statements presented in the questions of Socrates. Therefore, the dialogic process does not result in an exchange between conversational poles: previously, Socrates had intervened in the discursive material of his interlocutor. In its shape, the interrogation works with the asymmetry between interlocutors to produce different instances and a hierarchy of roles. The shape of the interrogation is imposed on its articulators. Also, a script of activities explains the hierarchy: initially, in the contact between discursive agents, it is assumed from the situation-problem that determines the meeting. There is a distribution of functions: Socrates asks and his interlocutor replies. On this response, Socrates questions him again in an attempt to show how the initial response, namely, his interlocutor's premise, has limited applicability. Such new questions insert the premise in correlated contexts as a way to test its efficacy. Proportional to this expansion of the applicability of the premise, we see the reduction of movement of the interlocutor's participation, which is limited to the role of corroborating what Socrates contends in his questions. The asymmetry between the discursive agents projects this complementary movement, which marks the extension of the acting. The continuity of Socrates' rise over his interlocutor is secured by the decrease of the discursive space of the interlocutor.

For this preliminary layout of the interaction between participants in the interrogation to become identifiable, Plato makes use of two procedures: the length of this conversation without exchanges, or this anti-dialogue, and its repetition. In the first instance, in practical terms, nobody would support the discursive situation imposed by the hierarchy and stability of roles for too long. Surveys about conversation show that an entire dynamic is enacted between the participants of a dialogue, forming an inter-individual context in which the frontiers between the speaker and the listener are constantly surpassed.[14] The participants in the dialogue thus act based on the dramaturgy that organizes the actions of the dialogue. The Socratic interrogation is thus identified by the way it arranges the interaction of the discursive agents. Hence, what matters more than the theme of the inquiry or the premise is the exercise of the formula, or the ratification of the model that determines the actions. Being figures, the characters of the Platonic dialogues expose not what they think about themselves or the universe but also expose themselves as references of appropriation and transformation of social performances.

The Socratic interrogation in the *Ion* points to the refutation of postures and promises that did not fit those supported and practiced by the conduit of such conversation without exchanges. Thereby, the *elenchus* is used as a filter, an emphasis of what should be done by refusing the values and actions of the non-requested, or the observational, target. It is not a matter of converting the interlocutor by changing his way of thinking but of demonstrating superiority in a distinguishable and organized manner by dealing with the other. Negotiation and inter-influence strategies are excluded from the experience of the interlocutors, to promote the reassurance of the same hierarchical nexus. What is excluded, then, is the interaction between the interlocutors *in praesentia* for a communal interaction of a second order. In the case of Ion, Socrates does not exchange or share anything with the rhapsode as he does with the members of the Platonic group. The incommensurability of the orders and plans of Ion and Socrates reinforces another receptive link by which the work is directed and from which we understand the dramaturgy of the dialogue. While manipulating the time

---

14 Sacks 1974, Sacks 1995, Goffman 1981, Goffman 1986.

of such interaction without interaction and extending the incommensurability between interlocutors, the dialogue reinvigorates the shapes of the organizational strategy used and the expectation horizon for which it is directed.

Secondly, this recourse in the Socratic questionnaire is recurrent, being used more than once in the sequence of the dialogue. In *Ion*, this is shown strongly: after the initial contact moment between the rhapsode and Socrates, we see that,

* the first interrogation (531a–532b), in which the starting point is the question of Socrates about whether Ion is too good (i.e., a specialist, skillful, and extraordinary) in his interpretation of Homer compared with the repertory of other writers, such as Hesiod and Archilochus;
* the second (532e–533c) discusses other arts, to ratify the hypothesis that Ion does not understand what he does, according to the modes of knowledge production in the Platonic community;
* the third (535b–535b) is connected to the "long" exposure of the magnetic theory of performance, of amplifying it; and
* the fourth (536e–541d) is centered in the references of Homer to specific non-artistic activities, interlaced by parts of the performed epic.

Such interaction reasserts the formulaic character of the procedure and emphasizes its identification with the Platonic community. At the same time, such integration between scheme and applicability approximates the Socratic questionnaire to a recourse widely used in the comedy of production, reception, and non-comic work processes, namely, improvisation. In the succession of encounter moments between the rhapsode and Socrates, the procedure is updated for each occasion. Thus, as a type of recourse to manipulate the interactions, the questionnaire takes the place of the reactions of the interlocutor or of the possible fluctuations between the members of the immediate dialogue. The reduction of the differences, of the disruptions in the interaction, is promoted by the use of contact forms that are imposed on the will of the interlocutor and reception.

Parry-Lord,[15] by way of approximation between the Homeric epic and the narrative singers of the Balkans, brought a pioneering comprehension of the relations among performance, improvisation, and textuality to classic studies. The formula character of the Homeric epic is expressed in the set of distinguishable orientation forms of contact between the performer and the audience. In the absence of a fixed text but under the circumstances of each contact, the forms would allow the confrontation of this reception dynamic. Collins[16] thus summa-

---

15 V. Mota 2010.

rizes such forms of improvisation or composition-in-performance as the following: material flexibility, building its length in light of the responses of the audience; repertoire amplification by means of adding new material; and competitive alignment between performers.

Thus, the use of formulas or schemes in performative activities ensures, for the performer and the audience, modes of participation in face-to-face interaction. The Socratic questionnaire enters the set of these recourses while presenting protocols to its performance which, when updated in asymmetric interactions, evidence its recognition.

Consequently, the activity of Socrates approximates that of the rhapsode: both work with situations of contact and interaction. The comic recognition of the procedure is a Platonic novelty. While making use of improvisational profile schemes with the purpose of parodying and degrading performative acts, Plato reasserts the superiority of his community and of the production and transmission of the knowledge processes he endorses. Hence, the Socratic questioning is a parody of a face-to-face contact situation, which is disfigured and redefined for the expectation horizons of the Platonic community.

After all, the questions do not serve the purpose of infusing knowledge or of transforming the interlocutor. The aporetic nature of many Platonic dialogues does not point to failure of persuasion before aporia; it unlinks the speakers and identifies to whom the dialogue is directed.

At this moment, we enter the second performative aspect of the Platonic dialogues, namely, its block structure. As has been discussed previously herein, the *Ion* is organized in the permutation between two sets of verbal activities: the schematic game of questions and answers and the blocks of Socratic assertions. That is, it is not based on the theme of a discursive unit that has the cohesion of the dialogue. There are discontinuities and juxtapositions of relatively independent moments that prevent a reading that summarizes the text into a full and unequivocal argumentative process.

Such cumulative paratactic logic projects another dimension of the comic and non-comic improvisational practice, namely, the variational rhapsodic composition, which does not work with conceptual hierarchies but with the relevance of each segment or block. The most important is an expanded effective presence, an always-renewed actuality, a focus of constant interest in what is current, as a way to make the performative game efficient. What is left behind is no longer important: what really matters is the image of the final process, developed by the interactivity of the procedures.

In the case of the *Ion*, the alternation between interrogations and full speeches is to confirm the expectations of the audience in the dialogue. This alternation is among the procedures of Socrates common to his group; also, Ion proved his ineptitude to assimilate such recourses, in the absence of another means of recourse other than ending the dialogue. This alternation, as it occurs in the dialogues and in the isolated speech blocks, manifests the lack of pertinence between the values and the cognitive horizons of the interlocutors placed in confrontation.

The technique of rhapsodic composition, or composition by blocks, highlights the focus on the discrete unit of events in succession without the selection and evaluation arising from a higher perspective, namely, from a narrator. In the work of the comic performer, such manipulation of contact formulas and blocks of events or situations determines its interactive activity with the audience.

Conclusion

As one can observe from reading the *Ion* attentively, many of its compositional aspects are better understood from the perspectives of Performance and Humor Research. It is worth mentioning that when we make use of references to comedy in other references that are apparently not studied or included in canons of comedy, we reach a hermeneutic degree of amplification of our perspective about the construction of serious and comic events. In other words, beyond the dichotomy, we start to see the comic as the non-serious or the serious as the non-comic. Such dichotomization assumes a type of essentialism, or an ahistorical, generic, and stable identification of ways to organize the events and its effects.

The possibility of substantiating an approach that explains Plato's comedy procedures directs us to a better understanding of the ways his group, in the rivalry with others, proposed an image of oneself parodically; these ways were exercised in the procedures that governed the dispute, presentation, and development of abilities during its meetings.

Works Cited

Bremer, J. *Plato's Ion: Philosophy as Performance*. North Richland Hillls: Bibal Press, 2005.
Charalabopoulos, N. Platonic Drama and its Ancient Reception. Cambridge: Cambridge University Press, 2012.
Collins, D. Homer and Rhapsodic Competition in Performance. *Oral Tradition*. 16(2001): 129–167.
Goffman, E. *Forms of Talk*. Philadelphia: University of Pennsylvania Press, 1981.
Goffman, E. *Frame Analysis*. Boston: Northeastern University Press, 1986.
Goldblatt, D. *Art and Ventriloquism*. London: Routledge, 2006.

Jones, J. A Complete Analysis of Plato's Philosophy of Humor. Link: http: //www.jon athonjones.com/papers/plato.pdf.

Latar, R. *The Basic Humor Process: A Cognitive-Shift Theory and the Case against Incongruity.* Berlin: Mouton de Gruyter, 1998.

Morreal, J. (Ed.) *The Philosophy of Laughter and Humor.* New York: State University of New York Press, 1986, pp. 188–207.

Morreal, J. Humor as Cognitive Play. *Journal of Literary Theory.* 3.2(2009): 241–260.

Morreal, J. *Comic Relief.* Chichester: Wiley-Blackwell, 2009 (MORREAL 2009a).

Mota, M. A performance como argumento: a cena inicial de Íon, de Platão. Revista *VIS.* 5 (2006): 80–92.

Mota, M. *A dramaturgia musical de Ésquilo.* Brasília: Editora UnB, 2008.

Mota, M. Performance e Inteligibilidade: Traduzindo Íon, de Platão. Revista *Archai* 2(2009): 183–204.

Mota, M. Nos passos de Homero: Performance como argumento na Antiguidade. Revista VIS (UnB), 9(2010): 21–59. Link: http: //www.ida.unb.br/revistavis/revista%20vis%20v9%20n2.pdf.

Mota, M. Pythagoras Homericus: Performance as Hermeneutic Horizon to Interpret Pythagorean Tradition. In: *Anais On Pythagoreanism.* Brasília, Archai, 2011, pp 293–306.

Nightgale, A. *Genres in Dialogue: Plato and the Construct of Philosophy.* Cambridge: Cambridge University Press, 2005.

Padilha, P. Convívio e triangulação Clownesca na potencialização do evento teatral: Substratos de uma montagem. *Cena em movimento.* 2(2011): 1–8. Link: http: //seer.ufrgs.br/cenamov/article/view/21632.

Perks, L.G. The Ancients Roots of Humor Theory. *Humor.* 25(2012): 119–132.

Puchner, M. *The Drama of Ideas. Platonic Provocations in Theater and Philosophy.* Oxford: Oxford University Press, 2010.

Raskin, V (Ed.). *The Primer of Humor Research.* Berlin: Mouton de Gruyter, 2009.

Sacks, H., Schegloff, E., and Jefferson, G. A Simpliest Systematics of the Organisation of Turn-taking for Conversation. *Language.* 50(1974): 696–735.

Sacks, H. *Lectures on Conversation.* Oxford: Wiley-Blackwell, 1995.

Shelley, C. Psychology of Humor. *Humor.* 16(2001): 351–367.

Scott, G.A. (Ed.) *Does Socrates Have a Method? Rethinking the Elenchus in* Plato's Dialogues and Beyond. Univesity Park: The Pennsylvania State University, 2002.

Soffredini, C. De um trabalhador sobre seu teatro. *Revista Teatro.* 1(1980).1–4.

Sofredini, R. and Pace, E. *Carlos Alberto Soffredini: Serragem nas veias.* Imprensa do Estado de São Paulo, 2010. Link: http: //www.aplauso.imprensaoficial.com.br.

Sommerstein, A.H. How to Avoid Being a Komodoumenos. *Classical Quarterly.* 46(1996): 327–356.

Sommerstein, A.H. *Talking about Laughter And Other Studies in Greek Comedy.* Oxford: Oxford University Press, 2009.

Worman, N. *Abusive Mouths in Classical Athens.* Cambridge: Cambridge University Press, 2011.

Mario Regali
Amicus Homerus: Allusive Art in Plato's *Incipit* to Book X of the *Republic* (595a – c)

Platonic scholarship has been characterized by an evaluation of the presence of Homer in the dialogues from as early as the work carried out by the Alexandrian philologists[1]. Apart from the controversial information advanced by Diogenes Laërtius regarding the ordering of the *corpus* in trilogies and the critical signs that led to conjecture as to the existence of an Alexandrian *ekdosis*[2], from the scarce remains that the sources contain an echo emerges, even if faint, of Aristarchus' interest in Homeric diction in Plato. As Francesca Schironi[3] has highlighted, it may be possible to recoup some traces of Aristarchus' work on the text of the dialogues from the Byzantine lexica: his work in this sense may be attributed precisely to Plato's pronounced tendency to reproduce some of the features of Homer's language. There is clear evidence of this in a scholion to the *Iliad* (in *Il.* IX 540, II p. 515 Erbse), which contains information about a work by Ammonius of Alexandria, a pupil of Aristarchus, entitled Περὶ τῶν ὑπὸ Πλάτωνος μετενηνεγμένων ἐξ Ὁμήρου, which Francesca Schironi translates as: "On the borrowings of Plato from Homer". In the eyes of the Alexandrians, therefore, Plato establishes a privileged link with Homer, a link that the grammarians can perceive particularly in the language and diction that Plato derives from Homer.

But it is no coincidence that the biographical tradition regarding Plato, the tradition that arose in the Peripatetic ambience, produced more than one anecdote based precisely on the relationship between Plato and Homer[4]. A long chain of sources going back to Dicaearchus, a first-generation Peripatetic, then down to Apuleius and Aelianus, and on to Olympiodorus and the Anonymous of the *Prolegomena*, attributes intense poetic activity to the young Plato, ranging from the dithyramb to the lyric and tragedy, as well as the *epos* (*An.* 14 Swift Riginos). This information is traditionally connected to a scene of great impact: that of Plato who, having listened to Socrates, burns his poetic output in public in front of Dionysus' theatre. Diogenes Laërtius recalls a verse, a hexameter that Plato is al-

---

[1] See Hunter (2012, p. 38: "No literary observation about Plato ia as common in antiquity as the philosopher's debt to Homer".
[2] See Lucarini (2010–2011), with bibliography.
[3] Schironi (2005).
[4] For the biographical tradition, see Swift Riginos (1976, pp. 17–21, 45–47, 197).

leged to have uttered as he watched his poems burn on the bonfire: Ἥφαιστε, πρόμολ' ὧδε· Πλάτων νύ τι σεῖο χατίζει (Diog. Laert. III 5: "Hephaistos, come this way, here is Plato, who has need of you"). A verse that is modelled on Homer's *Iliad:* in Book XVIII, after Hector has killed Patroclus and taken Achilleus' arms from him, Thetis, following the encounter with her son, reaches Hephaistos' abode, who will have to make new arms for Achilleus; there she is met by Charis, Hephaistos' wife, who lets Thetis sit on the throne. From this throne, Thetis calls Hephaistos to her aid: Ἥφαιστε πρόμολ' ὧδε· Θέτις νύ τι σεῖο χατίζει (392: "Hephaistos, come this way, here is Thetis, who has need of you now" trad. R. Lattimore). According to Diogenes Laërtius, or his source, Plato therefore turns from his activity as a poet by uttering a line by Homer, in which he substitutes the name of Thetis with his own. The ancient biography builds up an anecdote in which the last line of verse uttered by Plato is a hexameter, a line of verse by Homer that Plato re-elaborates by re-writing it with refined allusive artistry. Plato turns from the arms of the *epos*, abandons the hexameter, only to take up – like Achilleus – the new arms of dialogue, the literary genre that arose from the meeting with Socrates. Leaving aside the veracity of the episode, an image emerges of how Plato was seen in ancient criticism, an image that is confirmed in the dialogues of the *corpus:* Plato as *poeta doctus*, enjoying a privileged relationship with Homer[5]. This image is condensed by the anonymous writer of the *On the Sublime*, in the portrait he puts forward of Plato as Ὁμηρικώτατος, "most Homeric of authors", who draws infinite drafts from the Homeric wellspring (13,3)[6].

Modern criticism has continued the investigation of the ancients, starting with the work by Jules Labarbe who, in the aftermath of World War Two, analyzed Homeric quotations present in the dialogues[7]. This analysis, while valuable, states as a matter of policy that its exclusive aim is that of tackling problems concerning "critique verbale", that is, the links between the form of Homer's text cited by Plato and the Homeric text conserved in manuscript form. More recently, the field of critical investigation has expanded, moving beyond the history of Plato's and Homer's texts, to evaluate with increasing interest the literary strategy that Plato employs by means of the Homeric quotations[8]. In recent years the tendency has come to the fore to observe not only direct quotations, but also allusions to Homer's text independently of any direct quotation. On the basis of

---

[5] See the *status quaestionis* described by Erler (2007, pp. 29–30, 64–82).
[6] See Hunter (2012, p. 44).
[7] Labarbe (1949).
[8] After the seminal works of Benardete (1963) and Lohse (1964), see now Halliwell (2000), El Murr (2011), Yamagata (2012) and Regali (2013).

research by Fabio Massimo Giuliano[9], Diskin Clay[10], Patrick Gerald Lake[11] and Zacharoula Petraki[12], a complex picture emerges in which Plato's capacity to take on board both Homer's words and scenes in an innovative way is increasingly evident, moulding them to the dramatic requirements of his own philosophical writing.

It is our intention now to focus again on a renowned passage wherein, despite the absence of direct quotation, Plato establishes overt contact with the figure of Homer. In the opening of Book X of the *Republic*, Socrates once again suggests to Glaucon that they have a discussion on ποίησις, along the lines of Book III. Now, maintains Socrates, the rejection of the μιμητική part of poetry will become even more evident, once the parts of the ψυχή have been divided and separated (595a1-b1). Certain of the loyalty of his interlocutors in the *Republic*, who will not denounce him to the tragic poets or the other μιμητικοί poets, Socrates accuses poetry of giving rise to a damaging insult (λώβη) to the rational faculty (διάνοια) of those members of the public lacking the necessary medicine for an antidote: that is, to know (τὸ εἰδέναι) the essence of poetry. In reply to Glaucon's question, who requires further details regarding λώβη, Socrates makes a celebrated confession about the nature of his feelings towards Homer (595b8-c6):

> Πῇ δή, ἔφη, διανοούμενος λέγεις;
> Ῥητέον, ἦν δ' ἐγώ· καίτοι <u>φιλία γέ τίς με καὶ αἰδὼς</u> ἐκ παιδὸς ἔχουσα περὶ Ὁμήρου ἀποκωλύει λέγειν. ἔοικε μὲν γὰρ τῶν καλῶν ἁπάντων τούτων τῶν τραγικῶν πρῶτος διδάσκαλός τε καὶ ἡγεμὼν γενέσθαι. ἀλλ' οὐ γὰρ πρό γε τῆς ἀληθείας τιμητέος ἀνήρ, ἀλλ', ὃ λέγω, ῥητέον.
>
> "What do you have in mind when you say that?"
> "I'd better explain " I said, "though the affection and respect I have had for Homer since I was a child makes me very reluctant to say it. He seems to me to have been the original teacher and guide of all these wonderful tragedians of ours. All the same, no man should be honoured more than the truth. So as I say, I had better explain myself" (trad. T. Griffith, slightly modified)

The feelings that Socrates admits to in Homer's regard represent an obstacle to arriving at a definition of λώβη. Since his childhood, ἐκ παιδὸς, Socrates has been filled with affection and a sense of veneration towards Homer, φιλία and αἰδώς. Socrates explains these feelings as arising from the pre-eminent role that Homer plays as the first master and leader (ἡγεμών) of all the wonderful

---

9 Giuliano (2005).
10 Clay (2010).
11 Lake (2011).
12 Petraki (2011).

tragic poets. Despite the ties of affection that bind him to Homer, Socrates must arrive at a condemnation, since man should not be honoured more than the truth. Leonardo Tarán[13] dedicated a celebrated article to just this passage, investigating the success enjoyed by the sequence οὐ γὰρ πρό γε τῆς ἀληθείας τιμητέος ἀνήρ, a sequence which from Aristotle, down through Neo-Platonist channels, has reached also Roger Bacon and Thomas Aquinas, and on to Cervantes' *Don Quixote* and Sterne's *Tristram Shandy*: *Amicus Plato sed magis amica veritas*, with the alternative versions that Tarán traces with painstaking accuracy. The nexus φιλία καὶ αἰδώς, with which Plato describes Socrates' state of mind prior to the severe criticism of poetry that is developed in Book X, still remains to be explained. In recent studies attention has not been dedicated to the nexus offered by Socrates, except for a brief note by Ramona Naddaff who, in her book *Exiling the Poets*, points out that the nexus φιλία καὶ αἰδώς recalls a Homeric formula: "Socrates' own ironic reflection on his childish, cultivated *philia* and *aidos* for Homeric verse is couched in a phrasing itself echoing a Homeric formula"[14].

It is indeed surprising that, even after a cursory glance at the lexicon, neither the connection between the nouns φιλία and αἰδώς, nor the connection between the adjectives deriving from them, recur with any frequency in the literary tradition. In Plato's dialogues, the passage in Book X of the *Republic* that we are looking at is isolated: it is the only place in the *corpus* where φιλία and αἰδώς appear as a pair. But even in the literary output that precedes Plato, significantly Homer is the only one to offer a possible model for the nexus φιλία καὶ αἰδώς. In the *Iliad* and the *Odyssey* in fact, the adjectives φίλος and αἰδοῖος are said to a guest who is received in the welcoming-scenes, in particular to the world of the gods[15].

But, as will be seen, it is plausible that, rather than this formulaic use, Plato in the *Republic* accurately recalls an individual scene from the *Iliad*, thus weaving an allusive plot of some importance for the characterization of Socrates, in light of his relationship with Homer. Let us now observe the areas, which are not numerous, where the nexus appears in Homer.

In Book XVIII of the *Iliad*, in the scene that we have already briefly described, as it contains the line that, according to the anecdote conserved by Diogenes Laërtius, Plato is alleged to have recited in front of his burning poetry, Thetis is welcomed to Hephaistos' home by Charis (385–386):

---

[13] Tarán (1984).
[14] Naddaff (2002, p. 38 n.3).
[15] For the hospitality scenes in Homer, see Reece (1993, pp. 5–46).

> τίπτε Θέτι τανύπεπλε ἱκάνεις ἡμέτερον δῶ
> <u>αἰδοίη τε φίλη</u> τε; πάρος γε μὲν οὔ τι θαμίζεις.
>
> "Why is it, Thetis of the light robes, you have come to our house now? We honor you and love you; but you have not come much before this" (trad. R. Lattimore)

The same lines are then repeated in the following scene, uttered by Hephaistos to Thetis herself (424–425). The sequence αἰδοίη τε φίλη τε urbanely intends to manifest affection and respect for the goddess, whose requests Hephaistos is ready to grant[16]. Again in the *Iliad*, in Book XXIV, Zeus asks Thetis to allay Achilleus' ire: the gods, Zeus maintains, now think that after nine days they should recover Hector's body from Achilleus through deception by sending Hermes for it. But Zeus has called Thetis because he does not want to deny Achilleus his honour, in this way safeguarding the affection and respect of Thetis towards him (110–111)[17]:

> αὐτὰρ ἐγὼ τόδε κῦδος Ἀχιλλῆϊ προτιάπτω
> <u>αἰδῶ καὶ φιλότητα</u> τεὴν μετόπισθε φυλάσσων.
>
> "But I still put upon Achilleus the honor that he has, guarding your reverence and your love for me" (Trad. R. Lattimore)

The nexus also appears in the *Odyssey*, in a similar welcoming-scene among the gods. The very lines that in the *Iliad* are uttered by Charis and Hephaistos, who welcome Thetis to their home, are in Book V said by Calypso as she welcomes Hermes (87–88)[18]:

> τίπτε μοι, Ἑρμεία χρυσόρραπι, εἰλήλουθας,
> <u>αἰδοῖός τε φίλος τε</u>; πάρος γε μὲν οὔ τι θαμίζεις.
>
> "How is it, Hermes of the golden staff, you have come to me? I honor you and love you; but you have not come much before this" (Trad. R. Lattimore)

The nexus therefore constitutes the lynchpin of a typical scene: the welcome that the gods afford other gods who reach them[19]. Another item of some import for the scene Plato constructs in the *Republic* also emerges: Socrates confesses to

---

16 See Edwards (1991, p. 192: "the formular wording conveys readiness to attend to the visitor's wishes, affection, and the courteous implication that the visitor does not come often enough").
17 See Richardson (1993, p. 288: "'with the intention of preserving your respect and friendship in future': this could mean either Zeus's respect for her or viceversa, but more probably the former".
18 On the anomalies of Calypso's speech, see De Jong (2001, pp. 129–130).
19 See Arend (1933, pp. 36–37, 48–50).

a feeling towards Homer that evokes the respect given to a god. On the one hand, φιλία reveals a confidential type of relationship, the type of confidentiality that the gods have towards each other, in particular when they foresee that some request will be made of them by another god, as happens to Charis and Hephaistos with Thetis, or Calypso with Hermes, or when, as with Zeus with Thetis, they themselves make a direct request to another god.

Similar sequences are present, again in the *Odyssey*, even in relation to the world of men. In Book VIII, during the assembly of the Phaeacians, Athena infuses Odysseus with divine grace so that Laertes' son may be φίλος, δεινός and αἰδοῖος in the eyes of all the Phaeacians (18–22)[20]. In Book XI, in the dialogue with Alcinous that breaks up the story of *Nekya*, after Alcinous promises him gifts and grants safe passage for his return, Odysseus notes that the gifts will make him αἰδοιότερος καὶ φίλτερος, that is, they will gain him more respect and acceptance in the eyes of all the men who witness his return to Ithaca (358–361)[21].

However, as previously stated, it is plausible that Plato is not alluding in an indistinct way only to the formulaic nexus αἰδοῖός τε φίλος τε, but rather to an individual scene in the *Iliad* in Book X, on which he models the scene that he constructs in the *Republic* in order to illustrate the relationship between Socrates and Homer.

In Book X, during the night, fearful on account of the extraordinary feats that Hector has accomplished that very day, Agamemnon decides to consult Nestor, first among heroes, in order to work out a strategy with him that will save the Greeks (1–20). Agamemnon's brother, Menelaus, who has fallen prey to the same fears and cannot sleep, pays him a visit. Agamemnon carefully illustrates what his intentions are and what tasks Menelaus will be expected to carry out: he will have to summon Ajax and Idomeneus, while Agamemnon will go to Nestor (21–72). This Agamemnon does and confesses to him his anxiety: he fears for the fate of the Greeks, he cannot sleep, and he asks Nestor to accompany him to the guards to make sure that they are not sleeping, as he is concerned about a night incursion on the part of the Trojans (73–101). Nestor responds wisely, comforting him with Zeus' plan: the wise god will not let all Hector's plans be brought to pass, as he might fear at that moment. Instead, it will be Hector who suffers great anguish, even greater than that being suffered by Agamemnon,

---

[20] For the conferring of χάρις that causes the Phaeacians' admiration see Garvie (1994, pp.240–241).
[21] Heubeck & Hoekstra (1989, pp. 98–99) point out the courteous exaggeration of Odysseus who reassures Alcinous "that with the assurance of the πομπή and gifts to come he would gladly remain a year".

if only Achilleus will purge his heart of such bitter χόλος – the ire that now consumes it. Nestor pledges that he will assist Agamemnon in rallying the Greek leaders during the night. But Nestor, thinking here of Menelaus, points out that someone is needed to summon Ajax and Idomeneus, since their ships are far removed from those of the other leaders (103–113). At this point occur the lines that Plato recalls in the *Republic* (114–116):

ἀλλὰ <u>φίλον περ ἐόντα καὶ αἰδοῖον</u> Μενέλαον
νεικέσω, εἴ πέρ μοι νεμεσήσεαι, οὐδ' ἐπικεύσω
ὡς εὕδει, σοὶ δ' οἴῳ ἐπέτρεψεν πονέεσθαι

"But, beloved as he is and respected, I will still blame
Menelaos, even though you be angry, and I will not hide it,
for the way he sleeps and has given to you alone all the hard work"
(Trad. R. Lattimore)

Menelaus, says Nestor, should have been awake and praying for all the leaders, given the dire straits that they now find themselves in (116–118). However, as the reader of the *Iliad* knows, Menelaus is indeed already awake and carrying out the task that Nestor refers to, following the order given to him by his brother in the previous scene. In fact, Agamemnon reassures Nestor on this count: despite the fact that Agamemnon has on several occasions pressed Nestor to reprimand Menelaus for his indolence and the manner in which he must often be spurred to action by Agamemnon, on this occasion he is above reproach. He is already awake, already on his way to summon those very leaders selected by Nestor (119–127). Nestor is pleased, because Menelaus' role as commander will benefit: now no-one will raise his voice against him, no-one among the Greeks will disobey when Menelaus gives his orders (128–130).

In this scene in the *Iliad*, not only do we come across Plato's nexus φιλία καὶ αἰδώς in Nestor's words, for whom Menelaos is φίλος καὶ αἰδοῖος, as happens in the welcoming-scenes that we mentioned previously, but we also note a dramatic situation that is entirely similar: blame must be aportioned even when the person blaming has feelings of affection and respect towards the person being blamed. Like Nestor with Menelaus, in the *Republic* Socrates first demonstrates respect towards Homer, before criticizing him. We therefore find ourselves facing one of the not uncommon moments in which Plato characterizes Socrates by re-utilizing the profile of the heroes of the *epos*, by means of a re-visitation of some of the features of Homer's characters. Studies have shown several points of contact between Socrates and the heroic protagonists of Homer's poems: Achilleus, in particular in the *Apology*[22] (28b3-d4), and Odysseus, in the evident reference to *Nekya* in the *incipit* of the *Protagoras* (315b9–316b2)[23]. In the *Republic*, with the allusion to the scene in Book X of the *Iliad*, Plato must therefore intend to characterize Socrates as Nestor and in particular to illustrate the relationship between Socrates and Homer in light of the bond that Homer describes in Book X that exists between Nestor and Menelaus. But before analyzing the reasons that may have induced Plato to create in the *incipit* of Book X such a close bond with Homer, let us turn back to the points of contact between the two passages, between the scene with Nestor and Menelaus in the *Iliad* and the scene with Socrates and Homer in the *Republic*.

We have already mentioned the force with which the passage in Book X stands out among passages by Homer where the nexus between φιλία and αἰδώς appears, a force based on a similarity that is not limited to the verbal level, but rather involves the two scenes: the analogy between the two scenes of blame tempered by respect and affection that the character-mentor (Socrates-Nestor) feels towards the character-pupil (Menelaus-Homer). To return to the linguistic level, however, it is possible to identify further elements corroborating this. In the passages by Homer we have taken into consideration, both in the *Iliad* and the *Odyssey*, the formulaic nexus usually entails an inverted order compared to the nexus that Plato uses: Homer modulates the formula αἰδοῖός τε φίλος τε, depending on the syntactic context, in a varied manner, always, however, maintaining as unvaried the order between the two concepts: first the veneration and respect, the αἰδώς, then the affection and familiarity, the φιλία. This order is also reproduced in the only passage, in Book XXIV of the *Iliad*, where Homer varies the formulaic nexus by using the corresponding abstract nouns rather than the adjectives, αἰδώς and φιλότης (110–111). But the word order of the nexus that Plato attributes to Socrates is the opposite of that favoured by Homer: first φιλία, affection, then respect, αἰδώς. The only place where Homer's word order coincides with Plato's is in Book X of the *Iliad*, the scene with Nestor's rebuke to Menelaus: for Nestor, Menelaus is φίλος καὶ αἰδοῖος, not αἰδοῖος καὶ φίλος, just as Socrates feels φιλία καὶ αἰδώς for Homer. This is not a trifling distinction: in it may be seen a sign of the fact that the allusion to Homer is not generic, it does not vaguely recall the Homeric formula running through the typ-

---

22 See Montiglio (2011, pp. 42–43: "just as Achilles scorned death to avenge Patroclus, Socrates is ready to die – though for the sake of justice"). Clay (2000, pp. 56–59) states that Plato discovers "a new conception of heroism and a new paradigm for imitation in Socrates".
23 See Rutherford (1992), Capra (2001, 67–71) and Segvic (2006, pp. 255–257). For the link between Plato's *Nekyia* e and Protagoras's prophecy (361e) resembling Teiresias's words to Odysseus (XI. 90–137), see Corradi (2014).

ical welcoming-scenes among the gods; rather does it focus exclusively on the scene between Nestor and Agamemnon in Book X.

Furthermore, from the fact that φιλία precedes αἰδώς, there perhaps emerges a nuance in meaning, in significance, which is useful in order to understand the relationship between Nestor and Menelaus as a parallel with that between Socrates and Homer: between Nestor and Menelaus, φιλία is certainly more preponderant than respect, αἰδώς, namely, the fear deriving from veneration that dominates instead the frequently tense relationship among the gods who are taken up with safeguarding their own τιμή without undermining that of the other gods[24]. The rebuke that Nestor directs at Menelaus is mitigated by the affection of the wise hero instructing the younger one. Nestor's approach can clearly be seen in the subsequent exchange with Agamemnon, who has more than once asked Nestor for help in order to spur his younger brother to action on account of his tendency to idleness. It is no coincidence that, once he is reassured by Agamemnon that Menelaus is indeed awake, has already bestirred himself and is aware of the pressing need to rally the leaders during the night, Nestor is pleased and foresees that the Greeks will unhesitatingly acknowledge Menelaus as their commander. We will see shortly how this atmosphere is useful in order to understand Socrates' – if not Plato's – relationship with Homer.

However, once again in regard to the signals offered by the language Plato uses, let us also turn our attention, in light of the allusion in the scene with Nestor, to the definition that Socrates offers of Homer: "first master and guide of all these great tragedians", τῶν καλῶν ἁπάντων τούτων τῶν τραγικῶν πρῶτος διδάσκαλός τε καὶ ἡγεμών. For Homer, the term διδάσκαλος is easily comprehensible in relation to the tragedians, since they draw freely on the legacy of tales from the Homeric Cycle for their output; this concept is confirmed in several parts of the *Republic* (602b8–10; 605c11; 607a2–3) and then further developed by Aristotle in the *Poetics* (in particular 1459b2–7)[25]. But only here, in the *incipit* of Book X of the *Republic*, and in a passage a little bit further on that depends on this scene (598d7–8), does Plato attribute the title ἡγεμών to Homer. In the *Iliad* the term designates in a canonical manner the Greek heroes that have assembled

---

24 For this "prospective usage" of αἰδώς in Homer, see Cairns (1993, pp. 48–146, esp. 145: "explicitly... aidos in Homer is always concerned with the present (as respect for another) or the future (referring to future disapproval, or inhibiting future performance of action expressed by a verb in the infinitive").
25 See Goldhill (1991, pp. 170–174), who draws attention to "the link between Homer and the tragic poets in that both were performed at civic festivals" in Athens, and Murray (1996, pp. 188–189: "this is not just a reference to the fact that tragic plots tend to be taken from epic, but rather that Plato sees Homer as the originator of the dramatic method").

at Troy, heroes that are at the head of their respective troops of diverse provenance. It is no coincidence that the term appears in the lines that open and conclude the catalogue of Greek troops and their commanders, in the *Catalogue of Ships* in Book II: "these, then, were the leaders and the princes among the Danaäns" οὗτοι ἄρ' ἡγεμόνες Δαναῶν καὶ κοίρανοι ἦσαν (487 = 760; trad. R. Lattimore)[26]. ἡγεμών is therefore a title to be attributed to Menelaus, who is at the head of the Spartan troops (581–590), just as it should be attributed to Nestor, who is at the head of the troops from Pilo (591–602). In Plato's lexical choice, therefore, may be seen a further sign of the allusion to the scene in Book X of the *Iliad*: Homer is the tragedians' ἡγεμών, because Plato now uses for him Menelaus' model, when he is rebuked with affection and respect by Socrates, wearing Nestor's mask, the wise and elderly ἡγεμών guiding his pupil Menelaus.

Should our hypothesis prove to be right, it becomes necessary to ask oneself what literary strategy Plato is following in the *incipit* to Book X of the *Republic*, what intention lies behind the allusion to the scene from the *Iliad*. What emerges from the scene by Homer is that Plato re-elaborates the dynamic underpinning the relationship between master and pupil. Nestor is the wisest hero among the Greeks, significantly the guide that Agamemnon is now seeking, during the night recounted in Book X of the *Iliad*, because of the grave difficulties facing the Greek army. In the scene that opens Book X, Menelaus as a pupil is ready to act on Agamemnon's directions, while for Nestor he is a pupil in need of being corrected: his defects must be honed so that he may rise to the challenge of governing the army with a firm hand. In the scene from Book X between Nestor and Agamemnon, modern criticism has in fact discovered a moment in which the characterization of Menelaus is offered with remarkable clarity: not infrequently Menelaus shows that he is aware of his inferiority on the battle field and of living in his brother's shadow; the same brother who now, before Nestor, is protective of him[27]. A profile of Menelaus emerges that will be confirmed by Apollo in Book XVII, who in the dialogue with Hector describes him as a "feeble warrior", μαλθακὸς αἰχμητής (588)[28]. Faced with Menelaus' defects, however, both Nestor and Agamemnon are not harsh; rather do they show understanding and a wish to in-

---

[26] See Brügger, Stoevesandt & Visser (2010², p. 143).

[27] For the opening scene with Agamemnon and Menelaus see Sammons (2009, p. 34): "Agamemnon here shows an awareness that, apart from his own exercise of authority, Menelaus's contribution to the war effort depends on the willingness of the Acheans to help defend his slighted honor".

[28] Sammons (2009, pp. 27–41), follows the whole process through which Homer takes the reader in the *Doloneia* since the initial meeting between the brothers, showing Agamemnon's effort at each stage in protecting his brother's conduct, reputation and survival (1–240).

struct²⁹. Nestor is ready to rebuke, but in the sense of φιλία and αἰδώς; despite being grateful to Nestor for his solicitude, Agamemnon points out his brother's positive attributes, since on this occasion he has not been found lacking with regard to the task set him; Nestor shows his optimism in relation to the position of commander that the situation has thrust on Menelaus. These elements, if transposed to the scene in the *Republic*, are useful both for understanding the relationship between Socrates and Homer, and for gaining further confirmation of the image of Plato as *poeta doctus*, which those critics who are more sensitive to the literary component of the dialogues have observed, with results that have increasingly acquired consensus³⁰.

In the allusion to the scene from the *Iliad*, Socrates' superiority over Homer emerges, Socrates who wears Nestor's mask, the wisest of Greek heroes. For Homer instead, there is the mask of Menelaus, a hero whose defects have more than once had to be corrected by Nestor, as Agamemnon recalls. This state of apprenticeship develops, however, under the auspices of φιλία, the respect due to a ἡγεμών. In this way Socrates takes on, with respect to Homer and the poets, the role of master correcting his pupils' faults, in the sense of the ἀλήθεια that never comes second to τιμή, even if deserved, which must be kept for the great men. A further piece may be added to the mosaic of signs that studies have noted in Book X of the *Republic*, signs that lead to a different reading of the radical ban on μιμητική poetry from Socrates' ideal πόλις, as Fabio Massimo Giuliano has shown in his monograph on *Platone e la poesia*³¹, and more recently Stephen Halliwell, in his contribution to the miscellany *Plato and the Poets*³². In a circular structure, the same tone that emerges from the initial scene of Book X of the *Republic*, re-emerges at the end of the section containing the criticism of μιμητική poetry, following the definitive ban on Homer. The ban on ἡδυσμένη Μοῦσα now takes on the form of a defence of Socrates, whom the *logos* forced into expelling poetry (607b2–4). In order to escape the accusation of austerity and uncouthness, Socrates recalls an ancient dispute between philosophy and poetry (607b2-c4)³³. In a balanced approach, Socrates concedes the opportunity to defend itself even to the basest kind of poetry, which will be welcomed with relief provided it is capable of demonstrating that its presence in

---

29 Sammons (2009, p. 35 n. 35) points out that νεικέσω and νεμεσήσεαι in Book 10 "denote a mild, even playful, style of criticism among friends", while elsewhere in the *Iliad* they "imply forceful rebuke (cf. 4. 413, 2.. 224, 7. 95)".
30 Capra (2014) provides an up-to-date overview.
31 Giuliano (2005, pp. 118–132).
32 Halliwell (2011).
33 On the historical content of Socrates' remark see Most (2011).

the city is necessary (607c4-d3). Therefore, a defence connected also to poetry, with the objective of showing that poetry, even though it aims at giving pleasure, is useful for the city. This defence would be welcomed with relief by Socrates himself (607d4-e2). Plato builds up a judiciary metaphor in which, despite the context of the ban on poetry, Socrates too, who was initially a judge, is now charged with austerity and uncouthness. Socrates and poetry are therefore on the same level: both stand accused and then defend each other. It clearly emerges how Plato has the tendency to reduce the conflict between poetry and philosophy; it is no coincidence, following the judicial metaphor, that Socrates offers, on account of its relationship to poetry, the image of young love from which one has separated sorrowfully. Like those who have loved, but separated – even through force – from a love that is considered damaging, so too does Socrates, in whom the feeling of *eros* towards poetry was created because of the education he received in Athens, welcome with relief the absolution of poetry from his accusations. And even were poetry not capable of defending itself, Socrates would in any case continue to listen to it, while singing to himself like an enchantment the *logos* of the *Republic*, in order to avoid falling back into that youthful love (607e4–608a5). The converging defences of Socrates and poetry, along with the erotic language, are signs of Plato's tendency to identify a point of convergence between philosophy and poetry: a new agreement that overcomes the ancient dispute[34].

The reference to the scene from Book X of the *Iliad* fits harmoniously into this frame: like Nestor, Socrates is the wise hero who corrects and instructs Homer, his pupil. The new figure of the philosopher that Socrates' mask represents ejects Homer from the role that tradition had assigned him: that of παιδεία. Therefore, from Homer, master of the Greeks, to Homer, pupil of Socrates. Characterized by benevolence towards Homer, this passage marks the passing of the baton to Socrates, just as Nestor who, even when rebuking, shows respect and affection for Menelaus. The allusive art demonstrated by Plato through the writing of Socratic dialogues re-enforces the new consonance between poetry and philosophy, which find in the dialogues the common ground for a fertile exchange. After Socrates' examination, the masks of the dialogue give new life to Homer's heroes: this literary genre then recovers the communicative capacity of poetry with renewed functional vigour, at the service of the interlocking questions and answers that reproduce a shared search for ἀλήθεια, to which the highest τιμή must always be accorded.

---

[34] For the *Timaeus-Critias* as the outcome of this new agreement, cf. Regali (2012, pp. 142–147).

Works Cited

Arend, W 1933, Die typischen Scenen bei Homer, Weidmannsche Buchhandlung, Berlin.
Benardete, S 1963, 'Some Misquotations of Homer in Plato', *Phronesis* 8 (2), pp. 173–178.
Brügger, C, Stoevesandt, M & Visser, E 2010², *Zweiter Gesang (B). Band II. Faszikel 2: Kommentar*, in Bierl, A & Latacz, J (edd.). *Homers Ilias. (Basler Kommentar / BK)*, De Gruyter, Berlin-New York.
Cairns, D L 1993, *Aidōs. The Psichology and Ethics of Honour and Shame in Ancient Greek Literature*, Clarendon Press, Oxford.
Capra, A 2001, *Agon logon. Il Protagora di Platone tra eristica e commedia*, Edizioni Universitarie di Lettere Economia Diritto, Milano.
Capra, A 2014, *Plato's Four Muses. The Phaedrus and the Poetics of Philosophy*, Center of Hellenic Studies, Washington.
Clay, D 2000, *Platonic Questions. Dialogues with the Silent Philosopher*, The Pennsylvania State University Press, University Park.
Clay, D 2010, 'The Art of Platonic Quotation', in S Giombini & F Marcacci (eds.), *Il quinto secolo. Studi di filosofia antica in onore di Livio Rossetti*, Aguaplano, Passignano sul Trasimeno, pp. 329–338.
Corradi, M 2014, 'Platone al termine del *Protagora*: la profezia di una paideia possibile', in M. Vallozza (ed.), *Etica e politica: tre lezioni su Platone. Atti del Convivium Viterbiense 2013*, Università degli Studi della Tuscia, Viterbo, pp. 33–52.
Edwards, M W 1991, *Volume V: Books 17–20*, in G S Kirk (ed.), *The Iliad: a Commentary*, Cambridge University Press, Cambridge.
El Murr, D 2011, 'The *Telos* of our *Muthos*. A Note on Plato, *Plt.*, 277b6–7', *Mnemosyne* 64 (2), pp. 271–280.
Erler, M 2007, *Platon*, in H Flashar (ed.), *Grundriss der Geschichte der Philosophie. Die Philosophie der Antike*, II 2, Schwabe, Basel.
Garvie, A F 1994, *Homer. Odyssey. Books VI-VIII*, Cambridge University Press, Cambridge.
Giuliano, F M 2005, *Platone e la poesia. Teoria della composizione e prassi della ricezione*, Academia Verlag, Sankt Augustin.
Goldhill, S 1991, *The Poet's Voice. Essays on Poetics and Greek Literature*, Cambridge University Press, Cambridge
de Jong, I J F 2001, *A Narratological Commentary on the Odyssey*, Cambrige University Press, Cambridge.
Halliwell, S 2000, 'The Subjection of Muthos to Logos: Plato's Citations of the Poets', *Classical Quarterly* 50 (1), pp. 94–112.
Halliwell, S 2011, 'Antidotes and Incantations: Is There a Cure for Poetry in Plato's Republic?', in P Destrée, F-G Herrmann (eds.), *Plato and the Poets*, Brill, Leiden-Boston 2011, pp. 241–266.
Heubeck, A & Hoekstra, A 1989, *A Commentary on Homer's Odyssey. Volume II Books IX–XVI*, Clarendon Press, Oxford.
Hunter, R 2012, Plato and the Tradition of Ancient Literature. The Silent Stream, Cambridge University Press, Cambridge.
Labarbe, J 1949, *L'Homère de Platon*, Faculté de philosophie et lettres, Liège.
Lake, P G 2011, *Plato's Homeric Dialogue: Homeric Quotation, Paraphrase, and Allusion in the Republic*, Diss. Fordham, New York.

Lohse, G 1964, 'Untersuchungen über Homerzitate bei Platon', *Helikon* 4, pp. 3–28.
Lucarini, C M 2010–2011, 'Osservazioni sulla prima circolazione delle opere di Platone e sulle *Trilogiae* di Aristofane di Bisanzio (D.L. 3, 56–66)', *Hyperboreus* 16–17, pp. 346–361.
Montiglio, S 2011, *From Villain to Hero. Odysseus in Ancient Thought*, The University of Michigan Press, Ann Arbor.
Most, G 2011, 'What Ancient Quarrel between Philosophy and Poetry?', in P Destrée, F-G Herrmann, *Plato and the Poets*, Brill, Leiden-Boston 2011, pp. 1–20.
Murray, P 1996, *Plato on Poetry. Ion. Republic 376e-398b, Republic 595–608b*, Cambridge University Press, Cambridge.
Naddaff, R A 2002, *Exiling the Poets. The Production of Censorship in Plato's Republic*, The University of Chicago Press, Chicago-London.
Petraki, Z A 2011, *The Poetics of Philosophical Language. Plato, Poets and the Presocratics in the Republic*, De Gruyter, Berlin-Boston.
Reece, S 1993, *The Stranger's Welcome: Oral Theory and the Aesthetics of Homeric Hospitality Scenes*, University of Michigan Press, Ann Arbor.
Regali, M 2012, *Il poeta e il demiurgo. Teoria e prassi della produzione letteraria nel Timeo e nel Crizia di Platone*, Academia Verlag, Sankt Augustin.
Regali, M 2013, 'Il palazzo di Odisseo e la città di Socrate: la sezione sull'ἀλήθεια nel III libro della *Repubblica*', in N Notomi, L Brisson (eds.), *Dialogues on Plato's Politeia (Republic). Selected Papers from the Ninth Symposium Platonicum*, Academia Verlag, Sankt Augustin, pp. 325–329.
Richardson, N 1993, *Volume VI : Books 21–24*, in G S Kirk (ed.), *The Iliad: a Commentary*, Cambridge University Press, Cambridge.
Rutherford, R B 1992, 'Unifying the Protagoras', in A Barker & M Warner (eds.), *The Language of the Cave*, Academic Printing & Publishing, Edmonton, pp. 133–156.
Sammons, B 2009, 'Brothers in the Night: Agamemnon & Menelaus in Book 10 of the Iliad', *Classical Bulletin*, 85 (1), pp. 27–47.
Schironi, F 2005, 'Plato at Alexandria. Aristophanes, Aristarchus, and the philological tradition of a philosopher', *Classical Quarterly* 55 (2), pp. 423–434.
Segvic, H 2006, 'Homer in Plato's Protagoras', *Classical Philology* 101 (3), pp. 247–262.
Swift Riginos, A 1976, *Platonica. The Anecdotes Concerning the Life and Writings of Plato*, Brill, Leiden.
Tarán, L 1984, 'Amicus Plato sed magis amica veritas. From Plato and Aristotle to Cervantes', *Antike und Abendland* 30, pp. 93–124, now in Id., 2001, *Collected Papers (1962–1999)*, Brill, Leiden, pp. 1–46.
Yamagata, N 2012, 'Use of Homeric References in Plato and Xenophon', The Classical Quarterly 62, pp. 130–144

Fernando Muniz
Performance and Elenchos in Plato's Ion[1]

1. Goethe and Ion

Goethe considered *Ion* a pamphlet full of sarcasm[2]. The prestige of Goethe made his outraged reaction the paradigm for the reception of *Ion*. From Goethe on, *Ion* was considered either apocryphal, or an inexcusable mistake of Plato. However, Goethe identified, with insight, the presence of humor and irony in the dialogue, the "controversial thread" even though "hardly visible" in it. The recognition of an implicit motivation in the dialogue is one of the landmarks of Goethe's reading. He also provided general orientations for a contextualized presentation of *Ion*. One would understand not only what Plato was against but also what he was for. The understanding of this double aspect, according to Goethe, would be the proper way to introduce the dialogue. Assuming, again with Goethe, that we must determine what Plato says in *Ion* "seriously, joking or half-joking", I propose in this paper to follow the directions of Goethe – although only to reject his view that what Plato does in *Ion* is just an exercise in Aristophanic malice.

2. Images of poetry and the Rhapsode

The clarification requested by Goethe is no simple task. To separate the serious from the ironic, the criticism from the farce, is harder than it may have seemed to Goethe and to the tradition after him. An intricate subtext and a complex discourse interplay cause *Ion*, as Halliwell (2002, p. 41) says, to be the inverse of a doctrinal[3] dialogue. The motivation that moves the dialogue aims higher than what is established by it, and its subtext is "an attack on culturally widespread but unexamined, or insufficient substantiated, claims for the authority and wisdom of poets," (Halliwell, 2002, p. 41). The oblique character of this strat-

---

[1] This paper was also presented at Philosophy Department Colloquium Series at Northern Arizona University. For helpful comments, I thank to George Rudebusch and Julie Ann Piering.
[2] See Goethe, "Platão como partícipe da revelação cristã" in Muniz, 2011, pp.108–112.
[3] Halliwell (2002, p. 41): "In my view, briefly stated, is that Ion is the very reverse of a doctrinaire dialogue. It is a subtle Platonic exercise in the use of schematic dialectic to hint at much more that it ever states." [...] "[I]ts subtext is an attack on culturally widespread but unexamined, or insufficient substantiated, claims for the authority and wisdom of poets."

egy – employed by Plato to make the authority of rhapsodes and poets illegitimate – prevents direct access to the content of the dialogue and causes the aforementioned mistakes in reading. *Ion*, rightly understood, seems to be a milestone in the history of hermeneutics, being itself, by the complexity of its discursive game, an incitement to its own interpretation.

Another contextual fact contributes to mistakes in its interpretations. The poetry as treated in *Ion* is very different from how we understand it, or how it was understood by Goethe and the Romantics[4]. In oral-oriented ancient Greek culture, poetry was – though not exclusively – the main way of preserving the inherited tradition, and remained exercising this capital function even when writing, tied to the new emerging forms of knowledge, came to play an important role in composition and cultural transmission. In this context, the rhapsode carries an authority that covers almost all fields of knowledge. It's an encyclopedic authority, against which Plato fought a war even though not without ambiguity. If we consider these aspects, we cannot accept that the target of the *Ion* is just – as some commentators assume – to ridicule or demean a mediocre and silly rhapsode. The target of the *Ion* must be sought in the contrast established by the dialogue between two modes of communication: poetry and philosophy. I argue therefore that Plato, by attacking the communication mode of poetic performance, is deeply driven by its replacement by the Socratic *elenchos* as the ideal mean of communication for instruction and a guide to human life[5].

If the pros and cons that operate in the invisible dynamics of the dialogue are correctly identified (as Goethe suggested), it still remains for us (i) to know how the criticism of the poetic performance works, (ii) to identify which are the argumentative and dramatic means orchestrated by Plato to achieve this goal, and (iii) to show how such procedures are severally integrated into the overall strategy of the dialogue. I believe that the recognition of this strategy eliminates the sense of farce and fallacy that often come with superficial readings of the *Ion*. That feeling would be just the negative effect of the elaborate con-

---

[4] See Stern-Gillet (2004, p. 169): "Some historians of aesthetics [...] have sought to identify in it [Íon] the seeds of the post-Kantian notion of 'art' as non-technical making, and to trace to it the Romantic conception of the poet as a creative genius. Others have argued that, in the Ion, Plato has Socrates assume the existence of a techne of poetry. In this article, these claims are challenged on exegetical and philosophical grounds."

[5] I stand close to Yuni's position (2003): "Plato's dialogue Ion, which depicts a Homeric rhapsode in the middle to late fifth century, considers the manner in which poetic texts are received. Plato's irony is conspicuous; his purpose is clearly not historical. Rather he puts two modes of poetic reception in sharp contrast in order to illustrate their essential characteristics." (pp. 190–191).

struction of the dialogue.⁶ The positive reading that makes some of these aspects clearer for us reveals its ultimate goal. First, one of the distinctions we must recognize is the three images of poetry and oral poetic performance that appear superimposed on the dialogue.

The first image, the most plausible one (considering the evidence we have on the behavior of rhapsodes in ancient Greece) is built by the rhapsode himself. It highlights the empathetic nature of the performance, the emotional reaction of the audience, and the active participation of the rhapsode in the process of a performance. In 535b, for example, Ion recognizes that, especially when he sings some striking passages of the *Iliad* or the *Odyssey*, he is transported to the scenes narrated and becomes touched, with tears in his eyes, his hair bristling, his heart racing, etc. Socrates then asks if Ion realizes that the same thing is happening with the audience. Ion says he not only realizes it, but he needs to pay close attention to the spectators, and jokes: "If I do not make them cry, I will be the one to cry for having lost money." This image of the rhapsode as the one that controls the performance will be insistently ignored by Socrates throughout the dialogue. Ion is forced to identify himself with completely different images of his role, images produced by Plato out of elements taken from the tradition and the hermeneutic context of his time – even though he does so in order to highlight the traits that collaborate to disqualify the rhapsodes and the poets.

3. The Rhapsode as Hermeneutist of the Hidden Meaning

At the beginning of the dialogue, Ion arrives victorious from Epidaurus and runs into Socrates by chance. Immediately, the philosopher confesses to be envious of the rhapsodes. They would be worthy of envy because they are always beautifully dressed and familiar with the poets, especially Homer. The obvious irony in the envy assumed by Socrates encourages the reader to step on the shaky ground on which the plot of the *Ion* is built.

Flattered by the "confession" of Socrates, Ion now listens to the reasons given by Socrates to justify his envy: the rhapsodes "know by heart" (ekmanthanein) not only the verses (ta epe), but also "the thought" (dianoian) of the poet. This should be, he says, the fundamental condition for the proper performance of rhapsodes: "It is impossible for one to practice beautifully his craft if he does not 'understand' (suniemi) the meaning of the 'lines' of the poet (ta legomena)"

---

6 See also Kahn (1993, p. 378), Bloom (1987, p. 393): "Ion was caught in a sophistic argument".

(430c). With a terminology grounded in verbs of cognition (ekmanthanein, suniemi), Socrates presents a very different picture from the one more historically plausible in which Ion spontaneously recognizes himself. In this other image, he is called *hermeneus*, a translator of the thought of the poet to the audience. The ambiguity of the term *hermeneus* is the key to the dialogue. It designates, in this context, the holder of a semantic knowledge which enables one to translate from one language to another. *Language* is thus the hermeneutic paradigm that, by analogy, clarifies the nature of the skill of the rhapsode: the *object* of this technique is the meaning of the words or the intention (dianoia) of the poet. Thus the *translation* is the practical result of the activity of the rhapsode.

Surprisingly, Ion accepts this description of his craft. He states that he depends on this kind of knowledge, and adds, at 530c, that it was what gave he "more work (ergon) in my *technique*." But why would the rhapsode accept the role of a commentator on Homer? Were it not for the vanity of the rhapsode and the Platonic irony, this identification would be difficult to understand. (Actually, as we shall see, one of the tricks of the dialogue is to vary the image of the rhapsode with his own consent.) In classical Greece, as far as we know, the activity of the rhapsode is reduced to performance, and there is no room for comment or interpretive explanation. This identification accepted by Ion sounds a little off. As the oral tradition that supports the practice of the rhapsode does not make a clear distinction between composition and exhibition – every exhibition is a composition – it would not make sense to treat the oral poetic performance as a critical interpretive activity. Further in his speech, Ion – perhaps overwhelmed at being characterized as one that knows the thoughts of the poet – claims he has things to say *about* Homer that are more beautiful than what Metrodorus of Lampsacus, Stesimbrotos of Taso, among others, say. With this reference to the technical interpretation of Homer, especially the allegorical, Plato gives us a clear indication of the kind of thing he brings into play.

The word "allegory" – which literally means "to say something else" – appears after the classical period and has an interesting prehistory. At the end of the 6th century BC, some Homer admirers wanted to defend him from accusations of impiety and invented a reading procedure later called "allegory." Porphyry mentions this technique when he says that "unreasonable stories that Homer tells about the gods can be defended by appealing to his mode of expression, his *lexis*, thus ensuring that everything has been said in allegorical form."[7]

---

[7] See Ford (2002, p.70). Ford, nevertheless, associates Theagenes with rapsodes that, according to him, "also commented on the songs they performed" (p. 70). Ford uses the *Ion* as proof: "The rhapsode portrayed in Plato's Ion can recite passages from Homer on cue, but also can 'embel-

Also, according to Porphyry, that kind of defense of Homer would be very old and go back to Theagenes of Regium[8]. Theagenes and other staunch Homer supporters would be among those who tried to defend the author of the *Odyssey* from the attacks of rationalist detractors such as Xenophanes. As we can see, the famous quarrel between philosophy and poetry has deep roots.

Plutarch, at the beginning of our era, instructed us more precisely about the tactics of these hermeneutic advocates of poetry. According to him, allegory had originally another name. It was called *hyponoia* (*hidden meaning*), a term found in the fifth century in Thucydides, in Xenophon, and, what interests us, in Plato[9].

As he mentions allegory, Ion willingly inserts himself in the group of hermeneuts of *hyponoia*. Prompted by Socrates to identify his practice with the practice of a *hermeneus* – translator of the poets *dianoia* – the rhapsode accepts the role of mediator in a triadic mode of communication (poet – rhapsode – audience), assuming to have a kind of knowledge that underlies the paradigm of deciphering meaning. In order to show it clearly, Socrates asks him for an *epideixis* – a performance. When Ion says he is willing to do it, Socrates claims he does not have the time to watch it. As this refusal of *epideixis* is repeated by Socrates throughout the dialogue, readers should give the same emphasis Plato gives it. The poetic performance is excluded at the beginning by the mere dismissal of its presentation, but in the end, it is excluded by a redefinition of its meaning that will result in the disqualification of its (performative) style and the neutralization of its supposedly cognitive (poetic) content.

4. Performance and Elenchos

The translation of the term *epideixis* as performance reinforces the dialogue's ambiguous game. A *deixis* is a way of showing, of exposing; with the preposition *epi-*, the emphasis lies in its relationship with an audience – it means to show something before an audience. An *epideixis* is, therefore, a public display, a per-

---

lish' (kosmein) the poet by discoursing on his 'many fine thoughts' (polla kai kalla dianoiai, Ion 530d)." Ford took the Platonic text as an historical document that represents with accuracy the rhapsodes' activity. But, as Guthrie observes, the Ion is the only source for this conjecture. See next note.

[8] Guthrie (1975, p. 201): "Outside the Ion there is no evidence that these commentators were ever called rhapsodes, and the most reasonable conclusion is that Ion (who is otherwise unknown, and for all we know invented by Plato for his own purposes) is exceptional among rhapsodes in combining recitation with exposition."

[9] Thucydides (II. 41.4), Xenophon (Symp. iii, 6), Plato (Rep. ii, 378d).

formance. In this basic sense *epideixis* had, originally, a variety of forms. All had the same basic function, to "display or proof of an excellence or ability." At the end of the 5th and the beginning of the 4th century, the *epideixis* was still far from the kind of discourse set out by Aristotle as epideitic.[10]

On two other occasions, Socrates refuses to watch Ion's performance (530d and 536d). Moreover, when the rhapsode is asked to remember a passage from Homer, the philosopher interrupts his speech with a stern "enough!" (askei), and from then on, he himself quotes passages from Homer, relieving the rhapsode of his function. At the end of the dialogue in 541a, this tactic becomes even more evident when, not without some level of cruelty, Socrates complains that the rhapsode had not done the performance he asked for: "You have been unfair to me, Ion, promised me a performance, but did not do it." The ambiguous game of the *deixis* enables Socrates to tell Ion he didn't "show" what he had promised. In fact, Ion failed to make a "demonstration" of his discursive skills but only in the specific presentation mode of *elenchos;* he did not actually get a chance to even give it a try in a performance, as he was stopped by Socrates throughout the dialogue.

The contrast between *epideixis* and *elenchos* is a constant in the structure of the dialogue. The refusal of *epideixis* is always accompanied by a question, what allows the passage from the performance to the *elenchos*. Elenchos is distinct from *epideixis* as another public way of displaying something. Even though the dialectic is always restricted to two interlocutors, its public dimension is essential. And as the dialectical examination always takes place from what has been said and from the necessary consequences of what has been stated, the most appropriate Greek term to designate it is *apodeixis*, demonstration.

The denial of *epideixis* and the requirement of *apodeixis* are therefore complementary. It is that kind of statement that Socrates unceasingly demands from Ion instead of the performance. Consider a typical situation: Ion accepts the role of translator of Homer's *dianoia* – this implies that he must answer the question about the nature of this knowledge. The kind of question that allows the passage

---

10 Thomas, R. in Yunis (2003, pp. 173–4): "What form, or forms, does the display performance actually take? And what is the relation of oral performance to written text? We should not assume that the epideixis of the late fifth and early fourth centuries corresponded simply to Aristotle's epideictic genre of speeches (genos epideiktikon). Aristotle's definition belonged to a later, more text oriented period, when genres had crystallized and oral delivery had slightly different connotations. In the Rhetoric (3.12), he distinguished the 'agonistic style', which is for oral delivery, from the 'written style'; the agonistic style encompassed speeches for the assembly and for the courts, whereas the written style was epideictic: 'The epideictic style is most like writing for its objective is to be read' (Rhetoric 3.12.5)."

from the *epideixis* to the dialectical process of refutation is, in this case, the following: "Are you skilled only in Homer, or also in Hesiod or Archilochus?" Ion responds immediately: "I only speak well about Homer." That's the clue for the first refutation of Ion (531a–532c). "Does not Homer speak about the same things that other poets do?" Ion defends himself: "Homer actually does, but in a much better way." Socrates continues: "One who knows how to recognize what is well done, should not also acknowledge the badly done?" The conclusion is inevitable: if Ion is skilled in Homer's poetry, he must also be skilled in the poetry of other poets. Thus, Ion does not know what to say, he just "speaks beautifully and fluently about Homer, but in relation to others he stands in aporia not knowing what to say, with no interest." Socrates is then urged by Ion to explain this phenomenon. How can there be a knowledge which is irreducible in its specialty? The question points to a more appropriate response to the kind of experience provided by poetic performance.

5. The Rhapsode as Transmission Hermeneutist

At this moment, the dialogue symptomatically becomes a solemn monologue[11] (533d-534e). After stating he was unwise (532d: "You are the wise ones, the rhapsodes, actors, and all who sing poems"), Socrates exposes the wise doctrine of *enthusiasm* in an almost "enthusiastic" way. According to the doctrine, Ion is not practicing a *tekhne* when he sings Homer; he is doing it by the means of *theia dynamis* (divine power). This divine power is compared to a stone, a magnet that attracts an iron ring and transmits (entithesi) to it its own power of attraction, causing the ring to attract other rings and, in turn, transfer to them its strength, forming something like an integrated transmission circuit.

Thus a new image of the rhapsode and poet is created. Now the rhapsode is *entheos*, i.e., "he has a god within" and one link in the transmission chain emanated by divine power and therefore cannot be in possession of reason and cannot have *dianoia*. Divine intervention is understood here in an extreme manner: God expels the rhapsode mind out in order to possess the singer entirely.[12] This

---

[11] Stern-Gillet (2004 p.177): "[...] unlike most of the early dialogues, the Ion is not fully aporetic. Socrates is portrayed as being in a unusually loquacious mood, besides cross-examining his interlocutor and exposing his slow wit, he offers an alternative account of the genesis of poetry. This account, which is sandwiched between the two parts of the elenchus, is the pivot of the dialogue."
[12] Plato invents enthusiasm in this radical way. See Tigerstedt (1970), and Jacyntho Brandão in Muniz (2011).

new view on enthusiasm requires a new meaning for poetic communication and a new meaning for *hermeneus* – no longer "translator," but "transmitter." Thus, Plato invents the hermeneutics of magnetic transmission of meaning. Ion accepts gladly this new image. Called *hermeneus*, transmitter of divine messages, he claims to be touched by Socrates' words and grants. Flattered, he says: it is a divine privilege that good poets are the transmitters of messages from the gods to mortals. This allows Socrates to conclude "the rhapsodes have now turned into transmitters of the transmitters." Such successive transformation of the identity of the rhapsode is associated, as we shall see, to the proteic nature of poetry: mutability and incessant differentiation. Here are the three distinct images:

1. The performer rhapsode – aware of his resources and the effects he produce,
2. The hermeneus rhapsode – translator, commentator of Homer's dianoia or hyponoia,
3. The enthusiastic-rhapsode – possessed by gods and therefore transmitter-hermeneus, a ventriloquist's dummy of divinity.

The overlap of these images creates several problems for the interpretation of the dialogue. Some commentators[13] perceive this difficulty. Plato would have built many images of *Ions*, which could be either singer or commentator on Homer; either enthusiastic, or non-enthusiastic. The fact is that the only image the rhapsode spontaneously identified himself with was the figure of the skilled *performer*, an image he helped to build. He did not easily accept the image of a translator-commentator of Homer, nor of a transmitter in a trance. When he offers for the second time his performance to Socrates, Ion seems to finally say what he really thinks, "Had you heard me talking about Homer, you wouldn't believe I am possessed" (536d). But Socrates insists on his refusal of the performance: "Of course I want to hear it," he says, "but not before you answer a question." (536e). Again, it is a *minor question* that makes the passage from *epideixis* to *elenchos*.

---

[13] Yunis (2003, p. 191) "[...] he puts two modes of poetic reception in sharp contrast in order to illustrate their essential characteristics. When Ion performs Homer, he functions as the poet's surrogate, and his recitation of the text moves the audience to tears, terror, and amazement (Ion 535e). The audience's emotional reaction, which is pleasurable for them and wins the rhapsode admiration, enables them to experience vicariously the travails of Achilles, Odysseus, and the other characters. As if to signal the uncanny power of this performance, Plato ascribes it to divine inspiration (Ion 536b). This reaction to performed poetry was also described by the sophist Gorgias (Helen 9): "Those who hear it [poetry, poiesis] are overcome with fearful shuddering, tearful pity, and mournful yearning, and through the words [of the poetry] the soul experiences a feeling of its own over the good fortunes and ill-farings of other people and their affairs' (trans. McKirahan, adapted)".

6. Performance and hyponoia

Nowadays we know more about the bustling scene of poetry interpretation in the 5th century – when Ion mentions Metrodorus and Estesimbrotos he is referring to this scene[14]. Recent discoveries (Derveni Papyrus, 7.3–7) attest to the use of various techniques of interpretation such as analogy, etymology and allegory[15], as mentioned before. Such hermeneutic trends were built on the belief that it is impossible to understand the meaning of the poem at the time it is performed. This is said explicitly in the fragment of Derveni[16]. Techniques of poetry interpretation, such as *hyponoia*, among others, are generally critical responses to the public reception of poetry in the form of *epideixis,* oral performance, the original mode of presentation of poetry[17]. Fluidity and transparency, as conditions for poetic performance, imply the inseparability between the word and its meaning. These techniques tried to block just the emotional experience of fluidity and transparency through a minimal operation: to distinguish the word from its meaning. Once this principle is operating, a semantic depth is opened, several layers of the poet's *dianoia* are released, and what the poet "really" meant becomes a controversial subject. The authority of the poet's intention is both to legitimate certain interpretations and to refuse many others.

Prior to this, poetic performance did not allow any distance between the word and the meaning. When the gap between word and meaning was hermeneutically opened, there was no way to close it. Plato inherits and adopts this

---

14 Yunis (2003, pp. 193–4): "The evidence for these figures [Metrodorus and Estesimbrotos] and their work is meager, but it is clear that in the late fifth century they were prominent among those who began to interpret poetry in a way that had no regard for the experience of performed poetry. Metrodorus equated the Homeric gods and heroes with heavenly bodies and substances in an allegorical manner (DK 61.3–4). Stesimbrotus, a writer on contemporary fifth-century historical figures, also wrote about problems raised by the wording of Homer's text (FGrH 107 F 21–5)".
15 Laks A. and Most G. W (1997). Cf. Yunis (2003, pp. 195–6): "The best surviving extended example of poetic interpretation before Plato is the text preserved, imperfectly, on the Derveni papyrus. [...] The author interprets not Homer but a cosmogonic poem ascribed to Orpheus, distinguishes between the poem's words and its meaning".
16 Yunis (2003), pp. 196: "At one point, the Derveni author parenthetically explains the fact that the poem's true meaning has not been grasped by people who have heard the poem (20.2–3): 'It is not possible to hear and at the same time to learn the meaning of the words' ('para ou gar oion te akousai homou kai mathein ta legomena', trans. Laks and Most)."
17 See item 3.

general principle, but adapts it to his own interests.[18] Early in *Ion*, Socrates introduces the gap between word and meaning. His first tactical move is to force Ion into accepting the difference between the verses that he may know by heart and the *dianoia* of the poet. In *epideixis*, there is no way the spectators can distinguish what is said from the meaning of what is said. In this sense, for Plato, rhetoric[19] produces the same negative effect: the rhetorician shapes his compositions so that the audience is unable to consider what he says in a different way. Emotionally involved, the audience does not need to "understand" the meaning of the poetic word. Even though not everything is transparent in a poem, when there are opaque situations or expressions, they are ignored so that the poetic experience can keep its rhythm and fluency. The meaning of the performance is therefore built upon a stream of transparency, and any distance or obstacle blocks and nullifies the effect of meaning. All opacity that cannot be ignored interrupts the flow of emotional intensity – and is, potentially, *aporetic* and dialectic. The reception of the poetic performance is necessarily passive and uncritical. Under the doctrine of *enthusiasm*, the transmission of meaning must be effective through magnetic or viral ways, without any intellectual operation, with no inference and no deduction to stop its flow.

As we have seen, *epideixis* frontally opposes *apodeixis*. As a form of public display, *apodeixis* later became a model for philosophical proof. In the context we are dealing with, it had other distinguishing features. Used in preference to *epideixis*, the term *apodeixis* designates a means of display by evidence thus operating through inferences and deductions. It's by a promise to deliver an *apodeixis* that Herodotus introduces his work. In the Hippocratic treatises on the nature of man (ch 2.5.j), we read "I will show ... provide evidence ... to uncover the necessary causes" (*ego men gar apodeixo tekmeria parekho kai anankas apophaineo*). The translation of *apodeixo* here should be understood as "I will show in a decisive manner," which means to present evidence, proof and clear indications.

---

18 Yunis (2003), p. 190. "Historically, Thucydides and Plato reflect most clearly the explicit concern with hermeneutics – the systematic pursuit of understanding discourse – that arose around 400 bce in reaction to the changes then occurring in the way discourse was being composed and reaching its audience. The increased use of written texts, in addition to and alongside traditional modes of poetic and rhetorical performance, caused writers to consider how texts were and could be interpreted.4 Thucydides and Plato recognized that interpreting a written text was, in certain respects, different from interpreting orally delivered discourse. For written texts that have subtle didactic aims and require the reader to exercise critical thinking, as is the case with the texts of Thucydides and Plato, the reader's interpretive problem becomes acute. Insofar as such texts were new, so too were the corresponding problems of interpretation."
19 See Muniz (2011), chap. 3.2: A Retórica e a Potência da Aparência.

Elenchos, as a form of *apodeixis*, produces in its own way a gap between word and meaning[20]. Its characteristic feature is the question: what does *this* word mean? What does that person mean by that? (*ti legei*).[21] Transparency and opacity are opposite but complementary aspects of dialectic and *elenchos* engines. As there is always a meaning implied in everything that can be said and there is no speech that provides ultimate evidence, there is always opacity, obstacle, *aporia*. In *Apology* 21b, before the oracle of Delphi sent by God, Socrates asks "what did God mean by that?" Derived from oracular hermeneutics, *elenchos* is a model of critical reception. it seeks to analyze carefully the meaning of words, their implications, and what we can infer from them. For this reason, it is offered as a rational alternative for *epideixis* as the ideal form of ethical instruction.[22]

That said, we can see that in the poet/translator/audience triadic hermeneutic model the burden falls on the cognitive and intermediate functions of the translator. A qualitative difference articulates these three elements so that the operations of passage from one to another does take place without resistance, obstacles, opacities. Such *aporetic* limits need to be overcome, whether by the task of deciphering the thought of the poet, or in the form of communication of meaning to the audience. According to the *apodeitic* model, the poet sees, the poet conceives, the rhapsode translates and the audience receives.

In the Muse/poet/rhapsode/audience quaternary model, the differences between the links of the chain are no longer qualitative. The difference in the links is quantitative or one of degrees. From the Muse – the source – to the audience there is the same flow transparency of meaning. And even if you assume the possibility of a decrease in intensity in the passage from one link to the other, this reduction is quantitative. There is no intellectual operation of understanding of meaning that can qualify a reception as better or worse. The meaning simply passes – in the mode of affection and contagion – from one link to another in the chain with absolute fluency[23].

---

20 *Rep*, II, 378d5–8. See Lear (2006, p. 27): "hyponoia [...] is quite literally the under-thought. Indeed, it is an 'under-thought' in another sense: it enters de psyche beneath radar of critical thought".
21 *Gorg.*, 489d; *Rep.*, 331e; *Apol.*, 21b; *Symp.*, 200d; *Lach.*, 195d.
22 Yunis (2003), pp. 209–210. "When the poetic interpreters seek the meaning of a poem, they consider what the author of the poem intends; this is necessarily the absent author whom Plato finds so troublesome. In Thucydides' case, the author conspicuously calls attention to himself as author and to the 'clear view' of events that he promises the reader and makes available through critical reading. Plato, on the other hand, hides himself as author; he refrains from overtly signaling his presence or didactic purpose to the reader.
23 *Euporeia*, as can be seen at 533c, 536d.

7. Elenchos and Paradox

We can identify in *Ion* two forms of communication between gods and men: intensive magnetic communication, in which poets and rhapsodes are the transmitters, and another, dialectical communication, more connected to the philosophical practice, built from intellectual operations. Through the intensive[24] communication, the gods send "many beautiful things," but in the same action they prevent access to its primary discursive meanings; through the second, the demonstration, they make men aware of the true authors of poetry[25]: the gods. In this sense, they are opposing processes, although complementary: the demonstration proves that the intensive cannot be demonstrated. "The main evidence for this," says Socrates, "is the case of Tynnichus of Chalcis," which never produced a poem worthy of being remembered, although he composed the most beautiful poem in honor of Apollo. The most beautiful poems are taken as evidence of their divine origin. This is what Socrates says: "For a God, as I believe, demonstrates us (*endeixesthai*), leaving no doubt that these beautiful poems are neither human, nor the works of men, but divine and works of the gods." Poets would be nothing but transmitters of the gods, since they are wholly owned by them. Paradoxically, the most beautiful poem, produced by *enthusiasm*, is actually a demonstration that neutralizes it: "To provide demonstration (*endeiknymenos*) of that [poets are not the authors of the poems] God purposefully puts in the mouth of the most mediocre poet the most beautiful poem." (534d)

---

[24] French nietzscheanism, athough antiplatonic, reproduced, maybe unconsciously, Platonic distinctions. In Pourparlers (1990, p. 17), for example, Deleuze affirms "il ya deux manières de lire un livre", une manière classique et une manière intensive: "Ou bien on le considère comme une boîte qui renvoie à un dedans, et alors on va chercher ses signifiés [...] Ou bien l'autre manière : on considère un livre comme une petite machine a-signifiante ; [...] Cette autre lecture, c'est une lecture en intensité : quelque chose passe ou ne passe pas. [...] C'est du type branchement électrique. [...] Cette autre manière de lire s'oppose à la précédente, parce qu'elle rapporte immédiatement un livre au Dehors."

[25] In the *Apology*, Socrates says elenchos emerged from a Delphic oracle. Thus it is the oracle that lies at the origin of *elenchos*. And for irony is closely linked to the form of oracular speech, elenchos and irony are inseparable. When Socrates received the prophetic sentence from Chaerephon, he did not question the veracity of the oracle ("the gods are not allowed to lie"), but he found that the truth was not given in full. A hidden part of its meaning was to be discovered. Put another way, the oracle had to be put to the test. "What is the God saying by what he says? What is he pointing out?"- he wondered. Such issues are the engines of *elenchos*. The ironic aspect of *elenchos* is characterized by showing that the meaning is not always immediately revealed by what is manifested, and – exactly for that – it should be put to the test.

The answer to the question raised by Socrates ("Why does God take the reason out of these men and use them as his employees as he does with the prophets and diviners?") is crucial as it brings together and overlaps the two means of communication: the magnetically transmitted poetry is an *endeixis* from a deity, who thus gives a clear indication that there are poets who say valuable things, but it is the very divinity that speaks to us through them. From this point of view, the poem from Tynnichus of Chalcis is double-sided. On the one hand, it is an intervention of the Muse, able to mobilize an intensive communication circuit, but on the other hand, it is another type of sign – which does not reveal its hidden meaning without intellectual operations. In other words, the demonstration provided by Tynnichus's poem produces, on the surface, the magnetic effect, but in the depth, reveals the intent of the gods. Thus, the paradox exposed by the poem of Tynnichus of Chalcis – how can the best poem be produced by the worst poet? – is what motivates the research on poetry. Socrates equates this paradox with the oracle given by Apollo. What do the gods mean when they make Tynnichus sing the best poem? The best poem hides an *endeixis* in its *epideixis*: it shows that poets are not the authors and do not know what they are saying. If this interpretation is correct, we can finally explain the origin of Socrates' intriguing monologue: the doctrine of enthusiasm is the result of *elenchos*, an investigation into the enigma represented by the poem of Tynnichus.

8. Conclusion

In *Euthyphro*, 11b–c, Socrates says that Daedalus, the architect of the labyrinth, is his ancestor and he (Socrates) is part of a lineage of moving statues makers. This explains the fact that both "the statues of words" built by him as the ones built by his interlocutors always escape. The truth, in the context of *Euthyphro*, is so multiform, concealing and inaccessible as it is the marine deity, Proteus. In *Meno*, 97d–e, the *doxai* are compared again to the moving statues of Daedalus. This time, it is the *doxai* which must be chained so they do not escape and flee.

This idea is repeated at the end of *Ion*, 541e. "As Proteus, you evade from all sides and take the most varied forms" (*hosper ho Proteus pantodapos gigne strephomenos ano te kai kato*) – says Socrates to Ion. In Socratic dialogues, this extreme situation of impasse is described in the language of *plane*, of wandering. In *Ion*, it is the rhapsode and poetry that take many forms and escape as Proteus, without ever taking up a fixed form. Interestingly, the enchainment is used here, unlike the discursive enchainment suggested in *Meno*, as a metaphor for the immobilization of those who take part in a poetic performance. The chain links that form the magnetic circuit through which flows the stream of the Muse are now connected, but by the effect of *elenchos*, lack the necessary autonomy to talk about the meaning of poetry. The authority of poets and rhapsodes is reduced to mere means of transmission and thereby the meaning of the poetry is neutralized. Chained together, participants lose the "proteic" ability of poetry which allows them to escape assuming many forms. Immobilized, poets and rhapsodes no longer have the right to speak on behalf of the "many beautiful things" that are in poetry. The admirable things are restricted to the sphere of human experience, and because of this, they must be submitted to *elenchos*.

Works Cited

Deleuze, G. *Pourparlers*. Paris: Éd. de Minuit, 1990.
Dodds, E.R. *The Greeks and the Irrational*. Berkeley: University of Califórnia Press, 1951.
Ferrari, GRF Plato and Poetry. In: Kennedy, George A., ed. *The Cambridge History of Literary Criticism: I – Classical Criticism*. Cambridge: Cambridge University Press, 1989, pp. 92–148.
Ford, A. *The Origins of Criticism*. Literary Culture and Poetic Theory in Classical Greece.Princeton: PUP, 2002,
Fränkel, H. *Early Greek Poetry and Poetry: A History of Greek Epic, Lyric and Prose to the Middle of the Fifth Century*. Oxford: Basil Blackwell, 1975.
Havelock, E. A. *Preface to Plato*. Oxford: Basil Blackwell, 1963.
Halliwell, S. *The Aesthetics of Mimesis. Ancient texts and modern problems*. New Jersey: Princeton University, Press, 2002.
Laks A. and Most G. W. Studies on the Derveni Papyrus. Oxford: Clarendon Press, 1997.
Lear, J. Allegory and Myth in Plato's Republic p. 27. In Santas, G. (org.) Blackwell Guide to Plato's Republic. Oxford: Blackwell , 2006.
Murray, Penelope. Poetic Inspiration in Early Greece. *Journal of Hellenic Studies* 101 (1981), 87–100.
Muniz, Fernando. *A Potência da Aparência: um estudo sobre o prazer ea sensação nos Diálogos de Platão*. SP: Annablume, 2011.
—. (org.). A Arte do Entusiasmo. RJ: 7Letras, 2011.
Nagy, G. Early Greek Views of Poets and Poetry. In: KENNEDY, G., ed. *Cambridge History of Literary Críticism I*. Cambridge: Cambridge University Press, 1989, pp. 1–77.
—. *Pindar's Homer: The Lyric Possession of an Epic Past*. Baltimore; London: The Johns Hopkins University Press, 1990.
Ong, Walter J. *Orality and Literacy: The Technologizing of the Word*. London: Routledge, 1988.
—. *Rhetoric, Romance, and Technology: Studies in the Interaction of Expression and Culture*. Ithaca; London: Cornell University Press, 1971.
Pfeiffer, R. History of Classical Scholarship. Oxford: Clarendon Press, 1968.
Stern-Gillet, S. On (mis) interpreting Plato's *Ion*, *Phonesis*, vol. 49, n.2, 2004.
Tigerstedt, E.N. "Furor Poeticus": Poetic Inspiration in Greek Literature before Democritus and Plato. *Journal of the History of Ideas* 31 (1970), 163–78.

Verdenius, W.J. The Principles of Greek Literary Criticism. *Mnemosyne* 36 (1983), 14–59.
Yunis, H. Written Texts and the Rise of Literate Culture in Ancient Greece. Cambridge: CUP, 2003.

Mauro Tulli
Plato and the Catalogue Form in *Ion*

Socrates states in *Ion* that the master of τέχνη, in arithmetic or medicine for instance, may be a judge of both a negative and positive speech[1]. This certainly affects ποιητική (531d4–532b7). But, for the recitation or the interpretation, the text of Homer inspires Ion, while that of Hesiod and Archilocus makes him dull (532b8–c4). Socrates indicates why: Ion reacts to the text Homer and not to that of Hesiod and Archilocus because he is does not own τέχνη. In a well-defined field, τέχνη offers a model both for a positive and negative speech, it is a ὅλον that encompasses every type of opposition[2]. This is the result of research, σκέψις (532c5–d3). Ion believes it to be on the basis of knowledge, but Socrates emphasises it as an ἰδιώτης. Research, σκέψις, advances alongside common sense, τἀληθῆ λέγω (532d4–e4)[3]. This gives rise to a systematic development in terms of painting, sculpture and music, in particular the τέχνη of the flute, the τέχνη of the cithara, the τέχνη of song accompanied by the cithara and the τέχνη of rhapsodists (532e4–533c3).

A systematic development that has nourished more than a few doubts among scholars. Certainly, it is not rigorous, confusing as it does the judge with the author[4]. In a well-defined field, the judge of both a positive and negative speech is the author. The τέχνη by which the judge has the function of judge is but the indispensable τέχνη for painting, sculpture and music. But prior to the *Republic*, this is the concept of τέχνη. The necessity of establishing the boundary that separats τέχνη from τέχνη leads to a concrete flattening of the individual figures that Plato refers to. With regard to painting, sculpture and music, the author is indeed the judge or the judge is indeed the author.

In *Gorgias*, Plato immediately points out the central issue (449c9–450c2). Does rhetoric own a well-defined field, περὶ τί τῶν ὄντων τυγχάνει οὖσα? It makes little sense, however, to distinguish the judge: in *Laches*, the judge advances thanks to τέχνη, rather than following the majority's opinion (184d5–185b8). Unmasking the false, ἐξετάσαι, for medicine, politics and music, is a difficult task. In *Charmides* the judge of both a positive and negative speech is the author

---

[1] See Heitsch (1992, pp. 88–101).
[2] For the translation of ὅλον, Rijksbaron (2007, pp. 152–153).
[3] Giannantoni (2005, pp. 89–140) points out the essential role of τἀληθῆ λέγω for the portrait of Socrates in the *Apology*.
[4] See Janaway (1992, pp. 1–23): according to Capuccino (2005, pp. 171–206), the author possesses only a τέχνη, while the judge has ἐπιστήμη.

that possesses τέχνη, for the ἰατρός, the ἰατρός is the judge (169c3–171c10): the attempt to identify τέχνη for excellence in σωφροσύνη does not ensure a result, because it is sterile by means of σωφροσύνη to isolate the δίκαιον[5]. From this derives a concept of τέχνη lacking in nuance, tied to the concrete problem. And in *Ion* the concrete problem indicates τέχνη as ὅλον, that is, knowledge that encompasses every type of opposition: for the author or the judge[6]. A refusal of Hesiod and Archilocus is not plausible. Plato suggests a well-defined field both for the text of Homer and for that of Hesiod and Archilocus, a ὅλον for which the τέχνη, the ποιητική, for the author or the judge is unique[7].

A systematic development: painting, sculpture and music, τέχνη after τέχνη, with the τέχνη of the rhapsodists that Ion, who manages to re-experience the text of Homer and not that of Hesiod or Archilocus, does not own. Book II of the *Republic* offers a very similar passage (372c3–373d3): Plato suggests painting for τέχνη and, with the scheme in *Ion*, music, in particular the τέχνη of rhapsodists[8]. But a problem arises. The mode of articulation here lies in the framework of μίμησις. For painting, sculpture and music, a link with the μίμησις in *Ion* is missing[9].

The analytical solution is not convincing: Plato discovers the function of μίμησις in *Republic*, after the investigation in *Ion*. Certainly, by the end of *Ion* he arrives at πρέπον, that is, the appropriate speech for the slave and for the master, for the βουκόλος and for the κυβερνήτης, while passing over μίμησις (539d5–540d3)[10]. But the debate on μίμησις is already widespread before *Republic* and *Ion*, in the intellectual climate dominated by dramatic production. In *Thesmophoriazusae* Aristophanes' comic vein blossoms through μίμησις towards the effeminate Agathon (146–170), from μίμησις descends Damon's prompt support for music, with the canon of excellence, ἦθος (16 Lasserre)[11].

Criticism has mostly perceived an argumentative device. A link with μίμησις in *Ion* is missing because the function of μίμησις is not reconcilable with the friction between ἐνθουσιασμός and τέχνη[12]. Ion indicates the magnetic force of Homer, which comes down to us link by link from a god, and whose final victim

---

[5] On the ἰατρός in Plato, Vegetti (1995, pp. 3–48).
[6] See Cambiano (1966, pp. 284–305).
[7] In *Timaeus*, Socrates takes the role of the judge, thanks to the knowledge displayed in *Republic*: Regali (2012, pp. 43–56).
[8] On μίμησις and τέχνη in Book II of the *Republic*, Cerri (1996², pp. 35–66).
[9] See Diller (1971, pp. 201–219).
[10] Wilamowitz-Moellendorff (1969⁴, pp. 32–46) advances here with his biographical approach.
[11] On μίμησις before Plato and its echoes in Book III of the *Republic*, Tulli (2013, pp. 314–318).
[12] See Flashar (1958, pp. 36-54) and Halliwell (2002, pp. 37–71).

is the dreamy listener (533c4–535a5). But integrating the function of μίμησις into the function of ἐνθουσιασμός is not plausible. Plato underlines the condition of τέχνη for μίμησις in Book X of the *Republic* (600c3–602b11). Above and beyond *Ion*, Plato separates the τέχνη of creation, the τέχνη of usage and the τέχνη of μίμησις, leading to an ever-increasing discrepancy with the ideal[13]. Certainly, for the recitation or the interpretation of Homer the contribution of μίμησις is indispensable. The text of Homer for Book III of the *Republic* has its foundations in μίμησις, in particular in the μίμησις of the figures of the myth, Chryses or Agamemnon (392c7–393b3). The investigation of μίμησις which, on account of the fleeting material order of things, arises with the text of Homer, is similar in Book X of the *Republic*, following the pages on κλίνη, the triple bed (598d8–600c2)[14]. And Ion? He goes on, struck by ἐνθουσιασμός and lacking in τέχνη. But the result achieved in the recitation or the interpretation of Homer is positive. As far as μίμησις is concerned, a manageable field is lacking[15].

An argumentative device always occurs in relation to the overall literary setup. What argument may be put forward on the μίμησις compared to the ἦθος that Ion has? Criticism indicates in the *corpus* the importance of the individual figures that Socrates attracts in his research. Gorgias, Charmides, Protagoras or Timaeus: the plot that Plato offers depends on the individual figures[16]. The conflict between ἐνθουσιασμός and τέχνη, between blind, ineluctable adherence to the text of Homer and knowledge, fertile both for the text of Homer and that of Hesiod and Archilocus, is the code that animates Ion, which makes his ἦθος so concrete.

Painting, sculpture and music: the style gains pace, which, steady for painting, upbeat for sculpture, suffocates articulation for music: a vortex for the τέχνη of the flute, the τέχνη of the cithara and the τέχνη of rhapsodists. Studies here see a link with Democritus. The style has quickened in pace because Plato offers a resumé of an already widespread text, the *Mikros Diakosmos*[17]. Plutarch recalls for Democritus, with *De Sollertia*, a passage on song that does not omit the function of μίμησις: the τέχνη of song for the μίμησις of swan and nightingale (974a–d). With the support of Lucretius (V 1379–1435), the passage is mostly accredited to *Mikros Diakosmos* (68B154 DK)[18]. And a link with Democritus emerges in *Ion*, with unclear nuances, for ἐνθουσιασμός (68B18 DK). From this arises the

---

13 On the *Sophist* (218b6–221c5), Balansard (2001, pp. 118–139).
14 On the role of the κλίνη, Palumbo (2008, pp. 488–543).
15 See Pöhlmann (1976, pp. 191–208).
16 On the characterization of Socrates and the individual figures, Blondell (2002, pp. 1–112).
17 See Schweitzer (1932, pp. 20–31).
18 See Reinhardt (1960, pp. 114–132).

model: Plato proceeds with *Mikros Diakosmos* and stays silent in *Ion* on μίμησις, in Book II of the *Republic* on ἐνθουσιασμός, with a fertile selection. But the basis is weak. Plato in *Ion* certainly does not observe the result of ἐνθουσιασμός for painting, sculpture and music. It makes no sense to meditate in Book II of the *Republic* on the μίμησις that Plutarch claims for Democritus, on the μίμησις of swan and nightingale.

However, there is one problem: the author that Socrates indicates for painting, sculpture and music. For painting, Polygnotus, following the apprenticeship with his father, invited to Athens by Cimon, active in Delphi and, at the time of *Ion*, enjoying great fame for the psychological examination, the ἦθος, of the individual figures[19]. But, for sculpture, the systematic use of antedating emerges: before Theodorus of Samos, the εὑρητής for iron and bronze, Daedalus, celebrated in the *Iliad* for Knossos and Ariadne, for the χορός of dance (XVIII 590–606), and Epeius, praised in the *Odyssey* for the Trojan horse, deceitful wood (VIII 492–495, XI 523–532). Not Fidia, not Polykleitus, in *Protagoras* not forgotten (311a8–312b6)[20]. And finally, for music, the selection surprises: Olympus is the paradigm for the τέχνη of the flute, Socrates recalls Thamyris for the τέχνη of the cithara, in the *Iliad* mutilated for ὕβρις (II 591–602), Orpheus is the paradigm for the τέχνη of song, Socrates recalls Phemius for the τέχνη of rhapsodists, a symposium in the *Odyssey* between Telemachus and Penelope, with violence or sorrow (I 153–162, I 325–359). Why not Damon or Timotheos? A panorama mostly anchored to the text of Homer and to the time that the text of Homer suggests. By all means, Polygnotus. But for sculpture and music, the focus is on the origin, without the least consideration for the time, which does actually involve Socrates, for the classical production. The systematic use of antedating has an indisputable result: it collocates Ion among the figures of a glorious past, Daedalus and Thamyris or Epeius and Orpheus. It is not difficult to notice the shadows of the cultural climate that Ion offers[21]. Socrates underlines this. For painting, sculpture and music, the panorama, elaborated in the 4th century, established in the 5th, is dominated by archaic production, because Ion here possesses a paradigm for the recitation or the interpretation: the text of Homer.

The link with archaic production emerges immediately through form. Plato proceeds by means of parallel structures, with the repetition of more than one segment. It is a catalogue: the concept of τέχνη possesses a phonic strength and it is not difficult to notice, for painting, sculpture and music, a concrete

---

[19] For the references of Plato, Keuls (1978, pp. 88–109).
[20] See Tobin (1975, pp. 307–321).
[21] According to Murray (1996, pp. 104–112), "more than a little irony" shines here.

entry²². For painting, Plato recalls the result that he indicates for ποιητική. The sequence is very similar: ποιητικὴ γάρ πού ἐστὶν τὸ ὅλον (532c6–7) before γραφικὴ γάρ τίς ἐστι τέχνη τὸ ὅλον (532e4–5). Has Ion met a good and capable judge of painting, sculpture and music? Soon the flurry of questions on painting becomes more pressing, for painting ἤδη οὖν τινα εἶδες ὅστις (532e7), for sculpture with ἤδη τιν' εἶδες ὅστις (533a7), for music, and in particular for the τέχνη of rhapsodists, οὐδεπώποτ' εἶδες ἄνδρα ὅστις (533b7)²³. Ion states that the text of Hesiod and Archilocus induces torpor: οὔτε προσέχω τὸν νοῦν ἀδυνατῶ τε καὶ ὁτιοῦν συμβαλέσθαι λόγου ἄξιον, ἀλλ' ἀτεχνῶς νυστάζω (532b9–c1). The sequence is a paradigm for the judge that Ion certainly has not met. Plato recalls it for painting, νυστάζει τε καὶ ἀπορεῖ καὶ οὐκ ἔχει ὅτι συμβάληται (533a2–3), for sculpture with ἀπορεῖ τε καὶ νυστάζει, οὐκ ἔχων ὅτι εἴπῃ (533b4), for music, in particular for the τέχνη of rhapsodists, ἀπορεῖ καὶ οὐκ ἔχει συμβαλέσθαι (533c2–3). But for the recitation or the interpretation, the text of Homer kindles Ion: from εὐθύς τε ἐγρήγορα καὶ προσέχω τὸν νοῦν καὶ εὐπορῶ ὅτι λέγω (532c3–4) arises ἐγρήγορέν τε καὶ προσέχει τὸν νοῦν καὶ εὐπορεῖ ὅτι εἴπῃ (533a5) for painting. The model is polarized, marked by parallel structures: the crucial point here is δεινός, a term that Plato offers for painting, δεινός ἐστιν ἀποφαίνειν (532e8–9), for sculpture with δεινός ἐστιν ἐξηγεῖσθαι (533b2), for music, in particular after the mention of Olympus, with δεινός ἐστιν ἐξηγεῖσθαι (533b8)²⁴. Form pervades explanation after explanation. It is plausible at this stage to postulate a good capable judge only with regard to Polygnotus and Daedalus, Epeius and Theodorus? With emphatic force for painting, ἑνὸς μόνου (533a4): for sculpture a more balanced ἑνὸς πέρι (533b2).

But one may progress. In the frame of archaic production, the *incipit*, the exhortative λάβωμεν (532e4), recalls the invocation: for example the invocation that, in the *Iliad*, opens the catalogue of the ships (II 484–493) or that, at the end of the *Theogony* of Hesiod, makes the catalogue of women natural (1019–1022). And the *incipit* reaches us interwoven with the quantitative problem, ἁπασῶν, with the result of research, σκέψις (532c5–d3)²⁵. The catalogue indicates the style achieved through paratactic accumulation. With ἤ Plato separates the Daedalus, Epeius, Theodorus sequence (533a7–b2) and the Olympus, Thamyris, Orpheus, Phemius sequence (533b7–c1), with οὐδέ he underlines the result for music, in particular the τέχνη of the flute, the τέχνη of the cithara, the τέχνη

---

22 On the function of item, entry and rubric in a catalogue, Sammons (2010, pp. 3–22).
23 For similar questions in the text of Homer, Edwards (1980, pp. 81–105).
24 On δεινὸς ἐπαινέτης as adequate adulation of Ion, Lowenstam (1993, pp. 19–32).
25 For the quantitative problem in the invocation which opens the catalogue, Minton (1962, pp. 188–212) and De Sanctis (2006, pp. 11–33).

of song with the cithara and the τέχνη of rhapsodists (533b6–7): ἤ after ἤ, step by step, οὐδέ after οὐδέ, the discourse that Plato offers on ἐνθουσιασμός reaches us with plasitc force.

This discourse is rendered concrete by the systematic use of antedating. With the frame of ἐνθουσιασμός, Plato wishes to project Ion onto archaic production, connected with the god and the origin of inspiration. In the *Iliad*, knowledge, a knowledge of the past that the author does not own, reaches us from the abode of the god (I 1–7, II 484–493, II 760–762, XI 218–220, XIV 508–510). With the invocation, the author obtains knowledge, which is indispensable for the narration. Certainly, in the *Odyssey*, the direction is mostly similar (I 1–10, VIII 72–78, VIII 471–498, XVII 518–521). A knowledge that flows through invocation, which is a concrete favour by the god.

It is not difficult, however, to observe a sign of a rather important dynamic. Phemius is guided by νόος (I 345–349), Demodocus by θυμός (VIII 40–45). The implacable massacre descends on the μνηστῆρες and does not involve Phemius who in the song, even if constrained by the μνηστῆρες, is αὐτοδίδακτος: he possesses knowledge and does not neglect research (XXII 344–353)[26]. In the proem to the *Theogony*, the knowledge arrives unexpectedly to Hesiod (22–34). But it nevertheless arises from a selection, because the shepherd destined for song is not common on the barren slopes of Helicon. Criticism has perceived here an 'I' that, in the proem to the *Erga*, indicates in Zeus not just knowledge, but an ally for the rebuilding of a pact on the basis of δίκη (1–10)[27]. Tradition no longer has any sense. Soon, with the πανάριστος, the conscience of Hesiod goes beyond Zeus (293–297)[28]. But Parmenides brings it to the zenith. He transfers νόος, Phemius, and θυμός, Demodocus, to the proem, and indeed with the image of the ὁδός, collocates the πανάριστος of Hesiod there (28B1, 1–5 DK)[29]. In the proem, which in the code of archaic production contained the invocation. Parmenides passes beyond the shadows guided by θυμός: tradition offers the code to ensheath in solemn elegance the knowledge gained through research[30].

With the frame of ἐνθουσιασμός, Plato conceals a slow development. Ion indicates the magnetic force of Homer, which reaches down link by link from the god and eventually lights on the dreamy listener as victim. Plato certainly recalls the condition of the *Iliad*, through the invocation of the god for song, and the condition of the *Odyssey*, through the inspiration that the author without merit

---

[26] On the peculiar combination with the support of Zeus, Danek (1998, pp. 435–438).
[27] See Thalmann (1984, pp. 33–77).
[28] See Arrighetti (2006, pp. 3–27).
[29] For the relevance of this choice, Giuliano (2005, pp. 137–218).
[30] See Tulli (2000, pp. 65–81).

asks for. Daedalus and Thamyris or Epeius and Orpheus: a glorious past that Ion suggests because he is lacking in τέχνη and in thrall to the god. And the glorious past emerges through the form for excellence of archaic production: the catalogue. Phemius, αὐτοδίδακτος, is not reconcilable with the frame of ἐνθουσιασμός. Plato collocates Ion before Hesiod: Socrates is the πανάριστος of Hesiod, whose purpose is philosophy.

Works Cited

Arrighetti, G 2006, *Poesia, poetiche e storia nella riflessione dei Greci*, Giardini, Pisa.
Balansard, A 2001, *Technè dans les dialogues de Platon*, Academia Verlag, Sankt Augustin.
Blondell, R 2002, *The Play of Character in Plato's Dialogues*, CUP, Cambridge.
Cambiano, G 1966, 'Dialettica, medicina, retorica nel *Fedro* platonico', *Rivista di Filosofia* 57, pp. 284–305.
Capuccino, C 2005, *Filosofi e rapsodi*, CLUEB, Bologna.
Cerri, G 1996[2], *Platone sociologo della comunicazione*, Argo, Lecce.
Danek, G 1998, *Epos und Zitat*, Verlag der Österreichischen Akademie der Wissenschaften, Wien.
De Sanctis, D 2006, Tecnica compositiva nel *Catalogo* di Esiodo, in G Arrighetti & M Tulli (eds), *Esegesi letteraria e riflessione sulla lingua nella cultura greca*, Giardini, Pisa, pp. 11–33.
Diller, H 1971, 'Probleme des platonischen *Ion*', *Hermes* 83 (1955), pp. 171–187, now in *Kleine Schriften zur antiken Literatur*, Beck, München, pp. 201–219.
Edwards, M W 1980, 'The Structure of Homeric Catalogues', *Transactions of the American Philological Association* 110, pp. 81–105.
Flashar, H 1958, *Der Dialog Ion als Zeugnis platonischer Philosophie*, Akademie-Verlag, Berlin.
Giannantoni, G 2005, *Dialogo socratico e nascita della dialettica nella filosofia di Platone*, Bibliopolis, Napoli.
Giuliano, F M 2005, *Platone e la poesia*, Academia Verlag, Sankt Augustin.
Halliwell, S 2002, *The Aesthetics of Mimesis*, Princeton University Press, Princeton-Oxford.
Heitsch, E 1992, 'Die Argumentationsstruktur im *Ion*', *Rheinisches Museum* n. F. 133 (1990), pp. 243–259, now in *Wege zu Platon*, Vandenhoeck & Ruprecht, Göttingen, pp. 88–101.
Janaway, C 1992, 'Craft and Fineness in Plato's *Ion*', *Oxford Studies in Ancient Philosophy* 10, pp. 1–23.
Keuls, E C 1978, *Plato and Greek Painting*, Brill, Leiden.
Lowenstam, S 1993, 'Is Literary Criticism an Illegitimate Discipline? A Fallacious Argument in Plato's *Ion*', *Ramus* 22, pp. 19–32.
Minton, W W 1962, 'Invocation and Catalogue in Hesiod and Homer', *Transactions of the American Philological Association* 93, pp. 188–212.
Murray, P 1996, *Plato on Poetry*, CUP, Cambridge.
Palumbo, L 2008, *Mimesis*, Loffredo, Napoli.
Pöhlmann, E 1976, 'Enthusiasmus und Mimesis: zum platonischen *Ion*', *Gymnasium* 83, pp. 191–208.

Regali, M 2012, *Il poeta e il demiurgo*, Academia Verlag, Sankt Augustin.
Reinhardt, K 1960, 'Hekataios von Abdera und Demokrit', *Hermes* 47 (1912), pp. 492–513, now in *Vermächtnis der Antike*, Vandenhoeck & Ruprecht, Göttingen, pp. 114–132.
Rijksbaron, A 2007, *Plato, Ion*, Brill, Leiden-Boston.
Sammons, B 2010, *The Art and Rhetoric of the Homeric Catalogue*, OUP, Oxford.
Schweitzer, B 1932, *Xenokrates von Athen*, Niemeyer, Halle.
Thalmann, W G 1984, *Conventions of Form and Thought in Early Greek Epic Poetry*, Johns Hopkins University Press, Baltimore-London.
Tobin, R 1975, 'The Canon of Polycleitos', *American Journal of Archeology* 79, pp. 307–321.
Tulli, M 2000, Esiodo nella memoria di Parmenide, in G Arrighetti & M Tulli (eds), *Letteratura e riflessione sulla letteratura nella cultura classica*, Giardini, Pisa, pp. 65–81.
Tulli, M 2013, 'La μίμησις nel III libro della *Repubblica*: il rapporto di Platone con la tradizione', in N Notomi & L Brisson (eds), *Dialogues on Plato's Politeia*, Academia Verlag, Sankt Augustin, pp. 314–318.
Vegetti, M 1995, *La medicina in Platone*, Cardo, Venezia.
von Wilamowitz-Moellendorff, U 1969⁴, *Platon*, II, Weidmann, Dublin-Zürich.

Fernando Santoro[1]
Orphic Aristophanes at Plato's Symposium

Plato is a philosopher, so he is not ashamed of abstracting from private facts that which he believes as the universal truth. And Plato is a dramatic poet, in a way that, whether true or false, facts must consist of a wholeness of image and story. He is, therefore, a tributary author of Apollo and Dionysus. These two classical axioms guide our readings of the characters in Plato's dialogues. And each character is a private entrance to the understanding of his philosophical theater.

In this study, we are going to explore one of his most instigating, and therefore, controversial characters: Aristophanes, the comedy writer. It is about a central character at the *Symposium*, whose shadow also reaches other dialogues, either through clear references to his name and works, as in the Apology[2], or in less clear references imitating or pointing to his verses or poetic procedures, as in the delusional etymology of Cratylus[3].

Aristophanes is an important historical character of the 5th century Athenian culture, whose works were fairly well conveyed to us (eleven full comedies, from about forty he wrote). However, the character constructed by Plato in the dialogues not only has a real documented reference, namely that of a writer, it provides us textually with a style of speech, and also a discursive genre. Apart from the possibility of comparing the speech and actions of the character built by Plato with the works of the historic personality, this fact opens the possibility of constructing a particular reading of Plato's *Symposium* as a dialogue which not only depicts some 5th BC century Athenian high culture celebrities having a dialogue and making compliments to the god Eros, but also brings into play a friendly and yet loving dispute between the representatives of literary genres.

It is not surprising to readers and interpreters of the *Symposium* that a competition of speeches in it is composed of speeches which are not only the expression of their authors, but also representatives of discursive genres: the epic mythology, the medical art, Gorgias' rhetoric, the disproving dialectics, the initiatory mystique, comedy, tragedy, among many other genres which with interested eyes it can be interpreted. Not always is the correspondence between the discursive genre and the character univocal. In his speech, Socrates, for example, tries many genres like the fable, the dialectic disproof, the narrative mime... Nor

---
1 English translation by Collin Bowles, revised by Nicholas Riegel. I gratefully acknowledge the financial assistance of Capes (Brazil)/Cofecub (France) for this research.
2 18d. Cf. Santoro, F. "La citation des *Nuées* dans *l'Apologie de Socrate* de Platon" (2013).
3 Cf. Buarque, L. (2011).

does the speech made by the Platonic character necessarily correspond to the discursive genre in which the real character composes; so, the speech by Agathon, the acclaimed author of tragedy, is, by no means, a tragic speech, rather a perfectly structured encomium according to Gorgias' stylistic. Therefore, even if it is well established that the *Symposium* is an erotic duel of discursive genres, the interpretative contention among commentators for the identification of said genres and their implications inside the general sense of the dialogue is still interesting and even controversial.

With Aristophanes, we believe his Platonic character also has a complex construction which evades the univocity expected by the most current reading, according to which it is a character with comic gestures and speech.[4] Well, what else could one expect from a comedy writer? For though there is a clear comic character in Aristophanes' gestures and speech in the Symposium, I believe it is also possible to extract from there elements of other discursive genres and to investigate the Platonic proposals when constructing and giving life to that character in the dialogic theater of the *Symposium*. I still believe it to be a mistake, that not even the great Aristotle shirked from[5], to believe that the works necessarily mimic their author and that, therefore, the composition of comedies must born from a man of comic character. If so, and we deduce the author's character through the genre of the works, we probably would not get to the famous conclusion to which Socrates induces the resistant guests at the end of the Symposium: that the same author is able to write comedies and tragedies[6]. That conclusion is shown with the omission of the Socratic arguments and adds to the long list of Platonic enigmas, always with varied interpretations. For that enigma, I still cannot find anything better than the famous answer by Wilamowitz, that a so-called dramatic author is a self-reference to Plato himself and his dialectic art[7]. So we prefer to free the works from this interpretation

---

4 Cf. Wilamowitz-Moellendorff (1959), Platon: sein Leben und seine Werke, pp.307–308; Heinhardt (1989²) (2007 French translation, p.70); Strauss (2001) p.119.
5 *Poetics*, 48b.
6 Agathon, Aristophanes and Socrates are the only ones who still resist sleep and spend the night talking. In the morning Aristodemus finds them arguing whether the same man, through poetry, is able to write a comedy and a tragedy. Socrates makes them admit it so.
7 "For those oppositions, the artist who put the pictures side by side, mixed all their colors; Phaedo is laid out in completely dark tones, the symposium shines in colorful lights. But Socrates is the winner in both, winner over the others, over the world, because he won himself, raised as a hero by the power of Plato's poetry. Tragedy and comedy are complementary: only when we read them as such, we can reach the full understanding, the full pleasure." Wilamowitz-Moellendorff (1959), pp.307–308.

through the mimesis of the author's character and understand that the reasons can have their own course.

But let us not be fooled by another ruse of fiction: it is not about identifying Aristophanes' personality, the comedy author, with his genre of poetic writing or with any of his other characters. We are neither in the backstage of the theater of Athens nor examining one of Aristophanes' plays, but we are in the theatrical scene of a Platonic dialogue. Now, this might as well build Aristophanes's character in the *Symposium* as Aristophanes himself constructs a comic character. To some extent Plato does it, as if meeting the common expectations of seeing a comic comedy writer. However, to reiterate, we believe the Platonic character is more complex and other traits beyond comedy can be glimpsed in the *Symposium's* Aristophanes. We are not then going to worry so much about what is comic, which has already been very much addressed by Platonizing readers; rather, we are going to search for other discursive genres which are also represented by this Aristophanes.

A particularly interesting reading, in this line of investigation, is the one proposed by Lucas Soares (2002) in an article called "La concepción del poeta tragicômico en el Banquete de Platon". For him, the Platonic Aristophanes is the one who meets the aforementioned enigma of the poet able to write tragedy and comedy. Soares lists and describes the elements of comedy and tragedy comprising the character's speech like this. They are, on the tragic side: 1. The resource to mythology; 2. The hubris of ancient human nature; 3. Human beings as the gods' toys; 4. Eros' tragic conception as an attempt to restore the lost archaic integrity; 5. The intervention of practical reason in the erotic quest process; 6. The piety/impiety towards the gods. From the comic side he lists: 1. The physical movements of ancient human nature; 2. The conferences of the gods in the form of parody; 3. Pederasts and politics; 4. The reference to the relationship between Pausanias and Agathon and their effeminate characters.

Soares' reading points out the complex composition of the character's gestures and speech, with elements which can be attributed to comic and tragic genres. I would dispute whether it results in a tragicomic text or effect and whether it meets the suggestion of the poet idealized by Socrates. If Aristophanes is in the *Symposium* a character of tragic and comic traits, Plato is still the most dramatic poet responsible for the composition. In this sense we can include everything he does as a dramatic character in his characterization: his gestural interventions, such as hiccups, laughter and sneezes, his comments between the lines of the other guests and his encomium speech to Eros. On the other hand, if we do not see Aristophanes in his wholeness as a character, but only as a character characterized as a poet—meaning that at the moment he delivers his speech, the comic and tragic traits are sewn in the quilt of another discursive genre, a kind of cosmogonic narrative, a myth followed by a performance, analogous to the myth of Prometheus and Pandora, which Plato puts in the mouth of another of his characters: Protagoras, in the homonymous dialogue[8]—tragicomedy would then be deprived of many of its properly theatrical elements, even if the narrative is full of dramatic elements, such as the scenes of insurrection of men, conference of gods, punishment and reparation.

I would like to propose a different reading of the genre of speech which is represented by Aristophanes, which would also be able to include both the comic and tragic elements which are present in his encomium to Eros. The reading I suggest is previously announced by Socrates (177d-e), when the proposal made by Phaedrus and endorsed by Eryximachus is accepted by himself and the others:

> (1) "No one, Eryximachus", said Socrates, "will vote against you: I do not see how I could myself decline, when I set up to understand nothing but love-matters; nor could Agathon and Pausanias either, nor yet Aristophanes, who divides his time between Dionysus and Aphrodite; nor could any other of the persons I see before me.[9]
>
> Οὐδείς σοι, ὦ Ἐρυξίμαχε, φάναι τὸν Σωκράτη, ἐναντία ψηφιεῖται. οὔτε γὰρ ἄν που ἐγὼ ἀποφήσαιμι, ὃς οὐδέν φημι ἄλλο ἐπίστασθαι ἢ τὰ ἐρωτικά, οὔτε που Ἀγάθων καὶ Παυσανίας, οὐδὲ μὴν Ἀριστοφάνης, ᾧ περὶ Διόνυσον καὶ Ἀφροδίτην πᾶσα ἡ διατριβή, οὐδὲ ἄλλος οὐδεὶς τουτωνὶ ὧν ἐγὼ ὁρῶ.

Aristophanes is introduced as somebody whose vital occupation (*diatribe*) is fully dedicated around Dionysus and Aphrodite. In general it is only believed that Aristophanes is a man busy with theater and lust. With theater he surely is, but, apart from this mention, I do not know of any historic information that the comic writer has been a lustful man. I allow myself another more literal reading: Aristophanes deals with issues involving the gods Dionysus and Aphrodite, from the effective theological point of view. From the Greek theological point of view, it is obviously a question for the *theológoi*, which means, for the poets. He shows his theological perspective from the beginning of his speech, when he recriminates men for "not being sensitive to Eros' power, since if they had noticed it, they would build him the largest temples and altars and would make the greatest sacrifices".[10]

In this perspective I would like to read Aristophanes' speech as a speech coming from an Orphic-Dionysian background of wisdom. From said background

---

8 320c – 322e.
9 Translated by Lamb, W. R. M. (1925).
10 189c. ἐμοὶ γὰρ δοκοῦσιν ἄνθρωποι παντάπασι τὴν τοῦ ἔρωτος δύναμιν οὐκ ᾐσθῆσθαι, ἐπεὶ αἰσθανόμενοί γε μέγιστ' ἂν αὐτοῦ ἱερὰ κατασκευάσαι καὶ βωμούς, καὶ θυσίας ἂν ποιεῖν μεγίστας.

theatrical spectacles such as comedy and tragedy also originated, and for this reason comic and tragic elements are also found in his speech. This is not because he is innovating in the elaboration of a tragicomic genre, but because he is talking about from a common origin of many Dionysian manifestations and speeches. Aristophanes is one of the Dionysian voices speaking in Plato's *Symposium*.

Let us recollect Aristophanes' speech, firstly paying attention to the cosmogonic myth narrating the origin of human race. The myth told by Aristophanes is probably an origin of what will be amongst us a widespread conception of love: the attraction for the "soul mate". It is also the first image of the Platonic conception of desire and pleasure, as repletion of a lack, an idea which will be resumed in Socrates' speech[11] and also in the *Philebus*, which is about pleasures[12]. Aristophanes announces that to compliment Eros' powers it is necessary "to learn about human nature and its conditions". His myth narrates a genealogy of human race, in a structure very similar to myths of origin, such as Prometheus', which we have already noticed, or even Adam (to not only stay in the Greek tradition) – essentially tragic myths. First, men lived in an idyllic, powerful and self-sufficient prime condition; they were twice as strong and fast because they were twice as we are today: four legs, four arms, two faces on a head, four ears, two genitals... Their shape was spherical and made a full whole – *holon*. There were not two genders, but three: male, the son of the Sun; female, the son of the Earth; and the androgynous, the son of the Moon, with male and female features. As they were very powerful and self-sufficient, they arrogantly turned against the gods. This is another tragic element, as noted by Soares: hubris. Zeus punishes them by breaking them in two. To these amputations, Diotima's speech will make a reference in Socrates' speech. The description of ball men and the sewing surgery performed by Zeus and Apollo is completely achieved with figures and vocabulary of comedy, including somersaults, one-legged jumps, skin twitches, patched belly buttons, folds and rivets. After the surgery finished, the number of men doubled, but their power weakened to half and, the main thing, they were not self-sufficient anymore,

---

11 Socrates puts in Diotima's mouth a correction to Aristophanes' idea: The desire is not to complete a lack if that fullness is not beautiful. Making a clear reference to the image of the amputations that appear in the speech of the comedy writer (205e)Καὶ λέγεται μέν γέ τις, ἔφη, λόγος, ὡς οἳ ἂν τὸ ἥμισυἑαυτῶν ζητῶσιν, οὗτοι ἐρῶσιν· ὁ δ' ἐμὸς λόγος οὔτε ἡμίσεός φησιν εἶναι τὸν ἔρωτα οὔτε ὅλου, ἐὰν μὴ τυγχάνῃ γέ που, ὦ ἑταῖρε, ἀγαθὸν ὄν, ἐπεὶ αὐτῶν γε καὶ πόδας καὶ χεῖρας ἐθέλουσιν ἀποτέμνεσθαι οἱ ἄνθρωποι, ἐὰν αὐτοῖς δοκῇ τὰ ἑαυτῶν πονηρὰ εἶναι. Aristophanes still tries a replica (212c) but he is interrupted by the untimely entry of Alcibiades.

12 Cf. the *"Catártica"* chapter in Santoro (2007).

winning the current human condition of needy beings, who need to run after their satisfaction; they are not full wholes anymore, but incomplete beings. Breaking in two, there were only two genders left: male and female, because the androgynous also dissolved in both. Scattered halves, they ran to connect with their matches and when united they did not leave each other, and succumbed, inseparable, to inertia and starvation. Again the gods had to take action: so they changed the genitals of humans to the front, making the union of male and female genders generate the offspring, and, especially, making that union generate enjoyment and satisfaction in a way which allows the lovers to separate and to carry out the other errands of life. The Aristophanic wisdom is: pleasure is not what attracts lovers, but something which allows them, when fulfilled, to separate! Pleasure is not an end as an aim, a teleological end of a loving activity. Pleasure is an end as extreme, which consummates and ends the movement of desire; it is the eschatological end of desire. So that enjoyment is not what determines love, but only what allows the calm of that flame and thus seasons the moods of human nature. Love bearing enjoyment is what heals the indigence of prime division, at the same time allowing a harmonious life to each human soul mate. For this reason, Aristophanes' Eros is the most philanthropist god[13], the same feature usually attributed by the Greek to Prometheus. This loving union gets a very significant name from the poet. He calls it *sýmbolon*. The "symbol" is originally a medal-shaped pottery piece which friends break in two, as a sign of friendship and hospitality. Each friend has what complements the other. Aristophanes mentions the two values of symbolic love: *philia* – mutual friendship, and *oikeiotés* – intimacy, being at ease at home. So he provides the interpretative key of his mythical narrative, which will constitute his definition of love: "Therefore, Eros is the name of the desire and search for the whole." This sentence concentrates the nucleus of what we call Dionysian wisdom: the eternal coming back – the breaking of parts as a lack, the quest for the whole, the cathartic resolution in the whole – and that we will find in other poetical and even philosophical manifestations about Dionysus. To find it, let us examine the relationship between the cosmogonic myth of the origin of men delivered by Aristophanes of the *Symposium* and other cosmogonic myths. First let us compare it with the cosmogonic myth delivered by the choir of the Birds by Aristophanes, who is in this case the direct author and not Plato's character. There we will see more similarity of images than content, but from this comparison we will be able to find in Orphic cosmogonies and anthropogonies the model of speech which probably inspired the composition of the myth of the *Symposium*. Then we

---

13 189d ἔστι γὰρ θεῶν φιλανθρωπότατος.

will compare it to Orphic versions of the birth of Dionysus Zagreus, which are also myths about the origin of the human race and which seem to be the main inspiration of Platonic texts. Through this inspiration we will understand that Aristophanes is one of the many voices of Dionysus we find in the dialogue, the voice which starts the initiation rite in the *Symposium*, a rite which will continue in the voices of Diotima and Alcibiades – characters we will not discuss now.

As we already noted, Aristophanes is Plato's character who is subject to comparison with texts written by the historic personality. So that, for an understanding of the meaning of the character and the way Plato constructs it, the first clear step is to search for analoguous elements in the texts written by Aristophanes which are a legacy to us.

There is a passage in the choir of the comedy *The Birds*, which is in many aspects similar to the speech of the character of the *Symposium*. No one can help suspecting it guided Plato in the composition of the speech attributed to him. It is about a cosmogony, under the perspective of the birds, in which the prime generating element is an egg laid by the night and in which all gods are winged. Aristophanes explores the oviparous image in a comic manner, but the expression of cosmogonies with the images of an egg and winged gods, particularly love, is not new. In the poems by Empedocles[14] we find a criticism of that type of figuration of the gods, which supposes it is part of a traditional lineage of theogonies, although different from the Hesiodic lineage. Consider the choir of the comedy:

(2) The Birds 693–702

> At the beginning there was only Chaos, Night, dark Erebus, and deep Tartarus. Earth, the air and heaven had no existence. Firstly, black-winged Night laid a germless egg in the bosom of the infinite deeps of Erebus, and from this, after the revolution of long ages, sprang the graceful Eros with his glittering golden wings, swift as the whirlwinds of the tempest. He mated in deep Tartarus with dark Chaos, winged like himself and thus hatched forth our race, which was the first to see the light. That of the Immortals did not exist until Eros had brought together all the ingredients of the world, and from their marriage Heaven, Ocean, Earth and the imperishable race of blessed gods sprang into being. Thus our origin is very much older than that of the dwellers in Olympus. We are the offspring of Eros; there are a thousand proofs to show it. We have wings and we lend assistance to lovers. [15]

> Χάος ἦν καὶ Νὺξ Ἔρεβός τε μέλαν πρῶτον καὶ Τάρταρος εὐρύς·
> γῆ δ' οὐδ' ἀὴρ οὐδ' οὐρανὸς ἦν. Ἐρέβους δ' ἐν ἀπείροσι κόλποις
> 695 τίκτει πρώτιστον ὑπηνέμιον Νὺξ ἡ μελανόπτερος ᾠόν,

---

14 Cf. frag. 134 DK.
15 Anonym Transl. by Athenian Society, London (1912).

> ἐξ οὗ περιτελλομέναις ὥραις ἔβλαστεν Ἔρως ὁ ποθεινός,
> στίλβων νῶτον πτερύγοιν χρυσαῖν, εἰκὼς ἀνεμώκεσι δίναις.
> Οὗτος δὲ Χάει πτερόεντι μιγεὶς νύχιος κατὰ Τάρταρον εὐρὺν
> ἐνεόττευσεν γένος ἡμέτερον, καὶ πρῶτον ἀνήγαγεν εἰς φῶς.
> 700 Πρότερον δ' οὐκ ἦν γένος ἀθανάτων, πρὶν Ἔρως ξυνέμειξεν ἅπαντα·
> ξυμμειγνυμένων δ' ἑτέρων ἑτέροις γένετ' οὐρανὸς ὠκεανός τε
> καὶ γῆ πάντων τε θεῶν μακάρων γένος ἄφθιτον. Ὅδε μέν ἐσμεν
> πολὺ πρεσβύτατοι πάντων μακάρων ἡμεῖς. Ὡς δ' ἐσμὲν Ἔρωτος
> πολλοῖς δῆλον· πετόμεσθά <τε> γὰρ καὶ τοῖσιν ἐρῶσι σύνεσμεν

As opposed to the myth told in the *Symposium*, it is not about the origin of men (anthropogony) but the origin of gods from the primeval deities (theogony). However, we already have some important elements of the characterization of a Dionysian wisdom which also appears in the myth of the *Symposium*. First, the image of a primeval sphere, the cosmic egg similar to the first spherical and whole men. These men, in the myth of the *Symposium*, are direct children of cosmic entities: the sun, the earth and the moon; therefore they are round as them. The sphere and the cycle are recurrent images from the Dionysian wisdom. Besides, we have the presence of Eros with his power responsible for mixing all things and intertwining lovers. This model of cosmogonic theogony dates back to the Orphic theogonies such as Protogonos' (6th century B.C.), and the original deity which appears in the Orphic Hymns, with the same images of a primeval egg and winged powers. Let us see the hymn to Protogonos (a Hellenistic version from 3rd and 4th centuries).

(3) Protogonos

> O Mighty first-begotten [Protogonos], hear my pray'r, two-fold, egg-born, and wand'ring thro' the air, Bull-roarer, glorying in thy golden wings, from whom the race of Gods and mortals springs. Ericapæus [Erikapaios], celebrated pow'r, ineffable, occult, all shining flow'r. From eyes obscure thou wip'st the gloom of night, all-spreading splendour, pure and holy light hence Phanes call'd, the glory of the sky, on waving pinions thro' the world you fly. Priapus, dark-ey'd splendour, thee I sing, genial, all-prudent, ever-blessed king, with joyful aspect on our rights divine and holy sacrifice propitious shine. [16]

> Πρωτόγονον καλέω διφυῆ, μέγαν, αἰθερόπλαγκτον,
> ὠιογενῆ, χρυσέαισιν ἀγαλλόμενον πτερύγεσσι,
> ταυροβόαν, γένεσιν μακάρων θνητῶν τ' ἀνθρώπων,
> σπέρμα πολύμνηστον, πολυόργιον, Ἠρικεπαῖον,
> ἄρρητον, κρύφιον ῥοιζήτορα, παμφαὲς ἔρνος,
> ὅσσων ὃς σκοτόεσσαν ἀπημαύρωσας ὀμίχλην

---

[16] The Hymns of Orpheus. Translated by Taylor, Thomas (1792). University of Pennsylvania Press, 1999. (current edition)

πάντη δινηθεὶς πτερύγων ῥιπαῖς κατὰ κόσμον
λαμπρὸν ἄγων φάος ἁγνόν, ἀφ' οὗ σε Φάνητα κικλήσκω
ἠδὲ Πρίηπον ἄνακτα καὶ Ἀνταύγην ἑλίκωπον.
ἀλλά, μάκαρ, πολύμητι, πολύσπορε, βαῖνε γεγηθώς
ἐς τελετὴν ἁγίαν πολυποίκιλον ὀργιοφάνταις.

The construction of the cosmogonic myth of *The Birds* by Aristophanes follows the cosmogony present in Orphic myths in a form of parody, making use of images, cosmic entities and the Dionysian wisdom background of a happiness in the originating spherical whole. We can assume that to mimic Aristophanes, Plato had not chosen to reproduce any text by the comedy writer, but had used the same method to comically parody the same lineage of sources. He did not copy Aristophanes, but as a good playwright, he put himself in his own perspective of poetic composition. So, we believe that the anthropogonic myth told by the *Symposium*'s Aristophanes is directly built from Orphic anthropogonic myths, as well as the cosmogonic myth of the Birds is made from its cosmogonic myths.

The Orphic anthropogonic myth par excellence is Dionysus' dismemberment myth. Dionysus is the cosmic link between immortal deities and mortal beings. Dionysus is Life which renews in the cycles of nature: the seasons, the alternation of generations. In it death is not the end but the return to the starting point to a new beginning. This is the myth of Dionysus' dismemberment and resurrection which is latent in the myth of humans born from cutting in two halves, told by Aristophanes in the *Symposium*, with the same magic plot and its significant elements, even sometimes remixed. We do not have all the elements and the plot of the myth of death and resurrection of Dionysus Zagreus together in the same source. The text of the original theogony has not come intact to us, only traces in references and quotations. The most complete passage we found in Protrepticus by Clement of Alexandria, a Christian apologist from the 2nd – 3rd century who mentions it to exemplify the pagan savagery and punctuates the narrative with comments of censorship and ridicule.[17] It is conjectured that the contents to which Clement had access, called *Initiation* (*Telete*), a poem attributed to Orpheus, date back to a tradition which was possibly put in text by Onomacritus, a counselor of Pisistratus, in the 6th century B.C. Let us see the text by Clement:

---

17 For an analysis of the references to Dionysus in Clement of Alexandria's Protrepticus, cf. Jourdan (2006).

The mysteries of Dionysus are wholly inhuman[18]; for while still a child, and the Curetes danced around [his cradle] clashing their weapons, and the Titans having come upon them by stealth, and having beguiled him with childish toys, these very Titans tore him limb from limb when but a child, as the bard of this mystery, the Thracian Orpheus, says: – "Cone, and spinning-top, and, and fair golden apples from the clear-toned Hesperides." This was a common story among the infant gods: "Now the lofty Ida resounds with tinklings, that the boy may cry in safety with infant mouth. Some strike their shields with stakes, some beat their empty helmets. This is the employment of the Curetes, this of the Corybantes. The matter was concealed, and imitations of the ancient deed remain; the attendant goddesses shake instruments of brass, and hoarse hides. Instead of helmets they strike cymbals, and drums instead of shields; the flute gives Phrygian strains, as it gave before." And the useless symbols of this mystic rite it will not be useless to exhibit for condemnation. These are dice, ball, hoop, apples, top, looking-glass, tuft of wool. Athena, to resume our account, having abstracted the heart of Dionysus, was called Pallas, from the vibrating of the heart; and the Titans who had torn him limb from limb, setting a caldron on a tripod, and throwing into it the members of Dionysus, first boiled them down, and then fixing them on spits, "held them over the fire." But Zeus having appeared, since he was a god, having speedily perceived the savour of the pieces of flesh that were being cooked, —that savour which your gods agree to have assigned to them as their perquisite, assails the Titans with his thunderbolt, and consigns the members of Dionysus to his son Apollo to be interred.[19]

II, 17, 2–18, 1 (Kern, fr. 35) Τὰ γὰρ Διονύσου μυστήρια τέλεον ἀπάνθρωπα• ὃν εἰσέτι παῖδα ὄντα ἐνόπλῳ κινήσει περιχορευόντων Κουρήτων, δόλῳ δὲ ὑποδύντων Τιτάνων, ἀπατήσαντες παιδαριώδεσιν ἀθύρμασιν, οὗτοι δὴ οἱ Τιτᾶνες διέσπασαν, ἔτι νηπίαχον ὄντα, ὡς ὁ τῆς Τελετῆς ποιητής Ὀρφεύς φησιν ὁ Θρᾴκιος· κῶνος καὶ ῥόμβος καὶ παίγνια καμπεσίγυια, μῆλά τε χρύσεα καλὰ παρ' Ἑσπερίδων λιγυφώνων. Καὶ τῆσδε ὑμῖν τῆς τελετῆς τὰ ἀχρεῖα σύμβολα οὐκ ἀχρεῖον εἰς κατάγνωσιν παραθέσθαι· ἀστράγαλος, σφαῖρα, στρόβιλος, μῆλα, ῥόμβος, ἔσοπτρον, πόκος. Ἀθηνᾶ μὲν οὖν τὴν καρδίαν τοῦ Διονύσου ὑφελομένη Παλλάς ἐκ τοῦ πάλλειν τὴν καρδίαν προσηγορεύθη· οἱ δὲ Τιτᾶνες, οἱ καὶ διασπάσαντες αὐτόν, λέβητά τινα τρίποδι ἐπιθέντες καὶ τοῦ Διονύσου ἐμβαλόντες τὰ μέλη, καθήψουν πρότερον· ἔπειτα ὀβελίσκοις περιπείραντες "ὑπείρεχον Ἡφαίστοιο." Ζεὺς δὲ ὕστερον ἐπιφανείς (εἰ θεὸς ἦν, τάχα που τῆς κνίσης τῶν ὀπτωμένων κρεῶν μεταλαβών, ἧς δὴ τὸ "γέρας λαχεῖν" ὁμολογοῦσιν ὑμῶν οἱ θεοί) κεραυνῷ τοὺς Τιτᾶνας αἰκίζεται καὶ τὰ μέλη τοῦ Διονύσου Ἀπόλλωνι τῷ παιδὶ παρακατατίθεται καταθάψαι.

We also find a version of Dionysus' death by the Titans in the Dionysian by Nonnus of Panopolis, an Egyptian epic poet from the 3rd – 4th century:

(5) But he did not hold the throne of Zeus for long. By the fierce resentment of implacable Hera, the Titans cunningly smeared their round faces with disguising chalk, and while he contemplated his changeling countenance reflected in a mirror they destroyed him with an

---

18 Christian comment by Clement.
19 Translated by Schaff, Philip (1885).

infernal knife.[20] There where his limbs had been cut piecemeal by the Titan steel, the end of his life was the beginning of a new life as Dionysos.[21]

VI, 169–175 οὐδὲ Διὸς θρόνον εἶχεν ἐπὶ χρόνον• ἀλλὰ ἐγύψῳ
κερδαλέῃ χρισθέντες ἐπίκλοπα κύκλα προσώπου
δαίμονος ἀστόργοιο χόλῳ βαρυμήνιος Ἥρης
Ταρταρίῃ Τιτῆνες ἐδηλήσαντο μαχαίρῃ
ἀντιτύπῳ νόθον εἶδος ὀπιπεύοντα κατόπτρῳ.
ἔνθα διχαζομένων μελέων Τιτῆνι σιδήρῳ
τέρμα βίου Διόνυσος ἔχων παλινάγρετον ἀρχὴν

There are older references to the Orphic version of the birth of Dionysus dismembered by the Titans and resurrected, as in the historian Plutarch, 1st – 2nd century (*De Esu Carnium* 996c, *De E apud Delphos* 388E), in Diodorus Siculus, 1st century (*Biblioteca Historica*, III, 62; V, 75), in one of the Aristotelian Problems[22] (*Unpublished Problems*, III, 43), and in Euripides, 5th century B.C. (*Cretans*, fr. 472).

In the Orphic myth of *Initiation* (*Telete*), death and rebirth of Dionysus Zagreus immediately precede the appearance of men. Titans tear, cook, roast and eat Dionysus, except his heart collected by Athena (or Hermes) and the remains, which are buried by Apollo. Zeus destroys Titans. From their ashes or more probably from soot, men are born. Versions differ, but the result of Zeus' punishment of the Titans is always the dawn of mankind. In the 1st century, Dio Chrysostom refers to the myth by saying all men come from Titans' blood.[23] However, only after Olympiodorus, a neo-Platonic philosopher from the 6th century A.D., in his comment to Plato's *Phaedo*, do we have a more complete textual reference on the link between the crime committed against infant Dionysus, the Titans who sacrificed him, and the appearance of mankind. An anthropogony, as described by Aristophanes in the *Symposium*.

> (6) According to Orfeus, four kindgoms succeeded him. First, that of Uranus, after which Cronos castrated his father's genitles; after Cronos, Zeus reigned having promoted the father to Tartarus; and still after Zeus came Dionis, who they say conspired with Hera and

---

20 Cf. Eustakius, *On Illiad* II, 735.
21 Translated by...
Cf. XXVII, 228
22 *Unpublished Problems* added by Bussemaker to Bekker's edition were attributed to Aristotle (4th century B.C.) or his commentator Alexander of Aphrodisias (2nd – 3rd century A.D.), the authorship and date are still dubious, generally vaguely attributed to the Hellenistic period.
23 Letter XXX.

was cut to pieces by the Titans, having his flesh chewed by them. Zeus exploded with rage, and the matter that rose with the soot of the smoke gave rise to the birth of mankind.[24]

1.3. παρὰ τῷ Ὀρφεῖ τέσσαρες βασιλεῖαι παραδίδονται. πρώτη μὲν ἡ τοῦ Οὐρανοῦ, ἣν ὁ Κρόνος διεδέξατο ἐκτεμὼν τὰ αἰδοῖα τοῦ πατρός· μετὰ δὲ τὸν Κρόνον ὁ Ζεὺς ἐβασίλευσεν καταταρταρώσας τὸν πατέρα· εἶτα τὸν Δία διεδέξατο ὁ Διόνυσος, ὅν φασι κατ' ἐπιβουλὴν τῆς Ἥρας τοὺς περὶ αὐτὸν Τιτᾶνας σπαράττειν καὶ τῶν σαρκῶν αὐτοῦ ἀπογεύεσθαι. καὶ τούτους ὀργισθεὶς ὁ Ζεὺς ἐκεραύνωσε, καὶ ἐκ τῆς αἰθάλης τῶν ἀτμῶν τῶν ἀναδοθέντων ἐξ αὐτῶν ὕλης γενομένης γενέσθαι τοὺς ἀνθρώπους.

We assume Plato constructs the myth told by Aristophanes in the *Symposium* in the same way Aristophanes himself constructs the theogonical myth delivered by the *Birds*' choir: as a parody of parts of *Telete*, the Orphic poem of Initiation. The procedure is the same. The main difference is in the parts of the poem which are taken to make the parody. Aristophanes chooses the beginning of theogony, which shows the primeval deities Protogonos and Eros. Plato chooses the part about the last generation of divine power according to the Orphic narrative, in the part describing the dismemberment of Dionysus Zagreus carried out by the Titans, from whose ashes men emerged. Why does he choose this model? Surely because Plato's Aristophanes is one of the spokesmen of Dionysus in the *Symposium*. The whole *Symposium* is a Dionysian celebration, a collective rite of drinking wine, as the Greek word *sympósion* suggests. The body is prepared with food and drinks; initiation is performed with incantatory speeches praising a primordial cosmogonic god, until the time of the revelation reserved to the beginners, at the end of Diotima's speech and in Alcibiades' indiscretions. Aristophanes has a very important job in the rite, wearing the Dionysian mask of anthropogonic speech.

Let us see how Aristophanes' speech is constructed corresponding to the Orphic myth. The first relevant aspect is, as we already mentioned, the background of Dionysian wisdom: the integration of parts in the whole. The myth narrates the three stages of the cycle of cosmic return: first, the original and powerful whole; second, the crime resulting in the division of the whole in parts; third, the return and reintegration of the parts in the whole, by the effect of love. Mankind comes from the separation of a complete original condition; the human condition is not only mortal but also essentially needy. Love is the power able to meet this need and lead men again to lost integrity and to a much closer instance to the blessing of gods.

In the Orphic myth, the human condition results from a crime against Dionysus, committed by the Titans. Men are generated both from the remains of the

---

[24] Translated by Santoro (from Greek) and Bowles (to English).

Titans who committed the crime and from Dionysus', the swallowed victim. Both Dionysus' and Titans' flesh are disintegrated and reduced to soot which composes men. Crime and punishment provide the tragic aspect of this cycle of separation and reintegration which repeats in the myth of the *Symposium*. In Plato's myth, the arrogance of confronting gods comes from those double, round men, children of the stars, who being whole and complete, still do not have the manlike needy condition. Those double, giant men are analogue to Titans. Revenge and punishment come in the same way in both myths, with Zeus' drying and striking lightning. Healing also comes, in both myths, from Apollo, who collects the remains of Dionysus to bury them and fertilize the earth and who sews the skin cut from splitting halves.

The Platonic parody has a tragic plot, but the images, figures of speech and action are comical. The double men are not as monstrous as the Titans, but they are funny acrobats who roll on the ground. Apollonian healing is not a funereal ceremony but a funny sewing scene.

The only element we cannot find in the known traces *Telete's* anthropogonic myth is what differentiates the parts from the whole among male and female genders. On the other hand, there are versions (usually late) which show primeval deities such as Phanes and even Zeus and Dionysus in androgynous figuration[25]. But Aristophanes in the *Symposium* is a character of the dialogue who makes sure to value love between men and women, especially when he performs the myth he had just told, therefore being a fairly important element. We do not find the separation of the genders in the traces referring to the Orphic *Telete*. Bernabé (2010) notes that Phanes is described with his "genitals in the same anomalous display"[26] in the *Comment to Four Speeches* of Gregory of Nazianzus, wrongly attributed to Nonnus (Pseudo-Nonnus). As the reference is late, Bernabé prefers to attribute the similarity with Aristophanes' ball-men to chance or even to Platonic influence, and lists the passage between the doubtful references to Orphic poems[27]. However, the image of double beings which have male and female genders appear in another 5th century B.C. cosmogonic poem, in which love is a primordial power. This poem also shares the background of Dionysian wisdom of the relationship between the whole and the parts, although it often shows a critical distance from Orphic theogonies. It is the poem of a philosopher whose images appear in many Platonic myths and whose theories already inspired Eriximacus' speech in the *Symposium*. Curiously though, its name is

---

25 Cf. Orphic Hymns.
26 p.146.
27 On the other hand, Bernabé finds traces of the myth of Dionysus dismemberment in two other passages of the Laws: 701b and 854b (p. 234–242).

never mentioned. Let us see fragment 61 from the poem about the Origins, by Empedocles, located in the cosmogonic moment when the beings of monstrous aspect are generated, mixed beings, a moment preceding the generation of species as they are constituted in the present:

> (7) Many creatures were created with a face and breast on both sides; offspring of cattle with the fronts of men, and again there arose offspring of men with heads of cattle; and (creatures made of elements) mixed in part from men, in part of female sex, furnished with hairy limbs.[28]
>
> πολλὰ μὲν ἀμφιπρόσωπα καὶ ἀμφίστερνα φύεσθαι,
> βουγενῆ ἀνδρόπρωιρα, τὰ δ' ἔμπαλιν ἐξανατέλλειν
> ἀνδροφυῆ βούκρανα, μεμειγμένα τῆι μὲν ἀπ' ἀνδρῶν
> τῆι δὲ γυναικοφυῆ σκιεροῖς ἠσκημένα γυίοις.

The last observation on the relationship between the Aristophanic myth of the *Symposium* and the Orphic *Telete:* the name Aristophanes himself gives to his image of love as attraction between two halves of a whole: *sýmbolon*. The word, besides the image of the broken tessera which we already mentioned, clearly also evokes the symbolic performance of images. A primeval function of theogonical myths in Orphic initiation rites. An important part in initiation is the learning of Hermeneutics, for understanding of the meaning of rite symbols.

Aristophanes does not end his speech at the end of the myth, but he keeps on interpreting the images of the symbol according to the present facts. The comedy writer's language would not miss the opportunity of making fun of the living situation itself at Agathon's house. After symbolic love is explained in general, we still have to see how genders and individuals behave. There are two genders left: male and female; but three ways of loving union are left: one, of the majority, comes from the androgynous whole, it is the love between men and women; the male parts coming from the male whole love men similar to themselves, like the guests of the symposium; and the female parts coming from the female whole love women like them. Everyone loves according to a taste inherited by their primordial nature. Besides valuing love between men and women, he makes an ironic twist treating heterosexual as resulting from androgyny, whereas other come from pure genders. And he starts talking about love between men as not only pure, but the most audacious, brave and virile. The only one in the symposium who does not share the taste for pederasty, Aristophanes makes a mock-

---

[28] Translated by Freeman (1978), *Ancilla to the Pre-Socratic Philosophers*, pp.58–59. Cf. Também DK fr. 62, 63, 65, 67 e Parmênides DK fr. 17.

ing compliment to those who love the boys. "Some say they are shameless, but they are lying..." "the proof is that, once mature, they are the only ones who become men for politics." As a last joke alluding to the relationships of the attendees: "And I do not suppose Eryximachus was making comedy in the speech, as he was talking about Pausanias and Agathon..."

Works Cited

Aristophanes. (1912) The Eleven Comedies. Athenian Society.
Athanassakis, A. N. (1977) The orphic hymns. Missoula (Mont.), Scholars press.
Bernabé, A. (2011) Platão e o orfismo: diálogos entre religião e filosofia, São Paulo, Annablume, [translated by D. Xavier of (2010) Platón y el orfismo; diálogos entre religión y filosofia, Madrid, Abada].
Buarque, L. (2011) As Armas Cômicas: Os interlocutores de Platão no Crátilo, Rio de Janeiro, Hexis.
Burkert, W. (1983) Homo Necans: The antropology of Ancient Greek Sacrificial Ritual and Mith. Translated by P. Bing, Berkeley, U. Of California Press [translation of (1972) Homo Necans, Berlim, W. De Gruyter].
Burnet, J. (1900) Platonis Opera, Oxford.
Bussemaker, U. C. (1878) Problemata Inedita in: Aristotelis opera omnia: graece et latine cum indice nominum et rerum. t. IV, Paris, Ed. Ambrosio, Firmin-Didot.
Clay, Diskin, (1975) "The tragic and comic poet in the Symposium", Arion, New Series, Vol. 2, No. 2, pp. 238–261
Detienne, M. (1977) Dionysos mis à mort, Paris, Gallimard.
Dodds, E. R. (1959) The Greeks and the Irrational, Berkeley, U. Of California Press.
Ellinger, P. (1993) La Légende nationale phocidienne (BCH supp. 27, Paris) "La suie de la fumée des Titans", p. 147–163.
Freeman (1978), Ancilla to the Pre-Socratic Philosophers, Harvard University Press.
Hall, F.W. and Geldart, W.M., ed. (1906) Aristophanis Comoediae, Oxford University Press.
Jourdan, F. (2006) " Dionysos dans le Protreptique de Clément d'Alexandrie ", Revue de l'histoire des religions [on line], 3 | 2006, mis en ligne le 25 janvier 2010, consulté le 06 août 2012. URL : http://rhr.revues.org/5180
Guthrie W. K. C. (1952) Orpheus and Greek religion, Methuen & Co., Londres, [1935] 1952².
Reinhardt, K. (1989²) Platons Mythen, Göttingen, Vandenhoeck & Ruprecht GmbH & Co. KG, [Les mythes de Platon, french translation by Reineke, A.S., Paris, Gallimard, 2007]
Keydell, R. (1959) Nonni Panopolitani Dionysiaca, 2 vols., Berlin: Weidmann.
Mondésert, C. (1949²) Clément d'Alexandrie. Le protreptique, Paris, Cerf, Sources chrétiennes.
Nunes, C.A. (2001²) Platão, O Banquete (Ed. C.A.Nunes) Belém: Ed. UFPA.
Santoro, F. (2013) "La citation des Nuées dans l'Apologie de Socrate de Platon" in: Comédie et Philosophie: Socrate et les Présocratiques dans les Nuées d'Aristophane, org. Laks, A. & Cottone, Paris, Ed. D'Ulm, p. 193–206.
—— (2007) Arqueologia dos Prazeres, Rio de Janeiro, Objetiva.

Schaff, Philip (1885) Ante-Nicene Fathers. Fathers of the Second Century: Hermas, Tatian, Athenagoras, Theophilus, and Clement of Alexandria; Grand Rapids, Christian Classics Ethereal Library.

Strauss, L. (2001) On Plato's Symposium, Chicago, U. Of Chicago Press.

Taylor, Thomas (1999). The Hymns of Orpheus. Translated by Taylor, Thomas (1792). University of Pennsylvania Press.

Vogel, F., Fischer, K.T. (1964) Diodori bibliotheca historica, 5 vols., (post I. Bekker & L. Dindorf) Leipzig, Teubner, 1:1888; 2:1890; 3:1893; 4–5: 1906, Repr. 1964.

Wilamowitz-Moellendorff, Platon : sein Leben und seine Werke, (1959⁴) [1919], Zurich, Weidmann.

Westerink, L. G. (1976) The Greek commentaries on Plato's Phaedo, vol. 1 [Olympiodorus], Amsterdam, North–Holland.

Lamb, W. R. M. (1925) Plato. Lysis. Symposium. Gorgias. Translated by W. R. M. Lamb Loeb Classical Library.

Álvaro Vallejo Campos
Socrates as a physician of the soul

The Apology

In my contribution to this Symposium I would like to analyze Socrates as a character of the Platonic dialogues from the perspective of his conception of philosophy as therapy. I am going to distinguish three phases in the development of this idea: the definition of philosophy as ἐπιμέλεια (or θεραπεία) τῆς ψυχῆς in the so-called Socratic dialogues, and especially in the Apology, the transformation of philosophy into the art of politics in the Gorgias and the holistic therapeutics which Plato has put to work with the utopian character of the ideal city.

In the Apology we encounter a conception of philosophy which is completely bounded to Socrates as a recognizable character of Athenian culture at that moment. He was convinced that, if he wanted to maintain his commitment to justice in his own city and survive, "he must necessarily confine himself to private life (ἰδιωτεύειν) and leave politics alone" (μὴ δημοσιεύειν, Apol. 32a). Thus Socrates is, in his own words, a character who appears only on a private stage and whose philosophical project can be delivered only through a personal encounter with an interlocutor. We recall that his inner voice, the daímon, which used to dissuade him from certain acts, "debars him from entering public life" (31d), probably because it would have been a risk to his life, but also because he would have sacrificed it "without doing any good" either to himself or to the Athenian citizen. He has been perhaps the first philosopher to define explicitly and systematically with full consciousness philosophy as therapy of the soul in a way which calls up Epicure's assertion that "a philosopher's words are empty if they do not heal the suffering of man" (Usener 221).

I would like to comment on this philosophical project to clarify the differences with the development of Socrates' character as it appears in the Gorgias, which I believe to be one of the first dialogues where we find the most distinctive features of the Platonic Socrates[1]. The background of Socrates project in the

---

[1] Vlastos included the *Gorgias* in the group of the early or Socratic dialogues, although he recognized that "most present-day Platonists would agree that the G. is the last dialogue in this Group" (1991, p.48, n.4). In relation to the Socrates of the *Gorgias* I agree with Kahn, for, as he says (Kahn, 1996, 130), the Socrates who aspires to undertake the true political art (521c) "is no longer the ignorant Socrates of the *Apology*". See also Dodds, 1990, p.21. (Álvaro Vallejo Campos, Department of Philosophy II, University of Granada, avallejo@ugr.es).

Apology is determined by its nearness to rhetoric and medicine. The connection with the sophistical movement is perhaps not evident at first glance, but we must remember that Antiphon the Orator was credited with the invention of a method or Techne which consisted of an art intended to cure (θεραπεύειν) the afflictions or sufferings of the soul (87DKA6). He was supposed to cure these affections "by words" (διὰ λόγων), so that he could determine "the causes (τὰς αἰτίας) of the malady" and "prescribe the remedy". And Gorgias compares the art of rhetoric with medicine on declaring that "the power of logos has the same relation to the disposition of the soul as the disposition of drugs on the nature of bodies" (B 11.14).

Nevertheless, Socrates' conception of philosophy as ἐπιμέλεια (or θεραπεία) τῆς ψυχῆς has a normative instance in a double aspect, from an epistemological and a moral perspective, which relates it directly to medicine. This normative character of Socrates' practice, as defined in the Apology and the related dialogues, is what we might expect of the very notion of therapeía, which refers to the possibility of curing the disturbances of the soul or maintaining it in its proper and healthy state. From an epistemological viewpoint the normative aspects of the therapeutic understanding of philosophy are present in the unequivocal reference to intelligence and truth in Socrates' words (φρονήσεως δὲ καὶ ἀληθείας 29e) and from an ethical perspective the concept of ἀρετή is a key word that establishes an indissoluble link between the moral and the psychological or anthropological teleology of human nature which provides the fundament to the Socratic therapy. This is the great difference between the frequent comparisons with medicine which we find in rhetorical or sophistical texts and Socrates' intentions. For Gorgias the word φάρμακον is morally neutral, and it can equally mean remedy or poison, but this is not true of Socrates, who declares the necessary relation between the word therapeía and the existence of an end[2] and reminds us that we need a technician for the proper treatment of the soul (περὶ ψυχῆς θεραπεία, 185e), so that we can become "good and noble" (187a): this end is naturally the ἀρετή or excellence of the soul.

This proper condition of the soul which is the object of the Socratic therapy is the transcendental condition of all other goods, because, as he says, "wealth does not bring goodness, but goodness, that is, ἀρετή, brings wealth and all other good things, both to the individual and to the state"[3] (30b). Nevertheless, we cannot regard this supreme good as an exclusively moral good, for ἀρετή is not only moral excellence but rather that condition of the soul which brings

---

2 Cfr. *Laches* 185d.
3 Tredennick's translation (Hamilton, Cairns, 1982).

human nature to the perfection of its being. This will be very clear in the Gorgias where the noble and good soul is also happy (470e) and a soul that is not healthy is for that very reason "corrupt, impious, and evil" (479b–c). This is why Socrates says that justice is "medicine for wickedness" (478d), because wickedness represents for the soul "the greatest of evils" (478d) and injustice is called a "disease" (τὸ νόσημα τῆς ἀδικίας, 480b1) of the soul[4].

In relation to this therapy practiced by the Socrates of the Apology and the related dialogues, I would like to raise three questions: What method of therapeutic treatment is advocated by his conception of philosophy? What part of the subject is addressed? And finally, what scene can it be practiced in? The answer to the first question is too well known to require a detailed explanation[5], but we may remember in relation to this specific issue of Socrates as healer of the soul that he says to Charmides, that "the cure of the soul has to be effected by the use of certain charms" and that "these charms are fair words" (καλλοὶ λόγοι) by which temperance is implanted in the soul (157a)[6]. In the Apology Socrates gives a critical and negative version of his method that seems oriented to destroy the false beliefs of an ill society. Anyone who claims to be interested in these matters will be "questioned, examined and refuted" (29e). Socrates is "the stinging fly" appointed to the city by God and his method is intended "to rouse", "persuade" and "reprove" the citizens with regard to their consciousness.

In these terms the answer to the second question is already clear, for this is a method that can be addressed only to the intellectual and rational faculties of the human being: Socrates declares that his method is destined to awaken the interest of his fellow citizens in "truth and understanding" (29e). In the Protagoras the salvation of our lives depends on a science (ἐπιστήμη), capable of destroying the power of "appearances" which "leads us astray and throws us into confusion" (356d)[7]. The key which opens the path of a "good life" for us is "knowledge and a science of measurement" (357a).

Finally, regarding the third question, these are tasks which can be accomplished only in a private scene. It is true that the benefits of the Socratic method are intended for the whole city of Athens, but its aims and methods can be ach-

---

4 Woodhead's translation (Hamilton, Cairns, 1982).
5 I am referring to Socrates' "search for moral truth by question and answer" (Vlastos, 1994, p.4) without entering in the detailed description and in the philosophical complexities of the Socratic *elenchus*. See, on the different interpretations of Socrates' method, Tarrant, 2006, 254–272.
6 Jowett's translation (Hamilton, Cairns, 1982). On this καλλοὶ λόγοι and the rational nature of these Socratic charms, see Vallejo, 2000, 324–336.
7 Guthrie's translation (Hamilton, Cairns, 1982).

ieved only on a stage destined to practice a therapeutic action which consists of examining, refuting, and questioning a subject in order to activate the individual's intellectual powers. Socrates rejects explicitly, as we have seen, any intervention in politics that would have represented a risk for his own life, but especially, I presume, because this risk would have been assumed "without doing any good" either to himself or to the Athenian citizen[8].

The Gorgias

I have already quoted the Gorgias, because we still find in it many traits of the Socratic character that is known to us through the so-called Socratic dialogues. I see the Gorgias, nevertheless, as a transitional dialogue or (borrowing the terminology from C. Kahn) a "threshold dialogue", which opens the path clearly to the Platonic Socrates of the Republic. However, I do not accept C. Kahn's conjecture that the Gorgias was written before what he calls the threshold dialogues, which do not include this work, but a group formed by dialogues from the Laches and Charmides to the Meno and Euthydemus[9]. Nor can I agree with him when he denies "any fundamental shift in philosophical position" between the so-called Socratic dialogues, on the one hand, and the Phaedo and Republic, on the other. Although we can discern certain elements of continuity between the Gorgias and the Apology[10], such as I have noted in the preceding lines, I believe that we can also detect a very important shift in the conception of philosophy as therapy. For the Socrates of the Apology the main object of philosophy was the care of the soul, but now in the Gorgias this task, the τῆς ψυχῆς θεραπεία, is attrib-

---

[8] Naturally, as Ramtekar puts it, "there is a sense, a special Socratic sense, in which Socrates' moral engagement with individuals is political", but "this is not politics in the ordinary sense at all" (Ramtekar, 2006, p.215). Nevertheless, I would also admit that Socrates' critiques to Athenian democracy and his proposal of "professionalizing political rule", if it is genuinely Socratic and not a Platonic reconstruction, would have consequences for political thought (see, loc. cit. 223–226). A different thing is whether he drew himself these consequences. Perhaps Kraut is right when he refers to "conflicting elements in the early dialogues" (Kraut, 1984, p.244), for Socrates was critical of rule by the many, but he also saw a great value in critical inquiry and the intellectual freedom provided by the Athenian Democracy (see "Socrates and Democracy", loc.cit., 194–244).
[9] Although Vlastos included, as we have seen, the Gorgias in the group of the early dialogues, he has shown how many things, already present in this dialogue, are new in the path of the "metamorphofosis of Plato's teacher into Plato's mouthpiece" (Vlastos, 1994, p.37).
[10] Kahn (1996, 40) naturally acknowledges the difference between the Apology and the Gorgias and especially the unsocratic character of the moral téchnē alluded to in this dialogue.

uted to the political art, constituted by legislation and justice, which corresponds respectively to gymnastics and medicine, these taking care of the body: thus the counterpart of medicine in the case of the soul is not philosophy, without any further specification, but rather the political art (464b–c). The fundamental shift is in a certain sense recognized when Socrates now asserts that he is "one of very few Athenians, not to say the only one, engaged in the true political art" and that he alone "practices statesmanship" (521d). We could state in favour of a unitarian interpretation of the dialogues that, after all, the "true" political art is not so different from the practice of philosophy described in the Apology as tendance or care of the soul (28e-29a, 29d). But this is precisely the point that I want to question.

Various threads of continuity can still be observed. Philosophy is not neglected by Socrates; on the contrary, he declares to have being in love with philosophy all his life (481d, 482a) and this love is expressly contrasted with the love that Callicles professes to the Athenian demos. Nevertheless, now, paraphrasing Clausewitz's words, it could be said, as Dodds did[11], that philosophy seems to be the continuation of politics by other means, rather than its explicit rejection, as we have seen in the Apology. The aim of politics is still the same as Socrates' intention in the Apology, for the objective is "to make the Athenian citizens as good as possible" (521a), but the differences are evident, because in the Gorgias Socrates' project no longer consists only in examining other people and discussing virtue and other questions with them in the belief that life without examination is not worth living (38a). Now the therapeutic action must be applied directly to the city and Socrates refers to the necessity of proceeding to a θεραπεία τῆς πόλεως (521a, cfr.513e). The conversion of philosophy into a political art means that, although the objective is still the improvement of the citizens and the welfare of the soul, the method envisaged, as a plan to be implemented, and the scene are different, because the treatment has to be applied directly to the city and not to the individual. The illness now affects primarily the city, which is said to be "swollen and festering" (518e) and must be treated by the politician in the guise of a doctor (521a). The new Socrates is thinking that it is not enough to operate directly on the citizens and indirectly on the city, but the opposite: to heal the sufferings of mankind it is necessary first to practice a political art destined to operate on a diseased society. Naturally Socrates seems the same character, for the Gorgias presents him in discussion with Gorgias, Polo and Callicles, but his philosophical project has been radically altered: the scene destined to receive its direct action has changed. Now it will no longer consist in

---

11 Dodds, 1990, 384.

the cross-examinations of Socrates' interlocutors, questioning his fellow citizens, but in a new stage where the therapist must act through very different devices, for the patient has changed and so must the treatment methods.

A key sign of the dramatic change that has taken place is given by Socrates when he shows how to achieve the end of this πολιτικὴ τέχνη: it is like doing battle with the Athenians (διαμάχεσθαι Ἀθηναίοις, 521a). Socrates previously addressed his discourses only to those fellow citizens who would "profess to care" about the perfection of their soul (Apol. 29e), disregarding all the others, but now the therapeutic action must be practiced against the will of its patient. This patient, as we have seen, is the city, and the new statesmanship cannot provide her "with what she desires" (517b), but rather its aim consist in giving these desires "a different direction instead of allowing them free scope" (517b5). This means a fundamental turn in Socrates procedures, because the therapy must be applied to the citizens, "by persuading and compelling" them. We might ask how the Socrates of the Apology could have compelled any citizen to submit to the inquiries and refutations. We are naturally dealing with a complete transformation of the original Socratic project, which had in truth and intelligence and in the consent, freely given by his fellow citizens, the only way of practicing philosophy. It is easy to understand the change if we take into account that now the care has been converted into a medical treatment of a patient who is a different subject. The subject is a city that has developed a "sickness" (νόσος), "disregarding the rules of health" (518d) and these rules must be re-established even if the citizens do not wish to be submitted to that treatment and have to be forced, when persuasion fails. This situation is very naturally understandable as a political device, but it is absolutely incompatible with Socrates' conception of philosophy as tendance of the soul. "Persuading and compelling" seem to be antithetic, because persuading is possible for the Socrates of the Apology as a task which had to be accomplished "informing and convincing" (διδάσκειν καὶ πείθειν, 35c), but compelling means to force without the voluntary assent of those companions of Socrates whose friendship was necessary in the practice of his maieutic method.

The Therapy of Totality

I find no notable break between the Gorgias and the Republic, but it is clear that, in this work, some of the implications which involve the concept of the political art that Socrates is professing to practice in the Gorgias become evident and are fully developed. One of the most important ideas of this work, which sustains the whole building of the ideal city, is the philosopher ruler and, in my opinion, it is clear that this essential element of Plato's political philosophy is the development of the concept of a political art such as the one proclaimed in the Gorgias. In the Republic the philosopher is paradoxically the person who is supposed to possess this art and the one who is also frequently compared to a physician that has to treat the city as a patient suffering from its own diseases (VI 489b–c, VII 564c1). Although the first philosophical movement of this work is oriented to discovering justice as a good for the soul in itself, as we know, the discussion is redirected to the city as the larger scale where the quest will be more easily fulfilled. In the realm of the individual soul, justice continues to be conceived as a healthy state which results when "its principles are established in the natural relation of controlling and being controlled by one another"[12] (IV 444d). Establishing reason as the controlling power over the soul ensures justice as "a kind of health and beauty and good condition of the soul" (444d–e). But the same could be said about justice in the city. For, to discern the origin of justice and injustice in the state, we have to take into account, says Socrates, what it means to be a "healthy" (II 372e, 373b) or a "fevered state" (372e). This is also why in the Republic he can present the deviations of the ideal state, such as tyranny, democracy, oligarchy, and timocracy as "maladies of the state" (πόλεως νόσημα 544c; cfr. 556e, 563e–564a, 564b).

Definitively, the philosopher is established in the Republic as a lawgiver of the state and Plato makes a great effort to demonstrate why philosophers have been erroneously separated from government in the Greek states and confined to that private ambit where the Socrates of the Apology wished to remain. But this lawgiver of the state is at the same time "a good physician" (564c), although we cannot imagine a greater transformation of the character and his project which appeared in the Apology. Remembering his commitment to truth and reason, we now realize that the physician of the state is a very different character and that he has to conceive of the discourse not as a device intended to find the truth and dissolving all the false appearances through the cross-examination of his interlocutor. The new philosopher who is destined to act as a physician of the state will have to employ what Socrates calls "falsehood in words" as a medicine or φάρμακον useful to maintain the healthy condition of the state (382c, 389b). "It is obvious, says Socrates (389b), that such a thing must be assigned to physicians, and laymen should not have nothing to do with it". The philosopher kings "will have to make considerable use of falsehood and deception" (τῷ ψεύδει καὶ τῇ ἀπάτῃ), as it is recognized later in the work (459c).

Socrates' attitude in relation to truth has changed radically from the Apology to the Republic and this fundamental shift is correlative to the transformation of

---

[12] Shorey's translation (Hamilton, Cairns, 1982).

his character as a physician of culture. That is, in the Apology the therapeutic action of his philosophical enterprise was to be applied directly on his fellow citizens while the normative knowledge which was presupposed was relative to the soul and its healthy condition, but now the citizen is to receive the treatment indirectly through the mediation of the medical legislation which has to improve the conditions of life without necessarily involving the individual' s free will or conscious consent. The philosophical justification of the new practices that will be advocated come from a new conception of the human nature. The tripartite soul and the predominance of the irrational parts in most of the city would signify that not all persons are suitable "to be governed by the divine and the intelligent" (ὑπὸ θείου καὶ φρονίμου ἄρχεσθαι, 590d) principle dwelling within us to which the Socratic discourses were addressed. The abandon for most of the people in the ideal city of the Socratic intellectualism that founded all virtues on knowledge and intelligence signifies that, in the absence of the order that should be imposed by this divine principle from within, such order will have to be imposed from the outside (590d). Exterior reason, which resides in the philosopher ruler, will replace the interior order that Socrates sought to fundament through those καλλοὶ λόγοι "by which temperance is implanted in the soul" (Charm. 157a).

Every treatment presupposes, as we saw, a normative instance and the most profound transformation in my opinion takes place in the knowledge which is now involved. The philosopher kings who will act as physicians of the city are, as we know, a selected class, "the smallest part" of itself (428e), and the city will be wise as a whole by virtue of the knowledge (ἐπιστήμη) which resides exclusively in them, but, leaving aside this profound lack of symmetry between the individual and the city, I would like to examine the type of knowledge that functions as a normative instance of the therapeutic procedure of these physicians of society. This question is explicitly raised by Socrates and he declares that it is not a knowledge "about some particular thing in the city but about the city as a whole" (428c-d). The ontological status of this whole or of this unity which Socrates declares to be the greatest good for a state (462a–b) has been highly controversial. But it is evident that the philosopher who has to operate as a physician of culture has to bear in mind this whole in order to decide even about the life and death of the individual, as Socrates says in relation to a "political Asclepius" (407e) who "did not think worthwhile to treat" a patient when it was not going to be useful "either to himself or to the state". Leaving aside this controversial question about the ontological status of the unity of the state, which gave rise to Popper's critique of Plato's conception of the state as an organicist theory[13], I would like to concentrate on the knowledge of the whole that seems to me necessarily presupposed.

The question of the totality of the state is raised in the Republic when Socrates' interlocutors object (IV 419a, VII 519d) that the guardians of the state were not going to be very happy in a city which was controlled by them. Socrates' answer is that they were not considering how to obtain "the greatest possible happiness of any one class, but the possible greatest happiness of the city as a whole" (420b; 519e). I do not want to raise the question of the ontological status of this totality, but of the knowledge presupposed. I would like to recall two elucidating passages. The first is very important to clarify Plato's intentions about the philosopher rulers. Socrates establishes that the "first point of difference" between these lawgivers and ordinary reformers (501a) is that they will refuse to legislate unless they receive a clean slate or they will clean it themselves by erasing all the features of the previous state (501a–c). This is one of the essential features of the utopian thinking, as criticized by Popper[14] and analyzed by I. Berlin: the utopian therapeutic treatment would have to design the totality of the state[15], rebuilding the broken fragments into a perfect whole, as Berlin said, with the idea that "all the true answers, when found, must necessarily be compatible with one another and form a single whole"[16]. Naturally we do not have to follow Popper in all his critical details to realize that the Socrates of the Republic wants to redesign "the characters of men" (501c) through the establishment of a new state that presupposes the knowledge of "a heavenly model" (500e). This parádeigma implies a science of a totality which has to determine the life of the individual in a holistic way completely different from the Socratic therapeía exercised on the individual soul.

The second passage is quite illustrative of this feature of the new political therapy characteristic of the utopian model. Socrates is defending his model of an ideal state from the objection adduced by Adiemantus that in such a state the rulers would not be as happy as they could be in any other city under them (IV 419a). Socrates replies that his aim was not "the exceptional happiness of any one class but the greatest possible happiness of the city as a whole" (IV 420b). The philosopher as lawgiver and physician of culture has to

---

13 Cfr. Popper, 1966, vol.I, p.85f. (1981, 84–86); on this point, against the supposed organicism of Plato's theory of the state, see Vlastos, 1995, vol. II, 82 and Schofield, 2006, 220, but I think that Popper's case is by no means desperate; see, on Republic IV 420b-e, Brown, 1998, 21.
14 Cfr. Popper, 1966, vol.I, 169.
15 "Holistic or utopian social engineering" in Popper's words, cfr. Popper, 1961, 46f., 1966, vol. I, 160–172.
16 Cfr. Berlin, 1992, p.42.

place his therapeutic action under the perspective of the city as a whole (420c) and this action will determine the destiny and way of life of the individual. In the example of the statue given in this passage the painter has to proceed with an idea of the statue as a whole in order to paint the eyes or any other part, not to make each part as beautiful as possible but as beautiful as would correspond to its being a component of that whole. The perspective must be that of assigning to each part "what is proper to each" in order to make "the whole beautiful" (420e).

Criticizing the theory advocated by Grote and Popper that for Plato the state was conceived as an abstract unity or a superindividual whose happiness was distinct from the happiness of all the citizens, Vlastos affirmed[17] that in Plato's conception of the state the citizens imparted benefits to the community as something equivalent to imparting benefits to one another. Leaving aside once more the question of the ontological status of this entity, it seems evident that the philosopher who has to act as a physician to purge the city will have to determine the happiness of the individuals in accordance with his conception of this whole. Whatever its ontological status might be, it is clear that, from the perspective of the happiness achieved through the action of these lawgivers[18], the result is not equivalent to the sum of the happiness of each of the citizens, but that the way of life and happiness of these are determined by the knowledge of the whole. This is why they will have to be persuaded or even "constrained" (421c). Socrates is defining a kind of therapeutic action which has to operate by "harmonizing and adapting the citizens to one another by persuasion and compulsion" and, consequently, will create "such men in the state", "not that it may allow each to take what course pleases him, but with a view to using them for the binding together of the city" (VII 520a, Shorey's translation slightly altered). In this task, as a philosopher who has to design the whole and has to proceed with the corresponding knowledge, not only the guardians, but all the other citizens will be determined as farmers, potters or cobblers (420e–421a) by the glance of the philosopher directed at "the city as a whole" (εἰς τὴν πόλιν ὅλην βλέποντας, 421b). The happiness of each class and the way of life of its citizens is determined by its nature (421c), but this nature cannot be separated from what Socrates calls the development of the entire city and its good ordinance (οὕτω συμπάσης τῆς πόλεως αὐξανομένης καὶ καλῶς οἰκιζομένης, 421c), which is of course a result of the holistic knowledge of the philosopher. Each part of the state, the classes

---

[17] Vlastos, 1995, vol. II, p. 83.
[18] Cfr. *Republic*, IV 421a. See Brown, 1998, p. 21.

and the men who belong to them, is to be made happy, but, as L. Brown puts it[19], "with that happiness which it derives from its place in the polis as a whole".

Plato seems to have been fascinated by the therapeutic potency of the whole. We find three texts in Plato that belong to works probably written in very different and distant moments of his long career as a writer: all of them seem to underline the necessity of taking into account the totality. He is convinced in the Laws that "any physician or craftsman in any profession does all his work for the sake of some whole" (903c)[20]. In the Charmides, Socrates holds that "the reason why the cure of many diseases is unknown to the physicians of Hellas" is "because they disregard the whole" (156e). Charmides is interested in a remedy for curing his headache and Socrates sustains that it is not possible to cure the part without the whole, so that, following Zalmoxis, it would not be possible to cure the head without the body (156c) nor the body without the soul (156e). Thus the healer has to begin "by curing the soul" which seems to be the whole in which "all good and evil originates" and, as we know, the soul is cured through those charms and rational incantations of the Socratic logoi (157a).

Nevertheless, in the Phaedrus Socrates gives us another different account of the whole involved in medical treatments. In the context of the dispute against the technical character of rhetoric, Plato presents once more the art of medicine as a normative instance (270b) and Socrates affirms that just as medicine has to study the nature of the body, so rhetoric should study the nature of the soul, but that it is not possible to "understand the nature of the soul satisfactorily without the nature of the whole" (270c). This passage has been profoundly scrutinized in the secondary literature, because it is by no means clear what the nature of this whole is, not only in Plato's own intentions but in the supposed medical theory of the Hippocratic corpus to which he alludes. Scholars have given very different interpretations of this whole and have taken it as a reference to the universe, to the total environment, to the body as a whole or to the totality determined by the genus of any given object of definition[21]. I will not embark on the discussion of this highly controversial issue at this moment, but I agree with J. Mansfeld when he asserts that Plato places the dialectical study of soul within a larger context, which in his opinion is that of the dialectical study of reality as a whole[22]. Given the references to Pericles and Anaxagoras and the declared necessity that all arts have need of "discussion and high speculation about nature" (ἀδολεσχίας καὶ

---

19 Brown, 1998, 21.
20 Taylor's translation (Hamilton, Cairns, 1982).
21 Cfr. Isnardi Parente 1974, pp.497–8, Mansfeld, 1980, pp.341–362, Edelstein, 1987, pp.116–118, Vegetti, 1995, 102f.
22 Mansfeld, 1980, p. 352.

μετεωρολογίας φύσεως πέρι, 270a), it would be natural to assume that this *hólon* has a cosmological significance, but it could also be interpreted in a more general way as a universal methodological instance. In the Republic its political significance is evident: the tendance or care of the soul and the medical treatment advocated by Socrates as physician of culture cannot cure the soul without the purgation of the city and the treatment of the whole to which the soul belongs and this totality is the state. As a scholar has expressed it[23], the relevant whole for Plato in matters of health is the society at large. This version of the Socratic idea of the care of the soul with its epistemological presuppositions is so different from the project explained in the Apology that it offers one more perspective to affirm without hesitation that the Socrates of the Republic has been converted into a very different character from the one of the Socratic dialogues.

The nature of this whole which requires the treatment of the soul is also very different from the medical practices and the methodological treatments that we find in the Corpus Hippocraticum. Many scholars from Littré in 1839 to Vegetti in 1995 have conjectured that "the nature of the whole" mentioned in the Phaedrus was a reference to the Hippocratic treatise On Ancient Medicine (cfr. § 20 – 21), while others have referred it to Prognosticon (cfr. § 25), to Airs, Waters, Places, or to Regimen (§ 2.27), but I think that in all these cases it is a different whole which, despite its theoretical and speculative presuppositions, is to a high degree observationally and empirically founded and, most of all, it is a relational whole constituted by a determined constellation of particular factors that need to be observed. In other cases it is more a heuristic totality than a closed whole supposedly already known, as it is, on the contrary, in the Socrates of the Republic. The author of the treatise On Ancient Medicine affirms that medicine offers a good method for the science of nature and that "this knowledge is to be attained when one comprehends the whole subject of medicine properly", but he recognizes that we still have a long way to go until we attain it. It seems closer in its procedure to Popper's piecemeal social engineering than to the holistic conception which he rightly criticizes. On the contrary, the Platonic whole has a utopian character and this means that it has a normative instance, closed as the model of an ideal city and a "pattern laid up in heaven", the possibility and internal consistency of which is very poorly demonstrated, as we realize through the historical experience of all the other utopias that have been brought into reality. It could even be internally inconsistent, as I. Berlin has tried to show, with what he calls "the Ionian monism" which presupposes the compatibility of all values

---

23 W. Stempsey, 2001, 205.

in the perfect unity of the ideal society[24]. Nevertheless, the Socrates of the Republic, a different Socrates from that character in the Apology who wanted to remain far from a public realm, seems to be convinced that this whole to which we have to refer the medical treatment of culture constitutes a unity whose knowledge is possible to attain and that it is worth enough to sacrifice the autonomy of any individual person.

Works Cited

Berlin, I., "The Decline of the Utopian Ideas in the West", in I. Berlin, El Fuste Torcido de la Humanidad, Barcelona, 1992, 39–63; The Proper Study of Mankind, ed. by H. Hardy and R. Hausheer, London, 1998.
Brown, L., "How Totalitarian is Plato's Republic", in E.N. Ostenfeld (ed.), Essays on Plato's Republic, Aarhus, 1998, 13–27.
Dodds, E.R., Plato, Gorgias, Oxford, 1990 (1959).
Hipócrates, Tratados Hipocráticos, Introd., trad. y notas de C.García Gual, M.D.Lara Nava, J.A. López Férez, B. Cabellos Álvarez, Madrid, 2000.
Edelstein, L., Ancient Medicine: Selected Papers of L. Edelstein, Baltimore, 1987.
Hamilton, E. and Cairns, H., Plato, The Collected Dialogues, Princeton, 1982.
Isnardi Parente, M. in E.Zeller, -R.Mondolfo, La Filosofia dei Greci nel suo Sviluppo Storico, Parte II, vol. III/I a cura de M. Isnardi Parente, Florencia, 1974.
Kahn, C., Plato and the Socratic Dialogue, Cambridge, 1996.
Kamtekar, R., "The Politics of Plato's Socrates", in S. Ahbel-Rappe, R. Kamtekar, A Companion to Socrates, Oxford, 2006, 214–227.
Kraut, R., "Socrates and Democracy", in Socrates and the State, Princeton, 1984, 94–244.
Mansfeld, J., "Plato and the Method of Hippocrates", en Greek, Roman and Byzantine Studies, 1980, 21:4, 341–362.
Popper, K.R., The Open Society and Its Enemies, Princeton, New Jersey, fifth edition, 1966; The Poverty of Historicism, London, third edition, 1961.
Schofield, M., Plato, Political Philosophy, Oxford, 2006.
Stempsey, W., "Plato and Holistic Medicine", Medicine, Health Care and Philosophy, 2001, 4, 201–209.
Tarrant, H., "Socratic Method and Socratic Truth", in S. Ahbel-Rappe, R. Kamtekar, A Companion to Socrates, Oxford, 2006, 254–272.
Vallejo Campos, A., "Maieutic, epôidê and myth in the Socratic dialogues", in T.M. Robinson-L.Brisson, Plato, Euthydemus, Lysis, Charmides, Sankt Augustin, 2000, 324–336.
Vegetti, La medicina in Platone, Venecia, 1995.
Vlastos, G., Socratic Studies, Cambridge, 1994; "The Theory of Social Justice in The Polis in Plato's Republic", in Studies in Greek Philosophy, Princeton, 1995, vol. II, 69–103.

---

[24] Berlin, 1998, p.392.

Silvio Marino
The Style of Medical Writing in the Speech of Eryximachus: Imitation and Contamination[1]

In this article, I wish to stress the theme of the medical writing in the speech delivered by Eryximachus in the Symposium.[2] In the analysis of the style of writing and in the disposition of its contents, this example fits well in showing the skillful art of Platonic writing, that weaves texts and hypotexts together, creating numerous possible senses that the reader can catch and choose according to the object of the analysis he is developing.

In this discourse we can find that the style of medical treatises of the *Corpus Hippocraticum* is borrowed by Platonic discourse, imitating the medical one and, at the same time, intersecting it with the introduction of the philosophical discourse.

It is not possible here to analyze deeply all the connections between this speech of the *Symposium* and the treatises of the *Corpus Hippocraticum*; for this reason I would like to stress just three aspects that illustrate the retake of expositive and demonstrative schemes of medical treatises made by Plato:
1. The demonstration of the existence of the *techne iatrike* and its praise.
2. The principles which give life to the *kosmos* in this praise of the medical art are similar in both Eryximachus' speech and in *On Winds*.
3. The lexical and conceptual resemblance between Eryximachus' speech and the "physiological"[3] treatises of the C.H.

These three aspects will help to show the contamination and the reinterpretation of the medical discourse which Plato operates in the *Symposium*.

---

[1] I would like to thank here my friend Carl O'Brien for having revised the first English version of this article.
[2] For the reassessment of Eryximachus' speech, an important essay is the article by L. Edelstein, The Role of Eryximachus in Plato's Symposium, in "Transactions and Proceedings of the American Philological Association" 76 (1945), pp. 85–103.
[3] When I use the term "*physiological*" between inverted commas I mean that which concerns the *historie peri physeos*.

Medicine: Its Praise and the Demonstration of its Existence

At the beginning of his speech on love, Eryximachus recaps Pausania's discourse, which distinguished two *erotes*, two loves, a noble one and a vulgar one, making these two *erotes* the principles of reality. The opening of the speech deals with medicine in order to honor this *techne* (*presbeteuein*). This device produces a double praise: on one hand the praise of *eros*, the god present in everything, on the other hand the praise of the *techne* itself, the *techne* by which everybody can realize that in every being there is the presence of eros (*katheorakenai...ek tes iatrikes, tes hemeteras technes*, Symp. 186a7–b1).

Proposing a praise of the *techne* and stressing its importance, this speech agrees perfectly with the "epistemological" treatises of the *Corpus Hippocraticum*. If we look at these treatises, we can very quickly realize that one of the aim of the Hippocratic authors is to give a strong epistemological foundation to medicine. Actually the *techne iatrike* had numerous opponents, both on the popular plane (religious medicine), as well as on the philosophical one (sophists *in primis*). We can make a reference of this perspective by the treatises *On Ancient Medicine* and *On the Art*,[4] among all, to perceive this effort.

Furthermore, concerning the fact that *eros* is in everything Eryximachus states:

> it seems to me that it's an observation we can find out from medicine, our science [...].[5] (*Symp.* 186a7–b1)

This statement indicates that the method of medicine is valid also for the inquiry of all the things that exist, that is to say of the entire *physis*. The stress placed upon the correctness of the method by which we have to investigate nature, is also stressed by the author of *On Ancient Medicine*:[6]

---

[4] For the argumentation of the existence of medicine in *On the Art* see A. Jori, *Medicina e medici nell'antica Grecia*, il Mulino – Istituto Italiano per gli Studi Storici, Napoli 1996, capp. VII, VIII, IX. For the demonstration of the existence of medicine in *On Ancient Medicine* see Hippocrates, *On Ancient Medicine*, translated with introduction and commentary by Mark J. Schiefsky, Brill, Leiden-Boston, 2005, pp. 115–117; 133 ss.

[5] "καθεωρακέναι μοι δοκῶ ἐκ τῆς ἰατρικῆς, τῆς ἡμετέρας τέχνης".

[6] See Hippocrates, *On ancient medicine*, translated with introduction and commentary by Mark J. Schiefsky, cit., pp. 297–298 and 310 ss; J, Cooper, *Method and science in* On Ancient Medicine, in H. Linneweber-Lammerskitten e G. Mohr (eds.), *Interpretation und Argument*, Würzburg 2002, pp. 25–57.

I think that to know clearly nature in general no other source but medicine exists.⁷ (*On Ancient Medicine*, XX, 2, Jouanna p. 146, 9–11)

The words of Eryximachus are not just a praise of this *techne*, but also a clear demonstration of its existence. Stressing the fact that there are good physicians, good technicians, good *demiourgoi* – as Eryximachus does – is not just the praise of good physicians. Four times in the *Symposium*, there are expressions stating that the physician belongs to the art of medicine:

1. At 186c5, we find the term *technikos* and it is stated that whoever wants to be *technikos* has to impede the bad and sick parts of the body and to support the healthy ones (εἰ μέλλει τις τεχνικὸς εἶναι).
2. At 186c6–d1, the term indicating the physician is *iatrikotatos*, and it is the attribute of the physician to be able to distinguish (but the verb is significantly *diagignoskein*) the beautiful eros and the ugly one. Considered in its technical meaning, the verb *diagignoskein* indicates here exactly "to diagnose" the presence of both *erotes* (καὶ ὁ διαγιγνώσκων ἐν τούτοις τὸν καλόν τε καὶ αἰσχρὸν ἔρωτα, οὗτός ἐστιν ὁ ἰατρικώτατος).
3. Then, we have two occurrences of the expression *agathos demiourgos*: the first one is at 186d4–5, where it is said that the "good *demiourgos*" is the one who is able to engender (*eggenesthai*) the good *eros* where it ought to be and to remove the bad *eros* where it should not exist (ἐπιστάμενος ἐμποιῆσαι καὶ ἐνόντα ἐξελεῖν, ἀγαθὸς ἂν εἴη δημιουργός).
4. The second occurrence of *agathos demiourgos* is at 187d3–4, and it is used in relation to the specialist in music; here it is stated that in complicated situations a "good *demiourgos*" is needed (ἐνταῦθα δὴ καὶ χαλεπὸν καὶ ἀγαθοῦ δημιουργοῦ δεῖ).

Considered from a medical standpoint, the terminology used by Plato is extremely technical and gives rise to a strong conceptualization of *techne*.⁸ If we look at the Hippocratic treatises, we can find the use of the term "*demiourgos*",⁹ qualified as good or bad; and this term is employed in order to demonstrate the existence of the *techne iatrike*. It is not by chance that the majority of the occurrences of the stem *demiourg-* (noun and verb) are in *On Ancient Medicine* and in *On the Art*.

---

7 "Νομίζω δὲ περὶ φύσιος γνῶναί τι σαφὲς οὐδαμόθεν ἄλλοθεν εἶναι ἢ ἐξ ἰητρικῆς".
8 See G. Cambiano, *Platone e la tecniche*, Laterza, Roma-Bari 1991², pp. 35–45 and pp. 61–84.
9 For a different approach with respect to the works of Cambiano concerning the term *demiourgos*, see A. Balansard, *Technè dans les dialogues de Platon : l'empreinte de la sophistique*, IPS, Academia, Sankt Augustin, 2005.

If we consider *On Ancient Medicine*, the term *demiourgos* is always related to the expertise or incompetence. In the first occurrence, after the statement of the existence of medical *techne* – an art "that really is" (τέχνης ἐούσης, I, 1, Jouanna p. 118, 8) – the author states that "everybody praises greatly the good practitioners and the good professionals" (καὶ τιμῶσι μάλιστα τοὺς ἀγαθοὺς χειροτέχνας καὶ δημιουργούς, I, 1, Jouanna p. 118, 9–10). This discourse on the ἀγαθοὶ δημιουργοί leads to specifying the epistemological sense of competence and incompetence:

> Some practitioners are bad, while others are much better. This would not be the case if medicine did not exist at all and if nothing had been examined or discovered in it; rather, all would be equally lacking in both experience and knowledge of it, and all the affairs of the sick would be governed by chance.[10] (V.M. I, 2, Jouanna p. 118, 10–119, 1; transl. by M. Schiefsky)

In the third occurrence of "*demiourgos*", the author links medicine to all the other *technai*, showing that in all of them, it is possible to distinguish good and bad professionals; in this way, sharing the same characteristics of the other *technai*, medicine has the existence too.

But there is another text of the *Corpus Hippocraticum* showing specific affinities with Eryximachus' speech in relation to the organization of the subject and to the content: *On Winds*.[11]

First of all, as in the *Symposium*, there is praise of medicine, an art – as the author says – that gives pain and horrible views for the physician, whereas it gives relief to the patient, who can slip away from diseases and pains thanks to art (*dia technen*) (*On Winds* I, 1–2, Jouanna pp. 102–103).

As Eryximachus, the author of *On Winds* stresses the need of a technical intervention in hard cases, because only the mastery of the art can solve them, highlighting the distinction between professionals and laymen (δημότῃσιν, I, 3, Jouanna p. 103, 7; this is a term that – from a semantic point of view – is equiv-

---

10 "Εἰσὶ δὲ δημιουργοὶ οἱ μὲν φλαῦροι, οἱ δὲ πολλὸν διαφέροντες· ὅπερ, εἰ μὴ ἦν ἰητρικὴ ὅλως μηδ᾽ ἐν αὐτῇ ἔσκεπτο μηδ᾽ εὕρητο μηδέν, οὐκ ἂν ἦν, ἀλλὰ πάντες ἂν ὁμοίως αὐτῆς ἄπειροί τε καὶ ἀνεπιστήμονες ἦσαν, τύχῃ δ᾽ ἂν πάντα τὰ τῶν καμνόντων διοικεῖτο". For the relation *techne-tyche* cf. Hippocrates, *On ancient medicine*, translated with introduction and commentary by Mark J. Schiefsky, cit. pp. 5–13; A. Jori, *Medicina e medici nell'antica Grecia*, cit. pp. 317–332; Id., *Il caso, la fortuna e il loro rapporto con la malattia e la guarigione nel* Corpus hippocraticum, in Thivel, A.-Zucker, A. (éd.), *Le normal et le pathologique dans la Collection hippocratique. Actes du Xème colloque international hippocratique (Nice, 6–8 Octobre 1999)*, vol. 1, Publications de la Facultés des Lettres, Arts et Sciences Humaines de Nice-Sophia Antipolis, 2002, pp. 197–228.
11 On the contrary M. Vegetti, *La medicina in Platone*, Il Cardo, Venezia, 1995, p. 70, thinks that we are not allowed to compare Eryximachus' medicine to that of *On Winds* or of *Regimen*.

alent to ἰδιώτης, another word meaning the layman in many other treatises). From this standpoint, the terminology of *On Winds* and of *On Ancient Medicine* is very close and shows a common background: the proof of the existence of medicine, in *On Ancient Medicine*, is given by the qualitative difference of the physicians (and so, primarily by the difference between those who are physicians and those who are not). The verb used in *On Ancient Medicine* is *diaphero*, a verb used also in *On Winds* in a similar context:

> In these diseases [the most hidden and hard ones, *scil.*] competence mostly differs from incompetence.[12] (*On Winds* I, 3, Jouanna p. 103, 12–13)

We find the consideration that only a good physician can solve a difficult case both in *On Winds* and in *On Ancient Medicine* (IX, 4–5, with the example of the good and of the bad pilot): it is in difficult cases that the good physician clearly differs from the incompetent one.

The *techne iatrike*, in *On Ancient Medicine*, in *On Winds* and in Eryximachus' speech is, first of all, demonstrated as existent (remember the formula "*technes eouses*" of V.M.), and it is illustrated by the difference among professionals and laymen, good physicians and incompetent physicians. After this foreword shared by some treatises, Hippocratic texts get into the specific matter of the treatise, proposing their conceptions of the human body and of the pathogenic causes by which diseases start. And it is at this point that Eryximachus' speech becomes closer to *On Winds* than to *On Ancient Medicine*.

Praise of *eros*, Praise of *pneuma*, Praise of *logos*

The praise of medicine is joined to the praise of *eros*, a praise of the constituent principle of all the realities existing in the *kosmos*. In this way, Plato attributes Eryximachus' conception to a particular medical tendency, sharing the principles of the speculation *peri physeos* that starts with Ionian thinkers; a tendency contested by the author of *On Ancient Medicine*, but well documented by some Hippocratic treatises, *in primis*, by *Regimen*.

From this point of view, we are dealing with a particular medical perspective that does not refuse the "physiological" plane of discourse, but, on the contrary, that starts from this standpoint to propose a conception of living beings in general and especially of human beings. The principle of this "tendency" is that it is not possible to know a man, and therefore it is not possible to have an effect on

---

[12] "διαφέρει δ' ἐν αὐτοῖσι πλεῖστον ἡ πεῖρα τῆς ἀπειρίης"

him, if we do not know the nature of the whole (*holon*) to which man belongs and which encompasses him.

First of all, Eryximachus broadens the domain of *eros* to all the things that exist; in fact this god is in every body:

> in the bodies of all animals and in the plants that grow up on earth, and – so to speak – in all the things that are.[13] (*Symp.* 186a5–7)

Eros is within the constitution of all animated or inanimate things as the principle of their being; furthermore, *eros* is a god, a principle that reaches out both to the human level and to the divine one, including each level of reality, starting from the lower ones (inanimate things) right up to the highest ones (the gods themselves).

The medical discourse becomes "physiological" discourse; in fact Eryximachus states that:

> The nature of the bodies contains this double eros.[14] (*Symp.* 186b4)

Positing in this way only one φύσις for all bodies, Eryximachus' speech follows on from the medical treatises of the end of 5th century-beginning of the 4th century, and develops a physiology of the body, starting from the principle of the double *eros* (good and bad). By doing this, the physician of the *Symposium* sketches a theory of erotic fluxes that are in the human body and considers them as the origin of health and illness, identifying the principal aspects of this humoural physiology *sui generis* in the replenishment and in the emptying of the body. Medicine is – *apertis verbis* – "the science of erotic fluxes of the body in relation to replenishment and emptying (ἐπιστήμη τῶν τοῦ σώματος ἐρωτικῶν πρὸς πλησμονὴν καὶ κένωσιν)"[15]. The terms (πλησμονή and κένωσις) used here are very significant for the comparison which I am proposing here, because both terms are precisely used by the author of *On Winds* to indicate the way to cure diseases. Even if it is a common conception for ancient medicine, what is important to remark is that this is the only *locus* in the *Corpus Hippocraticum*

---

[13] "ἐν τοῖς ἄλλοις, τοῖς τε σώμασι τῶν πάντων ζῴων καὶ τοῖς ἐν τῇ γῇ φυομένοις καὶ ὡς ἔπος εἰπεῖν ἐν πᾶσι τοῖς οὖσι".
[14] "ἡ γὰρ φύσις τῶν σωμάτων τὸν διπλοῦν Ἔρωτα τοῦτον ἔχει".
[15] *Symp.* 186c6–7: "erotic fluxes" as Agathon says ("flussi erotici" as it's translated by M. Nucci, Platone, *Simposio*, Einaudi, Torino, 2009), since in 196a2 he says that *eros* has a fluid nature (ὑγρὸς τὸ εἶδος).

in which both terms are combined to describe the physiological dynamics of the body. In fact – the author states –

> The emptying is cured by replenishment and replenishment is cured by emptying.[16] (*On Winds* I, 4, Jouanna p. 104, 8–9)

The therapy through contraries is explicitly theorized in this treatise, just as in Eryximachus' speech medicine is the bearer of an erotic allopathy whose principle is to support the good *eros* against the bad one.

Both principles, *eros* and *pneuma*, flow through everything and unite the different parts of the *kosmos*. And from this point of view the praise of the respective principle is legitimized for both authors, a praise of the *dynamis* operated with a terminology very close to and which pertains to another important text, especially for Platonic philosophy: the *Encomium of Helen* by Gorgias.

In Eryximachus' speech it is well stated that

> Thus Love, conceived as a single whole, exerts a wide, a strong, nay, in short, a complete power: but that which is consummated for a good purpose, temperately and justly, both here on earth and in heaven above, wields the mightiest power of all and provides us with a perfect bliss; so that we are able to consort with one another and have friendship with the gods who are above us.[17] (*Symp.* 188d4–9)

The principal characteristic of *eros* is the power, properly the *dynamis*. But what has the greatest power, the *megiste dynamis*, is that *eros* aiming to good things and accompanied by wisdom and justice.

If we observe *On Winds* we can find for the *pneuma* the same characteristic underlined for *eros* in the description Eryximachus did:

> [Air, *scil.*] is the greatest sovereign in all things and dominates all things. It is right to contemplate his power.[18] (*On Winds*, III, 2, Jouanna p. 106, 2–4)

So, the power of the *pneuma* is in everything, even if it is not visible:

---

16 "πάλιν αὖ πλησμονὴν ἰᾶται κένωσις, κενώσιν δὲ πλησμονή".
17 Transl. by Harold N. Fowler, in Plato. Plato in Twelve Volumes, Vol. 9 translated by Harold N. Fowler. Cambridge, MA, Harvard University Press; London, William Heinemann Ltd. 1925. "Οὕτω πολλὴν καὶ μεγάλην, μᾶλλον δὲ πᾶσαν δύναμιν ἔχει συλλήβδην μὲν ὁ πᾶς Ἔρως, ὁ δὲ περὶ τἀγαθὰ μετὰ σωφροσύνης καὶ δικαιοσύνης ἀποτελούμενος καὶ παρ' ἡμῖν καὶ παρὰ θεοῖς, οὗτος τὴν μεγίστην δύναμιν ἔχει καὶ πᾶσαν ἡμῖν εὐδαιμονίαν παρασκευάζει καὶ ἀλλήλοις δυναμένους ὁμιλεῖν καὶ φίλους εἶναι καὶ τοῖς κρείττοσιν ἡμῶν θεοῖς".
18 "Οὗτος δὲ μέγιστος ἐν τοῖσι πᾶσι τῶν σωμάτων δυνάστης ἐστίν. Ἄξιον δ' αὐτοῦ θεήσασθαι τὴν δύναμιν".

however [air, scil.] is invisible to sight, but visible to the reason.[19] (*On Winds*, III, 3, Jouanna p. 106, 9–10)

This *megistos dynastes* is in everything and determines the cycle of seasons: in winter it becomes cold and dense (*psykron, pyknon*), in summer mild and calm (*prey, galenon*) (*On Winds* III, 3) just like the *erotes* of Eryximachus which determine the constitution (*systasis*) of the year. By finding a right *krasis*, the *erotes* give prosperity and health to men (*Symp.* 188a).[20]

The aspects of proximity between Eryximachus' speech and the medical discourse especially the one developed in *On Winds*, are various. I would like to show just a particular resemblance among this speech in the *Symposium*, in *On Winds* and, as I have already mentioned, the *Encomium of Helen* of Gorgias.

It has been already stressed that the terminology used in *On Winds* is close to the praise of the *logos* pronounced in this text of Gorgias.[21] The converging point of these three texts (*Encomium of Helen, On Winds* and Eryximachus' speech in the *Symposium*) that I would like to stress is the qualification given to the proper object of praise: *logos, pneuma* and *eros*.

It has been noted that Eryximachus attributes a *megiste dynamis* to *eros* and that the author of *On Winds* speaks about the *pneuma* as a *megistos dynastes*.

In Gorgias, we find the same characteristics of the *pneuma* – in *On Winds* – attributed to the *logos*:

> Logos is a great sovereign, which achieves the most divine works, with a very small and completely invisible body.[22] (*En. El.*, § 8)

In *On Winds* and in the *Encomium of Helen*, the respective principles praised are described by the same terms, thus creating a circle among these texts which determine conceptions of reality that are functionally similar, even if different in relation to the content:

1. *Eros, pneuma* and *logos* have a great *dynamis*.
2. *Logos* and *pneuma* are great sovereigns (*megas* and *megistos dynastes*).
3. *Logos* and *pneuma* are invisible (*aphanes* and *aphanestatos*).

---

[19] "Ἀλλὰ μὴν ἐστί γε τῇ μὲν ὄψει ἀφανής, τῷ δὲ λογισμῷ φανερός".
[20] M. Vegetti, *La medicina in Platone*, cit., p. 69–70, refers to *Airs, waters, places* I-II and XII, and to *Epidemics I* for the reference to seasons' *homonoia* and *krasis*.
[21] Cfr. J. Jouanna, *Notice* in Hippocrate, *Des vents – De l'art*, Les Belles Lettres, Paris, 2003 (ed. or. 1988), pp. 13–24.
[22] "λόγος δυνάστης μέγας ἐστίν, ὃς σμικροτάτωι σώματι καὶ ἀφανεστάτωι θειότατα ἔργα ἀποτελεῖ".

What is important to note is that these three principles are the basis of what reality really is; in the respective conceptions, they give form to and determine the reality.

For what concerns the *pneuma*, it is the primary cause of health and of all diseases of living beings. But it is the primary cause not only in the sense of a pathological etiology; it is the primary cause also from an ontological point of view, since nothing could be without it ("Without it, what could exist? Or from what it is absent? Or in what is it not copresent? ", *On Winds*, III, 3, Jouanna p. 106, 10–11: Τί γὰρ ἄνευ τούτου γένοιτ' ἄν; ἢ τίνος οὗτος ἄπεστιν; ἢ τίνι οὐ συμπάρεστιν;)

On another level of discourse, in the *Encomium of Helen*, the *logos* carries out a performative function of reality. Once the rift between things and the *logos* is established,[23] psychic reality becomes the battlefield in which the victory derives from persuasion. Now, this field is not exempt from analogies with the sphere of humoural medicine: Gorgias himself builds an image of the soul and of the changes that soul can have starting from the analogy between *psyche* and *soma* on one hand, and, on the other hand, between *logoi* and *pharmaka* (En. El. §14). In other words, the *logos* operates as a drug and it can give pleasure, scare, pain, instill courage, and this power, this *dynamis*, ensures that the *logos* "informs" the soul it is in contact with. Persuasion, indeed, adding itself to the *logos*, shapes also the soul as it likes.[24] (§13)

Through the considerations mentioned above, I would like to stress the way by which Plato operates more than a simple imitation of style and of contents; he substitutes the object of praise, the *megas dynastes*, identifying it in the *dialogos* and not in the *logos* of Gorgias. At this point, we can note that Plato mixes up medical discourse with his philosophy against the rhetoric of Gorgias.

Praise of eros or praise of the dialogos?

At the intersection of these three texts appears *el convidado de piedra*, as Tirso de Molina could say. The presence of the rhetorician of Leontini is very significant since in Eryximachus' speech there is not only the presence of medical terms, but also of terms precisely belonging to the Platonic theory of dialogical exchange.

---

23 Cfr. G. Casertano, *Sofista*, Guida, Napoli, 2004, pp. 53 ff.
24 "προσιοῦσα τῶι λόγωι καὶ τὴν ψυχὴν ἐτυπώσατο ὅπως".

In the comparison between medicine and music, introduced by an imprecise quotation of the fragment of Heraclitus DK 22b51 ("differing with itself, it is in concord with itself, as the harmony of the bow and of the lyre"), Eryximachus shows how these two arts follow the same methodology.

Now the activity of *eros* is to harmonize what is discordant:

> Harmony is consonance, and consonance is a kind of agreement; and agreement of things varying, so long as they are at variance, is impossible [...]. In all these cases the agreement is brought about by music which, like medicine in the former instance, introduces a mutual love and unanimity.[25] (*Symp.* 187b4–c4)

The terminology used here by Plato has not so much in common with the medical thought of the *Corpus Hippocraticum*. Συμφωνία occurs only three times (all of them in *Regimen*); ἁρμονία occurs seven times (four of them in *Regimen*); ὁμολογία occurs twice (but in *De decente habitu* and in the *Epistulae*); at last, there is no occurrence of ὁμόνοια.

Eryximachus' speech identifies a particular horizon of medical discourse, which belongs to the first book of *Regimen*,[26] the book where an explanation of the constitution of whole *kosmos* is proposed. Speaking about the particles composing man, indeed, the author of this treatise introduces medical discourse into the musical one:

> Since they [the particles, *scil.*] changed place and found a correct harmony that has musical ratios according to the three consonances, the fourth, the fifth, and the eighth, they live and grow up thanks to the same aliments they used before. But if they do not find the harmony, if the bass sounds are not in concord with the shrill ones in the first, in the second or in the eighth interval, since even if just one of them is deficient, the whole pitch is with no effect.[27] (*Regimen*, I, VIII, Joly, CMG, p. 132, 6–10)

---

[25] Transl. by Harold N. Fowler, cit.: "ἡ γὰρ ἁρμονία συμφωνία ἐστίν, συμφωνία δὲ ὁμολογία τις – ὁμολογίαν δὲ ἐκ διαφερομένων, ἕως ἂν διαφέρωνται, ἀδύνατον εἶναι·[...] τὴν δὲ ὁμολογίαν πᾶσι τούτοις, ὥσπερ ἐκεῖ ἡ ἰατρική, ἐνταῦθα ἡ μουσικὴ ἐντίθησιν, ἔρωτα καὶ ὁμόνοιαν ἀλλήλων ἐμποιήσασα".

[26] Cfr. E.M. Craik, *Plato and medical texts:* Symposium: *185c–193d*, in "Classical Quarterly" LI, 2001, pp.109–114; A. Thivel, *Eryximaque et le principe des contraires*, in "Cuadernos de filologia clàsica" (G) XIV, 2004, pp. 35–44.

[27] "χώρην δὲ ἀμείψαντα καὶ τυχόντα ἁρμονίης ὀρθῆς ἐχούσης συμφωνίας τρεῖς, συλλαβήν, δι' ὀξέων, διὰ πασέων, ζώει καὶ αὔξεται τοῖσιν αὐτοῖσιν, οἷσί περ καὶ πρόσθεν· ἢν δὲ μὴ τύχῃ τῆς ἁρμονίης, μηδὲ σύμφωνα τὰ βαρέα τοῖσιν ὀξέσι γένηται ἐν τῇ πρώτῃ συμφωνίῃ ἢ τῇ δευτέρῃ ἢ τῇ διὰ παντός, ἑνὸς ἀπογενομένου πᾶς ὁ τόνος μάταιος".

The way in which the discourse of *Regimen* establishes the analogy between the physiology of the body's components and the intervals of the pitches without announcing nor explaining it is very significant.

The need to interpret reality in terms of a relational structure brings the author of *Regimen* – again in the first book, in chapter XI – to propose one with no explicit referents, a structure able to be adapted to the most diverse realities.

> In fact, everything is similar even if they are dissimilar; everything is in concord even if they are not; everything is in dialogue even if they have no dialogue; everything has intelligence, even if they have not; the way of each thing is contrary even if it is in concord. The nomos and the physis, by which we do everything, are not in concord even if they are in concord.[28] (*Regimen*, I, XI, Joly pp. 134, 24–136, 1)

Eryximachus' speech and the passage quoted above aim to define a relational structure that could operate on different levels: from the singular bodily realities until the extra-individual ones (the dialogue and the political community). If we draw conclusions, the stress put by Eryximachus on the impossibility of an accord among dissimilar elements is of great relevance to Plato's philosophy.

Contamination of Models and Platonic Proposal

It is worth stressing the activity that *eros* produces through its *megiste dynamis*. Its *erga* consists in allowing a mutual coexistence and in making friends (*philoi*): not just human beings with one another, but also gods with men. But the function of *eros* is the same in each plane of reality of the *kosmos*. At a dialogical and political level producing coexistence and friendship among men means, at a physiological level, producing friendship among the parts of the body, as if to mean that the semantic horizon produced in a dialogue is functionally equal to the order established in a body, an order that is the sign of health. In this perspective, Eryximachus' medicine turns out to be a *techne* producing friendship (*philia*) at each level of reality:

> Indeed he must be able to make friends and happy lovers of the keenest opponents in the body.[29] (*Symp.* 186d5–6)

---

28 "πάντα γὰρ ὅμοια, ἀνόμοια ἐόντα· καὶ σύμφωνα πάντα, διάφορα ἐόντα· διαλεγόμενα, οὐ διαλεγόμενα· γνώμην ἔχοντα, ἀγνώμονα. ὑπεναντίος ὁ τρόπος ἑκάστων ὁμολογεόμενος. Νόμος γὰρ καὶ φύσις, οἷσι πάντα διαπρησσόμεθα, οὐχ ὁμολογεῖται ὁμολογεόμενα".
29 Transl. by Harold N. Fowler, cit.: "δεῖ γὰρ δὴ τὰ ἔχθιστα ὄντα ἐν τῷ σώματι φίλα οἷόν τ' εἶναι ποιεῖν καὶ ἐρᾶν ἀλλήλων".

Parts of the body, interlocutors in the dialogue and citizens in the city are the objects of an analysis and of an operation presupposing the same methodology deriving from the identity of the principle that acts in all these realities and from the "power" (*dynamis*) and the sovereignty that this principle possesses in relation to the *onta*.

After having shown the connections among the texts quoted, I would posit that Eryximachus' speech aims to introduce the theme of love in the theorization of the dialogue as a kind of information-communication, stepping forward as a different solution to the *logos* of Gorgias, *megas dynastes*, enchanter and poisoner of souls.

As we have noted, Eryximachus' medicine is presented through the characteristic of a dialogics intersecting different levels of reality (parts of body, of dialogue and of political community). By doing this, Plato needs to clarify what a creation of a *homonoia/homologia* means, specifying and interpreting the sense of the fragment of Heraclitus, and – especially – he needs to underline the political nature of this operation. In fact, if the term *homologia* is present along the entire *corpus platonicum*, it is not possible to state the same for *homonoia*. In the dialogues considered as authentic, this term occurs – besides these two occurrences in the *Symposium* – once in the *Statesman* and twice in the *Republic*: it is only the two occurrences in the *Symposium* which are in a non-explicitly political context. Significantly, unifying psychical and political levels, the political discourse in the *Republic* puts to work concepts we found in Eryximachus' speech, even if in two different perspectives: in the *Republic*, the political level is brought into physiology, whereas in the *Symposium*, the physiological level is brought into politics. In this dialogue, in fact, the description of erotic fluxes, that are present in everything, identifies a physiological plane coinciding with the political one; and – as we can say – with the Platonic one, which establishes the analogy between human body and political body.

The style of Eryximachus' speech is therefore a kind of *pastiche*, as Mario Vegetti says, in which, under the imitation of the style of medical writing, is introduced a plane of dialogical and political discourse, aiming at refusing both the rhetoric of Gorgias and his use of medical analogy. In the perspective in which we have looked at Eryximachus' speech, with its connection with medical treatises, Plato replaces the performative act of the *logos megas dynastes* of Gorgias with the informative-communicative act of the *dialogos* as the correct relational structure organized according to the principles of polarity and analogy.[30]

---

[30] Cf. G.E.R. Lloyd, *Polarity and Analogy: Two Types of Argumentation in Early Greek Thought*, Bristol Classical Press, 1966.

Esteban Bieda[1]
Gorgias, the eighth orator.
Gorgianic echoes in Agathon's Speech in the Symposium

After Agathon's speech in Plato's *Symposium*, Socrates takes a little time to make some comments about it. One of these comments is that the speech brought Gorgias to his memory (198c2–5). In this paper we intend to track down in three complementary levels the diverse reasons why this recollection took place: (A) regarding the *form* of the speech, we will try to show that there is an equivalence in how both Gorgias in his *Encomium to Helen* and the character of Agathon in the *Syposium* construct their respective *logoi*; (B) regarding the *style of writing*, we will see the frequent use in the poet's speech of the rhetoric resource of "saying things alike" (*isa legein*) usually ascribed to Gorgias; (C) finally, regarding the *contents* of both speeches we will try to show that many of the elements used by the sophist to praise the *logos* in his *Encomiun to Helen* (*EH*) may be found, more or less, in Agathon's praise of Eros. The article will try to show, thus, which are the precise elements that may have made Socrates remember Gorgias after listening to the tragic poet.

A. Form: cosmetic correspondences

Even when at first sight one might think that the speech of Agathon in Plato's *Symposium* has no formal relation with Gorgias' *EH*, the truth is that both speeches share not only the fact of being "*enkómia*"[2], but also a similar order regarding their formal organization. Let us consider the next six parts of both speeches: (i) the methodological guideline, (ii) the *status quaestionis*, mistakes of the predecessors and aim of the speech, (iii) the logical route to be followed, (iv) the development of the alternatives given in 'iii', (v) a summing up, (vi) a closure.

---

[1] A longer version of this paper was first published in *Elenchos* XXXI, 2, 2010, pp. 213–241.
[2] On the matter of the pair "*enkómion*"–"*épainos*", the difference between them is not that clear, at least in the *Symposium*, where Socrates uses both terms equally: see v.g. 199a3–6.

(i) The methodological guideline:

<u>EH</u>: paragraph 1 is a preface where the fundamental methodological guideline is given: the truth of the whole speech will be cosmetic: "order for a city is manhood, for a body is beauty, for a soul is wisdom, for an action is excellence, for a speech is truth" (*EH* § 1)[3]. The only "truth" in the *EH* lies on the formal order of the speech, *i.e.* in how the paragraphs connect with each other turning the whole into a perfectly coherent *lógos*[4].

<u>Agathon</u>: Agathon initiates his speech as follows: "but I, certainly, want to say, first, how (*hos*) it is necessary that I speak, and then speak" (194e)[5]. This brief methodological reference is fundamental regarding the way he is going to construct his speech in[6].

(ii) Status quaestionis, mistakes of the predecessors and aim of the speech:

<u>EH</u>: between paragraphs 2–5, Gorgias gives the *status quaestionis* of the issue he is about to deal with and makes a quick comment about the myth of Helen: her name was a synonymous with misfortune because of the "belief (*pístis*) of those who listened to poets, as well as because of the fame of her name that came to be remembrance of misfortunes"[7]. On the other hand, after mentioning the mistakes which those who preceded him in the topic of Helen would have made, Gorgias explicitly states his aim: "I want, after giving the speech some kind of logic (*log-*

---

[3] For the text of the *EH* we mainly follow the editions of Immisch (1927) and Untersteiner (1967). However, for the order of the paragraphs we use DK. We translate *"prâgma"* for "action" to keep the practical dimension of the latter, which Gorgias emphasizes when he refers it to *areté*.
[4] For the 'cosmetic' character of the truth in the *EH*, see Márcico (2007).
[5] Even when *"eipeîn"* is the infinitive used here in every occasion, it is not grammatical to translate it the same each time. In the next section of the paper we will analyze this characteristic gorgianic prose, almost impossible to translate to any modern language.
[6] According to Bury (1909, *"Introduction"*, § 3), "in his *speech* Agathon claims that he will improve on the *method* of his predecessors. In his attention to method he is probably taking a leaf out of the book of Gorgias, his rhetorical master and model".
[7] Something similar does Isocrates in his own *Encomium to Helen* when, after praising Gorgias for having written about Helen, he reproaches him that he was not coherent with the title of the *opusculum:* "for he <sc. Gorgias> says he has written an *enkómion* of her, but in fact he made an *apología* of what has been said by her" (14–15).

ismón tina), to stop the bad fame of the accusation, to show that the accusers lie, and, after showing the truth, cease ignorance"[8].

Agathon: "Everyone who has spoken before me does not seem to have praised the god <sc. Eros>, but to congratulate men because of the goods the god has been responsible for; however, no one said that the god gave those gifts because he is of a certain condition. [...] Then, it is fair that we praise, in the first place, Eros as he is, and then his gifts" (194e-195a). We can see how Agathon also mentions the mistakes of those who preceded him and, by doing that, gives a kind of *status quaestionis* at the moment when he will start his own *enkómion*. Finally, he insists on the methodological guideline[9].

(iii) Logical route to be followed:

EH: in paragraph 6 we find the possible alternatives regarding the subject of the speech. The different reasons why Helen might have traveled to Troy will constitute the logical route to be followed: "certainly, either because of the purposes of fortune, the designs of the gods and the decrees of necessity she <sc. Helen> did what she did, either because she was kidnapped with violence, or because she was persuaded with speech, or because she fell in love through sight" (§ 6)[10].

Agathon: after giving his methodological strategy, Agathon goes into action. In order to do that, he enunciates his own logical route: "well, if it is right and without offense to say it, I say that while all other gods are happy, Eros is happiest among them since he is <1> the most beautiful and <2> the noblest" (195a). After establishing that before worrying about the gifts that the god gives, it is necessary to understand his nature, Agathon states that that nature consists in

---

[8] The "truth" mentioned here is, of course, the one defined in paragraph 1: a *lógos* with *kósmos*. Therefore the intention of making to cease the ignorance by giving some *logismós* to his speech.

[9] For the typical strategy of rhetorics and oratory which is to discredit the words of those who spoke before about the same matter, see *v.g.* Isócrates, *Encomium to Helen* §§ 14–15, *Busiris* 222b, *Panegiric* 41b ss. and Bury (1909, *ad loc.*).

[10] Something similar may be found in the *Defense of Palamedes* (DP) § 5, when the hero presents the logical plan he is about to follow: "... I will show you in two different ways (*dià dissōn trópon epideíxo*) that <my accuser> does not speak truthfully. Certainly: <1> even if I wanted, I would not have been able to do it, and <2> if I was able, I would not have wanted to perform such actions". After that, he adds: "I go, in the first place, to that statement (*lógos*) that says that it is impossible that I do such a thing" (§ 6). Between paragraphs 6 and 12 he develops this first point. Then, between paragraphs 13 and 21 he develops the second alternative. In through paragraphs 22 and 27 Palamedes talks to his accuser. And finally, from paragraph 28 to 36 he talks to the judges to conclude his defense in paragraph 37.

being "the happiest" (*eudaimonéstatos*) god. After that, he gives two reasons why that happen: because he is the most beautiful (*kállistos*) and the noblest (*áristos*). The explanation of these two characteristics are the logical route to be followed in the rest of his speech.

(iv) Development of the alternatives given in (iii):

<u>EH</u>: between paragraphs 6–19 each of the alternatives given in the logical route is developed. The attention put by the sophist in the order of the speech makes sense, since it is there, in that *kósmos*, where the only chance of it being true lies. That is why in § 6 Gorgias deals with Fortune, gods and Necessity as possible causes of the trip; in § 7 he deals with violence; between § 8 and § 14 with *lógos*; and finally, between § 15 and § 19 he deals with *éros*.
<u>Agathon</u>: between 195a and 196b Agathon deals with <1> the beauty of the god: Eros is the most beautiful because he is <1.1> the youngest (*neótatos*) god, <1.2> delicate (*hapalós*), and <1.3> of a soft form (*hygrós tò eîdos*)[11]. Finally, in 196a the treatment of beauty is closed: "about the beauty of the god, these things are enough". Then, between 196b and 197c Agathon considers <2> the excellence of Eros with two arguments: <2.1> everyone serves Eros willingly (*hekón*) since he does not submit to anything; and <2.2> the fact that he embodies cardinal virtues.

(v) Summing up:

<u>EH</u>: in paragraph 20 Gorgias makes a brief summing up and, after that, he draws his conclusion: "then, how is it possible to consider lawful the charge against Helen, who did what she did either in love, persuaded through speech, kidnapped with violence, or coerced by a divine necessity? In any case, she escapes from the accusation". The logical route is revisited just to show the reader that each one of the alternatives anticipated in § 6 was developed and, after that, the conclusion is drawn: Helen must be acquitted[12].

---

11 See 195a-c, 195c-e y 196a-b for each of the three characteristics.
12 Something similar occurs in paragraph 37 of the *DP*: "I have said what is related to me. Now, I finish: certainly, to bring concisely to memory (*tò hypomnêsai*) the things said before through long <speeches> is reasonable before evil judges, but it is not even worthy of consideration that the first Greeks among the first Greeks <sc. his judges> do not pay attention or have not in their memory the things that have been said".

Agathon: in 197c1–3 Agathon sums up and draws his conclusion: "so, Phaedrus, I think that Eros first was, being himself mostly beautiful and noble, precisely because of this, responsible of other things like those for others". According to Bury (1909, "Introduction", § 3), "another mark of formal method is his <sc. Agathon's> practice of recapitulation".

(vi) Closure:

<u>EH</u>: in paragraph 21 Gorgias closes his speech by going back to the methodological guideline given in § 1: "I took out, through this speech, the infamy of a woman; I stayed in the norm (*nómos*) that I established at the beginning of the speech...". Finally, in his last words he mentions the famous "*paígnion*" that, according to some, proves that the whole *EH* might have been a mere rhetorical exercise or 'model' for the pupils of the sophist[13].

Agathon: in 197e we read: "be devoted to the god, Phaedrus, this speech of mine, speech that takes part, regarding some things, in the game, and regarding other things, as much as it is possible for me, in a measured seriousness (*spoudês metrías*)". We see an explicit reference to the end of the *EH* by mentioning the game.

In "C" we will deepen many of the things summarized so far. Let us focus, now, on the style of writing.

B. Style: the ἴσα λέγειν

Already from ancient times the gorgianic prose was considered to have a characteristic style, which was used not only by Gorgias. Philostratus refers to the poet Agathon with a verb created precisely to explain that style: "and Agathon, the tragic poet that comedy considers wise and elegant in diction, often, between the iambs, speaks like Gorgias (*gorgiázein*)" (*Vitae sophistorum* I.493). Nevertheless, this style is already mentioned in the *Symposium* after Pausanias' speech. Apolodorus is speaking: "after Pausanias paused –you see, the wise men teach me to say things alike (*ísa légein*)–, Aristodemus said that Aristophanes had to speak next..." (185c). The explanation between hyphens makes total

---

[13] According to Dover (1980, p.123), the reference to the "*paígnion*" makes of the *EH* a "a composition which is meant to be admired for its elegance, piquancy and skill, but is not a contribution to science or philosophy, let alone to practical politics".

sense in Greek, speaking of the sonority of the absolute genitive "*Pausaníou pausaménou*".

This way of speaking, this "*ísa legein*" characteristic of gorgianic prose, is present in some fragments of the historical Agathon –confirming what Philostratus tells us about him–, but also in the character of the *Symposium*. Let us see a few examples:

1) Gorgias:
   - <u>Defense of Palamedes</u> § 5: ὅτι μὲν οὖν οὐ <u>σαφῶς</u> <εἰδὼς> ὁ <u>κατήγορος κατηγορεῖ</u> μου, <u>σαφῶς οἶδα</u> · <u>σύνοιδα</u> γὰρ ἐμαυτῶι <u>σαφῶς</u> οὐδὲν τοιοῦτον πεποιηκὼς · [...] οὔτε γὰρ <u>βουληθεὶς ἐδυνάμην</u> ἂν οὔτε <u>δυνάμενος ἐβουλήθην</u> ἔργοις ἐπιχειρεῖν τοιούτοις.
   - <u>Encomium to Helen</u> § 11: <u>ὅσοι</u> δὲ <u>ὅσους</u> περὶ <u>ὅσων</u> καὶ <u>ἔπεισαν</u> καὶ <u>πείθουσι</u> δὲ ψευδῆ λόγον πλάσαντες. εἰ μὲν γὰρ <u>πάντες</u> περὶ <u>πάντων</u> εἶχον <u>τῶν <τε> παροιχομένων</u> μνήμην τῶν τε παρόντων <ἔννοιαν> τῶν τε μελλόντων πρόνοιαν, οὐκ ἂν <u>ὁμοίως ὅμοιος</u> ἦν ὁ λόγος, [...] ὥστε περὶ τῶν <u>πλείστων</u> οἱ <u>πλεῖστοι</u> τὴν δόξαν σύμβουλον τῇ ψυχῇ παρέχονται. ἡ δὲ δόξα <u>σφαλερὰ</u> καὶ <u>ἀβέβαιος</u> οὖσα <u>σφαλεραῖς</u> καὶ <u>ἀβεβαίοις</u> εὐτυχίαις περιβάλλει τοὺς αὐτῇ χρωμένους.

2) Historical Agathon
   - Frag. 3.4: <u>Κούρητες</u> εἶναι, <u>κουρίμου</u> χάριν τριχός.
   - Frag. 6: <u>τέχνη τύχην</u> ἔστερξε καὶ <u>τύχη τέχνην</u> –where we also find a chiasmus–.
   - Frag. 11: τὸ μὲν <u>πάρεργον ἔργον</u> ὡς <u>ποιύμεθα</u>, τὸ δ' <u>ἔργον</u> ὡς <u>πάρεργον ἐκπονούμεθα</u>.

3) Character of Agathon in the Symposium:
   - ἐγὼ <u>δὲ δὴ</u> βούλομαι πρῶτον μὲν <u>εἰπεῖν</u> ὡς χρή με <u>εἰπεῖν</u>, ἔπειτα <u>εἰπεῖν</u> (194e4–5).
   - ὧν ὁ θεὸς <u>αὐτοῖς αἴτιος · ὁποῖος</u>... (194e7).
   - λόγῳ διελθεῖν <u>οἷος οἴων</u> αἴτιος... (195a2–3).
   - φεύγων φυγῇ τὸ πάρος (195a8–b2).
   - ὁ γὰρ παλαιὸς λόγος εὖ ἔχει, ὡς <u>ὅμοιον ὁμοίῳ</u> ἀεὶ πελάζει. ἐγὼ δὲ Φαίδρῳ <u>πολλὰ ἄλλα ὁμολογῶν</u> τοῦτο οὐχ <u>ὀνολογῶ</u>... (195b5–6).
   - Ἔρως <u>οὔτ' ἀδικεῖ οὔτ' ἀδικεῖται οὔτε</u> ὑπὸ <u>θεοῦ οὔτε θεόν</u>, <u>οὔτε</u> ὑπ' ἀνθρώπου <u>οὔτε</u> ἄνθρωπον (196b6–7).
   - οὗτος δὲ ἡμᾶς ἀλλοτριότητος μὲν κενοῖ, <u>οἰκειότητος</u> δὲ <u>πληροῖ</u>, [...] <u>ἐν ἑορταῖς, ἐν χοροῖς, ἐν</u> θυσίασι γιγνόμενος ἡγεμὼν · <u>πραότητα μὲν πορίζων, ἀγριότητα</u> δ' <u>ἐξορίζων</u> · φιλόδωρος εὐμενείας, <u>ἄδωρος δυσμενείας</u> · [...] <u>θεατὸς σοφοῖς, ἀγαστὸς θεοῖς</u> · <u>ζηλωτὸς ἀμοίροις, κτητὸς εὐμοίροις</u> · [...] <u>ἐπιμελὴς ἀγαθῶν, ἀμελὴς κακῶν</u> · <u>ἐν πόνῳ, ἐν φόβῳ, ἐν πόθῳ, ἐν λόγῳ, κυβερνήτης, ἐπιβάτης, παραστάτης</u>... (197d1–e2).

C. Content of both speeches: encomium of lógos, encomium of Éros

Regarding the content of both speeches, we believe that a lot of what the character of Agathon says about Eros is also asserted by Gorgias about *lógos*. Let us see some of those similarities.

1. <u>195b–c</u>: after Agathon says that Eros is "the most beautiful" of the gods, we immediately found three of the four causes that Gorgias considers as possible reasons of Helen's trip to Troy in the *EH*. Of course, they do not have the same argumentative function as in the *EH*, but the fact is that there, they are at least mentioned. In 195b-c we read: "... I do not agree <with Phaedrus> when he says that Eros is older than Cronus and Iapetus. On the contrary, I hold that he is the youngest of all gods and always young, and also that the old facts regarding the gods narrated by Hesiodus and Parmenides took place (if they are true) by the action of Necessity, not of Eros (*Anánkei kaì ouk Éros*). For there would have been no gelding or fettering of each other, nor any of those various violences (*bíaia*), if Eros had been amongst them". Let us say one more time that in Agathon's argument, Necessity, Eros and violence are not used in the same way as in the *EH* (first, fourth and second cause respectively). Nevertheless, their appearance at the beginning of the speech does not seem hazardous: the same concepts echo in both speeches[14].

2. <u>195e</u>: Agathon says that Eros is "delicate" (*hapalós*) since he does not live neither on earth nor in the heads of humans, but in the softest things among beings (*malakótaton tôn óntōn*), this is: the characters and the souls (*ḗthē kaì psychaí*). This 'delicacy' of Eros that bonds him with the 'softness' of the souls is also present, in a way, in Gorgias' *EH*. The sophist uses two specific verbs when he is talking about the relation between *lógos* and the human soul: "*plássein*" and "*typoûn*". We find the first one in paragraph 11 with the *lógos* as its object: "and how many have persuaded how many about how many things, and <still> persuade <them>, by moulding a false *lógos*!". *Lógos* is, as well as the soul, something capable of being moulded, shaped and, because of that, implicitly 'soft' or 'malleable'. This *lógos* that can be moulded is precisely what moulds the souls of those who listen: "the persuasion that comes with *lógos* certainly modelled (*etypósato*) the soul as it wanted" (§ 13).

---

[14] Let us remember that our aim in the present paper is to try to explain what made Socrates recall Gorgias after hearing Agathon. The mention of three of the four causes of the *EH* is, in that sense, doubtlessly relevant.

3. 196a: besides this delicacy of Eros, Agathon adds that he is pliant or flexible or soft (*hygrós*)[15] of form (*eîdos*), something that lets him surround the souls and, by doing that, he can remain unseen (*lanthánein*). We also find this 'invisibility' in gorgianic *lógos*: "*lógos* is a powerful sovereign that with the smallest and mostly invisible body (*sómati aphanestátoi*) completes the most divine works" (§ 8).

4. 196a: The biggest proof of the symmetric and flexible aspect of Eros is his "*euschemosýne*", literally: his "good (*eû*)-figure (*schêma*)", "good-shape", his "harmony" or "proportion"[16].

This insistence on the harmonious shape of an Eros that is always at war with deformity and lack of harmony (*aschemosýne*) recalls the gorgianic definition of truth: a *lógos* is true when it has order (*kósmos*), when it is harmonic, formally organized and developed. The Eros of Agathon, just like the *lógos* of Gorgias, is an example of *euschemosýne*, this is: a reality that constitutes a *kósmos*. This is reinforced a few lines ahead when Agathon says that Eros is "*kósmos* of absolutely every god and man" (197e2)[17]: the relation between truth and *lógos* in the EH is equivalent to that between Eros and every man and god in the speech of Agathon.

5. 196c: "the sovereign laws of the city say that 'things that <someone> may agree with someone who acts willingly as well are just". The lines that Agathon quotes are ascribed by Aristotle (*Rhet.* 1406a22) to Alcidamas of Elea, an orator that is supposed to have been a disciple of Gorgias.

6. 197d–e: "in speech (*en lógoi*), <Eros> is pilot, sailor, a front-rank-man and also an excellent saviour". We can see that Eros is, regarding *lógos*, the most powerful sophist since he can hold every position: he can steer the dialectic ship and, "excellent saviour", bring it safely to a good harbour. When it comes to speech, there is nothing Eros cannot do. This omnipotence recalls, *mutatis mutandis*, that of gorgianic *lógos* defined as a "*dynástes mégas*", capable of completing "the most divine works" (*theiótata érga*). Likewise, we also read in 194e4 that Eros "participates in a song that sings charming the thought (*nóema*) of every god and man". This capacity to charm (*thélgein*) ascribed to Eros is ascribed by Gor-

---

15 We take this sense of "*hygrós*" as an antonym of "*sklerós*", "hard" (see 195e1). It is worthy to mention that the term has also erotic connotations that make it close even with "effeminate" (see Bailly *s.v.* II.6).

16 The connotation of "harmony" and "proportion" of the term may be found in the *Republic* 400c, where the *euschemosýne* and its opposite, the *aschemosýne*, are equivalent of the "rhythmic" (*eúrythmon*) and the "un-rhythmic" (*árrythmon*) respectively.

17 The context and the polysemy of the term make it very difficult to justify a final translation for "*kósmos*". Some other possible translations are "government" (Dover), "*honneur*" (Brisson), "ornato" (Juliá).

gias as well, but to *lógos:* "the enchantment inspired through words (*hai éntheoi dià lógon epoidaí*) leads to pleasure and moves away from pain" (§ 10).

7. 197e: Agathon finishes his intervention as follows: "be devoted to the god, Phaedrus, this speech of mine, speech that takes part, regarding some things, in the game (*paidiâs*), and regarding other things, as much as it is possible for me, in a measured seriousness (*spoudês metrías*)". We have already mentioned the coincidence with paragraph 21 of the *EH* and the "*paígnion*". But what about the "measured seriousness" that Agathon claims to have had in his speech?

It is important to recall the gorgianic definition of *poíesis:* "I consider and call absolutely every poetry 'speech with measure' (*lógon échonta métron*)" (§ 9). What does this definition have to do with what we are discussing? As Dover has shown meticulously, the speech of Agathon may be scanned just as if it were written in verse, which could also mean, according to gorgianic parameters, that it is a "speech with measure". Since, as Dover (1980, p. 124) says, "Plato has taken considerable trouble to give Agathon's peroration a poetic character in addition to caricaturing its 'Gorgianic' structure", that is: since the speech of Agathon is, apart from a rhetorically organized speech, a kind of poetry, *lógos échon métron*, it is likely that Agathon refers to the measured *poetic* seriousness of what in fact was a *rhetorical* game. After all, the character of Agathon is, just like Eros, a poet.

Conclusion

At the beginning of this paper we intended to track down the reasons why Socrates remembered Gorgias after hearing Agathon in the *Symposium*. Even when this may seem a pure speculative endeavour, we may think, why not, that maybe that was the intention of Plato: to cover up the allusion whom, over and over again if his dialogues, appears as a declared enemy. Why Plato decided to hide Gorgias behind Agathon is something unsolvable as well. One might answer that among those present there was already a *rhétor* like Phaidrus and not a composer of tragedies. Maybe the supposed theoretical rivalry between Socrates and Gorgias would have made the scene of a symposium shared by both of them implausible. Be that as it may, we do not expect to have *demonstrated* that behind the shoulders of the poet arises the head of the gorgianic Gorgon. We have rather wanted to give some elements that at least allow us to *insinuate* which were the possible reasons why Socrates recalls Gorgias after hearing Agathon: "because, certainly, his speech reminded me of Gorgias...".

Works Cited

Bieda, E 2008, 'Why did Helen travel to Troy? About the presence and incidence of fortune in Gorgias' Encomium to Helen', *Revue de Philosophie Ancienne* vol. XXVI, no. 1, pp. 3–24.

Brisson, L 2007, *Traduction, Introduction et Notes a Platon. Le Banquet*, Flammarion, Paris.

Bury, R G 190), *The Symposium of Plato*, W. Heffner and Sons, Cambridge.

Casertano, G 1986, 'L'amour entre lógos et páthos. Quelques considérations sur l' Helene de Gorgias', in B Cassin (ed), *Positions de la sophistique*, Vrin, Paris.

Cordero, N L 2000, 'Los atomistas y los celos de Platón', *Méthexis* vol. XIII, pp. 7–16.

Crockett, A 1994, 'Gorgias's Encomium of Helen: violent rhetoric or radical feminism?', *Rhetoric Review* vol. 13, no. 1, pp.71–90.

Diels, H & Kranz W 1952, *Die Fragmente der Vorsokratiker*, Weidmann, Berlin.

Dover, K J 1980, *Edition and Commentary on Plato's Symposium*, Cambridge University Press, Cambridge.

Hunter, R 2004, *Plato's Symposium*, Oxford University Press, Oxford.

Immisch, O 1927, *Gorgiae Helena*, Verlag von Walter de Gruyter & Co, Berlin und Leipzig.

Mársico, C 2007, 'Argumentar por caminos extremos: I) La imposibilidad de pensar lo que es; Gorgias y la instauración del criterio de verdad como coherencia de enunciados', in Castello, L A & Mársico, C T (eds), *El lenguaje como problema entre los griegos. ¿Cómo decir lo real?*, GEA, Buenos Aires.

Mazzara, G 1999, *Gorgia. La retorica del verosimile*, Academia Verlag.

Platón 2004, *Banquete*, Losada, Buenos Aires (intro., trad. & notes by V. Juliá).

Platón 1986, *Banquete*, in *Platón-Diálogos III*, Gredos, Madrid (trad. M. Martínez Hernández).

Platon 1951, *Le Banquet*, Les Belles Lettres, Paris (texte établi et traduit par L. Robin).

Platon 2007, *Le Banquet*, Flammarion, Paris (ed. by L. Brisson).

Robin, L 1951, *Introduction et notes a Platon. Le Banquet*", Les Belles Lettres, Paris.

Rowe, Ch 1998, *Plato: Symposium*, Aris & Phillips Ltd, Warminster.

Segal, Ch P 1962, 'Gorgias and the psychology of the lógos', in *Harvard Studies in Classical Philology* Vol.66, pp. 99–155.

Untersteiner, M 1967, *Sofisti, Testimonianze e Frammenti*, La Nuova Italia, Firenze.

Stokes, M C 1986, *Plato's Socratic Conversations*, John Hopkins University Press, Baltimore.

Beatriz Bossi
Plato's Phaedrus: A Play Inside the Play

> Anyone who fails to notice the element of comedy in this is, I fear, beyond help.
> Josef Pieper[1]

I.

It is usually thought that Socrates cannot abandon Phaedrus and go back across the river because his daimon forbids him to do so. This voice he hears when he is about to commit a shameful act, and Phaedrus is in need of a new speech on Eros, because the former ones do not offer a proper image of the God. Here I should like to show that Socrates' return has, in addition, a deeper meaning: Socrates cannot leave Phaedrus in his ignorance because he has something to teach his friend, and also because there is something he needs to know about himself. Socrates has to teach Phaedrus how a real lover acts towards his beloved, and by doing so, he has to learn whether he is able to master himself. This is a decisive moment in the dialogue, in which he reveals himself as a real teacher, who can transcend both the image of an erupting Typhoon who wants to devour his victim and also the image of a peaceful citizen, untouched by madness.

II. "Dear Phaedrus, where are you going and where do you come from?"(227a1)[2]

With this question, without further ado, the *Phaedrus* begins. It seems a simple question, just an innocent pretext for starting a conversation, but it could also be interpreted as a deliberate marker of a dynamic psychological process in which all of us find ourselves: we start from our beliefs and our ignorance, and we try to open ourselves up to new experience and to knowledge. The question is answered in the horizontal plane of space: Phaedrus says that he is going for a walk outside the walls, in order to take a rest. The walls protect, the walls enclose. The *pharmakon* heals, the *pharmakon* kills.

---

1 Pieper (1964, p. 33).
2 ὦ φίλε Φαῖδρε, ποῖ δὴ καὶ πόθεν;

The psychological response cannot be offered yet, but remains suspended, and the whole dialogue is, in a sense, an attempt to answer this initial question at two different levels: the level of speeches and the level of dramatic action. In the interaction, each character will receive some revelation about himself, and after the prayer and dismissal, will be able to go ahead in a different way.

The *Phaedrus* is composed of fine lace. In this dialogue, as well as in the *Lysis*[3], what the characters say and what happens in the dramatic action are the two sides of a single tissue. It is not just that Phaedrus reads a speech written by Lysias, about the appropriateness of pleasing a non-lover, but that Phaedrus himself is a prisoner of Lysias' snobbish rhetoric, which promotes pursuing maximum pleasure with minimal complications, while disguised as respect and discretion. And it is not merely that Socrates makes a speech similar to the previous one he had heard in order to please Phaedrus, but that Socrates cannot do anything else but pretend to agree formally to the speech, because he competes with Lysias for Phaedrus' attention, i.e., because he is, as he says later, "poisoned" by him (καταφαρμακευθέντος: 242e1).

However, there will come a moment in which Phaedrus himself, who gives the appearance of glowing with love for speeches, will want to learn from Socrates. He will leave behind the walls of empty words, and will let Socrates take him to the revelation of what the soul is like and of what it really wants. And he will find that he can, in imagination, ascend from the refreshing green spot beside the river along the heavenly paths of the gods to the true valley where souls are fed.

But to move Phaedrus on from his initial fascination, and to persuade him to make a change of course will require Socrates' strategic subtlety. And in spite of it, his first attempt will end in failure.

III. "If I don't know Phaedrus, I have forgotten myself" (228a5 – 6)[4]

The first game of flattery starts. Phaedrus tells Socrates that what he has to say is a matter of interest for him, and Socrates pleases him by saying he is eager to listen to him, at the extreme of sacrifice to himself, several times[5]. Phaedrus pro-

---

3 Bossi (2000).
4 εἰ ἐγὼ Φαῖδρον ἀγνοῶ, καὶ ἐμαυτοῦ ἐπιλέλησμαι.
5 He says he would follow him to Megara (227 d), and this strange Socrates, who looks like a foreigner to Phaedrus' eyes, says he could be led all over Attika by someone waving written

vokes him by putting Lysias' skills on a pedestal: he calls him δεινότατος, "the skillful" or also "the most terrible"[6] (228a1). He wants to be begged, and he pretends he cannot remember what the great Lysias wrote. Socrates reacts to this, aware as he is of the fact that Phaedrus knows the speech by heart and wants to show off, having met someone who is sick with passion for hearing speeches, a maniac like himself, a fellow who could lead him to ecstasy (συγκορυβαντιῶντα) (228b7).

Both characters are presented as united in their poetic madness, and we know how in Corybantic cults (ἐν τῇ τελετῇ τῶν Κορυβάντων) the initiate is enthroned amidst dancing and enthusiastic singing (cf. *Euthydemus* 277d). Such indeed will be the atmosphere of what lies ahead. After Lysias' speech is over, Socrates will find it "brilliant" (δαιμονίως 234d1), and will confess to having entered into Bacchic delirium with him (234d5: συνεβάκχευσα) when looking at his divine head as he was reading the speech. This Socrates is presented by Plato as if he were not able to say openly what he thinks about the content of the speech, and, apparently, will merely make a few formal comments. Why does he not do his job? Why does he not openly reject the content, or humiliate Phaedrus in order to teach him?

Phaedrus is dazzled by the speech of Lysias, and unable to undergo the test of refutation, while Socrates himself is drawn to enthrone Phaedrus, and cannot contradict him because he is under the effect of his venom. So much so that his daimon will have to intervene as the necessary antidote.

Socrates' words indicate that he knows his interlocutor so well that it would be necessary for him to forget who he is himself, if he were to ignore Phaedrus' purpose, which is none other than to provoke his admiration.

Later on, when he is about to leave Phaedrus in his ignorance and re-cross the river, the certainty about what the God deserves and what Phaedrus needs to know will force him to return. And just as he turned to Phaedrus, Socrates will return to himself. He will have to leave aside his narcissistic pain at Phaedrus' having fallen in love so blindly with the rhetoric of Lysias, and with the young man himself, and by revealing the mysteries of the Palinode to Phaedrus, he will have the chance to remind himself of them, and to become his best self.

---

speeches in front of him (230 d). This is surprising, for we know Socrates cannot stand long speeches (*Prot.* 334 d; *Gorg.* 449 b).

[6] Socrates will apply this very adjective to those who do not believe the evidence that love is a divine madness (245 b-c). He will also use it to describe Lysias' speech and his own first speech.

IV. "I investigate not these things but myself" (230a3)[7]

Socrates is worried about his true identity, because he has not been able to get to know himself, and therefore it seems ridiculous to him that he should investigate what he does not really care about, i.e. the beliefs and myths commonly accepted in the city. What he wants to know is whether he has become "a beast more convoluted and swollen (πολυπλοκώτερον καὶ μᾶλλον ἐπιτεθυμμένον) than Typhoon or a more peaceful and simpler creature, to whom a divine and clear lot (ἀτύφου μοίρας) is given by nature" (230a3–6)[8].

Socrates fears to have become a devious man, dominated by multiple and opposing desires, a proud, boastful, dangerous beast that destroys everything it touches. But he is not sure about this; maybe he has become a more civilized and simpler man, governed by a single principle, and able to participate in a divine destiny[9].

Socrates' concern may also be an advance notice of the image of the soul as a winged chariot: will this Socrates be a skillful charioteer able to drive his soul to his destiny, instead of competing with Lysias for Phaedrus' attention?

Although the atmosphere of seduction might suggest that Phaedrus is the potential youth beloved of Socrates, due to his age (between 30 and 40) he plays the part of lover[10], and this is manifested at the end of the dialogue: Phaedrus is Lysias' lover and Socrates is presented as Isocrates' (279b1–3). In line with this, Socrates fights, not for Phaedrus' love, but to take him away from the rhetoric of the Sophists[11]. Although this intellectual purpose is clearly there, we cannot ignore the deliberately charming atmosphere and the delicious games of praise and jealousy, especially manifest in the interludes, which indicate a rela-

---

7 σκοπῶ οὐ ταῦτα ἀλλ' ἐμαυτόν.
8 A Typhoon is a hundred-headed monster with a terrible voice, a fiery belch of smoke, manifested in the furious and devouring eruption of volcanoes (*Il.* II 782; *Theog.* 820 ff.).
9 In terms comparable to the tripartite scheme of the soul in the *Republic*, Socrates wonders whether what dominates himself is a multiplicity of appetites, combined with a pride always ready to rage over nothing (his spirited part), or whether his rational part is in control, able to tame the appetites, free from vain pretensions, and having access to divine, intellectual contemplation.
10 De Vries (1969, p. 6) points out how, even when Socrates calls him "young" (257 c 8) or "boy" (267 c 6), these forms denote Socrates' intention to emphasize the difference in age when addressing someone younger that himself.
11 There is no erotic relationship between Phaedrus and Socrates, according to De Vries (1969, p. 6); Gooch (1992, pp. 309–312); and Yunis (2011, p. 9), among other scholars.

tionship of complicity and close rivalry between the two friends, whose ups and downs mark the dynamic of the speeches.

So, from the very beginning, this Socrates does not appear to be the teacher who leads the discussion with mastery, refuting and teaching, as does the protagonist of the *Protagoras* or the *Gorgias*. This rather tentative Socrates probably does not know whether he will be able to persuade Phaedrus in the right direction, because he has tremendous concerns about his own personality. The announcement of his 'existential' doubts leads to ambivalent attitudes, and obviously Socrates is wounded by the exalted devotion of Phaedrus towards his beloved (cf. 234e).

One could be surprised or even feel irritated by a Socrates who, when giving his verdict on Lysias' speech, shows an evasive attitude. Firstly, led by a "Bacchic frenzy" provoked by Phaedrus' reading, he does not proceed directly to contradict him, but rather he 'enthrones' the speech by calling it "cool" or "inspired". Secondly, he is reluctant to judge the value of the content of the speech and only seems to notice its formal defects.

However, when Phaedrus provokes him by his view that Lysias' speech cannot be bettered (235b: 'nobody could ever speak about it more exhaustively or worthily than he has done'), Socrates disagrees and refuses to condescend to him, recognizing the superior value of other poets, such as the beautiful Sappho and the wise Anacreon, and other prose writers. He feels that his own 'breast is full', and that he could make another speech, addressed to the divine Phaedrus, different from the former one and not inferior to it: πλῆρές πως, ὦ δαιμόνιε, τὸ στῆθος ἔχων αἰσθάνομαι παρὰ ταῦτα ἂν ἔχειν εἰπεῖν ἕτερα μὴ χείρω (235c5–6), not because he had thought about these matters by himself, but because he has been suffused with other sources. This reference to Socrates' breast as full of inspiration is a clue from Plato that Socrates now feels courageous enough to start saying what he really thinks. Not because he is full of 'vain boastful smoke' like a Typhoon, but because he feels supported by a great tradition that says the opposite: 'love is madness'.

Phaedrus interprets this to mean that he will offer a better and longer speech, and enthusiastically promises a golden statue of both of them at Delphi. Socrates, in a fit of candor, calls him 'dearest' and 'really made of gold' if he thinks that he is claiming that Lysias was completely wrong, and that he himself can make a speech that is different on every point from his. That could not happen –he says- even to the worst possible author[12]. Why?

---

[12] Pieper (1964, p. 29) observes that irony adds certain difficulties to the conversation. Plato

I assume it is because Lysias' speech is partly right and partly wrong. So Plato is again warning us about the content of Socrates' next speech: to make it 'true' it must retain some parts and discard other parts[13]. In my view, Socrates is suggesting that, on the one hand, the praise of the serenity of the non-lover and the censorship of the lover's unreason will impress the audience as acceptable, topical points which nobody would dare to object to, (that could be organized in a better way) while, on the other hand, the arguments described as 'difficult to find' should be 'praised' as invention.

I think this praise is ironical. Lysias has offered a number of "not obvious" judgments that Socrates will fight. But he speaks in general terms, in a cautious way, so that Phaedrus does not feel scandalized, while the reader can anticipate his decision to dissent.

Phaedrus seems to have captured some irony in Socrates' words. After extolling Socrates for speaking in a measured way, he grants Socrates his ridiculous permission to "presuppose that the lover is sicker than the non-lover" and then, placing himself in a position to reward Socrates, he sets a condition: if Socrates is able to add anything of value to the former speech, he promises him a second statue, this time in Olympia.

Here again Socrates seems to realize that Phaedrus feels attacked, and that he simply wants to have the main thesis granted. So he returns to his humble attitude, and makes clear that he was only criticizing Phaedrus' beloved in order to tease him, and so this should not be taken seriously (236b5–8).

At this point Phaedrus returns Socrates his trap: "If I do not know Socrates is that I have forgotten myself", he says, because despite the misgivings of his friend, Phaedrus knows Socrates wants to speak. However, to be sure, he threatens him not to share any other speech with him ever in his life. Socrates follows him in the game and calls him "evil", and communicates to him his decision to

---

makes it look as though his main character is playing the fool when he is in fact building a powerful argument, and gives the impression of being enthusiastic when he is really being critical.

[13] "For example, to take the subject of his speech, who do you suppose, in arguing that the non-lover ought to be more favoured than the lover, could omit praise of the non-lover's calm sense and blame of the lover's unreason, which are inevitable arguments, and then say something else instead? No, I think, we must allow these points, and concede them to the speaker. In their case, we cannot praise their novelty but only their skilful arrangement, but in the case of arguments which are not inevitable and are hard to discover, the invention deserves praise as well as the arrangement": αὐτίκα περὶ οὗ ὁ λόγος, τίνα οἴει λέγοντα ὡς χρὴ μὴ ἐρῶντι μᾶλλον ἢ ἐρῶντι χαρίζεσθαι, παρέντα τοῦ μὲν τὸ φρόνιμον ἐγκωμιάζειν, τοῦ δὲ τὸ ἄφρον ψέγειν, ἀναγκαῖα γοῦν ὄντα, εἶτ' ἄλλ' ἄττα ἕξειν λέγειν; ἀλλ' οἶμαι τὰ μὲν τοιαῦτα ἐατέα καὶ συγγνωστέα λέγοντι· καὶ τῶν μὲν τοιούτων οὐ τὴν εὕρεσιν ἀλλὰ τὴν διάθεσιν ἐπαινετέον, τῶν δὲ μὴ ἀναγκαίων τε καὶ χαλεπῶν εὑρεῖν πρὸς τῇ διαθέσει καὶ τὴν εὕρεσιν (235 e 5–236 a 6).

speak with his head covered in order to end quickly and not to feel ashamed to look at him.

Before the Palinode, this Socrates seems to behave, in part, as a lover of flattery, fearful of drawing the enmity of Phaedrus, and acting in part not unlike the passionate lover Lysias combats, whose desire clouds his mind (233a).

The evasiveness of Socrates in this interlude, his typical admission of ignorance, his desire not to antagonize Phaedrus, and his fear of being ashamed in front of him, are commonly interpreted as anticipatory signs that the first speech of Socrates is an imitation of that of Lysias, formally improved but false and blasphemous in respect of content. Yet at every turn, interspersed with timid attitudes, we find that Socrates, in his outbursts of sincerity, also offers encrypted statements whose real goal is confrontation. This tremendous ambiguity in his attitude makes us think that Socrates feared his own Typhoon so much that he may have supposed that simply looking at Phaedrus could force him to say things to please his friend once more, instead of telling him the truth.

So, in my view, it is not in order to protect Phaedrus that Socrates covers his head, and certainly not because he will tell him what is not true, but on the contrary, to protect himself from the influence of Phaedrus[14], i.e. to say without hesitation what Phaedrus does not want to hear. The paradox is that Phaedrus, who apparently does not give any importance to the gesture, will listen, believing that Lysias' thesis has been granted.

In defense of the "limpid and civilized creature" who also dwells within him, Socrates covers his head, in order to open Phaedrus' mind to his views, even indirectly, by offering his friend some important clues, which are presented in the introduction to his first speech and I have summarized as follows:

1.) Socrates asks the Muses to help him; and
2.) He reveals the true intention of the "non lover" by telling a story:

> Now there was once upon a time a boy, or rather a youth, of great beauty: and he had many lovers. And among these was one of peculiar craftiness, who was as much in love with the boy as the others, but had made him believe that he was not in love. And once in pressing

---

14 Tejera (1992, p. 291) thinks that Socrates is blocked here: he is conquered by the eroticism of the situation, while resisting the sexuality of his answer. He observes that those scholars who do not perceive this point are unfair towards the self-control of Socrates, who has to make up a story about a pursuer and a pursued in order to put some distance between his own and Lysias' position; he mentions Schaerer (1938); De Vries (1969); Cooper (1938); Fowler (1914). Also for Helmbold and Holther (1952, p. 388) Socrates courts Phaedrus in an emotionally warm atmosphere, with multiple references to the *eros paidikos*.

his suit to him, he tried to persuade him that he ought to give his favours to a man who did not love him rather than to one who did (237b2–5)[15].

This way Socrates makes clear that the wily lover was just in love like the others, chasing the same thing as all of them: sexual pleasure;

3.) Socrates wants to come to an agreement on a definition of love, its nature and its power, in order to distinguish the lover from the non-lover: τῷ δὴ τὸν ἐρῶντά τε καὶ μὴ κρινοῦμεν. Thus, he presents two principles that govern and lead us: a natural appetite for pleasure and the learned opinion concerning the best, and he adds that these two principles are sometimes in agreement within us and are sometimes in a state of strife; and sometimes one, and sometimes the other has the greater power[16].

4.) Socrates also claims that:

> When opinion leads through reason toward the best and is more powerful, its power is called 'moderation' (σωφροσύνη; lit. 'being in your right mind' as Nehamas and Woodruff translate[17]) but when desire irrationally drags us toward pleasures and rules within us, its rule is called 'excess' (ὕβρις). Now excess has many names, for it has many members and many forms[18].

Like the Typhoon, it is multiple.

5.) Socrates adds that:

> The desire that overcomes rational opinion that strives toward the right, and which is driven to take pleasure in beauty, and again is strongly reinforced by its kindred desires for

---

15 ἦν οὕτω δὴ παῖς, μᾶλλον δὲ μειρακίσκος, μάλα καλός: τούτῳ δὲ ἦσαν ἐρασταὶ πάνυ πολλοί. εἷς δέ τις αὐτῶν αἱμύλος ἦν, ὃς οὐδενὸς ἧττον ἐρῶν ἐπεπείκει τὸν παῖδα ὡς οὐκ ἐρῴη. καί ποτε αὐτὸν αἰτῶν ἔπειθεν τοῦτ' αὐτό, ὡς μὴ ἐρῶντι πρὸ τοῦ ἐρῶντος δέοι χαρίζεσθαι.
16 ὅτι μὲν οὖν δὴ ἐπιθυμία τις ὁ ἔρως, ἅπαντι δῆλον: ὅτι δ' αὖ καὶ μὴ ἐρῶντες ἐπιθυμοῦσι τῶν καλῶν, ἴσμεν. τῷ δὴ τὸν ἐρῶντά τε καὶ μὴ κρινοῦμεν; δεῖ αὖ νοῆσαι ὅτι ἡμῶν ἐν ἑκάστῳ δύο τινέ ἐστον ἰδέα ἄρχοντε καὶ ἄγοντε, οἷν ἑπόμεθα ᾗ ἂν ἄγητον, ἡ μὲν ἔμφυτος οὖσα ἐπιθυμία ἡδονῶν, ἄλλη δὲ ἐπίκτητος δόξα, ἐφιεμένη τοῦ ἀρίστου. τούτω δὲ ἐν ἡμῖν τοτὲ μὲν ὁμονοεῖτον, ἔστι δὲ ὅτε στασιάζετον: καὶ τοτὲ μὲν ἡ ἑτέρα, ἄλλοτε δὲ ἡ ἑτέρα κρατεῖ (237 d 3- e 2).
17 Cooper (1997) ad loc.
18 δόξης μὲν οὖν ἐπὶ τὸ ἄριστον λόγῳ ἀγούσης καὶ κρατούσης τῷ κράτει σωφροσύνη ὄνομα: ἐπιθυμίας δὲ ἀλόγως ἑλκούσης ἐπὶ ἡδονὰς καὶ ἀρξάσης ἐν ἡμῖν τῇ ἀρχῇ ὕβρις ἐπωνομάσθη. ὕβρις δὲ δὴ πολυώνυμον —πολυμελὲς γὰρ καὶ πολυμερές (237 e 2–238 a 3).

beauty in human bodies, this desire, when it gains the victory, takes its name from the word for 'force' (ῥώμη), and is called 'love' (ἔρως).[19]

Plato invents this etymology here.

By introducing the distinction between appetite for pleasure, on the one hand, and right opinion concerning the best, on the other hand, and by claiming that the first one is called "love", what Socrates says from this point onwards, in imitation of Lysias' speech, refers to love in its ordinary, vulgar sense, i.e., egocentric sexual desire. This force, either when concealed by the non-lover or made manifest by the passionate lover, "has nothing beautiful or worthy in Socrates' view".[20]

However, it is important to observe that Socrates implicitly anticipates here the intellectual principle essential to the Palinode. Having defined ἔρως as sexual appetite, and having claimed that both the lover and the non lover share the same goal, setting aside their external behaviour, there is no difference concerning the quality of their feelings. But Socrates here also mentions 'right opinion concerning the best'. If this principle is essential to mankind, ἔρως cannot be mere passionate desire for sex, and divine erotic madness should include this 'non innate' opinion concerning the best, that the teacher should transmit to his beloved.

This Socrates, apparently too vulnerable, insecure, and amorous, is quite different from the unconvincing master of the early dialogues who would tire his interlocutors due to his arrogance and hidden desires of victory at all costs. This more human and closer Socrates has deployed subtle stratagems in order to reject Lysias' judgments categorically but indirectly. He even begins to suspect that perhaps he might beat his own Typhoon. But as he has spoken so discreetly he will have to go through the bitter experience of facing the fact that Phaedrus has not noticed that Socrates' speech actually contradicts that of Lysias.[21]

---

19 ἡ γὰρ ἄνευ λόγου δόξης ἐπὶ τὸ ὀρθὸν ὁρμώσης κρατήσασα ἐπιθυμία πρὸς ἡδονὴν ἀχθεῖσα κάλλους, καὶ ὑπὸ αὖ τῶν ἑαυτῆς συγγενῶν ἐπιθυμιῶν ἐπὶ σωμάτων κάλλος ἐρρωμένως ῥωσθεῖσα νικήσασα ἀγωγῇ, ἀπ' αὐτῆς τῆς ῥώμης ἐπωνυμίαν λαβοῦσα, ἔρως ἐκλήθη (238 b 7– c 4).
20 Sinaiko (1965, pp. 35–36) observes that this definition, based exclusively upon common opinion, lacks definite limits because Socrates does not specify that this is just one type of love, and that is why it turns out to be deceitful.
21 In this sense, the analysis of the psychological ambiguities of Socrates leads to the conclusion, advocated by Friedländer (1960, p. 207), that the first speech of Socrates, far from being limited to a formal review of the speech of Lysias, exposes the dangers of the speaker's message. In the same vein, Calvo (1992, p. 50) understands that this speech is 'deeply true'. And although

The speech of Lysias and the speech of Socrates agree verbatim in their rejection of possessive, manipulative love, and in the value of self-control. Three times Lysias emphasizes this aspect of the behavior of the non-lover: 1) he does not act out of necessity but deliberates willingly on the best (231a4–5), 2) he is master of himself, and chooses what is really best (232a4–6) and will not be dominated by Eros but by himself (233c1–2). However, in fact they do not really argue for the same thesis, but for opposite ones, since Socrates has realized that the non-lover is a liar who seeks the same as the passionate lover, i.e., mere sexual pleasure, unaccompanied by the friendship and consideration that Lysias claims the non-lover possesses (233a and 233c–d); he only uses apparent self-control to get more easily and effectively what he wants[22].

V. "Perhaps the attack may be averted" (238d6)[23]

Socrates finishes the preamble of his speech enthusiastically. He feels that while speaking he has suffered a divine transport (the place looks divine too, he is 'quite taken by the madness of the Muses", everything sounds like a dithyramb) and he attributes the cause of it all to Phaedrus. He asks Phaedrus to listen to what follows because, he says, "perhaps the attack (which threatens him) might be averted." That, however, is, according to Socrates, in the hands of God, and they must return to their boy.

In my view, Socrates feels helped by the divine Muses because he was able to speak frankly, by overcoming his fear of antagonizing Phaedrus.

At the beginning of the story, Socrates identifies the lover as the one who is dominated by desire, a slave of pleasure, and from that point onwards, nothing can be of worthy in the long description of his petty behavior with the beloved, which is summarized in the final judgment "as wolves want lambs, so lovers love young men" (ὡς λύκοι ἄρνας ἀγαπῶσιν, ὣς παῖδα φιλοῦσιν ἐρασταί: 241d1). Socrates ends the speech and flatly refuses to continue: "you will not hear another word from me," he says.

Phaedrus is stunned, because he expected Socrates to describe the advantages of pleasing the non-lover. It is clear that Socrates cannot do this, so he

---

Socrates will criticize it severely, judging that it is neither healthy nor true (242 e 5–243 a 1), he "does not deny, in retrospect, its content but only its lack of integration into a broader perspective" as Ferrari wrote (1987, p. 112).

22 I agree with Trabattoni (2011, p. 292) that both speeches say the same thing 'verbatim', but I disagree about his conclusion that they defend the same theses in depth.

23 ἴσως γὰρ κἂν ἀποτράποιτο τὸ ἐπιόν.

wants to get rid of him as soon as possible, and he gives him two justifications: 1) "the shortcomings for which we have blamed one, in the other are present as the opposite of them, as good qualities: ὅσα τὸν ἕτερον λελοιδορήκαμεν, τῷ ἑτέρῳ τἀναντία τούτων ἀγαθὰ πρόσεστιν." (241e5–6) and 2) "I have said enough about both of them" (241e7), so there is no need to make the discourse longer.

However, these justifications seem contradictory, because, if it is true that the non lover behaves well, Socrates has not spoken about him, and if the same criticism is applied to both of them, then it is not true that the non lover does well.

In my view, the second justification is understandable because in the introduction to his myth, Socrates has spoken of both of them: they both pursue their own pleasure. Therefore, we cannot conclude that one should please the non-lover, because both of them seek their own pleasure in an egocentric way, and since neither of them takes good care of the "beloved" (by appealing to his 'opinion concerning the best'), none of them deserves any compensation in terms of sexual pleasure. And though this is obvious to the attentive reader, it is not evident to Pheadrus.

As regards the first justification, it seems to suggest that if the non lover behaved contrary to the way the passionate lover acts, his conduct would be good. If selfish intruding passion is bad, the lack of it would turn out to be good. Let us observe that it is not necessarily the lack of any kind of passion which is to be rejected but the lack of selfish passion.

As it has become clear that for Socrates the non lover apparently controls himself but he is as selfish as the passionate lover and both of them are 'wolves', we can only infer that the opposite to what is objectionable to both characters is good. But that has not been said so far. Good divine passion has not entered the scene yet.

VI. "This way my story will meet the end it deserves, and I will cross this stream and leave before you put some further compulsion upon me" (241e8–242a2).[24]

When Socrates realizes that Phaedrus has not understood the message, for he does not accept that the non-lover is a fake, and apparently is not aware of the distinction between the opinion concerning the best and the desire for pleasure, he gives up.

Socrates no longer believes he can add anything else, since the seeds of his words have fallen on deaf ears. So Socrates desperately wants to leave. He has waged his own battle; has had the impression that he could beat his own Typhoon in a moment of exaltation when his clear-thinking part could tell the truth to Phaedrus; and had hoped that his friend would have understood the message. But despite his patience and special care not to oppose him straightforwardly, Phaedrus is convinced that the beloved should please the non-lover.

There are two forces that move the discourse's tension and dramatic action forward: uncertainty about the next step and confidence in the divine. This is the lowest moment in the dialogue, in which Socrates loses patience, and cannot bear further thought about Phaedrus' snobbish ideas. Uncertainty overcomes him, because, despite his strategy and efforts, nothing was enough to awaken Phaedrus from his delusion.

But has the masquerade ended? We all know the answer. The dialogue goes on. When Socrates starts crossing the river, Phaedrus appeals to the heat and the hour to persuade him to stay. Socrates turns round, gracefully praises his ability to convince, and reveals, to his amazement, that he is the cause of his coming back and making another speech. Phaedrus is happy that Socrates is no longer battling him, yet he does not understand his turnaround.

Socrates attributes his return to the fact that when he was crossing the river he felt the voice of his daimon preventing him from leaving, immediately guessed that he had committed some fault, and understood why he had felt a kind of anguish as he was speaking. Lysias' speech is as dreadful (δεινός) as the one Phaedrus made him give (242d4–5). This adjective can be translated as "terrible", "dangerous", "powerful", "skilled", and "clever".

---

24 καὶ οὕτω δὴ ὁ μῦθος ὅτι πάσχειν προσήκει αὐτῷ, τοῦτο πείσεται· κἀγὼ τὸν ποταμὸν τοῦτον διαβὰς ἀπέρχομαι πρὶν ὑπὸ σοῦ τι μεῖζον ἀναγκασθῆναι.

Now, Lysias' speech is terrible because it was false, and Socrates' speech is terrible because it was too "simple", and, to some extent, impious. Socrates has made a unilateral simplification of love, since he has taken it in its popular meaning, as mere appetite for sexual pleasure. In this respect, none of the speeches "said anything healthy or true" (242e5–243a2), because the partial view does not show the real nature of love and its greatness. Socrates feels guilty, and attributes his first speech to the pressure and poison of Phaedrus, who, being in love with Lysias, provoked his jealousy and rivalry.[25]

VII. Soc.: "Where is the boy to whom I was speaking? He should hear this also; if he does not, he may rush to please the non-lover. Phaed.: "Here he is, always by your side, very close, whenever you want him" (243e4–8).[26]

The love of friendship which Socrates feels for Phaedrus reveals itself, after the Socratic turnaround, as increasingly more serious, strong and committed. In general terms, we should not interpret the relationship between them as erotic.[27] On the one hand, because the dialogue ends by presenting them as two friends who have all in common, including the experience of being two adults who each love

---

[25] It is time to purify and sing the glories of authentic love, which is a divine madness that drives the soul to its true destiny, at the edge of the cosmos. The sight of beauty overwhelms the master with the sacred memory of Perfect Beauty, initiates the growth of new wings, and fills him with the overwhelming desire to lead the soul of the disciple, which he guesses is similar to his own, and also to the god he had elected in the celestial procession.

[26] ποῦ δή μοι ὁ παῖς πρὸς ὃν ἔλεγον; ἵνα καὶ τοῦτο ἀκούσῃ, καὶ μὴ ἀνήκοος ὢν φθάσῃ χαρισάμενος τῷ μὴ ἐρῶντι. οὗτος παρά σοι μάλα πλησίον ἀεὶ πάρεστιν, ὅταν σὺ βούλῃ.

[27] Nussbaum (1986, p. 204; p. 211) thinks that Socrates is the lover *par excellence*, and that Phaedrus is the pleasing beloved, and she takes this episode as an open confession of mad divine love between them. Gooch (1992, pp. 309–312) has tried to refute this interpretation by showing that the motive of the relationship is always friendship, and that, at the end of the dialogue, they do not plan to start a life in common but to return to their respective beloveds, not merely to appreciate their beauty but to take them towards the life of wisdom. Only when the lover controls the black horse can he see in his beloved the memory of perfect Beauty (who is sitting on her throne by Moderation), and it is their pure love what will make their souls acquire the wings necessary to ascend. See also De Vries (1969, p. 113).

their young ones, and on the other hand, because divine eros does not mark the reciprocal interaction between the two characters throughout the dramatic action; the intention of the palinode is to inspire Phaedrus towards a common object of heavenly worship. And yet these extraordinary tender words, perhaps the most critical in the dialogue, manifest their emotional overflowing in a kind of brief action in the action or "play inside the play". Socrates addresses Phaedrus as if he were his lover, while Phaedrus, solicitous, replies as if he were adopting the role of his beloved. Why?

From my point of view, this requirement of Socrates, in this peculiar circumstance, before starting his new song, is due to his deep desire to call Phaedrus to a different, more attentive attitude, in order to capture the meaning of the 'song's content'. In a sense, the rivalry game is over; Socrates wants no more competitive parodies. Phaedrus has been playing the distracted snob, the indifferent and superficial listener. But now Socrates attempts to cure his friend of his blindness, so Phaedrus needs to be in the right mood too[28]. And the paradox is that now he is ready to listen, to devote all his attention to his love-master, precisely because Socrates was about to leave him.

That said, I should like to add that, in my view, although the purpose of the relationship between the characters is not predominantly erotic, but didactic, this does not mean that it does not imply some elements that could be placed on the border line between what belongs to friendship and to the art of erotic relationships.

Is it because the topic of discussion is mad divine love that it requires a certain "passionate" tone? In a sense, but not only for this mimetic, formal, external reason.

Socrates describes a particular erotic relationship that is the highest and happiest a man can have, which implies that the lover should be full of divine madness. This revelation has direct and immediate consequences for their personal lives. Socrates is teaching Phaedrus to play the role of the lover with Lysias, but in order to do so, he himself has to assume the role of the lover with Phaedrus, to enable him not only to listen to the right description of love and acquire a desire for it, but also to imitate his own careful approach strategy, his emotional demands and, more importantly, his divine views as well. Only when Phaedrus acquires a taste of this real passionate love can he become inspired to become an authentic lover of someone else.

---

[28] Hackforth (1952, p. 53), against Friedländer, thinks that this is a mere game. Even so, one should try to clarify its meaning in the dramatic action.

So this special lover must be a double lover. He needs to be in love with philosophy in order to be able to take a philosophical character to his peak. This requires redirecting his relationship with Lysias, and, in the first place, compelling his beloved to rewrite his speech saying exactly the opposite: the beloved should give his favours to a lover rather than to a non-lover (243d5–7) because the lover is caring and is a teacher.

We are now able to understand why Phaedrus is the cause of the return of Socrates: Phaedrus needs to learn what true and liberated love is, in order to heal himself from the seduction of a fraud, for he could not escape from it by the mere criticizing of vulgar love. And he should learn it by means of another, mythic narrative and the loving care of Socrates himself[29]. He will learn because the story says the same thing as does the attitude of Socrates in the dramatic action.

In the framework of this dialogue, Plato lets Socrates persuade Phaedrus, and defends the role of the art of rhetoric. At this point his main character sets aside his jealousy, his desire for competition, and takes off the mask of condescension to literary, avant-garde, fashionable theses. He becomes brave enough to speak his mind to a Phaedrus who has surrendered, as a master-lover should do, without shame or fear. Only after Socrates masters his own attitude towards Phaedrus, is he able to recite the Palinode. He had to turn away for a second, he had to listen to his daimon, he had to master his Typhoon in order to let the 'limpid creature' within him say the words that could operate the change in Phaedrus, and plant the fertile seeds that could grow in his soul.

Thus, in general terms, the ideal that the dialogue proposes is not an intellectually rewarding life of loneliness, but a life that can only go up, if it has the guidance and care of the teacher who always turns back to tell new stories and pose the right questions, while he delights in contemplating the graceful beauty of the young man, and the way his soul is progressing. This is a life that is modeled after the divine procession, which takes only the minimum of essentials, and whose destiny is to evoke beautiful, elusive memories.

The Palinode will exert purification on both. In an effort to free Phaedrus from his vital and theoretical ignorance concerning true love, Socrates has released himself, through the mediation of his daimon, from the appetites and fumes that threatened him. His turnabout enables him to get to know himself and emerge as a true driver of souls.

---

[29] I do not agree with Griswold's thesis (1986, p. 71) that, in making a second speech, Socrates is more concerned with his own spiritual benefit rather than with that of Phaedrus.

But the Platonic ideal of love par excellence, i.e., an intellectual, emotional and sexual togetherness without genital relations, is not to be realized by Socrates and Phaedrus in their lives. The characters in the dialogue have helped to bring it out for the benefit of the reader. And they have done it so effectively, with their words so interwoven, with their attitudes, gestures and over-reactions so vivid, that they have made us believe –at least throughout the play inside the play- that they had fallen in love. The divine and terrible Plato managed to deceive us...for a while. At the end, he deliberately has let us go free from deception.

Works Cited

Bossi, B, 2000, 'Is the Lysis really aporetic?' in T. Robinson – L. Brisson, (eds.), *Plato, Euthydemus, Lysis Charmides, Proceedings of the V Symposium Platonicum, Selected Papers*, Academia, Sankt Augustin, pp. 172–179.

Calvo Martínez, T, 1992, 'Socrates's First Speech in the Phaedrus and Plato's Criticism of Rethoric', in L. Rossetti (ed.), *Understanding the Phaedrus, Proceedings of the II Symposium Platonicum*, Academia, Sankt Augustin, pp. 47–60.

De Vries, G J, 1969, *A Commentary on the Phaedrus of Plato*, Amsterdam.

Ferrari, G. R. F, 1987, *Listening to the Cicadas, A Study of Plato's Phaedrus*, Cambridge.

Friedländer, P, 1960, *Platon*, III, Berlin.

Gooch, P, 1992, 'Has Plato changed Socrates' heart in the Phaedrus?' in L. Rossetti (ed.), *Understanding the Phaedrus, Proceedings of the II Symposium Platonicum*, Academia, Sankt Augustin, pp. 309–312.

Griswold, C, 1986, *Self-knowledge in Plato's Phaedrus*, New Haven and London.

Hackforth, F. B. A. 1952, *Plato's Phaedrus*, Translated with an Introduction and Commentary, Cambridge.

Nussbaum, M, 1986, *The Fragility of Goodness*, Cambridge.

Pieper, J, 1964, *Love and Inspiration, A Study of Plato's Phaedrus*, London.

Sinaiko, H, 1965, *Love, Knowledge and Discourse in Plato: Dialogue and Dialectic in Phaedrus, Republic and Parmenides*, Chicago and London.

Tejera, V, 1992, 'The Phaedrus, Part I: A Poetic Drama', in L. Rossetti (ed.), *Understanding the Phaedrus, Proceedings of the II Symposium Platonicum*, Academia, Sankt Augustin, pp. 290–295.

Trabattoni, F, 2011, 'Un'interpetazione "platonica" del primo discorso di Socrate nel Fedro' in G. Casertano (ed.), *Il Fedro di Platone*, Napoli, pp. 285–305.

Yunis, H, 2011, *Plato, Phaedrus, Introduction and Commentary*, Cambridge.

Plato's Characters

Gabriele Cornelli
He longs for him, he hates him and he wants him for himself: The Alcibiades Case between Socrates and Plato

The central idea that we will here defend is that two different but complementary movements are at play within the skillful construction of the dramatic figure of Alcibiades in the interior of the Platonic dialogues: first, a deft rhetorical construction, strongly marked by an emphasis on Alcibiades' sexual *paranomia*, that is, on his deviant sexual behavior, which is in turn functional to a political strategy of memory control, regarding the posthumous defense of Socrates and his *paideia* as responsible for creating the ethical-political figure of Alcibiades.[1]

The chosen locus of research will precisely be Plato's Symposium, where *eros* and *paideia* draw the fabric of dramatic and rhetorical speeches and, especially, the beautiful picture of the relation between Socrates and Alcibiades.

In order to so do, we will focus, firstly, on two important facts, which are essential for the correct understanding of the dialogue, both of which appear at the beginning. First, it is said that Socrates, Alcibiades and the others (172b) were present at the famous banquet, and second, that the banquet and the erotic speeches of the participants were so celebrated as to attract the attention for several decades to come.[2]. One can thus collect from these first exploratory observations that the memory of that meal is thus the memory, far beyond the other symposiasts, and through the erotic speeches, of something very precise: that is, a particularly significant relationship, that between Socrates and Alcibiades.

The very structure of the dialogue leaves no doubt about the centrality of the relationship between the two: Diotima's speech would in fact seem the culmination of the discussion about love, from a theoretical point of view, and the dialogue could then end there. However, it is exactly at this point that Alcibiades,

---

[1] Thanks to Nicholas Riegel for his very generous and competent revision of the english text. A previous version of this paper has been already published in *Plato* journal 14 (2014).

[2] It certainly is the case of noting that in Xenophon's namesake *Symposium*, even if it is another banquet, this time in the house of the wealthy Callias of Athens, in Piraeus, held with the pretext of celebrating the recent victory at a pankration competition, in the Great Panathenaic of 422/3, of the young Autolycus, the son of a certain Licon, in the third part of it (ch. 8) Socrates says exactly one *erotikos logos* to signify the importance of that memory (according to Pinheiro 2011, 14–15).

mask of Eros and Dionysus, model lover, comes into play. In a way, it is possible to say that, playing with the lexicon of the *Symposium* itself, all the speeches longed and *missed* the entrance of the lover's own mask, the incarnation of Eros: Alcibiades. In his great literary skill, Plato seems to be able to converge all the speeches towards the final *mise en scène* of Alcibiades' entry.

Socrates' first speech (213d) after Alcibiades' entry sets the tone of the character: here Socrates expresses his fear of Alcibiades' *mania* and *philerastia*, that is, of his excesses in love.

> Agathon, see if you can defend me for the love for this man gave me no little trouble. From the moment I have fallen for him I am not even allowed to look or talk with one beautiful young man, he, overcome by jealousy and envy, makes incredible scenes, insults me and gets close to coming to blows. Please take care that this is not the case right now, and instead try to keep the peace between us, because I loathe both his *mania* as his pederasty (*Symp.* 213c – d):[3]

The plea for Agathon to control Alcibiades in his violent excesses in eros should not go unnoticed. The binding of erotica and violence is not only the character's card, but, as we shall see, his leitmotif throughout the dialogue.

With the excuse of having drunk too much wine, Alcibiades, significantly, refuses to continue the *erotikoi logoi* game, claiming to be able of speaking only about Socrates, and on this to want/to be able to tell only the truth (214c – d). With this speech of Alcibiades, therefore, the record of the conversation changes: from theory to history, from praise to the truth (a true Dionysiac, characterized by *mania* and *parrhesia* of drunkenness – *oinos alethes*, 217e: *in vino veritas*), from concepts to images (215a), being those of a life lived side by side (as in the case of military service), being, especially, those with great mimetic skill chosen to represent the real Socrates.

The very first image that Alcibiades uses is the one from the Sileni statues. The image goes beyond the approximation, widely perceived by ancient iconography, between the human typology of Socrates (some ugliness, fleshy lips, etc.) and the Silenus image. Here Alcibiades refers to something more precise, probably something that we know nowadays only through the Russian Matryoshkas statues, dolls that contain within them other dolls. The Sileni statues to which Alcibiades refers to, therefore, tend to be monstrous and tacky statues that once opened, reveal to contain within them statues of deities. In the same

---

[3] The translation is mine. But the translation of " blows " was suggested to me by Schiappa de Azevedo.

way – this is the moral of the image – Socrates would have been: a mask of himself, ugly and rude on the outside, but divine on the inside.

A detail from this image that often escapes the translators – Brisson, in this sense, well noticed it (1998, 217, N526): Alcibiades literally refers to statues that are in the laboratories of the *hermoglupheioi*, that is, the sculptors of herms (215B).

But this initial and veiled reference to the herms cannot be considered casual.[4] On the contrary, it inaugurates the Platonic politics of memory. In fact, Agathon's banquet would have happened a few months before this major event. On the morning of June the 8th, 415, it seems, it was found that all the herms had been mutilated, according to the testimony of Thucydides, "on the front" (*prosopa*, VI, 27, 3), which primarily means a mutilation of their sexual attributes. Placed at the entrances and exits of houses and temples, at intersections and at the city gates, the herms were – symbolically – entrusted with the protection of the city. The horror arisen by such tremendous sacrilege was boosted due to having been committed during a particularly critical juncture for Athens: the preparation for one of the most ambitious (and dangerous) military expeditions: that against Syracuse and its powerful allies. The suspicion of a sacrilegious act – one which also had a humorous side to it, so to speak – should usually fall upon the mess and brawl of some drunken youths. Plato seems, somehow, to want to endorse this version. In fact, the story of the very arrival of Alcibiades at the symposium at Agathon's house seems to contain a reference to suspicions that the Athenian people had come down on Alcibiades and his companions: while Socrates and the others spend the night drinking at home, and moderately, Alcibiades arrives at dawn, drunk and – that is what the text suggests – having wandered through Athens in an altered state. An Athenian would not need to use much fantasy in order to imagine Alcibiades and his drunken parties committing any sort of profanity. Plato's insistence on this version should also be one of the reasons for the telling of the second interruption of the banquet at the end of it (223b), held also by several other drunken youths. That is, Plato seems to insist presenting nights of rioting in the street, right at the time of the herms' mutilation, thus endorsing the lightest version of the motives that lay behind the sacrilege.

And yet, if this may seem a *non troppo* veiled admission of Alcibiades' and his party's guilt by Plato, freeing Socrates and his group of this suspicion, it is more likely that Plato is masking (after all, we are talking about the banquet,

---

[4] Likewise, Plato's game is probably present in the use by Alcibiades of the *hermaion* term, which also refers to herms, in order to describe his fate when he met Socrates (217a).

that is, of one most able game of masks) something more severe. Actually, in contemporary sources, the suspicion of desecration does not fall so much upon drunken youths: rather, a plot came more easily on people's mind, hatched up in an articulate manner, by groups intending to weaken the confidence of Athens and its democracy at a time so delicate in its history, wanting by this to restore oligarchy or tyranny.[5]

Let's see Thucydides' account on this matter:

> No one knew who had done this, but large rewards were offered by the state in order to find out who the criminals were, and there was also a decree passed guaranteeing immunity to anyone, citizen, alien or slave, who knew of any other sacrilegious act that had taken place and would come forward with information about it. The whole affair, indeed, was taken very seriously, as it was regarded as an omen for the expedition, and at the same time as evidence of a revolutionary conspiracy to overthrow the democracy (Thucydides, VI, 27, 3).[6]

Obviously, conspirators groups like these actually existed, as evidenced by the successive *staseis* that profoundly shaped the fifteen or twenty successive years of Athens' democracy. They were called *hetairias*, groups of friends, companions. The members were all of high social origin, and their meetings were usually associated with the ritual of the banquet and the symposium. That is, the suspicion falls exactly on top of a group like the one Plato sets in the *Symposium*, happily gathered a few months before the mutilation. In fact, several of these *hetairias* were charged and brought to trial, through the use of exceptional legal instruments such as the *eisaggelia*.[7] Athens starts to get obsessed with the risk of a return to oligarchy, or worse, to tyranny. Gradually – Thucydides is the main source on this issue – a rich, excessive, rebellious and powerful figure such as that of Alcibiades gets to meet all the conditions to concentrate on itself the fears of the democratic people. Thucydides states that plainly:

> As for Alcibiades, the same enemies of his who attacked him even before he set sail now renewed their attacks, and the Athenians took a serious view of the matter. Now that they thought they had discovered the truth about the Hermae, they were all the more inclined to believe that the sacrilege with regard to the mysteries, in which he was implicated, had

---

[5] Several contemporary commentators – Nails rightly notes (2002, 20) – seem to fall into the Platonic trap, and consider as a prank the case of the herms (prank: Dover 1970), underestimating motivations and political impacts of the gesture.

[6] Trans. R. Warner (1972).

[7] Cf. for the narration of events and the operation of emergency laws De Romilly (1995, 82).

been done by him as part and parcel of the same plot against the democracy (Thucydides, VI, 61: 1).[8]

But Alcibiades was never formally charged in relation to the case of the herms. However, within the climate of terror and slander prevailing while Alcibiades was preparing for the Syracusan expedition, there appears an explicit complaint against him of having committed another sacrilegious act: the accusation was that he participated in a parody of the mysteries, in a private home. Androcles tried to connect the two desecrations, the herms and the parody of the mysteries, as prologues to a threat to democracy. Plutarch thus reveals the defamatory intentions of Androcles:

> Androcles, the orator, presented as witnesses a few slaves and metics who accused Alcibiades and his friends of having mutilated other statues and of having parodied the mysteries under the effect of excessive drinking. It was said that a certain Theodoros played the harbinger, Pulition the torch bearer, Alcibiades the hierophant, and that the other elements of the group as spectators watched, playing the role of the initiated into the mysteries (Plutarch, *Alcibiades*, 19, 1–2).[9]

Although Alcibiades participation in the case of the herms was never proven, the association of the two sacrileges strongly marked Athens' public mind.[10] Thus, in fact, Thucydides describes the reaction of the Athenian people:

> These events had impressed themselves on the people of Athens and, recalling everything that they had heard about them, they were now in an angry and suspicious mood with regard to those who had been accused in connection with the mysteries; everything that had happened was, they thought, part of a plot aiming at setting up an oligarchy or a dictatorship (Thucydides, VI, 60, 1).[11]

The economy of this text does not allow us to monitor the troubled months that followed this complaint. Suffice to say that it was initially denied, and Alcibiades was able to travel as strategos, towards Syracuse. However, while in the middle of the expedition, a woman from a prominent family, Agariste, raised another version of the same charge of parody of the Eleusinian mysteries: but this time, it was alleged to have happened in the house of Charmides, member of Al-

---

8 Trans. R. Warner (1972).
9 The importance of the charge of Androcles to the fate of Alcibiades is also confirmed by Thucydides (VIII, 65, 2), on the occasion of the former's murder.
10 It is significant in this sense, Thucydides' (VI, 28, 1) mixing of the two charges, one regarding the desecration of the herms and the other regarding the parodies of the mysteries.
11 Trans. R. Warner (1972).

cibiades' *hetairia*. She accused him of playing the central role in it, the one of the high priest.[12] Considering the seriousness of the charge, a ship was immediately sent to Sicily in order to bring Alcibiades to stand trial in Athens. The rest is well known: the flight of Alcibiades marks his first betrayal and the exile.[13]

What matters most is that from this moment on, Alcibiades begins plausibly to be considered one of the major reasons for the defeat of Athens and the main cause of the crisis into which the city was plunged. And with him all those who belonged to his group. There is certainly nothing new in stating, as does Centrone, that "the proximity to so controversial a figure as Alcibiades was one of the real causes of the death of Socrates" (1999, xxxviii).[14] And the distrust of the city towards the groups of "philosophers" that remitted to him.

Nor does it surprise us that the so-called Socratics committed themselves, from this tragic moment on, to refuting the accusation of Socrates having been Alcibiades' mentor, to the point – as stated by Gribble – of reversing the charge: "*the allegation that Socrates corrupted Alcibiades, the charge made by society against philosophy, is not just refuted but turned on its head: it is society which corrupts Alcibiades and others like him*" (1999, loc. 394 Kindle Edition).

In the same way as the others Plato, also a Socratic, concerns himself with what might be called the Alcibiades' affaire (or the Alcibiades' Connection). Realizing there obviously was no way to deny the deep connection between Socrates and Alcibiades, he uses a most clever dramatic construction with the intention of operating a political intervention upon the memory of this relationship, that is, of rewriting history, thus producing another apology for Socrates, with the intent of relieving him of a more precise charge, which must have especially weighed upon Plato and upon Socrates' memory: of him having been Alcibiades' lover/mentor (trying to translate the broad vocabulary regarding the *erastes/eromenos* relationship).

The idea is obviously not novel. Already Gomperz (1905, 394) considers Alcibiades' speech as a response to Polykrates, who in the late 90's of the fourth century, that is, a few years after the death of Socrates, is thought to have written

---

[12] A comprehensive review of the charges can be found both at *About the mysteries* as well as at *About his return*, speeches that the also involved Aldocides writes during the last turbulent years af the fifth century.

[13] Nails (2002, 15) notes rightly that tradition knows two other recalls of Alcibiades and that they are often mixed one for the other.

[14] I devoted myself to the examination of these causes in a recent article published in the Proceedings of the 2008 *Socratica* Congress, to which I refer (Cornelli & Chevitarese 2010). Efforts to unravel the reasons for this conviction and death are certainly not irrelevant, although I must agree with Ferrari that this constitutes "a perhaps insoluble problem" (Ferrari 2007, 20).

an act of accusation against Socrates. The main witness to the existence of a *kategoros*, of an accuser identified by the critics as Polykrates, is Xenophon's *Memorabilia* (I, 2, 9).[15] Although Robin (1908) considered the possibility of this direct response to Polykrates as *toute gratuite* (1908, 60), and preferred, in the same case, to think of a polemic between Plato and Aristophanes, who would then have been considered by Plato "among Socrates' opponents, the one whose influence at that time was still worth fighting against" (1908, 61). The fact is that Plato, since he associated Socrates dramatically with Alcibiades, seemed to everyone to be feeling the need to defend him.

Socrates having the need of, somehow, being defended from Alcibiades is a recurrent *topos* in the dialogues. Consider, for example, the famous divine prohibition (*daimonion enantioma*) that prevented Socrates from speaking to Alcibiades at the beginning of *Alcibiades Major* (130a).

Not surprisingly, much of Alcibiades' speech in the *Symposium* tends to emphasize the defeat of Socrates' *paideia*, thus reinforcing the impression of a strong apologetic tendency. Socrates' very words, at the end of the praise, underline this defeat, when they attempt to debunk the prevarication, the use, the unfair exchange between Socrates' true and ephemeral beauty, which Alcibiades sought to carry out, in his own admission (218e). The term that Socrates uses to indicate this "forcing of the issue" of Alcibiades is very significant: *pleonektein*. Alcibiades is thus set in a context of violence and prevarication that describes those years of Athenian imperialism, and which Vegetti masterfully summarized using the concept of "anthropology of *pleonexia*" (Vegetti 2003).

Thus, in a large part, the praise of Socrates by Alcibiades can be considered more of an apology.

Let's, for example, think about the very use of the images of the Sileni statues, which illustrate the need to overcome the appearance, the historical and uncomfortable mask of Socrates, to look at a truth about his life and his legacy, which still remains hidden to the majority. For Alcibiades says "none of you know him" (216c–d). It is not difficult to see that through the voice of Alcibiades, Plato himself is saying this to Athens.

The apologetic sense is especially evident in Socrates' insistence, as the Alcibiades account goes, that he abandon *ta Athenaion pratto*, the political issues of Athens, to devote himself to the care of oneself (*emautos*). Obviously, both *in re* as in *post factum*, such an advice to abandon politics, when addressed to the great statesman, a true Athenian political animal, is doomed to failure, but it is functional to the politics of the Platonic memory, in his historiographical project,

---

[15] Xenophon refutes these accusations with the same force throughout ch. 2.

which is to mark a separation between Socrates and the Athenian *staseis* of his times.

The wonderful 221 and 222a pages, on the Socratic *logoi*, which metonymically participate in the image of the Silenus statue, which Alcibiades attributed to Socrates himself, so common on the outside, but divine on the inside, closes with the admission that these same speeches "tend towards, for those who want to become *kalo – kagatho*") (222a). That is, the *paideia* of Socrates, although it may seem *atopic*, is indeed deeply committed to the ideals of the *kalo–kagathia* that guide the Athenian *politeia*.

Thus, the problem is not Socrates' teachings, but, rather, Alcibiades' inability to overcome his *philotimia*, his love for the honors of the many (216b). This *philotimia*, of which Alcibiades is an almost paradigmatic example within the ancient world (according to Thucydides, *Alcibiades Major*, Plutarch, passim), on the one hand, moves him away from Socrates, thus escaping from his counseling, but on the other makes him feel ashamed of his own weakness. Giorgini (2005, 454) puts it well when he says that "without a doubt, the figure of Alcibiades represented the widest failure of both Athenian education and socratic pedagogy".

To explain Alcibiades' immunity to the Socratic *paideia*, in order to save Socrates from defeat, Plato makes use of a rhetorical strategy that comedy, oratory and Thucydides himself had already outlined: Alcibiades' *philotimia* and weakness would essentially indicate unequivocal *feminine* traits.

But this weakness of Alcibiades is not a simple association of immoderate demand for honors and wealth, with the parallel representation of the ethics of the feminine gender as necessarily connected to *philothimia* and to some weakness with respect to pleasure seduction. There is something more precise regarding the characterization of the *paranomia* of Alcibiades as a man, which makes him both feared and admired in the eyes of his contemporaries and even in the several centuries of tradition that followed. Once more Gribble rightly points out that "in the last ten years of the Peloponnesian War the constant ambivalence and indecision which characterized the Athenian attitude towards Alcibiades crucially undermined Athenian policy" (1999, loc. 61).

This indecision, a mixture of fear and attraction, is in a way the description of Athens' erotic relationship with Alcibiades. Aristophanes understood this well, when in The *Frogs* he makes Dionysus say that Athens "wants him, hates him and longs for him".[16] The meaning of this statement takes a very special connotation when you think that it was presented at the theater in the year

---

16 *Frogs* 1425: ποθεῖ μέν, ἐχθαίρει δέ, βούλεται δ' ἔχειν.

405, while Alcibiades was in exile and the war was almost lost, and that Dionysus is dramatically visiting, in the afterlife, the tragedians Aeschylus and Euripides.

It is Thucydides himself (VI, 15) who tells us of the great *paranomia* of Alcibiades, as the one which scandalized the Athenians (*oi polloi*) the most, regarding his *diaita*, his lifestyle. A *paranomia* which is described more precisely as *kata to eautou soma*, that is, regarding one's own body. Although you can certainly think of such excesses as the bodily pleasures of food and drinking, the expression refers more precisely to sexual deviancies (Gribble 1999 loc. 1094).[17] It is no accident that Antisthenes states that Alcibiades would be "*paranomos* towards women as well as regarding the remainder of his *diaita*" (Caizzi frag. 29).

Alcibiades' *paranomia* seems to carry within it a very precise sexual characterization. This is clearly shown by the large number of anecdotes, information and dramatic representations that characterize the tradition on the character.

Since childhood, according to Plutarch, Alcibiades' fame has been linked to female behavior. This is emblematic in the case of a famous fight, the central space for defining the male gender, in which Alcibiades surprisingly makes use of a bite:

> Once, when he found himself in trouble during a fight, in order not to fall, he brought towards his mouth the arms of the opponent that dominated him, and almost grabbed them from side to side. That one, dropping his prey, said: 'You bite, Oh Alcibiades, just like women do!' – and Alcibiades replied: 'No, just like the lions!' (Plutarch, Alcibiades 2, 2–3).[18]

Alcibiades' answer – "not as a woman, but like a lion!" – refers itself more immediately to another central passage of Aristophanes' comic reflection in *The Frogs*, on what to do with Alcibiades. The character Aeschylus actually says: "first of all, one should not raise a lion in the inner city. But if someone so does, then he must bend to its character" (1432–3). The lion, associated not only with the figure of Alcibiades, but more generally with an unruly and potentially dangerous social role within the community (in Homer, Achilles is a lion – *Il* . 18. 318–22), is in the fifth century Athenian context an image that immediately refers to the most feared tyrannical tendencies. Herodotus associates the

---

17 The proof is also a fragment of Eupolis (fr. 351 Kock), where, regarding both pleasures – drinking and sex –, Alcibiades stood out as much as to be considered practically the inventor of new forms of performance: πιπίνειν, something like getting back to drink in the morning and λακκοπρωκτία, idleness, licentiousness.

18 Translated by Maria do Ceu Fialho and Nuno Simões Rodrigues.

image of the lion with that of tyrants (V, 56; V, 92); and again Aristophanes, at the *Knights* (1037), speaks of a woman giving birth to a lion in Athens; Callicles, in Plato's *Gorgias*, compares the submission of the best and the strongest citizens to the city's laws to the one that is established in order to train young lions (*Gorg.* 483e).

This double feral and feminine imagery attributed to Alcibiades eventually pushes his representation more towards the wilderness than to the civilizing culture. Such a dichotomy between nature and culture is a strong mark of the rhetoric of gender. That is, as a lion and a woman Alcibiades flees from the moral norm and the established policy, outraging the social uses and threatening, in his irreducible difference and his ongoing challenge, the culture of sexual appearance promoted by the polis.[19]

In the political crisis of the late fifth century Athens, Alcibiades' sexual *paranomia*, therefore, plays a key role in the representation of an individual driven by his excesses and incapable of the *metron*, which has been established as the great democratic value (Darbo-Pechanski 2009, 51). Accordingly, this gender characterization reveals its inherent political connotation: "sexual pleasure is seen as the strongest and most dangerous of the desires of the body, hence its particular association with tyrants" (Gribble 1999 loc. 1094).

Thus, the very concept of *pleonexia*, which as we have seen was central to the political rhetoric of the late fifth century, turns out also to reveal an unprecedented gender connotation, referring to intemperance in sexual desires, in another example of the overlapping of the two areas.

That Alcibiades' sexual *paranomia*, his lack of masculinity, is primarily a political issue is also underlined by Gherchanoc: "*sa feminité est présentée comme un atout politique même si elle est du ressort de la critique*" (Gherchanoc 2003/4, 787).

A very well attested tradition portrays the young Alcibiades, in fact, as the favorite of many aristocratic lovers: always ready to be the object of the pleasure of others, not by constraint, but precisely because he is unable to control his own sexual desire. The same picture, indeed, emerges in the Platonic *Symposium*. See especially the statement (219b-d) regarding the ploy of "throwing himself under the covers" of Socrates to seduce him and spend the night with him.

A sexually deviant figure is a recipe for comedy, obviously. Aristophanes calls Alcibiades *euruproktos* (vagrant, *Acarn.* 716), while Eupolis represents the sexual role of Alcibiades as a woman's role (fr. 171 K-A).

---

[19] For a description of this culture of sexual appearance see Éloi & Dupont (2001).

But how to articulate this description with the one – also present in tradition – of Alcibiades as a *womanizer*? One must express, of course, a further hermeneutic caution: the short circuit suggested by this question may depend more on the modern description of gender relations, which not necessarily correspond to the same description within the ancient world. In fact, Davidson appropriately notes that, even more than his own passivity, his most feminine feature, according to ancient Greek ethics of gender, would be his inability to control his desire (Davidson 1997, 167–182). Likewise states Gribble (1999, loc. 1025), who thus solves the seeming contradiction just mentioned: "because the key issue in determining 'ethical gender' is the attitude of the subject to pleasure, even as active sexual agent the *kinaidos* remains assimilated to the feminine", especially when adulterous.[20]

The complex web of gender relations representation, when referring to the ancient world and, more precisely to Alcibiades, is far from the simple naturalizing dichotomy man/woman, if one assumes that an adulterer and a womanizer can be considered generally feminine. An ancient comic fragment by Ferecrates is in fact symptomatic of this gender perspective: "for not being a man (*aner*), Alcibiades, it seems, is now the husband (*aner*) of all women around him" (fr. 164 K–A). For not being a man, that is, for not controlling his desires – that one being the most defining representation of the male – Alcibiades is an adulterer.

Later tradition does not cease to collect several anecdotes that represent his specific sexual *paranomia* from the history of the trip to Abydos, in the company of his uncle Axioco, in which both are said to have slept with the same woman, Medontis, and to have claimed the paternity of the child that was from her born.

There is also the incident at Melos, where once again political and sexual excesses outrageously intertwined: after having decreed the mass enslavement of the inhabitants of the island of Melos (Thuc. V, 84ss), Alcibiades bought to himself a Melian woman and had a son with her. Andocides in his speech against Alcibiades, notes with revolt that the son of Alcibiades, born from a Melian slave within the context of the island's and its inhabitants' destruction, would most certainly be another enemy of Athens. With the result that Alcibiades therefore, as an Athenian general, is creating, with his sexual excesses, new enemies for the city (Andocides. *In Alcibiadem* 22–23).

Alcibiades dies fighting, referring conventionally to a *manly* death. However even in the traditions that mention his death, the representation of Alcibiades' femininity is strongly present. In fact, Plutarch, as is usual in his *Parallel*

---

20 Cf. Davidson (1997, 165).

Lives, at the end of the life of Alcibiades briefly symbolizes his existence in the final hours, using two representations unequivocally feminine (Plutarch 2011, 17). On the one hand, in the ultimate premonitory dream of his death, a courtesan applied cosmetics in him "and as if he was a woman, combed his hair" (39.2). On the other hand, after his death in battle, Alcibiades is dressed for the obsequies with woman's robes: "Timandra [his companion then] collected his corpse, wrapped it and covered it with her own clothes" (39.7). Therefore, the last image of Alcibiades refers symbolically to his gender *paranomia*.

However, probably the best description of Alcibiades gender *paranomia* can still be found in the very Platonic *Symposium*, in the reversal of roles between lover and beloved, a central *topos* to the economy of the dialogue as a whole: Alcibiades is the one in love with Socrates, and not vice versa (222b).

On page 213d quoted above, Socrates expressed his fear of Alcibiades' *mania* and *philerastia*. Alcibiades, in fact, mask and the very incarnation of Eros, is as powerful and surreptitious as him (205d). He is the paradigm of the tyrannical man, well described at the end of Book VIII of the *Republic*. But here in the *Symposium*, *eros tyrannos* is also reversed, as Alcibiades regrets twice having been put into slavery by Socrates, feeling obligated to love him: thus, the tyrannical man par excellence, he uses the adverb *andrapododos*, "like a slave", and the preposition *hypo*, "under", to show this subjection to Socrates (215Ee). Alcibiades says bluntly that sometimes he even has the desire to see Socrates dead, to get rid of this tyranny (216c). Certainly a *post factum* reference, gently tragic, from Plato to his already dead mentor, but also an affirmation of the nuisance that Socrates-Eros would have provoked at the Athenian polis elite, which Alcibiades is here representing.

The game of the reversal of roles serves simultaneously as a compliment, as high as possible, to Socrates as even superior to Eros himself and as the true incarnation of a philosopher, but also, once again, the reverse of the dramatic plot, serves to endorse the suspicions that Alcibiades, in his multiple *paranomiai*, was ultimately trying to achieve tyranny.

The introduction in the speech of Diotima of the theme of the mysteries' initiation can be analyzed in the same way as in the case of the presence of a lexicon linked to the herms. Mentioned already was the serious charge against Alcibiades of having participated in a parody of the mysteries, a charge that led to his first defection and "was a/the? source, not the least important one, of the defeat of Athens" (Thuc. VI, 15, 3). It is therefore impossible not to think that Plato, always a most able "weaver of words", has presented the discourse of Diotima, just before the entrance of Alcibiades, referring to a double initiation into the mysteries, having in mind the rhetorical plan of the scenic effect of this approach onto the figure of Alcibiades.

The rhetorical game of Plato, so clever and suggestive, designed along the lines above, ends up reinforcing the suspicions about Alcibiades, at the same time as it seeks an opposite effect: that is, the planning of a renewed apology for Socrates and his *hetairia*.

Socrates, at the end of the speech of Alcibiades, debunks the "satyric and Silenic drama" hidden behind the compliment: that is, the lover's intention of separating his beloved from Agathon, so that he can be with him (222c). All the rhetorical construction of the speech of Alcibiades would have thus been woven by an erotic story. As in much of ancient iconography, where Eros and Peitho appear side by side, the relationship between the two deities, love and persuasion, structures the whole *Symposium* dialogue, from the prologue to the speech of Alcibiades.

But this plot to hide is not only related to the charge that Socrates directs towards him at the end, that the praise was for other persuasion purposes. The thesis here proposed is that the story that Plato is hiding in his *logos sokratikos* – which is always *erotikos* par excellence – is that of an apology for Socrates, built with great literary skill, with plenty of implied references and lexical tricks. An apology that the *eromenos* Plato, in love with his mentor Socrates, judges to be only possible by "separating", albeit post-mortem, his memory from that of Alcibiades, within a precise and articulated strategy of memory policing. The latter will thus be the only one to blame for his own malpractices, including perhaps the very death of Socrates, which Plato would plausibly attribute largely to the fatal connection of the two.

The diverse representation of gender in the ancient Greek world, distinct from the dichotomy of male and female sex roles to which we are accustomed by our modernity, can reveal more precisely the rhetorical strategy of Plato in his use of Alcibiades' erotic *paranomia* as a symptom of a character politically dangerous because of his immoderate seduction exercised of Socrates and Athens.

This Platonic apology, which follows an investment on a policy of memory, is based, ultimately, in a clever rhetorical strategy, which emphasizes the now traditional sexual *paranomia* of Alcibiades, in order to make him guilty of an attempted excessive and outrageous seduction not only of Socrates, but of the polis. Reusing comic and oratorical/rhetorical motifs of his time, therefore, Plato deepens the *j'accuse* against Alcibiades, trying to withdraw him from the orbit of Socrates and the Socratics.

It is finally impossible not to notice that in facing Alcibiades' case this way, Plato himself acts according to the script of his character, Alcibiades: inspired by Eros and Peitho, he does "anything" to separate Socrates from the other *eromenos*. "With the intention that I love you and nobody else" (222d) – these are the words that Socrates directs to Alcibiades. But much of Plato's work, and especially the *Symposium*, is also an attempt to win Socrates over, to keep him only for himself, to rescue the memory of his beloved mentor, highly disputed in the literature of the beginning of the fourth century. Thus, the Socratic dialogues of Plato end up looking very much like the compliment of a lover – just like that of Alcibiades – that is, with a seductive declaration of love.

Fiction and reality, drama and authorship thus coincide, undoubtedly resulting in one of the most exciting and daring literary and philosophical works of all times.

Works Cited

Anthistenes. F. Decleva Caizzi. Antisthenis Fragmenta. Milan: Istituto Editoriale Cisalpino, 1966.
Aristophanes. N.G. Wilson. Aristophanis Fabulae. Oxford: Oxford University Press, 2007.
Casertano, G. (2007). Paradigmi della verità in Platone. Roma: Editori Riuniti.
Centrone, B. (1999). Introduzione a Platone Simpósio. Turin: Einaudi.
Cornelli, G. & Chevitarese, A. (2010). 'Socrate e Platone tra golpe oligarchico e restaurazione democratica (404–403 a.C.)'. In Rossetti, L. & Stavru, A. Socratica 2008. Studies in Ancient Socratic Literature. Bari: Levante ed.
Darbo-Pechanski, C. (2009) Ordem do corpo, ordem do mundo: aitia, tekmêrion, sêmeion, historion nos tratados hipocráticos do fim do século V antes de nossa era. In Peixoto, Miriam Campolina. A saúde dos antigos: reflexões gregas e romanas. São Paulo: Loyola.
Davidson, J. (1997) Courtesans & fishcakes: the consuming passions of classical Athens, London: Harper Perennial.
De Romilly, J. (1995) Alciabiade ou les dangers de l'ambition. Ed. de Fallois (quote from the Italian edition. Milan: Garzanti, 1997).
Dover, K.J. (1970) Excursus: The Herms and The Mysteries. In Gomme, A. W. & Andrewes, A. & Dover, K. J. A Historical Commentary on Thucydides. Vol. IV., Oxford: Clarendon.
Dupont, F. & Éloi, D. (2001) L'érotisme masculin dans la Rome antique. Paris, Berlin.
Eupolis. T. Kock. Comicorum Atticorum fragmenta, vol. 1. Leipzig: Teubner, 1880.
Ferrari, F. (2007). Socrates tra personaggio e mito. Milan: Rizzoli.
Gherchanoc, F. (2003). Les atours féminins des hommes: quelques représentations du masculin-féminin dans le monde grec antique. Entre initiation, ruse, séduction et grotesque, surpuissance et déchéance. In Revue Historique 4, n° 628, p. 739–791.
Giorgini, G. (2005). 'Il tiranno'. In Platone. Repubblica. Vol. VI, Libri VIII-IX. Traduzione e commento a cura di Mario Vegetti. Naples: Bibliopolis, 423–470.
Gomperz, T. (1905). Greek Thinkers. Vol. V: Plato. New York: Scribners.
Gribble, D. (1999) Alcibiades and Athens: A Study in Literary Presentation. Oxford: Clarendon (Kindle Edition).
Musti, D. (2001). Il simposio. Bari: Laterza, 2001.
Nails, D. (2002). The People of Plato. A Prosopography of Plato and Other Socratics. Indianapolis: Hackett/Cambridge.

Nucci, M. (2009). Note alla traduzione di Platone Simpósio. Turin: Einaudi.
Nussbaum, M. (1986). The Fragility of Goodness. Luck and Ethics in Greek Tragedy and Philosophy. Cambridge: Cambridge University Press.
Pherecrates. T. Kock. Comicorum Atticorum fragmenta, vol. 1. Leipzig: Teubner, 1880.
Pinheiro, A. E. (2011). Introdução a Xenofontes, Banquete – Apologia de Sócrates. Tradução do grego, introdução e notas Ana Elias Pinheiro. Classica Digitalia Brasil. São Paulo: Annablume.
Platonis Opera. Ed. John Burnet. Oxford: Oxford University Press, 1903.
Plutarch. Vidas Paralelas: Alcibíades e Coriolano. Tradução do grego, introdução e notas Maria do Céu Fialho e Nuno Simões Rodrigues. Classica Digitalia Brasil. São Paulo: Annablume, 2011.
Reale, G. (2005). Eros demone mediatore: il gioco delle maschere nel Simposio di Platone. Milan: Bompiani.
Robin, L. (1908). La theorie platonicienne de l'amour. Paris: Felix Alcan.
Rowe, Ch. (1998). Il Simposio di Platone: cinque lezioni sul dialogo e un ulteriore contributo sul Fedone. A cura di Maurizio Migliori. Sankt Augustin: Academia Verlag.
Thucydides. *History of the Peloponnesian War.* Trans. by R. Warner, with Introduction and Note by M. I. Finley. Penguin Books, London, 1972.
Vegetti, M. (2003). 'Antropologias da Pleonexía: Cálicles, Trasímaco e Gláucon em Platão'. Boletim do CPA. Ano VIII, n.16: 9–26.
Xenophon. Banquete – Apologia de Sócrates. Tradução do grego, introdução e notas Ana Elias Pinheiro. Classica Digitalia Brasil. São Paulo: Annablume, 2011.

Debra Nails[1]
Five Platonic Characters

The study of Plato is a veritable battlefield for multiple academic disciplines and popular discourses. Most notably, the continental and Anglo-American approaches to Plato have diverged over the past decade: reading different journals, assigning different translations, and hiring like-minded colleagues. Yet, for at least a decade, it has been a mere caricature of analytic philosophy to say that its method is to rip arguments out of their contexts in Plato's dialogues in order to represent them in propositional logic and assess their soundness. The corresponding caricature of the continental approach to Plato has become equally inappropriate: to say that Plato's philosophical dialectic is subordinate to a Heideggerian hermeneutic, the sensitive interpretation of dialogues read as wholes. I would like to preserve the rigor of the analytic approach while defending the view that Plato's literary craft was not mere window-dressing for schoolboys.

Plato's singular contribution, his achievement beyond pre-Socratic, sophistic, literary, and rhetorical precedents, was his doubly open-ended philosophical method, leading him to criticize most effectively even the beliefs he may have cherished most deeply. *Aporia* is one open end, well known to all; the other – and, to my mind, even more admirable – is Plato's refusal to allow even his most well-established starting points to be insulated from criticism. His dialogues are occasions to philosophize further, not dogmatic treatises.[2] Whatever views he held, however he expressed them, he requires us to perform our own intellectual labors and to reach our own conclusions by the best arguments we can muster. In that endeavor, we are well-advised to use whatever techniques are available to us, logical or literary. Within what Ruby Blondell has called the "insoluble paradox of our place at the crossroads of particularity and abstraction" (2002: 303), the collective effort to establish Plato's overarching view of human nature has diminished our regard for the particular human beings he features in his dialogues. My project here is to reestablish the importance of taking Plato's characterizations seriously on grounds that they are sometimes crucial to understanding what Plato is arguing.

---
[1] I am grateful for the friendship and the comments of our community in Brasília 2012, and for the support the IPS and UNESCO provided.
[2] This is the theme for which I argued in Nails 1995.

Appreciating the characters' individual roles within familial, social, and religious structures could deepen our understanding of some philosophical issues – human nature, epistemology, or justice and education in the polis. We have long used Athenian history and law to explain aspects of the dialogues that would otherwise be obscure.[3] All too often, however, we have contented ourselves with a phrase or two handed down from the nineteenth century about persons – a time when little was known and the texts were being established. Thanks primarily to classicists' early adoption of computer databases, we now know much more about Plato's characters than the old footnotes suggested, so the possibilities for understanding have been considerably extended.[4]

No one discusses the *Charmides* without mentioning Critias's future leadership of the Thirty, or the *Republic* without noting that Glaucon and Adeimantus are Plato's brothers. Some of Plato's dialogues, the *Laches* for example, assume a high level of familiarity with then-recent past events and the reputations of the persons represented – some of whom were still alive and active in Athens when Plato was writing his dialogues. I will focus on five actual people, two men and three women, whose lives and later reputations among Plato's audiences may be more important to understanding Plato's text than has previously been realized – but I have not selected the famous ones. What I hope to show is that the range of plausible interpretations of the texts, and the range of understandings of Plato's milieu, and perhaps that of Socrates as well, can be reduced and focused if a character had a career and a reputation in Athens already known to Plato's audience; discernible personalities matter to our interpretations, or so I shall attempt to establish.

I. Meno

Meno of Thessaly, son of Alexidemus,[5] became a mercenary general under the command of Cyrus. We meet him in Plato's dialogue when he is visiting Athens in late 402 as the guest of Anytus before he leaves on the military campaign that Xenophon will immortalize in the *Anabasis*. Meno was vicious. Xenophon is

---

[3] E.g. especially *Theaetetus*, *Euthyphro*, *Apology*, *Crito*, and *Phaedo*.
[4] The caveat is that we cannot confidently assume that what Plato's audience believed about a character is what happened to survive into our own time. We have before us a partial, fragmented record of ancient prosopography, so we cannot afford to be complaisant about the information that we have.
[5] Apart from his appearance in Plato's *Meno*, Meno appears in Xenophon's *Anabasis* 1.2.6–3.1, fragments 27–28 of Ctesias, and in Diodorus Siculus 14.19.8–9, 14.27.2–3.

pleased to list his vices with examples (greed, betrayal, hunger for power, deceit, malice, selfishness); he wasted the lives of his men, and he participated in their injustices, plundering the countryside. Xenophon counts Meno as having deserved the Persians' torture of him for a year before finally executing him by torture (*Anabasis* 2.6.21–29). Plato presents none of Xenophon's facts because, of course, none of this had happened yet in 402. What Plato's audience can surmise decades later is that – for all the talk of virtue – Meno was not made a better man by his conversation with Socrates. Meno is one of Socrates's tragic failures. Because Meno's malevolent behavior was still ahead of him, however, commentators in the philosophical traditions have had little to say about Meno's character, which is a mistake from the perspective I am taking here.

The *Meno* – and in this I follow Leibniz's *Discourse on Metaphysics* §26 – is not about virtue, excellence, *aretê*. It is about learning, inquiring by a method capable of leading one to valid inferences from true premises, to knowledge. In particular, the dialogue emphasizes learning as different from the transfer of information. Gorgias tried but failed to transfer information to Meno. Information-transfer can produce true beliefs, but it cannot produce knowledge and it is not a method practiced by Socrates, who adjusted his techniques to fit his interlocutors. Leibniz, a sensitive reader of Plato's dialogues, made light of those who took Plato's remarks on anamnesis literally, those who believed that Socratic priests and priestesses were conjuring immortal souls in possession of all knowledge. For Leibniz, anamnesis is learning, learning by inference from what is already known – familiar from Sherlock Holmes. Leibniz loved Plato's "beautiful experiment" with Meno's intelligent slave.[6] While the slave proves capable of learning, Meno does not. That contrast (and nothing about virtue) is the take-home message of Plato's *Meno*.

By my lights, what Plato does make explicit in the dialogue should be enough to put anyone on guard. And against what should we be defending ourselves? Against the view that the point of the dialogue is to identify the nature of virtue. Consider some of what Plato does tell us: (i) Aristippus is Meno's lover (*Meno* 70b) although, by Athenian standards, Meno is already too old to be a beloved; and it transpires that he still has more than one lover (76b).[7] (ii) If we can judge a man by the company he keeps, as Socrates says we might (95d–e) then we could also note that Meno's Athenian host, Anytus (90b), though a democrat when we meet him with Meno, had been an early supporter of the Thirty and had

---

[6] 'Boy' is a misnomer; Meno was not taking children on campaign with him, and elderly slaves —as in other cultures—were nevertheless called 'boy'.
[7] Xenophon adds that Meno also had a bearded beloved, Tharypus (*Anabasis* 2.6.28)—a further and double breach of convention.

even earlier invented a new way to bribe juries.[8] Later, he will be one of Socrates's three accusers.[9] (iii) Meno has trouble remembering and repeating what he is supposed to have learned from Gorgias. (iv) Socrates has to remind Meno that Meno's account of virtue as the ability to rule over people requires the modifier 'justly and not unjustly' (73d). (v) Socrates tells Meno, "you are forever giving orders in a discussion, as spoiled people do, who behave like tyrants as long as they are young" (76b). (vi) Plato's Socrates alludes to Meno's future failure to become better when he predicts, "you would agree, if you did not have to go away before the mysteries as you told me yesterday, but could remain and be initiated" (76e).[10]

In short, had we been a part of Plato's ancient audience, we would not seek to understand virtue by reading the *Meno* any more than we would now seek to understand virtue by reading a dialogue between some contemporary villain – Bashar al-Assad or George Bush – and a philosopher like Socrates.

II. Theaetetus

My second example of a misunderstood Platonic character whose actual biography can aid our understanding is the Athenian Theaetetus of Sunium, son of Euphronius, one of the great mathematicians of the ancient world,[11] though as ugly as Meno was beautiful. In this case, the received view of Theaetetus has had a misleading effect on the history of mathematics as well as on Platonic scholarship.

For most of the twentieth century, it has been thought that Theaetetus studied and taught mathematics in Plato's Academy and was Plato's associate there for nearly twenty years until his death in the Corinthian battle of 369,[12] and that Plato wrote the *Theaetetus* as a memorial to him when he died. I will explain in a moment why that poignant story is not possible, but I want first to say why we should care. In the twentieth century, cemented through the influence of Gregory Vlastos, major mathematical discoveries in the West were moved forward – into Plato's mature lifetime rather than that of Socrates; hence it was necessary to keep Theaetetus alive into the period that we have come to think of as Plato's

---

8 Pseudo-Aristotle, *Athenian Constitution* 27.5 and 34.3.
9 Socrates implicitly disparages Anytus by praising his father (90a–b) and then pointing out that such praiseworthy men are unable to bring up praiseworthy sons (93d–94c).
10 Translations of *Meno* are those of Grube as revised by Cooper.
11 Biographical material is adapted from Nails 2002.
12 Burnyeat 1990: 3. Translations of *Theaetetus* are from this edition of the dialogue.

maturity. According to Vlastos,[13] Plato discovered and was significantly changed by mathematics after writing his Socratic dialogues; the encounter with the mathematics of his associate, Theaetetus, marked a philosophical turning point for Plato's so-called theory of forms.

In fact, as argued in David Fowler's monumental *The Mathematics of Plato's Academy*, the claim makes no historical or biographical sense. When Theaetetus actually died, in 391, there was not yet an Academy of Plato. Plato learned mathematics as the other Athenian youths of his era did – and the mathematics he learned had already been established before and during the lifetime of Socrates. So much for a brief sketch of matters, the details of which I will now fill in on three fronts: evidence for the death of Theaetetus, the flawed account of the history of ancient mathematics, and the modern philosophical counterpart to that flawed ancient mathematical story. Along the way, one can see how Plato's dialogue has been interpreted and reinterpreted to fit such external constraints.

We know exactly when the Theaetetus takes place: in the months immediately preceding Socrates's death, at which time Theaetetus is *meirakion*, but on the young side, for he is not fully grown (155b); and Socrates says to the geometry master, Theodorus, "Look at the company then. They are all children but you" (168d). We also know that the dramatic frame of the dialogue, with Euclides and Terpsion, explicitly depicts Theaetetus's impending death. Plato tells us so.

There is no doubt either that Theaetetus was a very great mathematician whose work was codified in Euclid's *Elements* but, as often happens with known individuals from the ancient world, other mathematical discoveries whose authors were unknown were later ascribed to the known Theaetetus. The first scholium to book 13 of Euclid states, for example, that Theaetetus added the octahedron and icosahedron to the Pythagoreans' cube, pyramid and dodecahedron for the total of five regular solids (*Timaeus* 54d–55c). He was also credited with the two means of *Timaeus* (31b–32b), the mean of *Parmenides* (154b–d), incommensurability (*Meno*, *Theaetetus*), rational and irrational cube roots (*Theaetetus* 148b) and continuous quantities. The provenance of these attributions is uncertain. Understandably, the question began to be asked whether Theaetetus could have accomplished it all by 391, in less than a decade following Socrates's death.

In the 1910s, modern classical scholars began to suppose that he could not (Caveing 1996). They found a later battle in Corinth, a famous one in 369, and attached Theaetetus's death to that one, giving him twenty-two more years to

---

[13] Vlastos 1991 is a consolidation of his views, but they had been appearing in lectures and articles by then since the 1970s.

move mathematics forward. The suggestion was immediately and eagerly accepted, reinforcing a second important catalyst for re-dating the death of Theaetetus. Namely, from the eighteenth century, philosophers had a strong desire to make the *Theaetetus* the threshold for Plato's abandonment of forms as he "developed" and turned to the issues introduced in the *Statesman* and *Sophist*, dialogues with dramatic dates after the *Theaetetus* and with an overlap of characters.

I pause to note, though this is not the place to argue, that the *Theaetetus* does not abandon the forms. Forms are discussed there (185c–186d) as objects of knowledge – not of the senses – naming "being and not being, likeness and unlikeness, same and different; also one, and any other number applied to them...beautiful and ugly, good and bad...hardness...softness."[14] They are what is stable against Heraclitean flux.

Nevertheless, this direction of Platonic interpretation was comfortably supported by the claim that the mathematics of the *Theaetetus* is derived from Plato's time, not Socrates' – a claim based on the false premise that Theaetetus died in 369. The fact is that Theodorus, who was a rough contemporary of Socrates, made his discoveries by about 440, when both the concept and theorem necessary to prove similar rectangles by the method of anthyphairesis were available to him (Artmann 1994: 22). Neglecting that detail, historians of mathematics were swayed by a desire to locate and date ancient mathematical developments within the Academy itself; Fowler (1999: 360) says Theaetetus's death in 369 was "generally regarded as one fixed point, perhaps the only secure fixed point, in the shifting sands of the incommensurability issue" – yet he himself rightly doubted its truth. The year 369 for the death of Theaetetus raises four problems, explicit in Thesleff 1990: 149–50, that are together insuperable: (i) Athens was not mustering 46-year-old academics for hoplite combat in 369, (ii) Theaetetus's skillful soldiering (142b–c) was far more likely to have been exhibited when he was of military age, 24, than at 46. (iii) Euclides's 30-kilometer walk, from which he has just returned as the dialogue's frame begins, is more likely for a man of 59 than for a man of 81. (iv) The remark of Socrates that seems so prescient to Euclides and Terpsion, the query whether Theaetetus will live to grow up (142c–d), is appropriately applied to a man who dies before reaching 30, but not for one who reaches 46. Theaetetus died in 391, and the mathematics that fascinated Plato had already been established.

---

14 As John McDowell points out in the notes to his 1973 translation of *Theaetetus*, it is no good supposing that when Socrates reneges (183c) on his promise to discuss Parmenides (181a–b), he is merely postponing the discussion to the *Sophist*. The discussion of Parmenides in that dialogue is on a different subject.

Both the *Meno* and the *Theaetetus* are dialogues illustrating geometrical proof by the diagrammatic method. Our earliest texts use the term διάγραμμα for 'diagram' and 'proof' interchangeably, and both Plato and Aristotle continue that practice. While Socrates in the *Republic* distinguishes the methods of geometers from those of dialecticians, if I am right that the failing was in the practice – not the subject matter – then we are warranted in gathering the techniques of the mathematicians under the umbrella term 'dialectical method' – our most promising means of achieving such "pieces of knowledge"[15] as are possible for mortals. I take 'dialectical method' to be a flexible term in the dialogues. It is a bootstrapping method, a piecemeal method, the various techniques of which we use when we don't already have knowledge but desire it and seek it systematically.

Some of the mathematicians' methods are used often enough to ensure that we ought to take them as components of the dialectical method. Myles Burnyeat has made much of the first: (i) the crucial relationship between definition in mathematics and philosophy.[16] Glenn Morrow has explored further similarities between the *elenchus* and the procedures of the mathematicians; (ii) Socrates insists on deductive implication, tracing the *consequences* of common opinions, even in practical matters; (iii) avoidance of contradiction; and (iv) methodical, sometimes tedious, demonstration (Morrow 1970: 319–20). Most philosophers have shied away from saying that (v) the method of hypothesis was another key way in which *Socrates's* practice was like that of the mathematicians, though it is introduced as a geometer's method.[17] The passage implies knowledge of conic sections, and philosophers have generally considered that discovery *late*, despite the evidence of Democritus.[18] That brings me to …

A short history of mathematics in two parts: ancient and modern. Standard histories of ancient mathematics told the same tale from the Renaissance to the late twentieth century. Here is David Fowler's succinct version:

> The early Pythagoreans based their mathematics on commensurable magnitudes (or on rational numbers, or on common fractions m/n), but their discovery of the phenomenon of incommensurability (or the irrationality of the square root of 2) showed that this was inad-

---

[15] McDowell's translation, throughout the aviary section of the *Theaetetus*, for ἐπιστῆμαι; cf. the Rowe translation of *Symposium* 207e6, reserving 'branches of knowledge' or 'sciences' for μαθήματα. See now Benson 2012.
[16] See the introduction to his translation (Hackett, 1990), and Burnyeat 2000.
[17] *Meno* 86e4–87b2, where the hypothetico-deductive method is introduced, explicitly crediting the geometers.
[18] Morrow (1970: 313) argues that Democritus knew that a cone holds one-third the volume of a cylinder with the same base and height.

equate. This provoked problems in the foundation of mathematics that were not resolved before the discovery of the proportion theory that we find in Book V of Euclid's *Elements*.[19]

The story persisted – *persists* – despite the fact that many of its presuppositions did not pan out, as Fowler argues and Fernando Gouvêa seconds in his review. [20] First, the standard view was that Greek geometry was a de-arithmetized version of Babylonian arithmetized geometry. The latter seemed "more normal" to moderns in the West, but the study of books II and X of Euclid's *Elements* showed that cannot be so. The geometrical approach was independent and, as a result, incommensurability was not a foundational crisis in Greek mathematics but an interesting discovery that led to significant mathematics. Second, Greek arithmetic had no notion of common fractions as previously thought, but proceeded by parts so, for example, "one ninth of 2 is $1/6^{th} + 1/18^{th}$." Third, the Greek notion of 'proportion' (*a* is to *b* as *c* is to *d*) differed from the notion of 'ratio', and there were at least three competing definitions of 'ratio': from music theory, astronomy, and mathematics. Fourth, anthyphairesis, the method of reciprocal subtraction (similar to what is now called 'continued fractions') was of far greater importance than previously realized. Before the middle of the sixth century – that is, a hundred years before Socrates was born – architectural drawings were exact; materials were already available: not just wax tablets, but precisely planed marble slabs used in the building trades (Artmann 1994: 18).[21] Concepts too were available, though one of the matters still in some dispute is when proof was given for what was already intuited by working mathematicians – e.g., that the intersection of two straight lines yields equal angles. Where mathematicians dominate the history of their subject, proof is moved further back toward the sixth century; and Theodorus's fifth-century geometry lesson has been the locus for a library's worth of research in journals of geometry and history of science (see figures 1–3), as well as Wilbur Knorr's monograph on Theodorus's geometry lesson.

---

19 Fowler 1999: 356. The point is crucial to new claims that distinguish the second edition from the 1987 one.
20 My account of what is significant in Fowler 1999 is adapted from that of Gouvêa 1999.
21 Artmann discusses the sources, including *Philebus* 56b.

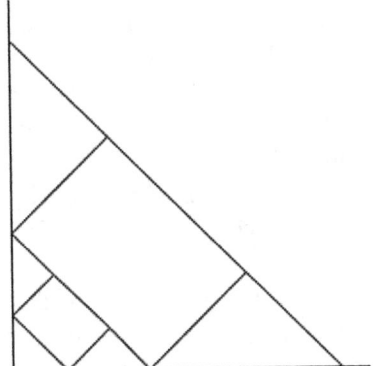

Fig. 1: Theodorus's proof by continued fractions in Theaetetus (Bindel 1962)

Fig. 2: Theodorus's spiral stops at step 17 to prevent the intrusion of √18 on √1 (Anderhub 1941)

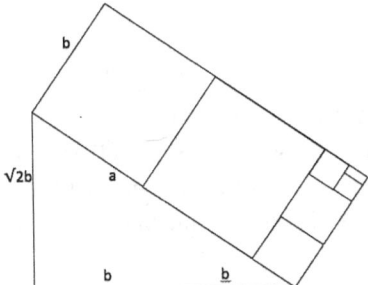

Fig. 3: Theodorus's proof by removing squares to prove similar rectangles by anthyphairesis (Artmann 1994)

There is a modern counterpart to the flawed ancient story. In the nineteenth century, as mathematicians explored the limits of infinite processes that defied the visual imagination, suspicion of geometrical intuition took hold. That "visual understanding actually conflicts with the truths of analysis" became dogma in the early twentieth century (Giaquinto 2007: 3–8). A host of arithmetized proofs for Theodorus's theorem appeared then – despite the clear text of the dialogue.[22]

---

22 Caveing (1996: 282): "…according to Vogt, 'Theodoros' lesson' was divided into two parts of which the geometrical one answers to the verb ἔγραφε [147d3], and the arithmetical one to the

Burnet in 1911 deprecated Socrates's use of a diagram in the slave's lesson, calling it "opposed to ... the process of good inquiry."[23] Heath's *History of Greek Mathematics* reflects what turns out to have been a benighted blip. The search for secure foundations for axiomatic systems spawned conflicting schools later in the twentieth century,[24] so the dogma did finally subside.[25]

Ancient philosophers, however, were *not* in the vanguard of all this activity. Scholars were under the sway of a just-so story about ancient Greek mathematics, and in the long shadow of Heath, so mathematical developments were pushed further toward the fourth century, a trend at its apex with Vlastos's view that Plato's discovery of advanced mathematics, as an adult with dialogues already written, marked a turning point. It now seems certain that it would be difficult to overemphasize the degree to which Socrates's generation was immersed in the visual and spatial thinking involved in geometrical proof. I do not mean Socrates was a mathematician, but that the evidence is great that whatever mathematical knowledge philosophers of the twentieth century attributed to Plato would as plausibly have been attributed to Socrates, an educated fifth century Athenian. The biography of Theaetetus is central to sorting out both the history of mathematics and the interpretation of Plato.

* * *

The literature on Plato's view of women flourishes, but works that evaluate the degree of Plato's feminism predominate, most of those based on explicit arguments about women in *Republic* 5,[26] with work on what women *symbolize* when encountered in Plato's dialogues taking a distant second place. In both

---

verb ἀποφαίνων: on the one hand mere constructions of lines, on the other logical proofs. But, according to classical Greek syntax, if a verb in the indicative mode is accompanied with another in the participle, the two ideas are linked, and the main one is borne by the participle, while the other points out only a modality of the action. So Plato means 'Theodoros proved by means of geometrical constructions...', that is the drawing of lines is part of the proof itself."

23 Brown (1971: 204n) cites Burnet's 1911 note to *Phaedo* 73a7, with approval.

24 Giaquinto (2007: 6) notes the phases: (i) Carnap's conventionalism measured "convenience and truthfulness; there is neither need nor possibility of establishing the axioms true and the rules valid." (ii) Quine's holistic empiricism trumped conventionalism but did not distinguish math and science: "Even professional mathematicians must await the verdicts of empirical science before they can justifiably assert the truth of their mathematical beliefs." And Gödel (1964) reasserted intuitionism.

25 Diagrammatic *proofs* (not mere illustrations) have begun to reemerge: cf. Brown 1999 and 2004.

26 There is extensive (more than the usual) overlap among these articles, chapters, and books; see Bluestone 1987 and Tuana 1994.

strands, however, the actual women of Plato's dialogues are themselves effectively suppressed. I support a third approach, rare but not entirely unknown: that the women represented in Plato's dialogues should be considered in their particularity – like the men. One need not insist that Plato's fourth-century representations of fifth-century women were perfectly accurate to value their philosophically informative function; but it is worth noting that, despite an overhaul of the Athenian legal code undertaken in 410 and completed for implementation in 403/2, the situation for women under the law remained virtually unchanged in Plato's lifetime; thus women of his fourth-century family[27] were subject to the same legal restrictions as those that had affected the women of Socrates's household.[28]

III. Diotima

Diotima of Mantinea, however, is not an Athenian. She is an exception to the rule of existing *contemporaneous* evidence confirming Plato's choosing his characters from among known persons,[29] making her a magnet for attention, though primarily insofar as she is conceived as a constructed stand-in for Socrates or Plato. There is a current and widespread assumption that Diotima is the *one* named character Plato invented out of whole cloth. David Halperin's famous title, "Why is Diotima a Woman?" suppresses the premise that Diotima was fabricated by Plato. As Hayden Ausland (2000: 186n11) has shown in striking detail,[30] however, "Diotima's fictionality is a modern development."

---

[27] Plato's mother was Perictione, daughter of Glaucon III; Potone, daughter of Ariston, was Plato's full sister. There is no record of Athenian women attending the Academy; the two women whose names are preserved, Axiothea of Phlius and Lasthenia of Mantinea, were from the Peloponnesus. Here and below, factual details derive from Nails 2002.

[28] Xanthippe of course, but others possibly as well (cf. *Phaedo* 116b). For present purposes, I leave aside the ubiquitous problem that affects the building of an account of the women in Plato's dialogues: sisters, in the absence of exact dates of birth, are often silently assumed to be younger than brothers. Further, despite the typical Athenian arrangement for girls-in-their-teens to marry men-in-their-thirties (Garland 1990: 210–213), the practice of scholars is to date children in relation to fathers, thirty years apart, without much regard for a woman's actual child-bearing span.

[29] Philebus is the only other.

[30] Ausland cites in evidence the testimonia in *Platonis Symposium*, ed. Otto Jahn, 2nd edn., Bonn: Marcum, 1875, 16–18; F. A. Wolf, *Platons Gastmahl*, Leipzig: Schwickert, 1782, xlvi (2nd edn. [1828], lxiv); and Plato's nineteenth century prosopographer, G. Groen van Prinsterer, *Prosopographia Platonica*, Leiden: Hazenberg, 1823, 125.

We are rightly suspicious of arguments from silence – not only because evidence has a way of turning up unexpectedly, but because we can be quite certain that we have such a small portion of the evidence – and a smaller portion for non-Athenian individuals than for most others of the late fifth and early fourth centuries. Yet the argument from silence has been the argument of choice that Diotima is not historical. There is a slightly more nuanced argument that is almost as common. Here's the version in the introduction to the Nehamas-Woodruff translation of the *Symposium*: "Diotima in her speech makes an allusion to the view Aristophanes has just presented at the banquet... This... suggests that even if Diotima actually existed, what she is represented as saying to Socrates cannot have been composed, as Socrates claims, long before the party during which he relates it."[31] But we do not know much about what he related. There is no certainty that Plato contrived the whole speech of Aristophanes *ex nihilo*. As with the book of Zeno in the *Parmenides*, or the speech of Lysias in the *Phaedrus*, it has often been noted that Plato's change of style and manner may well reflect his brilliance as an author, or his reconstruction of an existing original, or even his embedding of an original in his own text.[32] Moreover, the possibility that the story was not original with Aristophanes or Plato should not be dismissed lightly. The claim that Diotima could not in the late 440s have alluded to a speech that Aristophanes didn't make until 416 misses a point Dover made in 1966: Aristophanes, or Plato, was dressing up a folk tale, not inventing new material. There is a very similar ancient Indian myth of the original androgyne, suggesting Indo-European beginnings. If the story was not wholly original with Aristophanes, Plato's pointing to that fact in the Symposium may have been received as a mild comeuppance to Socrates's longtime accuser.[33]

A further point about Diotima: the secure dramatic date of Agathon's victory party, 416, and Socrates's claim that Diotima put off the Athenian plague for a decade, push his acquaintance with her back before 440 – when Socrates was an unattached young man in his thirties. That he might have learned *ta erôtika* from her, as he claims in the *Symposium* (201d), is no more refuted than confirmed by any available evidence. What is vexing is the insistence with which Diotima is so often assumed to be a pure fiction, Plato's creation. If the historical

---

[31] Nehamas and Woodruff, trr. 1989: xii, citing *Symposium* 204d–e, 212c.
[32] Ledger 1989: 103–4, 117, 124–25 (Lysias's speech in the *Phaedrus*, sometimes still listed among Lysias's sextant speeches), and 166 (Zeno's scroll from the *Parmenides*).
[33] After all, Aristophanes had been persistently critical of Socrates (423, ±418, 414, and 405), earning a mention in Socrates's speech before his jury. The present treatment of Diotima is a truncated version of a full article devoted to evidence for her existence and contribution (Nails 2015).

Socrates ever really mentioned learning from men and women, priests and priestesses, as Plato has him say more than once (cf. *Meno* 81a5–b1), or put names to any of them, would it be so very surprising that his young associates took note of it?

Whatever is going on with Diotima, we should not be reduced to assuming that she must be either non-existent or, *qua* stand-in for Plato, the fount of philosophical wisdom. She is represented as a mystagogue of the Eleusinian mysteries, and that gives us some idea of her role in society. Elsewhere in Plato, she would be ranked fifth among nine character types from philosopher to tyrant, right behind doctors.[34] We need to be paying more attention to what Diotima says, but not as Plato's mouthpiece.

The central roles of two foreign-born women – Diotima and Aspasia – both of whom Socrates said were his teachers – provide support for the argument that Plato viewed the intellects of women, when freed from the subjection of Athenian education and custom, as equal to those of men. Plato's *Symposium* and his *Theaetetus* introduce an epistemology that is more stable and more complex than the one attributed to Plato in the popular imagination: namely, the *Meno-Phaedo* doctrine that forms are recollected from our having apprehended them before we were born. Diotima, on the contrary, denies human immortality (212d5–7) and offers an epistemology that sounds much like physiology: human beings are capable of knowledge, just as they are capable of walking and talking. Men and women are pregnant in both body and soul, she says. Under the right stimulation, exercise for the body and *elenchus* for the psyche, limbs grow strong, vocabulary is acquired, and ideas develop. Human bodies, like those of other animals developing from infancy to old age, constantly replace their "hair or flesh or bones or blood" (207d); likewise, bits of knowledge are forgotten and must be studied anew in the course of a lifetime (208a). All desire, including intellectual curiosity, falls under her broad definition of 'erotic desire' (205b).

IV. Phaenarete

Phaenarete, wife of Sophroniscus and Chaeredemus. In the *Theaetetus*, Plato uses a woman, Socrates's midwife mother, Phaenarete, as a model in the process of intellectual development. As in the *Symposium*, one needs a guide to bring

---

[34] *Phaedrus* 248d3–4; cf. *Republic* 9.

one's ideas to birth, and Socrates describes himself as practicing his mother's art.[35]

I want to emphasize here a contribution that our background information about Phaenarete makes to our views of Plato's social and political philosophy. Cynthia Patterson (1998: 103–105, 133–137) takes a special interest in the innovations offered in Plato's *Laws* that address existing Athenian problems with inheritance of property, marriage, and adultery. As she details, the laws of inheritance proposed in the Platonic *Laws* are a significant improvement for women over the actual laws of Athens. Plato's revisions may owe something to the experience of the widows we find in the dialogues: Xanthippe, Aspasia, and Phaenarete. The experience of his own twice-widowed mother, Perictione, may also have had an effect, for she faced even fewer choices at the death of Plato's father, Ariston, than did Phaenarete when Sophroniscus died.

Phaenarete was married first to him, then to Chaeredemus, making Patrocles – whom Socrates mentions in the *Euthydemus* (297e) – his half brother. The career of Patrocles shows up in the records altogether later, indicating a rather wide gap, about twenty years, between the two sons of Phaenarete. That gap makes it unlikely that Sophroniscus left a will, bequeathing Phaenarete to someone else, as was his right. Our best evidence is that Socrates had already come of age when his father died. If so, Phaenarete was in a position unique within the Athenian legal code, allowed to choose whether to return to her father's household (or that of his heirs), or to remain in the house of Sophroniscus under the tutelage of her son Socrates. If Socrates had been a minor when his father died, Phaenarete would have been under the tutelage of Sophroniscus's nearest male relative, under well-defined regulations about degrees of kinship (Patterson 1998: 70–106). He would have had the power to give her in marriage, to marry her himself if eligible (i.e., if he was unmarried, or if he was married but childless and preferred to divorce his existing wife). Whatever Phaenarete chose, her dowry went with her to provide for her maintenance.[36]

---

[35] *Theaetetus* 149a. Plato's Socrates demonstrates some familiarity with the range of the midwife's knowledge, including the use of drugs (*pharmakeia*) and incantations for easing and causing pain, inducing birth, aborting the fetus, and cutting the umbilical cord. It should be noted that, in a society where infanticide was permissible for five days after birth, prohibitions on abortion would have made little sense. Until an infant was publicly acknowledged by its father in the *amphidromia* ritual that admitted the infant to the household (*oikos*), it had no status under law. Cf. Garland 1990: 93–4.

[36] See Harrison 1998: 1.38; MacDowell 1978: 88–9.

V. Unnamed of Athens

The unnamed Athenian first wife of Pericles then married Hipponicus.

It has long been the practice of translators and commentators to provide a sentence or thumbnail sketch of Plato's characters. Christopher Taylor's translation of Protagoras provides seven excellent sketches of famous characters from the dialogue, but there are no sketches of the other thirteen named characters. Another problem with the hallowed thumbnail sketch is that it does not show a character's relations to other people – but unrealistically presents persons as tiny "atomic careers." The Protagoras features three foreign sophists plus Protagoras's best student.[37] The conclave of sophists is so promising that three visitors have come into the Athenian urban area, the *astu*, from outlying demes across the Hymettos mountains.[38]

I want to concentrate on the other Athenians, those who live in or close to the walled center of the city. Host Callias is famous for paying a great deal of money to sophists; his house is in the Alopece deme, just southeast of the wall; so he and Socrates, as well as at least Hermogenes, and Callias's father, Hipponicus II,[39] are fellow demesmen, giving them special obligations to one another.[40] The others live within a three-mile radius. But there are closer and more interesting connections than precinct and proximity. It is not just failure to take seriously Plato's depiction of social life and relationships that has been at work in our not being able to fill in the missing social and political pieces of Socrates's life and those of his close associates. A longstanding obstacle has been that women have been ciphers to scholars, often not appearing on stemmata at all, though connections can be difficult to recognize or downright misleading without them. The stemma at figure 4, though very heavily abridged, illustrates some relations that are not normally noticed.

---

37 Protagoras of Abdera, Hippias of Elis, and Prodicus of Ceos; Protagoras's student is Antimoerus of Mende.
38 Philippides I is from Paeania, Phaedrus is from Myrrhinous, and Andron is from Gargettos. We do not yet know the demes for Agathon, though the presence of women in his house in Plato's *Symposium* makes an urban deme likely, or for Adeimantus, son of Cepis (a hanger-on of Alcibiades, making Scambonidae better than a mere guess).
39 It is interesting to note that Hipponicus II (d. ≤422) appears to have passed householder responsibilities on to his adult son, very like Cephalus with respect to Polemarchus in *Republic* 1.
40 On the demesman relation, see, for example, Plato *Laches* 180b–d (cf. 187d–e), *Apology* 33e, *Phaedo* 115c3; Aristophanes *Clouds* 1206–1210, 1322, *Ecclesiazusae* 1023–1024, 1114–1115, *Acharnians* 333, *Knights* 319–320, *Plutus* 253–254; and Lysias 16.14, 27.12.

The heavy arrow points to "unnamed" of Athens who was the wife of Pericles, then of Hipponicus II, though we do not know her name. She ties together the entire extended family. Without Plato's comment at *Protagoras* 315a1 that she is *homomêtrios*, we could not know that Callias's two maternal half-brothers are the sons of Pericles, both present in the dialogue. Callias's paternal half-brother is Socrates's frequent companion, Hermogenes, also present. Alcibiades – also present – is still Pericles's ward at the time of the dialogue, but he will later marry Callias's sister, Hipparete. Plato's own family is implicated too because Callias marries the daughter of Glaucon, Plato's great-granduncle.

By adding this unnamed woman to the picture, we can see that this is no arbitrary collection of visitors to the house of Callias, listening to sophists; this is the extended family of Pericles himself, visible as soon as the characters' familial relations are plotted on the page. The dialogue is set at the beginning of the Peloponnesian War, not long before Pericles's death and that of his sister and two eldest sons; and it makes the discussions in Plato's *Protagoras* of democracy, relativism, and education all the more pointed. For a modern parallel, think of the difference between a story of a conversation among high school students about prospective universities, and the story that the Kennedy clan once met in Hyannis Port to decide which university they would all attend and support.

* * *

We should not, of course, conclude too much from the historical facts Plato chose to allude to in his dialogues, but those facts show at least what he noticed and mentioned; and – together with his proposals for changes in inheritance laws – suggest that he *noticed* the conditions of women in Athens that made it so very unlikely that their intellects could be developed appropriately in the absence of training and education equal to men's. To return to my initial claim, it behooves us to pay attention to the people of Plato's dialogues as particular individuals, and in far greater depth than I can manage here. The fact that Plato's dialogues present us with specific individuals in conversation is something that we should take seriously. Platonic specificity is the unalterable basic condition of not only the dialogues but Plato's conduct of philosophy. We cannot reach the universal except by way of particulars; there is no unmediated apprehension of Platonic forms. So, although arguments can be addressed independently of the text, those arguments are not the dialogues – stripped of their context, they are not only no longer what Plato wrote, but no longer representative of how he does philosophy. I am not merely making the semantic point that 'dialogues' are, almost by definition, words plus context. Rather, I am saying

Five Platonic Characters — 313

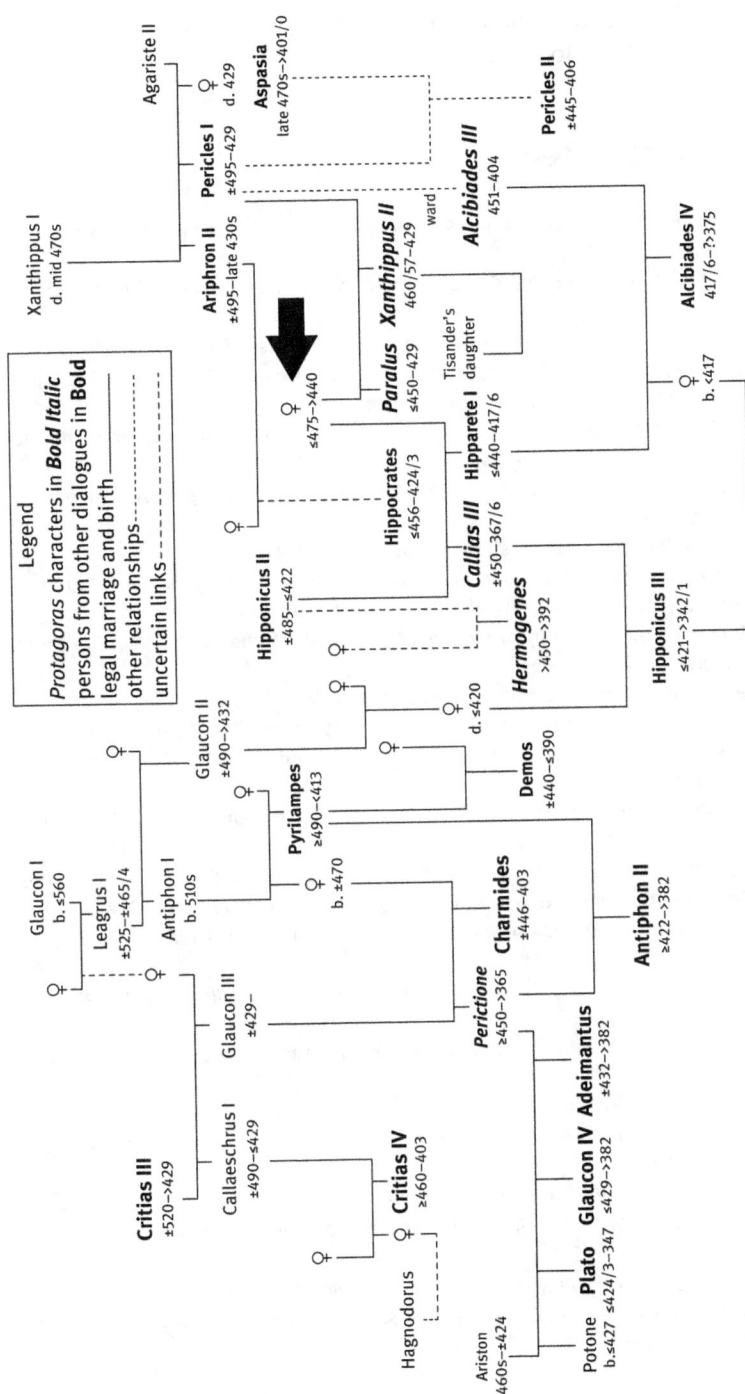

Fig. 4: Plato, Protagoras, abridged stemmata

that Plato's dialogues are irreducibly an interplay between particular and universal that we fail to confront to our peril.

Modern Works Cited

Anderhub, Jakob Heinrich 1941. *Joco-Seria aus den Papieren eines Reisenden Kaufmanns.* Wiesbaden: Kalle.
Artmann, Benno 1994. "A Proof for Theodorus' Theorem by Drawing Diagrams," *Journal of Geometry* 49.
Ausland, Hayden W. 2000. "Who Speaks for Whom in the *Timaeus-Critias?*" In Gerald A. Press, ed., *Who Speaks for Plato?*, 183–198. Lanham: Rowman and Littlefield, 2000.
Bindel, Ernst 1962. *Pythagoras.* Stuttgart: Freies Geistesleben.
Benson, Hugh H. 2012. "The Problem is not Mathematics, but Mathematicians: Plato and the Mathematicians Again," *Philosophia Mathematica* 20: 170–99.
Blondell, Ruby 2002. *The Play of Character in Plato's Dialogues.* Cambridge: Cambridge University Press.
— 2006. "Where is Socrates on the 'Ladder of Love'?" In Lesher et al., 147–178.
Bluestone, Natalie Harris 1987. *Women and the Ideal Society: Plato's* Republic *and Modern Myths of Gender.* Amherst: University of Massachusetts Press.
Brown, James Robert 1999. *Philosophy of Mathematics: An Introduction to the World of Proofs and Pictures.* New York: Routledge.
— 2004. "Peeking into Plato's Heaven," *Philosophy of Science* 71, 1126–1138.
Brown, Malcolm 1971. "Plato Disapproves of the Slave-boy's Answer," in *Plato's Meno* ed. Malcom Brown. Indianapolis: Bobbs-Merrill, 198–242. Reprinted from *The Review of Metaphysics* 20 (1967), 57–93.
Burnyeat, Myles 2000. "Plato on Why Mathematics is Good for the Soul," *Proceedings of the British Academy* 103, 1–81.
Caveing, Maurice 1996. "The Debate between H. G. Zeuthen and H. Vogt (1909–1915) on the Historical Source of the Knowledge of Irrational Quantities," *Centaurus* 38, 277–92.
Dover, Kenneth J[ames] 1989 <1978>. *Greek Homosexuality.* Cambridge: Harvard University Press.
— 1966. "Aristophanes' Speech in Plato's *Symposium.*" *Journal of Hellenic Studies* 86, 41–50.
Fowler, David 1999. *The Mathematics of Plato's Academy*, 2nd edn., Oxford: Oxford University Press.
Garland, Robert 1990. *The Greek Way of Life.* Ithaca: Cornell University Press.
Giaquinto, Marcus 2007. *Visual Thinking in Mathematics: An Epistemological Study*, Oxford: Oxford University Press.
Gödel, Kurt 1964. "What is Cantor's Continuum Problem?" in P. Benacerraf and H. Putnam, eds., *Philosophy of Mathematics: Selected Readings*, Cambridge: Cambridge University Press.
Gouvêa, Fernando Q. 1999. [review of Fowler 1999], *Mathematical Association of America* <http://mathdl.maa.org/mathDL/19/?pa=reviews&sa=viewBook&bookId=68671>, accessed 11 January 2011.

Halperin, David 1990. "Why is Diotima a Woman? Platonic Erôs and the Figuration of Gender." In *Before Sexuality: The Construction of Erotic Experience in the Ancient Greek World,* ed. David Halperin, John J. Winkler, and Froma I. Zeitlin, 257–308. Princeton: Princeton University Press.

Harrison, A. R. W. 1998 <c. 1968, 1971>. 2nd edn. with foreword by D. M. MacDowell. *The Law of Athens.* Vol. I: *The Family and Property.* Vol. II: *Procedure.* Indianapolis: Hackett Publishing.

Heath, Thomas Little 1921. *A History of Greek Mathematics.* Oxford: Clarendon.

Knorr, Wilbur 1975. *The Evolution of the Euclidean Elements: A Study of the Theory of Incommensurable Magnitudes and Its Significance for Early Greek Geometry.* Dordrecht: Reidel.

Ledger, Gerard R. 1989. *Re-counting Plato: A Computer Analysis of Plato's Style.* Oxford: Clarendon.

Leibniz, G. W. 1991 [1686]. *Discourse on Metaphysics,* tr. Daniel Garber and Roger Ariew, Indianapolis: Hackett Publishing.

MacDowell, Douglas M. 1978. *The Law in Classical Athens.* Ithaca: Cornell University Press.

Morrow, Glenn R. 1970. "Plato and the Mathematicians: An Interpretation of Socrates' Dream in the *Theaetetus* 201e–206c," *The Philosophical Review* 79: 3, 309–33.

Nails, Debra 1995. *Agora, Academy, and the Conduct of Philosophy.* Dordrecht: Kluwer.

—— 2002. *The People of Plato: A Prosopography of Plato and Other Socratics.* Indianapolis: Hackett Publishing.

—— 2015. "Bad Luck to Take a Woman Aboard." In *Second Sailing: Alternative Perspectives on Plato,* ed. Debra Nails and Harold Tarrant. Helsinki: Scientiarum Fennica.

Patterson, Cynthia B. 1998. *The Family in Greek History.* Cambridge and London: Harvard University Press.

Taylor, C. C. W., tr. 1976. *Protagoras.* Oxford: Clarendon.

Thesleff, Holger 1990. "Theaitetos and Theodoros," *Arctos* 24, 147–59.

Tuana, Nancy, editor. 1994. *Feminist Interpretations of Plato.* University Park: Pennsylvania State University Press.

Vlastos, Gregory 1991. *Socrates, Ironist and Moral Philosopher.* Cambridge: Cambridge University Press.

Francisco Bravo
Who Is Plato's Callicles and What Does He Teach?

Callicles is undoubtedly the Platonic character that has achieved the greatest autonomy from its author and has most influenced certain contemporary schools of thought.[1] It is indeed significant that his influence is felt even in our times.[2] As Dodds wrote in 1959[3], it is a strange irony of History that the presentation made by Plato of ideas he wanted to destroy, has actually contributed to their formidable renaissance in our days. It is therefore of great interest to reexamine this character's identity and the positions he defended. Who is he? What does he teach?[4] What does Plato attempt when he presents him? Being known only from *Gorgias* it is not plausible to answer to the question "who is he" before determining at least the gist of what he teaches.

I. Callicles and the Thesis of the Strongest's Rights

Callicles' "doctrines" range from a philosophy of philosophy to an extreme ethical hedonism, but the center of all these is his theory on justice. Interpreters agree that this is not a pure invention of Plato's, but a reflection of the doctrines bubbling at the time. But the author does not merely record them: the arguments advanced by his characters, Callicles in particular, are, as noted by G. B. Kerferd,[5] "composed and manipulated" by him, and we could add that "he is the producer, the production manager and the author of the script."

---

1 The nexuses between Callicles and Nietzsche has been particularly analyzed. A. Fouillée (1902: 96, 187) has done so in passing, others with more thoroughness. See specially W. Nestle (1912: 554) and Adolfo Menzel (1964).
2 cf. Menzel (1964: 23).
3 E.R. Dodds (1959: 390).
4 The "Thrasymachus" of the *Republic* has provoked in me the same line of questioning: "Who is and what does Thrasymachus, from the *Republic*, teach?", in *Estudios de Filosofía Griega*, Caracas, CEP/FHE, 2001, pp. 237–262.
5 Kerferd, (1981: 119).

The fundamental thesis defended by our character about the fair life is that the stronger should prevail over the weaker and have more than the latter.[6] Xerxes' actions, in recent Greek history, showed this. He invaded Greece with no other basis than his power, and the same point is shown regarding Darius' actions. Darius, Xerxes' father, subdued the weak Scythians based on the same principle of power. According to Callicles, both have acted "in accordance with the nature of what is fair (*katà physin tên toû dikaíou*),"[7] which, as such, is "a law of nature (*nómon tês phýseôs*),"[8] even though it opposes the city's laws. Callicles, thus, distinguishes natural law from State laws and argues that only the first one can be identified with the nature of what is fair, while the others are "rules contrary to nature (*nómous toùs parà phýsin hápantas*),"[9] and so being each one "most often contradict the other (*enantí'allêlois estín*)."[10]

We must, however, recall that it was not yet clear what a state law consisted of back then. "One gives the name of law – responds Pericles to Alcibiades' question – to any decision of the People's Assembly, made existent in writing, where it is determined what to do or not do."[11] Similar is the answer of Socrates to Hippias: "state laws are contracts or covenants made by the citizens, by which it is established and promulgated what should be done and what should be avoided."[12] In both descriptions, state laws are conventions established by the citizens "on what should be valid among them."[13] They are therefore subjective and vary from *polis* to *polis*.[14] But Callicles clarifies that they are not approved by the **whole** of the city, only by the **crowd**, since the wise men stick to what is in accordance with nature and the truth.[15] He, thus, fully embraces the antithesis between *nómos* and *phýsis*, probably introduced by Archelaus[16] and widely discussed in the 5th and 4th centuries.[17] Moreover, certain scholars[18] believe that

---

6 *Gorgias* 483 d 1–3 and 6.
7 *Gorg.* 483 e 4.
8 *Gorg.* 483 e 5.
9 *Gorg.* 484 a 6.
10 *Gorg.* 482 e 7–8.
11 Xenophon, *Mem.* I, 2, 40.
12 Xenophon, *Mem.* IV, 4.
13 Menzel (1964: 28).
14 This view is shared both by Callicles and Protagoras. Cf. *Teet.*, 177 d 1–4 and 172a-c.
15 Cf. Menzel (1964: 26). According to this author, Callicles approximates *phýsis* to reason, and thus equates natural law and rational law. Nevertheless, this idea would only achieve full development with the stoics. Through Cicero philosophy of law was finally imposed on Middle Ages and Modern times.
16 Diog. L., II, 16.
17 Cf. Bravo (2001: 15–42).

Callicles provides an original concept of this antithesis, and seem to place on his side Aristotle, linking him to our character,[19] noting that, "for these philosophers, that which is according to nature is the truth (tò alêthés) and what is under the law is the opinion of the crowd (tò toîs polloîs dokoûn)".[20] There are those, however, who believe that Callicles did nothing but "to reproduce the fundamental ideas of Hippias".[21] Against them, others feel that Hippias' *Ius naturale* is essentially different from the Calliclean *Ius naturale*. Let's recall the words Protagoras[22] puts in the mouth of the sophist from Elide: "Everyone here, he says, I consider as friends, as neighbors, as fellow citizens as according to nature (phýsei), but not to the law (ou nómoi). According to nature, indeed, the similar is a relative of the similar, but law, tyrant of men (týrannos tôn anthrôpôn), does violence to nature".[23] As seen, Hippias, like Callicles, also criticizes positive law in natural law's name. But he does not deny its validity as the latter. He rather advocates for "a senior law, an unwritten one",[24] which he explicitly names in his dialogue with Xenophon's Socrates[25] and which he attributes to the gods.[26] His *iusnaturalism* thus adopts a cosmopolitan, democratic and humanitarian direction. It is compatible to the written law, although above the latter. Callicles argues, in contrast, that all positive laws are "contrary to nature (parà phýsin hápantas[27])", and an invention of the weak to tame the stronger exponents of the law of nature (katà nómon ge tês phýseôs[28]). The weak, in effect, using the educational process, seize the strong ones from an early age, as if those were little lions (hôsper léontas) to be tamed, and model them using incantations, making them believe that "they must be each like the other (tò íson chrê échein)" and that "there we have the beautiful and the fair",[29] a tenor of Athenian democracy.

This is actually the target of Callicles' attacks, while for Protagoras, one of its oldest defenders, positive law is "the only justifiable form of government".[30] Ac-

---

18 Menzel (1964: 25).
19 Aristotle, *Soph. Elench.* 173 to 2 ss.
20 *Soph. Elench.* 173 to 16.
21 Cf. F. Dümmler, *Academica*, Huyesen, 1889, cit. by Menzel (1964) 30.
22 Cf. *Prot.* 337c-338b.
23 *Prot.* 337c7-d2.
24 Menzel (1964: 30).
25 *Mem.* IV, 4: "Do you know what does the expression 'unwritten laws' mean?" – "Yes, the ones that are uniformly observed in the whole country".
26 *Mem.* IV, 4: "I believe the gods made these laws for men".
27 *Gorg.* 484 a 5.
28 *Gorg.* 483 e 5.
29 *Gorg.* 484 a 1–3.
30 Cf. Menzel (1964: 10).

cording to the "Myth of Protagoras", cities themselves became possible thanks to Hermes, the messenger of Zeus, who brought men "decency and justice (*aidô te kaì díkên*[31])" and distributed these, not to only one or a few persons, as the art of music, but "to all" evenly (*epì pántas*[32]) as a first condition for life in society, which is the only true form of human life.[33] The conclusion of this Protagorean statement for democracy could not be sharper: "someone unable to participate in these gifts will be sentenced to death as a plague to the city" (322d4–5). According to the sophist from Abdera, Athenians firmly believe that "all men partake of justice".[34] For Herodotus, closely associated with him, "democracy is the world of equality (*isonomía*)".[35] Thucydides, undoubtedly influenced by Protagoras[36], Democritus[37] and even Euripides,[38] put in the mouth of Pericles the fundamental principle of the democratic State: "It serves – he says – the interests of the mass of citizens and not just a minority".[39] He then presents, as its fundamental elements, equality, freedom and the rule of law. Equality is held the most important element, and Pericles proclaimes that "all are equal before the law".[40] That is the principle Callicles tried to destroy.

Suppose, says he, that among the domesticated by democracy there emerges "a man sufficiently well endowed by nature as to shake (...) and throw away from him all the strings": "I'm sure – he maintains -, that, throwing to his feet our writings, spells and incantations", he, who was before our slave (δοῦλος)

---

[31] *Prot.* 322 c 2.
[32] *Prot.* 322 d 1.
[33] The "Myth of Protagoras" leads us to the idea that "natural state represents a life without any rights, without morality and without State", which goes contrary to Callicles' ideas. Protagoras' conclusion is that what is just "does not exist by nature, since it only happens through the laws approved by the people". Cf. Menzel (1964: 17–18).
[34] *Prot.* 323c1. This is what one understands from the translation by A. Croiset, Col. Budé, 1967.
[35] Cited by Menzel (1964: 10).
[36] Cf. Menzel (1964: 12, 14).
[37] Democritus also defends the democratic juridical thinking and the idea of the egalitarian State. He believes that democracy presupposes harmony (ὁμόνοια) among citizens. Cf. DK B 251.
[38] *The Suppliants* and *Phoenician Women* by Euripides show lovely praise to democracy. In the first one, Theseus agrees to rescue the corpses of the dead heroes, after a plead from his mother, but he wishes this would be "approved by the whole of the people (....)". "Because – he says – I made it a sovereign State, where all are free and have the same rights" (349–352). Addressing the herald from Thebes, he advises him that "our city is not in the hands of a sole man. It is its people who govern it. Money gives no advantages. The poor and the rich have equal rights" (404–408). Menzel (1964: 14) believes that these two tragedies may be considered as "literary models" of Pericles' Discourse.
[39] Thucyd. II, 1, 37; cf. Menzel (1964: 12).
[40] Thucyd. II, 1, 37.

would revolt and would then stand as our master (*despótês hêméteros*). And then "the just by nature would shine in all its glory (*to tês phýseôs dikaion*)"41.[41] Thus, instead of the principle of egalitarian democracy, Callicles presents the need of a **superman**, who would be the condition for natural justice to happen.[42]

II. Callicles' Allies

In support of its anti-egalitarian natural law (*iusnaturalism*), Callicles invokes an ode by Pindar expressing – he says – "the same thought I had when it claims that law, queen of all things (*nómos pantôn basileýs*) / justifies the driving force of all things / with its sovereign hand." And Pindar illustrates that idea with one of Heracles' feats, he who was the Greek model of the superman.[43] He, without paying for it or receiving it as a gift, seized a herd of oxen that belonged to Geryon,[44] claiming that under "natural justice, oxen and all the goods of the weaker and less brave man are property of the better and stronger one".[45] Thus, Pindar would have admitted the presence of natural law on Heracles' feat and was, thus, one of the first Greeks to defend it.[46] Callicles, meanwhile, uses this same Pindaric myth to apply, for the first time, for the advent of a superman

---

41 *Gorg.* 484 b 1.
42 Zarathustra's fundamental message is no different: "Ich *lehre euch den Übermenschen. Der Mensch ist etwas, das überwunden werden soll*". (F. Nietzsche, *Also sprach Zarathustra*, Prologue, 3).
43 Plato's *Symposium* (177b3) reminds us that Heracles was praised by some "sophists of value". He was obviously thinking about Prodicus' *Heracles*, mentioned by Xenophon *Mem.* II 21–34. Euripides considers him "the greatest of all heroes" (Heracles' *madness* 150).
44 Three-headed and three-bodied (up to his hips) giant, who lived on the island of Erytheia, at the outskirts of the Occident. His wealth consisted of herds of oxen kept by Eurytion and his dog Orthrus. Cf. P. Grimal (1994: 213).
45 *Gorg.* 484c2.
46 Plato seems to accept this understanding of the verses written by the author of *Epinikia*. Nevertheless, it seems unilateral and incomplete, since – according to Menzel (1964: 51) – it "omits the religious moment from the solution". Thus, "Heracles' victory over the giant Geryon is not due only to a stronger force, there is also a whole exteriorizing of divine will". Actually, Greek mythology is not clear on the reasons of Heracles' acts. It looks like the hero did not act so on his own will nor because he considered himself the strongest, but after Eurystheus' demand, who sent him "in order to bring back the precious oxen" of Geryon's (P.Grimal (1994: 246; cf. 213). Moreover, it seems that it was Eurystheus himself who gave Heracles these orders, either because he was so told by the gods, or because of the love shared between them, as a token of that love (a recognized Alexandrian tradition presents Heracles as Eurystheus' lover: cf. P. Grimal (1994: 187).

as the only way to restore the law of nature.⁴⁷ Curiously enough, Plato and Aristotle do not seem unaffiliated to this figure. It would, indeed, be legitimate to perceive some similarity between Callicles' superman and the ruler-philosopher of the Platonic state.⁴⁸ The Stageirite, on the other hand, does not rule out the hypothesis of an individual or group of individuals who, by their transcendent virtue become like a god among men (*hôsper gàr theón en anthrôpois*).⁴⁹ For these "supermen"⁵⁰- he holds – there is no law, but they themselves being the law,⁵¹ and it would be ridiculous to legislate for them, since they would reply with the words Antisthenes puts in the mouth of the lions when hares demand equality for all.⁵²

Let's go back to Plato. In addition to his thesis of the philosopher-king, who could evoke the superman of Callicles, there are, in the dialogues, other characters that seem to travel the same path as our character. And above all Thrasymachus,⁵³ whose main thesis is that what is fair is nothing but what is useful to the strongest (*toû kreítonos xymphéron*⁵⁴). However and contrary to Callicles, he concludes that the only right is the positive one,⁵⁵ determined in each case by the usefulness to the strongest.⁵⁶ At first glance, there appears an opposition to our character, because it excludes what is fair by nature. On the other hand, he coincides with Callicles by stating that positive law does not protect **all** citizens, but only the strongest.⁵⁷ Another character that comes close is Glaucon, chosen to expose the doctrine of some sophists, especially Thrasymachus.⁵⁸ Why did Plato give this task to his brother? Perhaps – says Menzel – "for the same reason he created the figure of Callicles, whose thoughts Glaucon is inti-

---

47 The idea of a superman or a superior man (*ho béltistos*) appears more than once on the Platonic dialogues. Cf., for example, *Rep.* IX, 590 d 1–2, where he is compared to the slave (*doúlos*), even though the advantages of him being "ruled by a divine and wise being (*hypò theíou kaì phromímou árchesthai*: 590 d 5.)" is stated, in opposition to Thrasymachus. Although Plato also believes that the best should line up the worst (cf. 590c-592a).
48 Cf. *Rep.* V 473 d; *Letter* VII, 326 b 1–4.
49 Aristotle. *Pol.* 1284 a 11.
50 J. Tricot (Aristote, *La Politique*, Paris, J. Vrin, p. 231) uses "surhommes" in his translation of 1284 to 10.
51 *Pol.*, III, 13, 1284 a 11.
52 *Pol.* 1284 a 17: "Where are your claws and teeth?". Cf. Aesop, *Fable* 241.
53 Cf. *Rep.* I 336 b ss, IX 590 d, *Laws* IV 714c.
54 *Rep.* 338 c 3.
55 Menzel (1964: 64).
56 Cf. *Rep.* 338 d-e.
57 Cf. Menzel (1964: 64).
58 Cf. *Rep.* 358 b-c. Glaucon wants to know "justice's and injustice's nature and the effects both produce within the soul they reside in" (358b4–5).

mately related to".⁵⁹ Given the disadvantages carried by both the perpetration and the suffering of injustice, he argues that the best thing to do was to establish mutual agreements to avoid each of these (*xýnthésthai allêlois mêt' adikeîn mêt' adikeîsthai*⁶⁰). Of these agreements were "born the laws and conventions of men among themselves" so that they are "the origin and essence of justice" (359a5), midpoint (*metaxý*) between the greatest goodness – injustice with impunity – and the greatest evil – "the inability to avenge" it (359a6–7). As seen, Glaucon does not merely comment on Thrasymachus: for the latter, law is an imposition made by the strongest, while for the former it is the result of a contract. This thesis makes him, as Menzel notes, "the forerunner of the idea of the social contract (*contractus socialis*)".⁶¹ However, he coincides with Callicles in considering that positive juridical order favors only the very weak and not the few "real men" (*alêthôs ándra*⁶²), which are the supermen. At the beginning of the story of the ring of Gyges, the statements are unequivocally Calliclean: the fair follows the same path as the unfair because, like him, he is driven by the incessant desire for more (*dià tên pleonexían*), that all nature pursues as a good (*ho pâsa phýsis diôkein péphyken ôs agathón*) and law diverts, by force, towards the respect for equality".⁶³

III. Who Is the Strongest?

Callicles' belief is that Socrates would accept his thesis if he himself would resign his own conception of philosophy and accepted Socrates'.⁶⁴ It is not my intent to take up the latter, akin to that of Isocrates' in several points⁶⁵, nor to dissect the Socratic refutation of his central thesis.⁶⁶ I will stick only to what Socrates puts at the center of the debate, namely, the concept of the 'strongest' (*tò kreîtton*). What Plato's spokesman tries to show is that the many weak can be stronger than the few strong. But what does Callicles mean by '*tò kreîtton*' (the strongest)? Does it mean the same as '*tò béltion*' (the best)? (488b9) Is it possible that the best partner with the weakest? (488c7). Callicles' negative response

---

59 Menzel (1964: 67).
60 *Rep.* 359 a 2.
61 Menzel (1964: 68).
62 *Rep.* 359 b 3.
63 *Rep.* 359 c 5–7.
64 *Gorg.* 484 c-d.
65 Cf. W. Jaeger, *Paideia* (1971: 662, 836).
66 Cf. *Gorg.* 487 a ss.

makes his opponent object that, regarding the reality of facts, the crowd (*hoi pólloi*) is naturally stronger and better than the individual (*toû henós*). It is, in fact, the crowd "that imposes its laws" (488d6–7), which are, therefore, "laws of the mighty" (488d7). Now, the crowd holds, contrary to Callicles, that "justice is equality" (*díkaion eînai tò íson échein*) rather than inequality and therefore "perpetrating injustice is uglier than suffering injustice" (489a3–4). Our anti-egalitarian natural law legislator cannot but admit that, yes, "this is what the crowd thinks" (489a8). This concession allows his opponent to conclude that the principle according to which perpetrating injustice is uglier than suffering it complies not only with the law (positive: *nómoi*), but also with nature (*phýsei*), and that therefore it is false that law and nature are contrary to each other (489b2–3). Given the risk of an unwanted recantation, Callicles claims that what he said is that 'better' and 'stronger' are (…) synonyms (489c2–3), but not at the level of worthless people, but that of the strong ones. This irritated loophole allows Socrates to conclude that, for his opponent, despite what he said, 'better' is not synonymous with 'stronger' (489d4). What do you mean, then, by the 'best'? (*ti pote legéis toùs beltíous;*)? "Who are the best"? (489e3). By any chance are they "the wisest" (*toùs phronimotérous*) (489e8)?

Callicles welcomes this suggestion with some enthusiasm and fits it with his thesis of the right of the strongest: "the fair, according to nature – says he now – is the best, that is, the most reasonable, the one who rules over the mediocre and have more than they do" (490a7–8). And then he reiterates that "the best is the wisest" (*tò phronimóteron beltío*: 490d2). What would be the order of things (*perì tinôn*: 491a4)?, asks his opponent. Not crafts wise, but in regard to political affairs. The best are, then, those engaged in them and who are wise and courageous in their management (491c6–7). But it remains to be determined if the best also govern themselves (*autòn heautoû árchonta*: 491d6), that is, as Socrates understands this, if "they dominate within themselves pleasures and impulses" (*ton hêdonôn kaì epithymían*: 491e1). This definition of self-government, far from pleasing our character, unleashes the harshest hedonism: to accept it, says he, would be to call wise the morons (*toû helithíous*) and to forget that our explanandum is "the beautiful and the fair according to nature" (*tò katà phýsin kalòn kaì díkaion*: 491e7). According to our nature, "to live well, one has to feed life with the strongest passions, instead of suppressing them" (491e9). Since such is not at their fingertips, the crowd claims that "intemperance is shameful" (*aischrón*) (492a5). Against such "human conventions against nature" (*tà parà phýsin synthêmata anthrôpôn*) and "worthy of nothing" (*oudenòs áxia*) (492c7–8) stands Socrates' opponent, who, however, praises his courage and frankness, and acknowledges that he has "clearly expressed what others think but do not dare say" (492d2–3). Then the problems on "how to live" (*pôs biotéon*: 492d5) and "who is happy and who is not" (*hóstis te eudaímôn estín kaì hostis mê:* 472c10), already debated with Polus, resurface. It is impossible to analyze the disjointed Platonic refutation of Callicles' sybarite hedonism.[67] There it is evident the existent gap between what is natural according to each of the interlocutors: Socrates sets it within the rational part of man, while Callicles sets it within the irrational.

IV. Who Is Callicles?

But who is this "somewhat mysterious figure" that has not left "trace in recorded history"[68] except from *Gorgias?* No doubt his identification can help us understand the Platonic way of philosophizing. We must, however, admit that there is not yet a satisfactory answer to the question here presented.[69] Nevertheless, it would be risky to argue that Plato "felt a secret sympathy for Callicles" and that this is, at heart, nothing more than "a portrait of Plato's self that Plato rejects".[70] Levinson rightly observes that "it is not correct to identify Plato with characters he himself abhors".[71] Apart from this hypothesis, which lies within subconscious psychology, there are three historical others: (1) Callicles is a historical character according to both his name and personality, (2) Callicles is Plato's invention from one extreme to the other, (3) His name was Plato's invention, but not the character itself, which is historically real. The first hypothesis, which was proposed by Wilamowitz,[72] seems untenable, since there is no reference to our character outside *Gorgias.* It is true that Aristotle mentions him as a defender of the antithesis *nómos-phýsis*[73] and Aulus Gellius[74] counts him among the enemies of philosophy, but both refer to the dramatic Platonic dialogue and not to a historical character. One could argue that Plato refers to several facts that seem to imply his existence: to his homeland (Acharneus[75]), to three of his friends (An-

---

67 Cf. F. Bravo (2007: 102–107).
68 W. K. C. Guthrie (1971: 102).
69 Cf. Menzel (1964: 113).
70 Guthrie (1971: 106). According to G. Rensi, cited by Levinson (1953: 471), "the Socrates-Callicles conflict in *Gorgias* is not a conflict between two individuals, but one that happens within just one mind set". E. R. Dodds (1959: 13 ss.) seems to accept this point of view when he says that "since Plato felt some sympathy for men of the Calliclean signature", his portrait of Callicles "has not only warmth and vitality but breathes out some affection plain of sorrow".
71 Levinson (1953: 472).
72 Wilamowitz-Möllendorf, *Platon* (1919: I, 208).
73 Cf. *Ref. Sof.*, 173 a 9.
74 A. Gellius, *Attic Nights*, book X, chap. 22.
75 *Gorg.* 495 d 5.

drotion, Lysander and Nausicydes[76]), who really existed, and to Demos, son of Pyrilampes, who would have been Callicles' lover.[77] Nevertheless, let's recall, along with Menzel, that Plato is both a philosopher and a poet, and, thanks to his dual nature, he was able to combine facts and fiction.[78] We must also rule out the hypothesis that Callicles is an outright invention of Plato's, as his doctrines transcend *Gorgias* and have been shared by other well-known writers: Pindar, already mentioned, Euripides, who develops the same doctrines as Callicles in *Phoenician Women*,[79] and especially Thucydides, as we shall see. There is still the third hypothesis, which is subject to novel discussion.

Who is behind the invented name of Callicles? Some historians, like Theodor Berg,[80] identify him with Charicles, one of the Thirty Tyrants. But Th. Gomperz timely notices that apart from this purely external onomastic similarity, Plato attributes to his character personality traits that conflict with Charicles' own.[81] Let's recall, with Menzel, that no one has mentioned the literary activities of this tyrant, while Socrates presents Callicles as one of the most learned men of his times.[82] Let's once again recall the spontaneity with which he turns to Pindar in order to support his natural law (*"iusnaturalism"*), and also to Euripides, so that he could illustrate the distinction between the two kinds of living.[83] One could argue that Charicles also defended the thesis of the right of the strongest, since that is what he exercised as a member of a tyrannical government. But he did act more on a political level than in a doctrinal one. For similar reasons, Otto Apelt's suggestion, that Callicles is none other than Alcibiades, has been rejected.[84] Alcibiades certainly had a dominant nature[85] and was, moreover, as our

---

[76] Cf. *Gorg.* 487c.
[77] *Gorg.* 481d-e.
[78] Menzel (1964: 114).
[79] Actually, *Phoenician Women* presents the confrontation of the two points of view: Jocasta's egalitarian "iusnaturalism", defended against her sons Eteocles and Polynices – "nature – says she – gave men the law of the equal rights" (tò gàr íson nómimon anthrôpois: 558) -, and the anti-egalitarian "iusnaturalism" of her sons (according to whom "one that attacks has the lawful right to oneself": 258; "mortals speak of equal rights, being those nothing than vain words, to be denied by the acts" (499–502); "if there is an error that can be justified it is the one committed because of royalty, admirable iniquity" (káliston adikeîn: 524–525).
[80] Th. Berg (1872–1877, vol. IV, p. 447).
[81] Th. Gomperz (1901: I, 577; cf. A. Menzel's (1964: 114) similar observation. Regarding the personality traits, see in particular *Gorgias* 487c.
[82] Menzel (1964: 115); cf. *Gorg.* 487b.
[83] Cf. *Gorg.* 485e-486a.
[84] Cf. Menzel (1964: 115).
[85] During the Peloponnesian War he was a marked defender of the Sicilian Expedition; notwithstanding, his urge for power led him to ally with the Lacedaemonians and the Persians.

character, Socrates'[86] friend, but, despite his reputation as an orator, it is not known either he ever exhibited literary tastes. Moreover, Alcibiades was present at Callicles' speech,[87] and this rules out the possibility *eo ipso* to identify the former with the latter. Add, following Menzel, that Callicles "was a strong supporter of the oligarchical thought and felt a profound contempt for the mass of the weak", while Alcibiades sought support for his plans within people's favor.[88]

Charicles and Alcibiades being weeded out, several historians identify Callicles with Critias, who, according to Guthrie, "seems to fit exactly the role of Callicles".[89] Especially, Menzel believes that he is "the embodiment of Plato's uncle" and that "the theory of the superman is, in a great extent, taken from his writings".[90] Before him, only Christian Cron[91] had looked upon such a hypothesis, but with arguments that seemed unconvincing to Menzel. What are those? This interpreter distinguishes between arguments and "evidence". The first indication that Callicles is Critias would be that the former appears as a host of Gorgias,[92] Critias teacher: such a presentation would be a way to insinuate his mental presence in the debate. The fact that Callicles is presented as a friend of Socrates'[93] would point to the same direction: Critias also was, even though bad friend and bad disciple, actually, because he joined the teacher and then departed from him because of mere political ambition[94] and, with his subsequent conduct, gave his enemies (mainly Polycrates[95]) weapons to accuse him of corrupting the youth.[96] A third evidence would be that, *testing* Xenophon,[97] Critias gives Socrates the same advice that Callicles does in *Gorgias* (490C, e): "you have

---

[86] *Gorgias* 481d3 presents him as his lover and 519a8 as his friend.
[87] Cf. *Gorg.* 481d3 and 519a8.
[88] Cf. Plutarch, *Parallel Lives*, Alcibiades, chap. 34.
[89] Guthrie (1971: 299).
[90] Menzel (1964: 115).
[91] Ch. Cron (1870), cited by Menzel.
[92] *Gorg.* 447b8.
[93] *Gorg.* 487d.
[94] Xenophon, *Mem.*, I, 2: "Ambition was his true life motivation". The rupture with Socrates happened when the former accused him of being "similar to a pig, because wanted to rub against Euthydemus, as pigs do against stones" (Xenophon, *Mem.*, I, 2, 12 ss.). Xenophon adds that "for this reason, Critias hated Socrates", and so, when he ended being part of the Thirty, "he recalled Socrates and prohibited him from teaching the art of discussion".
[95] Cf. J. Humbert (1930).
[96] Xenophon, *Mem.*, I, 2. When Xenophon talked about Critias and Alcibiades he said that "no one else has caused such harm to the State as they have. Because Critias was the greatest thief, violent and assassin, during the oligarchy; whereas Alcibiades was the greatest libertine, insolent and violent, during democracy".
[97] Xenophon, *Mem.*, I, 2, 37.

to avoid your favorite topics – says he: cobblers, builders, metal workers". Moreover – evidence number four – Xenophon alludes to Critias' passion for Euthydemus,[98] which recalls Callicles' own for Demos, son of Pyrilampes.[99] Finally, explaining his view of life, our character quotes Euripides' *Antiope*,[100] perhaps to evoke the close friendship between Euripides and Plato's uncle.[101] But beyond these indications, he puts forward several arguments. These focus on the personalities of Critias and Callicles, their political convictions and the literary production of the former. **(1) Common personality traits.** One of these would be given by the three qualities that are necessary to judge if someone has a good or bad life: knowledge, kindness and openness (*epistêmên te kaì eúnoian kaì parresían*[102]), which Socrates discovers in Callicles. Many Athenians can testify to the fact that he was a very educated character (487b6). Furthermore, he is gracious to Socrates (487b8), advising him, moved by friendship, to abandon philosophy as he conceived and practiced it.[103] Critias will do something similar when he rises to power, but not advising him, instead barring him from sharing his teachings.[104] Finally, Callicles openness has allowed him "to definitely state what others think, but dare not say" (492d2–3). These qualities also characterized Critias, who "participated in philosophical meetings, being considered profane among philosophers and a philosopher among the profane".[105] Philostratus says he "enjoyed an excellent education"[106] and Plato says in *Timaeus* (20 A5) that "he is not a novice in anything that concerns us". Another common feature of both characters is their courage.

Callicles argues that those who govern "are not only smart (*phrónimoi*) but also brave (*andreîoi*), since they are capable of running as planned and difficulties do not withdraw them from the task".[107] Critias said so in his works. Thus fighting the democrats, he "was killed by the hands of Thrasybulus and his sup-

---

98 Xenophon, *Mem.*, I, 2, 29.
99 Cf. *Gorg.* 481 d 5, 513 b 6.
100 Cf. *Gorg.* 484e, 485e ss.
101 The friendship between the two of them made some recent specialists attribute the *Sisyphus*' fragment to Euripides, and not to Critias, as does Sextus Empiricus (Adv. *Math.* IX, 54 = DK, 88 B 25) and the tradition that followed. Euripides did write a *Sisyphus*, now lost. Cf. Albrecht Dihle (1977) and Ch. Kahn (1997: 247–262).
102 *Gorg.* 487 to 2–3.
103 Cf. *Gorg.* 484c.
104 Cf. Xenophon., *Mem.*, I, 2, 12 ss.
105 *Scholas.*, ad. 1.
106 Philostratus, *Vitae sophistarum*, I, 168.
107 *Gorg.* 491b 2–4.

porters".¹⁰⁸ He has been criticized, it is true, for his cruelty. According to Philostratus, he "was the most wicked of all men who have become famous for their wickedness",¹⁰⁹ and according to Xenophon, he was "among the oligarchs, the falsest, the most violent and the most criminal".¹¹⁰ Critias and Charicles have been, among the Thirty, responsible for numerous executions. But Critias justifies himself by saying that "cruelty well used (...) is the one used for our own safety, looking, as far as possible, to become useful for the people".¹¹¹ **(2) common political beliefs. The two characters were avowed enemies of democracy.** According to Critias, democracy is the great enemy of oligarchy: "When we discover an enemy of oligarchy – he confesses – we use all the power there is to remove him from our path". "No middle ground is possible". Philostratus tells us that, in fact, he "collaborated with the Spartans with unprecedented tenacity, so that Attica [bastion of democracy] was depopulated of humans and became grazing land for cattle".¹¹² (3) Regarding Critias **literary production**,¹¹³ it should be noted that: (a) his taste for "categorical expressions and thoughts",¹¹⁴ which Callicles found to be equally pleasing, (b) his close links with Euripides,¹¹⁵ comparable with the constant attention Callicles throws at this tragic poet,¹¹⁶ and with Pindar, who is one of his greatest inspiring figures. To these literary similarities are added, by association, another common feature of the two characters, namely, the inconsistency in behavior and thinking. Callicles, prisoner of his dual love, the Athenian Demos and Demos, Pyrilampes' son, does not have, despite his talent (*kaíper óntos deinoû*: 481d7), the strength to say "no" when he does have to, and allows himself "to go back and forth" (*ánô kai kátô metaballoménon*: 481e1), at the mercy of his beloved's claim. Socrates re-

---

108 Philostratus, *Vitae sophistarum*, I, 168
109 Philostratus, *Vitae sophistarum*, I, 16.
110 Xenophon, *Mem.*, I, 2, 12.
111 Menzel (1964: 118).
112 Philostratus, *Vit. Soph.,I*, 16.
113 His most important works are the *Elegies*, the *Constitutions* (in prose and verse; among the last of them one should notice the ones about the Thessalians and about the Spartans), the *Aphorisms*, the *Homilies* and the *Tragedies* (among them *Sisyphus*).
114 Cf. Philostratus, *Vit. Soph.* II, 16.
115 He cites the following Euripides' phrase at *Tennes*: "Oh, there is no fair one among humans nowadays" (Stob., III, 2, 15). Cf. also the large Euripides' citation in his drama *Rhadamanthys*, collected by Stobaeus (Stob. II, 8, 12.). The ancient believed that Critias' three tragedies: *Tennes*, *Rhadamanthys* and *Pirithous*, were actually Euripides' works. Nowadays, it seems to be well demonstrated that Critias himself wrote a tragic tetralogy, which contains those drama and *Sisyphus*, which has also been attributed to Euripides.
116 Euripides' *Antiope* is several times cited, but only a few fragments remain: cf. *Gorg.* 485e, 489e2, 506b6.

proaches him for "never saying the same thing twice on the same object" (*oudépote tautà légeis perì tôn autôn:* 491b8). The "best and most powerful", for example, are sometimes the "strongest" (*ischyrotéros*), while other times the "wisest" (*phronimôtérous*) (491c1–2). And hedonic-wise, after maintaining that all pleasures are equally good, he suddenly accuses Socrates of speaking "as if he did not know, says he, that neither I nor anyone else forgot to distinguish between the best and the worst pleasures (*hôs men ... beltíous hedonás, tàs dè cheírous:* 499b7). This fickleness, logical and behavioral, repeats itself in Critias, who begins by turning to Socrates and accepting his teachings[117] and then, as he and Alcibiades believe themselves to be "more superior than their peers", "depart from him to devote themselves to politics, the only reason for his dealings with the teacher".[118] Equally incoherent was Critias regarding the political system: among the Thessalians, "he tried to establish democracy and armed, to this end, the "serfs" against their masters",[119] in Athens, however, "he established tyranny and was one of the Thirty".[120] No doubt the evidence and arguments presented by Menzel, which I have freely commented on, make plausible the identification of Callicles with Critias. They further help solve the worrisome problem of Plato's unwavering deference to his uncle: he never directly confronted him and he always gave him seats of honor, but not without overlooking his mistakes. By personifying them within Callicles, Plato found a good way to report them. But it would be an exaggeration to claim that Callicles is only Critias, as Menzel says. Among other things, it lacks in the speech of Callicles elements that are important in the thinking of Critias and, conversely, in Critias it lacks one of Callicles' most characteristic doctrinal features. I refer respectively to Critias' atheism and Callicles' hedonism. I will just speak about the Critian atheism. Following Sextus Empiricus it is commonly accepted that Critias scored the *Sisyphus*[121] remaining fragment containing the oldest explanation of the naturalist origin and evolution of religion. According to this, God is an invention of some clever ruler who aspired to the fear of His alleged omnipresence making evil go away in order to make social life more viable. Despite the importance that has been given to this hypothesis, Callicles does not pay it any attention, although the term "god" is repeated more than once in his discourse[122] and although he

---

117 His intervention in *Charmides* does so demonstrate. Cf., in particular, 169c3 ss.
118 Cf. Xenophon, *Mem.*, I, 2.
119 Xenophon, *Hel.*, II, 3, 36.
120 *Scholas.*, ad 1.
121 Sextus E., *Adv. Math.*, IX, 54, DK B 88b25. Recently, some researchers have doubted this attribution and have given it to Euripides. Cf. *supra*, note 109.
122 Cf. *Gorg.* 481b10, 458d1.

talks to Socrates about man's behavior towards the gods (*perì theoús*),[123] arguing that the uncontrollable "cannot be loved"[124] by them, but, on the contrary, can only be "punished by (them)".[125] Or if these references to divinity are not enough, Socrates comes to speak in these terms: "wise men say, Callicles, that heaven and earth, gods and men, are united by friendship, respect and order, moderation and justice, and therefore the universe is called the order of things, and not disorder or derangement".[126] It seems that, although Socrates has prompted him to take a stand before the divine, not once has Callicles given signs of sharing Critias' atheism. It would be a sign that there is not an equation between him and Plato's uncle, nor between him and any historical character, and that what the author of *Gorgias* wants to represent in him is not a historical figure, but a political-philosophical stance in vogue.

We could call it, with Guthrie[127] and Untersteiner,[128] "political realism". The term refers to the political action based on practical concerns rather than on ethical theories and principles.[129] This posture, incubated during the Peloponnesian War, is expressed in Thucydides[130] with singular strength, but also in the philosophical fragments of Critias, Lycophron, Alcidamas of Elaea and Thrasymachus of Chalcedon,[131] and literary works of Pindar and Euripides. Let's recall the discussions between envoys of Athens and representatives of Milos, an island that Athens wanted to federate by force.[132] The Athenians begin by stating that to resolve the conflict between them, they will not wield moral arguments because they know, like the Milonians, that "in the world of men, legal arguments have weight only to the extent that adversaries have equivalent means of coercion and, if not, the strongest use their power to the best of their game, while the weak have only to bend" (V, 89). Justice (*tò díkaion*) will not be complied,

---

123 *Gorg.* 507a8; cf. 507b3, 522d1.
124 *Gorg.*, 507e4.
125 *Gorg.*, 472e7, 525b5.
126 *Gorg.* 508a1.
127 W. K. C. Guthrie (1971: 84 ss).
128 M. Untersteiner (1967: II, 189 ss).
129 This type of politics has achieved a notable development in Modern Times. Its most important precursor is N. Machiavelli, specially in *The Prince*. According to him, the only concern a prince must have is to seek and maintain power, without taking in consideration ethical or religious concerns. Otto von Bismarck, in the 20th century, named this posture *realpolitik*. On the concept "political realism", see L. R. Oro Tapia (2009: 15–46). On the developments and existence of this line of thought, see R. A. Sanhuesa Carvajal (on line).
130 Cf. Bravo, (2001: 239).
131 Cf. M. Untersteiner (1967: II, 189–232).
132 Cf. Thucyd., V, 85–111.

only interest (*tò xymphéron*). However not mutual interest, but the strongest's, which is Athens. The Milonians note with surprise that "justice has nothing to do with the present discussion" and that what counts are the "utility considerations". Nevertheless, they do not rule out "the possibility, for whoever is in danger [and the Athenians may be], to appeal to the moral sense and fairness" (V, 90). But the Athenians affirm that the only thing that has brought them there is "the welfare of our empire" (V, 91), if they seem interested in "saving" Milos, know that they just want to "save" the "taxes" it can pay (V, 92). And since the Milonians, as a last resort, trust that "the gods will not allow" them to be in disadvantage, their opponents also point out that the gods "obey, for natural necessity (*hypò phýseôs anankaíon*), a law that forces them to dominate others whenever they feel the strongest" (V, 105). Among the gods, no less than men, "always (...) the strongest places the weakest under his thumb" (I, 76). And if the Milonians come to put their trust in the Lacedaemonians, their allies, they should remember that "there is not a people who is more flagrantly inclined to identify the agreeable with the good and its interest with justice" (*tà mèn hêdéa kalà nomízontai, tà dè xymphéron díkaion*) (V, 105). These few fragments show that the discourse of Callicles is not exactly an echo of the doctrines of Critias, but of the prevailing political realism, first formulated by Thucydides, especially in the speeches of Hermocrates of Sicily,[133] Pericles[134] and Cleon, the demagogue.[135] Thucydides, meanwhile, has been inspired by the ode of Pindar and has then inspired Euripides and Critias, one of the main representatives of the political realism. And what is even more important, he has been able to inspire the long struggle of Plato against Critias, first in *Gorgias*, through Callicles, then in the *Republic*, through the speech of Thrasymachus (336b–354b), seconded by Glaucon's (357th – 361b), and finally and repeatedly in the *Laws* (690c, 714c, 890a) It is important to state, together with some interpreters, that in this rich Greek literature, as revealed by the genius of Plato, did Nietzsche, in turn, inspire himself, he who was one of the leading representatives of contemporary political realism.

---

[133] Thucyd., IV, 60.
[134] Thucyd., II, 63.
[135] Thucyd., III, 39, 40.

Works Cited

Berg, Th., *Griechische Literaturgeschichte,* 1872–1877.
Bravo, F., "Quién es y qué enseña el Trasímaco de la *República*", in *Estudios de Filosofía Griega,* Caracas, CEP/FHE, 2001.
—, "La antítesis sofística *nomos-physis*", *Ibidem.*
—, "El *Gorgias* de Platón: ¿anti-hedonista o anti-relativista?", in M. Erler & L. Brisson (Eds.), *Gorgias – Menon. Selected Papers from the Seventh Symposium Platonicum,* Skt. Augustin, Academia Verlag, 2007.
Cron, *Beiträge zur Erklärung des platonische Gorgias,* Leipzig, G.B. Teubner, 1870.
Dihle, A., "Das Satyrspiel Sisifo", *Hermes* 105 (1977) 28–42.
Dodds, E.R., *Plato, Gorgias,* Oxford, Oxford University Press, 1959.
Dümler, F.D., *Academica,* Huyesen, 1889.
Fouillé, A., *Nietzsche et l' immoralisme,* 1902.
Gomperz, TH., *The Greek Thinkers,* London, Murray, I, 1901.
Grimal, P., *Diccionario de mitología griega y romana,* Barcelona, Ed. Paidos, 1994.
Guthrie, W. K. G., *The Sophists,* Cambridge, CUP, 1971.
Humbert, J., *Le pamphlet de Policrate et le Gorgias de Platon,* Paris, 1930.
Jaeger, W., *Paideia,* trans. by J. Xirau, Mexico, FCE, 1971.
Kahn, Ch., "Greek Religion and Philosophy in the *Sisyphus* Fragment" *Phronesis* 42, 3, (1997) 247–262.
Kerferd, G.B., *The Sophistic Movement,* Cambridge, CUP, 1981.
Levinson, R., *In Defense of Plato,* Cambridge (Mass.), Harvard University Press, 1953.
Menzel, A., *Kalikles. Eine Studie zur Geschichte der Lehre vom Rechte des Starken,* Wien und Leipzig, Franz Deuticke, 1922, Spanish translation by Mario de la Cueva, Mexico, UNAM, 1964.
Nestle, W., *Friedrich Nietzsche und die griechische Philosophie,* Neues Jahrbuch für die klassische Philosophie 29 (1912).
Oro Tapia, L.R., "En torno a la noción de realismo político", *Rev. Enfoques,* vol VII, n° 10 (2009) 15–46.
Sanhuesa Carvajal, R. A., "El realismo político: ¿un denostado desconocido?", *On line.*
Untersteiner, M., *I Sofisti,* Milan, L. Negri, 1967.
Wilamowitz-Moellendorff, *Platon,* Berlin, 1919.

Michele Corradi
Doing business with Protagoras (*Prot.* 313e): Plato and the Construction of a Character

In the ever-cogent *Platon*, Paul Friedländer states: "As Goethe is in Tasso *and* Antonio, so Plato is not only in Socrates – or in the disciples Charmides, Theaitetos, Alkibiades – but also, to a certain degree and manner, in the opponents of Socrates"[1]. The analogy with *Torquato Tasso*[2], Goethe's ambiguous drama, which hinges on the contrast between the figure of the Italian poet and that of the consummate secretary at the court in Ferrara, Antonio Montecatino, and concludes with a surprising twist that moved Wagner[3] to admit his inability to comprehend where right and wrong lay in the work, enables Friedländer to apprehend a crucial aspect of the personality and art of Plato. According to Friedländer, Socrates' struggle against his adversaries is to a certain extent a struggle of Plato against himself, against his own nature, "endowed with overabundant powers". For the German scholar, there is something in Plato of the ability and astuteness of the Eristics and Sophists, there is something of Callicles, "the 'Strong Man', something of his beloved Homer, and even something of Euthyphro's 'clerical piety'".

Certainly, these pages by Friedländer, characterized by word choices that are perhaps excessively marked by Existentialism[4], conceal concepts that have by now become established in the more modern exegetic tendencies regarding Plato, in particular in the so-called new "literary" approach[5]: Plato, heir to the Greek literary tradition, a discerning connoisseur of the mechanisms of tragedy and comedy, conceals himself behind his characters and allows his message to emerge through their interaction and dialogue, by means of the play of character – to use Ruby Blondell's acute expression[6] – which probably represents the best *mimesis* of the master's real and lively *synousia* with his disciples.

---

1 Friedländer (1964³ [1973²], pp. 166–67).
2 Goethe (1790 [1988], pp. 731–834).
3 In a letter to Mathilde Wesendonck of April 15th, 1859 (Wagner 1999, pp. 37–39).
4 On the relationship between Friedländer and Existentialism, see Giovanni Reale's preface to the last Italian translation of Friedländer's *Platon* (Reale 2004, pp. XI-XVI). Cf. also Trabattoni (2004², p. 310).
5 On this new approach to Plato's texts see Erler (2007, pp. 5–7).
6 Blondell (2002).

Opening up the gallery of characters, an incarnation of so many artistic projections of Plato's "I", Friedländer mentions, along with Agathon, the character of Protagoras, recalling him in particular for his love of "resounding speeches", which he shared with Plato.

Certainly, among Socrates' great adversaries, Protagoras is the one to whom Plato gives most space in his own output. In the *Protagoras*, Plato allows the Sophist about nine Stephanus pages (320c–328d = 80 C 1 DK). All the first part of *Theaetetus* (151d–187a) is dedicated to a discussion of the principle of the man-measure (80 B 1 DK) and in this same dialogue Socrates, like a ventriloquist, even lends his own voice to Protagoras who has returned from Hades to defend his position (166a–168c = 80 A 21a DK). Furthermore, there are references to Protagoras in many other works, explicit in *Cratylus* (385e–386a = 80 A 13 DK, 391b–c = 80 A 24 DK), *Euthydemos* (286b-c = 80 A 19 DK), *Hippias Major* (282d–e = 80 A 9 DK), *Meno* (91d–e = 80 A 8 DK), *Phaedrus* (267c = 80 A 26 DK), *Republic* (600c-e), *Sophist* (232d–233a = 80 B 8 DK), and implicit, as I have recently tried to demonstrate[7], in *Philebos* (62a-b) and *Letter VII* (343a).

Plato offers a complex portrait of Protagoras, which certainly does justice to the character's great stature. Ancient tradition underlined his special role among the protagonists of the dialogues, even going so far as to suggest a dependence on the part of Plato on Protagoras' works in the *Republic* (80 B 5 DK) and perhaps in the *Parmenides* (80 B 2 DK). In effect, in two passages of Plato's life (III 37 e 57), Diogenes Laërtius reports an interesting remark that goes back, through Favorinus (23 Mensching = 60 Amato), to Aristoxenus (67 Wehrli²): almost the whole of the *Republic*, Πολιτεία ... πᾶσα σχεδόν, seems to have already been written in Protagoras' *Antilogies* (80 B 5 DK), ἐν τοῖς Πρωταγόρου γεγράφθαι Ἀντιλογικοῖς. This remark can easily be inserted into a tradition, often hostile, which attributes plagiarism to Plato of the works of previous thinkers. Certainly, more in general, this appears to be a clear example of a tendency on the part of ancient literary criticism, which was anxious to identify the κλοπαί of authors from the past. In this sense, as an actual manifesto of widespread interest in the issue of plagiarism, the dense fragment of the Φιλόλογος ἀκρόασις by Porphyry (*apud* Eus. *PE* 10, 3, 1–25 = 410 F Smith) may be recalled. Right at this point, at the conclusion of the fragment, Porphyry confronts another of Plato's debts to Protagoras: Plato appears to have drawn on, perhaps in *Parmenides*,

---

7 Corradi (2012, pp. 216–24).

Protagoras' Περὶ τοῦ ὄντος, arguments against monist thinkers, πρὸς τοὺς ἓν τὸ ὂν εἰσάγοντας (80 B 2 DK)[8].

Certainly Aristoxenus, author of a Πλάτωνος βίος (61–68 Wehrli[2]), is probably not the most neutral source in regard to Plato[9]. From the fragments conserved, a critical approach emerges towards the philosopher. His studies may however be inserted fully within the scholarly activities of the Peripatetic, above all in the biographical arena. An activity focused on the works of the great authors of the past, with the aim of seeking out data useful in order to understand their personalities and reconstruct aspects of their lives. This activity did not conform to the criteria of modern historico-philological research, but inclined to imaginative reconstructions, often based on the so-called Chameleon method[10].

The analysis of what, with the apology in *Theaetetus* (166a–168c = 80 A 21a DK), the most important section is wherein Plato presents himself as Protagoras' spokesman, the great speech[11] in *Protagoras* (320c–328d = 80 C 1 DK), poses in any case a series of exegetic problems that confronts us with doubts that are not far removed from those that in all likelihood stimulated the curiosity of the ancient literary critics.

1. Memory of the μῦθος

The great speech of *Protagoras* (320c–328d) is structured in two sections, μῦθος and λόγος. In the first section Protagoras constructs a story on the origin of human society. This story starts from the original unhappy condition of mankind, up to the rise of the πόλις, and dwells on two subsequent interventions on the part of the divinity: that of Prometheus, who gives the gift of τέχναι to men, and that of Zeus who gives them a gift of αἰδώς and δίκη. In the λόγος section, Protagoras develops considerations on the educational commitment on the

---

8 Regarding the accusations of plagiarism towards Plato, see Dörrie, Baltes (1990, pp. 236–46). Cf. now also Corradi (2013, p. 82).
9 Dillon (2012) offers a recent contribution on the extant fragments of Aristoxenus' Πλάτωνος βίος. On Aristoxenus' biographical method, see Schorn (2012).
10 With regard to the so-called Chameleon method, cf. now Arrighetti (2008). A useful overview of the scholarly activity of the Peripatetics may be found in Montanari (2012). On the importance that biographical research assumes in that area, cf. Fortenbaugh (2007).
11 The label "great speech" for the μῦθος and the λόγος that the Sophist pronounces in *Protagoras* has become canonical above all starting with the introduction by Gregory Vlastos to the translation of the dialogue by Benjamin Jowett, revised by Martin Ostwald (Vlastos 1956 [1976], pp. 273–76).

part of Athens towards its young, as well as reflecting on the role of the Sophists and the function of punishment. Significantly, many of the elements developed in the great speech, which still come across as consistent overall with what we can reconstruct about Protagoras from the other testimonies in our possession, present aspects that are quite obviously Platonic. Just how much then of the extraordinary portrait of the Sophist that emerges is due to Plato's literary genius? The problem, however, may be put in diametrically opposite terms: is it possible to think that there really was a reflective influence exerted by his character, that is, by Protagoras on Plato?

We shall try here to put forward an answer that is at least plausible in regard to these considerations, by means of an analysis, in light of the most recent results arising from literary criticism, of some of the crucial points of the great speech in *Protagoras*. We shall then try to relate these, on the one hand, and where possible, to the testimonies concerning Protagoras in our possession, and on the other, to *loci paralleli* in Plato.

As is known, from a stylistic point of view, the μῦθος in the *Protagoras* presents unusual characteristics compared to the more usual style in Plato's myths; these confirm Philostratus' intuition (*VS* I 10, 4 = 80 A 2 Diels-Kranz), who was the first to grasp Plato's wish to mirror Protagoras' style in Protagoras' speech. Consider, for instance, the sequences already highlighted by Ludwig Friedrich Heindorf[12] or the choice of the λέξις εἰρομένη[13]. From the point of view of the content too, more than a few elements may in all likelihood be traced back to Protagoras. In recent times Bernd Manuwald[14] has carried out a series of in-depth studies on the *Protagoras*, and in particular on Prometheus' μῦθος: precisely in relation to the link between the μῦθος and the historical Protagoras, he has arrived at largely convincing results. It is plausible that Protagoras had in a lost work (which for Manuwald may well have been the Περὶ πολιτείας [80 B 8a DK] and not, as is generally supposed, the Περὶ τῆς ἐν ἀρχῇ κατα-

---

[12] Heindorf (1810, p. 505) recalls ἄοπλον ... φύσιν, σμικρότητι ἤμπισχεν, πτηνὸν φυγήν (320e). Cf. now Serrano Cantarín & Díaz de Cerio Díez (2005, pp. XLV–XLVI).
[13] Norden (1923², pp. 367–74). Bertagna (2012) highlights some specifics regarding the narrative structure of the μῦθος, which may have been conscious mirrorings of story-telling techniques proper to the archaic *epos*. While Morgan (2000, pp. 132–54) attempts to trace all the characters of Sophist epideictics in the μῦθος of *Protagoras*; Most (2012) shows how it already presents nearly all the typical features of myths present in Plato's mature work. However, insisting on a distinction between Sophistic and Platonic aspects may not be necessary. Cf. Manuwald (2003), who underlines the paradigmatic role that the μῦθος section of the *Protagoras* assumes for Plato.
[14] In particular Manuwald (1996), Manuwald (1999, pp. 168–236), Manuwald (2003) and Manuwald (2013).

στάσεως [80 B 8b DK]) already developed a mythological story on the origins of human civilization in order to illustrate the central role of πολιτικὴ τέχνη in its evolution, the superiority of this τέχνη compared to others and the space that the central role of πολιτικὴ τέχνη offers the Sophists' pedagogical activity. Indeed, some inconsistencies in the narration, in relation to subsequent developments in the dialogue, may be explained as the fruit of a rather complex process of adapting pre-existing material within the context of the dialogue. Manuwald insists for instance on the case of ὁσιότης: in the μῦθος this virtue, however non-explicit, clearly has origins prior to the gift of αἰδώς and δίκη by Zeus (322a); but subsequently it is considered on the same level as σωφροσύνη and δικαιοσύνη – terms that at the end of the μῦθος substitute the archaic and poetic αἰδώς and δίκη – which are necessary for the support of human communities (325a)[15]. Therefore, central to Protagoras' speech is the observation that all men possess to some extent σωφροσύνη and δικαιοσύνη, or at least that the possession of these virtues by all the members of a human community is the necessary condition for the existence of the community itself (322c–d, 323a–c, 324d–e, 325a–c, 326e–327a). This thesis, according to Manuwald, must have been the basis of Protagoras' politico-anthropological manifesto, just like the thesis of the man-measure (80 B 1 DK) represented his "erkenntnistheoretische *Credo*"[16]. It is precisely this link between the reflection on αἰδώς and δίκη and the principle of man-measure (80 B 1 DK) that appears to be decisive for the attribution of the theses advanced in the μῦθος to Protagoras, at least in the interpretation that Plato himself offers of it in the celebrated apology in *Theaetetus* (166a–168c = 80 A 21a DK): all men have real opinions and sensations, but just as the doctor substitutes πονηραί sensations with χρησταί sensations in the patient by means of medication, so does the Sophist, by means of his παιδεία, manage to direct opinions in the most useful direction. In a manner not dissimilar to the great speech in *Protagoras*, the Sophist acts on men who are in themselves endowed with αἰδώς and δίκη and therefore to some extent, at least potentially, participators in πολιτικὴ τέχνη, in order to perfect their natural talents and point them towards virtue[17].

---

15 Without falling into anachronism, Schlick (2012, pp. 40–43) perceives in the difficulty of conciliating the reflection on the religious phenomenon developed in the great speech with Protagoras' agnosticism (80 B 4 DK) one of the principal arguments against attributing the doctrines contained in it to the Sophist. In any case, as Brancacci (2013, pp. 66–67 n. 16) points out, in the great speech religion is confined to a pre-political phase in the evolution of mankind.
16 Manuwald (1996, pp. 124–25).
17 Cf. Corradi (2013a, p. 78 n. 25).

Important reflections on the link between the μῦθος in the *Protagoras* and the historical Protagoras have also been made recently by Mauro Bonazzi who, in Prometheus' μῦθος, perceives the desire to tackle literary tradition on the origins of humanity in decidedly innovative terms. This is particularly true for Hesiod, since this wish fits into the wide range of testimonies relative to Protagoras' critical commitment to poetry (80 A 25–30 DK)[18]. To return to a skilful intuition on the part of José Solana Dueso, it may be possible to perceive in the μῦθος in the *Protagoras* an exercise in ὀρθοέπεια on the part of the Sophist[19].

Manuwald and Bonazzi tend to some extent to signal the specificity of the μῦθος in the *Protagoras* compared to other texts on the origins and development of civilization dating back to the V century of which we are aware[20], in order to consider it a reflection on the nature of man and the opportunities of education. But Graziano Arrighetti, precisely through a study of the link with Hesiod and the literary tradition, has recently attempted to collocate it in the area of Plato's reflection on the origins of man and the organization of communities, by placing it in relation to *Politicus* and *Timaeus*, which definitely demonstrate a singular consonance with the speech made by Protagoras in the youthful dialogue[21]. Arrighetti in this case places himself on the same wavelength as Paul Friedländer, who offers a useful outline of the links between the μῦθος in the *Protagoras* and Plato's late works[22]. It is undoubtedly true also for the German scholar that, in Protagoras' μῦθος, motifs can be heard that later became important for Plato. In particular in the *Timaeus*, the function that was entrusted to Prometheus and Epimetheus in the μῦθος of the *Protagoras*, that of forming mankind, is entrusted to the lesser gods by the demiurge (41a–44c). Just as, in the *Prota-*

---

[18] See above all Bonazzi (2010, pp. 84–93) and Bonazzi (2012). It is probably no coincidence that in the dialogue (316d) Protagoras inserts Hesiod in the gallery of intellectuals who may have carried out the activity of Sophist prior to him, despite concealing this behind other professions. In this regard, after Brancacci (2002), cf. Boys Stones (2010, pp. 40–45). For Koning (2010, pp. 217–23) Protagoras' interest in Hesiod may be traced to "rhetorical puroposes".

[19] Solana Dueso (2011, pp. 5–23). On ὀρθοέπεια and Protagoras' literary reflection, cf. now also Corradi (2012, pp. 144–75) and Rademaker (2013). Calame (2012, pp. 134–36) tackles the links between μῦθος in the *Protagoras* and *Prometheus Bound*.

[20] Beresford (2013), however, underlines the aspects that Protagoras' μῦθος shares with Ionian rationalism. On its links with Democritus' anthropology, cf. Hourcade (2009, pp. 90–110). De Sanctis (2012) offers a wide-ranging overview of the theme of humanity at its origins in archaic poetry.

[21] Arrighetti (2013). Van Riel (2012) has made a recent attempt to identify the basis for the anthropological doctrine that Plato was to develop in subsequent dialogues in the μῦθος of the *Protagoras*.

[22] Friedländer (1964³ [1973²], pp. 176–77).

goras, mankind's body is formed from earth and fire and whatever may be combined with earth and fire, ἐκ γῆς καὶ πυρὸς μείξαντες καὶ τῶν ὅσα πυρὶ καὶ γῇ κεράννυται (320d), in the *Timeaus* the body of the world, whose matter has been borrowed in order to form mortal beings (42e-43a), is made up of fire and earth, between which the other elements, air and water, serve as "bonds" according to the laws of proportion (31b-32c). As has already been observed by Wilhelm Nestle, this μηχανᾶσθαι from the perspective of the σωτηρία of living beings that, in the μῦθος of the *Protagoras*, is attributed to Epimetheus (320e and 321a), in the *Timaeus* belongs to the demiurge and lesser gods (37e, 45d, 70c, 73c)[23]. Finally, while Epimetheus exhausts the δυνάμεις to be attributed to living beings before dedicating himself to man, the demiurge achieves the formation of the soul of the world by consuming the mixture of which it is composed (*Pr.* 321b: καταναλώσας; *Ti.* 36b: κατανηλώκει)[24].

If instead we consider the *Politicus*, what is immediately apparent in the celebrated myth narrated by the Eleatic Stranger in the dialogue (268d-274e) is that a close link may be deduced between origin of the world and origin of the state, much like what occurs in the μῦθος of the *Protagoras*[25]. When we come to the details, in this case too there are remarkable parallelisms between the two texts: the primitive men in the *Politicus* have nothing to cover themselves with and live naked, γυμνοὶ δὲ καὶ ἄστρωτοι (272a), just as in the *Protagoras* (321c) in the beginning man was naked, barefoot, with nothing to cover him, unarmed, γυμνός τε καὶ ἀνυπόδητος καὶ ἄστρωτος καὶ ἄοπλος – certainly curiously similar to Eros in Diotima's speech in the *Symposium* (203d: ἀνυπόδητος καὶ ἄοικος, χαμαιπετὴς ἀεὶ ὢν καὶ ἄστρωτος)[26]. In both stories a phase of history is examined dealing with the evolution of mankind, in which cities do not yet exist (*Prt.* 322b: πόλεις δὲ οὐκ ἦσαν; *Plt.* 271e: πολιτεῖαί τε οὐκ ἦσαν) and men succumb to wild beasts (*Prt.* 322b: ἀπώλλυντο οὖν ὑπὸ τῶν θηρίων; *Plt.* 274b-c: διηρπάζοντο ὑπ' αὐτῶν [sc. τῶν θηρίων]). For this reason, in the *Protagoras* Zeus fears that mankind will be destroyed, Ζεὺς οὖν δείσας περὶ τῷ γένει

---

[23] Nestle (1978[8], p. 93). With regard to the providential design aimed at the conservation of all species put forward by Epimetheus, cf. Demont (2011). Regali (2012, pp. 121–24) carefully considers the images with which Plato characterizes the creative action of the demiurge and lesser gods.
[24] Naturally it is impossible to cover the immense bibliography on the εἰκὼς μῦθος in the *Timaeus*. Regarding the contentious problem of its statute, cf. at least Burnyeat (2005) and, as the last in a series of contributions made by the scholar in this area, Brisson (2012).
[25] Nor is it possible, with regard to the myth in the *Politicus* to take into consideration the immense bibliography. A recent exegetic contribution has been made by Horn (2012). On the characters of the reconstruction of the past that the Eleatic Stranger offers here, cf. Tulli (1994).
[26] Cf. Serrano Cantarín & Díaz de Cerio Díez (2005 & p. 35 n. 4).

ἡμῶν μὴ ἀπόλοιτο πᾶν (322c). Similarly, the god in the *Politicus*, worried that the world will be overthrown by a storm of disorder and dissolve into the infinite sea of inequality, κηδόμενος ἵνα μὴ χειμασθεὶς ὑπὸ ταραχῆς διαλυθεὶς εἰς τὸν τῆς ἀνομοιότητος ἄπειρον ὄντα πόντον δύῃ, decides to invert its cycle (273d–e). Finally, in both myths the role of Prometheus is recalled, along with that of Hephaestus and Athena for the development of the τέχναι (*Prt.* 321c-d: ὁ Προμηθεὺς ... κλέπτει Ἡφαίστου καὶ Ἀθηνᾶς τὴν ἔντεχνον σοφίαν σὺν πυρί; *Plt.* 274c–d: πῦρ μὲν παρὰ Προμηθέως, τέχναι δὲ παρ' Ἡφαίστου καὶ τῆς συντέχνου)[27].

Certainly, there are illustrious precedents for Arrighetti and Friedländer among the ancient Platonists who perceived in the μῦθος of the *Protagoras* genuine elements of Platonic doctrine. As Harold Tarrant[28] recalls, in the *De Fortuna* (98d), Plutarch cites as an opinion of Plato's, κατὰ τὸν Πλάτωνα, the considerations on the condition of primitive man's disadvantage and want. And in a much more explicit way, in the *Platonic Theology* (V 24, pp. 87, 15–91, 18 Saffrey-Westerink), Proclus considers the μῦθος in the *Protagoras* to be an expression of Plato's thought. In it he finds proof for the identification of Zeus with the demiurge of the *Timaeus*. According to Proclus, in the pages of the *Protagoras*, Plato traces back to Zeus the παράδειγμα of πολιτικὴ τέχνη. In the same way it is the demiurge in the *Timaeus* who established the form of government permeating everything: the demiurge coincides therefore with Zeus[29].

2. From the *Protagoras* to the *Republic:* politics, παιδεία and poetry

As far as the more strictly political aspect of the great speech is concerned, Mario Vegetti, in returning to Aristoxenos' malicious observations, has underlined the link that reflections on the ideal πόλις in the *Republic* have with the great speech

---

[27] Cambiano (1991², pp. 200–4), despite underlining the undoubted affinities between the two myths, identifies two basic variants: in the *Politicus* a divine period of government is acknowledged preceding the phase in which the natural inferiority of man is manifested compared to animals, and intervention by Zeus aimed at resolving the conflict among men by means of the gift of πολιτικὴ τέχνη. On analogies and differences between the two myths, see now also El Murr (2013). The δόσις of fire on the part of Prometheus is recalled, in relation to the origins of dialectics, also in the *Philebus* (16c). On this, cf. Delcomminette (2006, pp. 91–96).
[28] Tarrant (2000, p. 76).
[29] An able presentation of the characters of Proclus' Platonic exegesis may be found in Helmig & Steel (2012). On Platonic tradition about the demiurge, cf. now Ferrari (2014).

in the *Protagoras* (320c–328c)[30]. According to the scholar, it is possible to create a parallel between the overcoming of the ἀδικία on the part of primitive men by means of αἰδώς and δίκη in Prometheus' μῦθος (322b–d) with the "genealogy of morality" that Glaucon puts forward in Book II of the *Republic:* for Protagoras as for Glaucon (358e–359a) a natural propensity to oppression is intrinsic to men[31]. For Glaucon, men establish a mutual pact not to commit nor have to undergo injustice. For Protagoras, men, despite being gifted with Prometheus' τέχναι, are not capable of living in a community without inflicting acts of injustice on each other, in so far as they lack πολιτικὴ τέχνη. For this reason Zeus makes them distribute αἰδώς and δίκη, so that good order may be established in the cities, along with constraints that link men in bonds of mutual friendship, πόλεων κόσμοι τε καὶ δεσμοὶ φιλίας συναγωγοί (322b–323a). In the interweaving of σωφροσύνη and δικαιοσύνη, which for Protagoras guarantees all citizens the right to participate in the political συμβουλή (323a), there may be perceived an anticipation of the results of Book IV of the *Republic:* while courage and wisdom may be found only in one part of the city, σωφροσύνη must permeate the whole city in order that harmony be established there (431–432a) and δικαιοσύνη must reign over it, so that every citizen may carry out their appointed task (433a–434c)[32]. Furthermore, both the great speech in the *Protagoras* and the political project in the *Republic* envisage the presence of two specialist elites in παιδεία. For Protagoras there exists a category of men, to which belongs the Sophist, which excels in the formation of πολιτικὴ τέχνη (328a–b). The philosophers of the *Republic* are described as an elite caste of educators that aspires however to the power to carry out a guiding role in the public παιδεία. This very reflection on the παιδεία is in any case the aspect that more than anything else likens the great speech in the *Protagoras* to the *Republic*. The essential function of music, literature and gymnastics in the formation of the young, emphasized by Protagoras (325d–326c), is in perfect accordance with what is established in Book III of the *Republic*. The connection between φύσις and παιδεία, which for Protagoras is the pre-requisite for successful formation (323c, 327b–c), is indispensable also according to pedagogical reflection in the *Republic*. Take, for instance, the considerations of Book IV (431c): only in a minority of the population, which excels

---

30 Vegetti (2004).
31 Vegetti (1998, pp. 163–69) identifies the strong influence of Antiphon's political thought in the theses put forward by Glaucon. For Reeve (2008), instead, Glaucon develops Thrasymachus' theses.
32 Brisson (2004) effectively highlights the link between the discussion on virtue in the *Protagoras* and the *Republic*. On the rather complex exegetic problems that the presentation of virtue raises in Book IV of the *Republic*, cf. now Rowe (2013).

in natural talents and formation, ἐν ὀλίγοις ... τοῖς βέλτιστα μὲν φῦσιν, βέλτιστα δὲ παιδευθεῖσιν, are simple and measured desires to be found. Or, the complex pages in Book VI on the characters of natural philosophy: certainly, even the most gifted souls, εὐφυέστατοι, if they are not educated in an appropriate manner, become wicked (491d–492a). Certainly, this theme in Plato is not limited only to the *Republic:* in the *Phaedrus* (269e–270a), Socrates, not perhaps without some irony, perceives in Pericles' speeches the result of a perfect union of natural talents and Anaxagoras' παιδεία; in the *Politicus* (308e–309a) the Eleatic Stanger presents these natural talents as a decisive element for obtaining a result in education. As far as the reflection on φύσις and παιδεία is concerned, it is however possible to establish a link with Protagoras' production. According to the anonymous writer of *De Hippomacho*, edited by Cramer in the *Anecdota Parisiensia*, in the lost Μέγας λόγος, Protagoras had tackled the issue, maintaining that in the didactic arena, both natural talents and practice are necessary (I 171, 31–172, 2 Cramer = 80 B 3 DK):

ἐν τῷ ἐπιγραφομένῳ Μεγάλῳ λόγῳ ὁ Πρωταγόρας εἶπε· 'φύσεως καὶ ἀσκήσεως διδασκαλία δεῖται' καὶ 'ἀπὸ νεότητος δὲ ἀρξαμένους δεῖ'[33].

As Vegetti points out, it is plausible that Protagoras be a significant presence in the *Republic*. Plato, however, goes beyond this presence by means of reference to a new order of absolute values, which precisely the central books of the *Republic* contribute to establishing. This order of absolute values is based on an ontology and epistemology that are clearly opposed to Protagoras' relativism.

In a contribution presented on the occasion of the IX Symposium of "The International Plato Society" in Tokyo, I attempted to develop Vegetti's conclusions concerning the link that Plato seems to have set up in the *Republic* with the reflection in the *Protagoras*, on the educational role of literary production[34]. This link is generally explained in any case in a plausible way as a shared refer-

---

[33] Without actually advancing the idea of a direct influence, Bonazzi (2009, pp. 461–62 n. 32) perceives the presence of similar concepts in the *Nicomachean Ethics* (1103b23–25 and 1104b11–13). On the polemical context to which his testimony refers, cf. Corradi (2012, pp. 15–31). As Brancacci (2013, pp. 83–84) rightly observes, Protagoras maintained that a natural disposition to acquire political virtue through education was intrinsic to man. More in general, with regard to the particular concept of φύσις, which seems to emerge from the great speech in the *Protagoras*, cf. Beresford (2013, pp. 148–61). On the role that natural talents play in the process of παιδεία for Plato, in particular in the *Republic*, useful considerations may be found in Cleary (2007 [2013], pp. 75–84).
[34] Corradi (2013).

ence to the educational practice of the time[35]. However, by observing more closely what is written in the *Protagoras* and the *Republic*, it is perhaps possible to better clarify the meaning that this link assumes from Plato's perspective.

Protagoras describes the path of the young Athenians' παιδεία in a very detailed manner (325c–326e): the youths, after having acquired language and their first concepts of morality at home, then learn writing and music from masters who, more than disciplines, occupy themselves with εὐκοσμία. To this end they pass on their knowledge of the works of the great poets, ποιητῶν ἀγαθῶν ποιήματα, since they contain a great deal of advice, νουθετήσεις, as well as many descriptions, eulogies and lots of praise of ancient heroes, πολλαὶ δὲ διέξοδοι καὶ ἔπαινοι καὶ ἐγκώμια παλαιῶν ἀνδρῶν ἀγαθῶν, so as to spur the young to a μίμησις of the favoured models[36]. In a similar way, the music teacher occupies himself with σωφροσύνη, teaching the works of other melic ἀγαθοί poets to the young, to be sung accompanied on the cithara. In this way, the rhythms and harmonies penetrate into the soul of the young, so they may become more mildmannered, ἡμερώτεροι, and, by becoming more harmonious and orderly, καὶ εὐρυθμότεροι καὶ εὐαρμοστότεροι γιγνόμενοι, trustworthy in word and action, χρήσιμοι … εἰς τὸ λέγειν τε καὶ πράττειν. Overall, in his life man needs εὐρυθμία and εὐαρμοστία. Along with the literary and musical παιδεία, there is gymnastics. Once studies have been concluded, the πόλις continues to educate its citizens to justice by means of laws and the punishment of those who infringe them.

The starting point of young people's educational formation, as outlined by Plato in Book II and III of the *Republic*, are μῦθοι, which mothers tell their children, and these μῦθοι are certainly inspired by the literary tradition. For Plato, only suitable μῦθοι ought to be selected, ἐγκριτέον[37]. Therefore those offering a negative image of the gods and heroes have to be excluded. The μίμησις must be limited from childhood to virtuous models, ἀνδρεῖοι, σώφρονες, ὅσιοι, ἐλεύθεροι, καὶ τὰ τοιαῦτα πάντα (395c). As far as the musical aspect is concerned, the παιδεία of the young only has to contain Doric harmony, which is capable of arousing determination and the Phrygian one, which is capable of inculcating non-violent behaviour (399a-c). Indeed, refined words, harmoniousness, elegance and rhythmic regularity contribute to the formation of

---

[35] For instance, in Giuliano (2005, pp. 39–40).
[36] Capuccino (2011, pp. 71–73) underlines the educational function that emulation has here for Protagoras. For Protagoras as for Plato the young have a tendency to perceive the protagonists of literary works as models to be admired and are therefore worth conforming their behaviour to. Cf. Lear (2011, pp. 212–13).
[37] On the role of κριτής in literary production, which the philosopher tends to assume in Plato's dialogues, cf. Regali (2012, pp. 53–56).

good character, εὐλογία ἄρα καὶ εὐαρμοστία καὶ εὐσχημοσύνη καὶ εὐρυθμία εὐηθείᾳ ἀκολουθεῖ (400d–e): in fact rhythm and harmony descend deep into the soul, imbuing it with beauty (401d–e)[38]. To literary and musical παιδεία corresponds an adequate physical education (411a–412a). In the *Republic* Plato therefore seems both to go into greater detail and apply discipline according to more rigid criteria than Protagoras set out in the dialogue by the same name. The link with Protagoras' words however is not limited to Book III. In Book X Plato develops his own criticism of poetry from the past, basing himself on an ontological criterion: art does not imitate being, but appearance, and for this reason it is τρίτον ... ἀπὸ τῆς ἀληθείας (602c). Poetry and in particular its greatest representative, Homer, have to be excluded from the ideal πόλις, wherein only artistic production capable of holding up positive models for imitation by its citizens may be accepted, ὅσον μόνον ὕμνους θεοῖς καὶ ἐγκώμια τοῖς ἀγαθοῖς ποιήσεως παραδεκτέον εἰς πόλιν (607a). At the end of his reflection on poetry, Plato therefore arrives at similar results to those of Protagoras, who placed contact with the production of great poets at the centre of young people's educational path, ποιητῶν ἀγαθῶν ποιήματα, full of νουθετήσεις, many descriptions, eulogies and lots of praise of ancient heroes, πολλαὶ δὲ διέξοδοι καὶ ἔπαινοι καὶ ἐγκώμια παλαιῶν ἀνδρῶν ἀγαθῶν, capable of spurring to imitation (325e–326a)[39].

As I had already pointed out in my contribution in Tokyo, in outlining the formative path of the guardians, Plato could not but bear in mind the reflection on literature developed by Protagoras: indeed, it is precisely in the *Protagoras* that Plato demonstrates his in-depth knowledge of it. With Protagoras' reflection on literature, Plato could find significant points of convergence. For both of them, poetry is the basis of the traditional παιδεία and the imitation of models put forward by literary texts as an efficacious educational tool. Both Plato and Protagoras, at least on the basis of the testimonies relative to its ὀρθοέπεια, underline the necessity of having a critical attitude towards poetry, and an accurate filter of texts in operation according to rigorous criteria.

---

[38] Pelosi (2010, pp. 14–67) correctly interprets musical παιδεία in the *Republic* as a process that aimed at the conditioning of young people's sensibility. More generally, on the central role of music in the pedagogical project of dialogue, cf. Schofield (2010).
[39] For Plato's reflection on μίμησις, Tulli (2013) reconstructs a fertile link with literary tradition. A recent contribution on the rather complex problem of the double treatment accorded to Book III and Book X has come from Casanova (2013). The hymns and encomia allowed in the ideal city probably indicate the same production as Plato. Cf. Gaiser (1984, pp. 103–23).

3. Punishment τοῦ μέλλοντος χάριν

Similar results also emerge from an analysis of another renowned passage of the great speech in the *Protagoras*, which has been attracting scholars' attention for some time now (323e–324c). In order to demonstrate that ἀρετή is held to be the fruit of ἐπιμέλεια, ἄσκησις and διδαχή, Protagoras develops reflections on the function of the punishment that come across as particularly innovative. According to Protagoras, nobody – unless he wants to commit an irrational vendetta, ἀλογίστως, on the same level as an animal, ὥσπερ θηρίον, – punishes whoever commits an injustice for the injustice committed. This is because it can in no way ensure that whatever has occurred not have occurred, οὐ γὰρ ἂν τό γε πραχθὲν ἀγένητον θείη. Punishment is meted out instead with an eye to the future, τοῦ μέλλοντος χάριν, so that whoever has committed an injustice not repeat his crime and other men, faced with the example afforded, not commit the same crime, ἵνα μὴ αὖθις ἀδικήσῃ μήτε αὐτὸς οὗτος μήτε ἄλλος ὁ τοῦτον ἰδὼν κολασθέντα[40]. Punishment therefore has a preventive purpose, it should deter, ἀποτροπῆς ... ἕνεκα. And – Protagoras emphasises – underpinning it lies the conviction that virtue may be acquired and taught, παρασκευαστὸν εἶναι καὶ διδακτὸν ἀρετήν.

This theme is taken up by Plato, for example in the *Gorgias* (525b) wherein Socrates first of all grasps the utility for whoever is being punished (he is improved and healed of his own injustice by means of the punishment), but he also emphasises the paradigmatic function of the punishment:

> προσήκει δὲ παντὶ τῷ ἐν τιμωρίᾳ ὄντι, ὑπ' ἄλλου ὀρθῶς τιμωρουμένῳ, ἢ βελτίονι γίγνεσθαι καὶ ὀνίνασθαι ἢ παραδείγματι τοῖς ἄλλοις γίγνεσθαι, ἵνα ἄλλοι ὁρῶντες πάσχοντα ἃ ἂν πάσχῃ φοβούμενοι βελτίους γίγνωνται[41].

The similarity with the extract of the *Protagoras*, also from a lexical point of view, is even more marked in Book XI of the *Laws* (934a–b). Despite occurring

---

[40] Denyer (2008, p. 112) connects the considerations developed here by Protagoras with Diogenes Laërtius' observation that the Sophist was the first to distinguish the μέρη χρόνου (IX 52 = 80 A 1 DK): originally they appear to have been inserted in to the context of a reflection on the differences between past and future. Saunders (1991, pp. 133–36) tends to play down the originality of Protagoras' position. Schlick (2012, pp. 30–32) raises doubts as to its historical consistency. Bonazzi (2010, p. 138 n. 9) collocates it however in a plausible way in the context of the radical humanism advanced by the Sophist.

[41] On the perspective, which is both philosophical and political, in which Plato appears to collocate the reflection on punishment in the myth of the *Gorgias*, cf. Sedley (2009).

in the context of a distinction between different types of guilt, the fruit of one's ἄνοια or others' persuasion, which is lacking in Protagoras' argument, the Athenian perceives how the punishment is not inflicted on the basis of the crime committed – in no case, in fact, may what has occurred, τὸ γεγονός, be ἀγένητον – but rather with a view to the future, τοῦ δ' εἰς τὸν αὖθις ἕνεκα χρόνον, so that both the person being punished and those who observe the punishment may abhor the nature of the injustice, ἢ τὸ παράπαν μισῆσαι τὴν ἀδικίαν αὐτόν τε καὶ τοὺς ἰδόντας αὐτὸν δικαιούμενον.

The repetition is striking, both in the extract from the *Laws* and in that of the *Protagoras*, of the truism, well-known in Greek literary tradition – Simonides (603 Page), Pindarus (O. II 15–17), Theognis (583–584), Sophocles (*Ajax*, 378 and the *Trachiniae*, 742–743), Agathon (39 F 5 Snell-Kannicht), Antiphon (87 B 58 DK) – indeed perhaps proverbial at this stage, according to which it is not possible for what has occurred not to have occurred[42].

As Richard Stalley has shown so persuasively, the distance between the position attributed to Protagoras and that maintained in other dialogues is not therefore so great[43]. In particular, the Protagoras of the *Protagoras* (323e–324c), the Socrates in the *Gorgias* (525b) and the Athenian of the *Laws* (934a–b) clearly collocate the punishment in a pedagogical context, sharing the conviction that the πόλις has the task of forming its citizens and that punishment plays a crucial role in this process.

4. An ἀγγεῖον for Protagoras' μαθήματα

From the series of excerpts that have been considered here, a sense of continuity clearly emerges between many points present in the great speech in the *Protagoras* and Plato's subsequent output. In several cases it has been possible to establish a point of contact with what may be reconstructed regarding the thought and figure of Protagoras from other available testimonies. In other cases the situation is more doubtful. Certainly, even if one were tempted to attribute a great deal to Plato's creative genius, the problem would still remain of ascertaining why Plato wished to make Protagoras a mouthpiece for doctrines and teachings that, from what emerges from other dialogues, Plato held to be valid. For this reason I believe it is plausible to think of the presence in Plato's output of a resumption, or

---

[42] Cf. Manuwald (1999, p. 208) and Schöpsdau (2011, p. 511).
[43] Stalley (1995).

at least a re-elaboration, of Protagoras' doctrines[44]. In any case, right in the initial section of the *Protagoras*, Plato himself, through Socrates, clearly theorized the possibility of acquiring μαθήματα from Protagoras when they may be judged as valid. Sure enough, within the dense exchange on the nature of the Sophist between Socrates and the young Hippocrates, who wishes to become a pupil of Protagoras (311b–314c), an exchange that is frequently interpreted, and understandably so, as a manifesto of Socrates' strongly critical approach towards the Sophists' παιδεία, Plato offers a criterion for the correct approach towards Protagoras' doctrines and teachings. The Sophists are presented, in a very similar way to that present in the *Sophist* (224c–d), as retail and wholesale merchants of μαθήματα, which they praise to the skies in order to sell them, ἐπαινοῦσιν μὲν πάντα ἃ πωλοῦσιν. Some of them may not know what, among the things they sell, is useful or dangerous for the soul of whoever buys it, τούτων ἀγνοοῖεν ὧν πωλοῦσιν ὅτι χρηστὸν ἢ πονηρὸν πρὸς τὴν ψυχήν. And the client will find himself in the same condition, unless by chance he happens to be a man ἰατρικός, who knows which among these doctrines is good and which bad, ἐπιστήμων τούτων τί χρηστὸν καὶ πονηρόν. This man may acquire them safely both from Protagoras or from anybody else, ὠνεῖσθαι μαθήματα καὶ παρὰ Πρωταγόρου καὶ παρ' ἄλλου ὁτουοῦν. As Michael Gagarin has already pointed out[45], this implies that Protagoras' doctrines may contain both useful and deleterious elements. So it is permissible to pick up useful contributions also from Protagoras. But how is the man ἰατρικός to act? In other words, how, without running a risk, is it possible to distinguish χρηστόν from πονηρόν in Protagoras' doctrines?

The analysis of two singular images utilized by Plato in this context may perhaps offer a key. The image of the man ἰατρικός, the doctor of the soul[46], which will certainly be greatly developed for example in celebrated pages of the *Gorgias* for the definition of rhetoric (463e–465d), may occupy a function that is similar to the image of φάρμακον in Book X of the *Republic*. When the discussion of po-

---

[44] For Van Riel (2012, p. 162) the Platonic character of many doctrines contained in the μῦθος does not negate a link with ideas of the historical Protagoras. Schlick (2012) is of the opposite opinion: Plato appears to attribute to Protagoras his own doctrine in order to better highght his own distance from the Sophist on a methodological level. In my opinion, Friedländer (1964³ [1973²], p. 177) is more plausible, who maintains: "Just as the general position of the Sophists is not only opposed to Socrates as something to be fought and overcome, but is, at the same time, a first approximation to the problems discussed, so the myth of the Sophist is a first hint – though not more than that – not altogether estranged from Plato's thoughts, but something that continues to grow within him throughout the years".
[45] Gagarin (1969).
[46] Desclos (1992, pp. 111–18) looks at the image of Socrates the "doctor" in *Protagoras*. Marino (2010, pp. 79–90) sees there the paradigm of the Hyppocratic τέχνη.

etry is taken up again at the beginning of the book (595a–b), Socrates underlines the necessity of not accepting imitative poetry in the ideal city. In fact, imitative poetry constitutes a λώβη for the διάνοια of whoever among the public is not in possession of a φάρμακον, that is to say, does not know its nature, τὸ εἰδέναι αὐτὰ οἷα τυγχάνει ὄντα. A φάρμακον that ought perhaps to be identified with the discussion itself that took place in the *Republic* on facilitating a correct and safe approach to the poets' texts, if not, as Stephen Halliwell[47] has recently maintained, with the knowledge of the true philosopher, whose paradigm has been outlined in the central books of the *Republic* as the pursuit of the idea of good. As in the case of poetry, the true philosopher may draw near to Protagoras' knowledge without risk, managing even to gain from it elements of manifest utility[48].

But it is perhaps possible to go even further. Continuing with the reading of the *Protagoras*, a curious image is encountered, put forward by Socrates (313e–314b). Socrates advises Hippocrates not to assimilate Protagoras' teachings, should he not be able to distinguish within them between what is advantageous and what is damaging. Taking up the parallelism again of the buying and selling of food, Socrates points out how, in the case of the teachings, the situation is much riskier compared to what occurs when dealing with food, γὰρ δὴ καὶ πολὺ μείζων κίνδυνος ἐν τῇ τῶν μαθημάτων ὠνῇ ἢ ἐν τῇ τῶν σιτίων. Whoever buys food wholesale from a merchant or retail, may place it ἐν ἄλλοις ἀγγείοις, in other containers, and bring it home before consuming it and ingesting it into one's body. In this way, a person may turn to an expert and enquire whether he may eat it, in what quantity and how, ἔξεστιν συμβουλεύσασθαι, παρακαλέσαντα τὸν ἐπαΐοντα, ὅτι τε ἐδεστέον ἢ ποτέον καὶ ὅτι μή, καὶ ὁπόσον καὶ ὁπότε. For this reason, buying food like this does not constitute a great risk. On the other hand, teachings may not be stored in another container, ἐν ἄλλῳ ἀγγείῳ, in order to be evaluated by an expert; once they have been assimilated, they penetrate the soul and whoever takes them on board, returns home either improved or damaged, ἀνάγκη καταθέντα τὴν τιμὴν τὸ μάθημα ἐν αὐτῇ τῇ ψυχῇ λαβόντα καὶ μαθόντα ἀπιέναι ἢ βεβλαμμένον ἢ ὠφελημένον. Therefore, for Socrates a container does not exist, an ἀγγεῖον capable of containing Protagoras' μαθήματα, a space in which they may be analysed without risk in such a way as to be able to choose useful doctrines and reject those that are dangerous. Certainly, as Lidia Palumbo[49] has noted, in the course of the dialogue, Hippocrates, with Socrates'

---

[47] Halliwell (2011).
[48] Notomi (2011) highlights the affinities that poet and Sophist present from the Platonic perspective.
[49] Palumbo (2004).

help, may get a taste of Protagoras' doctrines at no danger to himself. Socrates is therefore the ἰατρικὸς περὶ τὴν ψυχήν, capable of dealing correctly with Protagoras' μαθήματα. To all intents and purposes, cannot the container perhaps be identified with the same dialogue by Plato? An ἀγγεῖον that, in the literary pretence of the prologue of the *Protagoras*, for Socrates does not exist and cannot yet exist: it is Plato who, precisely in Socrates' name, has understood how it may be created[50]. Certainly, the image of the ἀγγεῖον does not always have a positive connotation in Plato. In the *Gorgias* (493e), for instance, the perforated container becomes a symbol for a life given over to pleasure. In the *Symposium* (175d) Socrates is ironic about a model of knowledge as if it were a decanting from a full container – in this case a κύλιξ – to an emptier one. In the *Phaedrus* (235c–d) it is Socrates himself however who becomes an ἀγγεῖον, even if of a type of knowledge that will be seen to be spurious: after having listened to Lisia's speech read by Phaedrus, Socrates declares that he knows the best speeches, whose authors, however, he does not exactly remember, perhaps Sappho, maybe Anacreon or some other prose writer. In fact, he feels his chest is full of λόγοι that are not the fruit of his learning, given his ignorance, but come from some other source, which he has been filled up with through listening, ἐξ ἀλλοτρίων ποθὲν ναμάτων διὰ τῆς ἀκοῆς πεπληρῶσθαι, like a vase, δίκην ἀγγείου[51]. And in the *Theaetetus* in any case an ἀγγεῖον is the cage in which ἐπιστῆμαι (197d–e) similar to birds accumulate from the earliest age[52].

---

50 Denyer (2008, p. 78) takes into consideration the hypothesis that a suitable container for holding the μαθήματα may be the book, only to reject it on the basis of Socrates' and Plato's well-known mistrust of writing. There is not sufficient space here to return to the *vexata quaestio* concerning Plato's judgement of the written word. Certainly, Gaiser (1984, pp. 31–54 and 103–123) claims a statute that is anything but marginal for the dialogue. In this regard, cf. at least Erler (2007, pp. 60–98, 416–18 and 486–97).
51 Concerning the image of the perforated jar in the *Gorgias*, cf. Dalfen (2004, pp. 376–77). Corrigan & Glazov Corrigan (2004, pp. 33–37) interpret the criticism of the transmission of knowledge as a simple passage of concepts that Socrates develops in the *Symposium* in the context of Plato's polemic against the Sophists. For the passage in the *Phaedrus*, Yunis (2011, p. 107) recalls Democritus (68 A 126a), according to whom hearing is like liquid filling a jar, ἀγγείου δίκην. For a convincing analysis of this passage, see now also Capra (2014, pp. 69–71). The image of dialogue as a container does not appear to be an *ex nihilo* creation by Plato: already in the VI *Istmica* (1–3), Pindarus conceives of his own ode as a crater of songs, κρατὴρ Μοισαίων μελέων, while in a fragment, attributed uncertainly to the poet (354 Snell-Maehler), reference is made to the opening, ἀνοῖξαι, of a πίθος ὕμνων. Cf. Nünlist (1998, pp. 199–205). On foodstuff metaphors, Curtius (1954² [2013²], pp. 134–36) offers a wide-ranging panorama from ancient times to the Latin Middle Ages.
52 On this famous analogy and its limits, cf. Ferrari (2011, pp. 103–4), who among other things offers an extensive bibliography on this topic.

In the new container represented by dialogue, Protagoras' μαθήματα may therefore been observed close up and studied without risk in the presence of Socrates, the doctor of the soul who, with his dialectic art, enables us to separate the χρηστόν from the πονηρόν. This χρηστόν, as we have already seen, is a precious legacy for Plato in the mature pages of the *Republic*, of the *Politicus* and the *Timaeus*, as well as the *Laws*, written in his in old age. This precious legacy gave rise to fruits that have a different taste to the one, perhaps still unripe, they had at the stall of the merchant Protagoras, because they have acquired maturity and flavour through the heat of the sun under whose rays Plato's art and thought have perceived the paradigm of ἀγαθόν.

Works Cited

Arrighetti, G 2008, 'Cameleonte peripatetico e gli studi sulla biografia greca', in P Arduini, S Audano, A Borghini, A Cavarzere, G Mazzoli, G Paduano & A Russo (eds), *Studi offerti ad Alessandro Perutelli*, vol. 1, ETS, Roma, pp. 63–69.

Arrighetti, G 2013, 'Il *Protagora* platonico, Esiodo e la genesi dell'uomo', *Athenaeum*, vol. 101, pp. 25–42.

Beresford, A 2013, 'Fangs, Feathers, & Fairness: Protagoras on the Origins of Right and Wrong', in J van Ophuijsen, M van Raalte & P Stork (eds), *Protagoras of Abdera. The Man, His Measure*, Brill, Leiden-Boston, pp. 139–62.

Bertagna, MI 2012, 'Sulla costruzione del racconto nel *Protagora* di Platone', *Antiquorum Philosophia*, vol. 6, pp. 91–100.

Blondell, R 2002, *The Play of Character in Plato's Dialogues*, Cambridge University Press, Cambridge-New York.

Bonazzi, M 2009, 'Protagoras d'Abdère', in J-F Pradeau (ed), *Les Sophistes*, vol. 1, Flammarion, Paris, pp. 45–90 e 443–72.

Bonazzi, M 2010, *I sofisti*, Carocci, Roma.

Bonazzi, M 2012, 'Il mito di Prometeo nel *Protagora:* una variazione sul tema delle origini', in F Calabi & S Gastaldi (eds), *Immagini delle origini. La nascita della civiltà e della cultura nel pensiero greco e romano*, Academia, Sankt Augustin, pp. 41–57.

Boys-Stone, GR 2010, 'Hesiod and Plato's History of Philosophy', in GR Boys-Stone & JH Haubold (eds), *Plato and Hesiod*, Oxford University Press, Oxford-New York, pp. 31–51.

Brancacci, A 2002, 'Protagora e la *techne sophistike*. Plat. *Prot.* 316 D-317 C, *Elenchos*, vol. 23, pp. 11–32.

Brancacci, A 2012, 'La pensée politique de Protagoras', *Revue de Philosophie Ancienne*, vol. 30, pp. 59–85.

Brisson, L 2004, 'La *Repubblica* specchio del *Protagora*. La lista di virtù necessarie al buon funzionamento della città', in G Casertano (ed), *Il Protagora di Platone: struttura e problematiche*, Loffredo, Napoli, pp. 317–27.

Brisson, L 2012, 'Why Is the *Timaeus* Called an *Eikos Muthos* and an *Eikos Logos?*', in C Collobert, P Destrée & FJ Gonzalez (eds), *Plato and Myth. Studies on the Use and Status of Platonic Myths*, Brill, Leiden-Boston, pp. 369–91.

Burnyeat, MF 2005 (2009), '*Eikōs muthos*', *Rhizai*, vol. 2, pp. 143–65, now in C Partenie (ed), *Plato's Myths*, Cambridge University Press, Cambridge-New York, pp. 167–86.

Calame, C 2012, 'The Pragmatics of 'Myth' in Plato's Dialogues: The Story of Prometheus in the *Protagoras*', in C Collobert, P Destrée & FG Gonzalez (eds), *Plato and Myth. Studies on the Use and Status of Platonic Myths*, Brill, Leiden-Boston, pp. 127–64.

Cambiano, G 1991², *Platone e le tecniche*, Laterza, Roma-Bari.

Capra, A 2014, *Plato's Four Muses. The Phaedrus and the Poetics of Philosophy*, Center for Hellenic Studies, Washington.

Capuccino, C 2011, 'Plato's *Ion* and the Ethics of Praise', in P Destrée & FG Herrmann (eds), *Plato and the Poets*, Brill, Leiden-Boston, pp. 63–92.

Casanova, A 2013, 'La *mimesis* platonica e la fondazione della *kallipolis*: gioco e serietà, coerenza e contraddizione', in N Notomi & L Brisson (eds), *Dialogues on Plato's Politeia (Republic)*. Selected Papers from the Ninth Symposium Platonicum, Academia, Sankt Augustin, pp. 330–35.

Cleary, JJ 2007 (2013), 'Cultivating Intellectual Virtue in Plato's Philosopher Rulers', in FL Lisi (ed), *The Ascent to the Good*, Academia, Sankt Augustin, pp. 79–100, now in J Dillon, B O'Byrne & F O'Rourke (eds), *Studies on Plato, Aristotle and Proclus. Collected Essays on Ancient Philosophy of JJ Cleary*, Brill, Leiden-Boston, pp. 73–97.

Corradi, M 2012, *Protagora tra filologia e filosofia. Le testimonianze di Aristotele*, Serra, Pisa-Roma.

Corradi, M 2013, 'Dal *Protagora* alla *Repubblica*: Platone e la riflessione di Protagora su letteratura e *paideia*', in N Notomi & L Brisson (eds), *Dialogues on Plato's Politeia (Republic)*. Selected Papers from the Ninth Symposium Platonicum, Academia, Sankt Augustin, pp. 82–86.

Corradi, M 2013a, 'Τὸν ἥττω λόγον κρείττω ποιεῖν. Aristotle, Plato, and the ἐπάγγελμα of Protagoras', in J van Ophuijsen, M van Raalte & P Stork (eds), *Protagoras of Abdera. The Man, His Measure*, Brill, Leiden-Boston, pp. 69–86.

Corrigan, K & Glazov-Corrigan, E 2004, *Plato's Dialectic at Play. Argument, Structure, and Myth in the Symposium*, The Pensylvania University Press, University Park.

Curtius, ER 1954² (2013²), *Europäische Literatur und lateinisches Mittelalter*, Francke, Bern, Eng. Tr. Princeton University Press, Princeton-Oxford.

Dalfen, J 2004, *Platon. Gorgias. Übersetzung und Kommentar*, Vandenhoeck & Ruprecht, Göttingen.

Delcomminette, S 2006, *Le Philèbe de Platon. Introduction à l'agathologie platonicienne*, Brill, Leiden-Boston.

Demont, P 2011, 'La *pronoia* divine chez Hérodote (III, 108) et Protagoras (Platon, *Protagoras*)', *Méthexis*, vol. 24, pp. 67–85.

Denyer, N 2008, *Plato. Protagoras*, Cambridge University Press, Cambridge-New York.

Desclos, ML 1992, 'Autour du *Protagoras*: Socrate médecin et la figure de Prométhée', *Quaderni di Storia*, vol. 36, pp. 105–40.

De Sanctis, D 2012, 'Ai tempi di Crono: il duplice volto dell'umanità primitiva in Omero e in Esiodo', in F Calabi & S Gastaldi (eds), *Immagini delle origini. La nascita della civiltà e della cultura nel pensiero greco e romano*, Academia, Sankt Augustin, pp. 17–39.

Dillon, J 2012, 'Aristoxenus' Life of Plato', in CA Huffman (ed), *Aristoxenus of Tarentum. Discussion*, Transaction, New Brunswick-London, pp. 283–96.

Dörrie, H. & Baltes, M. 1990, *Der Platonismus in der Antike. Grundlagen – System – Entwicklung*, vol. 2, *Der hellenistische Rahmen des kaiserzeitlichen Platonismus*, Frommann-Holzboog, Stuttgart-Bad Cannstatt.

El Murr, D 2013, 'Protagoras et l'âge de Zeus du mythe du *Politique*', in A Havlíček, J Jirsa & K Thein, *Plato's Statesman. Proceedings of the Eighth Symposium Platonicum Pragense*, Oikoumene, Prague, pp. 80–98.

Erler, M 2007, *Grundriss der Geschichte der Philosophie. Die Philosophie der Antike*, vol. II 2, *Platon*, Schwabe, Basel.

Ferrari, F 2011, *Platone. Teeteto*, BUR, Milano.

Ferrari, F 2014, 'Gott als Vater und Schöpfer zur Rezeption von *Timaios* 28C3–5 bei einigen Platonikern', in F Albrecht & R Feldmeier (eds), *Religious and Philosophical Concepts of Divine Parenthood in Antiquity*, Brill, Leiden-Boston, pp. 57–69.

Fortenbaugh, WW 2007, 'Biography and the Aristotelian Peripatos', in M Erler, S Schorn (eds), *Die griechische Biographie in hellenistischer Zeit*. Akten des internationalen Kongresses vom 26.–29. Juli 2006 in Würzburg, de Gruyter, Berlin-New York, pp. 45–78.

Friedländer, P 1964³ (1973²), *Platon*, vol. 1, de Gruyter, Berlin-New York, Eng. Tr., Princeton University Press, Princeton.

Gagarin, M 1969, 'The Purpose of Plato's *Protagoras*', *Transactions and Proceedings of American Philological Association*, vol. 100, pp. 133–64.

Gaiser, K 1984, *Platone come scrittore filosofico. Saggi sull'ermeneutica dei dialoghi di Platone*, Bibliopolis, Napoli.

Goethe JW 1790 (1988), *Torquato Tasso. Ein Schauspiel. Ächte Ausgabe*, Leipzig, Göschen, now in D Borchmeyer & P Huber (eds), *Sämtliche Werke. Briefe, Tagebücher und Gespräche*, vol. I. 5, *Dramen 1776–1790*, Deutscher Klassicher, Frankfurt/M., pp. 731–834.

Halliwell, S 2011, 'Antidotes and Incantation: Is There a Cure for Poetry in Plato's *Republic*?', in P Destrée & F-G Herrmann (eds), *Plato and the Poets*, Brill, Leiden-Boston, pp. 241–266.

Heindorf, LF 1810, *Platonis dialogi tres. Phaedo, Sophistes, Protagoras*, Nauck, Berolini.

Helmig, C & Steel, C 2012, 'Proclus', in EN Zalta (ed), *The Stanford Encyclopedia of Philosophy* (Summer 2012 Edition), <http://plato.stanford.edu/archives/sum2012/entries/proclus/>.

Horn, C 2012, 'Why Two Epochs of Human History? On the Myth of the *Statesman*', in C Collobert, P Destrée & FJ Gonzalez (eds), *Plato and Myth. Studies on the Use and Status of Platonic Myths*, Brill, Leiden-Boston, pp. 393–417.

Hourcade, A 2009, *Atomisme et sophistique. La tradition abdéritaine*, Ousia, Bruxelles.

Koning, HH 2010, *Hesiod: The Other Poet. Ancient Reception of a Cultural Icon*, Brill, Leiden-Boston.

Manuwald, B 1996, 'Platon oder Protagoras? Zur großen Rede des *Protagoras* (Plat. Prot. 320c8–328d2)', in C Mueller-Goldingen & K Sier (eds), Ληναϊκά. Festschrift für CW Müller zum 65. Geburtstag am 28. Januar 1996, Teubner, Stuttgart-Leipzig, pp. 103–31.

Manuwald, B 1999, *Platon. Protagoras. Übersetzung und Kommentar*, Vandenhoeck & Ruprecht, Göttingen.

Manuwald, B 2003, 'Der mythos im *Protagoras* und die Platonische Mythopoiie', in A Havlíček & F. Karfík (eds), *Plato's Protagoras. Proceedings of the Third Symposium Platonicum Pragense*, Oikoumene, Prague, pp. 39–53.

Manuwald, B 2013, 'Protagoras' Myth in Plato' *Protagoras:* Fiction or Testimony?', in J van Ophuijsen, M van Raalte & P Stork (eds), *Protagoras of Abdera. The Man, His Measure,* Brill, Leiden-Boston, pp. 163–77.

Marino, S 2010, 'Il dialogo e la cura dell'anima: un tentativo di lettura del *Protagora* attraverso il paradigma medico', in R Baldini (ed), *Le maschere di Aristocle. Riflessioni sulla filosofia di Platone,* Limina Mentis, Villasanta, pp. 67–114.

Montanari, F 2012, 'The Peripatos on Literature. Interpretation, Use and Abuse', in A Martano, E Matelli & D Mirhady (eds), *Praxiphanes of Mytilene and Chamaeleon of Heraclea. Texts, Translation and Discussion,* Transaction, New Brunswick-London, pp. 339–58.

Morgan, KA 2000, *Myth and Philosophy from the Presocratics to Plato,* Cambridge University Press, Cambridge-New York.

Nestle, W 1978^8, in W Nestle, H Hofmann, *Platon. Protagoras,* Teubner, Stuttgart.

Norden, E 1923^2, *Agnostos theos. Untersuchungen zur formengeschichte religioser Rede,* Teubner, Leipzig-Berlin.

Notomi, N 2011, 'Image-Making in *Republic* X and the *Sophist.* Plato's Criticism of the Poet and the Sophist', in P Destrée & F-G Herrmann (eds), *Plato and the Poets,* Brill, Leiden-Boston, pp. 299–326.

Nünlist, R 1998, *Poetologische Bildersprache in der frühgriechischen Dichtung,* Teubner, Stuttgart-Leipzig.

Palumbo, L 2004, 'Socrate, Ippocrate e il vestibolo dell'anima (un'interpretazione di *Prot.* 314c)', in G Casertano (ed), *Il Protagora di Platone: struttura e problematiche,* Loffredo, Napoli, pp. 86–103.

Pelosi, F 2010, *Plato on Music, Soul and Body,* Cambridge University Press, Cambridge-New York.

Rademaker, A 2013, 'The Most Correct Account: Protagoras on Language', in J van Ophuijsen, M van Raalte & P Stork (eds), *Protagoras of Abdera. The Man, His Measure,* Brill, Leiden-Boston, pp. 87–111.

Reale, G 2004, 'Il 'Platone' di Paul Friedländer, la sua importanza e la sua portata storico-ermeneutica', in P Friedländer, *Platone,* a cura di A Le Moli, introduzione di G Reale, Bompiani, Milano, pp. VII-XLV.

Reeve, CDC 2008, 'Glaucon's Challenge and Thrasymacheanism', *Oxford Studies in Ancient Philosophy,* vol. 34, pp. 69–103.

Regali, M 2012, *Il poeta e il demiurgo. Teoria e prassi della produzione letteraria nel Timeo e nel Crizia di Platone,* Academia, Sankt Augustin.

Richardson Lear, G 2011, '*Mimesis* and Psychological Change in *Republic* III', in P Destrée & F-G Herrmann (eds), *Plato and the Poets,* Brill, Leiden-Boston, pp. 195–216.

van Riel, G., 2012, 'Religion and Morality. Elements of Plato's Anthropology in the Myth of Prometheus (*Protagoras,* 320D–322D)', in C Collobert, P Destrée & FG Gonzalez (eds), *Plato and Myth. Studies on the Use and Status of Platonic Myths,* Brill, Leiden-Boston, pp. 127–64.

Rowe, C 2013, 'On Justice and the Other Virtues in the *Republic:* Whose Justice, Whose Virtues?', in N. Notomi & L Brisson (eds), *Dialogues on Plato's Politeia (Republic). Selected Papers from the Ninth Symposium Platonicum,* Academia, Sankt Augustin, pp. 49–59.

Saunders, TJ 1991, *Plato's Penal Code. Tradition, Controversy, and Reform in Greek Penology,* Oxford University Press, Oxford.

Schlick, AJ 2012, 'Der historische Protagoras in Platons gleichnamigem Dialog', *Museum Helveticum*, vol. 69, pp. 29–44.
Schofield, M 2010, 'Music All Pow'rful', in ML McPherran (ed), *Plato's Republic. A Critical Guide*, Cambridge University Press, Cambridge-New York, pp. 229–48.
Schöpsdau, K 2011, *Platon. Nomoi (Gesetze). Übersetzung und Kommentar*, vol. III, Buch VIII-XII, Vandenhoeck & Ruprecht, Göttingen.
Schorn, S 2012, 'Aristoxenus' Biographical Method', in CA Huffman (ed), *Aristoxenus of Tarentum. Discussion*, Transaction, New Brunswick-London, pp. 177–221.
Sedley, D 2009, 'Myth, Punishment and Politics in the *Gorgias*', in C Partenie (ed), *Plato's Myths*, Cambridge University Press, Cambridge-New York, pp. 51–76.
Serrano Cantarín, R & Díaz De Cerio Díez, M 2005, *Platón. Protágoras. Edición crítica, traducción, introducción y notas*, Consejo Superior de Investigaciones Científicas, Madrid.
Solana Dueso, J 2011, 'Protágoras y los poetas', *Convivium*, vol. 24, pp. 5–23.
Stalley, RF 1995, 'Punishment in Plato's *Protagoras*', *Phronesis*, vol. 40, pp. 1–19.
Tarrant, H 2000, 'Where Plato Speaks: Reflections on an Ancient Debate', in GA Press (ed), *Who Speaks for Plato? Studies in Platonic Anonymity*, Rowman & Littlefield, Lanham-Boulder-New York-Oxford, pp. 67–80.
Trabattoni, F 2004^2, *Scrivere nell'anima. Verità, dialettica e persuasione in Platone*, Filarete On Line, Milano, <http://www.studiumanistici.unimi.it/files/_ITA_/Filarete/154.pdf>.
Tulli, M 1994, 'La storia impossibile nel *Politico* di Platone', *Elenchos*, vol. 15, pp. 5–23.
Tulli, M 2013, 'La μίμησις nel III libro della *Repubblica*: il rapporto di Platone con la tradizione', in N Notomi & L Brisson (eds), *Dialogues on Plato's Politeia (Republic). Selected Papers from the Ninth Symposium Platonicum*, Academia, Sankt Augustin, pp. 314–18.
Vegetti, M 1998, 'Glaucone', in M Vegetti (ed), *Platone. La Repubblica*, vol. II, Libri II e III, Bibliopolis, Napoli, pp. 151–72.
Vegetti, M 2004, 'Protagora, autore della *Repubblica*? (ovvero, il 'mito' del *Protagora* nel suo contesto)', in G Casertano (ed), *Il Protagora di Platone: struttura e problematiche*, Loffredo, Napoli, pp. 145–58.
Vlastos, G 1956 (1976), 'Protagoras', in *Plato. Protagoras. Translated by B Jowett, Revised by M Ostwald and Edited, with an Introduction*, The Liberal Arts, New York, pp. VII-XXIV, now in CJ Classen (ed), *Sophistik*, Wissenschaftliche Buchgesellschaft, Darmstadt, pp. 271–89.
Wagner, R. (1999), *Sämtliche Briefe*, vol. 11, 1. April bis 31. Dezember 1859, herausgegeben von M Dürrer, Breitkopf & Härtel, Wiesbaden-Leipzig-Paris.
Yunis, H 2011, *Plato. Phaedrus*, Cambridge University Press, Cambridge-New York.

Marcelo D. Boeri
Theaetetus and Protarchus: two philosophical characters or what a philosophical soul should do*

Plato's spokesmen and Plato's voice

Plato speaks through his characters; even those characters who seem to be far from a view that we would attribute to Socrates (Plato) can be understood as speakers of Plato himself. When in the final section of the *Gorgias* the character Socrates discusses the Calliclean thesis of crude hedonism, nobody, I think, would be seriously willing to assume that Plato endorses Callicles' argument. But without a Callicles saying that the good can be identified with pleasure without qualification, Socrates could not deploy his arguments against that kind of hedonism. In the *Philebus* Plato does successfully show that a certain sort of pleasure can and should be incorporated into the good life, but in order to do that he must show first that the crude hedonism defended by Philebus and Protarchus (at the beginning of the dialogue) is not feasible.

The characters who appear to endorse sometimes antithetical positions in the dialogues (such as Protarchus and Socrates in the *Philebus*) may be understood as the means Plato makes use of to put difficulties to himself and thus to think that, after all, the dialogue is just a discourse (*logos*), a conversation the soul has with itself, since when one thinks, one dialogues, asks himself questions and answers, affirms and denies (*Theaetetus* 189e-190a; *Sophist* 263e). To be sure, when one debates with another, such a dialogue is not necessarily interior; but even in this case the question-answer method describes the movement of thought: thinking is dialoguing, conversing. It is the same procedure which allows one to think through an issue without having formulated it definitively.

I intend to discuss here two of these Platonic characters, namely, Theaetetus and Protarchus. In spite of their distinct personal characteristics they can be un-

---

* This is the expanded version of the lecture given at the colloquium "Plato's Styles and Characters" (Universidade de Brasilia, Brazil, August 20 – 24, 2012). I am grateful to the organizer of the conference, Gabriele Cornelli, for the invitation, and to Beatriz Bossi and Mauro Tulli for their remarks. I am also grateful to Michael Erler for his written comments, and Nicholas D. Smith for conversation on this topic. I am indebted both to Patricia S. Vulcano and Zachary Hugo for improving my English. The final version of this piece has been written with the support of Fondecyt project 1150067, Chile.

derstood as "philosophical characters", which I believe to be so for the following reasons: (i) they are willing to dialogue (and this is probably so because they take for granted that they can be wrong and hence they should modify what they believe). (ii) They note early on in the conversation that the dialogue permits one to observe from a different perspective what they themselves thought and, at least in some cases, they start to believe that there is reason to modify what they think (and this is not because of shame or because of an external pressure, say, but because of genuine conviction that what they believe is false); (iii) they also understand that they should not respond to Socrates (the great questioner of Plato's dialogues) with what he wishes to hear, but what they really believe to be true; (iv) finally, even though at the end of the conversation they are not completely certain with regard to the correct answer to the proposed question, they know that they have made some progress. If this is really so, there is reason to suspect that they have acquired an awareness, both of the limits of their own knowing and of the psychological change they have undergone after the dialogical debate. Naturally, all the points I have just listed actually are part of a set of common places in the dialogical practice, as we know from the dialogues. But in the development of my presentation I hope to show that the manner in which both Theaetetus and Protarchus can be regarded as good examples of such common places constitutes the conditions themselves of the philosophical dialogue.

Theaetetus and Protarchus as philosophical interlocutors

When one examines the character Theaetetus in the homonymous dialogue and the character Protarchus in the *Philebus*, an important point emerges with regard to the characters Theodorus and Philebus. A salient point of convergence between Theaetetus and Protarchus (two characters who, from the viewpoint of the characters themselves, appear to be very different) is that both end up taking the place of their respective mentors in conversation. It is true that the way in which Theodorus abandons the dialogue is considerably different from the manner in which Philebus does. However, they give up their place in conversation to their disciples on account of reasons that, from Plato's viewpoint, turn out to be unphilosophical.

Let us first examine the case of Theodorus: even though his participation in the *Theaetetus* is relevant at the beginning of the dialogue, he is reluctant to actively participate in conversation and in the process of research that he suspects such a conversation involves. First, Theodorus claims that he is unused to such kind of conversation and that, due to his age, his is not willing to accustom himself (*Theat.* 146b); later he justifies his retreat from the discussion asserting that he prefers to be a spectator and not to be dragged into the arena, so he does not have to struggle with someone younger and more supple (162b6–7: μὴ ἕλκειν πρὸς τὸ γυμνάσιον σκληρὸν ἤδη ὄντα, τῷ δὲ δὴ νεωτέρῳ τε καὶ ὑγροτέρῳ ὄντι προσπαλαίειν; see also 165a-b). In the previous passage (162a) Theodorus declares that he could not accept that Protagoras was refuted by what he (i.e. Theodorus) admits or acknowledges (δι' ἐμοῦ ὁμολογοῦντος); and immediately he adds that, against his own opinion, he may not oppose Socrates. Actually, this is Theodorus' justification for suggesting that Socrates should take up his dialogue with Theaetetus again, since "he was listening to Socrates very carefully". This remark produces Socrates' immediate reaction, who complains that if one attends a Spartan wrestling-school it would not be fair to be a spectator as other people exercise naked without stripping and showing one's own body (*eîdos*; Theaet. 162b).[1] The meaning of this comparison is clearly that, such as it is done in the wrestling-arena, one should exercise (or train) like the others. So Socrates' exhortation indeed points to the fact that Theodorus, just as Theaetetus, must be cooperative with the dialogue and should be an active participant in it.

There is a general sense in which the reasons provided by Theodorus to avoid participating in the debate seem to be reasonable; after all, he is not a professional philosopher, and the explanations Plato puts in his mouth for abandoning the discussion and the cooperative research process that such a debate presupposes appear reasonable if they are viewed from this perspective. Of course, Theaetetus is not a professional philosopher either, although, as Socrates has already noted, he possesses the ideal conditions to be so: in spite of the fact that at the beginning of the conversation Theaetetus has certain doubts, he finally decides to get involved in the debate. Yet, Theodorus probably also wants to retreat from discussion due to Socrates' intimidating style of addressing the audience which can be viewed as a way of announcing that the debate will be prickly, a situation in which Theodorus does not want to be involved. After the argument intending to show that knowledge (ἐπιστήμη) and wisdom (σοφία) are the same thing, Socrates challenges the audience again when he explains his puzzlement (ἀπορία), since he is unable to sufficiently understand

---

1 It is true that Theodorus plays a significant role in the discussion of Protagoras' theory (cf. 168c-183c). But Plato always shows Theodorus to be reluctant in the dialogue, and he intends to give a certain prominence to Theaetetus (see the final section of 183c).

what knowledge is. Before this statement he challenges the audience to answer his question (146a1: τί φατέ;), but there is complete silence (146a5: τί σιγᾶτε;). Certainly, one could think that after Socrates has said that the one who makes a mistake (or rather who always fails) will go to sit down like a donkey, the Socratic calling to dialogue and attempt to examine such a hard subject (knowledge) does not sound very friendly. By contrast, whoever makes it through without erring will be a king and will question whatever he or she wants. It is natural that no one should want to respond: the person who makes no assertions is the only one who is free from error. As we know, whoever dares to answer Socrates' questions chances being turned down and, apparently, being viewed as "the donkey who goes to sit down", and ridiculed. However, as is well known from the *Gorgias* onwards, Plato declares (through his spokesman Socrates) that to be refuted should not be understood as an insult; on the contrary, refutation is what guarantees that one is able to check his own view and, if necessary, to correct it.[2] But, of course, Socrates himself realizes he is being a little rude and immediately he attributes that to his "love of arguments"[3] and to his eagerness to make people converse and become friends and talkative to one another.[4]

Theodorus is the one who attempts to break up this tension, although his maneuver can be understood as an elegant strategy to swiftly retreat from debate: he, Theodorus, is not accustomed to this kind of discussion and, due to his age, he is not ready to become accustomed.[5] By contrast, it would be fitting for the young people around him to get involved in conversation, and if they do so they will improve and make progress. After saying that, Theodorus straightforwardly points to Theaetetus as the person Socrates should question (146b). Socrates already had the opportunity to talk to the young and promising Theaetetus, and now tries to persuade him to take the responsibility of conversation by arguing that he cannot distrust Theodorus, someone from whom Theaetetus admits having learned. And if he has recognized that he learns from him it is because he thinks Theodorus knows something. That is to say, if Theodorus takes Theaetetus

---

2 Plato, *Gorgias*, 458a2-b1. Cf. also *Euthydemus* 295a and *Sophist* 230b-e. It is true that in the *Sophist* 230d1–2 Plato makes emphasis on the fact that one's soul cannot be released from what prevents it acquiring knowledge until the one who refutes shames it by refuting it (πρὶν ἂν ἐλέγχων τις τὸν ἐλεγχόμενον εἰς αἰσχύνην καταστήσας). But maybe this is part of the shocking way with which Plato intends to move a person in order that such a person not believe that he or she knows what actually he or she does not know. Refutation as such has a therapeutic character insofar as the best thing to do is to rid one's soul of ignorance, which is badness.
3 *Theaet.* 146a6: ἐγὼ ὑπὸ φιλολογίας ἀγροικίζομαι.
4 Cf. also *Meno* 75d.
5 A similar scene can be seen in the *Laches* 194a6–7 (I owe this reference to Professor Michael Erler).

to be able to converse with Socrates, it is because Theodorus believes that he can do so. With his characteristic docility Theaetetus responds that he has to dialogue with Socrates since he was asked to do it, both by Theodorus and Socrates; anyway, if he makes a mistake, Theaetetus says, they will correct him (146c). This is a sign of trust on Theaetetus' part, who appears to assume that, even though he looks like a donkey, Socrates will take care of him. Probably Theaetetus thinks so because, although he just met Socrates, he notices that Theodorus, his mentor, trusts him. And if this is so, it must be true that, in spite of the initial manner (a little violent and intimidating) in which Socrates calls for dialogue, Socrates' purpose is to create conversation, to become friendly and talkative with the people he is conversing with.

Now if Plato really decides to leave Theodorus out of the conversation since said character realizes that his professional knowledge does not allow him to contribute to the debate, one should wonder why he, Theodorus, at the very beginning of the dialogue, makes the flagrant mistake of stating that his opinion has some worth even though he lacks the knowledge that would permit him to formulate a sound view. Theodorus asserts that Theaetetus is not handsome (καλός), but he resembles Socrates in the snubness of his nose and the bulging of his eyes (*Theaet.* 143e). When the young Theaetetus appears before Theodorus and Socrates, this one asks him to approach, so that he may examine for himself what sort of face he has (144d). This apparently trifling episode, which gives life to the dramatic plot in the introduction of the characters, is helpful to present for the first time one of the central topics of the dialogue: knowledge (ἐπιστήμη). In fact, in order to know whether or not Theodorus' view regarding the resemblance between Socrates and Theaetetus is well grounded one should look at Theodorus' expertise.

With regard to the resemblance of the faces, one should examine whether or not Theodorus speaks as a person who is a skilled draftsman (γραφικός). In other words, Theodorus' judgment is valuable if and only if it presupposes some form of expert knowledge related to what has been said, but insofar as he is not a skilled draftsman but a geometer, his opinion is not reliable (144e–145a). Therefore, knowledge is an indispensable condition for one's opinion to have some value. At any rate, one should appeal to charity in matching Theodorus' position to our own, since in fact it is he who acknowledges in Theaetetus the extraordinary qualities that make him the ideal interlocutor for Socrates: Theodorus introduces Theaetetus as a person who is unusually well-endowed by nature with the qualities of a philosopher: he is naturally good at remembering, quick to learn, high-minded, graceful, and so on. In addition to that he also is a person of an unbelievable gentle temper or docility.⁶ Maybe one should also grant Theodurus the fact that he often remains with Theaetetus when Socrates has raised a difficult problem; thus, it looks as if Theodorus' purpose is to encourage Theaetetus (*Theaet*. 165b), even though one could interpret Theodorus' attitude as a manner of running away and passing the problem to his disciple.⁷ However, if one is still charitable with Theodorus, one can continues to think that his intention is to support the young Theaetetus and accompany him in the middle of the dialectical storm. It seems to me that Theaetetus' docility should not be understood in the sense of someone who is willing to assent to everything that is said; of course, it is not the case that such a situation never occurs in the dialogue,⁸ but it would not be strange that Plato is thinking of the remark the Visitor makes to Socrates in the *Sophist*:

> "Well, Socrates, if the interlocutor submits to guidance easily and painlessly (ἀλύπως τε καὶ εὐηνίως προσδιαλεγομένῳ), it's easier in this way, to do it before someone else; but if that's not the case, by oneself (τὸ καθ' αὑτόν)" (transl. Benardete).⁹

An interlocutor who submits to guidance easily and painlessly is not (at least not necessarily) someone responding "yes" to anything; such a person can be someone who answers yes to what it is reasonable. In the *Sophist*, after the Visitor has persuasively and clearly argued that the soul will have no benefit from what is learned unless the person has eliminated the opinions that are impediments to what is learned, and such a person is "purified, believing he knows just what he does know and nothing else", Theaetetus responds that this "is the best and most moderate of states" (*Sophist* 230c-d). His answer is not a submissive "yes", but he is convinced that that is the case. A little earlier in the dia-

---

6 *Theaet*. 144a2–7: οὐδένα πω ᾐσθόμην οὕτω θαυμαστῶς εὖ πεφυκότα. τὸ γὰρ εὐμαθῆ ὄντα ὡς ἄλλῳ χαλεπὸν πρᾷον αὖ εἶναι διαφερόντως, καὶ ἐπὶ τούτοις ἀνδρεῖον παρ' ὁντινοῦν [...] οἵ τε ὀξεῖς ὥσπερ οὗτος καὶ ἀγχίνοι καὶ μνήμονες (on this passage cf. Ferrari 2011: 210, n.18). Theaetetus gathers several characteristics that, according to Plato, the guardian of the city should have (see *Republic* 487a; 490c; 494b; 503c, where "high-mindedness" –μεγαλοπρέπεια– is added as a distinctive quality of a philosopher). The philosopher must have a character that is both gentle and high-spirited at the same time" (πρᾷον καὶ μεγαλόθυμον ἦθος; *Rep*. 375c6–7. The argument intending to prove that these characterological features, apparently opposite, are possible starts at 375d10).
7 When at 165a-b a difficult matter is under discussion and Socrates is about to start questioning, he addresses Theodorus and asks him: "Shall I tell you how this might happen, or Theaetetus?" Theodorus responds that he should tell both of them, but the younger (i.e. Theaetetus) should answer, because if he slips up, it would be less embarrassing.
8 As noted by Blondell, when he is attacked, he is a "yes-man" (2003: 278).
9 *Sophist* 217d1–3.

logue, when the Visitor argues that there are two kinds of evils (κακίαι in the soul; 228d–e; wickedness –πονηρία– and ignorance: ἄγνοια), Theaetetus acknowledges that one should admit that these two kinds of evils exist, even though he hesitated to decide when Socrates was talking (*Sophist* 228e1–2: ἠμφεγνόησα). This suggests that Theaetetus was not immediately persuaded by Socrates, but upon reflection he became convinced that Socrates was right.

As already observed above, despite Theaetetus' doubts and hesitations as to whether he should get involved in the conversation, he eventually does so, unless Theodorus has been joking. It is true that the way in which Socrates urges Theaetetus to engage seriously in discussion looks a little intimidating ("Well then, it's time, my dear Theaetetus, for you to display and for me to examine"; transl. Benardete").[10] Socrates seems to be sure that the conversation will progress in the correct manner since he apparently trusts Theodorus' diagnosis with regard to Theaetetus' philosophical qualities. As I have just pointed out, Theaetetus is the one who doubts. This reveals the appropriate attitude that shows clearly that he does not presuppose knowing what he does not know (as we know, a quite different attitude is the one displayed by Protarchus at the beginning of his conversation with Socrates, even though this does not prevent him from being a reasonable interlocutor). As I have just remarked, the one who doubts is Theaetetus, and such doubting portrays a proper attitude insofar as it clearly shows the fact that he does not presuppose to know what he does not know. Socrates urges Theaetetus to trust and be firm about the original agreement.[11] In fact, it is Socrates himself who is responsible for giving confidence to Theaetetus when he recognizes that he also learns from Theodorus and from other people who understand questions of geometry. It is as if Socrates were saying to Theaetetus that he, the one who will lead the discussion and who, at least apparently, seems to possess the knowledge allowing him to ask the correct questions in order that the dialogue progresses, also learns from others or continues learning from other people.

As is very well known, the comparison Plato makes between Socrates and Theaetetus displays a unique detail of great intensity; of course, such a comparison presupposes a careful dramatic construction: like Socrates, Theaetetus' exterior look is ugly, and resembles Socrates in the snubness of his nose and the bulging of his eyes (even though those features are not so pronounced in him; *Theaet.* 143e8–a1). But just like in Socrates such an exterior ugliness contrasts

---

10 *Theaet.* 145b6–7: Ὥρα τοίνυν, ὦ φίλε Θεαίτητε, σοὶ μὲν ἐπιδεικνύναι, ἐμοὶ δὲ σκοπεῖσθαι·
11 It may be interesting to note that Socrates has not made any (explicit) agreement with Theaetetus, even though in this passage he refers to "what has been agreed" (145c3: τὰ ὡμολογημένα) and to the "agreement" (145c5: ὁμολογία).

with a beautiful interior: he possesses an extraordinary character as he goes smoothly, unfalteringly and affectively to his lessons and investigations and, despite the fact that his tutors have squandered his property, he is wonderfully open-handed about money (144b–d).¹² In addition to that, he recognizes his own ignorance (148b; 148e) and looks interested in maintaining the coherence of his speech (154c–e). He also shares the state of puzzlement (ἀπορία) characteristic of Socrates, a state characterizing the philosophical attitude in general (174c–d; 175b; 187d; 190e).¹³ It is pretty clear, it seems to me, that in the *Theaet.* 185e4–5 Plato is playing with the aesthetic-moral ambiguity of the word "beautiful" (καλός): in spite of his ugly look, Theaetetus is καλός, since the one arguing-speaking "beautifully" is "beautiful and good" (ὁ γὰρ καλῶς λέγων καλός τε καὶ ἀγαθός), that is, he is a good or distinguished person.¹⁴ Of course, arguing "beautifully" is arguing soundly, avoiding sophistical resources, saying what one really thinks, and admitting the consequences that follow from what one has taken to be true. This is why the one arguing well is both a praiseworthy and fine person (*Theaet.* 185e4). Interpreters have rightly suggested that Theaetetus, a fifteen or sixteen year old young man, is presented by Plato as the intellectual and human *alter ego* of Socrates.¹⁵

Unlike Theodorus (who avoids dialogue), Theaetetus is well disposed to discussion and is not afraid to make a mistake since, in the case he be wrong, he will surely be corrected (146c5: ἄν τι καὶ ἁμάρτω, ἐπανορθώσετε). If what one says is false and is refuted, and if one is able to understand that the refutation is sound, one should be pleased to be refuted. And this is so because falsehood and ignorance are evils. Perhaps one might suspect that the ignorance and stupidity Plato is speaking of in these kinds of passages cannot be ignorance in the sense of lack of certain cognitive contents. In the *Republic* 585b3–4, for instance,

---

12 Benardete (1984: I.159) understands differently this passage: Socrates really is ugly and his ugliness is that of an old woman and signifies the art he practices. But as Benaderte himself reminds, by his same art Socrates revealed that Theaetetus was beautiful.
13 On aporia as the first step in philosophical approach cf. Kahn 1996: 95–100; 178–180.
14 See also *Theaet.* 142b. There is a similar scene in the *Charmides*; Socrates, coming back to Athens, asks Critias if any of the young men had become distinguished for wisdom, beauty or both (*Charmides* 153d). The talented and handsome young man is Charmides, and, as in the introductory scene of the *Theaet.*, he has been practicing gymnastics, and impresses (both the youth and the elders) because of his beauty as well as his talent (see *Charmides* 154a-c, with the comments by Dover 1989: 55–56). Later on Socrates clarifies that Charmides' soul should be good by nature and that that means being "a very distinguished person" (καλὸς καὶ ἀγαθός; 154e4). Indeed Charmides, unlike Theaetetus, also is physically beautiful. For Socrates' erotic disposition towards the beautiful young men, see Plato, *Symposium* 216d.
15 See Palumbo 2000: 230; Blondell 2003: 261–62; 285.

ignorance (ἄγνοια) and stupidity (ἀφροσύνη) are understood as a sort of emptiness of the soul's state or condition (κενότης ἐστὶ τῆς περὶ ψυχὴν αὖ ἕξεως), in a very similar sense to the one just indicated. I mean, even though Theaetetus is aware that he can be mistaken, when he is asked "what is knowledge?", and answers "kinds of knowledge are what one could learn from Theodorus" (Theaet. 146c7–8), he also depicts a proper psychological condition which can be taken as a certain type of knowledge: the proper attitude or disposition to receive the needed objection that would permit him to correct his error. But there is another ingredient showing Socrates that Theodorus cannot be accused of committing perjury after he had noted Theaetetus' intellectual and human qualities: even though Theaetetus is aware of having an expertise, he is also aware of the limits of his own knowledge. In other words, although he is conscious that he possesses a specific type of knowledge, he does not believe to know what he actually does not know, let alone to be able to correctly answer a difficult question like "what is knowledge?" (148b). Theaetetus has the conviction that simply by virtue of possessing a specific knowledge he cannot assume that he knows other things, and this is so because each specific field of knowledge has its own objects. This shows, once again, the philosophical and human temper of Theaetetus, which makes him the ideal interlocutor for dialogue. Moreover, after he has provided his initial answer to the question "what is knowledge" and is refuted by Socrates (who in turn urges him again to endeavor to give a new answer) Theaetetus claims:

> "But know well, Socrates, it's often that I tried to make an examination of it, in hearing the questions that are reported as coming from you. But for all of that, I am myself incapable of either persuading myself that I say anything adequately or hearing someone else speaking in just the way you urge".

And Socrates replies:

> "The reason is, my dear Theaetetus, that you are suffering labor pains, on account of your not being empty but pregnant" (*Theaet.* 148e; transl. Benardete).[16]

Socrates probably gathers that Theaetetus is "pregnant" because he recognizes his incapability to properly respond to what was asked. In other words, Theaetetus acknowledges that he does not know, and such recognition is the first step to knowledge: not believing to know what one really does not know (*The-*

---

[16] On the analogy of the woman in labor to refer to the state in which the one who is experiencing a learning process see Bernadete 1984: I.99-I.103; Sedley 2004: 8–13.

aet. 210c), and, what maybe is more significant, the fact of being aware that possessing a knowledge does not enable one to believe that he or she knows another thing about which he or she does not have an expert knowledge. Theaetetus' attitude is decisive since, as Plato states, the worst form of ignorance is not knowing something and believing that one knows it.[17]

But what is the criterion necessary for knowing that one does not know? For, as Plato suggests, nobody believes that what he or she believes is false.[18] Obviously, I do not even plan to endeavor to respond that question, although the problem of self-knowledge be a promising path to investigate, such as is suggested in a memorable passage of the *Alcibiades I*, where Plato makes emphasis upon the relevance of distinguishing between caring for what belongs to oneself and caring for oneself (128a5–d7; 129e–130c; 130e–132a). If "oneself" is one's soul, one should attempt to know one's own soul (which means to know oneself, not what belongs to oneself), which is the state of mind in which one is.

If what I have been arguing is sound, it would be reasonable to admit that without a proper psychological disposition one will not even be willing to notice the power of an argument. This appears to be explicitly suggested by Plato when he states that those who live according to the unhappiest model (παράδειγμα), due to their folly and extreme foolishness (ὑπὸ ἠλιθιότητός τε καὶ τῆς ἐσχάτης ἀνοίας; *Theaet.* 176e5–177a1), will live with bad people and will be associated with evils. And given that they are terrible and wicked (δεινοὶ καὶ πανοῦργοι), they will surely take the suggestion that they should change their lifestyle as a recommendation coming from unintelligent people, even though actually they themselves are those who lack intelligence. It is pretty clear to me that the foolishness (which could be associated with "ignorance" in other parts of the dialogue; cf. *Theaet.* 176c) Plato is talking about here cannot be understood in the sense of lack of certain specific cognitive contents, but as a state of mind, a dispositional state, consisting in being unable to admit one's own mistake and hence believing to know what one actually does not know. Thus the ignorance Plato speaks of is the typical attitude of a person who is unable to doubt himself, no matter how powerful the objector's argument might be.

This last point is useful by way of transition to the discussion of the character Protarchus and his relation to Philebus. Maybe nobody would have any doubts about why one could consider Theaetetus to be a "philosophical character", although probably one does have such doubts with regard to Protarchus. First I would like to point out that Protarchus, unlike Theaetetus, already has

---

17 *Sophist* 229c1–5.
18 *Charmides* 166d; 167a. *Alcibiades I* 113b; 117b-118a. *Theaetetus* 171b4; 200a3. *Sophist* 228c-d.

a philosophical (and well defined) conviction; furthermore, he somehow believes himself to already be a philosopher. Perhaps this explains Protarchus' confident attitude from the very beginning of the dialogue as an active participant in the debate. As is usual in the argumentative strategy of Socrates, one should start by establishing certain basic agreements (ὁμολογίαι), to which the results of the discussion will have to fit in.[19] Socrates proposes to begin by the following agreement: each one will attempt to show a state or disposition of the soul (*Philebus* 11d4: ἕξιν ψυχῆς καὶ διάθεσιν) capable of providing a happy life to every human being. Once the two conflicting views have been summarized and clarified (*Philebus* 11b–c), Socrates is certain that the hedonists Philebus and Protarchus will endorse the state and disposition of pleasure; by contrast, Socrates will support the view of intelligence or wisdom. With regard to this assertion Protarchus responds with a natural and maybe emphatic "quite so" (11d10: Ἔστι ταῦτα). That is, from the very beginning of the dialogue Protarchus has already assumed the thesis of pleasure as his own.

On his part, Theaetetus is a geometrician and, even though he is well disposed towards the dialogue and portrays philosophical qualities, he does not presume to be a philosopher. What I would like to note is that, even if I think that both Theaetetus and Protarchus are two "philosophical characters", the manner in which Plato presents them in the respective dialogues where they are one of the central figures is quite different. The case of Theaetetus is relatively clearer, insofar as it is Plato himself the one who enhances his philosophical qualities. Protarchus, though, does not seem very docile, especially when the debate starts, but his attitude changes when he begins receiving the first of Socrates' onslaughts (particularly after the "mollusk argument", when Protarchus claims that the argument has left him "absolutely speechless for the moment"; 21d4–5: Εἰς ἀφασίαν παντάπασί με, ὦ Σώκρατες, οὗτος ὁ λόγος ἐμβέβληκε τὰ νῦν). Maybe this is the moment in which he starts to discover that the certainty he believed to have was actually quite weak, or that the fundamentals of his thesis were not as sure and reliable as he thought they were.

But before describing the philosophical characteristics of Protarchus I would like to reemploy the same strategy I previously used when I attempted to describe the philosophical traits that Theaetetus possesses. In order to bring Protarchus into the scene I shall compare, just as in the previous case, his attitude (disposed towards the dialogue, and even, one could say, his eagerness to obtain a certain prominence in the debate) to that of his mentor Philebus, who is reluc-

---

[19] On the agreement as the "basic consensus" of those who are involved in conversation cf. Erler 1991: 423, n. 9.

tant to keep conversing (Philebus even looks upset with Socrates). Naturally, this fact is not surprising at all, and one should suppose that it is part of a dramatic strategy carefully planned by Plato. One might imagine, for example, that this is due to the fact that Philebus has already been discussing the matters at stake and he does not wish to tolerate Socrates' objections, criticisms and arguments any longer. But in this case Plato explains the reasons of this situation from the beginning. The *Philebus* starts suddenly, taking again a conversation that was in progress. This accounts for the need to summarize the opposing views which is done both by Socrates and by Protarchus again later in the dialogue.[20] As is well known, this is one of the first interesting dramatic details in the *Philebus*: the dialogue starts *in medias res*, without any introduction, with a conversation that follows another one on the same topic (presumably the good), which has taken place just before and whose central difficulty has not been solved yet.[21] Socrates quickly attributes to Philebus the crude hedonist thesis; it is as if Plato pointed out that there already was a conversation on the topic at issue. After Socrates summarizes the two competing views, and asks Philebus if they have expressed themselves thus, Philebus responds with a laconic "Yes Socrates, exactly in that way" (*Phil.* 11c4). Immediately we learn that Protarchus will defend the cause of pleasure, as long as Philebus is not willing to keep dialoguing.[22] Philebus' refusal to keep dialoguing shows Protarchus that he is the one who must take the leading role in the defense of pleasure.[23] The next intervention of Philebus is in section 12a7–8, when Socrates states that if there is a state or condition that is superior both to the state of pleasure and that of wisdom, and if such a superior state shows itself more akin to pleasure, the life of pleasure will overcome that of wisdom, and that if this new state is more akin to wisdom, wisdom will overcome pleasure. Once Protarchus has accepted this strategy, Socrates asks Philebus what his opinion is about this matter, and Philebus categorically responds:

---

[20] *Philebus* 11b-c; Protarchus summarizes again the views on the good in 19c-d (cf. also the new summary of Socrates in 60a-b).
[21] See Bossi 2008: 224–225.
[22] *Philebus* 11c7–8: "the beautiful Philebus has backed down" (or "has surrendered": Φίληβος γὰρ ἡμῖν ὁ καλὸς ἀπείρηκεν).
[23] Thus it is indicated by Protarchus later when he suggests that Socrates not bother Philebus with his questions (15c8–9); surely Protarchus remembers that Philebus had already said (12b) that he released himself from any responsibility and that he invoked his goddess as a witness.

"I think and I will continue to think that pleasure completely wins. But you, Protarchus, you will know!"[24]

It seems to me that this kind of recalcitrant attitude explains the fact that Plato leaves Philebus out of the debate. As is clear, Philebus is a dramatic construction of Plato, whose intention may be to describe a certain sort of character that is not necessarily hard to find: the character of the one who prefers to keep dogmatically his or her beliefs and views without considering them in the light of the dialogical discussion.[25] The way in which Philebus persists in his belief and his refusal to allow the others to examine his view reveals an unphilosophical attitude on Philebus' part. By contrast, in Plato's view the healthy philosophical attitude and the commitment to the dialogue presupposes being able to review one's own beliefs and, if necessary, to change them. Philosophical beliefs are liable to be modified by an argument; if Philebus' attitude were correct, the object of discussion would become a doctrinal object or rather a dogmatic object of investigation, which is the same thing as saying that the problem of good requires no more research. However this approach sounds strongly anti-Platonic, for not only has Plato pointed out to us that philosophical beliefs can be modified by argument (*logos*), but also that in order to modify our beliefs by argument we need to transform our own soul's state. But all of this would be possible for someone who is willing to take care of what follows (at least whenever it follows) from the starting points of his or her own *logos*. However this somewhat presupposes one's willingness to review one's own beliefs: against ignorance and foolishness there is not any possible argument.[26]

Even though Philebus does not participate much in the dialogue (much less than Theodorus in the *Theaetetus*, indeed), he remains attentive to the discussion ("as a sleeping dog") and eventually he adds some remarks, annoyed by

---

24 *Philebus* 12a7–8: μοὶ μὲν πάντως νικᾶν ἡδονὴ δοκεῖ καὶ <u>δόξει</u>· σὺ δέ, Πρώταρχε, αὐτὸς γνώσῃ.
25 Or, as Gadamer proposes to read the passage, Philebus *refuses to discuss his thesis* making use of logical argumentation, a thesis that in the spirit of a dialogical treatment always presupposes receiving criticism and is potentially refutable (1999: 187). On the relevance of dialogical method (understood as refutation) in Davidson, see Natali (2007: 139–40) and Davidson (2005: 252–4).
26 That ignorance (ἄγνοια) should be understood as a state or condition is said by Plato himself (cf. *Philebus* 48c2: Κακὸν μὴν ἄγνοια καὶ ἣν δὴ λέγομεν ἀβελτέραν ἕξιν). Of course, this is not new in Plato: in the divided line διάνοια, νοῦς, νόησις and εἰκασία are states, conditions (ἕξεις) or affective states (παθήματα; indeed of the soul). See *Republic* 511d-e.

the direction the conversation takes.²⁷ For example, in passage 17c–e, when Socrates attempts to show the way in which the one-multiple distinction can be applied to determine what being an expert in a discipline (such as grammar or music) ²⁸ is, Protarchus enthusiastically gives his assent to Socrates' account.²⁹ Apparently, Protarchus talks to Philebus, who is on his side. Philebus responds that Socrates has argued (spoken) well, but anyway he does not see why Socrates is bringing up this point now. After a brief digression, Socrates tries again to answer Philebus' doubt; but the one who notes what Socrates means is Protarchus. In fact, he claims that what Socrates is doing is asking about the kinds of pleasure (19b). The interesting detail that, once again, Plato emphasizes in a fresh dramatic turn (which describes Protarchus' philosophical attitude and his collaboration with the dialogue) is focused on the manner in which Protarchus becomes again the main interlocutor of Socrates and, hence, puts aside Philebus as a valid partner for conversation. According to Protarchus, he (who had been acting as the replacement of Philebus in the defense of pleasure) would be making a fool of himself in asking Philebus to respond to such a difficult question (18e–19a). Protarchus' attitude shows again his commitment to the role he has taken in the defense of pleasure and in the relevant function that his participation plays in order that the dialogue progress.³⁰ There is even a passage where Philebus excludes himself from the dialogue: in 27e–28b a decisive conversation between Socrates and Philebus takes place; Philebus accepts that both pleasure and pain should be put among what admits "the more", for

> "pleasure would not be the whole good if it were not unlimited by nature, both in quantity and intensity" (27e).

---

27 See Frede 1996: 218. Philebus' sporadic interventions are for complaining that he does not understand (18a), or in order to protest that even though his goddess (Aphrodite) cannot be identified with the good, Socrates' god (Apollo; 22c) cannot be identified with it, either. In the same line Philebus complains to denounce that Socrates is praising his god.

28 A sound spoken by a person is a single thing, and yet is also indeterminate in number. But we are not wise because of this, but because of knowing how many species of sound there are, and of which kind they are (this is what makes us grammarians; cf. *Philebus* 17b). The same thing occurs with music: sound is a single thing, but there are kinds of sound (height and depth), which also shows that it is multiple. But what makes us experts in music is understanding (or knowing) how many intervals of sound there are with regard to what is height and depth, how many combinations, and so forth (17c-d).

29 "Philebus, it seems to me that Socrates has perfectly argued what has been said now" (17e7–8: Κάλλιστα, ὦ Φίληβε, ἔμοιγε τὰ νῦν λεγόμενα εἰρηκέναι φαίνεται Σωκράτης).

30 At any rate, Philebus never disappears completely from the scene; in fact, there are some passages where Socrates talks to him directly (cf. 26b; 27e).

When Socrates asks him in which genus wisdom, knowledge and intelligence should be put "without sacrilege", Philebus complains that Socrates is praising his own god. Socrates replies that Philebus is praising Aphrodite, but the question must nonetheless be dealt with. Protarchus claims that he is right; then Philebus reminds Protarchus that he had chosen to speak on his behalf (28b6). Protarchus admits that he is puzzled and asks Socrates (not Philebus) to be his interpreter. Both Philebus' withdrawal from the conversation and Socrates' understanding give a new thrust to the dialogue. I think that what I have said so far is enough to show how and why Plato leaves Philebus out of the discussion and to depict the philosophical character of Protarchus. Once Philebus has stated that he thinks and will continue to think that pleasure always wins and has shown his intention to not keep dialoguing in an active way, Protarchus notes that Philebus should no longer take it upon himself to agree or disagree with Socrates. Interestingly Philebus freely chooses to relinquish any and all responsibility. But whether or not Philebus consents, Protarchus is interested in moving on with the discussion (*Philebus* 12a–b). Protarchus attitude, if compared to Philebus', is quite different: first, because he quickly notes that if Philebus backs down and is not willing to continue discussing, Philebus will have no authority with regard to the fixed agreements, or as a the "official" speaker in favor of pleasure. This is a way of saying that Protarchus is aware that a certain agreement should be established as a necessary condition of the dialogue and of assuming the responsibility in the defense of pleasure in the contest for the good. In fact, as is well known, in the Platonic dialogues it is usual to emphasize the previous agreements among the speakers, agreements that will have to be kept for the sake of coherence of argument.[31] Second, Protarchus disposition is relevant because he takes seriously the dialectical mechanism that compels one to check one's own beliefs; even though Protarchus is not disposed to easily abandon his position, he is ready to review the scope of his thesis after Socrates' first attempt at refutation has taken place. Moreover, Protarchus claims to return to the question-answer method when he realizes that the matter is hard to explain (24e) and, in spite of Socrates' attacks, he does not lose his good disposition towards the dialogue. A paradigmatic case of this is shown in section 15d–16a, where Socrates criticizes the ambiguous use of language and the generally ludic attitude of which young people are so fond. They have no mercy, Plato says, on their father or mother or on any other of their audience (15e–16a). Protarchus reacts to such comment by noting that they are a crowd of young people,

---

[31] See as way of example *Gorgias*, 461b; 468e; 482d; 487e; 495a (with the comments by Erler 1991: 431–32). *Theaetetus* 145c2–5; 159c14; d6; 164a5–7 *et passim*.

and stating that Socrates' remark is a little insulting; however, Protarchus claims to have understood Socrates' concern and that he will endeavor to keep the discussion free of such upsets, in addition to the fact that he is willing to accompany Socrates in his path, "a gift from the gods to human beings" (16c). This good disposition towards the dialogue once again reveals Protarchus' philosophical attitude.

At the beginning of the debate Protarchus shows himself to be confident with regard to his view: the good is pleasure without qualification. It appears to me that Protarchus' initial confidence cannot be compared to the confidence Theaetetus starts acquiring when after a brief initial doubt he begins conversing with Socrates and, so to speak, he relaxes himself and feels more confident. As I indicated above, it is clear that Socrates notes Theaetetus' doubt and encourages him to keep moving on; besides, Theaetetus seems to trust his master and what Theodorus believes about Socrates. But Protarchus' confidence is different from Theaetetus': Protarchus is confident because he appears to be convinced that there is no way to refute his hedonism. In 12c Socrates opens a new front for discussion in order to try to show that pleasure and the good cannot be identified without qualification, and he observes that "he knows that pleasure is varied" (or "diversified"; 12c4: τὴν δὲ ἡδονὴν οἶδα ὡς ἔστι ποικίλον). In fact, pleasure takes all sorts of forms, which somehow are unlike each other.[32] The argument he provides for demonstrating this is simple but forceful: both the temperate and the intemperate person are pleased, but it is obvious that what pleases the one and the other are different things (12d). Naturally, Protarchus finds this account a little outrageous, and this is so because what in his view finally counts is that those pleasures come from opposite things. But those pleasures, *qua* pleasures, are not different. By contrast, Socrates believes that, even though from a general viewpoint the whole is a unity, from the point of view of the parts some are as opposite as they can be: black and white are two species of color (two "parts" of the genus color). *Qua* colors they are the same, since both of them are "color"; but at the same time they are dissimilar, as they are the species of color most opposite of each other. The same thing occurs in the case of pleasure: the pleasures of the temperate and intemperate people are the same thing *qua* pleasures; but from a specific viewpoint, they are as opposite as they can be (12e–13a). Protarchus, of course, is firm in his position and believes that this type of argument cannot damage his thesis; but if one recognizes, as Protarchus implicitly does at the beginning (and later explicitly; 13c), that given that one is dealing with dissimilar things, calling them with a different name,

---

[32] 12c7–8: μορφὰς δὲ δήπου παντοίας εἴληφε καί τινα τρόπον ἀνομοίους ἀλλήλαις.

then, it is reasonable to assume that not every pleasant thing is a good, which does not mean to say that the pleasing things are displeasing (13a–b). Regardless of Socrates' argument against crude hedonism, what concerns me is Protarchus' attitude before Socrates' objection: (i) he is not willing to abandon his position for, as he himself puts it, the person who states that pleasure is the good could not be disposed to admit or tolerate that someone says that some pleasures are good and others bad (13b–c); (ii) even having clarified this point, Protarchus admits that pleasures are dissimilar from each other and that some of them are opposite (although he makes it clear that not *qua* pleasures). (iii) When Socrates introduces the one-multiple problem (whose application is seen later; 18d ff.) he addresses a powerful attack to the young men, who are fond of making use of an ambiguous use of the language (15d-16a), as if one's treatment with language were a mere entertainment or a game.[33] Socrates' remark can be grasped (as in fact Protarchus grasps it) as an elegant way to say that the hedonist view is a childish position resorting to improper uses of language. Note that it is Protarchus who asks Socrates moderate the tone of confrontation in order that the dialogue be possible. That is, Protarchus understands Socrates' tone as agonic or polemic, i.e. as unphilosophical.[34] But as it can be seen in what follows in the text, Protarchus is still well disposed to continue discussing, since he declares to recognize Socrates' concern, in addition to the fact that he has no problem in eliminating what preoccupies Socrates and that he (Protarchus), along with the others (surely the silent audience), will accompany him as far as possible.

The mollusk argument is a fantastic piece which combines both dramatic and philosophical ingredients; the argument identifies neither wisdom nor those distinct intellectual abilities with the good or the good life. What the argument actually shows is that without such capacities one would not even be able to postulate the possibility that pleasure is the good, for one would be unable to know if he is enjoying a pleasure, or if a certain sensory state can be recognized as pleasant or not (this makes clear the necessity of possessing at least true opinion). Memory, on its part, guarantees that one can remember that in the past one was enjoying a pleasure, and calculation guarantees that one will be able to enjoy a pleasure in the future. These three ingredients, which are the Socratic

---

33 On the ambiguous expression τῶν λόγων … πάθος (*Phil.* 15d7–8) cf. Casertano 1999: 408; Pradeau, 2002 (note *ad loc.*).
34 There is a similar scene in *Theaet.* 167e-168c, where Protagoras (in his defense) tells Socrates not to confuse verbal struggle (ἀγωνιζόμενος) with a genuinely philosophical conversation (διαλεγόμενος), without ill will or hostility, and in a kind spirit (168b2–3: οὐ δυσμενῶς οὐδὲ μαχητικῶς ἀλλ' ἵλεῳ τῇ διανοίᾳ).

candidates to win the competition for the good, are at least a necessary condition of pleasure and, if this is so, it cannot be true that Protarchus cannot be in need of anything but the greatest pleasure to be happy (*Phil.* 21a).[35] As it can be seen later (21d–e), although with less emphasis, Socrates applies the same argumentative strategy to show that the good life requires pleasure. On the other hand, there are also some dramatic ingredients that one should not overlook: as I already pointed out, at the beginning of the dialogue Protarchus' confidence and, in a certain way, arrogance is noteworthy. To be sure, with absolute confidence he has been defending the thesis that the good is pleasure, or that the best life style is the pleasant life. Obviously, the point is not that one cannot defend hedonism as a philosophical view, but Protarchus' initial attitude in this respect depicts a certain naturalness and evidence that require examination and justification. This is why Protarchus' question of whether he would accept to live his entire life enjoying the greatest pleasures turns out to be unusual, although it is quite clear that the question seems definitely outrageous to Protarchus. However, Socrates' argument persuasively shows that it is untrue, as Protarchus had supposed, that pleasure is enough to decide whether or not he is really living a good life.[36] Towards the end of the argument, both seriously and jokingly, Socrates suggests that the one who is willing to defend Protarchus' view will live a mollusk life or the life of those sea animals that live in shells, the most stupid and ignorant of all, according to Plato (*Timaeus* 92a–b).[37]

After this first blow Protarchus looks a little overwhelmed ("this argument has left me absolutely speechless for the moment"), and after Socrates' argument he is not so confident; but the dialogue as a method of joint research to find the truth must continue (at the beginning of the dialogue Socrates reminds Protarchus that they are not engaged in rivalry (οὐ δήπου ... φιλονικοῦμεν), but they have to be allies for what is nearest to the truth (τῷ δ' ἀληθεστάτῳ δεῖ που συμμαχεῖν; 14b5–7). Refutation (in case the mollusk argument can be considered as a refutation of Protarchus' view) as a therapeutic method has started to change Protarchus' disposition in the right direction. This does not mean that Protarchus should change his mind, but rather he must be able to allow the oth-

---

35 See 63d and 65c, where it is clear enough that the greatest pleasures are the sexual ones, even though probably not the sexual pleasures without qualification, but the sexual pleasures lacking measure.

36 One might interpret the mollusk argument as an *ad hominem* argument, but indeed it is helpful to show that the life of pleasure is neither a sufficient (or self-sufficient) nor a perfect life, two necessary conditions of the happy life, as was agreed at the beginning of the debate (20c-21a).

37 On the example of the mollusk, see Lefèbvre 1999.

ers (and he himself) to scrutinize his view. Clearly Socrates notes that Protarchus is overwhelmed; this is why Socrates immediately replies: "Let us not be softened, let's turn now to examine the life of intellect" (21d6–7). One might understand this remark in two ways: Socrates shows that his own view should be scrutinized as well, and that it eventually can be objected (this way producing a certain confidence in the overwhelmed Protarchus). But the phrase "Let us not be softened" (Μήπω τοίνυν μαλθακιζώμεθα) can be a way of saying "let us not be mollusks, let us not be the most stupid and ignorant animal living in shells"[38] (which does not sound very friendly, even though it can be taken to be part of the serious game Socrates is playing).

It is true that Socrates does not devote much time to the examination of his own thesis, even though it is clear that he appears to agree, along with Protarchus, that a lifestyle in which one possesses any kind of wisdom, intelligence, knowledge and memory without participating in the slightest pleasure (or pain) does not constitute a choice-worthy life (21d–e). This is what in the dialogue permits to introduce a third type of life (the mixed life), which is presented as a position that overcomes both the life of pleasure and that of wisdom (22a). At this point Socrates is willing to give up, and he admits that his model of the good life does not lack difficulties, either (how would the life of a person who does not feel pleasure or pain be... it would be the life of a person without feelings of any kind).[39] Then he suggests the type of life which is made up of a mixture of both lives. Protarchus' conclusion before this new perspective leaves no doubts that, even if he is still a little overwhelmed, he wishes to move on, concluding that "of the three possible lives before us, two of them are neither adequate nor worth choosing for a human being or a beast" (22a–b). It is probably just at this point that Protarchus understands the eligibility requirement (that Socrates early introduces in conversation; 18e), a requirement that must be satisfied by anything that purports to be a suitable candidate in the contest for the good. The argument by itself was already enough to warn a well-intentioned and collaborative interlocutor that his view at least needed to be nuanced; but the dramatic ingredient enhances the dramatic force of the argument, as Protarchus, rejoicing in his hedonism, is unwilling to allow himself to be confused with a mollusk or a sea animal living in a shell.

Once Protarchus has ruled out the life of pure intelligence or knowledge as eligible, a life in which there is no pleasure or pain, he admits that pleasure

---

38 See *Timaeus* 92b–c.
39 *Philebus* 21e2: ἀλλὰ τὸ παράπαν ἀπαθὴς πάντων τῶν τοιούτων. This is a kind of life that Aristotle (maybe thinking of this passage of the *Philebus*) does not accept either (see Aristotle, *Eudemian Ethics* 1230b13–14).

seems to have been beaten by Socrates' argument. But he also makes the interesting point that the life of reason cannot claim the first prize, either (22e–23a). That is, after Socrates' comparison of the hedonist life to the life of a mollusk, Protarchus has taken a beating, but he is not completely overcome yet. It is clear that the argument has shown that a life of pleasure without qualification is not self-sufficient or perfect (two basic requirements of the good; 20d–21d), but it has not proved that a life of pure intelligence and knowledge, deprived of any pleasure, fulfills these requirements.

From that moment Protarchus is increasingly collaborative and active in the dialogue, and although in some passages he seems to be a "yes-man", he continues to make his way into a healthy dialogical attempt to find the truth. When Socrates notes that Aphrodite realizes the excess and evil of all things and that there was in them no limit to pleasures and indulgences, and when the goddess established law and order as determinants of such pleasures and indulgences, Protarchus entirely agrees that it is so (*Philebus* 26b–c). [40] But this does not mean, I submit, that Protarchus is willing to assent to all that Socrates says. Much later in the dialogue (36e), after Socrates' question, Protarchus admits that no one –asleep or awake, in a state of madness or delirium– believes that one is feeling pleasure when one is not, or thinks oneself distressed about something when one is not. All of us, Protarchus adds, have supposed that it is so (ὑπειλήφαμεν; 36e10). Then Socrates asks if such an assumption is right or not, or if it should be examined if it is; Protarchus has no doubt that the view should be scrutinized (Σκεπτέον, ὥς γ' ἐγὼ φαίην ἄν; 36e13). The character Protarchus continues to defend his thesis that there cannot be false pleasures; however he also is willing to admit that his view should be examined.

Maybe he still remembers his experience at the beginning of the discussion, when he stated that he would have no need of any other thing if he had pleasure. Moreover, after Socrates provides his image of the soul as a book and explains the role of memory as a scribe writing speeches in our souls, Protarchus says

---

[40] As it is clear, at this moment Protarchus is not yet so sure about his crude hedonism, and even though he sometimes presents objections against Socrates' view, he is already disposed to grant some basic points against hedonism (in 65c-d he is even more emphatic: "pleasure is the greatest impostor of all" ... "Pleasures are like children who lack the least bit of intelligence"). Kraut (1992: 26) is too strict when he suggests that at the beginning Socrates wins the discussion to a recalcitrant Protarchus who later becomes a "yes-man", whose role is to seek clarifications. D. Frede's position (who thinks that Protarchus plays an active role at the end of the discussion) is much more nuanced. There is probably a reason to believe that Protarchus is more than that: as Frede herself recognizes (1992: 442), there are passages (*Philebus* 36c) in which Protarchus still offers a stubborn resistance to Socrates' claims.

that he seems that this is so because he accepts what has been said (ἀποδέχομαι τὰ ῥηθέντα οὕτως; 39b1–2). That is to say, he accepts what Socrates says because apparently he admits that what has been said has passed the dialogical test. At this point of the dialogue Protarchus has already incorporated the Platonic teaching that beliefs should be subject to the joint effort of the dialogical conversation.

Epilogue: the dialogue as a cooperative work

At the outset of this paper I pointed out that the characters of Plato's dialogues can be understood as his spokesmen, whether or not Plato agrees with all the views defended by his characters. He invented a way of doing philosophy in which he himself is never entirely committed to the "I say" level. Both Theaetetus and Protarchus are sometimes accused of being "yes-men". But it is arguable, I think, that it is not necessarily something bad to be a "yes person" at a certain point of the debate: on the one hand, there are questions whose answer is so obvious that they require a "yes" as a response. On the other hand, one might respond "yes" but not in order to escape from the attack of the question or to avoid being ridiculed if one gives a wrong answer. Rather, such an answer can be the result of the joint examination that both Theaetetus and Protarchus, understood as philosophical characters collaborating in the investigation, conduct with Socrates.

Works Cited

Blondell, R. *The Play of Character in Plato's Dialogues*, Cambridge, Cambridge University Press, 2002.

Bossi, B. *Saber gozar. Estudios sobre el placer en Platón*, Madrid, Trotta, 2008.

Casertano, G. "*Écrire et peindre dans l'âme. Le statut du Logos dans le Philèbe*", in Dixsaut, M. (dir.), *La fêlure du plaisir. Études sur le Philèbe de Platon*. 1 Commentaires, Paris, Vrin, 1999, 403–21.

Davidson, D. "*Dialectic and Dialogue*", in Davidson, D., Truth, Language, and History, Oxford, Oxford University Press, 2005, 251–259.

Dover, K. *Greek Homosexuality*, Cambridge-Massachusetts, Harvard University Press, 1989, (First ed. 1978).

Erler, M. *Il senso delle aporie nei dialoghi di Platone. Esercizi di avviamento al pensiero filosofico*, Italian trans. Milano, Vita e Pensiero, 1991.

Ferrari. F. Platone. *Teeteto* (Introduzione, traduzione e commento di Franco Ferrari. Testo Greco a fronte), Milano, BUR (Classici Greci e Latini), 2011.

Frede, D. "*The Philebus: The Hedonist's Conversion*", in Gill, C. – McCabe, M. M. (eds.), *Form and Argument in Late Plato*, Oxford, Clarendon Press, 1996, 213–48.

Gadamer, H.G., *Die Idee des Guten zwischen Plato und Aristoteles*, in Gadamer, H. G., Gesammelte Werke 7. Griechische Philosophie III, Tübingen, J. C. B. Mohr (Paul Siebeck), 1999.

Kahn, C. *Plato and the Socratic Dialogue. The Philosophical Use of a Literary Form*, Cambridge, Cambridge University Press, 1996.

Lefèbvre, D. "*Qu'est-ce qu'une vie vivable ? La découverte de la vie mixte dans le Philèbe, 20b–22b*", in Dixsaut, M. (dir.), *La Fêlure du plaisir*, Études sur le Philèbe de Platon, I, Commentaires, Paris, Vrin, 1999, 61–88.

Natali, C. "*Due dissertazioni scritte in fretta. Gadamer e Davidson sul Filebo di Platone*", in Méthexis XX, Sankt Augustin, Academia, 2007, 113–43.

Palumbo, L. "*Struttura narrativa e tempo nel Teeteto*", in Casertano, G. (a cura di), *La struttura del dialogo platonico*, Napoli, Loffredo, 2000, pp. 225–37.

Pradeau, J.-F. Platon. *Philèbe* (Introduction, traduction et notes), Paris, Flammarion, 2002.

Christian Keime
The Role of Diotima in the *Symposium*: The Dialogue and Its Double

I would like to examine what appears to be an exemplary case of the intimate connection between philosophical content and literary form in Plato's dialogues: the way Socrates, in the *Symposium*, after having discussed for a while with his table companion Agathon, chooses to praise *Eros* (201d1–212c3).[1] Unlike the former orators, the dialectician does not deliver a speech in his own name but reports the theory of a priestess, Diotima of Mantinea, who allegedly initiated him to the mysteries of *Eros*. Moreover, instead of reporting the theory through a long monologue, he embeds Diotima's words into a dialogue which involves Socrates himself, when he was younger. Why Diotima? Why a reported dialogue? Here are the two questions I intend to address jointly.

Until now, most of the studies focused on the first question (why Diotima ?) and proposed three major answers. The first one is that Plato introduced the character because she was a philosopher who historically existed and taught Socrates.[2] The second interpretation, which is the prevailing one, considers that Diotima is a literary device that represents the philosopher par excellence: as such she conveys to the audience of the banquet, and to the readers of the book, what the philosophers, Socrates and Plato, really think deep down about matters of love.[3] On this reading, the use of a mouthpiece may be accounted for through different motives: (1) investing the theory with prestige and authority;[4] (2) enabling Socrates to preserve his mask of ironic ignorance and to remain polite as he contradicts his host Agathon;[5] (3) showing that Plato was emancipated from Socrates' thought.[6] As a priestess and a woman, Diotima may also (4) symbolize what philosophy owes to the religious paradigm of inspi-

---

[1] My thanks to Ruby Blondell, Luc Brisson, Paul Demont, Étienne Helmer, Stéphane Jettot, and Elizabeth Rowley-Jolivet for their helpful comments on an earlier draft of this paper.
[2] Taylor 1949, pp. 224–25; Wider 1986, pp. 45–8; Waithe 1987, pp. 101–9.
[3] See McPherran 2006, p. 91, n. 43.
[4] Kranz 1958, p. 80; Sier 1997, pp. 3 & 8; Frisbee Sheffield (2012, p. 134) considers the figure of Diotima as Socrates' "euporetic *alter ego*".
[5] This is the most commonly given reason. See Robin 1929, pp. XXV-XVI & LXXVI; Bury 1932, p. XXXIX; Cornford 1950, p. 71; Wippern 1965, p. 126; Allen 1991, p. 46; Sier 1997, p. 9.
[6] Hermann 1839, p. 523; Vlastos 1981, p. 21; Reeve 2004, p. 96, and 2006, p. 135.

ration[7] or (5) to the feminine paradigm of pregnancy.[8] A third strand of interpretation takes in earnest the comparison Socrates draws between the priestess and the 'accomplished sophists' (οἱ τέλεοι σοφισταί, 208c1) and notes that her manners as well as many points of her theory confirm such an identification.[9] In this respect, far from being the representation of the true philosopher and the faithful mouthpiece of Socrates and Plato, Diotima may be used to play ironically upon and to ridicule the pretended omniscience of the sophists, or to parody the earlier speeches.[10] Plato may also use this mask to distance himself from some points of her theory, particularly her view of immortality (207d – 209e).[11] The colorful sophist, finally, may be the key element of a general poetic enterprise, which consists in challenging Aristophanes or trying to create a new literary genre.[12]

The purpose of this paper is not so much to contradict these explanations as to suggest a new one which may help to reconcile some views that are outwardly contradictory, in particular the views that Diotima is a philosopher and that she is a sophist. I shall argue that with Diotima Plato acts just like his legendary father Apollo[13] who, according to the famous Heraclitean fragment, οὔτε λέγει οὔτε κρύπτει ἀλλὰ σημαίνει.[14] His intention is neither to communicate directly through her mouth and her appearance what *eros* and philosophy are, nor to hide ironically or poetically what he or Socrates truly thinks. His purpose is rather to show how a philosopher can communicate his philosophical knowledge when he has to speak or write within an enunciative situation that does not altogether suit the practice of philosophy. Thanks to Diotima, Socrates and Plato deliver a lesson in communication besides a lecture on *eros*.

However, as such, Diotima is part of a larger tool of communication, that is, the whole dialogue between her and the younger Socrates, reported by Socrates himself. Thus, if we recall the two questions I asked initially – Why Diotima ?

---

[7] Ficino 2002, pp. 127 & 150 – 1; Friedländer 1964, pp. 157 – 9; Rosen 1968, pp. 203 – 20; Nussbaum 1979, pp. 144 – 5; D Frede 1993, p. 415; Fierro 2003, p. 46; Evans 2006; Horn 2012b, pp. 2 & 13, Sampson 2013, pp. 104 – 7.
[8] Ast 1816, p. 312; Dover 1980, p. 145; Halperin 1985 & 1990; Lesley 1992; Brisson 1998, pp. 63 – 4; Corrigan & Glazov-Corrigan 2004, pp. 114 & 116; Hobbs 2006, p. 264.
[9] Wilamowitz 1919, p. 298; Neumann 1965, pp. 33 – 59; Dover 1980, p. 145; Rutherford 1995, p. 192.
[10] Stallbaum 1857, p. 147; Nails 2006, pp. 184 – 5; Wildberger 2012, p. 21.
[11] Neumann 1965, pp. 33 – 5 & 41; Rowe 1999, pp. 250 – 6; Erler 2003, p. 162; Corrigan & Glazov-Corrigan 2004, pp. 142 – 3.
[12] Gold 1980; Erde 1976, p. 161.
[13] See Woodbridge 1929, p. 2; Plato was said to be born on Apollo's birthday (Diog. Laert. 3. 2).
[14] 22 B 93 DK.

Why a reported dialogue ? –, in order to propose a new answer to the first one, we must first and foremost answer the second one, a question that has not been investigated enough by modern scholars.

I. The dialogue and its double

The function of the reported dialogue may appear conspicuously if we first look at the similarities between the protagonists of this conversation[15] (Diotima and the younger Socrates) and those of the dialogue in which this conversation is embedded – Socrates, who reports the conversation, and his audience. The latter are mainly Agathon, and more generally all the earlier speakers to whom this speech is indirectly addressed. Each character in this fiction (Diotima and the young Socrates) appears to be a combination of Socrates and his audience at the symposium.

I.1. Diotima

To begin with Diotima, the very content of her theory seems be a compromise between the point of view of the dialectician Socrates and that of his main addressee, Agathon, particularly insofar as she seems to consider that the soul is as perishable as the body.[16] Another point is her attitude to the nature of the supreme idea which the initiate is to behold at the end of the philosophical ascent: the form of Beauty and not the form of Good.[17] However, within the limits of this paper I cannot discuss the content of Diotima's speech in the depth it deserves. I shall focus on the formal features of the discourse and study how, in the way she delivers her theory, the priestess mediates between the purposes of the philosopher and the expectations of his audience.

The 'father of the speech'[18] is not Socrates but Phaedrus who proposed through his constant complaints to Eryximachus that *Eros*, as a great god,

---

15 To be precise, one should speak of conversations, since Socrates summarizes several meetings with Diotima (περὶ τῶν ἐρωτικῶν λόγους ποιοῖτο, 207a5–6).
16 207e-208a; compare with *Phaedo* 72e-84b. On this question, see Hackforth 1950, pp. 43–5, Luce 1952, pp. 137–41 and D Frede 2012, pp. 154–6.
17 212a; compare with *Prot.* 351b-357c, *Rep.* VI 507c-509d, *Phil.* 20d. On these apparent inconsistencies with 'platonism' see Neumann 1965, pp. 33–59.
18 πατὴρ τοῦ λόγου, 177d5.

should be the subject of a laudatory ode.¹⁹ Such an epideictic mode of expression matches the tastes and the skills of all the former speakers, particularly of Agathon who is characterized by Socrates as a master of public discourse²⁰ and a follower of Gorgias.²¹

But delivering an *encomium* contradicts Socrates' own inclinations in two main respects: firstly a eulogy is a long speech and secondly it intends to communicate in a dogmatic way the ideas of the speaker to the public.²² The dialectician may indulge in long speeches (μακρολογία), admittedly, as it is the case in the *Phaedrus*, but he always uses this mode of expression as a second best way designed to meet the expectations of his interlocutors.²³ When Socrates has the choice of weapons, he prefers to use dialogue in the form of short questions and short answers (βραχυλογία).²⁴ This is the best way to teach the truth about anything since it prevents the participants from branching off and loosing sight of the question of essence.²⁵ Moreover, genuine Socratic teaching amounts to questioning the student so that he finds a universal and transcendent truth by himself.²⁶

In the *Symposium*, although Socrates agrees to the initiative of Eryximachus and Phaedrus, he still exhibits his preference for *brakhulogia* and dialectical inquiry. When Agathon is about to speak, Socrates leads him into a question-and-answer discussion, but the dialectician is soon called to order by Phaedrus who reminds him of the rules of the game:

> Phaedrus broke in and said 'My dear Agathon, if you answer Socrates' questions (ἐὰν ἀποκρίνῃ Σωκράτει), it'll no longer matter to him in the slightest how any of the things we're

---

19 See 177a-d. 'laudatory ode' translates ὕμνους καὶ παίωνας (177a5–7), ἐγκώμιον (177b1) and ἔπαινος (177b3, d2).
20 194b: Socrates congratulates him for his splendid display of eloquence in the theatre.
21 198c: according to Socrates, Agathon borrowed the beautiful vacuity of his eulogy from the sophist.
22 Of course, another non-philosophical feature of such a eulogy is that it does not primarily intend to tell the truth, as Socrates puts it (198d-199a); see Nightingale 1993, pp. 116–17. I will address the issue later.
23 See *Phaedr.* 236d-237a and 241e-242b: Socrates describes himself as the hostage of Phaedrus, the young lover of rhetoric.
24 See *Prot.* 328e-329b, 334e-335c; *Gorg.* 449b-c, 461d-462b; *Hipp. Min.* 364b-c; *Soph.* 217c-218a.
25 The "What is it?" question. See *Prot.* 335b: Socrates describes *brakhulogia* as "διαλέγεσθαι ὡς ἐγὼ δύναμαι ἕπεσθαι".
26 See *Meno* 81a-e, 85b-86c; *Theaet.* 150c-d. On Socrates' preference for *brakhulogia*, see Dixsaut 2001, pp. 17–21 and Longo 2007, p. 265. On the opposition between *makrologia* and *brakhulogia*, see Dixsaut 2013, pp. 11–17. According to M Frede (1992, p. 207) this distinction is primarily one of modes of discourse and of argument, rather than one of style.

doing here turn out – so long as he has someone to converse with (διαλέγηται), especially someone beautiful. I myself enjoy listening to Socrates conversing (διαλεγομένου), but it's my business to see to our encomium to Love and get the required speech from each one of you (ἀποδέξασθαι παρ' ἑνὸς ἑκάστου ὑμῶν τὸν λόγον); so when the two of you have paid your dues to the god, then you can have your conversation (διαλεγέσθω).' (*Symposium* 194d, trans. CJ Rowe, modified[27])

After Agathon's speech, and before reporting the theory of Diotima, Socrates asks Phaedrus for a provisory dispensation (199b) and interrogates Agathon again (199c-201c). At the end of this question-and-answer session, that turned out to be a refutation (ἔλεγχος), Socrates emphasizes that the universal truth and not himself is responsible for the outcome of the cross-examination:

'I am unable, Socrates, to argue against you (σοὶ ἀντιλέγειν),' said Agathon; 'let it be as you say.'
'No, it's rather the truth (τῇ ἀληθείᾳ), beloved Agathon,' Socrates said, 'that you can't argue with, since there's nothing difficult about arguing against Socrates.' (201c)

This statement is consistent with what Socrates says to the tragic poet at the outset of the drinking party: contrary to what Agathon imagines, real knowledge cannot be transferred between two minds as water flows from a cup to another:

Agathon (…) said 'Come here, Socrates, and recline beside me (παρ' ἐμὲ κατάκεισο), so that I can also have the benefit of contact with that bit of wisdom of yours (τοῦ σοφοῦ ἁπτόμενός σου ἀπολαύσω), the bit that came to you in the porch. It's clear that you found (ηὗρες) what you were looking for, and have it in your possession (ἔχεις); you wouldn't have come away before you had.' Socrates sat himself down and said 'It would be a good thing, Agathon, if wisdom were the kind of thing that flowed (ῥεῖν) from what is fuller (ἐκ τοῦ πληρεστέρου) into what is emptier in our case (εἰς τὸ κενώτερον ἡμῶν), if only we touch each other (ἁπτώμεθα ἀλλήλων), like the water in cups which flows from the fuller into the emptier through the thread of wool.' (175c–d)

Agathon's prejudices are typical of a follower of the sophists, since these educators consider that their knowledge can be exchanged on the market place like any kind of goods.[28]

Now, when Socrates exposes the bulk of his theory through the mouth of Diotima, he combines his favourite mode of expression (question and answer), and the methodological choices of his audience (continuous oration). Diotima plays

---

[27] All the following texts and translations of the *Symposium* are from Rowe 1998, with modifications in the translation.
[28] Cf. *Prot.* 313c-d and *Soph.* 224c-e; see Nightingale 1995, pp. 43–9; Nails 2006, p. 196; Brisson 2006, pp. 250–1.

the part of the older Socrates – she is supposed to have brought against her ignorant interlocutor the arguments which Socrates has just put to Agathon:

> 'So it's the account she gave that I'm going to try to describe to all of you, starting from what has been agreed between myself and Agathon (ἐκ τῶν ὡμολογημένων ἐμοὶ καὶ Ἀγάθωνι), and doing it all myself, in whatever way I can manage it. (...) I myself was saying to her other things of pretty much the very sort that Agathon was saying to me just now (ἐγὼ πρὸς αὐτὴν ἕτερα τοιαῦτα ἔλεγον οἷάπερ νῦν πρὸς ἐμὲ Ἀγάθων), that Love was a great god, and was of beautiful things; and she then set about examining me by means of the very arguments I was using with Agathon (ἤλεγχε δή με τούτοις τοῖς λόγοις οἷσπερ ἐγὼ τοῦτον), with the outcome that Love was neither beautiful – by my own account – nor good.' (201d–e)

She first interrogates the young Socrates in a typically Socratic manner, that is to say in the form of *brakhulogia* (201e–207c), as the older Socrates has done up to then with Agathon.[29] Yet, this first section includes a myth (203b–204a) and at the end of the conversation Diotima expounds her doctrine in a long didactic monologue, without the aid of further questioning (207c–212a).[30] Then she adopts the tone of a mystagogue or a schoolmaster who claims to reveal the truth to an ignoramus, as if Socrates could directly seize what *eros* truly is just by listening passively to her speech.[31] Incidentally, Socrates compares her to the sophists at the very moment when she tells him 'εὖ ἴσθι': 'and I said: "Well now, most wise (σοφωτάτη) Diotima: is what you say really true?" Like the accomplished sophists (ὥσπερ οἱ τέλεοι σοφισταί), she said "You can be sure of that (εὖ ἴσθι), Socrates." (208b–c)[32]

To reply to an interlocutor (Agathon) he characterized as the mouthpiece of a great sophist (Gorgias), Socrates reports the lesson of a teacher he compares to the great sophists.[33] And if we remember in addition that mystery religion was

---

[29] Rehn (1996, pp. 82–3) emphasizes this point.
[30] FCC Sheffield (2006a, p. 45) has already noticed that Diotima's myth is a way to compromise with her (and Socrates') audience.
[31] See *Symp.* 204d1–2 (πειράσομαί σε διδάξαι), 206b5–6 (Οὐ μεντᾶν σέ ... ἐθαύμαζον ἐπὶ σοφίᾳ καὶ ἐφοίτων παρὰ σὲ αὐτὰ ταῦτα μαθησόμενος), 207a5 (ἐδίδασκέ με), 207c6–7 (διδασκάλων δέομαι ... μοι λέγε καὶ τούτων τὴν αἰτίαν καὶ τῶν ἄλλων τῶν περὶ τὰ ἐρωτικά).
[32] According to RG Bury (1932, note ad 208c), 'ὥσπερ οἱ τέλεοι σοφισταί' should be translated as 'in true professorial style'. Bury notices that the link between the didactic form of the speech and the characterization of Diotima as a sophist had already been noticed by Wolf (1782), Hommel (1834), Schleiermacher (1807) and Ast (1816). See also Stallbaum 1857, p. 147: 'Ridet sophistas, de quibuslibet rebus ita disputantes, ut videri vellent earum veritatem *prorsus habere perspectam atque exploratam*' (my italics).
[33] In fact, the didactic *form*, not the content, of Diotima's speech is sophistic. As Ruby Blondell reminded me, this didactic mode used by the sophists is not exclusively or intrinsically sophis-

particularly fashionable among the Athenian elite of the time,[34] Diotima, both as a sophist and as a priestess of a mystery cult who tells a myth,[35] is principally the mouthpiece of Socrates' audience. If Socrates deliberately intended to craft an ambivalent character, thanks to whom his mute audience could speak as loudly as himself, it is no accident that Diotima sparks such controversy among scholars.

I.2 Socrates as a young interlocutor

As for the younger Socrates who replies to Diotima, he may be considered for different reasons as a similar hybrid character. Like Agathon in front of the older Socrates, he plays in front of Diotima the role of the student, and when Socrates starts reporting the dialogue, he claims that he had formerly given Diotima the same answers as Agathon (201e3–5).[36] Like Agathon, this younger Socrates is supposed to be around thirty years old.[37] He seems to share with the poet his ignorance about *eros*, since he considers Diotima as the "master of truth"[38] she claims to be, and he describes himself as the ignorant and passive recipient of her knowledge.[39]

However, in his way of discussing, this young man proves to have an attitude towards knowledge which is the opposite of that of Agathon. In a passage formerly quoted, the tragic poet visibly considered Socrates' refutation as an offence, he shamefully admitted defeat and retreated into silence:

---

tic: it is a direct heir of traditional Greek methods of education, which are authoritarian and paternalistic. See Blondell 2002, pp. 95–9.

34 See Strauss 2001, p. 15 and Nails 2006, pp. 202–3. In the days following the party, Phaedrus, Alcibiades, and Acoumenus, the father of Eryximachus, were accused of profaning the Eleusinian mysteries; see Andocides 1.11–16 & 18 and Thucydides 6.28. As Debra Nails (2006, pp. 184–5 & 193) argues against Martha Nussbaum (1986), Plato does not conflate philosophy and mystery religion.

35 After Theon of Smyrna, many commentators have pointed out that Diotima describes the ascent to the divine beauty metaphorically as the successive stages of the initiation rites of a mystery religion (209e-212b). See Dupuis 1892, pp. 21–3; Jaeger 1961, p. 132; Riedweg 1987, pp. xii & 192; Evans 2006.

36 σχεδὸν γάρ τι καὶ ἐγὼ πρὸς αὐτὴν ἕτερα τοιαῦτα ἔλεγον οἷάπερ νῦν πρὸς ἐμέ.

37 Socrates claims to have met Diotima about ten years before the plague that struck Athens in 430 BC. At that time (440) Socrates was about thirty years old, that is to say the age of Agathon at the date of the drinking party (416). See Athenaeus, *Deipn.* 217a; Robin 1929, p. XLV; Sier 2012, p. 55, n. 4; Nails 2002, pp. 8–10.

38 I borrow this phrase from Marcel Detienne (1967).

39 See above, n. 31.

> 'I am unable (οὐκ ἂν δυναίμην), Socrates, to argue against you (σοὶ ἀντιλέγειν),' said Agathon; 'let it be as you say (ἀλλ' οὕτως ἐχέτω ὡς σὺ λέγεις).'
>
> 'No, it's rather the truth (τῇ ἀληθείᾳ), beloved Agathon,' Socrates said, 'that you can't argue with, since there's nothing difficult about arguing against Socrates. And now I'll leave you alone (Καὶ σὲ μέν γε ἤδη ἐάσω).' (201c-d)

Contrary to Agathon, the young Socrates, when refuted by Diotima with the same arguments, proved to be able to reply, even though he did so in a naïve way. He carried on interrogating, and thanks to this active stance, his teacher carried on discussing with him:

> 'And she then set about examining me by means of the very arguments I was using with Agathon, with the outcome that Love was neither beautiful – by my own account – nor good. Then I said "What do you mean Diotima (πῶς λέγεις, ἔφην, ὦ Διοτίμα)? Is Love then ugly and bad?"
>
> 'She said "Take care what you say! (οὐκ εὐφημήσεις;) Or do you suppose that whatever is not beautiful is necessarily ugly?..." (201e)

Afterwards, Socrates didn't stop asking (202a2, d8, e2, 203a9, 204c8, 205b7 etc), objecting (202b6–7, 208b8–9) or expressing reservations (205b3, 206e6). In the presence of Diotima, the young Socrates was obviously motivated by a curiosity and a critical mind that foreshadowed what he was to become, and later proved to be in the discussion with Agathon: a dialectician in love with knowledge, who interrogates over and over. While the young Socrates is characterized as a naive man similar to Agathon, he is endowed, contrary to Agathon, with a "philosophic nature" (ἡ φιλόσοφος φύσις, *Republic* III 410e1).[40] And it is thanks to this active attitude that the young man squeezed out of Diotima her theory about *eros*.

Thus, similarly to Diotima, the young Socrates appears as a mixed character, midway between the grown-up philosopher (Socrates) and his naive addressee (Agathon). While Diotima is the philosopher considered from the poet Agathon's point of view, the young Socrates is the portrait of the poet as a young philosopher.

But why does Socrates express his views through such a dramatic device, that matches the sophistication of a postmodern meta-fiction?

---

[40] Monique Dixsaut (1985, pp. 129–86) demonstrated that the 'philosophic nature' is essentially erotic.

II. The function of Diotima and the reported dialogue: a communication tool.

These preliminary observations may help us to understand the function of the dialogue reported by Socrates, that is, to deliver a lesson in communication besides a lecture on *eros*. This lesson can be divided into three points: thanks to the characters of Diotima and the young Socrates, (1) Plato and Socrates show that they must adapt their lesson to their addressees, (2) they show what value a lesson expounded in the form of a didactic monologue may have and (3) what value a teaching delivered in the form of a reported dialogue may have.

II.1. Adapting to the interlocutor.

By talking through the mask of a priestess and a sophist, Socrates compromises with his interlocutors' viewpoint: he addresses them in a form that gives intelligibility and authority to his theory. By doing so, the dialectician implements the instructions he gives in the *Phaedrus*: a true orator, that is to say a good dialectician,[41] must know the truth about both his subject matter (262c) and the soul of his addressee (269e–272b).[42] When he knows how this soul is likely to be affected, he can administer convincing *logoi* to it as a good doctor adapts his drugs to the bodily constitution of his patient:

> [Socrates:] Since the power of speech is in fact a leading of the soul (ψυχαγωγία), the man who means to be an expert in rhetoric must know (εἰδέναι) how many forms (εἴδη) the soul has. Thus their number is so and so (τόσα καὶ τόσα), and they are of such and such kinds (τοῖα καὶ τοῖα), which is why some people are like this, and others like that; and these having been distinguished in this way, then again there are so many forms of speeches (λόγων αὖ τόσα καὶ τόσα ἔστιν εἴδη), each one of such and such a kind. People of one kind are easily persuaded (εὐπειθεῖς) for one sort of reason by one kind of speech to hold one kind of opinion, while people of another kind are for these reasons difficult to persuade (δυσπειθεῖς). (*Phaedrus* 271c–d, trans. CJ Rowe (2005), modified)[43]

Socrates argues in the *Meno* (75c-76e) that this rule applies to short dialectical exchanges (βραχυλογία) as well as to rhetoric (μακρολογία): to answer dialectically (διαλεκτικώτερον ἀποκρίνεσθαι, 75d5–6) the philosopher may borrow the-

---
41 True rhetoric is equivalent to philosophy (*Phaedr.* 261a4–5) and dialectic (*Phaedr.* 266b3–c1).
42 About both aspects, see Ayache 2002, p. 153.
43 On this passage, see Macé 2006, pp. 159–61. Cf. *Phaedr.* 277b5–c6.

ories from thinkers his interlocutor is prone to believe (in this instance, Gorgias and Empedocles), even if, as a philosopher, he himself strongly disagrees with these views.[44]

This implies that the words of the dialectician are to be read necessarily as a synthesis between his own point of view and his listener's particular set of beliefs. In Plato's dialogues speaking is, as Montaigne puts it, "half his who speaks, and half his who hears"[45]. We may also say that the words of the dialectician have the "dialogical" value Mikhail Bakhtin brought to light in the monologues of Dostoyevsky's heroes[46]: the discourse integrates with the interlocutor's viewpoint it conflicts with. Just like the daemon *Eros*, described by Diotima as an intermediate (μεταξύ) between ignorance and knowledge (202a), the discourse of the dialectician who reports this description, must be regarded not as a wise *logos*, but as a *metaxu* between the knowledge of the dialectician and the point of view of his addressee, who proved to be somewhat ignorant.

There is no alternative to this enunciative strategy. The dialectician who wants to communicate the truth must use language, that is to say a set of images (*Cratylus* 430a–432d), and a good image, a true image, must fit the point of view of the beholder in order to let him catch a glimpse of the truth.[47]

However, while the dialectician is always forced to compromise, he can show that he does so, he can present the discourse he delivers in a form that does not make misleading implicit claim as to the status of this discourse. When Socrates cannot only interrogate, but has to teach in a dogmatic way, he always lets us know that he is not speaking in his own name, and uses "dialogical" mouthpieces who always prove to be in some way the expression of the interlocutors' prej-

---

44 Socrates – 'with friends who wish to converse with each other (ἀλλήλοις διαλέγεσθαι), as in our case, a gentler answer (πρᾳότερόν πως ἀποκρίνεσθαι) is indicated, one more suited to dialectic (διαλεκτικώτερον). It is more dialectical (διαλεκτικώτερον) not only to answer what is true (τἀληθῆ), but to do so in terms which the questioned person further agrees that he knows (δι' ἐκείνων ὧν ἂν προσομολογῇ εἰδέναι ὁ ἐρωτώμενος). So that's how I'll try to answer you.' (...). 'Then would you like me to answer you in the manner of Gorgias (κατὰ Γοργίαν ἀποκρίνωμαι), which would be easier for you to follow (ἀκολουθήσαις)?' (...) Meno – 'Your answer, Socrates, seems to me excellently put.' Socrates – 'No doubt because it is put in a way you're accustomed to (σοὶ κατὰ συνήθειαν εἴρηται). (...) It is an answer in the high poetic style (τραγική), Meno, and so more agreeable to you (ἀρέσκει σοι) than my answer about figure (...) But yet, son of Alexidemus, I myself am convinced the other answer was better (οὐκ ἔστιν ὡς ἐγὼ ἐμαυτὸν πείθω, ἀλλ' ἐκείνη βελτίων)'. (*Meno* 75d-76e)
45 "La parole est moitié à celuy qui parle, moitié à celuy qui l'escoute." Montaigne, *Essais*, 3. 13.
46 Bakhtin 1984. For a definition of dialogism, see Bres 2005, pp. 47–62.
47 On the inescapability of mimetic language, see Kosman 1992, pp. 91–2 and Sayre 1992, p. 231. On the adaptation to the audience in Plato's dialogues, see Robb 1997, p. 31; Wolfsdorf 2004, pp. 31–7; Hobbs 2006, pp. 258 & 267.

udices on the subject. Since all Socrates' interlocutors are typical examples of the assumed readers of Plato's dialogues – that is to say ordinary ladies and gentlemen, well-off Athenians who received a good but not a philosophical education[48] – this strategy of explicit adaptation is designed to warn both the audience and the readers against their own prejudices.

II.2. Limits and good usage of a didactic monologue

One of these prejudices is to assume like Agathon that one could become wise about matters of *eros* by merely hearing or reading Diotima's didactic monologue. Such an assumption fits the natural expectation of any listener or any reader. Yet, it contradicts not only Socrates' habits, as seen before, but the model of communication delivered by Diotima herself through her theory of love. Indeed, according to this theory, the process of learning requires an active and autonomous learner: the soul gives birth itself to its own wisdom when it comes across a beautiful person, a beautiful branch of knowledge or beauty itself, and not by learning a lesson from an outside authority:

> [DI. –] "All human beings, Socrates, are pregnant (κυοῦσιν), both in body and in soul, and when we come to be of the right age, we naturally desire to give birth (τίκτειν ἐπιθυμεῖ). We cannot do it in what is ugly, but we can in what is beautiful. (...) If ever what is pregnant approaches something beautiful (καλῷ προσπελάζῃ), it becomes gracious, melts with joy, and gives birth and procreates; but when it approaches what is ugly, it contracts, frowning with pain, turns away, curls up, and fails to procreate, retaining what it has conceived, and suffering because of it. This is why what is pregnant and already full to bursting feels the great excitement it does in proximity to the beautiful, because of the fact that the beautiful person frees it from great pain. For, Socrates," she said, "love is not, as you think, of the beautiful.
> [SO. –] Well, then what is it of?
> [DI. –] Of procreation and giving birth in the beautiful (Τῆς γεννήσεως καὶ τοῦ τόκου ἐν τῷ καλῷ)." (*Symposium* 206c–e)

And further:

> "For in fact", she said, "there are those who are pregnant in their souls still more than in their bodies, with things that it is fitting for the soul to conceive and to bring to birth. What then are these things that are fitting? Wisdom and the rest of virtue (φρόνησίν τε καὶ τὴν ἄλλην ἀρετήν). (...) When someone is pregnant with these things in his soul, from youth on, by divine gift, and with the coming of the right age, desires to give birth and procreate (τίκ-

---

[48] See Bury 1932, p. LVII; Rowe 1998, p. 9; Sheffield 2006b, p. 23.

τειν τε καὶ γεννᾶν ἤδη ἐπιθυμῇ), then I imagine he too goes round looking for the beautiful object in which he might procreate; for he will never do so in what is ugly." (209a–b)

In order to become wise, one must be previously pregnant with wisdom and crave to give birth to it. In other words, one cannot acquire knowledge of anything without being primarily in love with this knowledge. Thus, if a student wants to draw any knowledge of love from a theoretical description similar to that of Diotima, he or she must know love primarily in an empirical way: he or she must be in love with the knowledge of love. And since the very knowledge of love is empirical, the very efficacy of Diotima's theoretical account can only consist in fostering this empirical knowledge already present in the soul of the interlocutor.[49]

Since Socrates declares that, thanks to Diotima, he has become "expert in matters of love alone" (οὐδέν φημι ἄλλο ἐπίστασθαι ἢ τὰ ἐρωτικά, 177d7–8)[50] we must consider that, in spite of appearances, despite his modest confession ("I didn't know anything") and Diotima's claim ("I will teach you everything"), the young man already carried in his soul, even unconsciously, this empirical knowledge of *eros*. This implies also that Diotima and her lesson, in the manner of a beautiful person and a *kalos logos* (210d5), were the cause, but not the source of Socrates' knowledge: Diotima's discourse was for Socrates a chance to give birth to a science already embryonically present in his soul.

This interpretation of Diotima's lesson, and of the way Socrates supposedly benefited from it, may look over-subtle, but it is the only way to align straightforwardly what Socrates and Diotima claim to be with the theory of knowledge they champion.

Moreover, this reading is supported by the literary device through which Socrates delivers his lesson: the reported dialogue. By putting the theory into the mouth of a suspicious sophist who lectures on *eros* as a master of truth, that is to say in a most un-erotic manner, Socrates and Plato mean the passive recipients of this lesson (Agathon and the reader) not to adopt Diotima's views uncritically as theirs, and not to rely exclusively on her speech if they want to acquire a full knowledge of *eros*.

---

[49] Commentators have already pointed out that Diotima's discourse as such cannot convey true philosophical knowledge, that is, knowledge of the forms: see Rosen 1968, pp. 256 & 264; Nails 2006, p. 184; Scott & Welton 2008, pp. 156–7; Belfiore 2012, pp. 145–6; Wildberger 2012, pp. 30–2. On the empirical nature of a genuine knowledge of love, see Scott & Welton 2000, p. 152, n. 8.
[50] See also 201d5 (ἣ δὴ καὶ ἐμὲ τὰ ἐρωτικὰ ἐδίδαξεν) and 207a5 (Ταῦτά τε οὖν πάντα ἐδίδασκέ με).

On the other hand, by representing this priestess teaching the young Socrates, and not Agathon, Socrates and Plato lead us to understand which kind of interlocutor is likely to benefit from this teaching and to achieve full erotic knowledge. The audience listening to or reading Diotima's lesson know Socrates as a grown-up philosopher and can guess from what Socrates has turned out to be the very nature of his science about *eros*, which he claims to have drawn out from Diotima. Indeed, after meeting the lecturing priestess, Socrates did not become a priest himself, nor a schoolmaster devoted to rote learning and repeating factual truths, about *eros* or any other subject-matter. He did not become a theoretician of love but, above all, a practitioner of the love of knowledge, "a lover (ἐραστής) of the processes of division and bringing together" (*Phaedrus* 266b3–5),[51] a man passionately involved in the infinite quest for truth who calls into question others' certainties in order to communicate to them the *eros* of knowledge, rather than the theoretical knowledge of *eros*. As Diotima herself says, *Eros* in its very nature is not a god and as such is not beautiful, since he is a desiring agent, the lover and not the object of love, the instrument and not the aim of the search for divine forms, especially the form of beauty (204c4–5).[52] Hence, there is no cause for postulating the existence of any Idea of love, similar to the Idea of good or virtue,[53] and this explains why the best theoretical account Socrates can give of *eros* is a mythical description delivered through the mouth of a priestess (203b–204a), a *mûthos* that can convey no more than an *orthê doxa*.

Now, although the young Socrates appeared to totally lack this theoretical knowledge of love, he proved, in front of Diotima, that he already knew love in an empirical way: as he questioned Diotima, he acted, contrary to Agathon, as a budding philosopher.

We can infer from all these elements that the real virtue of Diotima's lecture was to be a beautiful rather than a true *logos*.[54] This *kalos logos* helped Socrates to recognize the value of the desire for knowledge he carried within his soul, and to devote this desire to the search for the essences. Thanks to Diotima, Socrates gave birth to his own science of *eros*, that is to say his διαλεκτικὴ τέχνη (*Phaedrus* 276e5). This ancillary value of Diotima's speech is perfectly consistent, on the reader's part, with the function Socrates grants to the books in the *Phaedrus*:

---

51 Τούτων δὴ ἔγωγε αὐτός τε ἐραστής, ὦ Φαῖδρε, τῶν διαιρέσεων καὶ συναγωγῶν, ἵνα οἷός τε ὦ λέγειν τε καὶ φρονεῖν. On this passage, see Macé 2010, p. 73.
52 See also *Rep.* V 476c-477b, 478c–480a.
53 See Rosen 1968, p. 210; Sheffield 2006b, p. 44; Borges de Araújo 2012, p. 27.
54 By the way, as he congratulates Diotima on her myth, he doesn't say "ὀρθῶς" or "ἀληθῆ λέγεις" but "καλῶς γὰρ λέγεις" (204c7).

written words must be used as mere reminders (ὑπομνήματα, 276d3) for a person who already knows.[55]

Therefore, the complex embedded dialogue form used by Socrates and Plato in the *Symposium* cannot be considered as a mere vehicle for the conveyance of Socratic or Platonic theory of love. The literary feature is integral to the theory in three respects: it prevents the reader from misunderstanding (1) the nature of Socrates' wisdom about love (it is an empirical, rather than a theoretical knowledge), (2) the nature of love itself (it is an active force striving for knowledge rather than a passive object of knowledge) and (3) the nature of any good teaching on love (one must communicate the *eros* of knowledge rather than the knowledge of *eros*).

Furthermore, the embedded dialogue shows that the effectiveness of the lesson depends on the philosophical nature of its addressee, and on the use this addressee is willing to make of it. At this point, we encounter once again Montaigne's view that speaking is a shared experience: Plato's dialogues show not only that a lesson makes sense if it compromises with the point of view of the addressee, as seen above, but also that this lesson is efficient, and even true, iff the addressee uses it correctly.[56] In this respect, the sophistic nature of Diotima's speech is relative to the nature and the attitude of her public. This is why the priestess is only compared to, and not plainly identified with, the sophists.[57] Diotima is a sophist insofar as her lesson meets a public as passive and complacent as the pupils of the sophists.

II.3. The virtue of dialogue

To conclude, Socrates enunciative practice can be considered as the demonstration of the advantage of reporting dialogues rather than addressing an audience in one's own name. This may provide important clues to Plato's literary practice.

Staging in front of Agathon an image of himself dressed up as a dialectician, Socrates encourages him to get right into the part, to identify himself with the young Socrates, that is, to awaken from his shameful muteness and go on discussing with Socrates. The dialogue reported by Socrates has the same function as the discussion carried on with the young slave in front of Meno (*Meno* 82b–85b): it is a methodological parenthesis, a metacommunication sequence – Gregory

---

[55] See also *Phaedr.* 275c5-d2 & 278a1. Cf. Sayre 1992, p. 231.
[56] This view is close, albeit not identical, to Wittgenstein's second theory of language (Wittgenstein 1953, p. 43: "Die Bedeutung eines Wortes ist sein Gebrauch in der Sprache.")
[57] ὥσπερ οἱ τέλεοι σοφισταί, 208c1.

Bateson would call it a metalogue[58] – whose purpose is to help Socrates' main interlocutor (Meno or Agathon) to go beyond *aporia*, and convince him that he can and must become active again in order to find the truth by himself. Therefore, we can consider that Socrates intends to affect Agathon in the way he was himself affected by Diotima's didactic monologue, and to communicate the *eros* of knowledge rather than the knowledge of *eros*.

Yet, in the presence of an interlocutor whose philosophical *eros* proved to be completely dormant, Socrates cannot use a mere didactic monologue, for the admirer of Gorgias would take it at face value as a sophistic lesson. To stir up his interlocutor, Socrates embeds the monologue in a dialogue that is both a critical and a protreptic tool. As Socrates emphasizes in his concluding words, his own purpose is less to teach than to urge his audience to honour *eros* in the form he described it, that is, as a desire for knowledge. His purpose is to lead his audience, particularly Agathon, towards philosophical inquiry:

> 'since I am persuaded (πεπεισμένος), I try (πειρῶμαι) to persuade (πείθειν) everyone else too that for acquiring this possession[59] one couldn't easily get a better co-worker (συνεργὸν) with human nature than Love is. That's why I declare that everyone must honour (τιμᾶν) Love, and I myself honour (τιμῶ) what belongs to him and practise it (ἀσκῶ) more than anyone, and call on everyone else to do so (καὶ τοῖς ἄλλοις παρακελεύομαι), and both now and always I eulogize the power and courage of Love to the best of my ability.' (212b)

The result of this method is provisionally positive: like Meno, Agathon after the "metalogue" takes up discussing with Socrates again and until the end of the night (221d–223d). But as in the *Meno* this positive result is a flash in the pan: thanks to the distancing function of the narrative, the reader, by hindsight, is aware that for lack of serious philosophical education and practice Agathon will spend his last years not as a dialectician interrogating himself and his fellow citizens about virtue and justice, but as a poet in exile singing the praises of a tyrant.[60] As in many dialogues, the discussion between Socrates and his contemporaries is full of promise but proves to be, in the long run, a complete educational failure.[61]

---

58 According to G Bateson (1972, p. 21) "A metalogue is a conversation about some problematic subject. This conversation should be such that not only do the participants discuss the problem but the structure of the conversation as a whole is also relevant to the same."
59 That is, the contemplation of the idea of beauty.
60 Archelaus of Macedonia. See Brisson 1998, p. 25 and Nails 2006, p. 205. On the retrospective irony created by the elaborate process of transmission, see Halperin 1992, p. 100.
61 See Whitlock-Blundell 1992, p. 133 & 171.

Therefore, the actual effectiveness of Socrates' method must not be merely considered at the level of the oral exchange between Socrates and his interlocutor, but at the level of the literary communication between Plato and his readers. While the young Socrates is a double of Agathon, both Agathon and the young Socrates are doubles of the reader, since they are two kinds of addressee of the lesson about *eros*.[62] To use a concept investigated by Umberto Eco, we could say that each character is a *lector in fabula*[63]: Agathon, as a passive recipient and a typical product of the traditional education, is the reader's most obvious double; Socrates as the double of this double, is a more indirect image. But since the reader can compare the opposite attitudes of these two images of himself, he is prompted to distance himself from his obvious double, and to identify rather with Socrates. Thus, Socrates may be considered as a portrait of the reader – as well as of Agathon – as a young dialectician. While Agathon is called to leave his passive position of hearer, the reader is indirectly prodded into leaving the book he or she is currently reading in order to practise philosophy. Like the dialogue reported by Socrates, the dialogue written by Plato intends to transmit both the theoretical knowledge of *eros* and the *eros* of knowledge,[64] by engaging his addressee in a complex process of mimetic pedagogy, a "play of character" already studied by Ruby Blondell.[65]

This erotic purpose and this call to identification is not by any means the only common point between Socrates' and Plato's practices of the reported dialogue. Just as Socrates makes known those to whom Diotima's theory is addressed, Plato, before having the dialectician speak, always makes his audience speak. By characterizing this audience dramatically and stylistically, he shows with what characters and beliefs the dialectician is going to compromise. In the *Symposium*, this may explain the function of the first speeches delivered about *eros*, from Phaedrus to Agathon, an issue that still sparks controversy among scholars.[66] In my view, one function of these discourses – though not the only one – is to show whom Socrates is going to address and to adapt to.

---

[62] On the dialogues' portraying Plato's intended readership, see Gordon 1996, pp. 259–78; Wolfsdorf 2004, p. 30; Reeve 2006, p. 138.

[63] Cf. Eco 1979.

[64] This conclusion is similar to that of David Halperin (1992, p. 119–29), but my point is quite different: according to Halperin, the *eros* communicated by the dialogue is a hermeneutic desire to understand a literary text, not a philosophical desire to search after the essences; in addition, this desire is supposed to be stimulated by the insoluble contradictions of the text, not, as I consider, through a precise mimetic strategy of identification.

[65] See Blondell 2002, pp. 39, 46–8, 80–94.

[66] See Rowe 2006, p. 21 and Sheffield 2006b, p. 24.

Furthermore, in order to make it plain that the dialectician's discourse is adapted and belongs to the listener as well as to the speaker, Plato lets his favourite mouthpiece (Socrates) either interrogate his audience or act as a performer who, when he undertakes to expound a theory, never does it in his own person, but uses such dialogical masks as the character of Diotima. In this way, he shows that he adapts to his audience and that, in spite of appearances, he still makes his audience speak. The character of Socrates is used by Plato as the character of Diotima is used by Socrates: as a way of showing that his discourse is addressed to an audience and that the expression of his knowledge is relative to the enunciative situation. This is why Socrates may be considered as a mouthpiece for the author but cannot be confused with him: Socrates is not merely Plato, but a figure of Plato expressing himself within a given enunciative context, and explicitly adapting his discourse to a definite audience.[67] Whereas Socrates interlocutors are *lectores in fabula* whose function is to show us how we are expected to read, Socrates, although he is talking, can be viewed as a *scriptor in fabula* whose function is to show how Plato writes.

If this interpretation is correct, Socrates' discourse must always be considered as ironical and always requires a critical reader who takes into account the literary characteristics of the dialogical framework, even when and especially when, this discourse appears to be delivered in a dogmatic way.

However, this interpretation implies at the same time that Platonic and Socratic irony must not be considered, as they are traditionally, as a way of concealing anything.[68] In Plato, irony is rather a means of exhibiting what kind of enunciative strategy the dialectician has to implement when he expresses himself. In Plato, the purpose of the ironist is far from misleading anyone: irony aims to prevent the audience from any kind of misunderstanding about the way they must listen to or read the discourses of the philosopher.[69]

---

[67] As LA Kosman (1992, p. 75) puts it, one should discuss Platonic ventriloquy rather than Platonic silence: "the ventriloquy we call drama, or more generally, literature: not the simple renunciation of or withdrawal from speech, but the *displacement* of speech, its *projection* into a created other."

[68] In this respect, I do not follow the esoteric interpretation of the Milan-Tübingen school.

[69] See Wildberger 2012, p. 33: "Ebenso (...) zielt wahre Sokrates-Rezeption nicht auf Sokrates selbst, sondern auf das Gebären in Sokrates. Das gleiche gilt natürlich auch für Platon-Rezeption. *Wer immer nur Leser bleibt, hat verloren.*" (my italics). See also Reeve 2006, p. 138.

Works Cited

Allen, RE 1984, *The Dialogues of Plato*, I, Yale University Press, New Haven.
— 1991, *The Dialogues of Plato*, II, Yale University Press, New Haven.
Anton, JP 1974, 'The Secret of Plato's *Symposium*', *Southern Journal of Philosophy* 12, pp. 277–93.
Ast, F 1816, *Platons Leben und Schriften*, Weidmann, Leipzig.
Ayache, L 2002, 'Hippocrate, l'ultime recours contre Socrate (*Phèdre*, 270c)', in Dixsaut, M & Brancacci, A (eds), *Platon source des présocratiques. Exploration*, Vrin, Paris, pp. 151–167.
Bakhtin, M 1984 [1963], *Problems of Dostoyevsky's Poetics*, ed. & trans. C Emerson, University of Minnesota Press, Minneapolis.
Bateson, G 1972, *Steps to an Ecology of Mind*, University of Chicago Press, Chicago.
Belfiore, E 2012, *Socrates' Daimonic Art: Love for Wisdom in Four Platonic Dialogues*, Cambridge University Press, Cambridge.
Borges de Araújo, A Jr. & Cornelli, G (eds) 2012, *Il Simposio di Platone: un banchetto di interpretazioni*, Loffredo, Napoli.
Borges de Araújo, A Jr 2012, 'Eros: direzione e effetti', in A Borges de Araújo Jr & G Cornelli (eds) 2012, pp. 15–31.
Blondell, R 2002, *The Play of Character in Plato's Dialogues*, Cambridge University Press, Cambridge.
Bres, J 2005, 'Savoir de quoi on parle : dialogue, dialogal, dialogique ; dialogisme, polyphonie...', in J Bres, PP Haillet, S Mellet, H Nølke & L Rosier (eds), *Dialogisme et polyphonie. Approches linguistiques. Actes du colloque de Cerisy*, Bruxelles, 2005, pp. 47–62.
Brisson, L 1998, *Platon, Le Banquet*, GF-Flammarion, Paris.
— 2006, 'Agathon, Pausanias, and Diotima in Plato's *Symposium*: Paiderastia and Philosophia', in J Lesher, D Nails & FCC Sheffield 2006, pp. 229–51.
Bury, RG 1932, *The Symposium of Plato*, 2nd edn, Heffer, Cambridge.
Cavarero, A 1995, *In Spite of Plato: A Feminist Rewriting of Ancient Philosophy*, Routledge, New York.
Cornford, FM 1950, 'The Doctrine of Eros in Plato's *Symposium*', in FM Cornford, *The Unwritten Philosophy and Other Essays*, Cambridge University Press, Cambridge.
Corrigan, K & Glazov-Corrigan, E 2004, *Plato's Dialectic at Play: Argument, Structure, and Myth in the* Symposium, Pennsylvania State University Press, University Park.
De Luise, F 2012, 'Il sapere di Diotima e la coscienza di Socrate. Note sul ritratto del filosofo da giovane', in A Borges de Araújo Jr & G Cornelli (eds) 2012, pp. 115–38.
Detienne, M 1967, *Les Maîtres de vérité dans la Grèce archaïque*, Maspero, Paris.
Dixsaut, M 1985, *Le Naturel philosophe. Essai sur les Dialogues de Platon*, Vrin, Paris.
— 2001, *Métamorphoses de la dialectique dans les dialogues de Platon*, Vrin, Paris.
— 2013, 'Macrology and digression', in G Boys-Stones, D El Murr & C Gill (eds), *The Platonic Art of Philosophy*, Cambridge University Press, Cambridge, pp. 10–27.
Dover, KJ 1980, *Plato: Symposium*, Cambridge University Press, Cambridge.
Dupuis, J 1892, *Théon de Smyrne. Exposition des connaissances mathématiques utiles pour la lecture de Platon*, Hachette, Paris.

Eco, U 1979, *Lector in fabula. La cooperazione interpretativa nei testi narrativi*, Bompiani, Milano.
Erde, EL 1976, 'Comedy and Tragedy and Philosophy in the *Symposium:* An Ethical Vision', *Southwestern Journal of Philosophy* 7, pp. 161–7.
Erler, M 2003, 'To Hear the Right Thing and to Miss the Point: Plato's Implicit Poetics', in AN Michelini (ed), *Plato as Author. The Rhetoric of Philosophy*, Brill, Leiden & Boston, pp. 157–73.
Evans, N 2006, 'Diotima and Demeter as Mystagogues in Plato's *Symposium*', *Hypatia*, vol. 21, n. 2, pp. 1–27.
Ficino, M 2002 [1469], *Commentarium in convivium Platonis*, ed. & trans. P Laurens, Les Belles Lettres, Paris.
Fierro, MA 2003, *Plato's Theory of Desire in the 'Symposium' and the 'Republic'*, Durham Theses online, < http://etheses.dur.ac.uk/4110/>
Frede, D 1993, 'Out of the Cave: What Socrates Learned from Diotima', in RM Rosen & J Farrel (eds), *Nomodeiktes, Greek Studies in Honor of Martin Ostwald*, University of Michigan Press, Ann Arbor, pp. 397–422.
— 2012, 'Die Rede des Sokrates: Eros als Verlangen nach Unsterblichkeit (204c7–209e4)', in C Horn 2012a, pp. 141–57.
Frede, M 1992, 'Plato's Arguments and the Dialogue Form', in JC Klagge & ND Smith 1992, pp. 201–19.
Friedländer, P 1964, *Platon*, I, de Gruyter, Berlin-Leipzig.
Gold, BK 1980, 'A question of Genre: Plato's *Symposium* as Novel', *Modern Language Notes* 95, pp. 1353–9.
Gordon, J 1996, 'Dialectic, Dialogue, and Transformation of the Self', *Philosophy & Rhetoric*, vol. 29, n. 3, pp. 259–78.
Hackforth, R 1950, 'Immortality in Plato's *Symposium*', *Classical Review*, vol. 64, n. 2, pp. 43–5.
Halperin, DM 1985, 'Platonic Eros and what Men Call Love', *Ancient Philosophy* 5, pp. 161–204.
— 1990, 'Why is Diotima a Woman', in D Halperin, *One hundred Years of Homosexuality and Other Essays on Greek Love*, Routledge, New York & London, pp. 113–51.
— 1992, 'Plato and the Erotics of Narrativity', in JC Klagge & ND Smith 1992, pp. 93–129.
Hermann, KF 1839, *Geschichte und System der platonischen Philosophie*, Winter, Heidelberg.
Hobbs, A 2006, 'Female Imagery in Plato', in J Lesher, D Nails & FCC Sheffield 2006, pp. 252–71.
Hommel, A 1834, *Platonis convivium*, Fleischer, Leipzig.
Horn, C 2012a (ed), *Platon: Symposion*, Akademie Verlag, Berlin.
— 2012b, 'Enthält das *Symposion*, Platons Theorie der Liebe?', in C Horn 2012a, pp. 1–16.
Jaeger, W 1961, *Early Greek Christianity and Greek Paideia*, Belknap Press of Harvard University Press, Cambridge.
Klagge, JC & Smith, ND (eds) 1992, *Methods of Interpreting Plato and His Dialogues*, Clarendon Press, Oxford.
Kosman, LA 1992, 'Silence and Imitation in the Platonic Dialogues', in JC Klagge & ND Smith 1992, pp. 73–92.
Kranz, W 1958, 'Platonica', *Philologus* 102, pp. 74–83.

Leitao, DD 2012, *The Pregnant Male as Myth and Metaphor in Classical Greek Literature*, Cambridge University Press, Cambridge & New York.
Lesher, J, Nails, D & Sheffield, FCC (eds) 2006, *Plato's* Symposium. *Issues in Interpretation and Reception*, Center for Hellenic Studies, Washington, DC.
Lesley, A 1992, 'The Politics of Pleasure: Female Sexual Appetite in the Hippocratic Corpus', *Helios* 19, pp. 72–91.
Longo, A 2007, *L'art du questionnement et les interrogations fictives chez Platon*, trans. A Lernould, Mimesis, Milan.
Luce, JV 1952, 'Immortality in Plato's *Symposium*: A Reply', *Classical Review* 66, pp. 137–41.
Macé, A 2006, *Platon, philosophie de l'agir et du pâtir*, Academia, Sankt Augustin.
– 2010, *L'Atelier de l'invisible. Apprendre à philosopher avec Platon*, Ère, Alfortville.
McPherran, ML 2006, 'Medicine, Magic, and Religion in Plato's *Symposium*', in J Lesher, D Nails & FCC Sheffield 2006, pp. 71–95.
Nails, D 2002, *The People of Plato. A Prosopography of Plato and other Socratics*, Hackett, Indianapolis & Cambridge.
– 2006, 'Tragedy Off-Stage', in J Lesher, D Nails & FCC Sheffield 2006, pp. 179–207.
Neumann, H 1965, 'Diotima's Concept of Love', *The American Journal of Philology*, vol. 86, n. 1, pp. 33–59.
Nightingale, AW 1993, 'The Folly of Praise: Plato's Critique of Encomiastic Discourse in the *Lysis* and the *Symposium*', *Classical Quarterly* 43, pp. 112–30.
– 1995, *Genres in dialogue. Plato and the Construct of Philosophy*, Cambridge University Press, Cambridge.
Nussbaum, M 1979, 'The speech of Alcibiades: A reading of Plato's *Symposium*', *Philosophy and Literature*, vol. 3, n. 2, pp. 131–72.
– 1986, *The fragility of goodness. Luck and ethics in Greek tragedy and philosophy*, Cambridge University Press, Cambridge.
Reeve, CDC 2004, 'Sôkratês Erôtikos', in Karasmanis, V (ed), *Socrates: 2400 Years Since His Death*, European Cultural Centre of Delphi, Athens-Delphi, pp. 94–106.
– 2006, 'A Study in Violets: Alcibiades in the *Symposium*', in J Lesher, D Nails & FCC Sheffield 2006, pp. 124–46.
Rehn, R 1996, 'Der entzauberte Eros: *Symposion*', in T Kobusch & B Mojsisch (eds), *Platon: Seine Dialoge in der Sicht neuer Forschungen*, Wissenschaftliche Buchgesellschaft, Darmstadt, pp. 81–95.
Riedweg, C 1987, *Mysterienterminologie bei Platon, Philon, und Klemens von Alexandrien, Untersuchungen zur antiken Literatur und Geschichte* 26, de Gruyter, Berlin & New York.
Robb, K 1997, 'Orality, literacy and the dialogue form', in RE Hart & V Tejera, *Plato's Dialogues: The Dialogical Approach*, Edwin Mellen Press, Lewiston, NY, pp. 29–64.
Robin, L 1929, *Platon, Le Banquet*, Les Belles Lettres, Paris.
Rosen, S 1968, *Plato's Symposium*, Yale University Press, New Haven.
Rowe, CJ 1998, *Plato: Symposium*, Aris & Phillips, Warminster.
– 1999, 'Socrates and Diotima : Eros, Immortality, and Creativity', in JJ Cleary and GM Gurtler (eds), *Proceedings of the Boston Area Colloquium in Ancient Philosophy* 14, Brill, Leiden, Boston & Köln, pp. 239–59.
– 2005, *Plato: Phaedrus*, Harmondsworth, Penguin.
– 2006, 'The *Symposium* as a Socratic Dialogue', in J Lesher, D Nails & FCC Sheffield 2006, pp. 9–22.

Rutherford, RB 1995, *The Art of Plato*, Duckworth, London.
Sampson, K 2013, 'The Philosophical Significance of the Figure of Diotima', *Norsk filosofisk tidsskrift*, vol. 48, n. 1, pp. 100–11.
Saxonhouse, AW 1984, 'Eros and the Female in Greek Political Thought: An Interpretation of Plato's *Symposium*', *Political Theory* 5, pp. 5–27.
Sayre, K 1992, 'A Maieutic View of Five Late Dialogues', in JC Klagge & ND Smith 1992, pp. 221–43.
Schleiermacher, F 1807, *Platons Werke*, II, Reimer, Berlin.
Scott, GA. & Welton, WA 2000, 'Eros as Messenger in Diotima's Teaching', in GA Press (ed), *Who Speaks for Plato ? Studies in Platonic Anonymity*, Rowman & Littlefield, Lanham, MD, pp. 147–59.
— 2008, *Erotic Wisdom: Philosophy and Intermediacy In Plato's 'Symposium'*, State University of New York Press, Albany, NY.
Sheffield, FCC 2006a, *Plato's Symposium: The Ethics of Desire*, Oxford University Press, Oxford.
— 2006b, 'The Role of the Earlier Speeches in the *Symposium*: Plato's Endoxic Method?', in J Lesher, D Nails & FCC Sheffield 2006, pp. 23–46.
— 2012, '*Symposium* 201d1–204c6', in C Horn 2012a, pp. 125–140.
Sier, K 1997, *Die Rede der Diotima. Untersuchungen zum Platonischen 'Symposion'*, Beiträge zur Altertumskunde 86, Teubner, Stuttgart & Leipzig.
— 2012, 'Die Rede des Pausanias (180c1–185c3)', in C Horn 2012, pp. 53–69.
Stallbaum, G 1857, *Platonis opera omnia*, Hennings, Gotha-Erfurt.
Strauss, L 2001, *On Plato's Symposium*, Chicago & London, University of Chicago Press.
Taylor, AE 1949, *Plato the Man and His Work*, 6th edn, Methuen, London.
Vlastos, G 1981 [1969], 'The Individual as an Object of Love', in G Vlastos (ed), *Platonic Studies*, Princeton University Press, Princeton, NJ, pp. 1–34.
Waithe, ME 1987, 'Diotima of Mantinea' in ME Waithe (ed), *A History of Women Philosophers*, I, Martinus Nijhoff, Dordrecht & Boston.
Wersinger, AG 2012, 'La voix d'une 'savante': Diotime de Mantinée dans le *Banquet* de Platon (201d-212b)', *Cahiers 'Mondes anciens'* online, vol. 3, retrieved 13 july 2012, <http://mondesanciens.revues.org/index816.html>
— 2013, 'Diotima and *kuèsis* in the Light of the Myths of the God's Annexation of Pregnancy', in *Proceedings of the X Symposium Platonicum : 'The Symposium'*, Pisa, 15–20 July 2013, p. 134–10.
Wider, K 1986, 'Women philosophers in the Ancient Greek World : Donning the Mantle', *Hypatia*, vol. 1, n. 1, pp. 21–62.
Wilamowitz-Moellendorff, U von 1919, *Platon I*, Weidmann, Berlin.
Wildberger, J 2012, 'Die komplexe Anlage von Vorgespräch und Rahmenhandlung und andere literarisch-formale Aspekte des *Symposion* (172a1–178a5)', in C Horn 2012, pp. 17–34.
Wippern, J 1965, 'Erôs und Unsterblichkeit in der Diotima-Rede des *Symposions*', in H Flashar und K Gaiser (eds), *Festgabe für W Schadewalt*, Neske, Pfullingen, pp. 123–9.
Whitlock-Blundell, M 1992, 'Character and Meaning in Plato's *Hippias Minor*', in JC Klagge & ND Smith 1992, pp. 131–72.
Wittgenstein, L 1953, *Philosophische Untersuchungen*, Basil Blackwell, Oxford.
Wolf, FA 1782, *Platons 'Gastmahl': ein Dialog*, Schwickert, Leipzig.

Wolfsdorf, D 2004, 'Interpreting Plato's early dialogues', in D Sedley (ed), *Oxford Studies in Ancient Philosophy* 24, Oxford, pp. 15–40.
Woodbridge, FJE 1929, *The Son of Apollo*, Houghton Mifflin Company, Boston-New-York.

Contributors

Esteban Bieda received his Doctorate in Philosophy (Ph.D.) from the University of Buenos Aires. He is a researcher at the Consejo Nacional de Investigaciones Científicas y Técnicas (CONICET) and Professor of the History of Ancient Philosophy and Classical Greek in the Faculty of Philosophy and Letters at the University of Buenos Aires and the University of San Martin. Among his recent publications are *Aristóteles y la tragedia* (Buenos Aires, Altamira, 2008), and *Platón. Apología de Sócrates – Critón* (Buenos Aires, Winograd, 2014. Bilingual edition, with Introduction, Translation, Notes and an edition of the Greek Text). He is editor, in collaboration, of the volumes, *Expresar la phýsis. Conceptualizaciones antiguas sobre la naturaleza* (Buenos Aires, UNSAM Edita, 2013), and *Diálogos interepocales. Confluencias y divergencias entre la filosofía antigua y la contemporánea*, (Buenos Aires, Rhesis, 2014). He is also author of numerous articles on philosophy and classical Greek culture.

Marcelo D. Boeri is Professor of Ancient Philosophy at Universidad Alberto Hurtado (Philosophy Department, Chile). He has been Assistant Professor in the Departments of Classical Letters and Philosophy at the Universidad de Buenos Aires, Fellow at the National Council for Scientific and Technological Research (CONICET, Argentina). After receiving his Ph.D. in philosophy from the University of Salvador (Argentina), he was appointed Associate and Independent Researcher (1996–2003) at CONICET. He has been visiting researcher at Georgetown University (1994–95), Junior Fellow at Harvard's Center for Hellenic Studies (1999–2000), Brown University (2009), and Fellow of the John Simon Guggenheim Foundation (2008–2009). He has served as co-editor of *Méthexis: International Journal for Ancient Philosophy* (1999–2008); since 2007 he is a member of the Editorial Board of the International Plato Studies (IPS). He has published books, papers, and critical reviews (both in Spanish and English) on Plato, Aristotle, and the Stoics.

Beatriz Bossi is Associate Professor of Ancient Philosophy at the Universidad Complutense de Madrid and Associate Researcher for the Scientific and Technological Council of Argentina (1980–1995). Among her publications are *Virtud y Conocimiento en Platón y Aristóteles* (2000); *Saber Gozar: Estudios sobre el Placer en Platón* (2008). She is author of more than forty articles on Greek philosophy to publications in Argentina, Chile, USA, Ireland, Germany, Italy and Spain.

Franciso Bravo received his Doctorate in Philosophy from the University of Paris (Sorbonne). He is Professor at the Central University of Venezuela (UCV), where he is Director of the Center for Classical Studies (CECLA). He is a member of the International Institute of Philosophy (Paris), and Co-President of the International Plato Society. His recent publications include *Ética y Razón*, Caracas, 2a. ed., 2009, and *Las ambigüedades del placer. Ensayo sobre el placer en la filosofía de Platón*, Sankt Augustin, Academia Verlag, 2003. Trad. portuguesa, Ed. Paulus, 2009.

Álvaro Vallejo Campos is Professor of Ancient Philosophy at the University of Granada (Spain), where he has been teaching since 1992. His courses and main published work has been in ancient Greek philosophy. He has written books on Plato (*Mito y Persuasión en Platón; Platón, el Filósofo de Atenas*) and Aristotle (*Aristóteles: Fragmentos*) and published articles and essays concerning the Sophists as well as different aspects of Platonic dialogues, and on the reception of Greek philosophy by contemporary authors (Nietzsche, Heidegger, Gadamer, Berlin). He has translated into Spanish Plato's *Theatetus* and the fragments of Aristotle's lost works (Biblioteca Clásica Gredos).

Gabriele Cornelli is associate professor of Ancient Philosophy at Universidade de Brasília, Brazil. Coordinator of the Archai UNESCO Chair since 2001, former President of the Brazilian Classical Studies Society and now President of the International Plato Society. Among his publications are *In Search of Pythagoreanism* (DeGruyter, 2013), *On Pythagoreanism* (DeGruyter, 2013) and *Plato and the City* (Academia Verlag, 2010). He has held a Fellowship from Universidade de Coimbra (Portugal) and Honorary Professorship from University of Stellenbosch (South Africa).

Michele Corradi Michele Corradi is Attaché Temporaire d'Enseignement et de Recherche at Aix-Marseille University (Institut d'Histoire de la Philosophie, E.A. 3276). He is the author of *Protagora tra filologia e filosofia. Le testimonianze di Aristotele* (Pisa-Roma 2012) and of many articles on Greek literature and ancient philosophy.

Michael Erler (Lehrstuhl für Klassische Philologie I (Graezistik), University of Wuerzburg). Professor Erler's research areas include classical and Hellenistic literature, their relation to philosophy, and their tradition in imperial times. Among his recent book publications are *Epikur – Die Schule Epikurs-Lukrez* (1994), *Epikureismus in der späten Republik und der Kaiserzeit* (2000), *Pseudoplatonica* (2005, with S. Schorn and K Döring), *Platon* (2006), *Platon* (2007; ital. 2008;

port. 2012), *Die Griechische Biographie in Hellenistischer Zeit* (2007, with S. Schorn), *Menon und Gorgias* (2007 with L. Brisson), *Philosophie der Lust* (2012, with W. Rother), *Argumenta in Dialogos Teil 2* (2012, with A. Neschke-Hentschke) and *Argument und literarische Form in antiker Philosophie* (2013, with Jan Erik Heßler). He has published various articles on Greek drama, hellenistic literature, Plato and Platonism, Epicurus and Epicureanism, and Augustine.

María Angélica Fierro currently works as Associate Researcher at the National Council for Scientific and Technological Research (CONICET), Argentina. She has given seminars on Ancient Philosophy in Argentina and abroad. She got her Doctor of Philosophy degree at the University of Durham, United Kingdom with a thesis on Plato's theory of desire in the Symposium and the Republic. She has worked as Associate Lecturer for the Open University, United Kingdom where he taught Philosophy, Humanities and Ancient Greek. She has published several papers and chapters of books on Ancient Philosophy.

Mary Louise Gill is David Benedict Professor of Classics and Philosophy at Brown University. She is the author of *Aristotle on Substance: The Paradox of Unity* (Princeton, 1989), co-translator and author of the *Introduction, Plato: Parmenides* (Hackett, 1996), and author of *Philosophos: Plato's Missing Dialogue* (Oxford, 2012), and of numerous papers on Plato and Aristotle. She is co-editor of three anthologies of papers on ancient philosophy, *Self-Motion: From Aristotle to Newton* (Princeton, 1994), *Unity, Identity, and Explanation in Aristotle's Metaphysics* (Oxford, 1994), and *A Companion to Ancient Philosophy* (Blackwell, 2006).

Gilmário Guerreiro da Costa has a Degree in Philosophy (1995), MA in Literature (1999) and Ph.D. in Literature (2005), all from the University of Brasilia. He is a Professor and assessor in the Department of Philosophy at the Catholic University of Brasilia. In 2012 he started a postdoctoral research fellowship at the University of Brasilia. In December 2013 he was awarded a scholarship (CAPES-Brazil) to attend Coimbra University, where he started a second postdoctoral research fellowship. He is a Member of Archai Group (the plural origins of Western thought) in the Department of Philosophy at the University of Brasilia, the Brazilian Society of Platonists (SBP), and the Brazilian Society for Classical Studies (SBEC). He works in the areas of philosophy of art, aesthetics and politics, literary theory, comparative literature, and literary criticism.

Raúl Gutiérrez is Professor of Ancient Philosophy, Metaphysics and Philosophy of Religion at the Catholic University of Peru (Lima). He is the author of *Schelling: Apuntes Biográficos* (1990) and *Wille und Subjekt bei Juan de la Cruz* (2003) and editor of *Los Símiles de la República VI-VII de Platón* (2003). Together with Hugo Ochoa Disselkoen he has published an annotated Spanish translation of the correspondence between Kant, Fichte, Schelling and Hegel (2011). Since 2009 he is the General Editor of *Areté. Revista de Filosofía*. He is also the Chairman of the Asociación Latinoamerica de Filosofía Antigua (ALFA) and a member of the International Plato Society. He has published papers on Plato, Neoplatonism, and Medieval Platonism. He is currently working on a book on Plato's Republic.

Christian Keime passed the 'Agrégation' in classical literature (a competitive entry examination of the French national Education) and is holder of a master 2 in Ancient Philosophy. He teaches comparative literature in the Catholic University of Angers and is currently working on a PhD about Plato's *Symposium* in the University of Cambridge.

Graciela E. Marcos de Pinotti (PhD University of Buenos Aires, 1991) is Professor of Ancient Philosophy at University of Buenos Aires and a researcher of CONICET (National Scientific and Technical Research Council) in Argentina. She is the author of numerous articles on Plato and the older Sophists. Her books include *Gorgias: Encomio de Helena. Introducción, traducción y notas* (2011) and *Platón ante el problema del error* (1995). She has coedited *Diálogo con los griegos. Estudios sobre Platón, Aristóteles y Plotino* (2004) and *El surgimiento de la phantasía en la Grecia Clásica. Parecer y aparecer en Protágoras, Platón y Aristóteles* (2009).

Silvio Marino is an Italian researcher in Ancient Philosophy and a Professor of History and Philosophy at Italian High School. He received his PhD from the University of Naples "Federico II", under the monitoring of Giovanni Casertano, with a dissertation about the relations between the form of the Platonic dialogue and ancient medical thought. During this period he studied in Paris at the C.N.R.S. (U.P.R. 76), under the monitoring of Prof. Michel Narcy (2009–2010). He then had a post-doctoral position at the University of São Paulo (USP) and of Campinas (UNICAMP), under the monitoring of Prof. Marco Zingano and Prof. Fatima Evora, for a research concerning the medical and biological background of Platonic political perspective. He has published articles both in reviews and books and participated in several congresses and seminars in South America and Europe.

Marcus Mota is Professor of Theatre History at University of Brasilia, Brazil. Besides several articles on Performance and Classics, he has published *The Musical Dramaturgy of Aeschylus* (University of Brasilia Press, 2008), and *In Homer Steps: Essays on Performance, Philosophy, Dance and Music* (Annablume, 2013). He also directs the Laboratory of Dramaturgy (LADI) where musical plays based on Classical subjects are created and staged.

Fernando Muniz is Doctor of Philosophy at the Federal University of Rio De Janeiro (UFRJ/1982–1999). He is currently Associate Professor in the Department of Philosophy at the Universidade Federal Fluminense/UFF. Some publications: (with George Rudebusch) "Philebus 15b: A Problem Solved." *Classical Quarterly*; "Pleasure and Deficiency of the Sensible World in Plato." *Southwest Philosophy Review*. Ed. J. K. Swindler (16:2. Jul/2000); *A Potência da Aparência: um estudo sobre o prazer e a sensação nos Diálogos de Platão* (2011) and *O Filebo de Platão* (2012).

Debra Nails is Professor of Philosophy at Michigan State University. Her areas of research include Plato, Spinoza, and procedural justice in the academy. She serves as Book Review Editor for the *Journal of the History of Philosophy* and is a member of Committee A—Academic Freedom and Tenure of the American Association of University Professors.

Mario Regali is Fellow of the "Dipartimento di Scienze dell'Antichità e del Tardoantico" at the Bari University "Aldo Moro". He is the author of *Il poeta e il demiurgo. Teoria e prassi della produzione letteraria nel Timeo e nel Crizia di Platone* and of many articles on Critias, Plato, Epicurus and the Greek grammarians.

Dino De Sanctis is Research Fellow of Greek Literature at the Università di Pisa. His interests are Archaic epic, relationship between Greek comedy and Plato, Epicureanism, and Literary Papyrology. His "*Le voci di Elena: ricerche sul personaggio narratore nell'Iliade e nell'Odissea*" is about to be published in the Biblioteca di Studi Antichi, Serra editore, Pisa/Roma.

Fernando Santoro is Professor of Philosophy at Universidade Federal do Rio de Janeiro, Researcher of the Collège International de Philosophie and Director of the OUSIA laboratory on classical philosophical studies. He is editor of *Anais de Filosofia Clássica* on-line, and author of *Arqueologia dos Prazeres* (2007), *Os Filósofos Épicos: Xenófanes e Parmênides: fragmentos* (2011).

José Trindade Santos is Professor of Philosophy (retired) at the University of Lisbon (Dept. of Philosophy), having read Ancient Philosophy from 1977 to 2004; and Professor at the Universidade Federal da Paraíba (retired) since 2004.

Samuel Scolnicov † (1941–2014) was Professor emeritus of Philosophy and of Education at The Hebrew University of Jerusalem, founding member and President of the International Plato Society from 1998 and 2001. He is the author of *Plato's Philosophy of Education, Platão e o problema educacional, Plato's Parmenides*, and of books and articles on Greek philosophy, and on philosophy of education. His *Euthydemus: Language and Ethics* is about to be published in the Lecturae Platonis series.

Lucas Soares is a doctor of philosophy from the Universidad de Buenos Aires and researcher for the Consejo Nacional de Investigaciones Científicas y Técnicas (CONICET). Professor of History of Ancient Philosophy at the Faculty of Philosophy and Letters at the Universidad de Buenos Aires. He is the author of the books *Anaximandro y la tragedia* (Biblos), *Platón y la política* (Tecnos), and articles on subjects relating to the aesthetics and politics of Greek philosophy.

Mauro Tulli Mauro Tulli, former President of the International Plato Society, organised the X Symposium at the University of Pisa in July 2013. He is Full Professor of Greek Literature, Director of the Department of Philology, Literature and Linguistics and Member of the Academic Senate at the University of Pisa. Currently President of the Italian University Council for Greek Literature, he published many research papers on Papyri and Tradition of Greek Literature, Epic, the Relationship between Literature and Philosophy, Rhetoric.

Citations Index

Aesop
– Fab. 241
Agathon
– 39 F 5 Snell-Kannicht
Andocides
– In Alcibiadem 22–23
Anonymous
– De Hippomacho (I 171, 31–172, 2 Cramer = 80 B 3 DK)
Antiphon (the Orator/Sophist?)
– 87 B 58
– 87DKA6
Aristophanes
– Acharnians, 19-20, 333, 658, 716
– Birds 407-408, 693-702
– Clouds 32-33, 225, 1206-1210
– Assemblywomen 1023-1024, 1114-1115,
– Frogs, 686, 1425, 1432-3
– Knights, 319-320, 1037
– Plutus 253-254
– Thesmophoriazusae 25-26, 146-170
Aristotle
– Athenian Constitution 27.5, 34.3
– Eudemian Ethics 1230b13-14
– Metaphysics IV
– On the Soul B5,417a28-30
– Poetics 48b, 1447b11, 1459b2-7
– Politics 1284,
– Rhetoric 1406a22
– Sophistical Refutations 173
Aristoxenus of Tarentum
– Life of Plato 61–68 Wehrli
Athenaeus
– Deipnosophistae 217a, 384
Aulus Gellius
– Attic Nights X,22

Ctesias
– frgs. 27–28

Democritus
– DK B 251
Dicaearchus
– PHerc. 1021, col. I Dorandi

Dio Chrysostom
– Letter XXX
Diodorus Siculus
– 3.62, 5.75, 14.19.8–9; 14.27.2–3
Diogenes Laertius
– Lives of Eminent Philosophers 3.56–62

Empedocles
– 61, 134 DK.
Euripides
– Cretans fr. 472
– Electra 779-783
– Phoenician Women 258, 499-502, 524-525, 558
– The Suppliants 349-352, 404-408
Eusebius Caesariensis
– PE 10, 3, 1–25 = 410 F Smith

Gorgias
– Encomium of Helen DK82B11
– Defense of Palamedes

Herodotus
– VII.139
Hesiod
– Works and Days 1-10, 293-297
– Theogony 22-34, 98, 820
– Catalogue 1019–1022
Hippocrates
– On Ancient Medicine 20-21
– On Airs 1.1-2
– On Regimen 2.27
– Prognostics 25
Homer
– Iliad 1.1-7, 2.484-93, 2.591-602, 2.760-762, 2.782, 9.540, 10.1-101, 10.116-130, 11.218-220, 14.508-510, 18.385-386, 18.392, 18.590-606, 24.110-111
– Odyssey 1.1-10, 1.153-162, 1.170, 1.325-359, 3.267, 4.17, 5.87-88, 7.238, 8.18-22, 8.40-45, 8.72-82, 8.471-98, 9.252, 9.523-532, 11.363, 12.189-91, 12.260-402, 10.14-16, 17.518-521, 19.104-105, 22.344-353

Horace
- Ars Poetica 333
- Epistles 1, 2, 3

Isocrates
- Busiris222b
- Encomium to Helen 14-15
- Panegiric 41b

Lucretius
- V1379-1435

Pindar
- I. 6.1-3
- N. 8.49
- O. 2.15–17

Philostratus
- Vitae Sophistarum 1, 168, 1.493, 2.16

Plato
- Apology 19c, 23a-b, 24e10, 28b3-d4, 28e-29a, 29d, 29d7-8, 29e, 30b, 32a, 33e, 35c
- Charmides 135a1-b4, 153d, 154a-c, 154e4, 156c, 156e, 157a, 157b-c, 166d, 167a, 169c3-171c10,
- Cratylus 385e-386a, 386d, 388c, 429b, 429d-430a, 430a-432d,
- Critias 110d5-d8, 120d6–121a6, 121a7–b7, 121b7–c5
- Crito43a-b
- Euthydemus 274d-e, 276b-c, 277d, 280b-c, 283e-284c, 284c3-4, 285d-286b, 286b-c, 293b, 295a, 295b5, 295c, 295e8, 297e, 303b,
- Euthyphro 2a1-2b10, 13a-c,
- Gorgias 447b8, 449b-c, 449c9-450c2, 458d1, 461d-462b, 466b, 472e7, 473b10-11, 481b10, 481d-e, 482, 483d1-3, 483d6, 483e, 484a1-3, 484a5, 484b1, 484c2, 484c-d, 484e, 485e-486a, 487a, 487b, 487c, 487d, 489e2, 491b2-4, 493a, 495d5, 499d, 506b6, 507a8, 507b3, 507e4, 508a1, 511c-513a, 513b6, 519a8, 522d1, 523a, 525b5,
- Hippias Major 281a1-b1, 289e6,
- H. Min. 364b-c
- Ion 530a1-b3, 530b1, 530d, 531a1-2, 531a3, 531b9-c1, 531d4-532b7, 532b, 532b8-c4,

532c3-4, 532c5-d3, 532d4-e4, 532e-533c, 533a2-3, 533a4, 533b4, 533b8, 533c2-3, 533c4-535, 535b, 535d1-3, 535e, 536e, 538b-539e, 539d5-540d3, 540d, 541d,
- Laches 180b-d, 185d, 187d-e, 194a6-7
- Laws 690c, 701b, 714c, 845b, 890a, 903c, 934a-b,
- Lysis 203a1-b1
- Menexenus 234a1
- Meno 70b, 73d, 75c, 75d, 76b, 76c, 76e, 79e-82b, 80, 81a5-b1, 82b-85b, 85b-86c, 86e4-87b2, 90b, 91d, 95d-e,
- Parmenides 126a, 135c5, 136b1-c5, 137a5-6, 154b-d, 160b5-b6, 160b6-c5, ,
- Phaedo 246d, 57a-59c, 58c, 58d, 58e-59a, 59b, 65a, 66b-d, 69b-c, 69d, 72e-84b, 82e, 85d, 87a7-9, 89b9-c4, 94b, 100a, 101c, 100e-103a, 115a,
- Phaedrus 227a1, 228a1, 228a5-6, 228b7, 229c, 230a3-6, 233a, 234d1, 234d5, 234e, 235b, 235c5-6, 236b5-8, 236d-237, 238d6, 241e5-6, 241e7, 241e8-242a2, 242d4-5, 242e1, 242e5-243a2, 243e4-8, 243d5-7, 245a, 245b-246a, 246a-b, 246c, 246d, 246e-247a, 247a, 247b, 247c-d, 248b-c, 248c-e, 248e, 249a, 249b, 250b-c, 250c-d, 250d-252a, 252c, 253b, 253d, 253e-254b, 254b-c, 257a, 257b, 257c, 261a, 264a5, 264c, 265d, 266b-d, 267c, 269b, 269e-270a, 270b, 272c-d, 275a, 275b-c, 275d, 276d, 277a-c, 277b-c, 277d, 278a, 279b1-3,
- Philebus 11b-c, 11c4, 11c7-8, 11d-4, 11d10, 12a7-8, 12b, 15c8-9, 16c, 17b, 17c-d, 18a, 18e-19a, 19b, 21e2, 26b-c, 27e-28b, 28b6, 36c, 36e, 48c2, 56b, 62a-b,
- Protagoras 309a1, 309d3, 311a8-312b6, 311b-314c, 313e-314b, 315a1, 315b9-316b2, 316a5, 316d, 320e, 321a, 320c-328d, 321c-d, 322a, 322b, 322c2, 322d1, 323a-c, 323c1, 323e-324c, 324d-e, 325a-c, 325d-326c, 326e-7a, 327b-c, 328a-b, 328e-329a, 333d, 334d, 334e-335c, 335d2-5, 336d6–e4, 337c-338b, 347c3-e1, 351b-357c, 356d, 357a, 358e-359a, 361e,
- Republic 328a-b, 335c5–334b6; 335b2-d13; 336b, 338c3, 338d-e, 340d1–342e11; 345c7–347a6; 349d13–350c11, 348b8-

350c11, 350c12–352d2, 352d2–354a7, 358b4–6, 358b-c, 358e-359a, 359a2, 359b3, 359c5-7, 366d7-e9, 367d8-e1, 368c7–369a3, 370a-c, 375a-376c, 375c6-7, 375d10, 383a-c, 394d, 395c, 399a-c, 400d-e, 401d-e, 410e, 411a-412a, 414b, 431-432a, 432c7–8, 432d3, 433a4–9, 433d, 434d4, 434d9, 434e3-4, 435b1-2, 435b-e, 435d1, 435d8, 436a8-b3, 436b8, 436e8–437a2, 437a4-6, 437a6, 441a, 442b, 443c1, 443c4–5, 444d-e, 445b6, 445c, 498d, 449c4, 449c7-8, 449d4, 449e7, 450b1, 450b5, 450c-d, 452e5, 453a1-4, 453b2-3, 453b10-c1, 453d-e, 453d9-11, 454a5-7, 454c, 454c7-8, 454d1, 454d-e, 455b4-c2, 455d6-e2, 456c4, 456e, 457b7, 457c1-2, 457c4-5, 457d9, 458a-b, 458b3-5, 458c-461e, 461b1-7, 461d7, 461e7-8, 462a2, 462a9-b3, 462c-d, 462e, 463a-b, 463b10-c7, 463c-d, 463e3-5, 464b8-c4, 464d3-5, 464d7-465b4, 465b5-10, 465d, 465e-466b, 466c-d, 466d6-469b4, 471c6–7, 471c8-e2, 472a3-4, 472b7-c3, 472c3-4, 472c4-5, 472d9-473b2, 473a5-b1, 473c6-7, 473c11, 473d1-3, 474b3-c7, 475e9-476a7, 476a, 484b3-6, 484d1-3, 484d5-7, 485a1-2, 485a4-8, 485a10-487a8, 487a-502c, 500c2–5, 503a7-b1, 507b2-7, 507c-509d, 509c7-10, 510b, 510c3, 510c6–7, 510d1, 510d2, 511a, 511b4-5, 511b6-7, 511b7-c1, 511d-e, 518b-519a, 523d8-e1, 533a3, 533c7-d1, 534b8-c3, 354c1-2, 537c2-3, 537c7, 540c1-3, 543b, 545c5, 545c6-7, 564c, 581b, 582d, 585b3-4, 590b, 590d1-2, 590d5, 595a-b, 596a, 600c-e, 602c, 607a, 611b10-c7, 617e,
- Statesman 257a1-c5, 258a3-4, 258b1-c2, 271e, 272a, 273d-e, 274b-c, 274c-d,
- Sophist (sph) 216a1, 216d3-217b4, 217c3-7, 232d, 237b-239c, 238b4-5, 238c10-11, 238b6-8, 239b10, 240a-b, 244b, 244d, 251e9, 252b5, 252c5, 252c6-9, 257b-259b, 258b, 259d9-e2, 259e, 262a1-2, 262c, 262d, 263a-e, 263e-264a,
- Symposium 172a1-5, 172b-e, 173b, 173c, 174d-175c, 175d, 175e7-9, 183e6-184a4, 185d2-3, 185c, 185d-e, 186a5-7, 186a7-b1, 186b4, 186c6-7, 186d5-6, 187b4-6, 187b4-c4, 188a, 188d4-9, 189a, 193b5-6, 194a1-4, 194e4-5, 194e7, 195a2-3, 195a8-b2, 195b-c, 196b6-7, 197d1,e2, 198c2-5, 198d7-199a3, 199b2-5, 201c8-9, 201d, 201e2-7, 202e3-203a4, 203d, 204d-e, 205a-206a, 206b3-8, 206c-e, 207a4-5, 207c5-7, 207e6, 210a-212a, 212b, 212c-d, 213b, 213c-d, 215e, 216c, 216d, 219b-d, 222b, 222c, 223b,
- Theaetetus 142c-143a, 143b, 143e, 144a2-7, 142b, 144b-d, 144d, 145a, 145b6-7, 145c3, 145c5, 146a6, 146b, 146c, 148b, 148e, 149a, 152c, 152d2-4, 152d7-8, 154c-e, 157b3-c2, 162a, 162b6-7, 165a-b, 166a-168c, 170d, 171a6-d8, 171a9, 171b1-2, 171b10-11, 171c5-7, 171a9, 171b7, 172a-c, 173c, 174c-d, 175b, 177d1-4, 181a-b, 182d-4, 183a5-6, 183b4, 183c, 183e5-184a2, 185c-186d, 185e4-5, 187d, 189e-190, 190e, 197d-e, 210d4,
- Timaeus 17a1-5, 17c1-19a9, 19b1-2, 19b3-c8, 19c8-9, 19e2-8, 20a1-b1, 20b1-7, 20e1-3, 21a1-3, 21a8-b1, 22c1-23d1, 24d6-25c6, 25c6-d6, 27a2-b6, 27b, 28c, 29c-d, 30d, 336b, 7c6-38c3, 85b5-90d7, 90e1-92c3,

Plutarch
- Alcibiades 2.2-3, 19.1-2, 34, 39.2, 39.7
- De Esu Carnium 996c,
- De E apud Delphos 388e
- De sollertia Animalium 974a-d

Quintilianus
- 9.2.44

Sextus Empiricus
- Adv. Math. IX, 54 = DK, 88B25
- P. 2, 128a1

Simonides
- 603 Page

Solon
- frg. 1 Diehl=13 West

Sophocles
- Ajax 378
- The Trachiniae 742–743

Stobaeus
- 2.8, 12
- 3.2, 15

Theocritus
– 7.7-26
– 14.1-7
– 15.1-10
Theognis
– 583–584

Thucydides
– 1.22, 1.140, 2.1.37, 2.63, 2.65, 3. 39-40, 4.58-64, 4.60, 5.84, 5.85–111, 6.7, 6.15.3, 6.27.3, 6.28.1, 6.60.1, 6.61.1, 6.76, 8.65.2

Xenophon
– Anabasis 1.2.6–3.1, 2.6.21–29,
– Memorabilia 1.2.9-12, 1.2.29-40, 2.21-34, 4.4
– Historia Graeca (Hel) 2.3.36

Author Index

Academicorum Index 132
Acumenos 125
Adam, J. 215
Adeimantus 16 f., 20, 29, 36, 298, 311
Aegisthus 127
Aeschines 132
Aeschylus 110, 289
Agamemnon 127, 178 f., 181–183, 205
Agariste 285
Agathon 52, 64, 67–71, 125, 204, 212–214, 224, 246, 253–261, 282 f., 293, 308, 311, 336, 348, 379, 381–386, 389–394
Ajax 178 f., 348
Alcibiades 52, 63, 65, 68, 71, 112, 128, 215, 217, 222, 281–294, 311 f., 326 f., 330, 366, 385
Alcidamas 260, 331
Alcinous 124, 126, 178
Alexander of Aphrodisias 221
Alexidemus 298, 388
Allen, R. E. 85, 379
Anacreon 267, 351
Anaxagoras 237, 344
Anaximander 5
Andocides 291, 385
Andrieu, J. 119
Androcles 285
Andron 311
Antisthenes 289, 322
Anton, J. P. 396
Anytus 298–300
Aphrodite 68, 214, 370 f., 376
Apollodorus 66 f., 150
Archelaus 318, 393
Archilochus 169, 193
Ares 58
Ariadne 206
Aristippus 299
Aristodemus 67, 121, 150, 212, 257
Ariston 307, 310
Arrighetti, G. 129, 208, 337, 340, 342
Artmann, B. 302, 304 f.
Asclepius 128, 234
Aspasia 309 f.

Augustine 5
Autolycus 281
Axiothea 307
Ayache, L. 387

Bailly, A. 260
Bakhtin, M. 165, 388
Balansard, A. 205, 243
Barthes, R. 66
Bateson, G. 393
Battegazzore, A. M. 128
Benardete, S. 174, 362–365
Beresford, A. 340, 344
Berg, Th. 326
Bernabé, A. 223
Bertagna, M. I. 338
Blondell, R. 103, 122, 130, 205, 297, 335, 362, 364, 379, 384 f., 394
Bluck, R. S. 105, 113
Bluestone, N. H. 306
Bonazzi, M. 340, 344, 347
Bowie, A. 104
Bowles, C. 211, 222
Brancacci, A. 339 f., 344
Bremer, J. 159 f.
Brink, C. O. 107
Brisson, L. 58, 63, 260, 283, 341, 343, 379 f., 383, 393
Broadie, S. 40, 54
Brochard 63
Brown, L. 94, 235–237, 306
Buarque, L. 211
Burkert, W. 225
Burnet, J. 48, 122, 306
Burnyeat, M. 42, 119, 300, 303, 341
Bury, R. G. 63 f., 254 f., 257, 379, 384, 389

Cabrera, I. 78
Cairns, D. L. 181, 228 f., 233, 237
Calame, C. 340
Callias 281, 311 f.
Callicles 6, 122, 231, 290, 317–332, 335, 357
Calvo, T. 271

412 — Author Index

Cambiano, G.   204, 243, 342
Campbell, L.   33
Campese, S.   120
Capra, A.   126, 180, 183, 351
Capuccino, C.   130, 203, 345
Casanova, A.   346
Casertano, G.   249, 373
Cassin, B.   70
Caveing, M.   301, 305
Cebes   9
Centrone, B.   128, 131, 286
Cephalus   120, 122, 311
Cerri, G.   204
Chaeredemus   309 f.
Chaerephon   124, 198
Charalabopoulos   157
Charicles   326 f., 329
Cherniss, H. F.   7
Chevitarese, A.   286
Chryses   205
Cicero   5, 318
Cimon   206
Circes   127
Clay, D.   37 f., 40 f., 103, 121, 124, 175, 180
Cleary, J. J.   344
Clement of Alexandria   219
Cleon   332
Clinias   8
Collins, D.   169
Cooper, J. M.   242, 269 f., 300
Cornelli, G.   2, 281, 286, 357
Cornford, F. M.   8, 33, 40, 43, 63, 77, 83, 379
Corrigan, K.   63, 351, 380
Croiset, A.   320
Crombie, I. M.   7, 84
Ctesippus   126
Curtius, E. R.   351
Cyrus   298

Dalfen, J.   114, 351
Damon   204, 206
Danek, G.   208
Darbo-Pechanski, C.   290
Darius   318
Davidson, J.   33, 291, 369
de Jong, I. J. F.   104, 126, 177

de Romilly, J.   284
de Vries, G. J.   266, 269, 275
Decleva Caizzi, F.   289, 294
Delcomminette, S.   342
Deleuze, G.   70, 198
Democritus   12, 205 f., 303, 320, 340, 351
Demodocus   208
Demont, P.   341, 379
Descartes   5
Desclos, M. L.   349
Desjardins, R.   10
Detienne, M.   385
Dicaeopolis   125
Diehl, E.   38, 43
Diels-Kranz   338
Dihle, A.   328
Diller, H.   204
Dillon, J.   337
Dilthey, W.   143
Dionysius   43, 70
Dionysodorus   8
Dionysus   70, 173, 211, 214, 216 f., 219 – 223, 282, 288 f.
Diotima   52, 63, 65, 68 f., 215, 217, 222, 281, 292, 307 – 309, 341, 379 – 381, 383 – 395
Dixsaut, M.   142, 155, 382, 386
Dodds, E. R.   227, 231, 317, 325
Dostoyevsky, F.   388
Dover, K. J.   66, 257, 260 f., 284, 308, 364, 380
Dropides   38, 42

Echecrates   105 – 107, 110 – 112
Edelstein, L.   237, 241
Edwards, M. W.   177, 207
Eggers Lan, C. E.   58
Epicrates   124
Epimetheus   340 f.
Eratosthenes   107
Erebus   217
Erler, M.   2, 103 – 106, 111 – 113, 115, 119, 174, 335, 351, 357, 360, 367, 371, 380
Eros   49 – 52, 211, 213 – 218, 222, 246, 248, 253, 255 – 257, 259 – 261, 263, 272, 282, 292 f., 341, 379, 381, 388, 391
Eryximachus   64, 67 f., 71, 121, 214, 225, 241 – 252, 381 f., 385

Eteocles   326
Eucleides   106, 114
Eurycles   85
Eurystheus   321
Eurytion   321
Euthydemus   6–8, 10f., 91f., 96, 230, 265, 310, 327f., 360
Euthyphro   6, 122, 199, 298, 335

Fantuzzi, M.   108
Ferrari, G. R. F.   22, 59, 125, 272, 286, 342, 351, 362
Fialho, M. C.   289
Ficino, M.   380
Flashar, H.   128, 204
Fortenbaugh, W. W.   337
Fouillée, A.   317
Fowler, H. N.   91, 247, 250f., 269, 301–304
Friedländer, P.   33, 271, 276, 335f., 340, 342, 349, 380

Gadamer, H. G.   73, 143f., 154, 369
Gagarin, M.   349
Gagnebin, J. M.   138–140, 146f.
Gaiser, K.   133, 346, 351
Gallop, D.   105
Garland, R.   307, 310
Garvie, A. F.   127, 178
Gastaldi, S.   121
Gentzler, J.   23
Geryon   321
Gherchanoc, F.   290
Giannantoni, G.   203
Giaquinto, M.   305f.
Gill, M. L.   1, 33, 37f., 40, 89
Giorgini, G.   288
Giuliano, F. M.   132, 175, 183, 208, 345
Glaucon   16f., 20, 29, 36, 121, 154, 175, 298, 307, 312, 322f., 332, 343
Glazov-Corrigan, E.   63, 380
Goethe, J. W.   149, 187f., 335
Goffman, E.   168
Goldblatt, D.   166
Gomperz, T.   286, 326
Gooch, P.   266, 275
Gorgias   47, 64, 104, 110, 122f., 148, 194, 203, 205, 211f., 227–233, 247–249, 252–254, 256–261, 267, 290, 299f., 317f., 325–327, 331f., 347–349, 351, 357, 360, 371, 382, 384, 388, 393
Gow, A. S. F.   132
Gregory of Nazianzus   223
Gribble, D.   286, 288–291
Grimal, P.   321
Grinswold   60
Grube, G.   63, 300
Guariglia, O.   84
Guattari, F.   70
Guthrie, W. K. C.   33, 63, 191, 229, 325, 327, 331
Gutiérrez, R.   1, 15, 21f., 28
Gyges   323

Hackforth, F. B. A.   276, 278
Hackforth, R.   58, 59, 61, 381, 397
Halliwell, S.   20, 22, 24, 47, 103f., 106, 113, 174, 183, 187, 204, 350
Halperin, D. M.   103, 106, 307, 380, 393f.
Hamilton, E.   228f., 233, 237
Harrison, A. R.   310
Havlicek, A.   116, 354
Heath, M.   306
Heidegger, M.   66
Heinaman, R.   84
Heindorf, L. F.   338
Heitsch, E.   125, 130, 203
Helen   194, 247–249, 253–256, 258f.
Helios   108
Helmig, C.   342
Hera   58, 220f.
Heracles   124, 321
Heraclitus   5, 79, 250, 252
Hermae   284
Hermann, K. F.   379
Hermes   69, 177f., 221, 320
Hermocrates   33, 35–38, 40–43, 121, 332
Hermogenes   69, 311f.
Herrmann, F. G.   185, 186, 353, 354, 355
Hestia   58
Hicks, R. D.   33
Hieronymus   126
Hippocrates   242, 244, 349f.
Hipponicus   311f.
Hippothales   126

Hobbs, A.   380, 388
Hoffmann, E.   11
Hommel, A.   384
Hordern, J. H.   132
Horn, C.   341, 380
Hourcade, A.   340
Hude, K.   40
Humbert, J.   327
Hunter, R.   103, 106–108, 132, 173 f.
Hylas   5

Iago   6
Iapetus   259
Ion   128–132, 157–171, 187–196, 198 f., 203–209
Isnardi Parente, M.   237

Jaeger, W.   323, 385
Janaway, C.   203
Jocasta   326
Johansen, T. K.   40, 43
Jones, H. S.   38, 40, 157
Jori, A.   242, 244
Jouanna, J.   243–245, 247–249
Jourdan, F.   219
Jowett, B.   229, 337

Kahn, C.   15, 23, 63, 119, 129, 189, 227, 230, 328, 364
Kanayama, Y.   23
Kannicht, R.   103, 107, 109 f., 348
Kant, I.   12, 69
Kerferd, G. B.   317
Keuls, V.   206
Kierkegaard, S.   65
Klagge, J. C.   116, 397, 399
Klooster, J.   132
Knorr, W.   304
Kock, T.   289
Köhnken, A.   104
Kosman, L. A.   388, 395
Krämer, M.   11, 15
Kraus, W.   107
Kraut, R.   230, 376
Kullmann, W.   112
Kyoung-Lee, M.   90

Lacan, J.   66
Lamb, W. R. M.   214
Lampert, L.   123
Lampetie   108
Lasthenia   307
Latacz, J.   108
Latar, R.   172
Ledger, G. R.   308
Lefèbvre, D.   374
Leroux, G.   20
Lesher, J.   75, 116, 314, 396, 398, 399
Lesley, A.   380
Lispector, C.   138
Lowenstam, S.   207
Luce, J. V.   381
Lucretius   205
Lycidas   131
Lycophron   331
Lysander   326

MacDowell, D.   310
Machiavelli, N.   331
Maehler, H.   108, 351
Malcolm, J.   83
Männlein-Robert, I.   120
Mansfeld, J.   237
Manuwald, B.   338–340
Maricus   124
Mársico   71, 74, 254, 262
Martinelli Tempesta, S.   126
Martínez Hernández, M.   74, 262
Mazzara, G.   262
McCabe, M. M.   47
McDowell, J.   78, 302 f.
McGibbon, D.   56
McKenzie, M. M.   60
McPherran, M. L.   379
Medontis   291
Meletus   122
Menandros   132
Menzel, A.   317–323, 325–327, 329 f.
Migliori. M.   14, 62, 73, 74, 295
Miller, M.   33
Minton, W. W.   207
Montaigne, M.   5, 388
Montanari, F.   337
Morgan, K. A.   103, 119, 122, 338

Morreal, J.   172
Morrow, G.   303
Murr, D. E.   174, 342
Murray, P.   119, 181, 206
Musti, D.   294
Muthmann, F.   104

Nails, D.   2, 36–38, 42, 122, 284, 286, 297, 300, 307f., 380, 383, 385, 390, 393
Narcy, M.   72, 81
Natali, C.   369
Nausicydes   326
Nesselrath, H.-G.   33, 40
Nestle, W.   317, 341
Neumann, H.   380f.
Nietzsche, F.   5, 65, 72, 317, 321, 332
Nightingale, A. W.   73, 119, 157, 382f.
Norden, E.   338
Nucci, M.   246
Nunes, B.   138
Nussbaum, M.   63, 71, 73, 149, 275, 380, 385

Odysseus   107–109, 123f., 126f., 178, 180, 194
Olson, S. D.   125
Olympiodorus   173, 221
Onomacritus   219
Orestes   127
Orpheus   195, 206f., 209, 218–220
Osborne, C.   63
Ostenfeld, E. N.   50, 58
Ostwald, M.   337
Owen, G. E. L.   7, 94

Padilha, P.   160
Padilla, M.   130
Palamedes   255, 258
Palumbo   205, 350, 364
Panagiotou, S.   33
Pandora   214
Panopea   126
Paschalis, M.   116
Pasquali, G.   120
Patrocles   310
Patterson, C.   310
Pausanias   64, 67f., 70, 213f., 225, 257

Payne, A.   69, 132
Pelosi, F.   346
Penelope   206
Penner, T.   22, 123
Pericles   237, 311f., 318, 320, 332, 344
Perictione   307, 310
Perks, L. G.   165
Petrucci, F.   128, 131
Phaenarete   309f.
Phemius   206–209
Pherecrates   295
Philippides   311
Philodemus   132
Philonous   5
Philostratus   257f., 328f., 338
Phlius   307
Pindar   114, 321, 326, 329, 331f.
Pinheiro, A. E.   281
Pinotti, G.   1, 77, 81
Piraeus   36, 121f., 281
Pirithous   329
Pithus   122
Polemarchus   20, 311
Polus   64, 325
Polygnotus   206f.
Polynices   326
Popper, K. R.   234–236, 238
Poratti, A.   58
Porphyry   190f., 336
Powell, J. E.   38, 40
Pradeau, J.-F.   373
Praxinoa   132
Proclus   38, 43, 342
Prodicus   311, 321
Prometheus   214–216, 337f., 340, 342f.
Protagoras   6f., 12, 37, 39, 77f., 80–82, 86, 96, 121, 127f., 180, 205f., 214, 229, 267, 311–313, 318–320, 335–352, 359, 373
Protarchus   357f., 363, 366–377
Protrepticus   219
Puchner, M.   157
Puente, F. R.   141f.
Pylades   127
Pyrilampes   326, 328f.

Raalte, M. V.   352, 353, 355
Rademaker, A.   340

Radke, G. 104
Reents, E. 103
Reeve, C. D. C. 63, 343, 379, 394 f.
Rehn, R. 384
Reinhardt, K. 205
Rhadamanthys 329
Richardson Lear, G. 355
Ricoeur, P. 143 f., 149 f.
Riegel, N. 2, 211, 281
Riginos, A. S. 104, 173
Rijksbaron, A. 128, 203
Robin 58, 287, 379, 385
Robinson, T. M. 80
Rodrigues, N. S. 289
Rosa, G. 150
Rosen, R. M. 63, 73, 380, 390 f.
Rossetti, L. 103
Rowe, C. J. 48, 50, 58, 60, 123 f., 303, 343, 380, 383, 387, 389, 394
Rutherford, R. B. 154 f., 180, 380

Sacks, H. 168
Sammons, B. 124, 182 f., 207
Sanctis, D. d. 2, 119, 207, 340
Sanhuesa Carvajal, R. A. 331
Sansone, D. 123
Santoro, F. 2, 211, 215, 222
Sappho 267, 351
Sattler, B. 33, 40, 42
Saunders, T. J. 347
Schiefsky, M. J. 242, 244
Schirren, T. 111
Schleiermacher, F. 384
Schlick, A. J. 339, 347, 349
Schofield, M. 235, 346
Schorn, S. 337
Schweitzer, B. 205
Schwinge, E. R. 104, 110
Sedley, D. 58, 79, 347, 365
Serrano Cantarín, R. 338, 341
Sheffield, F. 379, 384, 389, 391, 394
Shorey, P. 233, 236
Sier, K. 379, 385
Silenus 282, 288
Simichidas 131
Simmias 9
Simplicio 5

Sinaiko, H. 271
Sisyphus 328–330
Slings, S. R. 124
Smith, N. D. 336, 357
Soares, L. 1, 63, 213, 215
Socrates 5 f., 8–13, 15, 17 f., 20–22, 24–31, 34–38, 40–44, 47–50, 52, 59 f., 63–72, 78, 82, 89 f., 97, 103, 105 f., 110–114, 119–131, 137, 146 f., 150, 152, 154, 158–163, 165–170, 173–184, 188–194, 196–199, 203–206, 209, 211–215, 227–239, 253, 259, 261, 263–278, 281–283, 286–288, 290, 292–294, 298–304, 306–312, 318 f., 323–331, 349, 351, 357–365, 367 f., 370–377, 379–395
Soffredini, C. 160
Solana Dueso, J. 340
Sommerstein, A. 162
Stallbaum, G. 380, 384
Stalley, R. 348
Stavru, A. 103
Steel, C. 342
Steinthal, H. 62
Stempsey, W. 238
Stokes, M. C. 69
Stork, P. 352, 353, 355
Strauss, L. 212, 385
Szlezák, T. A. 11, 18, 22, 31, 47

Tarrant, H. 33, 229, 342
Tasso, T. 335
Taylor, A. E. 33, 43, 218, 237, 311, 379
Tejera, V. 269
Telemachus 126, 206
Telete 219, 221–224
Tennes 329
Terpsion 301 f.
Theodorus 34, 206 f., 301 f., 304 f., 358–365, 369, 372
Thesleff, H. 10 f., 302
Thrasybulus 328
Thrasyllus 33
Thrasymachus 15, 17, 317, 322 f., 331 f., 343
Thyonicus 132
Timandra 292
Timotheos 206

Tobin, R.   206
Trabattoni, F.   145, 272, 335
Tsitsiridis   128
Tynnichus   198f.
Typhoon   263, 266f., 269–271, 274, 277
Tyrtaios   109

Uranus   67f., 221

Valentin, A.   148
Vallejo Campos, A.   2, 47, 227
van Riel, G.   340, 349
Vegetti, M.   26, 120, 146, 204, 237f., 244, 248, 252, 287, 342–344
Verdenius, W. J.   128
Vidal-Naquet, P.   40
Vlastos, G.   10, 89, 227, 229f., 235f., 300f., 306, 337, 379

Wagner, R.   335
Waithe, M. E.   379
Walker, I.   122

Westerink, L. G.   342
Wilamowitz-Moellendorff, U.   40, 204, 212
Wilson, N. G.   15
Witlock-Blundell, M.   393, 399
Wittgenstein, L.   5, 392
Wolf, F. A.   307, 384
Woodbridge, F. J. E.   380
Woodruff, P.   131, 270, 308

Xanthippe   307, 310
Xenophanes   109, 191
Xerxes   318

Yunis, H.   192, 194–197, 266, 351

Zalmoxis   237
Zarathustra   321
Zeno   308
Zeus   41, 43, 51, 58, 108, 124, 127, 177f., 208, 215, 220–223, 320, 337, 339, 341–343

Subject Index

abandon 30, 55, 57, 152, 174, 234, 263, 287, 302, 328, 358, 371, 373
ability 23, 57, 97, 103, 167, 192, 200, 274, 300, 335, 393
absence 41, 43, 130 f., 147, 150, 169, 171, 175, 234, 307, 312
absolute 20, 23, 82 f., 85 f., 146, 197, 258, 344, 374
abstraction 143, 149, 297
academia 139, 243
academy 126, 133, 139, 300–302, 307
accordance 16 f., 21, 24 f., 31, 79, 153 f., 236, 318, 343
accusation 137 f., 145, 183 f., 190, 255 f., 285–287, 337
acquaintance 56, 105, 308
acquisition 57, 120, 131
action 31, 35 f., 53, 55, 93, 148, 153–155, 157 f., 160 f., 167 f., 179, 181, 198, 211, 216, 223, 230–232, 234, 236, 254 f., 259, 264, 274, 276 f., 306, 318, 331, 341, 345
activity 51, 148, 154, 162, 165–167, 170 f., 173 f., 190 f., 216, 250 f., 306, 337, 339 f.
actor 70, 155, 193
adaptation 388 f.
adornment 139
adultery 310
advice 9, 115, 287, 327, 345
aesthetic 144, 148 f., 364
aesthetics 188
affection 113, 148, 175–177, 179–182, 184, 197, 228, 325
afterlife 289
agent 158, 160 f., 163, 167 f., 291, 391
agnosticism 339
agonistic 70, 89, 192
agreement 19, 22, 24, 27, 58, 64, 81, 165, 184, 250, 270, 323, 363, 367, 371
aidos 176, 181
aisthesis 148
ambiguity 124, 151, 188, 190, 269, 364
anairesis 21

analogy 17–19, 164 f., 180, 190, 195, 249, 251 f., 335, 351, 365
analysis 8, 15, 18 f., 69, 95, 104, 113, 131, 138, 141, 147, 174, 219, 241, 252, 271, 305, 337 f., 347, 349, 351
anamnesis 299
androgyny 224
animal 24, 41, 56, 246, 287, 309, 342, 347, 374 f.
anthropology 287, 340
antiplatonic 198
antithesis 92, 318 f., 325
apodeixis 192, 196 f.
aporia 85 f., 140, 170, 193, 197, 297, 364, 393
appearance 22, 29, 64, 69, 112, 128, 151, 153, 162, 221, 229, 233, 259, 264, 287, 290, 298, 346, 380, 390, 395
archetype 58, 159–161
arete 15 f., 153
argument 2, 6, 8 f., 15–21, 24, 26, 28 f., 47–49, 59, 70 f., 77–84, 86, 90–96, 105, 113 f., 150, 164–166, 189, 205, 212, 242, 256, 259, 268, 297, 306, 308 f., 312, 317, 327 f., 330 f., 337, 339, 348, 357, 359 f., 362, 366–369, 371–376, 382, 384, 386
art 1, 16 f., 23, 30, 50, 72, 137, 140, 149–151, 153–155, 159, 163 f., 169, 173, 184, 211 f., 227 f., 231–233, 237, 241–244, 248, 250, 276 f., 310, 320, 327, 335, 346, 352, 364
assembly 38, 41, 108, 148, 178, 192, 318
atheism 330 f.
Athens 35–37, 40–43, 70, 119–126, 128–131, 162, 181, 184, 206, 213, 229, 281, 283–288, 290–293, 298, 302, 310–312, 330–332, 338, 364, 385
audience 7, 33 f., 42 f., 98, 104, 106–111, 114, 160–167, 169–171, 189–191, 194, 196 f., 268, 298–300, 359 f., 371, 373, 379, 381, 383–385, 388 f., 391–395
author 1 f., 6 f., 13, 42, 63, 107 f., 111, 114, 138, 141, 144 f., 148 f., 154 f., 164, 174,

191, 195, 197–199, 203f., 206, 208f., 211–213, 216, 238, 242, 244–248, 250f., 267, 301, 308, 317f., 321, 331, 336f., 351, 395

backstage 213
banquet 105, 127, 213, 281, 283f., 379
beautiful 7, 12, 53, 55, 57, 69, 121, 131, 148, 154, 190, 198, 200, 215, 236, 243, 255–257, 259, 267, 271, 277, 281f., 299f., 302, 319, 324, 364, 368, 382–384, 386, 389–391
belief 58, 80, 90, 97, 195, 229, 231, 254, 263, 266, 297, 299, 306, 323, 329, 369, 371, 377, 388, 394
bendideia 120f.
blame 122, 179f., 268, 293
body 18, 25, 48f., 51f., 54f., 57, 63, 68, 177, 222, 231, 237, 243, 245–248, 251f., 254, 260, 289f., 309, 341, 350, 359, 381, 389
book 2, 15, 21, 31, 33f., 37f., 42, 50, 138, 148, 150, 152–154, 173–178, 180–184, 204–206, 250f., 254, 292, 301, 304, 306, 308, 325, 343–347, 349–351, 376, 379, 391, 394

category 109, 343
catharsis 148
cause 25, 29f., 54, 68, 79, 107, 110f., 113, 164, 178, 187f., 196, 228, 245, 249, 256, 259, 272, 274, 277, 286, 368, 390f.
celebration 71, 222
chaos 40, 141, 217
character 1f., 5f., 21, 34–38, 41f., 64, 67–71, 73, 95, 103, 126, 130, 142, 144, 147–150, 154f., 157, 159, 161f., 168f., 179f., 187, 194, 211–214, 216f., 223, 227f., 230f., 233–235, 237–239, 253f., 258f., 261, 264f., 268, 273, 276–279, 282, 289, 293, 297–300, 302, 307, 309, 311f., 317–319, 322, 324–329, 331, 335f., 338, 341f., 344, 346, 349, 357f., 360–362, 364, 366f., 369, 371, 376f., 379, 381, 385–387, 394f.
children 20, 22, 24–27, 30, 36, 72, 218, 223, 299, 301, 307, 345, 376

choir 216f., 222
cithara 203, 205f., 208, 345
citizen 15, 25f., 35f., 70, 125, 130f., 163, 227, 229–232, 234, 236, 252, 263, 284, 290, 318–320, 322, 343, 345f., 348, 393
coexistence 165, 251
cognitive 34, 89f., 97, 159, 164f., 171, 191, 197, 364, 366
comedy 69, 125, 127, 131f., 152, 157f., 160, 163, 165f., 169, 171, 211–213, 215, 217, 219, 224f., 257, 263, 288, 290, 335
commentator 188, 190f., 194, 212, 221, 284, 299, 311, 385, 390
communication 114, 144, 188, 191, 194, 197–199, 252, 380, 387, 389, 394
competition 60, 71, 211, 277, 281, 374
conclusion 8f., 12, 19, 24, 29, 34, 47, 52, 60, 81–83, 90, 95–97, 114, 131, 159, 171, 191, 193, 199, 212, 251, 256f., 261, 271f., 297, 320, 336, 344, 375, 394
contrary 12, 38, 59, 78, 86, 89, 92, 95, 110, 154, 163f., 231, 238, 244f., 251, 259, 269, 273, 283, 309, 318–320, 322, 324, 331, 360, 383, 386, 391
conversation 5, 8, 34, 36, 65f., 72f., 97f., 103, 105f., 111–113, 146, 149, 168, 263, 267, 282, 299, 312, 357–361, 363, 367f., 370f., 373, 375, 377, 381, 383f., 393
cosmogony 217, 219
creation 40, 72, 167, 205, 252, 308, 351
culture 2, 137, 148, 188, 211, 227, 234f., 238f., 290, 299

daimon 263, 265, 274, 277
dance 71, 206
death 5, 11, 13, 20, 29f., 42f., 49, 58, 105, 112f., 127, 147f., 152, 180, 219–221, 234, 286, 291–293, 300–302, 310, 312, 320
debate 97, 104, 109, 141f., 151, 204, 323, 327, 357–361, 367, 369, 372, 374, 377
deity 199, 218
democracy 37, 41–43, 230, 233, 284f., 312, 319–321, 327, 329f.
demos 29, 231, 326, 328f.

Subject Index — 421

description   24, 49, 51 f., 54, 58, 60, 80, 91, 110, 112, 126, 190, 215, 229, 247, 252, 272, 276, 288, 290–292, 318, 345 f., 388, 390 f.
desire   28 f., 51–57, 59, 68 f., 131, 151, 215 f., 232, 266, 269–272, 274–277, 290–292, 302 f., 309, 323, 340, 344, 389, 391, 393 f.
device   1, 33, 59, 91, 104, 114, 124, 137, 204 f., 232 f., 242, 379, 386, 390
diairesis   23
diaita   289
dialectic   9, 15 f., 18–23, 27 f., 30, 35, 60, 70, 79, 89, 97, 112, 120, 124, 130, 150, 155, 166 f., 187, 192, 196 f., 211 f., 260, 297, 342, 352, 387 f.
dialogue   1 f., 5–13, 18, 20, 33–35, 38, 40–42, 49 f., 59 f., 63–67, 69–73, 80, 82, 89–91, 94–98, 103–112, 114 f., 119–126, 128–133, 137–143, 145–152, 155, 157–163, 166–171, 173 f., 176, 178, 182–184, 187–194, 199, 211–214, 217, 223, 227–231, 238, 243, 251 f., 261, 263 f., 266, 271, 274–278, 281 f., 287, 292–294, 297–303, 305–307, 310–312, 314, 319, 322, 325, 335–337, 339–341, 345 f., 348, 350–352, 357–377, 379–382, 385, 387–390, 392–394
dianoia   17–19, 21, 189–196
dichotomy   140, 149, 171, 290 f., 293
disciple   72, 92, 260, 275, 327, 335, 358, 362
discourse   5, 16, 22, 48–50, 55, 63–69, 71–73, 77, 79, 86, 93, 96 f., 138 f., 144, 155, 164, 187, 192, 196, 208, 232–234, 241 f., 244–246, 248–252, 273 f., 292, 297, 299, 320, 330, 332, 357, 381 f., 388, 390, 394 f.
divine   16, 29, 41, 47 f., 51–53, 55–58, 68 f., 107, 178, 193 f., 198, 218, 222, 234, 246, 248, 256, 260, 265–267, 271–278, 283, 287 f., 321 f., 331, 342, 385, 389, 391
doctrine   7, 11, 47, 66, 77–83, 91, 97, 145, 193, 196, 199, 309, 317, 322, 326, 332, 339 f., 342, 348–351, 384
dogma   305 f.
doxa   7, 12, 21, 24, 90, 151, 391

drama   5 f., 37, 72, 137, 140, 145, 147, 150, 293 f., 329, 335, 395
dramatic   5, 34, 37 f., 40, 50, 52, 63, 65, 73, 104 f., 114, 137 f., 149, 151 f., 155, 175, 179, 181, 188, 204, 211–214, 232, 264, 274, 276 f., 281, 286, 289, 292, 301 f., 308, 325, 361, 363, 368–370, 373–375, 386
dynamis   193, 247–249, 251 f.

education   1, 26, 29 f., 36, 42, 153, 155, 184, 288, 298, 309, 312, 328, 340, 344, 346, 385, 389, 393 f.
epic   107–109, 124, 152, 169, 181, 211, 220
epideixis   191–197, 199
epistemology   97, 298, 309, 344
epos   119 f., 124, 131, 173 f., 179, 338
ergon   15–17, 22 f., 190
essence   21, 29, 144, 153, 155, 175, 323, 382, 391, 394
evil   18, 24 f., 30, 51, 152, 229, 237, 256, 268, 323, 330, 363 f., 366, 376
existence   49, 51 f., 54–57, 59 f., 77, 80, 82–84, 86, 93, 97, 140, 143, 160, 173, 188, 217, 228, 241–245, 287, 292, 308, 325, 331, 339, 391
experience   24, 28, 65–67, 73, 80, 107, 119 f., 123, 131, 140, 143, 148 f., 151, 160, 168, 193–196, 200, 204, 238, 244, 263, 271, 275, 310, 376, 392
expression   1, 22, 30, 48 f., 52, 54, 59, 78, 82–84, 91, 139, 154, 157, 190, 196, 211, 217, 243, 289, 319, 329, 335, 342, 373, 382 f., 388, 395

fabula   394 f.
failure   9, 41, 155, 170, 264, 287 f., 299 f., 311, 393
false   9, 77, 79 f., 92 f., 95, 154, 167, 203, 211, 229, 233, 259, 269, 275, 302, 324, 358, 364, 366, 376
fear   29, 127, 152, 154, 178, 181, 263, 266, 269, 272, 277, 282, 284, 288, 292, 330, 341
female   22, 24, 27, 68, 215 f., 223 f., 289, 293

fiction   121, 131, 138, 140, 147, 213, 294, 308, 326, 381, 386
foreigner   126 f., 130, 264
formula   168–171, 176 f., 180, 245
fragility   148, 150
friendship   177, 216, 232, 247, 251, 272, 275 f., 297, 328, 331, 343

gender   68, 215 f., 223 f., 288–293
genre   1, 6, 64, 66, 69–73, 101, 119, 121, 132, 149, 152, 157, 160, 174, 184, 192, 211–215, 380
gesture   131, 137 f., 140, 148, 150, 212 f., 269, 278, 284
god   36, 41, 47 f., 50–52, 55–59, 66–69, 108 f., 128, 152–154, 176–178, 181, 190, 193–195, 197–199, 204, 208 f., 211, 213–218, 220, 222 f., 229, 242, 246 f., 251, 255–257, 259–261, 263–265, 272, 275, 319, 321 f., 330–332, 340–342, 345, 370–372, 381, 383 f., 391
goddess   36, 120 f., 177, 220, 368, 370, 376
good   6, 8 f., 12, 16, 20 f., 23–28, 30 f., 41, 50, 52–54, 56 f., 59 f., 69, 71, 91, 108, 112, 114, 122, 128, 132, 148, 154, 169, 194, 207, 219, 227–231, 233 f., 236–238, 243–247, 255, 260, 273, 302, 306, 321, 323, 328, 330, 332, 343, 346, 349 f., 357 f., 361, 364, 368–376, 381, 383 f., 386–389, 391 f.
government   20 f., 35, 110, 233, 260, 319, 324, 326, 342
grammar   73, 370
grammarian   33, 173, 370
greed   35, 41 f., 299
gymnasium   123

happiness   25, 123, 219, 235–237
harmony   63, 65, 67 f., 250, 260, 320, 343, 345 f.
health   43, 67 f., 232 f., 238, 246, 248 f., 251
heaven   56–60, 108, 217, 238, 247, 331
hedonism   317, 324 f., 330, 357, 372–376
hegemony   161, 167
hermeneutics   138, 143 f., 188, 194, 196 f., 224
holistic   227, 235 f., 238, 306

homonoia   248, 252
honor   105, 121, 177, 182, 198, 242, 288, 330
hospitality   176, 216
hostility   373
hubris   40, 213, 215
humor   157, 171, 187
hymn   218, 223, 346
hyponoia   191, 194 f., 197
hypothesis   9, 15, 18 f., 21–29, 80, 85, 90, 146 f., 153, 169, 182, 303, 322, 325–327, 330, 351

iconography   282, 293
identity   23, 37 f., 43, 79, 93 f., 124, 129, 150, 154, 166, 194, 252, 266, 317
ignorance   130, 154, 255, 263, 265, 269, 277, 351, 360, 363–366, 369, 379, 385, 388
image   15–23, 26, 29, 31, 47, 50, 53–55, 64, 93, 119, 125, 147 f., 150 f., 153 f., 163, 170 f., 174, 183 f., 187, 189 f., 193 f., 208, 211, 215–219, 223 f., 249, 263, 266, 282 f., 287–290, 292, 341, 345, 349–351, 376, 388, 392, 394
imitation   151–153, 180, 220, 241, 249, 252, 269, 271, 346
inspiration   108, 164, 194, 208 f., 217, 267, 380
intelligence   30, 90, 228, 232, 234, 251, 366 f., 371, 375 f.
invention   103, 228, 268, 317, 319, 325 f., 330
irony   9 f., 125 f., 131, 137, 150, 152 f., 187–190, 198, 206, 267 f., 317, 344, 393, 395
irrational   12, 53–55, 57, 91, 110, 234, 301, 325, 347

judgement   21, 70, 132, 351
justice   15–19, 23–26, 29, 31, 37, 42, 68, 113, 138, 145, 180, 227, 229, 231, 233, 247, 298, 317, 320–324, 331 f., 336, 345, 393

katharsis   113, 148
knowledge   28–31, 34, 53, 55 f., 59–61, 79, 89–91, 95, 97, 109, 112, 120, 129 f., 137,

Subject Index — 423

139 f., 142, 145, 151, 153–155, 159 f., 162 f., 169 f., 188, 190–193, 203–205, 208, 229, 234–236, 238 f., 244, 263, 299, 302 f., 306, 309 f., 328, 345 f., 350 f., 359–361, 363, 365 f., 371, 375 f., 380, 383, 385 f., 388–395

language 2, 5, 10–12, 16, 19, 48, 77–80, 82–86, 138–141, 144 f., 150, 152, 173, 181, 184, 190, 199, 224, 254, 345, 371, 373, 388, 392
laughter 152, 157, 213
law 5, 7, 24, 26, 28, 33, 70, 72, 122, 140, 154, 223, 237, 260, 284, 290, 298, 307, 310, 312, 318–324, 326, 332, 341, 345, 347 f., 352, 376
lawgiver 233, 235 f.
legislation 24, 26, 31, 231, 234
limit 20, 53, 66, 144, 154, 197, 271, 305, 351, 358, 365, 376, 381, 389
literary 1, 3, 5, 7, 50, 61, 63, 72 f., 119–121, 126, 131 f., 138–140, 152, 155, 173 f., 176, 182–184, 205, 211, 277, 282, 293 f., 297, 320, 326–329, 331, 335–338, 340, 344–346, 348, 351, 379 f., 390, 392, 394 f.
literature 2, 5, 109 f., 115, 138 f., 144, 155, 237, 294, 306, 332, 343, 346, 395
logos 11, 13, 20, 31, 89 f., 92–94, 140, 145–147, 183 f., 228, 245, 248 f., 252 f., 281, 293, 357, 369, 388, 390 f.
love 5, 28 f., 48–52, 54–58, 63–68, 70–73, 125, 132, 177, 184, 214–217, 222–225, 231, 242, 247, 250, 252, 255 f., 263–278, 281 f., 286, 288, 292–294, 299, 321, 326 f., 329, 336, 360, 379, 382–384, 386, 389–393

madness 263, 265, 267, 271 f., 275 f., 321, 376
male 22, 24, 68, 215 f., 223 f., 289, 291, 293, 310
mania 282, 292
mask 182–184, 222, 277, 282–284, 287, 292, 379 f., 387, 395
material 140, 159, 161, 167, 170, 205, 300, 304, 308, 339

memory 23, 29, 38, 141, 147, 253, 256, 275, 281, 283, 286 f., 293 f., 337, 373, 375 f.
message 6, 40, 42 f., 194, 271, 274, 299, 321, 335
metaphor 139, 145, 148, 184, 199, 351
mimesis 7, 132, 140, 152, 213, 335
mind 5, 7, 16, 18, 22–24, 48, 51, 53, 63–66, 70, 91, 98, 106, 110 f., 113, 132, 153, 175 f., 193, 234, 269 f., 277, 284 f., 292, 297, 325, 346, 366, 374, 383, 386
model 26, 49 f., 72 f., 95, 120, 126, 132, 140, 157, 159 f., 164 f., 168, 176, 178, 182, 196 f., 203, 206 f., 216, 218, 222, 235, 238, 251, 254, 257, 282, 309, 319–321, 345 f., 351, 366, 375, 389
monologue 5, 160, 193, 199, 379, 384, 387–389, 393
moral 5 f., 58, 81, 228–230, 283, 290, 331 f., 364
mortal 49, 51 f., 54–58, 84, 108, 194, 218 f., 222, 303, 326, 341
motivation 54 f., 121, 187, 284, 327
movement 9, 58 f., 78 f., 94, 97, 130, 137, 139 f., 144 f., 149, 168, 213, 216, 228, 233, 281, 357
muse 163 f., 197, 199 f., 269, 272
music 203–208, 243, 250, 304, 320, 343, 345 f., 370
myth 1, 8, 47–51, 57, 60 f., 125, 144, 149, 154, 205, 214–219, 221–224, 254, 266, 273, 308, 320 f., 338, 341 f., 347, 349, 384 f., 391

narration 7, 52, 60, 104–109, 111, 113 f., 124, 208, 284, 339
narrative 1 f., 8, 40, 72, 103 f., 106 f., 109–112, 114, 120, 122, 150, 152 f., 169, 211, 214, 216, 219, 222, 277, 338, 393
nature 8, 16, 22–24, 27–31, 37, 43, 47, 50, 54, 60, 63, 65 f., 68, 72 f., 78, 90 f., 93, 95, 98, 112, 129, 137, 141, 153, 170, 175, 189 f., 192, 194, 196, 213, 215 f., 219, 224, 228 f., 234, 236–238, 242 f., 246, 252, 255, 266, 270, 275, 290, 297–299, 318–324, 326, 335, 340, 348–350, 361, 364, 370, 381, 386, 390–393

nomos 251
novel 5, 72, 92, 103, 106, 144, 286, 326

ode 321, 332, 351, 382
oligarchy 37, 41, 43, 233, 284f., 327, 329
ontology 97, 344
oracle 124, 197–199
orator 60, 65–67, 69, 124, 228, 253, 260, 285, 327, 379, 387
oratory 255, 288
origin 1, 33, 35, 40, 67, 141, 198f., 206, 208, 215–218, 224, 233, 246, 284, 323, 330, 337, 339–342

paideia 281, 287f., 323
pain 25, 68, 90, 93, 110, 112–114, 244, 249, 261, 265, 310, 365, 370, 375, 389
palinode 47–49, 265, 269, 271, 276f.
paradigm 26, 57f., 119, 127, 143, 180, 187, 190f., 206f., 292, 349f., 352, 379f.
paradox 137, 144, 198f., 269, 276, 297
paranomos 289
parody 163, 167, 170, 213, 219, 222f., 285, 292, 380
peace 25, 38, 71, 81, 125, 158, 282
pederasty 224, 282
performance 55, 57, 70, 157f., 160, 162, 164, 166–171, 181, 187–196, 199, 214, 224, 289
peripatetic 132, 173, 337
persuasion 137, 163, 165, 170, 232, 236, 249, 259, 293, 348
philosopher 1, 16, 24, 27–31, 33–37, 42f., 56f., 60, 72, 78, 84, 98, 104, 112, 115, 120, 137–139, 142–145, 147, 151–154, 184, 189, 192, 211, 221, 223f., 227, 232–236, 286, 292, 300, 302f., 306, 309, 319, 322, 326, 328, 337, 343, 345, 350, 359, 361f., 367, 379–381, 386–388, 391, 395
philosophy 1f., 5, 7f., 12, 27–31, 37, 47, 53, 55, 65f., 69–73, 77, 84, 96, 103, 106, 137–139, 141f., 145–147, 150, 154f., 158, 183f., 187f., 191, 209, 227–232, 247, 249, 251, 257, 277, 286, 297, 303, 310, 312, 317f., 323, 325, 328, 344, 377, 379f., 385, 387, 394

physis 15–17, 22f., 141, 242, 251
platonism 145f., 381
play 1, 54, 63–65, 67, 69, 71, 104, 132, 137, 144f., 154, 159, 163, 175, 188, 190, 211, 213, 263, 266, 276, 278, 281f., 290, 335, 344, 347f., 359, 370, 376, 380, 383, 385, 394
pleasure 25, 29, 53, 103, 106f., 109–115, 148–150, 184, 212, 215f., 249, 261, 264, 270–275, 288–291, 324, 330, 351, 357, 367–376
pleonexia 15, 41, 287, 290
poet 35, 71f., 107, 109f., 114, 129, 147, 152–154, 164, 174–176, 181, 183, 187–191, 193–200, 211, 213f., 216, 220, 253f., 257, 261, 267, 326, 329, 335, 345f., 350f., 383, 385f., 393
poetry 1f., 37, 47, 67, 72, 103f., 107, 109f., 119f., 123, 126, 129, 131, 142, 148, 151, 153–155, 175f., 183f., 187–189, 191, 193–195, 198–200, 212, 261, 340, 342, 346, 350
poiesis 148f., 194
politics 37, 42, 70, 146, 153, 203, 213, 225, 227, 230f., 252, 257, 283, 287, 330f., 342
portrait 33f., 122, 174, 203, 325, 336, 338, 386, 394
praise 35, 107, 152, 154, 241–245, 247–249, 253, 255, 266, 268, 274, 282, 287, 293, 320, 324, 345f., 349, 379, 393
principle 12, 18f., 21, 25, 36, 77f., 195f., 233f., 241f., 245–249, 252, 266, 270f., 318, 320f., 324, 331, 336, 339
procedure 9, 12, 17f., 21f., 27, 72f., 89, 137, 139, 143, 148f., 151, 157f., 160, 162f., 166–171, 188, 190, 211, 222, 232, 234, 238, 303, 357
progress 72, 145, 166, 207, 358, 360, 363, 368, 370
prolepsis 1
public 16, 31, 81, 92, 151, 161–164, 173, 175, 191f., 195f., 227, 239, 285, 343, 350, 382, 392
pupil 91, 119, 173, 180, 182–184, 257, 349, 392

Subject Index — 425

rational   13, 42, 48, 113, 140, 144, 175, 197, 229, 237, 266, 270, 301, 303, 318, 325
reaction   113, 152, 169, 187, 189, 194, 196, 278, 285, 359
reason   1, 12f., 16f., 20, 25, 31, 33, 44, 48–51, 53f., 57, 85, 91, 97, 105, 110, 113, 147, 151, 154, 158, 180, 189, 193, 197, 199, 213, 215f., 229, 233f., 237, 241, 248, 253, 255f., 259, 261, 270, 276, 283, 286, 318, 321f., 326f., 330, 341, 343, 346, 348, 350, 358f., 365, 368, 376, 379, 385, 387
recognition   20, 170, 187f., 365
refutation   24, 29, 68f., 77f., 80, 82f., 86, 92, 95, 168, 193, 232, 265, 323, 325, 360, 364, 369, 371, 374, 383, 385
religion   58, 330, 339, 384f.
reminiscence   119, 145f., 150
rhapsode   128–131, 162–170, 187–194, 197–200
rhetoric   2, 50, 59f., 64, 66, 70, 72, 104, 106, 108, 111f., 139, 145, 192, 196, 203, 211, 228, 237, 249, 252f., 255, 264–266, 277, 290, 349, 382, 387
rhythm   126, 160, 196, 345f.
ridicule   152, 188, 219, 380
ritual   284, 310
role   1, 17, 26, 38, 58, 63f., 68, 71, 97, 103, 122, 132, 141, 144, 158, 161, 163f., 166–168, 175, 179, 183f., 188–192, 203–205, 241, 276f., 285f., 289f., 292f., 298, 309, 327, 336, 338f., 342–346, 348, 359, 368, 370, 376, 379, 385
ruler   24f., 27, 37, 232, 234f., 322, 330

sacrifice   122, 127, 214, 218, 239, 264
sarcasm   187
satire   161–163
scene   13, 43, 119, 121–126, 128, 131f., 137, 147, 149f., 152, 158, 173, 175–184, 189, 195, 213f., 223, 229, 231, 261, 273, 282, 360, 364, 367, 370, 373
scholar   1f., 33, 36–38, 42, 47, 80, 147, 154, 203, 237f., 266, 269, 301, 306f., 311, 318, 335, 340f., 343, 347, 381, 385, 394

science   8, 143, 229, 235, 238, 242, 244, 246, 257, 303f., 306, 390f.
sculpture   203–207
seduction   150, 155, 266, 277, 288, 293
sexual   53, 55, 57, 68, 270–273, 275, 278, 281, 283, 289–291, 293, 374
shame   54, 277, 358, 360
singer   107–109, 169, 193f.
slave   121, 204, 272, 284f., 291f., 299, 306, 320, 322, 392
song   107, 109, 190, 203, 205f., 208, 260, 276, 351
sophia   70, 244
sophist   5, 7f., 30, 33–35, 37, 65, 77, 80–84, 86, 89, 91–98, 109f., 128, 131, 150–152, 194, 205, 242, 253, 256f., 259f., 266, 302, 311f., 319–322, 335–340, 343, 347, 349–351, 357, 360, 362f., 366, 380, 382–385, 387, 390, 392
sophos   52, 89
soul   6f., 10f., 15–21, 25f., 29, 37, 41, 48–59, 61, 67f., 89, 95, 110, 149, 153, 194, 215f., 227–235, 237f., 249, 252, 254, 259f., 264, 266, 275, 277, 299, 309, 322, 341, 344–346, 349f., 352, 357, 360, 362–367, 369, 376, 381, 387, 389–391
spectacle   54, 121, 125, 162f., 215
speech   10, 26, 28, 30, 35, 38, 40, 48, 50, 52, 59f., 63, 66, 70, 82, 84, 86, 112, 125, 148, 150, 153, 157, 159–162, 170f., 177, 190, 192, 197f., 203f., 211–217, 222–225, 241f., 244–257, 259–261, 263–265, 267–269, 271f., 274f., 277, 281f., 286–288, 291–293, 308, 327, 330, 332, 336–344, 347f., 351, 364, 376, 379–384, 387, 390–392, 394f.
stage   5, 23, 71, 122, 128, 146f., 182, 207, 222, 227, 230, 232, 348, 385
state   24, 26, 33, 35, 38, 40f., 48f., 55, 64–66, 89f., 92f., 95, 132, 138, 141f., 145, 174, 176, 180, 183, 187, 190, 203, 207, 228, 231, 233–236, 238, 242, 244, 246f., 252, 254f., 270, 283f., 289, 291, 301, 318, 320, 322, 327f., 332, 335, 341, 362, 364–369, 373, 376

stem 65, 143, 147, 243
stemma, stemmata 38, 42, 311
stoics 318
story 8, 35, 38, 40f., 47, 91, 105–112, 114, 121, 128, 150, 178, 211, 220, 269, 272, 274, 277, 283, 293, 300f., 304–306, 308, 312, 323, 337–339
stranger 5, 25, 131, 151, 341
style 1–3, 49, 65, 72, 95, 120, 133, 183, 191f., 205, 207, 211, 241, 249, 252f., 257, 308, 338, 357, 359, 374, 382, 384, 388
symposium 7, 12f., 49, 51–53, 55, 63–67, 69–73, 104–107, 112, 121, 150, 206, 211–213, 215–219, 221–224, 227, 241, 243f., 246, 248, 250, 252f., 257f., 261, 281–284, 287, 290, 292–294, 303, 307–309, 311, 321, 341, 344, 351, 364, 379, 381–383, 389, 392, 394

teacher 175, 230, 263, 267, 271, 277, 309, 327, 330, 345, 384, 386
techne 188, 228, 241–245, 251
telos 31
temporality 137, 139, 141f., 147f.
tetralogy 329
theater 160, 211–214, 288
theogony 207f., 218f., 222
theory 8, 49f., 53, 65, 78, 89, 97, 109, 141, 145, 163f., 169, 235–237, 246, 249, 282, 301, 304, 317, 327, 359, 379–381, 383, 386f., 389f., 392, 394f.
therapy 227–230, 232, 235, 247
tone 123f., 129, 131f., 183, 212, 276, 282, 373, 384
topos 141, 287, 292
tradition 1f., 97, 101, 103f., 106f., 110f., 114f., 119, 157f., 160, 162f., 165, 167, 173, 176, 184, 187–190, 208, 215, 219, 267, 286, 288–291, 299, 321, 328, 335f., 340, 342, 345f., 348

tragedy 69, 72, 127, 131, 137, 149, 152f., 155, 173, 211–213, 215, 335
transmission 163, 170, 188, 193f., 196, 200, 351, 393
treatise 5, 65, 72, 196, 238, 241–243, 245–247, 250, 252, 297
trilogy 33, 41f., 68
truth 9, 13, 18, 29f., 38, 47, 50–57, 59, 61, 63–66, 69, 73, 77, 79, 81f., 84, 89, 92–96, 103, 105, 137f., 140f., 143, 146f., 149, 153, 175f., 198f., 211, 228f., 232f., 253–255, 260, 269, 274, 282, 284, 287, 302, 305f., 318f., 374, 376, 382–388, 390f., 393
tyche 244
tyranny 41–43, 233, 284, 292, 330

unity 15, 21f., 25, 72, 82f., 85f., 96, 104, 142, 145f., 234, 236, 239, 372
universe 49, 55, 58–60, 168, 237, 331

victim 204, 208, 223, 263
violence 67, 81, 206, 255f., 259, 282, 287, 319
virtue 10, 16, 18, 27–29, 31, 36, 41, 52, 66, 68, 80, 113f., 137, 151, 231, 234, 256, 299f., 322, 339, 343f., 347, 365, 389, 391–393
vision 19, 40, 52, 57, 90, 148
voice 73, 85, 151, 179, 215, 217, 227, 263, 266, 274, 287, 336, 357

weakness 23, 130, 288
wine 222, 282
wisdom 51–55, 67f., 70, 113, 154, 187, 214, 216, 218f., 222f., 247, 254, 275, 309, 343, 359, 364, 367f., 371, 373, 375, 383, 389f., 392
witness 71, 157, 178, 285, 287, 368

youth 29, 126, 151, 266, 269, 283f., 301, 327, 345, 364, 389

www.ingramcontent.com/pod-product-compliance
Lightning Source LLC
Chambersburg PA
CBHW070747230426
43665CB00017B/2278